THE HANDBOOK
OF DERIVATIVE
INSTRUMENTS

THE HANDBOOK OF DERIVATIVE INSTRUMENTS

Investment Research, Analysis, and Portfolio Applications

2nd Edition

Atsuo Konishi
Sumitomo Bank Capital Markets, Inc.

Ravi E. Dattatreya
Sumitomo Bank Capital Markets, Inc.

IRWIN
Professional Publishing®
Chicago • London • Singapore

Times Mirror
Higher Education Group

Library of Congress Cataloging-in-Publication Data

The handbook of derivative instruments : investment research, analysis, and portfolio applications / Atsuo Konishi, Ravi E. Dattatreya, [editors].
    p.   cm.
  Includes bibliographical references and index.
  ISBN 1-55738-867-9
  1. Derivative securities. 2. Investment analysis. 3. Portfolio management.   I. Konishi, Atsuo.   II. Dattatreya, Ravi E.
HG60-24.3.H37   1996
332.6—dc20   95–47699

Printed in the United States of America

1 2 3 4 5 4 6 7 8 9 0 BS 3 2 1 0 9 8 7 6

Dedication

To my wife, Mitsuyo,
                    Atsuo Konishi

To my wife, Goda,
                    Ravi E. Dattatreya

Table of Contents

Chapter One

Introduction

A. Konishi
Sumitomo Bank Capital Markets, Inc.

Ravi E. Dattatreya
Sumitomo Bank Capital Markets, Inc.

YIELD OF DREAMS

The early 1990s saw an explosion in the use of derivative products, especially the over-the-counter variety. Most of the growth came from the investment community rather than corporations, the traditional users. We can trace the roots of this phenomenal growth to several factors that influenced investors. Interest rates in the United States fell to historically low levels across all maturities. Suddenly, many investors found that the returns on their fixed-income portfolios were barely noticeable. The traditionally high-quality, high-yield area of mortgage-backed securities also was affected severely. As mortgage lenders began to offer low-cost or no-cost refinancing, home owners began to prepay their loans at rates much higher than levels assumed by investors. That left only one other area to consider for yield-seeking investors: junk bonds. However, astute investors are always cautious of subjecting the entire capital to credit risk in return for a few basis points of extra yield. After all, credit risk is difficult to measure and manage.

This is where derivatives provided an alternative. Derivative-embedded securities, called structured notes,[1] allowed investors to achieve high yields in most foreseeable scenarios. Credit risk was replaced by market risk. In

---

1 For a detailed discussion of structured notes, see *The Structured Note Market* by Scott Peng and Ravi El Dattatreya (Chicago: Irwin Professional Publishing, 1995).

addition, investors could select their type and leverage (i.e., degree) of market risk. Most often, any risk was limited to the size of the coupon received. Clearly, the technological advancement in theoretical modeling and computer implementation, and the level of comfort and confidence that dealers had in such models and systems, fueled the use of such derivatives.[2]

BREAKTHROUGH OR BREAKDOWN?[3]

The gold rush mentality is only natural in anything that is good, especially in the financial markets with their excellent infrastructure where the participants eagerly service the herd for a fee. The contagious desire for high returns at low levels of credit risk soon attracted a large number of investors. Many of these investors had excessive amounts of structured notes in their portfolios. The risk in these notes, at first limited to the coupon flow, expanded to include the principal payment. As investors clamored for greater yields, derivatives began to be introduced at higher levels of leverage.[4]

Not all corporate liability managers were immune to this demand for high returns or, equivalently, lower interest costs. They were able to execute the derivative portions of these structured notes in the form of structured swap transactions. The hedging context of the corporate treasury provided some form of protection from mark-to-market scrutiny.

A majority of structures depended on two very reasonable assumptions, which, if true, would have provided the promised or expected returns to the investors. The first was that the relationships among the currencies in the Exchange Rate Mechanism (ERM) of the European Monetary System (EMS) was stable. The second major assumption was that the interest rates in the United States would remain low. Unfortunately, neither of these assumptions held true. The ERM broke down in late 1992. U.S. interest rates moved upward in the same dramatic manner as their earlier march downward. These mistaken assumptions resulted in well-publicized losses

---

2 Add to this the often excessive margins enjoyed by the dealers in such transactions.

3 This phrase is attributed to golf pro Robert Wenz. You can sell a golfer anything, he says, referring to a common belief among golfers that the latest equipment (or gimmick) can improve their scores. We have a queasy feeling that not all of us in the financial markets are immune to a similar gullibility.

4 Derivative-embedded securities (i.e., structured notes) have elements of both the physical or cash security and the derivative. At high levels of leverage, the derivative portion dominates the risk characteristics of the security.

at many financial institutions and corporations, many of which went into default. What began as a breakthrough in the development of hedging and trading tools seemed like a breakdown of the financial system.

Many good and bad things have resulted from this saga. On the good side, we see an increased awareness of derivatives on the part of corporate management and the general public.[5] There is increased understanding of the need for judicious risk management. Some standards of risk measurement, such as value-at-risk, are beginning to emerge and are finding wider usage. Investors are wary of any black-box investment that they do not fully understand. There is some realization that if something looks too good to be true, it probably is. More and more participants are appreciating the importance of education at all levels—from the boardroom to the trenches. There is now more price transparency and more disclosure of the risks involved. End users try to rely more on themselves and less on the dealer selling the derivative. More corporations and investing institutions are putting in place hedging, risk management, or "derivative" policies and procedures. Such policies, whether perfect or not, provide guidance to the officers who deal in these markets every day.

There have been negative effects of the meltdown as well. We saw corporations terminating swap contracts, even genuine hedges, simply to say that they have no derivatives on their books. A large number of participants put in place policies eliminating the use of derivatives altogether. Other policies require so much senior management attention that the reaction time of a hedger has been lengthened from minutes or hours to days or even weeks—a crippling development in a rapidly changing and volatile market. Others want to do only plain vanilla transactions, eschewing all advantages of innovation.[6]

There also has been stifling legislative and regulatory scrutiny of derivative markets. If each one of us, for example, purchased puts for hedging, as the regulators would have us do, who would sell them to us in the resulting one-sided market?

Notwithstanding all of these developments, derivatives are here to stay. They are simply too useful, too influential, and too entrenched in the financial markets to disappear or even take a backseat.

---

5   One derivative dealer said that he no longer has to explain to this grandmother what he does for a living.

6   This is not altogether limiting because, fortunately, the meaning of "plain vanilla" keeps advancing periodically.

BACK TO BASICS

A derivative is commonly defined as a financial instrument whose value depends in some way on the values of other more basic underlying securities. Examples are futures on the long Treasury bond and a call option on IBM stock. Not too long ago, these derivatives played a secondary role in finance. They were used mainly for hedging (e.g., the short sale of a future or purchase of a put option to hedge a long position in the underlying security). Derivatives were also used by some investment managers to enhance returns, perhaps by selling covered call options on an existing portfolio. With such a limited application, many participants had the choice of learning about these derivatives or totally ignoring them. Needless to say, the latter choice was the more popular one.

Today, the situation is dramatically different. Derivative products dominate the financial markets. The types of derivatives has increased several fold. A variety of futures and options are available in almost every market. In most cases, the size of the derivative market is much larger than the size of the underlying or "cash" market itself. The influence of derivatives on the basic market is so great that the latter now follows the former. For example, many bond traders look to the Treasury futures markets in order to price Treasury bonds. The large size of the futures market and the corresponding superior liquidity and higher frequency of trading means that a trader has greater confidence in the futures price as a representation of the current market level rather than the price indication for a cash bond. As far as pricing is concerned, therefore, the roles of the derivative and the underlying security seem to have been reversed: The price of the underlying security now responds to the price changes in the derivative.

Derivatives also interconnect different markets. For example, swaptions (options on interest rate swaps) can replicate call options in corporate bonds; currency forwards relate exchange rates and interest rates in different currencies; the so-called quanto and CMT contracts can connect interest rates in different currencies and different maturities. This property also leads derivatives to influence pricing by allowing for arbitrage when price imbalances occur.

There are many reasons for the success of derivatives. In a world of advanced communications, speed is everything. Market players constantly receive new information. To act on this information, they automatically gyrate toward the derivative market because it offers speed of execution and an acceptable transaction cost in addition to other advantages such as anonymity. It is simply cheaper and faster to deal in derivatives. Liquidity is a property of a market that feeds on itself because a liquid market naturally attracts greater participation and thus achieves greater liquidity.[7]

Another important reason for the success of derivatives is the ability of a large portion of the market to quickly and reliably price them. The rapid advances in modeling and mathematical techniques and their general availability have brought an unprecedented level of comfort and confidence to the valuation of derivatives. The valuation technology will continue to play a major role in the further development of these markets in the future. A major goal of this book is to introduce several of these techniques to the reader.

In the past, many of the risks in traditional financial activities—for example, the optionality in the single premium deferred annuity (SPDA) product of the insurance industry—have largely been ignored. The major reasons for this have been (1) that these risks are complex and difficult to quantify and (2) there was very little that one could do about these risks. The recently developed modeling technology and the ability to create complicated instruments in the derivatives area have enabled us not only to quantify but also to hedge and manage these complex risks.

Derivative products are not limited to exchange-traded instruments nor are they conceptually new. Options have always been an integral part of the financial markets in the form of advance loan commitments, prepayment rights, and insurance contracts. Where exchange-traded instruments do not exist or have been slow to develop, other types of markets have sprung up. The stripped zero-coupon market is an excellent example. Another is the interest rate swap market, which began modestly to arbitrage the credit spreads in different markets and is today one of the most dynamic derivative markets in the world, approaching $8 trillion in size. In line with this phenomenon, the usual exchange-traded products, such as futures and options, as well as others such as convertible bonds and interest rate swaps, are covered in this book.

In the current environment dominated by derivatives, therefore, market participants do not have any alternative but to gain a good understanding of how derivative products work. Derivatives, fortunately, are not necessarily always more complex than cash securities. For example, bond futures and options on bond futures are more easy to model and value than

---

7 Where credit and legal concerns exist, as in the swap market, adequate advances, such as credit risk reducing techniques (e.g., netting and offsetting) and standardized documentation, have helped.

many cash instruments such as callable bonds and mortgage-backed securities. In several cases, we can look at a derivative, such as a bond option, as representing the simpler building blocks of a cash security, such as a callable bond. This interpretation of derivatives becomes more clear if we view any security as a collection of parameters or properties such as duration and convexity. Often, a derivative highlights or embodies a single property with all other properties playing minor roles. Thus, we can use derivatives to change the character of a portfolio without adding excess bulk. For example, by purchasing bond futures we can increase the duration of a portfolio without increasing the current market value of the portfolio or without adding to the investment. The bond future thus represents the *essence* of a bond's price volatility or duration. Similarly, an option on a bond or the bond future can add a great amount of convexity to a portfolio, but for a much smaller cash investment than is possible with a cash bond. Also, the option, not the bond, can add convexity without at the same time significantly increasing the duration of the portfolio. In this context, we can think of derivatives as condiments that can be used to prepare a portfolio to our taste.

Generally, a successful derivative must represent the broad market. By so doing, it will appeal to most participants in that market. Second, it must closely follow an existing security without duplicating its function exactly. Third, the underlying securities themselves must be reasonably liquid. Finally, there should not be too much drag due to regulatory, accounting, legal, and tax issues. The long bond future is an excellent example of a successful derivative. It is attractive to a large number of participants because it broadly represents long-term interest rates represented by the large and liquid long Treasury bond market. Long bond futures are not an exact duplicate of a position in any one long bond, yet they are close enough to such a position that they naturally attract arbitrageurs. Arbitrageurs can use futures positions to trade against bond positions and thus will provide the other side for those who use futures for hedging.

In financial activities, a methodology for the valuation of the different securities is an essential requirement. Invariably, this methodology includes a set of implicit or explicit assumptions about the market. We call the methodology and its assumptions a *framework*. A framework should satisfy many different requirements, including tractability and computational ease, but there are two fundamental requirements in a framework. The first is that the assumptions in the framework should not be self-contradictory; that is, the framework should have *internal consistency*. Second, the framework should agree with market realities. We call this property *external consistency*. The ideal situation of course is one in which a single, consistent, universal framework can be used to value all securities, including the various derivatives. In the study of derivative products, one should look for the building blocks and the insight necessary to construct a suitable framework. The insight gained in such a study is far more valuable than the detailed knowledge of contractual particulars, numerical procedures, and arcane techniques. Often, application to derivatives can highlight and expose weaknesses in commonly used rules of thumb and ad hoc procedures. For example, the still-popular use of yield as a measure of value fails totally when applied to futures and options because there are no well-defined fixed cash flows for derivatives. Derivative products are an excellent touchstone for analytical frameworks.

Exhibit 1–1 illustrates the capital market concept. It starts at the bottom with simple securities in the equity, fixed-income, money market, and foreign exchange areas. It ends at the top with portfolio management. The implication is that every activity in finance can be viewed as a portfolio management activity. The conceptual network between the goal (portfolio management) and the starting point (basic securities) is spanned essentially by derivative securities. Thus, we believe that the basic securities are only the starting point on the financial landscape, and that the derivative products are an integral part of the portfolio management process.

Derivative products began their reign of the financial markets with the introduction of financial futures and options in the early seventies, and their dominance is expected to continue for a long time into the future— albeit perhaps with a few bumps along the way. Given these factors, it behooves us to gain a good working knowledge of the market for derivatives. We should also strive to obtain a level of insight into the behavior of derivatives in response to changes in the market environment. It is the goal of the following chapters to provide the reader with this knowledge and insight.

A ROAD MAP

The chapters in this book are broadly divided into four parts. Note, however, that by necessity some chapters do not fit strictly into any particular category while others span the topics of two or more parts. The first part covers interest rate derivatives.

EXHIBIT 1-1
Capital Markets Concept Chart

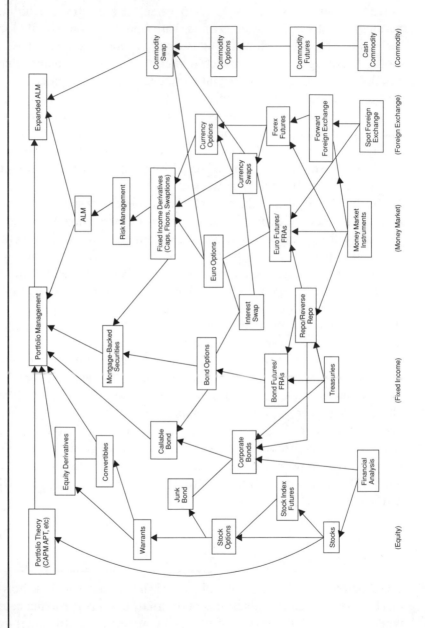

We start with Satish Swamy's descriptive discussion of the interest rate futures and options contracts traded on the Chicago Mercantile Exchange (Chapter 2). This chapter is based on material provided by the CME, and is revised and updated by the author. Even though the main thrust of this book is concept and framework oriented, the contractual details cannot be ignored. Chapter 2 is also a very good introduction to interest rate futures and options for the beginning reader. It includes a discussion of the Eurodollar futures contract, which is among the most successful.

Another successful futures contract is the Treasury long bond contract, which is traded on the Chicago Board of Trade. This contract has some degree of complexity in that it allows a number of Treasury bonds to be delivered and also provides some flexibility in the timing of the delivery. These characteristics are collectively called delivery options. Though largely ignored in the initial days of futures modeling, this feature has recently gained popularity among researchers mainly because of advances in computer and modeling technology. Chapter 3 deals with the long bond futures contract and the similar note futures contract. Galen Burghardt, Terrence Belton, Morton Lane, and John Papa describe how to use these futures for hedging purposes.

Eurodollar futures prices are rough indicators of the forward rates prevailing in the market. They are not accurate indicators mainly because of the daily mark to market and daily variation margin flow. Briefly, when rates move higher, a short position in futures has margin inflow that can be invested at the higher rate; when rates fall, the corresponding margin outflow can be funded at the lower rate. Thus, a short position in futures has an advantage that increases with the size and frequency of rate movements.[8] This advantage, similar to the convexity property of options, makes it deviate a little from the forward rate when priced into the future. Bill Hoskins and Galen Burghardt cover this effect in more detail in Chapter 4.

In the next chapter, Galen Burghardt, Liz Flores, and James Horning cover details of hedging and trading with municipal bond futures. Working with municipal hedging vehicles, whether exchange-traded futures or over-the-counter swaps, is always interesting because the tax treatment varies for

---

8 The price of this convexity also depends on the number of days to maturity of the future. In fact, it increases rapidly as the maturity increases. Other factors are correlations among rates at different parts of the yield curve. These effects and the convexity property can be quantified by means of a simple binomial model of the future contract.

different parts of a transaction. The effects of this difference should be carefully analyzed.

The interest rate swap is a fascinating derivative product that has developed into a multibillion dollar global market without any help or hindrance from the established exchanges. Indeed, as exchange-traded derivatives such as futures and options gained acceptance, the word *derivative* has been applied mostly to over-the-counter contracts such as swaps. In Chapter 6, Ravi E. Dattatreya, Raj E. S. Venkatesh, and Vijaya E. Venkatesh introduce this captivating market to the beginning reader.

Indexed amortization swaps (IAS)[9] and their applications are addressed next (in Chapter 7 by Bjorn Pettersen and Vijay Raghavan and in Chapter 8 by Ramine Rouhani of CDC Investment Management Company). These swaps are amortizing. The amortization rate itself is variable and is indexed to market parameters (e.g., LIBOR). One of the interesting contributions of the derivative markets has been to create acceptable alternatives to mortgage-backed securities. The major advantage of the indexed notes is that they remove an entire layer of uncertainty, represented by a prepayment model, that haunts investors in mortgage-backed securities.[10] In contrast, the indexed amortizers need no leap of faith[11] in a prepayment model and can be analyzed completely in any interest rate scenario with a simple spread sheet. We believe that the concept of indexed amortization in its present form or something newer has a great deal of potential.

One sector of the mortgage market that is influenced significantly by prepayment variations is the servicing industry. Some of the recent derivative instruments that were developed to feed the exploding structured note market are finding new applications, such as hedging of the complex risks in this industry, that cannot be adequately handled with traditional, nonderi-

---

9 We prefer a slightly different, more descriptive terminology for these: IVAR (indexed variable amortization rate) swaps and notes.

10 The risk in this uncertainty was realized in a painful way by investors during the recent bond market rally when most, if not all, prepayment models failed to anticipate the unprecedented prepayment rates, requiring major jiggering of these models. One reason for this failure is that the models take into account only the behavior of the borrower, not the lender. During the rally, lender behavior changed dramatically as lenders initiated refinancing activity with zero-cost transactions. Investors and traders who did not patch their prepayment models correctly got whipsawed again in early 1994 when rates rose quickly.

11 Prepayment modeling will always be less than scientific because too many factors are involved with too much slippage between cause and effect.

vative instruments. Laurie Goodman covers the hedging of servicing income in Chapter 9.

Fischer Black, Emanuel Derman, and William Toy then present a simple model to value interest rate options in Chapter 10. The Black-Derman-Toy model has already become a widely accepted classic. To model debt options, we have to assume how interest rates behave. A reasonable and relatively simple approach assumes that the yield curve at any point in time can be fully determined by knowing one independent variable.[12] In many such models, known as one-factor models, the independent variable can be interpreted as the short-term rate. The model discussed in this chapter is such a one-factor model. The main input data for this model is the current yield curve, but it has an innovation: It also uses the volatilities at various maturities as input and generates an interest rate process consistent with these volatilities. It uses the binomial approach for numerical computation that was first used with options by William Sharpe and later popularized by John Cox and Mark Rubinstein. The model satisfies the internal and external consistency conditions reviewed above. The internal consistency condition places several restrictions on the relative movements of rates at different maturities and their corresponding volatilities. Therefore, it is sometimes possible that a consistent binomial tree cannot be generated with a given set of data representing the yield levels at various maturities (i.e., the discount function) and the corresponding volatilities.[13]

The philosophy apparent in this chapter is to eschew complexity for its own sake; the authors demonstrate that the simple one-factor model can be extended to include a variety of details, such as a volatility structure.[14] Thus there is no need nor any obvious justification for the computational and data-gathering complexity associated with multifactor models. The one-factor model is complicated enough.

---

12 See, for example, Ravi E. Dattatreya and Frank Fabozzi, *Active Total Return Management of Fixed Income Portfolios,* revised ed. (Chicago: Irwin Professional Publishing, 1995).

13 This happens because the number of degrees of freedom available in a binomial model is not sufficient to handle an arbitrary set of input data. A multinomial but still one-factor model can perhaps provide more flexibility.

14 Though not discussed in this chapter, this model is used not only for the valuation of fixed-income options. It can also be used to determine the value of securities whose cash flow is not fixed (e.g., inverse floaters) and to determine horizon returns under various scenarios as well as the probability of those scenarios.

In Chapter 11, Fischer Black and Piotr Karasinski take this concept one step further. Their model allows for independent specification of mean reversion behavior of short-term rates. In addition, it is more flexible and has some computational advantages.

Part I concludes with Chapter 12 by Satyajit Das on Range Floaters. These are floating-rate structured notes with the coupon set high if a market indicator (e.g., LIBOR) is within a range, low otherwise. A very large amount of such notes have been issued over the past few years.

Part II deals with equity derivatives. It has been said that the 1990s will be the decade of equity and equity derivatives just as the 1980s were dominated by debt and interest rate derivative products. We expect a significant amount of innovation and attention to modeling in the equity market during the next few years.

This part begins with a descriptive presentation of stock index futures and options traded on the Chicago Mercantile Exchange. The stock index future discussed here joins the Eurodollar future and the long bond future as one of the most successful futures contracts. In Chapter 13 Satish Swamy has revised and updated material provided by the CME.

As we mentioned earlier, the key difference between forward contracts and futures contracts is that the latter are settled daily, resulting in variation margin flows. This feature affects hedge ratios and in general introduces some uncertainty in all futures transactions. It is usually addressed by a technique called tailing. In Chapter 14 Ira Kawaller and Timothy Koch examine the tail hedge as it applies to stock index futures and show how to manage the associated cash flow risk.

To most practitioners, the derivative products market really started in the early seventies with the introduction of exchange-traded stock options and the contemporaneous development of the Black-Scholes-Merton option model. The original arbitrage argument used in this model will continue to be a major concept driving all modeling activity in finance. In Chapter 15, Richard Bookstaber examines the modern approaches to modeling stock options and their applications. This is a very useful introduction for the beginning reader.

In Chapter 16, Jim Crawford analyzes equity-linked notes, which are not unlike convertible bonds and have both debt and equity plays. This is followed by Ron Slivka's discussion in Chapter 17 of equity derivative applications.

Perhaps the most neglected security in the area of modeling has been the convertible bond. The complexity of two independent variables—the stock price and interest rates—has no doubt been an important reason for this lack of attention. We believe, however, that the convertible is an underutilized capital-raising tool, especially in the United States where the convertible has some attractive tax benefits associated with it. As new structures that highlight these benefits, such as the zero-coupon convertible, are introduced, this market should grow significantly. Also, the convertible provides a smooth transition from the debt-laden 1980s to the 1990s and beyond where, we believe, equity will be king. In Chapter 18, Dan Rissin introduces the convertible bond market. In concluding the part on equity derivatives, Tom Ho develops an elegant approach to pricing this elusive instrument in Chapter 19.

Part III covers currency derivatives. Currencies play in a liquid market of gigantic proportions. The uncertainties of the strengths of different economies and the tendency of some governments to manipulate free market forces provides for an exciting and vibrant trading environment.

This part deals mainly with the discussion of currency futures and options. These currency products have not yet fully realized their potential in the portfolio management arena. However, as financial businesses become more global in nature, as participants become more comfortable with currency risk, and as regulating entities wake up to the rapidly developing world of derivatives, the use of currency products should increase in depth and breadth. In Chapters 20 and 21, David DeRosa covers the various instruments and applications in this market, including spot, forward, and futures contracts, and options.

One of the effects of the recent trend toward globalization of the capital markets is the increased interest in international equity portfolios. In Chapter 22, Fischer Black derives some interesting results in the area of optimizing currency risk and reward in such portfolios.

Part IV covers risk management, the fashionable new phrase in financial markets. Whereas traditional risk management dealt mainly with the risk in a portfolio of assets or liabilities, we now have to worry about two other aspects as well: (1) the risk of the risk-reducing tools (i.e., derivatives) and (2) the risk of the providers of these tools.[15] The chapters in Part IV cover all three aspects.

In Chapter 23 Steven Allen examines how a derivative provider should view the market risk in its portfolio. This is usually not a major concern be-

---

15 That is, the credit risk of, or exposure to, derivative dealers.

cause sophisticated professionals generally manage the portfolios of providers. However, some oversight is necessary because subtle risks persist, portfolio sizes are large, and the potential for large losses and gains exists.

The next chapter addresses the important subject of tools and techniques for analyzing derivatives. In Chapter 24, Ravi E. Dattatreya and Raj Pundarika propose the use of interest rate risk management as an integral part of a comprehensive program. They also recommend the application of the *risk point method* to accomplish the Four Ms of risk management: measurement, monitoring, modification, and management. The risk point method has other related applications in investment management, such as the replication of bond indexes and immunization.[16]

In Chapter 25, Leslie Rahl and Tanya Beder tackle the various issues that must be addressed by end users of risk management tools. Next, Azam Mistri offers a fresh approach to corporate exposure management in Chapter 26. Here you will find some guidelines for escaping from what he calls "conventional confusion" and for developing effective corporate risk management policies, which have become a must in light of recent disclosures of derivative-related losses by several corporations.

The rest of Part IV covers credit risk, especially OTC derivatives such as swaps. In Chapter 27, Gregg Whittaker and Sumita Kumar introduce the reader to the new and developing world of credit derivatives. This is an important area and will grow in size over the next few years. One trend that will fuel this growth is the desire of major banks to shed their assets to achieve more comfortable asset/capital ratios.

The next two chapters cover how swap dealers handle credit risk. In Chapter 28, Gus Moore shows how a dealer might measure and manage the credit risk in its swap portfolio. Credit risk has received increased attention recently not only because of the failure of a few counterparties[17]—the shocks from which, fortunately, have been absorbed with little disruption—

---

16 The risk point method as presented here does not include correlation risk, given its *ceteris paribus* approach. Nor does it incorporate the effect of differential volatility of different sources of risk. Fortunately, the latter effect can be easily accommodated, resulting in volatility-adjusted risk points (VARPS). In addition, it is possible to combine the currently popular value-at-risk (VAR) concept with the risk point approach to obtain value-at-risk corresponding to each source of risk.

17 Failure of a swap dealer is not expected to create a major problem because even a dealer with a large portfolio has mostly offsetting cash flows and contracts. That is, a dealer portfolio, large in gross amount, is usually small in net amount. The resilient nature of the dealer network reminds us of the Internet, which also can easily withstand the failure of a node.

but also because of the increased exposure to counterparties due to large positions that have been building up over the years. A portfolio approach to credit risk can actually decrease the perceived exposure because of netting of offsetting positions. In this sense, the portfolio approach is aggressive. However, we can only be conservative at a cost.

In Chapter 29, which concludes this part, Jennifer White shows how a swap dealer can use credit enhancement by way of special-purpose vehicles to minimize credit risk and thus attract end users.

Part V covers the investment, hedging, and trading strategies in derivative products. The coverage is by no means exhaustive; however, the chapters do provide the reader with a few of the applications possible with derivatives.

In their option model, Black and Scholes made several simple assumptions that are known not to hold strictly. Yet, the market prices of stock options exhibit remarkable agreement with the Black-Scholes model. In Chapter 30, Fischer Black provides tips on how to use the holes in the Black-Scholes model to trading advantage.

In Chapter 31, Tom McAvity discusses how the insurance industry has liabilities that include optionlike features which can be effectively hedged with more structured swaps and other derivative products.

Satyajit Das covers structured investments, discussed earlier, in Chapter 32. These are hybrids, commonly known as *structured notes,* that combine traditional forms of fixed-income investment with exotic options and swaps. The reason for their existence is the need for yield enhancement without attendant credit risk,[18] as well as the need for new and unusual risk-return patterns. Structured notes can also be used as hedges in many situations, for example, the single-premium deferred annuity (SPDA) product in the insurance industry or the unusual risks of a mortgage investment.

One of the major applications of derivatives (especially futures) in investment management has been in asset allocation. It has been said that the manner in which assets are allocated to different market segments has more influence on the returns than on any other decision. In Chapter 33, Roger Clarke describes how futures and options can be used for tactical asset allocation in an efficient manner.

---

18 Mortgage-backed securities also offer higher promised yield with little credit risk. In this context, structured notes are alternatives to mortgage-backed securities.

Portfolio efficiency and optimization is a frequent goal of investment managers. Fischer Black and Robert Litterman describe techniques of optimizing a global portfolio in Chapter 34.

Insurance derivatives are a brand-new addition to the industry. As the number of natural disasters seems to be on the rise, this kind of derivative has taken on more interest. In Chapter 35 Joseph Cole and Richard Sandor look at hedging and trading opportunities with insurance derivatives. Here is a classic case where hedging is possible by one group, the insurance companies, only if there is another group willing to speculate (or invest, if you prefer).

We all know that convexity is good in an investment, but how do you profit from it? Laurie Goodman explains in Chapter 36 how to convert convexity into tangible dollars. This is followed by an analysis of inverse floaters by Laurie Goodman, Jeffrey Ho, and Linda Howell in Chapter 37.

Adjustable-rate mortgages (ARMs) have become very popular in the United States, especially with their low initial teaser rates.[19] Lenders who fund ARMs with floating rate financing are exposed to the risk of the periodic caps embedded in them as well as the uncertain prepayment behavior. In Chapter 38, Venkat Ramdev, Lev Borodovsky, and Matthew Baber show how a lender can restructure ARMs with appropriate hedges.

The prepayment function is the most important component of any mortgage model. In Chapter 39, Jeffrey Ho specifies a simple, generalized form of the prepayment function and examines the results as applied to spread analysis.

Traditional option structures are memoryless in the sense that the value of the option depends on the prevailing values of market parameters, but not on the sequence of values attained (i.e., path followed) by the parameters in the past. There are many options in the market that are not memoryless. The periodic caps in an ARM are one example. These are called path-dependent options. John Hull and Alan White present efficient procedures for valuation of these in Chapter 40.

The book concludes with K. Ravindran's chapter on exotic options. Our word processor's thesaurus offers several synonyms for the word *exotic,* including alien, foreign, imported, fascinating, romantic, strange, unusual, outlandish, and wondrous. In the financial world, however, exotic most

---

19 With the new zero-point mortgages, one viable strategy is to refinance every year to obtain the attractive teaser rates again and again.

often simply means "new."[20] The current crop of exotic options is made possible by the dramatic development of mathematical models that can be used to price and hedge these instruments as well as the level of comfort that traders and users have attained in using these models. In addition to the investment community's need for new and varied risk-reward profiles, exotics also fulfill two hedging needs. They allow for more complete hedging of actual risks in liabilities (e.g., insurance contracts). Second, they can result in more cost-effective hedges through their ability to select the particular risks to be hedged. Ravindran takes a building-block approach that we mentioned earlier. This concept has wide applicability and can bring together the entire derivative market.

A SAD NOTE

As we prepare to go to press, we learn of the sad news that Fischer Black passed away on August 30, 1995. Fischer has always been a good friend and a strong supporter of our book projects. He has contributed no less than five articles for this handbook. We have enjoyed our varied discussions on financial topics both in person and on the Internet. The last debate (this one in cyberspace) was about the possibility of negative interest rates in Japan. He will always occupy a special place in our hearts.

ACKNOWLEDGMENTS

First, we thank all of our contributing authors who patiently stayed with us over the extended time that it took to bring the book to a final form. We also thank several authors who worked on articles that were not included in this volume for various reasons beyond their control. We also thank all of our associate editors for enthusiastically accepting the invitation to contribute long hours of work and tons of political capital.

We also wish to thank Kenji Kita of Sumitomo Bank Capital Markets, Inc., New York, for providing assistance and for his encouragement throughout this long project. We acknowledge the help of Joyce Frost and Sumita Kumar in reading drafts of parts of the book.

---

20 Not so long ago, the plain vanilla swap was an "exotic" transaction.

Finally, we thank Ashwani Fodar, an MBA student at the Columbia University Business School, who interned at SBCM through the summer and fall of 1995. He performed an admirable job proofreading the manuscripts and managing the entire process efficiently. He was instrumental in the preparation of this book.

I

INTEREST RATE DERIVATIVES

Chapter Two

Short-Term Interest Rate Futures, Options, and Trading Strategies

Satish Swamy
Lincoln Investment Management

One of the most successful and exciting innovations in the history of the futures markets has been the emergence of interest rate futures contracts. The International Monetary Market (IMM), a division of the Chicago Mercantile Exchange (CME), introduced the trading of interest rate futures in 1976. Since then, the value of the futures in transferring financial risk has been widely recognized and financial futures trading has experienced explosive growth. The open interest by the summer of 1995 had exceeded $23 trillion (face value) of underlying financial instruments, up from $800 billion in 1990. Furthermore, the interest rate futures market has come to represent about one-half of the entire futures market, and most industry experts expect the continued growth of the futures market to center around these financial instruments.

The International Monetary Market has successful contracts with very short maturities, trading contracts for three-month Treasury bills, one-month LIBOR, and three-month Eurodollar time deposits. In 1976 the IMM introduced the three-month Treasury bill futures contract, the first interest rate futures contract based on a money market instrument. Its success indicated the need to transfer short-term interest rate risk.

In 1984, Eurodollar futures contracts identical to those traded on the CME began trading on the Singapore International Monetary Exchange

(SIMEX). Under a linked clearing program called the Mutual Offset System, Eurodollar futures can be traded on one exchange and held or liquidated at the other. Because SIMEX is open when the CME is closed, traders have access to an extended trading day. Options on Eurodollar futures were introduced on the Index and Options Market (IOM) division of the CME in 1985, and options on T-bill futures were opened in 1986. Options, used separately or in combination with the futures, offer additional trading flexibilities and positioning choices.

This chapter will discuss the Treasury bill, Eurodollar, and LIBOR futures contracts and options on futures. The different speculating and hedging strategies are also discussed for the inquisitive trader.

THE UNDERLYING "CASH" MARKETS

The money market instruments on which CME interest rate futures contracts are based (sometimes referred to as the "cash markets") include U.S. Treasury bills and Eurodollar time deposits. All are separate, yet interdependent.

Treasury Bills

Treasury bills are discounted, noncallable securities that are issued, guaranteed, and auctioned by the U.S. Treasury, generally with maturities of 13, 26, or 52 weeks. The 13-week U.S. Treasury bill (T-bill) futures contract at the CME relates to the interest rate for a deferred delivery of a T-bill with 13 weeks remaining until maturity and a face value of $1 million.

Eurodollars

Eurodollars are U.S. dollars on deposit with banks or bank branches outside the United States. The CME's Eurodollar time deposit futures contract reflects the offered rate for a three-month, $1 million deposit, commencing the third Wednesday of the contract month.

One-Month LIBOR

LIBOR is the acronym for the London Interbank Offered Rate, a reference rate for dealing in Eurodollar time deposits between commercial banks in the London interbank market. The CME's LIBOR contract is analogous to the Eurodollar contract, but it pertains instead to a one-month, $3 million deposit.

THE FUNDAMENTALS OF SHORT-TERM INTEREST RATE FUTURES TRADING

All CME interest rate futures contracts are traded using a price index, which is derived by subtracting the futures' interest rate from 100.00. For instance, an interest rate of 5.00 percent translates to an index price of 95.00 (100.00 − 5.00 = 95.00). Given this price index construction, rising interest rates imply a falling contract price. Therefore, to profit from declining interest rates, you would buy the futures contract (or in trading terminology, "go long"); to profit from a rise in interest rates, you would sell the contract ("go short").

The design of most CME interest rate futures contracts feature a minimum price move, or "tick," of 0.01; however, the one-year T-bill has a minimum tick equal to one-half of 0.01. Gains or losses, therefore, are calculated simply by determining the number of ticks moved, multiplied by the value of the tick. For the dollar-denominated contracts (Eurodollar, LIBOR, and the 13-week and one-year T-bill futures) the tick value is $25. Thus, a price move from 95.00 to 95.01 in the case of the Eurodollar, for example, would mean a $25 gain for the long position, and a $25 loss for the short position; a full percentage point change in interest rates—equivalent to a 1.00 change in the futures price—would translate to $2,500.

Before buying or selling a futures contract, a trading account must be established that includes depositing performance bond with a broker—either a cash deposit or another form of collateral. These funds serve as a good faith deposit, guaranteeing performance of the financial obligations that can arise from initiating a futures position. After satisfying this requirement, an order can be placed with the broker. The price at which the broker transacts the buy or sell order becomes the "entry" price; at the end of trading on that day, the contract value is "marked to market." Each day the trade remains open (i.e., as long as it is not liquidated by an offsetting trade), the position incurs a profit or a loss based on the difference between the entry price and the "settlement" price. A cash payment is applied to the trading account if the position realizes a profit; if the position incurs a loss, cash must be paid out of the account. If daily losses cause the trading account to fall below a certain level, further funds will be required to maintain the contract position.

At expiration, CME 13-week Treasury bill futures are settled by physical delivery. That is, any open position after termination of trading on the last trading day would be required to make or take delivery of a cash market T-bill priced at the final futures settlement price. For the remaining interest rate futures contracts (Eurodollars, LIBOR, and one-year T-bills), no physical delivery takes place. These contracts are said to be "cash settled." Following the last trading day, a final mark-to-market adjustment is made, and the contracts simply cease to exist. By contract design, this last mark-to-market process ensures convergence between futures and cash interest rates.

HEDGING WITH SHORT-TERM INTEREST RATE FUTURES

When an investor takes a hedged position in interest rate futures, the idea is to offset an existing interest rate risk. Fundamentally, the hedger in interest rate futures attempts to take a futures position that will generate a gain to offset a potential loss in the cash market. On the other hand, this also means that the hedger takes a futures position that will generate a loss to offset a potential gain in the cash market. In this section, we will discuss the concept of hedging with interest rate futures.

A Simple Long Hedge

Let's assume that on September 15 a short-term money manager is expecting to receive $985,500 to invest in 90-day T-bills six months from now. Current yields on T-bills are 6 percent. The money manager finds out that the yield curve is flat and, as a result, the forward rates are also 6 percent. Based on current economic views, the manager feels that 6 percent rates are attractive and decides to lock in that rate by "buying to open" one T-bill futures contract maturing in March (someday in the third week), which happens to be the day that the requisite funds would become available for investment. Therefore, with the current yield of 6 percent, the portfolio manager expects to be able to buy $1 million face value of T-bills, which can be shown as follows:

$985,538.36 = $1,000,000/(1.06) ^ 0.25.

The manager executes the hedge and waits for March 15. On that day (March 15), the 90-day T-bill yield has fallen to 5 percent, confirming the money manager's intuition that rates might fall. Consequently, $1 million face value of 90-day T-bills is now worth:

$987,876.55 = $1,000,000/(1.05) ^ 0.25.

To complete the futures hedge, the manager "sells to close" (just before the futures contract matures), making a profit of $2,338.19 (985,538.36–987,876.55). However, in the spot market, the cost of $1,000,000 face value of 90-day T-bills has risen from $985,538 to $987,876, generating a loss of $2,338. However, the futures profit exactly offsets the cash market loss for a zero change in wealth.

Hedging a Forward Borrowing Rate

In late September, a corporate treasurer projects that cash flows will require a $1 million bank loan on December 15. The contractual loan rate is 1 percent over the three-month Eurodollar rate (LIBOR) on that date. LIBOR is currently 5.45 percent. The December Eurodollar futures, which can be used to lock in the forward borrowing rate, are trading at 94.25, implying a forward Eurodollar rate of 5.75 percent (100.00 – 94.25). By selling one December Eurodollar futures contract, the corporate treasurer hopes to ensure a borrowing rate of 6.75 percent for the three-month period beginning December 15. This rate reflects the bank's 1 percent spread above the rate implied by the futures contract.

By December 15, the exisiting Eurodollar rate rises to 7.3 percent, and the December futures price declines to 92.8 (reflecting a 7.2 percent rate). As a result, the treasurer's interest payment to the bank is $20,750 for the quarter ($1,000,000 × 8.3 × 1/4 year). However, the decline in the futures price produces a profit on the short futures of $3,625 (that is (94.25 – 92.8) × $2,500). So the net interest expense for this quarter is $17,125 for an effective annual rate of 6.85 percent.

This example illustrates that the realized cost of funds may differ somewhat from the cost of funds anticipated at the time the hedge was initiated. The difference can be accounted for by the difference between the spot market LIBOR rate and the rate implied by the futures contract at the time the hedge was liquidated. The LIBOR rate was 10 basis points higher than the rate implied by the December futures contract on December 15, accounting for the 10 basis point differential between anticipated and realized cost of funds. In this case, the difference worked against the hedger, but in other situations the difference may prove beneficial. In general, this hedging inaccuracy, called "basis risk," is minimized the closer the loan pricing date is to the delivery date of the futures contract.

Cross-Hedging

The asset manager who knows that funds will be available for investment beginning on some forward date may buy futures to establish a rate of return for this investment. Also, the liability manager who plans for a forthcoming debt issuance can prearrange funding costs by selling interest rate futures. In either case, the manager may hedge even if his or her risk does not involve precisely the same instrument that underlies a futures contract. For example, although short-term interest rate futures contracts are traded only for 91-day T-bills and Eurodollars, a manager with a portfolio of, say, commercial paper could still benefit by employing a "cross-hedge." In such cases, the hedge manager must allow for less than perfect hedge performance.

Consider the case of the treasurer of a large corporation that has decided to issue $2 billion worth of 90-day commercial paper in three months. The outstanding 90-day commercial paper of the firm yields 7 percent or 2 percent above the current 90-day T-bill rate of 5 percent. Fearing that rates might rise, the treasurer decides to hedge against the risk of increasing yields by entering the interest rate futures market. This is an example of a cross-hedge.

In general, a cross-hedge occurs when the hedged and hedging instruments differ with respect to (1) risk level, (2) coupon, (3) maturity, or (4) the time span covered by the instrument being hedged and the instrument deliverable against the futures contract. What this really implies is that the vast majority of all hedges in the interest rate futures markets are cross-hedges. The hedge being put on by the treasurer is a cross-hedge because the commercial paper and the T-bill differ in risk. Assuming that the commercial paper is to be issued in 90 days ensures that the commercial paper and the T-bill delivered on the futures contract cover the same time span.

Therefore the treasurer decided to sell 2,000 T-bill futures contracts to mature in three months. The futures price for this contract is $1,971,076.72, which implies a futures yield of 6 percent. This is different from the current 90-day T-bill yield of 5 percent. At maturity, if the futures yield remains at 6 percent, the trade incurs no gain or loss on the futures contract.

In the cash market, the 90-day commercial paper spot rate at the end of the hedging period has become 8 percent, not the 7 percent that was the original 90-day spot rate at the initiation date of the hedge. Since the treasurer thought he was "locking-in" the 7 percent spot rate, he expected to receive $1,966,455,175 for the commercial paper issue. But the commercial paper rate at the time of issue is 8 percent, so the corporation receives only $1,961,887,304. There appears to be a loss of $4,567,871 in the cash market. The treasurer may have thought that he was locking in the prevailing spot rate of 7 percent at the time the hedge was initiated, but this assumption was totally unwarranted. By hedging the issuance of the commercial paper, the treasurer should have expected to lock in the three-month forward rate of 90-day commercial paper.

Modifying Maturities

Asset managers can lengthen the effective maturity of short-term investment assets by buying futures contracts and shorten the effective maturity of those assets by selling futures contracts. Liability managers can achieve the same effects by doing the opposite, that is, selling futures to lengthen their liabilities and buying futures to shorten them.

For either assets or liabilities, hedging serves as an alternative to restructuring the portfolio in the cash markets. The use of futures may be attractive when physical restructuring is not possible (e.g., term deposits cannot be bought back prior to their maturity dates). It also may be cheaper to use futures because transaction costs in the futures markets may be lower than those in cash markets or liquidity conditions in the cash market would result in substantial market penalties.

Exhibit 2–1 demonstrates the use of futures to shorten the effective maturity of a Treasury bill from 174 days to 83 days so that the 83-day yield is locked in. Exhibit 2–2 shows how to extend the maturity of an 83-day Treasury bill and fix a rate of return over a longer period. (All rates and prices shown are hypothetical, and the two examples are independent. Also note that daily marking to market is ignored.)

Both of these examples show the purchase of the asset on the day the maturity-altering futures transaction takes place. The analysis is identical if the investment or liability is already in the portfolio. The manager merely determines the market price of the instrument of that day.

By phrasing the examples in terms of buying the T-bills, the examples show that managers can also use futures to improve performance without changing the basic maturity structure of their portfolios. Referring again to Exhibit 2–1, if on April 1 the manager held the June 23 bill with 83 days to maturity and if that bill provided a yield of less than 10.25 percent, he or she improves performance by selling that bill and entering the cash/futures combination shown in that exhibit. Analogously, in Exhibit 2–1, the man-

EXHIBIT 2–1
Shortening a Treasury Bill's Maturity

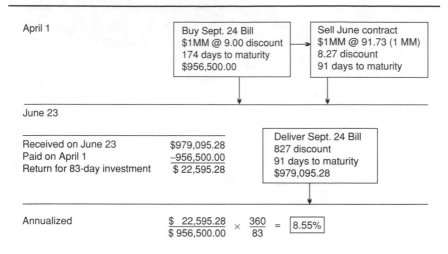

| April 1 | Buy Sept. 24 Bill
$1MM @ 9.00 discount
174 days to maturity
$956,500.00 | Sell June contract
$1MM @ 91.73 (1 MM)
8.27 discount
91 days to maturity |

June 23

Received on June 23	$979,095.28	Deliver Sept. 24 Bill 827 discount 91 days to maturity $979,095.28
Paid on April 1	−956,500.00	
Return for 83-day investment	$ 22,595.28	

Annualized $\quad \dfrac{\$\ 22,595.28}{\$\ 956,500.00} \times \dfrac{360}{83} =$ $\boxed{8.55\%}$

EXHIBIT 2–2
Extending a Treasury Bill's Maturity

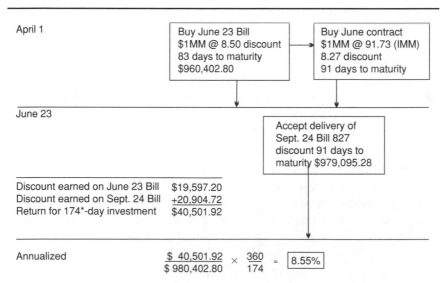

| April 1 | Buy June 23 Bill
$1MM @ 8.50 discount
83 days to maturity
$960,402.80 | Buy June contract
$1MM @ 91.73 (IMM)
8.27 discount
91 days to maturity |

June 23

| | | Accept delivery of
Sept. 24 Bill 827
discount 91 days to
maturity $979,095.28 |

Discount earned on June 23 Bill	$19,597.20
Discount earned on Sept. 24 Bill	+20,904.72
Return for 174*-day investment	$40,501.92

Annualized $\quad \dfrac{\$\ 40,501.92}{\$\ 980,402.80} \times \dfrac{360}{174} =$ $\boxed{8.55\%}$

*Ignores the potential of interest income on the discount from June 23 to Sept. 24

ager who held a September 24 bill earning less than 8.55 percent is better served by the cash/futures combination that results in that same maturity.

SPECULATING WITH SHORT-TERM INTEREST RATE FUTURES

Case 1: Naked speculation. In this strategy, the long trader is betting that interest rates will fall so that the price of the futures will rise. On the other hand, the short trader is betting that interest rates will rise so that the futures price will fall. Consider an example.

If a trader expects interest rates to go up (and subsequently, bond prices to come down) with new economic numbers indicating inflation, then she would decide to "sell to open" 1 Dec 95 Eurodollar futures at 94.25 on August 1, 1995. One week later, after leading economic indicators have been released, interest rates go up and on August 8, 1995, the Dec 95 Eurodollar futures are trading 93.85. The trader decides to "buy to close" 1 Dec 95 Eurodollar future at 93.85 for a profit of 40 basis points. The total profit realized would be $1,000 (40 × $25).

Case 2: Spread speculation—The case of the T-bill and Eurodollar (TED) spread. In this kind of speculation, we might expect to find a widening of the yield spread between T-bill deposits and Eurodollar deposits. This widening yield spread would reflect the changing perception of the risk involved in holding Eurodollar deposits (in the face of potentially very large loan losses). In August 1995, assume that the yields for the Mar 96 T-bill and Eurodollar futures contracts are 5.34 and 5.76 percent respectively. If the full riskiness of the banks' position due to an international crisis has yet to be understood, we might expect the yield spread to widen. This would be the case whether interest rates were rising or falling. To take advantage of this belief, a trader could sell the Mar 96 Eurodollar contract and buy the Mar 96 T-bill contract.

Since the trader expects the yield spread to widen, the trader sells the Eurodollar contract and buys the T-bill contract index values of 94.66 and 94.24. Later, in December 1995 for example, the yield spread of the example has widened, with T-bill yields having moved up slightly so the spread has widened by 35 basis points, implying a profit of $875 on the trade.

In this interesting example, it should be emphasized that people are aware about the different kinds of problems faced by financial institutions such as large banks in international lending. With efficient media and other forms of communication, information travels very fast with modern day technology. When a trader is putting on the above mentioned trade, he or she is actually betting against the market that the spreads will widen further. This spread relationship is quite popular as the "TED spread" (Treasury-Eurodollar).

THE FUNDAMENTALS OF OPTIONS ON INTEREST RATE FUTURES

The potential risk in futures, despite the commensurate opportunity, may be undesirable for some investors. An alternative could be to select a CME option on interest rate futures. Purchasing an option involves all the benefits of futures with an added measure of security: maximum risk exposure established in advance, equal to the price of the option.

The CME offers options on all of its interest rate futures contracts. These option contracts grant the right to take a futures position at a stated price on or before the option's expiration date. A call option is the right, but not the obligation, to buy (go long) the underlying futures at a specific "exercise" or "strike" price; a put option is the right, but not the obligation, to sell (go short) the underlying futures at a specific strike price.

Both calls and puts have fixed expiration dates. For example, a 95.00 strike June call on a Eurodollar futures contract gives the option holder the right to purchase a June Eurodollar futures contract at a price of 95.00 any time until the call's expiration in mid-June.

For each option expiration, calls and puts are listed at several strike prices. Each strike represents a distinct option, just as calls and puts are distinct. To close out a purchased 95.00 strike June call position, you would sell the same call. Puts and calls are listed for trading with strike prices at every 25 basis points. For example, the available strikes could be at 95.00, 95.25, 95.50, 95.75, and so on. Performance bond is not required to buy an option. Instead, you would pay the premium, or price, in full for the call or the put at the time of the trade. This premium is found by multiplying the traded price of the option, which is expressed in index points (e.g., 1.00) times a multiplier of $2,500.

If you choose to offset the option before expiration, you can sell it back, in which case the gain or loss would simply reflect the price change over your holding period. If you exercise the option into a futures position, a performance bond would then be required—the same as for any futures position. Finally, if at expiration the option has no value, the position can be left to expire without taking any further action.

HEDGING WITH OPTIONS ON INTEREST RATE FUTURES

Case 1. Whenever T-bill or Eurodollar futures can be used to lock in a rate, options on futures can be substituted to guarantee a rate floor or ceiling. As an alternative to a long futures position, which predetermines a forward investment return for an asset, a long call can be substituted. The call gives the right to buy the futures contract at a stated price. This provides a floor for the asset return while preserving the opportunity for better performance. On the other hand, instead of taking a short futures position to predetermine a liability rate, a long put option can provide protection. The put gives the right to sell the futures at a stated price, providing a ceiling for the liability rate while preserving the opportunity for a lower cost of funds.

The floor or ceiling rate provided by the option is determined by its strike price and the premium paid. The "strike yield" (100 minus the option strike price) is adjusted to reflect the cost of the option. For example, suppose the following prices are used from *The Wall Street Journal* of Monday July 31 (see Appendix 2–A).

To summarize the listing, consider the September contracts.

Sep Eurodollar futures	94.24
Sep 94.00 strike call	0.27
Sep 94.25 strike call	0.09
Sep 94.00 strike put	0.03
Sep 94.25 strike put	0.10

Under these conditions, the user of the futures contracts locks in a target LIBOR of 5.76 percent (100.00 − 94.24)—an asset return if long or a liability cost if short. Subject to basis risk, this yield is locked up whether market rates rise or fall over the hedge period.

Using the 94.00 strike call to hedge a floating-rate investment, a hedger guarantees a minimum LIBOR return of 6 percent for a cost of 27 basis points. In other words, the realized minimum LIBOR return is 5.73 percent as a worst case (6.00 − 0.27).

If the rate falls below 6.00 percent, futures prices rise and the call option increases in value. The fallen investment rate on the asset is supplemented by the profit on the call to ensure a minimum net return of 5.73 percent. On the other hand, if the rate rises above 6 percent, the option is worthless at expiration, and the investor simply loses the cost of the option and receives the higher market rate on the asset.

Using the 94.25 strike call, the investment hedger establishes a minimum LIBOR return of 5.66 percent (100.00 − 94.25 − 0.09). Why use the 94.25 strike call rather than the 94.00 strike call when the 94.00 strike call offers a higher minimum return? The question goes to an important trade-off consideration.

While it is true that the 94.00 strike call provides a more attractive worst-case scenario, it does so for a larger up-front cost. The purchase of the 94.00 strike call cost $675 for this protection ($25 × 27 bp), while the cost of the 94.25 strike call is only $225 ($25 × 9 bp).

To hedge floating rate liabilities, put options present an analogous set of choices. A short futures contract establishes a forward LIBOR of 5.76; the 94.00 strike put provides a ceiling range of 6.03 percent (100.00 − 94.00 + 0.03) for the risk of $75 ($25 × 3 bp); and the 94.25 strike put provides a 5.85 percent (100.00 − 94.25 + 0.1) ceiling rate for the risk of $250 ($25 × 10bp).

Options offer a special advantage for hedging contingent liabilities or investments. If it is not certain whether funds are needed or available, interest rate options can secure a rate at the lowest risk. If the contingency eventually is not realized, forward or futures hedging commitments present sizable losses. The potential loss on long puts or calls, on the other hand, is limited to their purchase price, which is known in advance.

Case 2. The concept of "protective put" can be applied to hedge short-term interest rates. Let's assume, for example, that an issuer (or an investor) who is planning to sell 182-day commercial paper wants to be protected against any significant increase in the commercial paper rate. Since the 182-day commercial paper is highly correlated with six-month LIBOR, the six-month Eurodollar futures options contract will be used as the hedging vehicle. In this example, the settlement date for the futures contract coincides with the planned sale date of commercial paper.

Because the "underlying security" for the Eurodollar contract is the six-month LIBOR rate on the day the contract settles, the commercial paper seller uses a regression to establish the relationship between 182-day commercial paper (CP) and six-month LIBOR. Over a recent period, the regression gave the following results:

CP rate = .27 percent + .94 × LIBOR

The commercial paper rate is thus projected to equal the six-month LIBOR rate times .94, plus 27 basis points. Using this equation, the commercial paper seller can calculate the hedge ratio and the effective strike rate in terms of a commercial paper rate (as opposed to a LIBOR strike rate). For example, consider a put option on Eurodollar futures struck at 94.00, or 6 percent. To have meaning to the commercial paper seller, this strike must be translated into an equivalent commercial paper rate. Using the regression equation, this is easy:

CP rate = .27 percent + .94 × 6 percent = 5.91 percent

Thus, the Eurodollar option struck at 6 percent is roughly equivalent to an option on 182-day commercial paper struck at 5.91 percent. Obviously, we can go the other way as well. Given a desired strike rate for commercial paper, the equivalent six-month LIBOR rate can easily be found.

Suppose the commercial paper seller feels that 5.91 percent is about the right strike price and offers the right amount of protection. Thus, the 94.00 put is the option to buy. The remaining question is, how many puts should the hedger purchase? That is, what is the hedge ratio for the futures options hedge? The hedge ratio for this, or any, futures options hedge can be derived the same way as the hedge ratio for the futures hedge. The futures hedge ratio for short-term instrument is given by:

Hedge ratio = Yield beta × (PVBP of the hedged security/PVBP of the futures contract)

The relative price values of a basis point is obviously 182/182 = 1.0. Thus the hedge ratio is 0.94.

The cost of the puts can be easily added in to see the total effect of buying protection. Prices for Eurodollar puts are quoted in basis points and, like the Eurodollar futures contract, carry a value of $25 per basis point per contract. For example, if the commercial paper seller pays 15 basis points for each put, the dollar price is 15 × $25 = $375 for each option. However, as the hedge ratio indicates, for each $1 million of commercial paper, the seller must buy 0.94 options; therefore given a basis point cost per option, the total cost of option protection per million is 0.94 × 15 × $25 = $353. In terms of an incremental interest expense for the 182-day paper, $353 is equivalent to 14.1 basis points. However, if interest rates are low on the sale date, the Eurodollar options expire worthless and the commercial paper seller has no need for the insurance. The cost of the options lowers the effective sale price of the paper, and the effective sale rate for the paper is exactly 14.1 basis points higher at low interest rates than it would have been without the hedge.

Case 3. Suppose a financial manager has access to funding at three-month LIBOR plus 25 basis points, and she wants to put a limit on how this rate rises by the time she borrows in September. In effect, she wants insurance that pays off if rates increase but does not generate losses if rates fall. A Eurodollar put serves this purpose.

At the time of the decision (let's say July 1), three-month LIBOR is 5.75 percent, the September Eurodollar futures are trading at 93.60 (6.40 percent), and the 94.00 strike put is trading at .72. At these prices, this put provides a maximum cost of funds equal to 6.97 percent (100.00 – 94.00 + .72 + .25, where .25 reflects the spread above LIBOR).

When the put is purchased in July, the manager knows what she can expect in September. If LIBOR at the time is less than 6 percent, the put expires worthless and the manager simply borrows at LIBOR plus 25 basis points. Of course, she has to add the initial .72 cost of the put option to her total cost, but even with that expense it is never higher than 6.97 percent (6.00 + .25 + .72).

In the event that LIBOR rises above 6 percent, the price of the futures contract declines and the put has intrinsic value at its expiration equal to LIBOR minus 6 percent. Suppose, for example, LIBOR rises to 8.5 percent at the expiration of this option contract. In this case, the cost of funds from the bank is 8.75 percent (reflecting the 25 basis points spread) for an interest cost of $21,875 per million for the quarter ($1,000,000 × .0875 × 1/4 year). The final value of the 94.00 – strike put is $6,875 ((94.00 – 91.25) × $25). The profit on the put, $6,875 less its initial cost (72 bp. × $25 = $1,800), is deducted from the interest expense. Net interest expense thus is $16,800 per million for the quarter ($21,875 – 6,875 + 1,800) . On an annualized basis, the effective rate is calculated as:

$$\frac{16,800}{1,000,000} \times \frac{360}{90} = 6.72\%$$

It is important to note that this rate results regardless of how high market rates rise.

USING DIFFERENT SHORT-TERM INTEREST RATE INSTRUMENTS

Banks, security dealers, and other financial firms were the early users of financial futures and options for managing their interest rate exposures. Interest rate contracts are an obvious and effective risk management tool where uncertain interest income and expense are integral parts of a business.

Interest expense is an important expense component in nearly any type of business because interest rate volatility can have a major impact on earnings and cash flows. Any firm with a substantial interest rate exposure—temporary or permanent—should investigate the risk-minimizing benefits that financial futures and options can provide. The money market comprises the markets for short-term, heavily traded credit instruments with maturities of less than one year. Money market instruments include Treasury bills, commercial paper, bankers' acceptances, negotiable certificates of deposit (CDs), Federal funds, and short-term loans collateralized by such securities ("repos"). The markets for these instruments are distinct but interdependent. Their respective interest rates reflect general credit conditions with adjustments for differences in credit risk and liquidity.

The money market has expanded rapidly in recent years because of changing economic conditions. Volatile interest rates have advanced the rate of financial innovation. With the development of money market funds, small investors no longer were locked out of the money market by large minimum transaction barriers.

As both corporate and individual funds sought higher money market returns, negotiable CDs and Eurodollar time deposits (both developed in the 1960s) became key funding sources for banks. Floating rate deposits, a response to the growth of money market funds, further reduced a bank's core of stable-rate funds. As the banks found it necessary to pay money market rates for lendable funds, they became reluctant to make fixed-rate loans of longer maturities. So, even companies too small to participate in the commercial paper or Eurodollar market became indirect money market borrowers through bank loans based on floating rates.

Corporations today are making more aggressive use of cash management techniques. No longer willing to leave balances as unproductive, non–interest-earning demand deposits, the corporate cash manager places funds in short-term or overnight securities that have little or no credit risk. As these markets have become more liquid, corporate debt managers borrow in the commercial paper or Eurodollar markets when they offer a price advantage.

T-bills as an Important Money Market Instrument

U.S. Treasury bills are the foundation of the money markets because of their unique safety and liquidity. As direct obligations of the U.S. Treasury, they are considered risk-free debt instruments. Changes in the yields on T-bills reflect "pure" interest rate movements, free of the credit concerns that may dominate price movement in riskier securities. The most common maturity, 91-day (or 13-week) T-bills, are auctioned weekly by the U.S. Treasury.

The aggregate volume of T-bills outstanding has more than quadrupled in 15 years due to large government deficits. As a result, a large and active dealer network has developed. Dealers—who transact their own business over the telephone—buy and sell securities for their own accounts, arrange transactions with customers and other dealers, and buy debt directly from the Treasury for resale to investors. There are fewer than 40 primary dealers in T-bills, about a third of which represent commercial banks. Dealers, whose chief assets are inventories of T-bills, tend to be highly leveraged because they can easily borrow against those inventories.

Eurodollar Time Deposits as an Important Avenue to the International Market

As recently as 1970, the Eurodollar market, which now is perhaps the world's center of attention for dollar-denominated short-term interest rate trading, barely existed. Today, after more than 25 years—and partially as a result of the demand for dollar-denominated trade outside the United States and restrictive bank regulations within the United States—the total value of Eurodollar deposits outstanding has grown to more than $20 trillion. The International Swap Dealers Association found that by the end of 1994, there were nearly $25 trillion outstanding over-the-counter (OTC) derivative instruments such as interest rate swaps, caps, and floors. Most of these are tied somehow to a Eurodollar interest rate. Furthermore, at the CME the portfolio equivalent value of Eurodollar futures and options outstanding (open interest) by the end of 1994 was around $20 trillion.

Eurodollar time deposits are money market securities with a distinction. The deposit is not transferable and cannot be posted as physical collateral. However, Eurodollars are a very important part of the money markets because any short-range maturity date is always available for taking or placing deposits. A bank or corporation that has deposited Eurodollar funds can, at any point, borrow for the same maturity date. The effect is the same as the sale of a security because the funds are available again; the difference is that both transactions remain on the books until maturity date.

Being more risky, Eurodollar deposits typically have a higher interest rate than US Treasury bills. As direct obligations of the U.S. Treasury, T-bills are considered risk-free debt instruments. Eurodollar deposits are direct obligations of the commercial banks accepting the deposits and are not guaranteed by any government. Although they are considered low-risk investments, Eurodollar deposits are not risk free.

Since the Eurodollar futures contract was introduced by the CME in 1981 along with the Treasury bill futures contract, spreading between these two (the simultaneous purchase of one contract and sale of the other) has become increasingly popular. The reason for trading the TED (Treasury-Eurodollar) spread is to take action based on an opinion of what will happen to the rate differential between the two instruments.

The TED spread is a "quality play." One takes action on an opinion that, all else being equal, the gap between rates required for U.S. treasury bills and rates required for Eurodollar time deposits will widen or narrow. As the gap in rates moves, so does the gap in the prices of the respective futures instruments. If the gap in rates widens, then the gap in prices widens, and vice versa.

WHAT IS A "MARKET VIEW"?

Participating in short-term interest rate futures or options markets calls for a judgment on the direction of interest rates or, more specifically, three-month and one-year Treasury bills, one- and three-month Eurodollar deposits. In general, interest rates rise because the demand for funds exceeds the supply of funds at prevailing interest rates. As a result, rates typically rise during periods of economic expansion and tend to decline when the economy slows. If the inflation rate rises, the interest rate tends to rise to compensate investors for the decline in real returns.

Expectations of the direction of interest rate changes and the overall health of the economy also play a role in interest rate determination, influencing the plans and behavior of both those who supply funds (savers) and those who use funds (consumers and investors).

A crucial consideration underlying changes in interest rates is an assessment of economic policy. Central banks (in particular, the Federal Reserve Board and the Bundesbank) affect interest rates through monetary policies.

Government fiscal policy (spending and taxing practices) is also a major influence, affecting the overall supply and demand for funds and, ultimately, interest rates.

The various forces affecting short-term interest rates rarely operate in concert. As a consequence—even when backed with the best information, logic, and judgment—a trade can be undone by seemingly perverse money market behavior or simply inopportune timing. These are the complications, however, that bring both risk and commensurate reward to the aggressive investor.

CONCLUSION

Futures and options on futures provide alternatives for turning a market view into a market position. Suppose you want to profit from declining interest rates; two choices would be (1) to buy an interest rate futures contract or (2) to buy a call option. Both will produce a profit if interest rates fall (sufficiently). Each alternative will have a different outcome, however, depending upon how much and how fast interest rates actually change. In a similar fashion, to position for an interest rate rise, the two comparable choices would be (1) to sell an interest rate futures contract or (2) to buy a put option.

With the futures contract, the opportunities and risks are symmetric. A futures position could realize virtually unlimited profits; but it could result in virtually unlimited losses. On the other hand, a long options position offers something like insurance. If you've made the incorrect trading decision, your loss is limited to the original price of the option.

Additionally, the option buyer is confronted with yet another trade-off: A higher priced option will foster a larger payoff if your view proves to be correct. If you are wrong, however, the more expensive option translates into a larger loss. All options buyers must see at least some favorable price move in the underlying futures contract, just to break even. This required threshold movement is diminished, however, as you shift to successively more expensive options. A good way of viewing this issue is to realize that when holding options to expiration, a call would make money only if the underlying futures price rose above the strike price, plus the premium paid for the option; a put would make money only if the underlying futures price fell below the strike price, by the price paid for the option.

Short-term interest rate contracts give individual investors and money managers equal footing in the wholesale money markets. They can be used to minimize investment risk or to increase interest rate market exposure. The individual, the businessperson, and the banker no longer need be passive victims of interest rate circumstance. By using these futures and options, alone or in combination, each has the ability to determine a position in the market, control capital risk, and seek opportunity.

Appendix 2–A
Understanding Futures and Options Prices

Trading activity can be monitored daily in the business pages of most major newspapers. Exhibits 2–3 and 2–4 are illustrations from *The Wall Street Journal* of Monday, July 31, 1995. The numbers on Exhibit 2–3 refer to the numbered explanation below:

Futures

1. Contract delivery months that currently are traded.
2. Prices represent the open, high, low, and settlement (or closing) price for the previous day.
3. One day's change in the settlement price.
4. The interest rate implied by the settlement price.
5. One day's change in the future's interest rate equal and opposite to change in the settlement prices.
6. Number of contracts traded in the previous two trading sessions.
7. The number of contracts still in effect at the end of the previous day's trading session. Each unit represents a buyer and a seller who still have a contract position.
8. The total of the right column and the change from the prior trading day.

Options:

1. Most active strike prices.[*]
2. Expiration months.[*]
3. Closing prices for calls and puts.
4. Volume of options transacted in the previous two trading sessions. Each unit represents both the buyer and the seller.

---

[*] Note that further option expirations and strike prices usually will be available. Check with a broker for quotations.

EXHIBIT 2–3
Eurodollar Futures

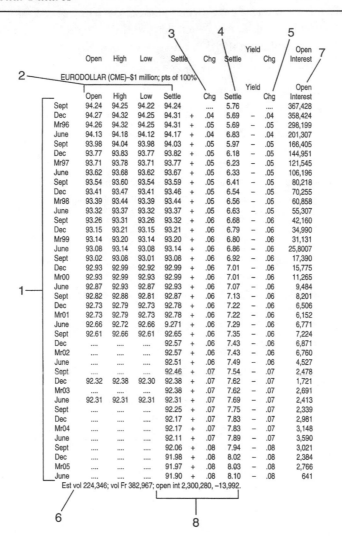

	Open	High	Low	Settle	Chg	Yield Settle	Chg	Open Interest
EURODOLLAR (CME)–$1 million; pts of 100%								
	Open	High	Low	Settle	Chg	Yield Settle	Chg	Open Interest
Sept	94.24	94.25	94.22	94.24	....	5.76	....	367,428
Dec	94.27	94.32	94.25	94.31	+ .04	5.69	– .04	358,424
Mr96	94.26	94.32	94.25	94.31	+ .05	5.69	– .05	298,199
June	94.13	94.18	94.12	94.17	+ .04	6.83	– .04	201,307
Sept	93.98	94.04	93.98	94.03	+ .05	5.97	– .05	166,405
Dec	93.77	93.83	93.77	93.82	+ .05	6.18	– .05	144,951
Mr97	93.71	93.78	93.71	93.77	+ .05	6.23	– .05	121,545
June	93.62	93.68	93.62	93.67	+ .05	6.33	– .05	106,196
Sept	93.54	93.60	93.54	93.59	+ .05	6.41	– .05	80,218
Dec	93.41	93.47	93.41	93.46	+ .05	6.54	– .05	70,255
Mr98	93.39	93.44	93.39	93.44	+ .05	6.56	– .05	60,858
June	93.32	93.37	93.32	93.37	+ .05	6.63	– .05	55,307
Sept	93.26	93.31	93.26	93.32	+ .06	6.68	– .06	42,160
Dec	93.15	93.21	93.15	93.21	+ .06	6.79	– .06	34,990
Mr99	93.14	93.20	93.14	93.20	+ .06	6.80	– .06	31,131
June	93.08	93.14	93.08	93.14	+ .06	6.86	– .06	25,8007
Sept	93.02	93.08	93.01	93.08	+ .06	6.92	– .06	17,390
Dec	92.93	92.99	92.92	92.99	+ .06	7.01	– .06	15,775
Mr00	92.93	92.99	92.93	92.99	+ .06	7.01	– .06	11,265
June	92.87	92.93	92.87	92.93	+ .06	7.07	– .06	9,484
Sept	92.82	92.88	92.81	92.87	+ .06	7.13	– .06	8,201
Dec	92.73	92.79	92.73	92.78	+ .06	7.22	– .06	6,506
Mr01	92.73	92.79	92.73	92.78	+ .06	7.22	– .06	6,152
June	92.66	92.72	92.66	9.271	+ .06	7.29	– .06	6,771
Sept	92.61	92.66	92.61	92.65	+ .06	7.35	– .06	7,224
Dec	....	....	....	92.57	+ .06	7.43	– .06	6,871
Mr02	....	....	....	92.57	+ .06	7.43	– .06	6,760
June	....	....	....	92.51	+ .06	7.49	– .06	4,527
Sept	....	....	....	92.46	+ .07	7.54	– .07	2,478
Dec	92.32	92.38	92.30	92.38	+ .07	7.62	– .07	1,721
Mr03	....	....	....	92.38	+ .07	7.62	– .07	2,691
June	92.31	92.31	92.31	92.31	+ .07	7.69	– .07	2,413
Sept	....	....	....	92.25	+ .07	7.75	– .07	2,339
Dec	....	....	....	92.17	+ .07	7.83	– .07	2,981
Mr04	....	....	....	92.17	+ .07	7.83	– .07	3,148
June	....	....	....	92.11	+ .07	7.89	– .07	3,590
Sept	....	....	....	92.06	+ .08	7.94	– .08	3,021
Dec	....	....	....	91.98	+ .08	8.02	– .08	2,384
Mr05	....	....	....	91.97	+ .08	8.03	– .08	2,766
June	....	....	....	91.90	+ .08	8.10	– .08	641

Est vol 224,346; vol Fr 382,967; open int 2,300,280, –13,992.

5. The number of option contracts (each unit represents both a long and a short) that were still open at the end of the previous day's trading session.

EXHIBIT 2–4
Treasury Bills and LIBOR Futures

TREASURY BILLS (CME)–$1 mil.; pts of 100%

	Open	High	Low	Settle	Chg	Discount Settle	Chg	Open Interest
Sept	94.65	94.67	94.65	94.65	....	5.35	....	8,350
Dec	94.72	94.78	94.72	94.77	+ .04	5.23	– .04	9.737
Mr96	94.68	94.73	94.67	94.73	+ .05	5.27	– .05	2,177

Est vol 11,189; vol Fr 1,548; open Int 20,279, –278.

LIBOR–1 MO. (CME)–$3,000,000; points of 100%

	Open	High	Low	Settle	Chg	Settle	Chg	
Aug	94.15	94.15	94.14	94.14	....	6.86	....	19,446
Sept	94.24	94.26	94.24	94.24	....	5.76	....	5,658
Oct	94.31	94.31	94.31	94.31	....	5.69	....	1,706
Nov	94.32	94.32	94.32	94.32	....	5.68	....	835
Dec	94.20	94.21	94.19	94.23	+ .02	6.77	– .02	582
Ja96	....	....	....	94.45	+ .04	5.55	– .04	75

Est vol 1,219; vol Fr 3,922; open Int 28,401

EXHIBIT 2–5
Eurodollar Options

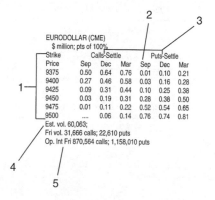

EXHIBIT 2–6
LIBOR Options

LIBOR - 1 Mo. (CME)
$3 million; pts. of 100%

Strike Price	Calls-Settle			Puts-Settle		
	Aug	Sept	Oct	Aug	Sept	Oct
9425	0.01	0.08	....	0.12	0.09	0.14

Est vol 5 0 calls 0 puts
Op Int Fri 574 calls 1,089 puts

Appendix 2–B
Interest Rate Futures and Options Contracts

EXHIBIT 2–7
Chicago Mercantile Exchange
Interest Rate Futures and Options Contract Highlights— *Three-Month*
Eurodollar Time Deposits

Futures	Options on Futures
Ticker Symbol	
ED	Calls—CE; Puts—PE
Contract Size	
$1,000,000	One ED futures contract
Price/Premium Quotation	
IMM index points	
Strike Prices	
NA	.25 intervals, e.g., 94.25, 94.50, 94.75
Minimum Price Fluctuation (Tick)[1]	
.01 = $25.00/contract	
Price Limits	
None for regular trading hours[2]	
Contract Months	
Mar., June, Sept., Dec.	Mar.
Trading Hours[2,4] (Chicago Time)	
7:20 A.M.–2:00 P.M. (Last day: 7:20 A.M.– 9:30 A.M.)	7:20 A.M.–2:00 P.M. (Last day March Quarterly: 7:20 A.M.–9:30 A.M.)
Last Day of Trading	

Futures: The second London business day immediately preceding the third Wednesday of the contract month.

Exhibit continues

EXHIBIT 2–7
continued

Futures	*Options on Futures*

Ticker Symbol

March Quarterly Cycle Options: Second London business day immediately preceding the third Wednesday of the contract month; **Serial Options** (Jan., Feb., Apr., May, July, Aug., Oct., and Nov.): Friday immediately preceding third Wednesday of contract month; **Mid-Curve Options:** (Mar., June, Sept., Dec.): Friday immediately preceding third Wednesday of contract month.

Futures Final Settlement: Cash settlement to CME survey of London interbank market. Consult your broker or the CME for specific procedures.

Options Exercise: An option may be exercised until 7:00 P.M. (Chicago time) on any business day the option is traded. An option that is in-the-money and has not been exercised prior to the termination of trading shall, in the absence of contrary instructions delivered to the Clearing House by 7:00 P.M. on the day of termination of trading, be automatically exercised.

---

[1] An option trade may occur at the value of a half-tick (cabinet).
[2] This contract also is traded on the GLOBEX® system. Contact your broker or the CME for specific GLOBEX trading hours and price limits.
[3] Options on ED futures are listed for all 12 calendar months. March quarterly-cycle and serial options are exercisable into the March-quarterly, quarter-end futures contract. For example, Jan, Feb and Mar options are exercisable into the March futures contract. At any point in time, you can choose from options that expire in the next three calendar months, plus five March-quarterly expirations and two 2-Year and two 5-Year Mid-Curve option expirations.
[4] Trading will end at 12:00 noon on the business day before a CME holiday and on any U.S. bank holiday that the CME is open.

EXHIBIT 2–8
Thirteen-Week U.S. Treasury Bills

Futures	Options on Futures
Ticker Symbol	
TB	Calls—CO; Puts—PQ
Contract Size	
$1,000,000	One T-bill futures contract
Price/Premium Quotation	
IMM index points	
Strike Prices	
NA	.25 intervals, e.g., 93.00, 93.25, 94.50
Minimum Price Fluctuation (Tick)[1]	
.01 = $25.00/contract	
Price Limits	
None for regular trading hours[2]	
Contract Months	
Mar., June, Sept., and Dec.	
Trading Hours[2,3] (Chicago Time)	
7:20 A.M.–2:00 P.M. (Last day: 7:20 A.M.–10:00 A.M.)	7:20 A.M.–2:00 P.M.
Last Day of Trading	

Futures: The business day immediately preceding the first delivery day (first day of contract month that issuance of new 13-week bill coincides with 13 weeks to maturity in old one-year bill).

Options: The last business day of the week preceding by at least six business days the first business day of underlying contract month.

Exhibit continues

EXHIBIT 2–8
continued

Futures Final Settlement: Physical delivery of 13-week U.S. Treasury bills; contact your broker or the CME for specific procedures.

Options Exercise: An option may be exercised until 7:00 P.M. (Chicago time) on any business day the option is traded. An option that is in-the-money and has not been exercised prior to the termination of trading shall, in the absence of contrary instructions delivered to the Clearing House by 7:00 P.M. on the day of termination of trading, be automatically exercised.

---

[1] An option trade may occur at the value of a half-tick (cabinet).

[2] This contract also is traded on the GLOBEX® system. Contact your broker or the CME for specific GLOBEX trading hours and price limits.

[3] Options on ED futures are listed for all 12 calendar months. March quarterly-cycle and serial options are exercisable into the March-quarterly, quarter-end futures contract. For example, Jan, Feb and Mar options are exercisable into the March futures contract. At any point in time, you can choose from options that expire in the next three calendar months, plus five March-quarterly expirations and two 2-Year and two 5-Year Mid-Curve option expirations.

[4] Trading will end at 12:00 noon on the business day before a CME holiday and on any U.S. bank holiday that the CME is open.

EXHIBIT 2–9
One-Month LIBOR

Futures	*Options on Futures*
Ticker Symbol	
EM	Calls—EM; Puts—EM
Contract Size	
$3,000,000	One LIBOR futures contract
Price/Premium Quotation	
IMM index points	
Strike Prices	
NA	.25 intervals, e.g., 94.25, 94.50, 94.75
Minimum Price Fluctuation (Tick)[1]	
.01 = $25.00/contract	
Price Limits	
None for regular trading hours[2]	
Contract Months	
All 12 calendar months[3]	
Trading Hours[2,4] (Chicago Time)	
7:20 A.M.–2:00 P.M. (Last day: 7:20 A.M.–9:30 A.M.)	
Last Day of Trading	

The second London bank business day immediately preceding the third Wednesday of contract month.

Futures Final Settlement: Cash settlement to CME survey of London interbank market. Contact your broker or the CME for specific procedures.

Options Exercise: An option may be exercised until 7:00 P.M. (Chicago time) on any business day the option is traded. An option that is in the money and has not been exercised prior to the termination of trading shall, in the absence of contrary instructions de-

Table continues

EXHIBIT 2–9
continued

livered to the Clearing House by 7:00 P.M. on the day of termination of trading, be automatically exercised.

---

[1] An option trade may occur at the value of a half-tick (cabinet).
[2] This contract also is traded on the GLOBEX® system. Contact your broker or the CME for specific GLOBEX trading hours and price limits.
[3] Options on ED futures are listed for all 12 calendar months. March quarterly-cycle and serial options are exercisable into the March-quarterly, quarter-end futures contract. For example, Jan, Feb and Mar options are exercisable into the March futures contract. At any point in time, you can choose from options that expire in the next three calendar months, plus five March-quarterly expirations and two 2-Year and two 5-Year Mid-Curve option expirations.
[4] Trading will end at 12:00 noon on the business day before a CME holiday and on any U.S. bank holiday that the CME is open.

GLOSSARY

add-on yield Standard yield calculation for Eurodollars; relates annualized interest to original principal.

asset-liability management The process by which a bank or institution monitors its portfolio of assets and liabilities to control company-wide interest rate exposure. There are three standard measures: gap analysis, which measures the mismatch in discrete time intervals; ratio analysis, typically rate-sensitive assets divided by rate-sensitive liabilities; and profit sensitivity, a measure of predicted changes in profit from a six-month or one-year interest rate increase of 100 basis points.

basis The price or yield difference between a futures contract and the underlying cash instrument; the primary risk in a hedge is a basis shift.

call option An option that gives the holder the right to enter a long futures position at a specific price and obligates the seller to enter a short futures position at a specific price, if he is assigned for exercise.

clearing house An adjunct to a futures exchange through which transactions executed on the floor of the exchange are settled by a process that matches purchases and sales. A clearing organization also is charged with the proper conduct of delivery procedures and the adequate financing of the entire operation.

convergence The movement of a futures price toward the price of the underlying cash instrument as the delivery date approaches (the basis with the deliverable instrument approaches zero). Until the settlement date draws near, there is a natural difference between the cash and the futures price because of the cost of carry.

cost of carry The cost of holding a commodity, including financing cost, storage, and security. In the case of interest-paying securities, a negative cost of carry (benefit of carry) exists when the security yields in excess of the short-term financing cost.

cross-hedge Hedging a cash market position with a futures contract for a different, but price-related commodity. Example: hedging commercial paper with Eurodollar futures.

daily settlement The cash adjustment required by futures participants who are charged for losses or credited for gains at the end of each trading day.

discount yield Some money market instruments, principally T-bills and commercial paper, are priced on the basis of a discount from par value. The ratio of the annualized discount to the par value is the discount yield.

exercise (strike) price The price at which the futures transaction takes place if the option holder exercises the option.

forward contract A contractual agreement between two parties to exchange a commodity at a set price on a future date; differs from a futures contract because most forward commitments are not actively traded or standardized, are not marked to market, and carry a risk from the creditworthiness of the other side of the transaction.

futures contract A standardized contract, traded on an organized exchange, to buy or sell a fixed quantity of a defined commodity at a set price in the future. Positions easily can be closed or offset by taking the other side in the open outcry auction.

gap analysis A technique to measure interest rate sensitivity. Assets and liabilities of a defined interest-sensitivity maturity are netted to produce the exposure in established time intervals. Rate sensitivity liabilities are subtracted from assets. A positive (negative) result denotes a positive (negative) gap. With an overall positive (negative) gap, an institution is exposed to falling (rising) interest rates.

hedge An attempt to reduce risk by either (1) taking a futures or option position opposite to an existing or anticipated cash position or (2) shorting a security similar to the cash position.

hedge management Monitoring a hedge for basis risk and the changing sensitivity of the cash position.

hedge ratio The number of futures or options contracts used in a given hedge.

intrinsic value The value of the option if it were exercised immediately. It is the amount that the futures price is higher than a call's exercise price; or the amount that the futures price is below a put's exercise price.

LIBOR London Interbank Offered Rate on Eurodollar deposits traded between banks. The IMM's Eurodollar deposit contract is based on the three-month LIBOR.

long hedge A hedge in which the futures contract is bought (a long position). Long hedges can be used to protect the investment of future cash flows (anticipatory) and to shorten the interest-sensitivity duration of a liability.

money market The market in which short-term instruments are issued and traded. Money market instruments have a maturity of one year or less and include T-bills, commercial paper, CDs, Banker's acceptances, and repurchase agreements.

put option An option that gives the holder the right to enter a short futures position and obligates the seller to enter a long futures position at a specific price if he or she is assigned for exercise.

short hedge A hedge that involves the selling (shorting) of a futures contract. A short hedge guards against a price decrease in the underlying commodity; a short position in interest rate futures protects the hedger from rising rates.

time value The part of the option price that is not intrinsic value. It is the risk premium demanded by the option seller, and it depends on the relationship of the futures price to the exercise price, the volatility of the futures price and the amount of time remaining until expiration.

volatility The degree of price fluctuation in the futures contract. Volatility is commonly defined as one standard deviation of price moves over a one-year period, expressed as a percentage of the current price. One standard deviation added to and subtracted from the current futures price describes the range, which encompasses two-thirds of all price moves in the sample.

REFERENCES

Chicago Mercantile Exchange. "Using Short-Term Interest Rate Futures and Options." Chapter 2 in *The Handbook of Derivative Instruments—Investment Research, Analysis and Portfolio Applications.* A. Konishi and R. Dattatreya, eds. Chicago, IL: Probus Publishing, 1991.

Fabozzi, Frank. *Fixed Income Mathematics.* Chicago, IL: Probus Publishing, 1993.

Fabozzi, Frank, ed. *The Handbook of Fixed-Income Securities,* 4th ed. Chicago, IL: Probus Publishing, 1995.

Hull, John C. *Options, Futures and Other Derivative Securities,* 2nd ed. Englewood Cliffs, NJ: Prentice Hall, 1993.

Chapter Three

Hedging with Bond and Note Futures[*]

Galen D. Burghardt
Dean Witter Reynolds

Terrence M. Belton
JP Morgan Futures

Bond and bond futures prices rise and fall together. As a result, bond futures can be used as a vehicle for trading the general level of bond prices without trading the bonds themselves. Bond futures, therefore, can be used to hedge the price exposure in a bond position. Hedging with bond futures, however, requires an understanding of how the futures contract works.

A widely held misconception about Treasury bond futures is that the contract is based on a 20-year, 8 percent coupon Treasury bond. In fact, bond futures are based on a deliverable basket of Treasury bonds with widely different price and yield characteristics. Furthermore, a short bond futures position contains a number of valuable strategic delivery options that affect the behavior of the futures price.

Even though bond futures have no yield, bond futures prices can be linked to the yields on the underlying basket of deliverable bonds. Thus, if we trace these linkages, we can calculate the dollar value of a basis point ($DV01$), the yield value of a 32nd, or the duration of a futures contract where the

---

[*] Reprinted from *The Treasury Bond Basis*, rev. ed., by Galen D. Burghardt, Terrence M. Belton, Morton Lane, and John Papa (Burr Ridge, IL: Irwin Professional Publishing, 1994), pp. 89–117.

yield that is changing is the yield of a given deliverable bond. With these values, we are equipped to calculate hedge ratios.

In this chapter, we lay out the mechanics of what we think is the best way to reckon hedge ratios using Treasury bond and note futures. Along the way, we explain what you have to know about the concept of duration and what it means to impute a duration to a futures contract. We show you how to calculate "option-adjusted durations" or "option-adjusted $DV01$s," and how they are used in practice to calculate hedge ratios. We also explain the logic behind two widely used rules of thumb and what the shortcomings in these rules of thumb are. We finish the chapter with some evidence that supports our belief that option-adjusted hedge ratios are better than thumb-rule hedge ratios.

DURATION

Duration, as defined by Macaulay, is a weighted average of the times remaining to various cash flows where the weights are the relative present values of those cash flows, or:

$$\text{Macaulay duration} = \sum \frac{tP_tC_t}{P}$$

where t is the time between now and a cash flow (measured in years), $P_t = 1/(1 + r_t)^t$ is the price of a \$1 zero-coupon bond that matures t periods from now; C_t is the amount of cash flow to be paid or received t years from now; and P is the market price of the entire instrument. Measured this way, the units are years. For example, a 10-year Treasury note might have a duration of seven years.

Measured in years, Macaulay's duration is of no particular use to anyone. Transformed, however, duration has several useful properties, including:

- Its use as a risk measure.
- Its additivity.
- Its use in calculating hedge ratios.

It is used widely in managing bond portfolios.

Risk measure. To get a useful measure of the sensitivity of a bond's price to a change in its yield, we define *modified duration* as:

$$\text{Modified duration} = \frac{\text{Macaulay duration}}{1 + \dfrac{r}{f}}$$

where r is the annualized yield on the instrument and f is the payment frequency (e.g., $f = 2$ for a Treasury instrument to reflect semiannual coupon payments). In this form, duration is the link between yield changes and price changes. In particular,

Percent price change $\approx$ Modified duration $\times$ Yield change

where the yield change is expressed in percentage points. Hence, modified duration tells us the percent change in the price of a bond for a one-percentage-point (100-basis-point) change in the bond's yield.

For example, on August 6, 1992, the 9⅞s coupon Treasury bond maturing November 15, 2015, had a modified duration of 10.25. At 2 P.M. Chicago time its price was 126-19.25/32nds (or 126.6016) to yield 7.449 percent to maturity. Its full price including accrued interest was 128.9361. A modified duration of 10.25 indicates that a one-percentage point increase in the bond's yield would cause its price to fall by 10.25 percent of its full price, or 13.22 [= 0.1025 × 128.9361] points. If the yield on this bond increased 10 basis points to 7.549 percent, the bond's modified duration indicates that the bond's price would fall by approximately 1.322 points, or slightly more than ⁴²⁄₃₂.

Additivity. A second helpful property is that the duration of a cash bond portfolio is simply a weighted average of the durations of the component bonds. The weights are the relative holdings, at market prices, of the bonds in the portfolio. For example, a portfolio containing $50 million market value of a bond with a duration of 10 and $100 million market value of a bond with a duration of 6 has a duration of:

$$7.3 = \frac{(\$50 \times 10 + \$100 \times 6)}{(\$50 + \$100)}$$

Hedge ratio. Because of the relationship between a bond's or note's duration and its dollar value of a basis point, durations can be used in quick and easy hedge calculations. If the purpose of a hedge is to offset the price exposure in a portfolio, then the number of futures contracts that the hedger holds, when multiplied by the change in the value of one futures contract, should equal the negative of the change in the value of the portfolio

EXHIBIT 3–1
Futures Hedge Algebra

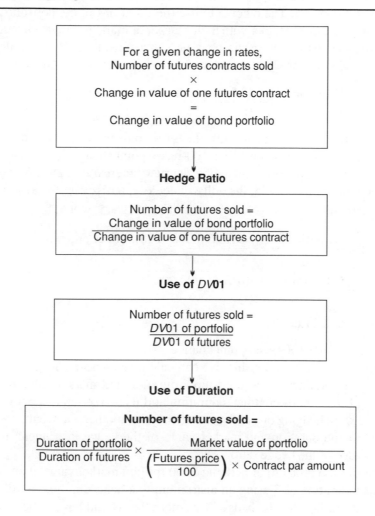

For a given change in rates,
Number of futures contracts sold
×
Change in value of one futures contract
=
Change in value of bond portfolio

Hedge Ratio

Number of futures sold =
$$\frac{\text{Change in value of bond portfolio}}{\text{Change in value of one futures contract}}$$

Use of *DV*01

Number of futures sold =
$$\frac{DV01 \text{ of portfolio}}{DV01 \text{ of futures}}$$

Use of Duration

Number of futures sold =

$$\frac{\text{Duration of portfolio}}{\text{Duration of futures}} \times \frac{\text{Market value of portfolio}}{\left(\dfrac{\text{Futures price}}{100}\right) \times \text{Contract par amount}}$$

to be hedged. If this condition is met, then the hedger will make as much on the hedge as is lost on the portfolio or will lose as much on the hedge as is made on the portfolio.

Either way, as shown in Exhibit 3–1, the appropriate number of futures to sell to hedge a long bond position is found simply by dividing the change in the value of the portfolio for any given change in yields by the change in the value of one futures contract. This can be done in either of two ways.

One way is to calculate the hedge ratio directly by dividing the dollar value of a basis point of the portfolio by the dollar value of a basis point for one futures contract. The other is to use the durations of the portfolio and the futures contract together with their market or market-equivalent values. What allows you to do this is that an issue's or a portfolio's $DV01$ is roughly proportional to the product of its duration and market value—in particular:

$$DV01 \approx \frac{\text{Duration} / 100 \times \text{MarketValue}}{100}$$

where the dividing through by 100 reflects the convention of stating duration as the percent change in value for a 100-basis-point change in the yield. For example, with a full price including accrued interest of 128.9361 and a modified duration of 10.25, the dollar value of a basis point for $1 million face or par amount of the $9\frac{7}{8}$s of November 15, 2015, would be:

$$DV01 \approx \frac{(\text{Duration} / 100) \times (\text{Full price}/ 100) \times \text{Face amount}}{100}$$

$$= \frac{0.1025 \times 1.289361 \times \$1,000,000}{100}$$

$$= \$1,321.60$$

or $132,160 for a 100-basis-point change.

Armed with this relationship, we can calculate the same hedge ratio by dividing the product of the portfolio's duration and market value by the product of the futures contract's duration and its market-equivalent value. Or, if we were hedging one cash instrument with another, we would use the product of the duration and market value of the hedge instrument in the denominator of the hedge ratio.

Consider the problem of hedging $100 million market value of an issue that has a duration of 5 using an instrument that has a duration of 10. The number of millions of the hedge instrument that would have to be sold or shorted would be calculated as:

$$\text{Amount to sell} = \frac{5 \times \$100 \text{ million}}{10 \times \$1 \text{ million}}$$

$$= \frac{\$500}{\$10}$$

$$= 50$$

That is, the hedger would sell $50 million of the hedge instrument to off-set the interest rate exposure in the portfolio. A check on this hedge can be made by calculating the duration of the hedged portfolio, which would be:

$$\text{Hedged portfolio duration} = \frac{(5 \times \$100) - (10 \times \$50)}{\$100 - \$50}$$

$$= 0$$

DURATION OF A FUTURES CONTRACT

Fitting bond futures into this hedging framework poses two challenges, both stemming from the fact that bond futures have neither periodic cash payments nor a yield to maturity. This means that bond futures have no market value in the same sense that a bond or note has a market value. Also, it means that we cannot calculate the duration of a futures contract as we do a cash bond.

We meet the first challenge simply by treating a bond or note futures contract for the purpose of measuring price risk as if it has the portfolio-equivalent value of $100,000 face value of an actual bond or note ($200,000 for the two-year note contract). Thus, if the futures price were 105, the portfolio-equivalent value of the futures contract would be $105,000. In other words, the price risk in one futures contract would be the same as the price risk of $105,000 market value of a bond or note with the same duration. One must still be careful in reckoning the duration of a portfolio that contains bond and note futures, however. As we show at the end of this chapter, bond and note futures contribute price risk to a portfolio but no market value. As a result, their portfolio-equivalent values appear in the numerator of the duration calculation but not in the denominator. See Exhibit 3–12 on page 80 for an example.

We meet the duration challenge by linking the price sensitivity of the futures contract to a change in the yields of the deliverable bonds. Once we have established the relationship between the price of the futures contract and the yields of the deliverable bonds, we can tie *changes* in the futures price directly to *changes* in the cheapest to deliver bond's yield. Thus, we can calculate the duration of a futures contract directly by dividing the percent change in the futures price by the change in the yield of the cheapest to deliver bond.

OPTION-ADJUSTED HEDGE RATIOS

The link between the futures price and the price of the cheapest to deliver bond or note can be written as:

$$\text{Futures price} = \frac{\text{CTD price} - \text{Carry} - \text{Delivery option value}}{\text{CTD factor}}$$

where CTD price is the price of the cheapest to deliver bond or note and CTD factor is its conversion factor. This is an especially useful way of expressing this relationship because it highlights what is needed to capture the effect of a change in the yield of the cheapest to deliver on the futures price. Namely, in addition to determining the effect of a yield change on the price of the cheapest to deliver, we also have to reckon its effect on the value of carry and the value of the short's strategic delivery options.

Option-adjusted futures prices. The first step in calculating an option-adjusted duration for bond futures is to project futures prices over a range of bond yields. We do this by calculating price, carry, and delivery option value for each deliverable bond over a range of yields. At each yield level, we determine the cheapest to deliver bond and project the futures price using the pricing equation shown above.

A sample of the output of our futures projection model is shown in Exhibit 3–2, which shows three price/yield change relationships for April 4, 1990. One is for the converted price (spot price divided by conversion factor) of the 14s of November 2006; one is for the converted price of the 7¼s of 2016; and one is for the projected futures price. Bond yields at the time this exhibit was drawn were in the neighborhood of 8.5 percent to 8.75 percent, and we have drawn the chart for yield changes of 100 basis points up and down from those levels.

The projected futures price/yield relationship should look right in several respects. Note, for example, that the projected futures price is lower than either of the converted bond prices at every yield level. Part of the difference is the effect of carry. Much of the difference, however, and especially at yield levels where uncertainty about the cheapest to deliver bond is greater, is the value of the short's strategic delivery options.

Note, too, that at extremely low yields, the futures price behaves very much like the price of the 14s, a low-duration bond. At low yields, the chances that a low-duration bond will be cheapest to deliver are high, and the weight given the delivery of a high-duration bond is low. Thus, at low yields, the futures contract has a low duration.

EXHIBIT 3–2
Projected Treasury Bond Futures Price

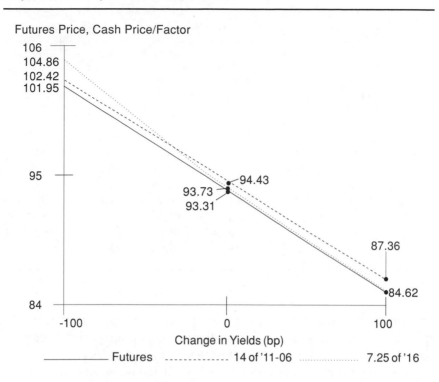

Futures Price, Cash Price/Factor

In contrast, the projected futures price behaves much like the price of the 7¼s when yields are high. Thus, at high yields, the futures contract has a high duration. For that matter, if yields had been 100 basis points higher than they were on April 4, there would have been no difference between the futures price and the converted price of the 7¼s of 2016. Carry on this issue was negligible, and the short's strategic delivery options would have been worthless.

At the crossover point, which falls about 30 basis points lower than the level of yields on April 4, uncertainty about the deliverable bond is high, and the sensitivity of the futures price is somewhere between that of the two bonds.

Futures convexity. In one important respect, the shape of the futures price/yield relationship is radically different from the price/yield relationship of a conventional bond. In bond parlance, bonds exhibit "posi-

EXHIBIT 3–3
Theoretical Futures Prices at Various Yields *(April 4, 1990)*

	Bond		10-Year Note		5-Year Note	
Yield Change (basis points	*Yield of 11.75 off '14-09*	*Theoretical Futures Price (decimal)*	*Yield of 8.00 of 8/99*	*Theoretical Futures Price (decimal)*	*Yield of 7.75 of 2/95*	*Theoretical Futures Price (decimal)*
+100	9.74	84.62	9.57	90.41	9.57	94.08
+50	9.24	88.89	9.07	93.32	9.07	95.87
+20	8.94	91.54	8.77	95.10	8.77	96.96
+10	8.84	92.43	8.67	95.69	8.67	97.32
0	8.74	93.31	8.57	96.26	8.57	97.69
−10	8.64	94.20	8.47	96.87	8.47	98.05
−20	8.54	95.07	8.37	97.46	8.37	98.42
−50	8.24	97.68	8.07	99.18	8.07	99.51
−100	7.74	101.95	7.57	101.93	7.57	101.34

tive convexity," which means that their prices become more sensitive to changes in yields as yields fall. Bond futures, in contrast, exhibit negative convexity over a wide range of yields; that is, bond futures prices become less sensitive to changes in yields as yields fall and more sensitive to yield changes as yields rise.

The difference in their behavior influences the effect of a change in yields on the durations of the two instruments. For example, an increase in yields reduces the duration of a coupon bond. In contrast, an increase in yields can increase the duration of a futures contract.

The same theory, though with different deliverable issues, works for Treasury note futures as well.

Exhibit 3–3 shows projected prices for Treasury bond futures and for both 10-year and 5-year Treasury note futures. The bond futures prices are shown against hypothetical yields for the $11\frac{3}{4}$s of '14-09, the 10-year contract against hypothetical yields for the 8s of August 1999, and the 5-year contract against hypothetical yields for the $7\frac{3}{4}$s of February 1995.

Option-adjusted durations. These price/yield relationships were used to calculate the durations shown in Exhibit 3–4. For example, if we define futures duration for a 100-basis-point move up and down in the yield

EXHIBIT 3–4
Option-Adjusted Durations for June Bond and Note Futures (April 1990)

	Bond		10-Year Note		5-Year Note	
Duration Calculated Over	*4/4/90*	*4/16/90*	*4/4/90*	*4/16/90*	*4/4/90*	*4/16/90*
± 10 bp	9.47	9.54	6.13	6.27	3.73	3.77
± 20 bp	9.47	9.53	6.13	6.26	3.73	3.77
± 50 bp	9.42	9.47	6.09	6.22	3.72	3.76
± 100 bp	9.29	9.31	5.98	6.12	3.72	3.74
CTD:						
Duration	8.52	9.66	6.36	6.31	3.86	3.83
Coupon	(11.75)	(10.625)	(8.0)	(8.0)	(7.75)	(7.75)
Next CTD:						
Duration	9.78	9.93	6.01	6.31	3.63	3.60
Coupon	(10.625)	(9.25)	(8.875)	(7.875)	(8.25)	(8.25)

of an underlying bond, we find that the duration of the June bond futures contract on April 4 was 9.29 [= $100 \times (101.95 - 84.62) / (2 \times 93.31)$].

Exhibit 3–4 provides a number of useful insights. Notice, for example, that the duration of the bond futures contract on April 4 is higher than the duration of the cheapest to deliver. This is because the futures price projections put a high weight on the likelihood that a high-duration bond will be cheapest to deliver at expiration.

Notice, too, that the duration of the cheapest to deliver rose much more dramatically than did the duration of the futures contract between the 4th and the 16th. This is because yields rose over the period and brought about a shift in the cheapest to deliver from the 11¾s to the 10⅝s. (You can see as well that the increase in yields reduced, as it should have, the duration of the 10⅝s between the 4th and the 16th.)

Also, the practical hedger should notice that the duration estimate depends on how wide a range of yield changes is used. In this case, estimated futures duration is higher for smaller changes than for larger changes. For most hedging problems, the duration estimates based on 10- or 20-basis-point yield changes might be more appropriate than the estimate based on a 100-basis-point swing in either direction.

Calculating option-adjusted hedge ratios. Using the option-adjusted duration of a futures contract or its option-adjusted $DV01$ is simplicity itself. Consider the problem of hedging the 8s of November 2021 on August 7, 1992. As shown in Exhibit 3–5, its modified duration was 11.51 percent against a full price of 108.3444. The dollar value of a basis point for the issue was $124.68 per $100,000 face value. At the bottom of Exhibit 3–5, we see that the option-adjusted duration of the September 1992 futures contract was estimated to be 10.44 percent against a futures price of $105^4/_{32}$s. The option-adjusted $DV01$ of the futures was estimated to be $109.75. Notice that the option-adjusted $DV01$ equals the portfolio-equivalent value of the futures contract times its option-adjusted duration (divided by 100 to produce the change for a one basis point change in yield), or:

$$\$109.75 = \$105,125 \times \frac{0.1044}{100}$$

With this, we can calculate a hedge ratio for the 8s either by using durations or by using dollar values of a basis point. If we use durations, the hedge ratio per $100,000 face amount of the 8s would be calculated as:

$$\text{Hedge ratio} = \frac{\$108,344 \times 0.1151}{\$105,125 \times 0.1044}$$

$$= 1.136$$

which is the number shown in column 11 of Exhibit 3–5. If we use the dollar value of a basis point, the hedge ratio per $100,000 face amount is simply:

$$\text{Hedge ratio} = \frac{\$124.68}{\$109.75}$$

$$= 1.136$$

The answers are the same, of course, because the two approaches are simply different ways of solving the same problem.

STANDARD RULES OF THUMB

For several years, the industry has relied on two rules of thumb for determining hedge ratios. Both rules of thumb are based on the assumption that the futures price is driven by the price of the cheapest to deliver. The reasoning behind the rules of thumb is comparatively simple and straightforward, but as we will show in this section, the two thumb rules are not

EXHIBIT 3-5
Deliverable Notes and Bonds (Delivery Month: September 1992)

2-year note futures = 106 2/32nds
5-year note futures = 108 31/32nds
10-year note futures = 108 8/32nds
Bond futures = 105 4/32nds
RP = 3.35%

Price data = 8/6/92
Trade data = 8/7/92
Settlement date = 8/10/92
First delivery date = 9/1/92 (Days remaining = 22)
Futures expiration date = 9/21/92 (Days remaining = 42)
Last delivery date = 9/30/92 (Days remaining = 51)

Note/ Bond	Coupon	Maturity	2:00 P.M. Cash Price (32nds)	Conversion Factor	Basis (32nds)	Yield	Yield Value of a 32nd	Dollar Value of a Basis Point	Modified Duration	Option-Adjusted Hedge Ratio	Cash Price + Accrued Interest (decimal)	Carry in Dollars per Day	Carry in 32nds per Day	Total Carry in 32nds to Last Delivery Day	Implied RP Rate to First Delivery Day	Implied RP Rate to Last Delivery Day
(1)	(2)	(3)	(4)	(5)	(6)	(7)	(8)	(9)	(10)	(11)	(12)	(13)	(14)	(15)	(16)	(17)
T	5.000	06/30/94	101.1250	0.9518	11.24	4.224	0.01722	18.14	1.78	1.049	101.9477	41.00	0.1312	6.691	−0.84	2.37
T	8.500	06/30/94	107.2300	1.0078	23.50	4.202	0.01654	18.89	1.74	1.092	108.6658	129.86	0.4158	21.193	−3.41	2.88
T02	4.250	07/31/94	99.3050	0.9371	15.17	4.274	0.01669	18.73	1.87	10.82	100.0686	22.37	0.0715	3.651	−3.60	0.81
T	6.875	08/15/94	104.3000	0.9803	27.92	4.289	0.01586	19.70	1.82	1.139	108.2806	90.40	0.2892	14.753	−7.13	0.55
T	8.625	08/15/94	108.0800	1.0108	30.31	4.304	0.01555	20.10	1.79	1.162	112.4440	135.19	0.4326	22.062	−6.45	1.62
T	8.500	09/30/94	108.1250	1.0091	40.59	4.346	0.01466	21.31	1.91	1.232	111.4562	129.16	0.4133	21.079	−11.12	−0.53
F	6.125	12/31/96	102.1125	0.9334	20.48	5.513	0.00800	39.07	3.79	0.934	103.0340	70.56	0.2257	11.516	−4.35	1.43
F	6.250	01/31/97	102.2100	0.9368	18.38	5.570	0.00786	39.74	3.86	0.950	102.8261	74.15	0.2378	12.102	−3.19	2.00
F	6.750	02/28/97	104.1825	0.9542	18.95	5.599	0.00765	40.82	3.80	0.976	107.5622	86.48	0.2767	14.113	−2.90	2.34
F	6.875	03/31/97	104.3175	0.9582	18.51	5.635	0.00752	41.55	3.87	0.993	107.4717	88.35	0.2827	14.418	−2.51	2.49
F	6.875	04/30/97	104.3000	0.9574	19.55	5.666	0.00741	42.16	3.95	1.008	106.8431	87.40	0.2797	14.263	−3.06	2.26

Table continues

EXHIBIT 3-5
continued

(1) Note/ Bond	(2) Coupon	(3) Maturity	(4) 2:00 P.M. Cash Price (32nds)	(5) Conversion Factor	(6) Basis (32nds)	(7) Yield	(8) Yield Value of a 32nd	(9) Dollar Value of a Basis Point	(10) Modified Duration	(11) Option-Adjusted Hedge Ratio	(12) Cash Price + Accrued Interest (decimal)	(13) Carry in Dollars per Day	(14) Carry in 32nds per Day	(15) Total Carry in 32nds to Last Delivery Day	(16) Implied RP Rate to First Delivery Day	(17) Implied RP Rate to Last Delivery Day
F	6.750	05/31/97	104.1250	0.9520	20.88	5.690	0.00733	42.65	4.03	1.019	105.7001	86.07	0.2754	14.046	-3.82	1.92
F	6.375	06/30/97	102.2875	0.9367	26.48	5.686	0.00728	42.91	4.14	1.025	103.6087	76.82	0.2458	12.537	-7.05	0.38
F05	5.500	07/31/97	99.0875	0.9013	33.92	5.669	0.00733	42.63	4.29	1.019	99.4229	56.94	0.1822	9.292	-12.03	-2.11
N07	7.000	04/15/99	104.1075	0.9501	47.60	6.195	0.00563	55.47	5.20	0.790	106.5736	92.08	0.2946	15.028	-16.38	-3.39
N	9.125	05/15/99	115.2075	1.0562	42.07	6.249	0.00524	59.67	5.07	0.849	117.8057	138.34	0.4436	22.577	-10.69	-0.30
N	6.375	07/15/99	101.0450	0.9163	62.44	6.169	0.00557	56.10	5.52	0.798	101.5910	78.70	0.2518	12.843	-25.29	-7.42
N	8.000	08/15/99	109.2175	0.9998	46.44	6.273	0.00527	59.34	5.23	0.845	113.5698	116.76	0.3736	19.055	-14.40	-2.19
N	7.875	11/15/99	108.2925	0.9934	44.11	6.323	0.00515	60.68	5.48	0.864	110.7758	110.91	0.3549	18.101	-13.41	-1.83
N	8.500	02/15/00	112.1525	1.0269	42.07	6.383	0.00493	63.45	5.44	0.903	116.6098	127.83	0.4090	20.862	-11.63	-0.85
N	8.875	05/15/00	114.2225	1.0486	37.90	6.437	0.00475	65.82	5.64	0.937	116.7935	132.49	0.4239	21.622	-9.16	0.28
N	8.750	08/15/00	114.0025	1.0425	37.03	6.481	0.00466	67.07	5.67	0.955	118.2626	133.25	0.4264	21.746	-9.01	0.35
N	8.500	11/15/00	112.1575	1.0291	34.95	6.518	0.00459	68.01	5.94	0.968	114.5017	124.43	0.3981	20.307	-8.35	0.53
N	7.750	02/15/01	107.2375	0.9849	36.06	6.549	0.00462	67.57	6.06	0.962	111.5107	111.72	0.3575	18.233	-9.99	-0.34
N	8.000	05/15/01	109.1000	1.000	34.00	6.582	0.00449	69.63	6.26	0.991	111.2038	113.91	0.3645	18.590	-8.60	0.29
N	7.875	08/15/01	108.1225	0.9920	31.96	6.625	0.00443	70.57	6.29	1.004	112.2121	114.55	0.3666	18.694	-7.90	0.61
N	7.500	11/15/01	105.2250	0.9684	27.96	6.663	0.00442	70.77	6.58	1.007	107.4762	103.79	0.3320	16.939	-6.48	1.09
N10	7.500	05/15/02	106.0250	0.9672	44.12	6.642	0.00424	73.75	6.84	1.050	107.8512	103.44	0.3310	16.882	-14.12	-2.22

Table continues

EXHIBIT 3–5
continued

Note/Bond (1)	Coupon (2)	Maturity (3)	2:00 P.M. Cash Price (32nds) (4)	Conversion Factor (5)	Basis (32nds) (6)	Yield (7)	Yield Value of a 32nd (8)	Dollar Value of a Basis Point (9)	Modified Duration (10)	Option-Adjusted Hedge Ratio (11)	Cash Price + Accrued Interest (decimal) (12)	Carry in Dollars per Day (13)	Carry in 32nds per Day (14)	Total Carry in 32nds to Last Delivery Day (15)	Implied RP Rate to First Delivery Day (16)	Implied RP Rate to Last Delivery Day (17)
B	10.375	11/15/12–07	128.1625	1.2053	57.62	7.253	0.00286	109.40	8.35	0.997	130.9606	160.06	0.5121	26.122	−14.75	−1.96
B	12.000	08/15/13–08	144.0775	1.3544	59.55	7.277	0.00255	122.55	8.17	1.117	150.0774	194.01	0.6208	31.662	−12.85	−0.96
B	13.250	05/15/14–09	157.0650	1.4763	64.23	7.283	0.00232	134.59	8.39	1.226	160.3356	210.85	0.6747	34.411	−12.40	−0.75
B	12.500	08/15/14–09	150.0900	1.4110	62.40	7.294	0.00239	130.89	8.37	1.193	156.3595	202.07	0.6466	32.977	−12.97	−1.01
B	11.750	11/15/14–09	143.0625	1.3452	57.00	7.305	0.00246	127.06	8.70	1.158	145.9732	183.46	0.5870	29.940	−12.09	−0.74
B	11.250	02/15/15	141.1600	1.3350	37.06	7.427	0.00219	142.82	9.72	1.301	146.9705	176.05	0.5633	28.731	−5.55	2.00
B	10.625	08/15/15	134.2525	1.2728	31.55	7.443	0.00226	138.46	9.89	1.262	139.9556	165.20	0.5286	26.960	−4.21	2.55
B	9.875	11/15/15	136.1925	1.1958	28.58	7.449	0.00236	132.20	10.25	1.205	128.9361	148.36	0.4747	24.212	−3.84	2.60
B	9.250	02/15/16	119.2300	1.1308	26.99	7.459	0.00246	126.82	10.21	1.156	124.2167	141.61	0.4531	23.111	−3.92	2.59
B	7.250	05/15/16	97.1850	0.9211	23.92	7.468	0.00288	108.43	10.92	0.988	99.2921	104.61	0.3347	17.073	−5.18	1.83
B	7.500	11/15/16	100.0925	0.9470	23.54	7.472	0.00280	111.54	10.93	1.016	102.0622	108.83	0.3482	17.761	−4.61	2.10
B	8.750	05/15/17	114.1100	1.0800	25.88	7.469	0.00251	124.70	10.71	1.136	116.4124	129.44	0.4142	21.125	−4.02	2.45
B	8.875	08/15/17	115.2500	1.0935	26.47	7.472	0.00247	126.37	10.52	1.151	120.0968	135.02	0.4320	22.035	−4.14	2.46
B	9.125	05/15/18	118.2600	1.1216	28.94	7.468	0.00239	130.57	10.79	1.190	120.9698	135.39	0.4332	22.096	−4.85	2.10
B	9.000	11/15/18	117.1375	1.1087	28.08	7.474	0.00240	130.17	10.89	1.186	119.5574	133.31	0.4265	21.756	−4.65	2.18
B	8.875	02/15/19	116.0025	1.0952	28.00	7.478	0.00242	129.23	10.74	1.177	120.3234	134.81	0.4313	22.000	−4.80	2.16
B	8.125	08/15/19	107.1350	1.0135	28.09	7.481	0.00256	122.13	10.97	1.113	111.3728	122.28	0.3912	19.956	−5.91	1.64

Table continues

EXHIBIT 3–5
continued

Note/ Bond (1)	Coupon (2)	Maturity (3)	2:00 P.M. Cash Price (32nds) (4)	Conversion Factor (5)	Basis (32nds) (6)	Yield (7)	Yield Value of a 32nd (8)	Dollar Value of a Basis Point (9)	Modified Duration (10)	Option-Adjusted Hedge Ratio (11)	Cash Price + Accrued Interest (decimal) (12)	Carry in Dollars per Day (13)	Carry in 32nds per Day (14)	Total Carry in 32nds to Last Delivery Day (15)	Implied RP Rate to First Delivery Day (16)	Implied RP Rate to Last Delivery Day (17)
B	8.500	02/15/20	111.2575	1.0549	29.07	7.482	0.00246	126.94	10.95	1.157	115.9379	128.46	0.4110	20.965	-5.79	1.71
B	8.750	05/15/20	114.2550	1.0829	30.62	7.476	0.00240	130.23	11.14	1.187	116.8655	129.02	0.4128	21.056	-6.08	1.54
B	8.750	08/15/20	114.2700	1.0829	32.12	7.477	0.00239	130.61	10.97	1.190	199.0986	132.47	0.4239	21.619	-6.78	1.29
B	7.875	02/15/21	104.2300	0.9859	34.43	7.473	0.00257	121.79	11.22	1.110	108.5481	117.96	0.3774	19.251	-9.37	0.11
B	8.125	05/15/21	107.2350	1.0140	36.40	7.466	0.00250	125.11	11.41	1.140	109.6552	118.75	0.3890	19.380	-9.73	-0.07
B	8.125	08/15/21	107.2600	1.0138	39.58	7.463	0.00249	125.52	11.23	1.144	111.7634	121.92	0.3901	19.897	-11.30	-0.72
B30	8.000	11/15/21	106.1450	1.0000	42.50	7.453	0.00251	124.68	11.51	1.136	108.3444	116.57	0.3730	19.024	-12.84	-1.43

Option-Adjusted futures duration ($/BP)

2-Year	5-Year	10-Year	Bond
1.63 (34.61)	3.84 (41.84)	6.49 (70.25)	10.44 (109.75)

entirely consistent with each other and can produce what we think are highly inadequate hedge ratios in a number of important applications.

Rule of Thumb #1

The dollar value of a basis point for a futures contract is equal to the dollar value of a basis point for the cheapest to deliver *divided by* its conversion factor.

Rule of Thumb #2

The duration of a futures contract is equal to the duration of the cheapest to deliver bond.

The algebra that supports the first rule of thumb is based on the assumption that the futures price converges to the converted price of the cheapest to deliver issue at expiration. At expiration, then, we know that:

$$\text{Futures price} \approx \frac{\text{CTD price}}{\text{CTD factor}}$$

The relationship is approximate because of the small amount of carry and the value of the switch options that exist at expiration. From this relationship, the first rule of thumb follows immediately, because:

$$\text{Futures price change} \approx \frac{\text{CTD price change}}{\text{CTD factor}}$$

almost by definition.

The second rule of thumb can be derived approximately from the first by dividing both sides by the futures price. The effect of dividing the left-hand side by the futures price is to produce a number equal to:

$$\frac{\text{Futures price change}}{\text{Futures price}}$$

which is the percent change in the futures price. On the right-hand side, we would have:

$$\frac{(\text{CTD price change} / \text{CTD factor})}{(\text{CTD price} / \text{CTD factor})}$$

which simplifies to:

$$\frac{\text{CTD price change}}{\text{CTD price}}$$

after the factors cancel. Thus, we know that the percent change in the futures price is approximately equal to the percent change in the cheapest to deliver's price at expiration. Because a bond's duration is the percent change in its full price for a one-percentage point change in its yield, we can conclude that the duration of the futures contract at expiration is nearly the same as the duration of the cheapest to deliver bond.

The chief difference, which can matter a lot, is that the relationship between a bond's duration and its dollar value of a basis point (for $100 par amount of the bond) is given by:

$$DV01 \approx \frac{(\text{Duration} / 100) \times \text{Full price}}{100}$$

$$DV01 \approx \frac{(\text{Duration} / 100) \times (\text{Price} + \text{Accrued interest})}{100}$$

Consider what this means for the duration rule of thumb. Convergence at expiration allows us to argue that the percent change in the futures price will equal the percent change in a bond's clean price, or price net of accrued interest. But, because a bond's clean price is lower than its full price, which includes accrued interest, the percent change in a bond's clean price, for any yield change, is always higher (except on coupon payment dates when accrued interest equals zero) than the percent change in a bond's full price. As a result, the percent change in the futures price at expiration will be greater than the cheapest to deliver's duration. Just how much greater depends on how much interest has accrued on the bond.

Put differently, the second rule of thumb imputes too small a duration to the futures contract, and the resulting hedge ratio will be larger than it should be. Again, just how much larger depends on the relative relationship between a bond's full price and its clean price. For a bond with a coupon of 9 percent, for example, its full price could include as much as 4.5 points of accrued interest. If the bond were trading at par, the hedge ratio would be 4.5 percent too large.

The Rules of Thumb in Practice

To see how these rules of thumb might be used in practice, suppose we want to hedge $10 million face or par amount of the $5\frac{1}{2}$s of July 31, 1997. As shown in Exhibit 3–5, its market price on August 6, 1992, was 99-8.75/32nds. Its full price including accrued interest was 99.4229. Its modified duration was 4.29 and its $DV01$ per $100,000 face amount was $42.63, or $4,263 for the full $10 million.

How many of the September five-year Treasury note futures would you need to hedge the \$10 million position in the $5\frac{1}{2}$s?

To use the rules of thumb, we need to identify the cheapest to deliver note. With an implied repo rate of 2.49 percent, the $6\frac{7}{8}$s of March 31, 1997, were cheapest to deliver. The relevant data for this issue include:

$$\text{Futures price} = 108 - 31/32\text{nds}$$

$$\text{Factor} = 0.9582$$

$$DV01(\text{per }\$100,000\text{ face}) = \$41.55$$

$$\text{Modified duration} = 3.87$$

Using the rule of thumb, we would calculate that

$$\text{Futures } DV01 = \frac{\text{CTD } DV01}{\text{CTD factor}}$$

$$= \frac{\$41.55}{0.9582}$$

$$= \$43.36$$

$$\text{Futures duration} = \text{CTD duration}$$

$$= 3.87$$

To calculate the hedge ratio using the first rule of thumb, we would divide the $DV01$ of the portfolio by the $DV01$ of the futures contract—

$$\text{Hedge ratio \#1} = \frac{\text{Portfolio } DV01}{\text{Futures } DV01}$$

$$= \frac{\$4,263}{\$43.36}$$

$$= 98.32$$

which would require you to short 98 five-year Treasury note futures contracts.

Important note. This rule of thumb is the working rule that Bloomberg uses when you request a hedge ratio. As shown in Exhibit 3–6, if you had asked Bloomberg on August 6, 1992, to hedge \$10 million of the $5\frac{1}{2}$s of July 1997 using the September 1992 five-year note futures contract, it would have suggested shorting 98 contracts. It arrived at this

EXHIBIT 3–6
Bloomberg PDA Screen

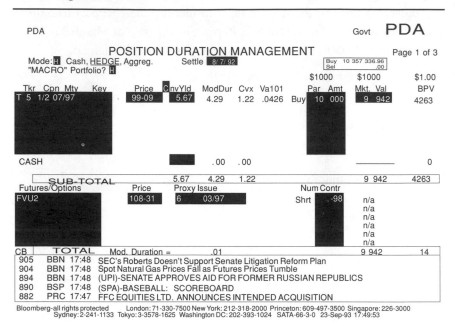

answer by noting first that the cheapest to deliver note was the $6\frac{7}{8}$s of March 1997 (see box labeled Proxy Issue) and that its dollar value of a basis point was $0.04155 per $100 face amount of the issue. Combining this *DV*01 with its September 1992 conversion factor of 0.9582, Bloomberg calculated the *DV*01 for the September 1992 futures contract as 0.0434 [= 0.04155 / 0.9582] per $100 face value of the contract, or $43.40 per contract. Given a *DV*01 of $4,263 for a $10 million position in the issue, Bloomberg calculates a hedge of 98.22 [= $4,263 / $43.40] contracts, which is rounded to 98.

If we calculate the hedge ratio using the second rule of thumb, we would divide the product of the portfolio's market value and its duration by the product of the portfolio-equivalent value of the futures contract and its duration. Given a full price including accrued interest of 99.4229, the market value of $10 million face amount of the $5\frac{1}{2}$s would be $9,942,290. As shown at the top of Exhibit 3–5, the five-year Treasury note futures price was $108\frac{31}{32}$ (or 108.96875). Because the nominal face value of the futures contract is $100,000, the futures contract can be treated as if it has a market value of $108,968.75. Thus, the hedge ratio calculation would appear as follows:

$$\text{Hedge ratio\#2} = \frac{(\$9,942,290 \times 4.29)}{(\$108,968.75 \times 3.87)}$$

$$= 101.14$$

which would require you to short 101 note futures contracts.

Why are the answers different? The difference between the two hedge ratios reflects two fine points that are worth touching on. The first is the correct application of duration. The second is the role of carry in driving a wedge between the spot and futures prices.

Consider the duration issue first. Correctly used, a bond's or note's duration is applied to its full price, which is its clean price plus any accrued interest. Because the clean price, which is also the quoted price, is less than the full price, the result of dividing the cheapest to deliver issue's $DV01$ by its clean price is a percentage price change that is larger than the issue's duration would suggest. In our example, the cheapest to deliver's modified duration is 3.87. If we apply this to its full price of 107.4717, we find a $DV01$ of 0.04159, or 4.159 price points for a 100-basis-point change in the note's yield. A price change of 4.159 price points, however, represents a 3.96 percent change in the note's clean price, or price net of accrued interest.

Because the convergence argument indicates that the percent change in the futures price should be nearly equal to the percent change in the cheapest to deliver's clean price, we can see that the effective duration of the futures contract can be substantially higher than the cheapest to deliver's duration. In this example, with a full price of 107.4717 and a clean price of 104.99219, the effective duration of the futures contract should really be 3.96 [= 3.87 x (107.4717 / 104.99219)]. By understanding the effective duration of the futures contract, the rule of thumb produces hedge ratios that are too high. In this case, the calculated hedge ratio is overstated by a little over 2 percent. In other words, if the true hedge ratio were 100, the calculated hedge ratio using this rule of thumb would be 102.33 [= 3.96 / 3.87], or a little more than two contracts too high.

Now consider the wedge between the futures price and the converted price of the cheapest to deliver. Before delivery, the relationship between the futures price and the cheapest to deliver's price is:

$$\text{Futures price} = \frac{\text{CTD price} - \text{CTD Basis}}{\text{CTD factor}}$$

where the basis in a positive yield curve setting is definitely positive. With this relationship, if we calculate the *percent* change in the futures price while holding the basis constant, we see that

$$\frac{\text{Futures price change}}{\text{Futures price}} = \frac{\text{CTD price change}}{\text{CTD price} - \text{CDT basis}}$$

Because the denominator in the right-hand side of this expression is smaller than the cheapest to deliver's price, the percent change in the futures price is greater than the percent change in the cheapest to deliver's price. How much greater? In this example, the issue's price is 104.99219 and its basis is 18.51/32nds, or 0.5784 price points. Thus, the percent change in the futures price should be 1.0055 [= 104.99219 / (104.99219 – 0.5784)] times the percent change in the issue's clean price. The difference is not much, but the effect is to understate the effective duration of the futures contract by another half a percent or so, and that is all we need to reconcile the difference between the two hedge ratios.

Other Pitfalls

Lest you feel tempted to cast out the second rule of thumb in favor of the first, you should know that both rules of thumb suffer from two further deficiencies. Neither allows for the effect of changes in carry on the hedge ratio, and neither allows for changes in the value of the short's strategic delivery options.

Complicating effects of carry on hedge ratios. Net carry accounts for much of the spread between spot and futures prices in bond and note futures, and an appreciation of how carry behaves as yields change is important for proper hedge construction. Paying careful attention to carry is especially important for those who use two-year and five-year Treasury note futures for hedging.

The best way to see how carry can affect a hedge ratio is to begin with the relationship between the futures price and an issue's spot price, which we write as:

$$\text{Futures price} = \frac{\text{Spot price} - \text{Carry} - \text{Option value}}{\text{Factor}}$$

This can also be written as:

$$\text{Futures price} = \frac{\text{Forward price} - \text{Option value}}{\text{Factor}}$$

The advantage of looking at the futures price this way is that we can see more clearly that it is the change in the issue's forward price, not its spot price, that drives a change in the futures price. If, for the purpose of focusing on carry, we hold the value of the short's delivery options fixed, then we can write the change in the bond's forward price as:

Forward price change = Spot price change − Change in carry

for a given change in yields. To determine the effect of a change in yields on carry, note that carry is defined as:

$$\begin{aligned}
\text{Carry} &= \text{Coupon income} - \text{Financing cost} \\
&= \frac{C}{2} \times \frac{Days}{N} - \text{Full price} \times RP \times \frac{Days}{360}
\end{aligned}$$

where C is the annual coupon on the note, *days* is the actual number of days remaining to delivery, N is the actual number of days in the coupon period, and RP is the repo or financing rate. For the purpose of this example, we assume that there is no intervening coupon payment between today and delivery. If there is, the principles are the same, but the execution is slightly more difficult.

You can see from the definition of carry that a change in yields can affect carry in two ways. First, a change in the bond's yield will certainly affect the bond's full price. For any given level of the repo rate, a decrease in the bond's yield will cause its full price to rise and, as a result, the total cost of financing the position to rise. Thus, a decrease in the bond's yield will tend to cause carry to fall because of its effect on the bond's price. At the same time, it is unlikely that a change in bond yields would be accompanied by no change in the RP rate. Rather, if bond yields fall, repo rates are likely to fall as well. And a fall in the repo rate will tend to decrease the cost of financing the position and, thus, will tend to cause carry to increase.

Given the relative sizes of those offsetting effects of yield and repo rate changes on carry, what you assume about the relationship between the two can have a profound effect on the way you calculate a hedge ratio. Consider the two-year note on August 6. The cheapest to deliver note was the $8\frac{1}{2}$s of June 1994, which had a full price of 108.6658 and a $DV01$ of $18.89 per $100,000 par value of the issue. With 51 days to delivery and a 3.35 RP

rate, total carry to delivery on the issue was $662.28 per $100,000 of the issue (21.19/32nds).

Now consider two exercises. In the first, we lower the yield on the note 1 basis point while holding the repo rate fixed at 3.35 percent. If we do this, the cost of financing the position to delivery would increase by $0.09 (i.e., nine cents) per $100,000 par value of the issue. As a result, carry would fall by $0.09, and the forward price would increase by $0.01898 [= ($18.89 − (−$0.09)) / $1000] per $100 to reflect the $DV01$ of the note and the decrease in net carry. Put differently, the $DV01$ of a forward position in $100,000 par value of the issue would be $18.98, in contrast to the $18.89 for a spot position in $100,000 of the issue. These two changes are very close to each other, and the ratio of the forward price change to the spot price change is 1.005 [= $0.01898 / $0.01889], which is very close to 1.

In the second exercise, we lower both the yield on the note and the repo rate 1 basis point. If we do this, the cost of financing the position to deliver actually decreases by $1.45, so that the change in the forward price would be $0.01744, or $17.44 per $100,000 of a forward position in the note. Here the difference in the change of the spot price and the change in the forward price is much more pronounced. The ratio of the change in the forward price to the change in the spot price is only 0.923 [= $0.01744 / 40.01889], which is quite a bit different from 1. In this case, ignoring the effect of carry on the behavior of the forward price and in turn on the futures price would overstate the price sensitivity of the futures contract by about 7.7 percent. In other words, the hedge ratio obtained by using the $DV01$ of the cheapest to deliver's spot value would be too small by 7.7 contracts for each 100 in the hedge.

The effects of carry for the full range of Treasury futures contracts is shown for August 6, 1992, in Exhibit 3–7. The effect on net carry of changing the issue's yield while holding the repo rate fixed increases with the $DV01$ of the note or bond. This is simply because a change in the issue's yield has a larger effect on the value of what has to be financed if the issue is a bond than if it is a note. Also, the incremental effect on carry of a change in the repo rate is substantially larger than the simple effect of a change in the issue's yield. This reflects nothing more than the fact that a 1 basis point change in the repo rate is a very large fraction of the repo rate, while the $DV01$ is a comparatively small fraction of the price of any of these issues.

Finally, the problem of ignoring carry is relatively more important for the note contracts than for the bond contract. As Exhibit 3–7 shows, ignoring carry can throw off a hedge ratio involving two-year Treasury note futures

EXHIBIT 3–7
Effect of a One Basis Point Drop in Yield per $100,000 Face Value (August 6, 1992)

Treasury Futures ContractRB(CTD)	Change in Value of Spot Position (per $100,000 par value)	Change in Carry		Change in Value of Forward Position		Ratio of Change in Forward Value to Change in Spot Value	
		RP rate Fixed	RP Rate Change Equals Yield Change	RP Rate Fixed	RP Rate Change Equals Yield Change	RP Rate Fixed	RP Rate Change Equals Yield Change
	(1)	(2)	(3)	$(4)=(1)-2$	$(5)=(1)-3$	$(6)=(4)/(1)$	$(7)=(5)/(1)$
2-year (8-1/2s of 6/94)	18.89	-0.09	+1.45	18.98	17.44	1.005	0.923
5-year (6-7/8s of 3/97)	41.55	-0.20	+1.33	41.75	40.22	1.005	0.968
10-year (7-1/2s of 11/01)	70.77	-0.34	+1.19	71.11	69.58	1.005	0.983
Bond (9-7/8s of 11/15)	132.20	-0.63	+1.20	132.83	131.00	1.005	0.991

by 7 to 8 percent of the size of the hedge when there are 51 days to expiration. For the bond contract, the difference might be as much as 1 percent. The difference can be accounted for by the substantially different $DV01$s of the issues in the different deliverable sets. The cheapest to deliver into the bond contract had a $DV01$ of $132.20 per $100,000, while the cheapest to deliver into the two-year note contract had a $DV01$ of only $18.89. As a result, even though the effect of yield changes on carry was not so very different for the two issues, the relative effect was much greater for the two-year note than for the long-term bond.

Changes in the cheapest to deliver. The second problem with the rule of thumb hedge ratios is that they do not reflect the influence of switches in the cheapest to deliver bond on futures prices. Consider the problem of hedging $100 million of the $8\frac{1}{2}$s of February 2020 on May 31, 1990, the day before the U.S. Labor Department's monthly payroll announcement. At the close of business on May 31, the total $DV01$ on the portfolio was $105,760. Exhibit 3–8 shows that the cheapest to deliver into the June 1990 futures contract was the $7\frac{1}{2}$s of November 2016. The $DV01$ per $100,000 face value of the $7\frac{1}{2}$s was $92.96, and its June 1990 conversion factor was 0.9453. Using the first rule of thumb, the imputed $DV01$ for the June 1990 futures contract would have been $98.34 [= $92.96 / 0.9453]. The hedge ratio given by the first rule of thumb, then, would have been about 1,075 [= $105,760 / $98.34] contracts.

Bond prices rose the next morning in response to a weak employment number, and the $7\frac{1}{2}$s of November 2016 were replaced by the $11\frac{3}{4}$s of '14-09 as the cheapest to deliver. (You should satisfy yourself that replacing a high-duration bond with a low-duration bond makes sense when yields are falling and bond prices are rising.) The effect of this shift in the cheapest to deliver on the hedge ratio produced by the first rule of thumb was striking. Dividing the $DV01$ of the $11\frac{3}{4}$s by its conversion factor gives a $DV01$ for the futures contract of $83.60 [= $114.11 / 1.3649], which is about 15 percent lower than it was the day before. With a new $DV01$ for the $8\frac{1}{2}$s of $108,640 and a futures $DV01$ of $83.60, the hedge ratio calculation on June 1 would have yielded a short position of 1,300 [= $108,640 / $83.60] contracts.

Does a 20 percent increase in the hedge ratio in response to less than a point and a half increase in bond prices make sense? We think not. Although the change in the hedge ratio is in the right direction, the change is much

EXHIBIT 3–8
Hedge Ratios and Shifts in the Cheapest to Deliver

Cheapest to Deliver Bond

Date	Futures Price (32nds)	Issue	Factor	Duration	DV01 per $100,000	DV01/ Factor	8.5 of '20 DV01
5/31/90	92-29	7.5 of '16	0.9453	10.52	$92.96	$98.34	$105,760
6/1/90	94-12	11.75 of '14-09	1.3649	8.80	$114.11	$83.60	$108,640

Hedge Ratio Calculation

Date	Hedge Ratio	Hedge Contracts
5/31	$\dfrac{\$105,760}{\$98.34}$	1,075
6/1	$\dfrac{\$108,640}{\$83.60}$	1,300

too abrupt and much too large. As yields fall and bond prices rise, the futures price should be more heavily influenced by the price behavior of low-duration bonds. Or, as yields rise and bond prices fall, futures prices should behave more like the prices of high-duration bonds.

The change in the price behavior of a futures contract should be gradual, however, and should depend on the likelihood of a shift in the cheapest to deliver. If the market is close to a switch point between a high-duration bond and a low-duration bond, bond futures should behave like a blend of the two bonds. Moreover, the weights attached to the two bonds' behavior should reflect their respective likelihoods of being delivered. The rule-of-thumb approach to hedging assumes that the current cheapest to deliver is certain to remain cheapest to deliver, no matter how close the market is to a crossover point. And, once the crossover point has been passed, even if only by a basis point in bond yields, the rule-of-thumb approach to hedging assumes that the new cheapest to deliver is now a sure thing.

Are the mistakes that one makes using the rule-of-thumb approach to hedging serious? The evidence in Exhibit 3–9 suggests that they can be. The solid line charts the duration of whatever bond happened to be the cheapest

EXHIBIT 3–9
Duration of Cheapest to Deliver Bond and 10-year Note (Lead Contract)

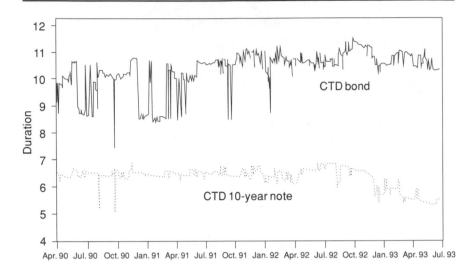

to deliver on each day between April 1990 and July 1993. The dotted line tracks the duration of the cheapest to deliver note into the 10-year Treasury note contract. Although we find periods of comparative stability in the duration of the cheapest to deliver, we also encounter periods of frequent and large changes in duration because of shifts in the cheapest to deliver. These were periods when yields were either very volatile or very close to critical crossover points. Either way, these were periods during which rule-of-thumb hedging would have required an extraordinary amount of hedge rebalancing and, we think, would have resulted in less than the best possible hedges combined with unnecessarily large transaction costs.

HORSE RACE OF HEDGE RATIOS

The real test of which is better—an option-adjusted hedge or a thumb-rule hedge—is in performance. To illustrate the difference between the two, we ran a horse race between option-adjusted hedge ratios and the hedge ratios produced by the first rule of thumb. To run this race, we used beginning-of-the-week bond and futures price data for June 1989 to March 1990. For each week that the lead bond futures contract had at least one month remaining to expiration, we calculated two hedge ratios for each of five bonds. Each hedge was then held for one month. No effort was made to adjust the hedge ratios. Altogether, we were able to look at the behavior of 27 hedges over the nine-month period for each of the five bonds. The results are shown in Exhibit 3–10.

Throughout this period, the average hedge ratio using the option-adjusted futures method was lower than the hedge ratio using the cheapest to deliver approach. This need not have been the case. For example, in a high-yield environment, the duration of the cheapest to deliver could be higher than the duration of the futures contract. As it happened in this case, however, the cheapest to deliver bond had a relatively low duration but stood a good chance of being replaced by a high-duration bond as cheapest to deliver. Thus, the option-adjusted futures model placed a comparatively high weight on a high-duration bond being the cheapest to deliver.

More Accurate Hedges

The hedge errors indicate that the projected futures approach produced the more reliable hedge. With one exception—the 14s of '11-06—the option-adjusted futures approach gave us smaller errors than did the conventional cheapest to deliver approach. Over the set of five bonds, the average hedge

EXHIBIT 3–10
Comparison of Hedge Effectiveness (June 1989 to March 1990)

Portfolio	Average Hedge Ratio Using[1]		Average Hedge Error Using[2]	
	Cheapest to Deliver Duration	Option-Adjusted Duration	Cheapest to Deliver Duration	Option-Adjusted Duration
10.75 of '05	11.9	11.0	9.0	4.5
14.0 of '11-06	14.7	13.5	5.6	6.3
12.5 of '14-09	14.9	13.7	7.7	2.6
7.25 of '16	11.7	10.8	10.9	6.0
8.875 of '19	14.0	12.9	16.2	9.7
Equally Weighted Portfolio	13.4	12.4	9.9	5.8

[1] Number of contracts to short per $1 million holdings of bonds.
[2] Absolute value of gain or loss on hedged portfolio (in 32nds). 1/32 equals $31.25 on $100,000 portfolio.

error for the option-adjusted futures approach was about half as large as the error produced by using the duration of the cheapest to deliver.

The experienced hedger may find fault with this kind of horse race, because hedges in the real world are adjusted as yields change to reflect the changing durations of both the position to be hedged and the duration of the hedging instrument. Thus, the hedge errors reported for the conventional hedge are larger than they would have been in practice.

To be fair, however, the hedges based on the option-adjusted futures approach would have been adjusted as well. Thus, the hedge errors reported for the projected futures approach are overstated too.

What should be clear, however, is that the cheapest to deliver approach nearly always understates or overstates the duration of the futures contract. The option-adjusted futures approach provides an unbiased estimate of futures duration. Thus, the hedge error in using the conventional approach should be larger than the hedge error in using the option-adjusted futures approach, no matter how small the change in yields. As a result, even though the hedge errors in using the conventional rules of thumb can be kept down by adjusting the hedge from time to time, they can never be as small as they are with the option-adjusted futures approach.

More Stable Durations

A second source of comfort in the option-adjusted duration approach to hedging is the greater stability exhibited by the option-adjusted duration of bond and note futures contracts over time. Exhibit 3–11 shows that the option-adjusted durations of the long-term Treasury bond and 10-year Treasury note futures contracts varied over time, as one would expect. If you compare the behavior of the option-adjusted durations shown in Exhibit 3–11 with the thumb-rule durations shown in Exhibit 3–9, however, you will find that the option-adjusted durations were considerably more stable.

Lower Transactions Costs

A beneficial side effect of using option-adjusted hedge ratios is that the resulting hedges can be substantially less costly to maintain when yields fluctuate around levels at which there are changes in the cheapest to deliver. At such a level, a small change in the level of yields can cause a huge shift in the futures duration provided by the conventional rules of thumb. At such

EXHIBIT 3–11

Option-Adjusted Duration of Bond and 10-Year Note Futures Contract (Lead Contract)

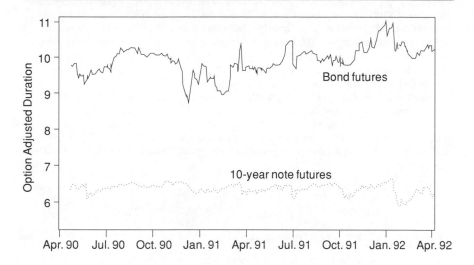

times, the rules of thumb dictate correspondingly huge changes in the size of a hedge. If yields fluctuate very much around critical crossover points, the conventional rules of thumb can produce a great deal of unnecessary trading. In contrast, option-adjusted hedges require comparatively little tending and so would save greatly on transactions costs.

EXHIBIT 3–12
Measuring Duration with Futures in a Bond Portfolio

For calculating price exposure, a futures contract is treated as if it has a portfolio-equivalent value of $100,000 par value of bonds. Thus, a futures price of 93 would produce a portfolio-equivalent market value for one futures contract of $93,000. If the duration of the futures contract were 8, a 100-basis-point increase in the yield of the underlying bond would cause the futures price to fall 8 percent, or 7.44 [= 93 × 0.08] points. Under the terms of the contract, this would be a loss of $7,440 to the long and would have to be paid through the clearinghouse in the form of variation margin to the short.

When calculating the duration of a portfolio, however, you must remember that a futures contract ties up no cash and has no net liquidating value. In other words, no money changes hands when a long or short position in a futures contract is established, and no money is either required or released when a futures position is unwound or offset. In practice, this means that the duration of a portfolio that contains bond futures (or note futures) is calculated as:

$$\text{Portfolio duration} = \frac{\left(\begin{array}{c} \text{Bond} \\ \text{duration} \end{array} \times \begin{array}{c} \text{Bond} \\ \text{market} \\ \text{value} \end{array} \right) + \left(\begin{array}{c} \text{Futures} \\ \text{duration} \end{array} \times \begin{array}{c} \text{Futures} \\ \text{Market–Equivalent} \\ \text{value} \end{array} \right)}{\text{Bond market value}}$$

In other words, the hypothetical market value of the futures position is used in reckoning price exposure, which is used in the numerator of the duration calculation. Only the actual net liquidating value or cashing-out value of the portfolio, however, is used in the denominator.

For example, consider a portfolio that contains $100 million market value of bonds and notes and 200 *short* futures at a market price of 90. For the purpose of calculating exposure to yield changes, the futures would be treated as if they have a market value of $18 million [= 200 x $90,000]. If the duration of the cash bond and note portfolio were 5 and the duration of the futures contract 8, the duration of this particular portfolio would be:

$$\text{Portfolio duration} = \frac{(5 \times \$100) + (8 \times -\$18)}{\$100}$$

$$= \frac{\$500 - \$144}{\$100}$$

$$= 3.56$$

## Chapter Four

The Convexity Bias in Eurodollar Futures

Galen Burghardt
Dean Witter Reynolds

Bill Hoskins
Dean Witter Reynolds

There is a systematic advantage to being short Eurodollar futures relative to deposits, swaps, or FRAs. Because of this advantage, which we characterize as a convexity bias, Eurodollar futures prices should be lower than their so-called fair values. Put differently, the three-month interest rates implied by Eurodollar futures prices should be higher than the three-month forward rates to which they are tied.

The bias can be huge. As Exhibit 4–1 shows, the bias is worth little or nothing for futures that have less than two years to expiration. For a futures contract with five years to expiration, however, the bias is worth about 17 basis points. And for a contract with 10 years to expiration, the bias can easily be worth 60 basis points.

The presence of this bias has profound implications for pricing derivatives off the Eurodollar futures curve. For example, a five-year swap yield should be about 6 basis points lower than the yield implied by the first five years of Eurodollar futures. A 10-year swap yield should be about 18 basis points lower. And the differential for a five-year swap five years forward should be around 36 basis points. (These estimates are explained in Exhibits 4–10, 4–14, and 4–15.)

These are big numbers. A 6-basis-point spread is worth more than $200,000 on a $100 million five-year swap. An 18-basis-point spread is worth about $1.2 million on a $100 million 10-year swap.

EXHIBIT 4–1
Convexity Bias

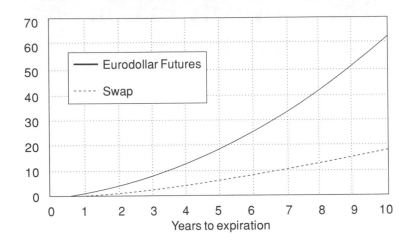

Although the swaps market has begun to recognize this problem, swap yields still seem too high relative to those implied by Eurodollar futures rates. (See Exhibit 4–16.) If so, then there is still a substantial advantage in favor of being short swaps and hedging them with short Eurodollar futures. Also, because the value of the convexity bias depends so much on the market's perceptions of Eurodollar rate volatilities, one should be able to trade the value of the swaps/Eurodollar rate spread against options on forward Eurodollar rates. The convexity bias also affects the behavior of the yield spreads between Treasury notes and Eurodollar strips.

Students of Eurodollar futures pricing should like this note. The standard approach to estimating the value of the convexity bias (also known as the financing bias) has been bound up in complex yield curve simulations and option pricing calculus. Although such methods can yield reasonable enough answers, we show how the problem can be solved much more simply. For that matter, anyone armed with a spreadsheet program and an understanding of rate volatilities and their correlations can estimate the value of the convexity bias without recourse to expensive research facilities.

The difference between a futures contract and a forward contract is more pronounced for Eurodollar futures, swaps, and FRAs than for any other commodity. In particular, there is a systematic bias in favor of short

Eurodollar futures relative to deposits, swaps, or FRAs. As we show, the value of this bias is particularly large for futures contracts with expirations ranging from five to ten years. The purpose of this note is to show

- Why the difference is so important for Eurodollar futures
- How to estimate the value of the difference
- What trades can do about the difference

What we find is that the implications for swaps traders and those who manage swaps books are particularly important. Given the rate volatilities that we have observed over the past four years or so, it seems that market swap yields should be several basis points lower than the implied swap yields that one calculates from the rates implied by Eurodollar futures prices. Judging by current spreads between these rates, it appears that the swaps market has not fully absorbed the implications of this pricing problem. As a result, there still appear to be profitable opportunities for running a book of short swaps hedged with short Eurodollar futures. By the same token, this pricing problem raises serious questions about how a swaps book should be marked to market.

INTEREST RATE SWAPS AND EURODOLLAR FUTURES

Interest rate swaps and Eurodollar futures are driven by the same kinds of forward interest rates. But the two derivatives are fundamentally different in one key respect. With an interest rate swap, cash changes hands only once for each leg of a swap and then only in arrears. With a Eurodollar futures contract, gains and losses are settled every day. As it happens, the difference in the way gains and losses are settled affects the values of swaps and Eurodollar futures relative to one another. In particular, there is a systematic bias in favor of a short swap (i.e., receiving fixed and paying floating) and against a long Eurodollar futures contract. Or, one can think of the short Eurodollar position as having an advantage over a long swap. Either way, because swap prices are so closely tied to Eurodollar futures prices, it is important to know how much this bias is worth.

The easiest way to understand the difference between the two derivatives is through a concrete example that compares the profits and losses on a forward swap with the profits and losses on a Eurodollar futures contract.

A Forward Swap

A plain vanilla interest rate swap is simply an arrangement under which one side agrees to pay a fixed rate and receive a variable or floating rate over the life of the swap. The other side agrees to pay floating and receive fixed. The amounts of money that one side pays the other are determined by applying the two interest rates to the swap's notional principal amount.

The typical swap allows the floating rate to be reset several times over the swap's life. For example, a five-year swap keyed to three-month LIBOR would require the value of the floating rate to be set or reset 20 times—once when the swap is transacted and every three months thereafter. One can think of the swap as having 20 separate segments with the value of each segment depending on the swap's fixed rate and on the market's expectation today of what the floating rate will be on that segment's rate setting date.

The starting point for our example is the structure of Eurodollar futures prices and rates shown in Exhibit 4–2. These were the final settlement or closing prices on Monday, June 13, 1994. Each of the implied futures rates roughly corresponds to a three-month period. The actual number of days covered by each of the futures contracts is shown in the right-hand column.

Now consider a swap that settles to the difference between a fixed rate and the value of three-month LIBOR on March 15, 1999. On June 13, 1994, this would be a forward swap whose rate setting date is four and three-fourths years away and whose cash settlement date is a full five years away. To make the example more concrete, suppose that the forward swap's notional principal amount is $100 million. Suppose too that the fixed rate for this swap is 7.83 percent, which is the forward value of three-month LIBOR implied by the March 1999 Eurodollar futures contract. This may not be strictly the correct thing to do, but throughout this note we use futures rates in lieu of forward rates because we have much better information about the futures rates. Although the purpose of this note is to explain why the two rates should be different, we can use the behavior of futures rates as an excellent proxy for the behavior of forward rates.

The Value of a Basis Point

Under the terms of this forward swap, if the value of three-month LIBOR turns out to be 7.83 percent on March 15, 1999, no cash changes hands at all on June 14. For each basis point that three-month LIBOR is above 7.83 percent, the person who is long the swap (i.e., the person who pays fixed

EXHIBIT 4–2
Structure of Eurodollar Futures Rates *(June 13, 1994)*

	Eurodollar futures			
Quarter	*Expiration*	*Price*	*Implied Futures Rate (percent)*	*Days in Period*
1	6/13/94	95.44	4.56	98
2	9/19/94	94.84	5.16	91
3	12/19/94	94.14	5.86	84
4	3/13/95	93.91	6.09	98
5	6/19/95	93.61	6.39	91
6	9/18/95	93.36	6.64	91
7	12/18/95	93.12	6.88	91
8	3/18/96	93.08	6.92	91
9	6/17/96	92.98	7.02	91
10	9/16/96	92.89	7.11	91
11	12/16/96	92.74	7.26	91
12	3/17/97	92.72	7.28	91
13	6/16/97	92.63	7.37	91
14	9/15/97	92.55	7.45	91
15	12/15/97	92.42	7.58	91
16	3/16/98	92.42	7.58	91
17	6/15/98	92.34	7.66	91
18	9/14/98	92.28	7.72	91
19	12/14/98	92.16	7.84	91
20	3/15/99	92.17	7.83	91

Swap payment on: 6/14/99

Note: Given these rates, the price of a $1 zero-coupon bond that matures on 6/14/99 would be .70667, and its semiannual bond equivalent yield would be 7.0658 percent.

and receives floating) receives $2,527.78 [= (0.0001 × (91/360)) × $100,000,000] on June 14, 1999. For each basis point that three-month LIBOR is below 7.83 percent, the person who is long the swap pays $2,527.78.

Thus, the nominal value of a basis point for this swap is $2,527.78, with the cash changing hands five years in the future.

Eurodollar Futures

The futures market has based much of its success on a single operating principle: that is, all gains and losses must be settled up at the end of the day—in cash. This is as true of Eurodollar futures as it is of any futures contract.

Consider the March 1999 Eurodollar futures contract. When it expires on March 15, 1999, its final settlement price will be set equal to 100 less the spot value of three-month LIBOR on that day. Before expiration, the Eurodollar futures price will be a function of the rate that the market expects. If there were no difference between a futures contract and a forward contract, and if the market expected a forward rate of 7.83 percent, for example, the futures price would be 92.17 [= 100.00 − 7.83]. If the market expected 7.84, the futures price would be 92.16. That is, a 1-basis-point increase in value of the forward rate produces a 1-tick decrease in the futures price.

Under the Chicago Mercantile Exchange's rules, each tick or .01 in the price of a Eurodollar futures contract is worth $25. This is true whether the futures contract expires 10 weeks from now, 10 months from now, or 10 years from now. The nominal value of a basis point change in the underlying interest rate is always $25.

Reconciling the Difference in Cash Flow Dates

We now have two cash payments that are tied to the same change in interest rates. For the particular forward swap in our example, a 1-basis point change in the expected value of three-month LIBOR for the period from March 15 to June 14, 1999, changes the expected value of the swap settlement on June 14 by $2,527.78. At the same time, a 1-basis-point change in the same rate produces a $25 gain or loss that the holder of a Eurodollar futures contract must settle today. The difference in timing is illustrated in Exhibit 4–3.

The simplest way to reconcile the timing difference is to cast the two amounts of money in terms of present values. Eurodollar futures are easy to handle. Because gains and losses are settled every day in the futures market, the present value of the $25 basis point value on a Eurodollar futures contract is always $25.

The present value of the $2,527.78 basis point value for the swap can be determined using the set of futures rates provided by a full strip of Eurodollar futures. For example, if we suppose that $1 could be invested on June 13, 1994 at the sequence of rates shown in Exhibit 4–2—for example, 4.56 percent for the first 98 days, 5.16 percent for the next 91 days and so on —

EXHIBIT 4–3
Cash Consequences of a Change in a Forward Rate

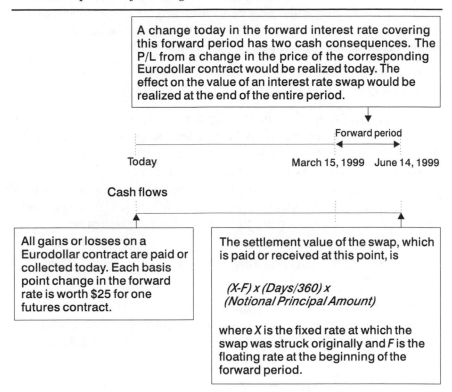

A change today in the forward interest rate covering this forward period has two cash consequences. The P/L from a change in the price of the corresponding Eurodollar contract would be realized today. The effect on the value of an interest rate swap would be realized at the end of the entire period.

Forward period

Today   March 15, 1999   June 14, 1999

Cash flows

All gains or losses on a Eurodollar contract are paid or collected today. Each basis point change in the forward rate is worth $25 for one futures contract.

The settlement value of the swap, which is paid or received at this point, is

(X-F) x (Days/360) x
(Notional Principal Amount)

where *X* is the fixed rate at which the swap was struck originally and *F* is the floating rate at the beginning of the forward period.

the total value of the investment would grow to $1.41509 by June 14, 1999. Put differently, the present value in June 1994 of $1 to be received in June 1999 would be $0.70667 [= $1/$1.41509]. This is shown at the bottom of Exhibit 4–21 as the price of a zero-coupon bond with five years to maturity. At this price, the present value of $2,527.78 five years hence would be $1,786.30 [=$2,527.78 × 0.70667].

Hedging the Forward Swap with Eurodollar Futures

Given these two present contracts values, 71.45 [=$1,786.30/$25.00] Eurodollar futures would have the same exposure to a change in the March 1993 three-month forward rate as would $100 million of the forward swap. For someone who is short the swap (i.e., receiving fixed and paying floating), the appropriate hedge against a change in the forward rate would be a short position of 71.45 Eurodollar futures. Considering what has gone into this calculation, the number of Eurodollar futures needed to hedge any leg of a swap whose floating rate is three-month LIBOR would be:

Hedge Ratio =
NPA × [.0001 × Days/360] × Zero-Coupon Bond Price/$25

where *NPA* is the swap's notional principal amount, or $100 million in our example. The .0001 represents a 1-basis-point change in the forward rate. *Days* is the number of days in the period, which is 91 in our example. The *zero-coupon bond price* is the price today of a bond that pays $1 on the same day that the swap settlement is paid. In our example, the swap settlement is five years away, and the price of such a bond is 0.70667. The $25 is simply the present value of a basis point for a Eurodollar futures contract.

The Other Source of Interest Rate Risk in the Forward Swap

Because any gain or loss on the swap is realized only at the end of the term, a swap can have unrealized asset value. In particular, the present value of a short position in the forward swap in our example can be written as:

Swap Value =
NPA × [(X − F) × Days/360] × Zero-Coupon Bond Price

where *X* is the fixed rate at which the swap was struck originally and *F* is the current market value of the forward rate. From this we can see that the unrealized asset value of a swap depends both on the difference between the swap's fixed rate and the forward rate and on the present value of a dollar to be received on the swap's cash settlement date.

The practical importance of this expression is that there are really two sources of interest rate risk in a forward swap. The first, which we have dealt with already, is uncertainty about the forward rate, *F*. The other is uncertainty about the zero-coupon bond price, which reflects uncertainty about the entire term structure of forward rates extending from today to the swap's cash settlement date. If the forward rate is below the fixed rate, for example, the person who is receiving fixed and paying floating has an asset whose value is reduced by a general increase in interest rates. To get complete protection against interest rate risk, the swap hedger not only must offset the exposure to changes in the forward rate, but also exposure to changes in the term or zero-coupon bond rate. The simplest way to hedge against exposure to changes in zero-coupon term rates it to buy or sell an appropriate quantity of zero-coupon bonds whose maturity matches that of the swap.

Interaction between the Two Sources of Risk

Now we have come to the heart of the difference between a swap and a Eurodollar futures contract. With Eurodollar futures, the only source of risk is the forward or futures rate. When the futures rate changes, the holder of the futures contract collects all of the gains or pays all of the losses right away. The holder of the swap, on the other hand, faces two kinds of risk—a change in the forward rate and a change in the term rate.

To see why this matters, consider what happens to a short swap and a short Eurodollar position if all 20 of the three-month spot and forward rates from June 1994 through March 1999 either rise or fall by 10 basis points. The results of such an exercise are shown in Exhibit 4–4. Note, first, that the $17,863 gain on the short Eurodollar position when the March 1999 futures rate rises 10 basis points is the same as the $17,863 loss when the futures rate falls 10 basis points.

Similarly, the nominal loss on the short swap—$25,278—when the March 1999 forward rate rises is equal to the nominal gain when the forward rate falls. However, the present values of the gain and the loss on the swap are not the same because because the price of the zero-coupon bond falls when the forward rates rise and rises when the forward rates fall. Taking the rates in Exhibit 4–2 as our starting point, the price of the zero-coupon bond falls to $0.70315 per dollar when all of the forward rates increase 10 basis points. The price of the zero increases to $0.71020 when all of the forward rates fall 10 basis points. (Because of differences in compounding conventions, the semiannual bond equivalent yield on the zero-coupon bond changes by 10.3 basis points when the various forward rates change 10 basis points.)

With these changes in the price of the zero-coupon bond, the present value of the loss on the swap if all rates rise 10 basis points is $17,774 [=$25,278 × 0.70315], while the present value of the gain on the swap if rates fall 10 basis points is $17,952. As a result, we find that the short Eurodollar position makes $89 more than is lost on the swap if all forward rates rise and loses $89 less than is gained on the swap if interest rates fall.

EXHIBIT 4–4
Swap and Eurodollar Futures P/Ls

Interest Rate Changes			Short Swap P/L			
Forward Rate	Term Rate on Zero-Coupon Bond	Nominal Value (as of 6/14/99)	Price of Zero-Coupon Bond	Present Value (as of 6/13/94)	Short Eurodollar P/L	Net
(basis points)			(notional principal amount = $100 million)		(71.45 contracts)	
10	10.8	($25,278)	0.70315	($17,774)	$17,863	$89
0	0	0	0.70667	$0	$0	$40
–10	–10.3	$25,278	0.71020	$17,952	($17,863)	$89

A familiar way of depicting this comparison is provided in Exhibit 4–5. A short swap, which requires the holder to pay a floating or variable rate such as three-month LIBOR while receiving a known fixed rate, is much the same as owning a bond that is financed with short-term money. The price/yield relationship for such a position exhibits what is known in the fixed-income trade as positive convexity. That is, the price increases more when yields fall than the price falls when yields rise. In our example, the increase in the swap's price was $17,952 while the decrease in its price was only $17,774. A Eurodollar futures position, on the other hand, exhibits no convexity at all. Each basis point change in the forward rate is worth $25 today no matter what the level of the interest rate. The short Eurodollar position makes $17,863 for a 10-basis-point increase in rates and loses $17,863 for a 10-basis-point decline in rates.

Because of the difference in the convexities of the two instruments, a short swap hedged with a short position in Eurodollar futures benefits from changes in the level of interest rates. As shown in Exhibit 4–5, the difference in convexities for the forward swap in our example is worth $89 if rates rise 10 basis points and $89 if rates fall 10 basis points.

Trading the Hedge

Exhibit 4–5 provides an especially useful way to illustrate the nature of the trade. For example, if interest rates fall 10 basis points, the hedger of the short swap is $89 ahead of the game. At this point, the hedger could (in

EXHIBIT 4–5
The Convexity Difference between Swaps and Eurodollar Futures

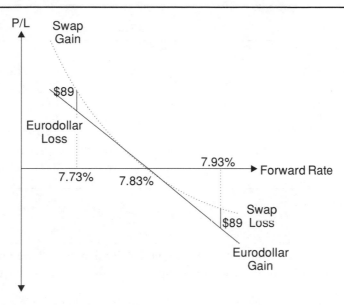

principle, if it weren't for the costs imposed by bid/asked spreads and brokerage) close out the position and pocket the $89. On the other hand, the hedger could view this as a vehicle for trading Eurodollar futures that would eventually accumulate a substantial amount of money. Notice that as rates fall, the number of futures needed to hedge the position increases, which requires selling the additional contracts at a higher price. On the other hand, as rates rise, the number of futures needed to hedge the position falls, which requires the hedger to cover some of the short futures by buying the excess contracts at a lower price.

HOW MUCH IS CONVEXITY BIAS WORTH?

The difference in the performance of a swap and the performance of a Eurodollar futures contract depends on three things:

- The size of the change in the forward rate
- The size of the change in the term rate (or zero-coupon bond price), and
- The correlation between the two.

EXHIBIT 4–6
Net P/Ls for a Short Swap Hedged with Short Eurodollar Futures

Zero-coupon yield change (bp)	*Forward rate change (bp)*				
	–10	*–5*	*0*	*5*	*10*
10	($86)	($43)	$0	$43	$86
5	($43)	($22)	$0	$22	$43
0	$0	$0	$0	$0	$0
–5	$43	$22	$0	($22)	($43)
–10	$86	$43	$0	($43)	($86)

Note: Based on Eurodollar futures rates in Exhibit 1.

These points are illustrated in Exhibit 4–6, which shows the net hedge P/L on our $100 million forward swap for a variety of different possible rate changes.

If both rates rise 5 basis points, the net P/L is $22. If both rates rise 10 basis points, the net gain is $86, or nearly four times as much. (The net gain in this instance is less than the $89 produced by the example illustrated in Exhibit 4–4 because the term rate has only changed by 10 basis points rather than the 10.3 basis points produced by a parallel shift in all three-month spot and forward rates.) Also, if the forward rate rises 10 basis points while the zero-coupon rate rises only 5 basis points, the net P/L is $43. From this we can conclude that the value of the convexity difference is greater when interest rates are volatile than when they are stable.

Exhibit 4–6 also allows us to see the importance of correlation. The net P/Ls are positive if the two interest rates both rise or both fall. If one rate falls while the other rises, the hedged position actually loses money. If one rate changes while the other does not, there is neither a gain nor a loss.

Moreover, if the zero-coupon yield is just as likely to rise as it is to fall no matter what happens to the forward rate, the expected or average net P/L is also zero. For example, if the forward rate increases 10 basis points, the net P/L is a gain of $86 if the zero-coupon rate also increases 10 basis points. The net P/L is a loss of $86, though, if the zero-coupon rate falls 10 basis points. If the probability of the zero-coupon rate rising is a half no matter

EXHIBIT 4–7
Changes In 5-Year Term Rates vs. Changes in the 4.75-year Futures Rate
(Weekly Interval, 7/10/92 through 7/1/94)

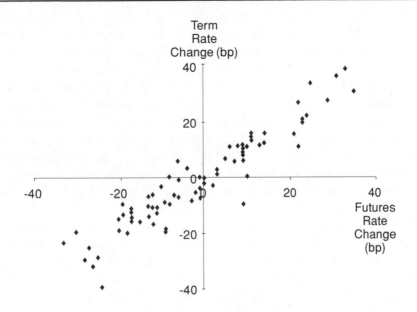

what happens to the forward rate, then the expected or probability weighted average gain would be zero.

How Correlated Are the Rates?

As it happens, forward interest rates and their respective term or zero-coupon rates tend to be very highly correlated. Eurodollar futures rates and strips can be used to estimate the correlation. Exhibit 4–7 shows, for example, the relationship between changes in three-month rates four and three-fourths years forward and changes in five-year zero-coupon term rates. The correlation is not perfect, but with only a few exceptions, increases in the forward rate are accompanied by increases in the term rate, and decreases in the forward rate are accompanied by decreases in the zero-coupon term rate.

Estimating the Value of Convexity Bias

To get a rough idea of how much the convexity bias might be worth, we used actual Eurodollar futures data to calculate hedge one-week P/Ls for three-month forward swaps with two years and five years to final cash settlement. The calculations were much like those summarized in Exhibit 4–4. In particular, we used 1-week changes in the price of the eighth contract in an eight-contract strip to represent the change in a three-month forward rate one and three-fourths years forward. We used all eight rates implied by the eight-contract strip to calculate two-year zero-coupon bond prices and then calculated the one-week price changes associated with one-week changes in the two-year term rate. For the longer-dated forward swap, we used the change in the price of the 20th contract in a 20-contract strip to represent the change in a three-month forward rate four and three-fourths years forward and all 20 rates in the strip to calculate the price of a five-year zero-coupon bond.

The results of these exercises for the three-month swap one and three-fourths years forward are shown in Exhibit 4–8. The results for the three-month swap four and three-fourths years forward are shown in Exhibit 4–9. In both cases, the hedge P/L has been divided by the number of futures contracts in the hedge so that the results are expressed in dollars per Eurodollar futures contract. In other words, Exhibit 4–8 shows the distribution of hedge P/Ls per futures for contracts that would have had one and three-fourths years to expiration, while Exhibit 4–9 shows the distribution of hedge P/Ls per futures for contracts that would have had four and three-fourths years to expiration.

Three things stand out. First, both relationships look a lot like long straddles or strangles in Eurodollar options. While the resemblance is close, the net P/L relationships in Exhibits 4–8 and 4–9 are much more like parabolas than are straddle and strangle P/Ls. Even so, the optionlike quality of a swap hedged with Eurodollar futures is pronounced.

Second, the convexity is more pronounced for the three-month swap four and three-fourths years forward than for the three-month swap one and three-fourths years forward. This is natural enough. Longer-dated swaps exhibit greater convexity than do shorter-dated swaps, and that is what we are seeing in these two exhibits.

Third, the distribution of outcomes looks about right. As one would expect, most of the realized outcomes involved fairly small changes in the

EXHIBIT 4–8
Hedge P/L for a Three-Month Swap 1.75 Years Forward
(Weekly gains per futures contract, 1/5/90 through 7/1/94)

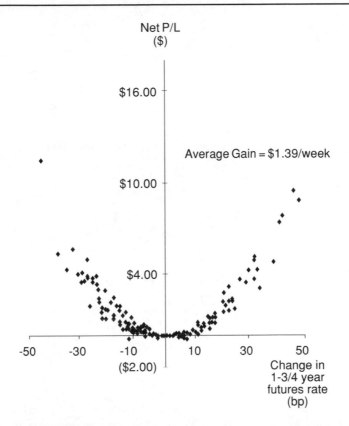

forward rate and correspondingly small net P/Ls on the hedged position. Only some of the changes were very large.

Calculating the Value of the Bias

Given the outcomes plotted in Exhibits 4–8 and 4–9, it is now a simple matter to calculate the average net P/L. Exhibit 4–8 shows that the average outcome amounted to $1.39 per Eurodollar contract per week for futures with one and three-fourths years to expiration. Exhibit 4–9 shows that the

EXHIBIT 4–9
Hedge P/L for a Three-Month Swap 4.75 Years Forward
(Weekly gains per futures contract, 7/10/92 through 7/1/94)

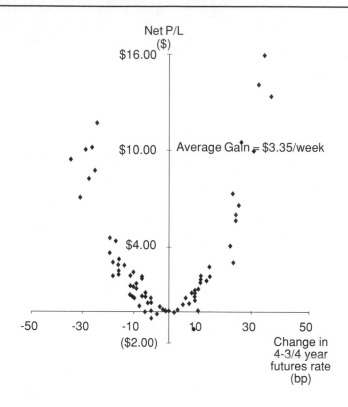

average hedge P/L was $3.35 per Eurodollar contract per week for futures with four and three-fourths years to expiration.

RECONCILING THE DIFFERENCE BETWEEN A SWAP AND A EURODOLLAR FUTURES CONTRACT

If you've been thinking ahead, you may see in all of this the makings of a free lunch. Exhibits 4–8 and 4–9 show all upside and no downside. As it happens, if Eurodollar futures prices were simply 100 less the appropriate forward rates, one could make money easily enough simply shorting swaps and hedging them with short Eurodollar futures. Unhappily for the swaps community, Milton Friedman was right in reminding us that there is no such thing as a free lunch—at least not for long.

If there is an advantage to being short Eurodollar futures, then one should be willing to pay for the advantage. The interesting questions then are how much this lunch should cost and how one should pay.

How to Pay for the Advantage

How one pays for the advantage is comparatively easy to describe. To make the P/L distribution shown in Exhibit 4–8 a fair bet, the whole distribution would have to be shifted down $1.39 for the week. To make the distribution in Exhibit 4–9 a fair bet, the whole distribution would have to be shifted down $3.35.

The easiest way to do this is to allow the futures rate to drift down relative to the forward rate. This would cause the futures price to drift up relative to the value of the swap. At the right rate of drift, the hedger who is short the swap and short futures would expect to give up $1.39 per week or $3.35 per week due to drift but would make it back on average because of convexity differences. In other words, the futures rate implied by any Eurodollar futures price must start out higher than its corresponding forward rate and drift down to meet it at futures contract expiration. For what we are doing, however, it makes no particular difference how one rate converges to the other. The futures rate can fall to meet the forward rate, the forward rate can rise to meet the futures rates, or the two rates can converge to one another. They are all the same to us.

If the presence of a convexity bias means that the futures rate should be higher than the forward rate, then we have to be careful about how we calculate the so-called fair value of a futures contract. The market convention is to define the fair value of the futures as 100 less the value of the forward rate. Considering the value of the bias in favor of short Eurodollar futures, the fair value of the futures contract should be lower than is provided by the conventional definition. How much lower depends on the value of the convexity bias.

Translating the Advantage into Basis Points

In Exhibit 4–8 we found that the average net hedge gain for the three-month swap one and three-fourths years forward was $1.39 per week per futures contract. At $25 per basis point for a Eurodollar contract, this means that the rate of drift for a Eurodollar futures contract with one and three-fourths years to expiration would have to be about .056 [=1.39/25] basis points per week to compensate for the convexity bias. Over the span of a quarter, the drift would have to be about .73 basis points.

In Exhibit 4–9, we found that the average net hedge gain for the three-month swap four and three-fourths years forward was $3.35 per week per futures contract. Using the same arithmetic, the rate of drift for the Eurodollar contract with four and three-fourths year remaining to expiration would have to be .13 basis points per week or about 1.74 basis points per quarter.

To determine how much the difference should be between a three-month rate four and three-fourths years forward and the three-month interest rate implied by a Eurodollar futures contract with four and three-fourths years to expiration, the problem boils down to one of tracking a contract step by step and adding up the drift as the contract approaches expiration.

A WORKABLE RULE OF THUMB

There are a number of ways to determine the value of the convexity bias. One is the empirical approach illustrated in Exhibits 4–8 and 4–9. This is a perfectly good approach if one simply wants to look back and reconcile the historical differences between swaps and Eurodollar futures. The problem with this approach, however, is that it hides the assumptions that go into reckoning the value of the bias and makes it hard to adjust your estimates of the bias as your views about rate volatilities and correlations change.

Another approach is to undertake extensive and complex yield curve simulations that would allow you to estimate the cumulative gains associated with trading a hedged swap book or with financing the mark-to-market gains or losses on a futures contract.[1] Such interest rate simulations can produce reasonable results, but the equipment seems much too heavy for the job and may well obscure what is really going on.

The good news is that the problem can be tackled with relatively light tools. The value of the convexity bias really depends on only three things: the volatility of the forward rate, the volatility of the corresponding term rate, and the correlation between the two. As it happens, the value of the drift in the spread between the futures and forward rates that is needed to

---

1 This is the approach taken in *The Financing Bias in Eurodollar Futures*, which is contained in Chapter 7 of Burghardt, et al., *Eurodollar Futures and Options: Controlling Money Market Risk* (Chicago, IL: Probus Publishing, 1991).

compensate for the advantage of being short Eurodollar futures can be expressed as:

$Drift$ = standard deviation of forward rate changes

   × standard deviation of zero-coupon bond returns

   × correlation of forward rate changes with zero-coupon bond returns

where *Drift* is the number of ticks that the rate spread has to fall during any given period to compensate for the convexity bias. Those who want to know where this expression comes from will find an explanation along with tips on how to apply the rule in Appendix 4–A.

Applying the Rule of Thumb

Exhibit 4–10 provides examples of how to apply this rule to Eurodollar futures contracts with times to expiration ranging from three months to ten years. Consider, for example, the lead futures contract, which has three months remaining to expiration. The annualized standard deviation of changes in the lead futures price (or rate) is shown as 0.92 percent or 92 basis points. (Notice that this is an absolute and not a relative rate volatility like those quoted for Eurodollar options.) The annualized standard deviation of returns on a zero-coupon bond with an average of four and one-half months to maturity (the zero begins the quarter with six months to maturity and ends the quarter with three months remaining) is shown as 0.35 percent, or 35 basis points. This standard deviation is itself the product of the standard deviation of changes in the yield on the zero-coupon bond and the zero's time to maturity, which is also its duration. The historical correlation between these two changes is shown as .9945, which is about as highly correlated as anything can be. Taken together, we find that the required drift over a quarter of a year would be calculated as

$Drift = [0.92\% \times 0.35\% \times 0.9945]/4$

   $= 0.08$ basis points

In other words, for a Eurodollar futures contract with three months left to expiration, the rate of drift expressed in basis points per quarter would be 0.08 basis points. That is, the spread between the futures and forward rates would have to converge at this rate to compensate for the value of the convexity differential.

The Importance of Time to Contract Expiration

If we do the same exercise for a futures contract that has six months left to expiration, we find that the required quarterly rate of drift in the price or the rate is 0.19 basis points [= $1.03\% \times 0.74\% \times 0.9824 / 4$], which is over twice as fast. The higher rate of drift is the combined effect of slightly higher rate volatilities, a very slightly lower correlation, and a very much higher duration of the zero-coupon bond.

As we saw in Exhibits 4–8 and 4–9, the value of the convexity bias depends directly on the convexity of the forward swap that is associated with the futures contract. This depends in turn on the price sensitivity of the zero-coupon bond that corresponds to the swap's maturity. Because the price of a zero-coupon bond with five years to maturity is more sensitive to a change in its yield than is the price of a zero with two years to maturity, the value of the bias is greater for a Eurodollar futures contract with four and three-fourths years to expiration than for a contract with one and three-fourths years to expiration.

The rule of thumb captures this effect nicely because the standard deviation of a zero-coupon bond's return is simply the product of the standard deviation of the zero's yield and its duration. If its yield is reckoned on a continuously compounded basis, then a zero-coupon bond's duration is simply its maturity. The result is a higher rate of drift for contracts with longer times remaining to expiration. For example, the rate of drift for a contract with five years to expiration is shown in Exhibit 4–10 to be about 1.5 basis points per quarter. For a contract with 10 years to expiration, the rate of drift is nearly 3 basis points per quarter.

The Cumulative Effect of Drift

We know that when the futures contract expires, its final settlement price will be set equal to 100 less the spot value of three-month LIBOR. As a result, the implied futures rate and the spot rate have to be the same at contract expiration. We also know that the implied futures rate before expiration should be drifting down relative to the corresponding forward rate so that the two meet on contract expiration day.

The question, then, is how much different the futures and forward rates should be at any time before expiration. The answer is found simply by adding up the quarterly drift estimates, which is what we have done in the last column of Exhibit 4–10. For example, if a futures contract with three months to expiration is drifting at a rate of 0.08 basis points per quarter,

EXHIBIT 4-10
Calculating the Value of the Convexity Bias

(1) Years to Futures Expiration	Annualized Standard Deviations		(4) = (1) + 1/8 Average Years to Zero Maturity (avg. duration)	(5) = (3) × (4) Annualized Standard Deviation	(6) Correlation of Eurodollar Rate Changes and Zero Returns†	Convexity Bias (bp)	
	(2) Eurodollar Rate Changes	(3) Zero Yield Changes*				(7) = (2)×(5)×(6)/4 per Quarter	(8) Cumulative Bias
1/4	0.92%	0.92%	3/8	0.35%	0.9945	0.08	0.08
1/2	1.03%	1.18%	5/8	0.74%	0.9824	0.19	0.27
3/4	1.12%	1.33%	7/8	1.16%	0.9726	0.32	0.59
1	1.18%	1.42%	1 1/8	1.60%	0.9646	0.45	1.04
1 1/4	1.22%	1.42%	1 3/8	1.95%	0.9581	0.57	1.61
1 1/2	1.23%	1.37%	1 5/8	2.23%	0.9527	0.65	2.26
1 3/4	1.23%	1.30%	1 7/8	2.44%	0.9484	0.71	2.97
2	1.22%	1.24%	2 1/8	2.64%	0.9448	0.76	3.73
2 1/4	1.21%	1.20%	2 3/8	2.85%	0.9419	0.81	4.54
2 1/2	1.20%	1.17%	2 5/8	3.07%	0.9396	0.86	5.40
2 3/4	1.18%	1.15%	2 7/8	3.31%	0.9377	0.92	6.32
3	1.17%	1.14%	3 1/8	3.56%	0.9363	0.98	7.30
3 1/4	1.16%	1.13%	3 3/8	3.81%	0.9352	1.04	8.34
3 1/2	1.15%	1.12%	3 5/8	4.06%	0.9344	1.09	9.43
3 3/4	1.14%	1.12%	3 7/8	4.34%	0.9339	1.16	10.59
4	1.14%	1.12%	4 1/8	4.62%	0.9336	1.23	11.82

Table continues

101

EXHIBIT 4-10
continued

Years to Futures Expiration	Annualized Standard Deviations		Average Years to Zero Maturity (avg. duration)	Annualized Standard Deviation	Correlation of Eurodollar Rate Changes and Zero Returns†	Convexity Bias (bp)	
	Eurodollar Rate Changes	Zero Yield Changes*				per Quarter	Cumulative Bias
(1)	(2)	(3)	(4) = (1) + 1/8	(5) = (3) × (4)	(6)	(7) = (2) × (5) × (6) / 4	(8)
4 1/4	1.13%	1.11%	4 3/8	4.86%	0.9335	1.28	13.10
4 1/2	1.13%	1.11%	4 5/8	5.13%	0.9336	1.35	14.45
4 3/4	1.12%	1.11%	4 7/8	5.41%	0.9339	1.42	15.87
5	1.12%	1.11%	5 1/8	5.69%	0.9342	1.49	17.36
5 1/4	1.11%	1.12%	5 3/8	6.02%	0.9348	1.57	18.93
5 1/2	1.11%	1.12%	5 5/8	6.30%	0.9354	1.64	20.57
5 3/4	1.11%	1.12%	5 7/8	6.58%	0.9361	1.71	22.28
6	1.11%	1.12%	6 1/8	6.86%	0.9369	1.79	24.07
6 1/4	1.11%	1.12%	6 3/8	7.14%	0.9378	1.86	25.93
6 1/2	1.11%	1.11%	6 5/8	7.35%	0.9388	1.92	27.85
6 3/4	1.11%	1.12%	6 7/8	7.70%	0.9398	2.01	29.86
7	1.11%	1.12%	7 1/8	7.98%	0.9409	2.08	31.94
7 1/4	1.11%	1.11%	7 3/8	8.19%	0.9420	2.14	34.08
7 1/2	1.10%	1.11%	7 5/8	8.46%	0.9432	2.21	36.29
7 3/4	1.10%	1.11%	7 7/8	8.74%	0.9444	2.27	38.56
8	1.10%	1.11%	8 1/8	9.02%	0.9457	2.34	40.90

Table continues

EXHIBIT 4–10
continued

Years to Futures Expiration	Annualized Standard Deviations		Average Years to Zero Maturity (avg. duration)	Annualized Standard Deviation	Correlation of Eurodollar Rate Changes and Zero Returns†	Convexity Bias (bp)	
	Eurodollar Rate Changes	Zero Yield Changes*				per Quarter	Cumulative Bias
(1)	(2)	(3)	(4) = (1) + 1/8	(5) = (3) × (4)	(6)	(7) = (2) × (5) × (6) / 4	(8)
8 1/4	1.10%	1.10%	8 3/8	9.21%	0.9470	2.39	43.29
8 1/2	1.09%	1.09%	8 5/8	9.40%	0.9484	2.44	45.73
8 3/4	1.09%	1.09%	8 7/8	9.67%	0.9497	2.51	48.24
9	1.09%	1.09%	9 1/8	9.95%	0.9512	2.57	50.81
9 1/4	1.09%	1.09%	9 3/8	10.22%	0.9526	2.64	53.45
9 1/2	1.08%	1.09%	9 5/8	10.49%	0.9540	2.71	56.16
9 3/4	1.08%	1.08%	9 7/8	10.67%	0.9555	2.75	58.91
10	1.08%	1.08%	10 1/8	10.94%	0.9570	2.82	61.73

* Zero-coupon yield continuously compounded.
† Equals correlation of Euro$ rates and zero-coupon yield changes.

then the futures and forward rates would have to be 0.08 basis points apart if they are to meet exactly at expiration. On the other hand, if a futures contract with six months to expiration is drifting at a rate of 0.19 basis points per quarter for the first three months of its life and then at a rate of 0.08 basis points for the last three months of its life, the total drift in the contract's price would be 0.27 [= 0.08 + 0.19] basis points for the entire six months. The bias for the next contract out would be .59 [= .08 + .19 + .32] basis points, and so on down the list.

For short-dated futures contracts, all of this work adds up to comparatively little. For a contract with one year to expiration, for example, the total cumulative value of the bias adds up to only 1.04 basis points. Considering everything else that the market has to worry about, this is really nothing.

On the other hand, the adding up of these little bits of drift per quarter has a profound effect on the spread between futures and forward rates for contracts with several years to expiration. For example, the cumulative value of the bias for a contract with five years to expiration is about 17 basis points. For a contract with 10 years to expiration, the cumulative value of the bias is more than 60 basis points.

How Sensitive Are the Estimates to the Assumptions?

The rule of thumb makes it clear that the value of the bias is directly related to three things: the volatility of the forward rate, the volatility of the zero-coupon bond or term rate, and the correlation between the two. Because the rate of drift is calculated simply by multiplying these numbers together, the required rate of drift is directly proportional to the value of each of these three things. If forward rate volatility doubles, the value of the bias doubles too. If term rate volatility doubles, the value of the bias doubles as well. If both double, the value of the bias quadruples. If both rate volatilities were increased by 10 percent, the value of the bias would be increased by 21 percent. In other words, the value that anyone places on the convexity bias depends clearly on his or her views about interest rate volatility.

To get an idea of how changeable these three key variables could be, we used Eurodollar futures data to estimate them for different time periods. The results of these exercises are shown in Exhibits 4–11, 4–12, and 4–13. The peculiar look of these exhibits—i.e., the reason the lines have different lengths—is because the Chicago Mercantile Exchange has added futures

FIGURE 4–11
Standard Deviation of Eurodollar Futures Rate Changes (annualized)

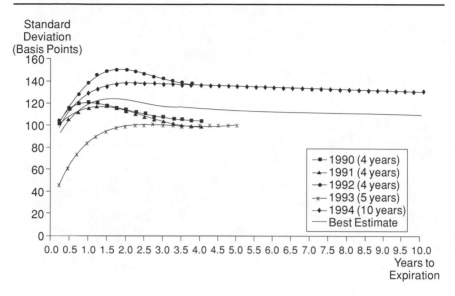

contracts with longer times to expiration in more or less discrete chunks. For example, from 1990 to 1992, futures contracts extended out to four years, and so our estimates of rate volatilities and correlations for these years are limited to horizons of four years. By the middle of 1992, however, the CME had listed the "golds," which had five years to expiration. Then, by the end of 1993, the exchange had listed contracts with expirations extending out a full 10 years.

Even with the mixed collection of data that were available to us, the results are instructive. Consider first the volatility of forward rates, which is represented by the standard deviation of Eurodollar futures rates in Exhibit 4–11. The annualized standard deviation of a three-month rate four years forward in 1993 was around 100 basis points, or 1 percentage point. In 1994, the annualized standard deviation of a four-year forward rate was closer to 140 basis points. In Exhibit 4–10, we used 114 basis points or 1.14 percent to reckon the value of the convexity bias for a futures contract with four years to expiration. (See Exhibit 4–10, column 2.) The estimate of 114 basis points was taken from the solid, unmarked

FIGURE 4–12
Standard Deviation of Term Yield Changes *(annualized)*

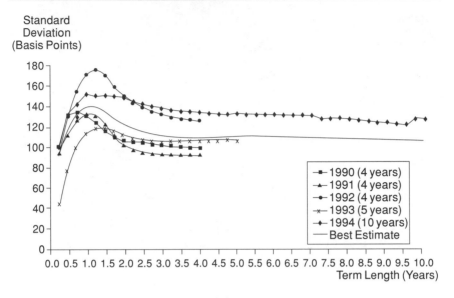

Note: Yield changes are continuously compounded.

line in Exhibit 4–11 that extends all the way out to 10 years. This line represents our best guess about the structure of forward rate volatilities for the years 1990 through August 1994.

Because the value of the convexity bias is directly proportional to the standard deviation of forward rates and the standard deviation of term rates, the ranges of these standard deviations shown in Exhibits 4–11 and 4–12 impart substantial range to the possible value of the bias. For example, based on our best estimate of rate volatilities over the past five years, we reckoned that the value of the bias was 17 basis points for a contract with five years to expiration. Because the rule of thumb is linear in rate volatility, we can easily estimate the bias for higher or lower levels of rate standard deviations. For example, if we scale both forward and term rate standard deviations up by 15 percent (a reasonably high estimate given the volatility experience we saw in Exhibits 4–11 and 4–12), the bias would increase to about 22 basis points [= $17 \times (1.15) \times (1.15)$]. On the other hand, if we scale both standard deviations down by 15 percent (to a low estimate), the value of the bias would decrease to about 12 basis points [= $17 \times (.85) \times (.85)$]. So, the true value of the bias for a contract with five years to expiration could easily vary between 12 and 22 basis points, depending on the market's assessment of rate volatility.

Of the three key variables, the correlation between changes in forward and zero-coupon bond rates seems to be the most stable. To get a feel for these relationships, we calculated the correlations between changes in Eurodollar strips rates and changes in the rate implied by the last contract in the strip. As shown in Exhibit 4–13, the lowest of these correlations appears to have been in the low 90s or upper 80s, while the highest have been in the upper 90s. We used correlations in the mid-90s to construct the estimates in Exhibit 4–9. Given the range of correlations shown in Exhibit 4–13, changes in correlation from one year to the next would increase or decrease the value of the convexity bias by 3 or 4 percent, which is less than a basis point for a contract with four years to expiration and only two or three basis points for a contract with 10 years to expiration.

Practical Considerations in Applying the Rule

One of the good things about the way we approach the problem of valuing the convexity bias is that anyone with a spreadsheet program and an understanding of rate volatilities and correlations can do the job. To do the job right, however, requires some attention to detail. For those who want to try their hand at it, follow the guidelines provided in Appendix 4–A.

THE IMPORTANCE OF BIAS FOR PRICING TERM SWAPS

The swaps industry is accustomed to pricing swaps against Eurodollar futures, chiefly because Eurodollar futures prices are thought to provide the most accurate and competitive market information about forward rates. The reasoning behind such a practice is solid because the futures market is more heavily scrutinized by interest rate traders than either the cash deposit market or the over-the-counter derivatives markets.

The problem now, however, is that swaps traders are gaining a heightened appreciation for the importance of the convexity difference between swaps and Eurodollar futures. Several years ago, when futures expirations only extended out three or four years, this was not much of a problem.

FIGURE 4–13
Correlation of Eurodollar Rates and Term Rates

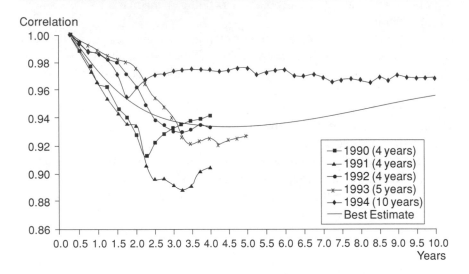

Today, with futures expirations extending to 10 years and with longer-dated swaps trading more actively, the problem of reconciling the differences has become more acute. The effect of the convexity bias on the pricing of swaps against Eurodollar futures is illustrated for term swaps with various maturities in Exhibit 4–14.

The interest rates shown in the second column represent the spot and implied Eurodollar futures rates on June 13, 1994. If we take these rates at face value and ignore the value of the convexity differences, we can calculate two kinds of term rates. One is the Eurodollar strip rate, which is the same as the rate for a zero-coupon bond with a maturity equal to the length of the strip. Another is an implied swap yield. Examples of both are shown in columns 5 and 6.

For example, the zero-coupon rate for a five-year Eurodollar strip is shown as 7.06 percent. The swap rate next to it is 6.98 percent. The reason for the difference, which is described in Appendix 4–B, is that a five-year Eurodollar strip gives equal weight to all 20 of the three-month rates that go into its calculation. An implied five-year swap rate, however, gives greater weight to the nearby forward rates than it does to the more distant

EXHIBIT 4–14
Eurodollar and Swap Convexity Bias

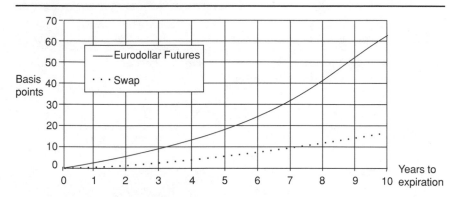

Convexity-Adjusted Swap Yields

	Eurodollar Rates (MM A/360)			Calculated Term Yields SA 30/360)			
Years to Expiration	Futures Market	Convexity bias (bp)	Convexity Adjusted	Euro-dollar Strip*	Implied Swap	Convexity Adjusted Swap	Swap Convexity Bias (bp)
(1)	(2)	(3)	(4) = (2) – (3)	(5)	(6)	(7)	(8)
Spot	4.56	0.00	4.56				0.00
1/4	5.16	0.08	5.16				0.02
1/2	5.86	0.27	5.86	4.95	4.95	4.95	0.04
3/4	6.09	0.59	6.08				0.14
1	6.39	1.04	6.38	5.51	5.50	5.50	0.23
1 1/4	6.64	1.61	6.62				0.41
1 1/2	6.88	2.26	6.86	5.89	5.87	5.87	0.59
1 3/4	6.92	2.97	6.89				0.83
2	7.02	3.73	6.98	6.18	6.16	6.15	1.08
2 1/4	7.11	4.54	7.06				1.37
2 1/2	7.26	5.40	7.21	6.40	6.36	6.34	1.66
2 3/4	7.28	6.32	7.22				1.99
3	7.37	7.30	7.30	6.57	6.52	6.50	2.32
3 1/4	7.45	8.34	7.37				2.68
3 1/2	7.58	9.43	7.49	6.71	6.66	6.63	3.05
3 3/4	7.58	10.59	7.47				3.44

Exhibit continues

EXHIBIT 4–14
continued

Years to Expiration	Eurodollar Rates (MM A/360)			Calculated Term Yields SA 30/360)			
	Futures Market	Convexity bias (bp)	Convexity Adjusted	Euro-dollar Strip*	Implied Swap	Convexity Adjusted Swap	Swap Convexity Bias (bp)
(1)	(2)	(3)	(4) = (2)–(3)	(5)	(6)	(7)	(8)
4	7.66	11.82	7.54	6.84	6.78	6.74	3.83
4 1/4	7.72	13.10	7.59				4.25
4 1/2	7.84	14.45	7.70	6.96	6.88	6.84	4.68
4 3/4	7.83	15.87	7.67				5.13
5	7.91	17.36	7.74	7.06	6.98	6.92	5.58
5 1/4	7.97	18.93	7.78				6.06
5 1/2	8.09	20.57	7.88	7.16	7.07	7.00	6.55
5 3/4	8.06	22.28	7.84				7.06
6	8.10	24.07	7.86	7.25	7.15	7.07	7.57
6 1/4	8.14	25.93	7.88				8.11
6 1/2	8.24	27.85	7.96	7.34	7.22	7.13	8.65
6 3/4	8.19	29.86	7.89				9.21
7	8.21	31.94	7.89	7.41	7.28	7.19	9.77
7 1/4	8.22	34.08	7.88				10.36
7 1/2	8.30	36.29	7.94	7.48	7.34	7.23	10.95
7 3/4	8.24	38.56	7.85				11.57
8	8.24	40.90	7.83	7.54	7.39	7.27	12.18
8 1/4	8.25	43.29	7.82				12.83
8 1/2	8.33	45.73	7.87	7.60	7.44	7.30	13.47
8 3/4	8.27	48.24	7.79				14.13
9	8.29	50.81	7.78	7.64	7.48	7.33	14.79
9 1/4	8.31	53.45	7.78				15.48
9 1/2	8.37	56.16	7.81	7.69	7.52	7.35	16.16
9 3/4	8.33	58.91	7.74				16.87
10	8.35	61.73	7.73	7.74	7.55	7.38	17.58

* Calculated from futures market Eurodollar rates on June 13, 1994.

rates. As a result, if the forward rate curve slopes upward, the implied swap rate is lower than the strip rate.

There is no need to take the futures rates at face value, however. If we are confident in our estimates of the value of the convexity bias, then we can adjust each of the futures rates before calculating the swap rates. No adjustment would be required for the spot rate. An adjustment of 0.08 basis points for the first of the Eurodollar futures rates is too small to have a noticeable effect. The adjustment to the rate implied by the futures contract with five years to expiration, however, is 17 basis points. As shown in columns 3 and 4 of Exhibit 4–14, the convexity-adjusted futures rate would be 7.74 [=7.91 – .17] percent. Similarly, the convexity-adjusted futures rate for the longest dated futures contract, which had 10 years to expiration, would be 7.73 [=8.35 – .62] percent to reflect an adjustment of 62 basis points.

These convexity-adjusted futures rates are a much better reflection of the forward rates implied by Eurodollar futures prices and are the rates that we use to calculate what we call convexity-adjusted implied swap rates. For example, the five-year swap rate implied by the adjusted futures rates would be 6.92 percent, which is 6 basis points less than the 6.98 percent that one would get using the raw, unadjusted rates. The 10-year swap rate would be 7.38 percent, which is 17 basis points less than the 7.55 percent obtained from the unadjusted futures rates.

In other words, if our estimates of the convexity biases are reliable, then a five-year swap rate should be about 6 basis points lower than the rate implied by raw Eurodollar futures rates. A 10-year swap rate should be about 17 basis points lower. Put differently, if one wants to know whether swap yields are rich or cheap relative to Eurodollar futures, the convexity-adjusted yield spreads are the standards against which the market spreads should be compared.

Biases in Forward Swap Rates

The market for forward swaps seems to have been growing recently. For example, one can find more or less active markets for five-year swaps five years forward, or for two-year swaps eight years forward. For such swaps, the convexity bias can loom fairly large.

Exhibit 4–15 shows what the bias would be for a wide range of spot and forward swaps given the volatility and correlation assumptions that we have used. Along the top row, for example, are the calculations for spot swaps

EXHIBIT 4–15
Convexity Bias in Forward Swaps (bp)

Years forward	Swap term (years)									
	1	2	3	4	5	6	7	8	9	10
Spot	0.23	1.08	2.32	3.83	5.58	7.57	9.77	12.18	14.79	17.58
1	1.99	3.49	5.23	7.21	9.44	11.88	14.55	17.42	20.48	
2	5.11	7.05	9.25	11.71	14.39	17.32	20.46	23.78		
3	9.16	11.58	14.30	17.24	20.43	23.85	27.47			
4	14.22	17.22	20.42	23.90	27.61	31.52				
5	20.48	23.94	27.71	31.73	35.95					
6	27.70	31.81	36.14	40.69						
7	36.28	40.91	45.77							
8	45.93	51.13								
9	56.76									

(Six month LIBOR, SA 30/360)

with terms ranging from 1 to 10 years. The numbers in this row are the same as those in the right hand column of Exhibit 4–14. Along the second row are the biases for swaps that begin one year in the future. For example, the value of the convexity adjustment for a five-year swap that begins one year in the future is about 9 basis points. In contrast, the value of the convexity bias for a five-year swap that begins five years in the future would be about 36 basis points.

THE MARKET'S EXPERIENCE WITH CONVEXITY BIAS

Exhibit 4–16 provides an interesting look at how the market's appreciation for convexity bias has grown over the past couple of years. We used data on five-year swap rates to calculate the spread between market swap rates and the swap rates that can be calculated using Eurodollar futures rates. The solid line represents the spread between market swap rates and the swap rates implied by convexity-adjusted futures rates. The dashed line represents the spread between market swap rates and the swap rates implied by the raw unadjusted futures rates. Notice that in 1992, the spread between the market and raw implied swap rates was around zero. In other words, in

EXHIBIT 4–16
Spreads between Market and Implied Swap Yields

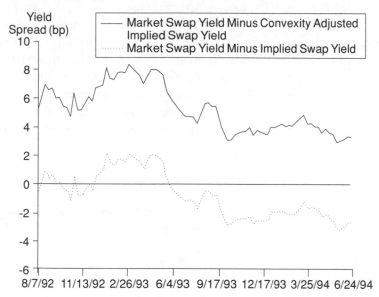

Note: Five-year swap rates courtesy of NationsBand-CRT.

1992, swaps appear to have been priced right on top of the Eurodollar futures rate curve. At the same time, the spread between market swap rates and the convexity-adjusted implied swap rates was around 6 basis points.

Since then, these spreads have fallen. Market swap rates now tend to trade below those that are implied by raw, unadjusted Eurodollar futures rates. At the same time, the spread between market and convexity-adjusted rates has been drifting down toward zero. In both cases, the drop in the spread suggests that the swaps market is adapting to the value of the bias in short Eurodollar futures relative to short swaps. But the adaptation appears to be incomplete. Given our estimates of the value of the convexity bias, there still seems to be some advantage in hedging a short swaps book with short Eurodollar futures.

NOW WHAT?

The natural question to ask now is what can be done with this information. Several possibilities come to mind.

Running a Short Swaps Book

Given the size of the swaps market, the value of knowing how to price swaps correctly against Eurodollar futures prices is enormous. If a five-year swap is mispriced by as little as 2 or 3 basis points against Eurodollar futures, the mispricing is worth about $80,000 on a $100 million swap. If a 10-year swap is mispriced by as little as 5 basis points, and our conversations with swaps traders suggests that this is possible, the mispricing is worth about $350,000 on a $100 million swap. These are large enough amounts of money and suggest that there is a lot at stake. For one thing, it suggests that a swaps desk can still make money by shorting swaps and hedging them with short Eurodollar futures.

Marking a Swaps Book to Market

Not that bank comptrollers and risk managers need any more to worry about, but the value of the convexity bias between swaps and Eurodollar futures raises a big question about how a derivatives book should be marked to market. The standard for many banks is to mark its swaps to market using Eurodollar futures rates. This standard makes good sense because Eurodollar futures prices are the result of a much more open and competitive market process than are swap yields in the over-the-counter market. The problem we find now, however, is that Eurodollar futures prices produce forward rates that are higher than the forward rates that should be used to value swaps.

This leaves comptrollers and risk managers with a difficult choice. One approach is to stick with raw, unadjusted futures rates. The advantage to this approach is that the rates are easy to calculate and to document and no one can tinker with them. The disadvantage to this approach is that the true value of the swaps book is misstated.

The other approach is to make what seems like a reasonable allowance for the value of the convexity bias. This has the advantage of providing better estimates of the value of the swaps book and of providing correct incentives for a swaps desk. The disadvantage is that convexity-adjusted Eurodollar futures rates depend so much on assumptions about rate volatilities.

Volatility Arbitrage

Because the spread between swap and Eurodollar rates should depend on expected interest rate volatilities every bit as much as the prices of caps and swaptions, one should be able to detect differences in implied rate volatilities and to construct trades that profit from differences between the two markets. For example, the spread between a five-year swap yield and the swap yield implied by a five-year strip of Eurodollar futures can be used to impute an expectation about interest rate volatilities from the perspective of swaps and Eurodollar traders. The price of a five-year interest rate cap, on the other hand, reflects that market's expectations about interest rate volatilities over the same period. A sharp trading desk should be able to arbitrage differences between the two markets' implied rate volatilities.

Evaluating Term TED Spreads

A trade that has gained considerable popularity over the past few years has been to spread Treasury notes against strips of Eurodollar futures. In practice, the market has viewed this trade as a way of trading the yield spread between private bank paper and Treasury paper. Now we find that the rates implied by Eurodollar futures prices reflect a convexity bias, which means that these trades have a volatility component as well. For notes with 5 to 10 years to expiration, the value of the convexity bias can loom fairly large. The imputed credit spread between the yield on a five-year Eurodollar strip and a five-year Treasury note really should be about 6 basis points narrower than it appears to be. In light of the comparatively tight spreads at which Eurodollars have been trading against Treasury notes anyway, such an adjustment would make the imputed credit spread appear to be paper thin rather than merely narrow.

Appendix 4–A
DERIVING THE RULE OF THUMB

The rule of thumb for calculating the rate of drift in Eurodollar rates relative to forward rates stems directly from calculating the expected gain when a forward swap is hedged with Eurodollar futures and applying the "no free lunch" principle.

Swap Value

The net present value of a forward swap that receives fixed and pays floating for a three-month period is:

$$NPV = NPA \times (X - F) \times (Days / 360) \times P_z$$

where NPA is the swap's notional principal amount, X is the fixed rate at which the swap is struck, F is the forward rate, *days* is the actual number of days in the swap period to which the floating and fixed rates apply, and P_z is the fractional price of a zero-coupon bond that matures on the swap payment date (which is *days* following the swap rate setting date). The interest rates in this expression are expressed in percent (i.e., 7 percent would be .07). If we multiply and divide this expression by \$1,000,000 as well as by 90, we get:

$$NPV = (NPA / \$1MM) \times [(X - F) \times 10,000]$$

$$\times [(Days / 90) \times (90 / 360) \times \$100] \times P_z$$

which is fairly messy but allows us to arrive at:

$$NPV = (NPA / \$1 \text{ MM}) \times (X* - F*) \times (Days / 90) \times \$25 \times P_z$$

in which $X*$ and $F*$ are expressed in basis points. We also find the \$25, which corresponds nicely to the value of a tick or basis point on a Eurodollar futures contract. The value of Days/90 compensates for the actual length of the swap period.

When a typical swap is transacted, we being with $X* = F*$ so that the net present value of the swap is zero. When interest rates change, both $F*$ and P_z change, and both contribute to the swap's profit or loss.

Swap P/L and Hedge Ratio

For a change of $\Delta F*$ in the forward rate and ΔP_z in the price of the zero, the profit on the forward swap is:

$$NPV = -(NPA / \$1MM) \times (Days / 90) \times \$25 \times \Delta F* \times (P_z + \Delta P_z)$$

Because the change in the value of one Eurodollar futures contract is equal to $-\$25 \times \Delta F*$, the number of futures contracts needed to hedge against unexpected changes in rates would be:

$$Hedge\ Ratio = -(NPA / \$1MM) \times (Days / 90) \times P_z$$

This hedge ratio makes sense. The minus sign indicates that the hedger must short the contracts, $NPA/\$1MM$ captures the nominal number of contracts required, Days/90 reflects the importance of the day count in the swap, and P_z provides the present value correction for the difference in timing of the cash flows on the futures and the swap.

Eurodollar P/L

Given this hedge ratio, the profit on the short Eurodollar futures position would be:

$$(NPA / \$1MM) \times (Days / 90) \times P_z \times (\Delta F* + Drift) \times \$25$$

where Drift represents the systematic change in the Eurodollar futures rate relative to the forward rate needed to compensate for the convexity difference between the swap and the futures contract.

Expected Hedge P/L

To eliminate any possibility of a free lunch in this hedge, the expected profit of the hedged swap must be zero. Put differently, the expected profit on the swap must exactly offset the expected profit on the Eurodollar position. Because the $[(NPA /$ $1MM) \times (Days / 90) \times $25]$ is common to both the profit on the swap and the profit on the Eurodollar position, this part of both expressions cancels out. The result of setting the two combined profits equal to zero and rearranging shows us that:

$$E[\Delta F* \times (P_z + \Delta P_z)] = E[P_z \times (\Delta F* + Drift)]$$

where $E[]$ represents the market's expectation today of whatever is contained inside the brackets. Because P_z is a known number, we can solve for the drift by dividing through by P_z within the expectations to get:

$$E[Drift] = E[\Delta F* \times (\Delta P_z/P_z)]$$

If we combine this expression with the fact that the average move in forward rates and term rates will be zero and use the formula for correlation, we arrive at the rule of thumb:

$$E[Drift] = stdev(\Delta F*) \times stdev(\Delta P_z/P_z) \times correlation \ (\Delta F*, \Delta P_z/P_z)$$

This rule of thumb assumes nothing, by the way, about the distribution of rate changes.

Practical Considerations

- The drift is expressed in basis points per period if the standard deviation of $\Delta F*$ is in basis points per period.

- To use volatilities from the options market, relative or percentage rate volatilities must be converted to absolute rate volatilities by multiplying by the level of the interest rate.

- $\Delta P_z/P_z$ is the *unexpected* return on a zero-coupon bond over the period. It should be expressed as a fraction (for example, as 0.015). The easiest way to compute the standard deviation of $\Delta P_z/P_z$ is to break it into two parts: the standard deviation of the zero's continuously compounded yield and duration. (See Appendix 4–B for the method used to compute continuously compounded zero-coupon yields from Eurodollar future rates.)

- The length of the period over which you calculate changes in rates is not terribly important as long as the duration for the zero-coupon bond is chosen to be its average years to maturity over the period. A period of one day would be theoretically correct, because mark to market actually occurs daily in the futures market. But this would be computational overkill. Using a quarterly period produces almost the same result as daily calculations with a lot less work.

Appendix 4–B
CALCULATING EURODOLLAR STRIP RATES AND IMPLIED SWAP RATES

Eurodollar Strip Rates

A Eurodollar strip is a position that contains one each of the contracts in a sequence of contract months. For example, a one-year strip might contain one each of the June 94, September 94, December 94, and March 95 contracts. A two-year strip would contain these plus one each of the June 95, September 95, December 95, and March 96 contracts. The rates implied by a strip of Eurodollar futures prices together with an initial spot rate can be used to calculate the terminal value of $1 invested today. For example:

$$TWT = [1 + R_0 \, (D_0/360)] \times [1 + F_1(D_1/360)] \times \ldots \times [1 + F_n(D_n/360)]$$

where

TW_T is the terminal value (i.e., terminal wealth) of $1 invested today for T years.

R_0 is spot LIBOR to first futures expiration

F_1 is the lead futures rate [=100 lead futures price]

F_n is the futures rate for the last contract in the strip

D_i is the actual number of days in each period, $i = 0, \ldots, n$

From this value of terminal wealth, we can calculate Eurodollar strip rates in several forms including money market, semiannual bond equivalent, and continuously compounded. All three are zero-coupon bond rates implied by a strip of Eurodollar futures prices.

Money Market Strip Yield

The money market strip yield is the value of R_{MM} that satisfies:

$$[1 + R_{MM}(365 / 360)]^N \times [1+R_{MM} (D_f / 360)] = TW_T$$

where N is the whole number of years in the strip and D_f is the number of days in a partial year at the end of the strip.

Semiannual Bond Equivalent Yield

The semiannual bond equivalent strip yield is the value of R_{SA} that satisfies:

$$[1 + R_{SA} / 2]^{2T} = TW_T$$

which provides R_{SA} as:

$$R_{SA} = [TW_T^{\frac{1}{(2T)}} - 1] \times 2$$

Continuously Compounded Yield

For computing returns on zero-coupon bonds, continuously compounded yields are the most convenient because the duration of a zero-coupon bond is equal to its maturity when yield changes are continuously compounded. The continuously compounded yield is the value of R_{CC} for which:

$$e^{T \times R_{cc}} = TW_T$$

where e is the base for natural logarithms. This can be solved as:

$$R_{CC} = In\ (TW_T) / T$$

where In() is the natural log.

Zero-Coupon Bond Price

The price of a $1 par value zero-coupon bond that matures at T is:

$$P_z = 1/TW_T$$

Implied Swap Rates

A conventional fixed/floating interest rate swap typically is priced as if it contains a long position in a floating rate note and a short position in a fixed-rate note. At the time of the transaction, the fixed and floating rates are set so that the net present value of the swap is zero. If the initial floating rate is set equal to the market rate for the term of the floater—for example, equal to three-month LIBOR if the swap has three-month reset dates—then one can assume the hypothetical floater would

trade at par. As a result, one can assume that the fixed rate on the swap must be set
so that the hypothetical fixed-rate note would also trade at par. The swap yield is
simply the coupon rate that would accomplish this. For example, the swap yield
for a one-year swap with semiannual reset dates would be the value of C that
satisfied the following:

$$[C/2 \times P_6] + [(C/2 + 100) \times P_{12}] = 100$$

where P_6 is the price of a zero-coupon bond that matures in 6 months, and P_{12} is
the price of a zero-coupon bond that matures in 12 months. If one happens to be
pricing a swap on a futures expiration date, the zero-coupon prices would be
calculated as:

$$P_6 = 1 / \{[1 + F_1(D_1 / 360)] \times [1 + F_2 (D_2 / 360)]\}$$
$$P_{12} = 1 / \{[1 + F_1 (D_1 / 360)] \times [1 + F_2 (D_2 / 360)]$$
$$\times [1 + F_3 (D_3 / 360)] \times [1 + F_4 (D_4 / 360)]\}$$

and so forth. Note that F_1 and F_2 appear both in P_6 and P_{12} and F_3 and F_4 appear
only in P_{12}. From this, one can see that the swap yield implied by a sequence of
Eurodollar futures rates is a weighted average of these rates that gives greater
weight to the nearby rates than to the more distant rates.

Chapter Five

Hedging and Trading with Municipal Bond Futures

Galen Burghardt
Dean Witter Reynolds

Liz Flores
Dean Witter Reynolds

James Horning
Dean Witter Reynolds

The Chicago Board of Trade's municipal bond futures contract has been an especially useful tool for both hedgers and traders. The municipal bond market may be large, but the markets for individual issues can be extremely illiquid. To limit losses in a falling market, portfolio managers must choose between selling bonds or selling municipal bond futures contracts. Often enough, there have been no firm bids for the bonds themselves, so that the futures contract has afforded the only reasonable form of protection.

Also, one cannot short municipal bonds because of the tax-exempt coupon, but one can short the futures. There is a large and active population of traders who have views either on the level of municipal bond yields or on the relationship between taxable and tax-exempt bond yields. For many of these traders, the municipal bond futures contract is the only tool available for taking advantage of these views.

Anyone who wants to hedge or trade with the contract, however, should know something about how the contract works in practice. Consider, for example, the spread between municipal bond and Treasury bond futures prices, which is known as the MOB spread (see Exhibit 5–1). This spread has tended over the years to drift downward and frequently hits new lows,

EXHIBIT 5–1
MOT (Munis over Bonds) Spread in 32nds

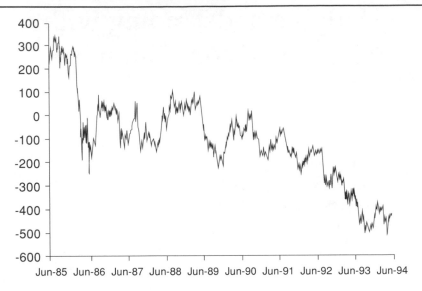

not because tax-exempt yields have been rising steadily relative to the taxable yields on Treasury bonds, but because of a built-in tendency for *The Bond Buyer* Index of municipal bond prices, to which the futures contract settles in cash at expiration, to drift down over time. One of the purposes in this chapter is to explain the reasons for the index's downward drift.

We also show how to reckon the effective duration and the dollar value of a basis point for a municipal bond futures contract. Even though one cannot hedge a municipal bond position or trade a yield spread without such information, it is more difficult than one might suppose to get reliable estimates of these measures of futures price sensitivity. To arrive at the duration and *DV*01 of the futures contract, one must know how to determine the fair value of the futures price, which we also show how to do.

Municipal bond futures can be an extremely useful tool for hedging municipal bond positions and for trading spreads between taxable and tax-exempt bond yields. To hedge or trade successfully, though, one has to know how to reckon the duration or dollar value of a basis point for the futures contract and whether futures are rich or cheap. To do this correctly, requires a special understanding of the relationship between municipal bond futures prices and the prices of cash bonds in the municipal market. Our purpose is to lay out these key relationships and to explain how to determine:

- The fair price of a municipal bond futures contract.
- The proper hedge ratio for cash municipal bonds.
- The proper weighting for a MOB (muni over bond) spread.

Once we have done this, we will look at opportunities for trading the municipal bond futures basis, muni calendar spreads, and the MOB spread.

THE MUNICIPAL BOND FUTURES CONTRACT

Key contract specifications for the Chicago Board of Trade's municipal bond futures contract are shown in Exhibit 5–2. Notice that the last day of trading coincides with the expiration of Treasury bond and note futures and that the nominal size of the contract is $100,000, so that one price point is worth $1,000 and a 32nd is worth the standard $31.25. Notice, too, that the contract is settled at expiration in cash rather than through the delivery of any bonds. The final settlement price is simply the value of *The Bond Buyer* Index (BBI) of municipal bond prices on that day, and all positions that are still open at the close of trading on the last day are marked to market at that price.

Because the futures price converges at expiration to the value of the BBI, the business of pricing municipal bond futures and of determining how sensitive the futures price is to a change in municipal bond yields centers on an understanding of the following:

- How the BBI is calculated and maintained over time.
- How municipal bond prices respond to changes in yields.
- How spot and forward municipal bond prices are related.

CALCULATING THE BBI

The Bond Buyer Index (BBI) is a measure of the prices of comparatively new issues of municipal bonds. The 40 bonds whose prices went into the value of the index on June 1 are shown in Appendix 5–A. The index is calculated as:

EXHIBIT 5–2
Key Contract Specifications:
Long-Term Municipal Bond Index Futures

Trading unit	$1,000 times the closing value of *The Bond Buyer* Municipal Bond Index. A price of 90–00 reflects a contract size of $90,000.
Price quotation	Points ($1,000) and thirty-seconds of a point; for example, 85-16 equals 85 16/32.
Tick size	One thirty-second (1/32) of a point ($31.25 per contract)
Daily price limit	3 points ($3,000 per contract) above or below the previous day's settlement price (expandable to 4 1/2 points)
Contract months	March, June, September, and December
Last trading day	Seventh business day preceding the last business day of delivery month
Settlement	Municipal Bond Index futures settle in cash on the last day of trading. Settlement price equals *The Bond Buyer* Municipal Bond Index value on that day.
Trading hours	7:20 A.M. to 2:00 P.M. (Chicago time), Monday through Friday. On the last trading day of an expiring contract, trading in that contract closes at 2:01 PM.
Ticker symbol	MB

$$BBI = Coefficient \times \sum_{i=1}^{40} \frac{Price_i}{Factor_i} \times \frac{1}{40}$$

where $Price_i$ is the i-th bond's cash price, $Factor_i$ is the approximate hypothetical price at which the i-th bond would yield 8 percent to its first par call date (typically 12 years from issuance), and *Coefficient* is a number that is recalculated each time new bonds are substituted for old bonds, so that the simple act of making the substitutions does not change the value of the index.

In practice, *The Bond Buyer* reviews the composition of the bonds in the index every two weeks and, given a set of well-defined criteria, throws out older bonds and replaces them with more recently issued bonds. On average, five or six bonds are replaced every two weeks. However, as many as 16 have been replaced at one time. As we will see, this periodic refreshing of the index imparts some downward drift to the index over time.

A PRICE/YIELD RELATIONSHIP FOR THE BBI

A price/yield relationship for the BBI stems directly from the price/yield relationships of the individual bonds in the index.

Pessimistic Pricing Practices

Municipal bonds in the BBI all contain call features that allow an issuer to redeem a bond either at par or at a premium to par before the bond matures. A typical issue, for example, might have a maturity of 30 years, a 10-year period during which the bond cannot be called, and a schedule of prices at which the bond can be redeemed or called during the remainder of its life. Typically, when a bond is first callable, it can be redeemed only if the issuer pays a premium over par (e.g., 102). Thereafter, the call price drifts down over time until the bond can be redeemed by the issuer at par. Appendix 5–A provides information about the call provisions of the various bonds in the index on June 1.

The issuer's right to redeem the bond is a call option that gains in value as yields fall. From the investor's standpoint, an investment in a municipal bond can be thought of as a long position in a noncallable tax-exempt bond and a short position in whatever call options are embedded in the bond. The business of pricing municipal bonds, then, comes down to pricing noncallable bonds and various options on those bonds.

Our understanding of the pricing practice in the municipal market indicates that the option pricing part of this problem is very straightforward. If the bond is trading at a discount to par, the call options are considered worthless and the bond is priced to par. If the bond is trading at a premium to par, the options are considered to be fully in the money and the bond is priced to the call date—either first premium call or first par call—at which the bond's price is lowest. In the parlance of the municipal bond market, the bonds are "priced to worst," where worst is from the investor's viewpoint.

Exhibit 5–3 shows what a typical price/yield relationship looks like if a bond is priced this way. Three price/yield relationships are shown. One relationship assumes that the bond is priced to maturity, one that the bond

EXHIBIT 5–3
Price/Yield Relationship for a Typical Municipal Bond

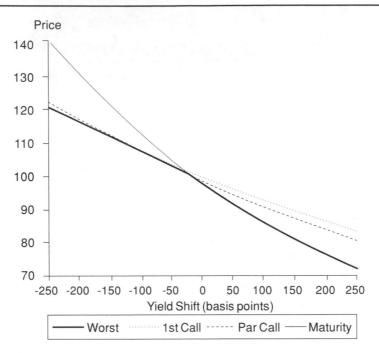

is priced to its first call at par, and one that the bond is priced to its first premium call. In such a setting, if the bond's yield is higher than its coupon, then the lowest of the three valuations would be produced by assuming that the bond is carried all the way to maturity. If the bond's yield is lower than its coupon, then the lowest of the three prices corresponds to one or the other of the call dates. If the bond's yield is slightly lower, then the lower valuation is produced by assuming that the bond is carried to its first par call date. If the bond's yield is sufficiently low, however, then the lower valuation is produced by assuming that the issuer will be willing to pay the premium at the bond's earliest possible call date.

The result of chaining together the lowest segments of each of the three price/yield relationships is a kinked relationship that gives the impression of strong negative convexity. Even though the various segments of the relationship exhibit positive convexity, the overall price/yield relationship is dominated by the shifts from one price/yield relationship to another when the bond is trading at or slightly above par.

To people who are accustomed to valuing embedded options, this approach to valuing the issuer's prepayment or redemption rights may seem a bit rough and to afford opportunities for refinement.

The Bonds Used in Calculating the BBI

Whether this extreme approach to pricing individual municipal bonds is strictly true likely does not matter much when constructing a price/yield relationship for an index based on 40 different bonds. Reckoning a price/yield relationship for the BBI is a simple matter of producing price/yield relationships for the 40 bonds whose prices are used in calculating the index and then calculating the index for each level of yields. Given the actual bonds used in calculating the BBI on June 1, 1994, Exhibit 5–4 shows the results of such an exercise. Notice that averaging the prices tends to iron out any kinks in the individual price/yield relationships.

The result is a fairly smooth relationship that exhibits interesting convexity properties. As shown in Appendix 5–A, most of the bonds in the BBI on June 1 were trading at a discount to par, and only a few were trading at a slight premium. Thus, most of the bonds in the BBI were priced to maturity and were trading at yields well away from the points at which they might be priced to call. As a result, for any increase in yields, the BBI's price/yield relationship could be expected to exhibit positive convexity. In the other direction, yields would have to fall by about 50 basis points before the individual bonds' call features would come into play and impart negative convexity to the relationship.

THE BBI'S TENDENCY TO DRIFT DOWN OVER TIME

The BBI tends to drift downward for reasons that have nothing to do with the level of yields; any effort to reckon a fair futures price must take index drift into account. Downward drift in the index is produced by the combined effect of the negative convexity in municipal bonds and *The Bond Buyer's* practice of substituting recently issued bonds for bonds that have been in the index for a while.

As noted above, the BBI is calculated by averaging the converted prices of the 40 bonds in the index and then multiplying this average by a coefficient:

EXHIBIT 5–4
Price/Yield Relationship for **The Bond Buyer** *Index*

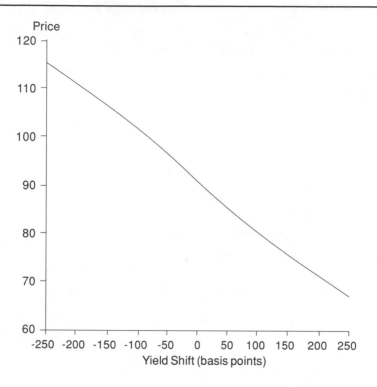

$$\text{BBI} = Coefficient \times \sum_{i=1}^{40} \frac{Price_i}{Factor_i} \times \frac{1}{40}$$

Now consider what happens when a new bond, which likely is trading close to par, is substituted for an older bond, which may well be trading at a premium to or a discount from par. In particular, suppose that bond yields start at point *A* in Exhibit 5–5 and fall to point *B*. The value of the index, tracking the rise in the price of a bond that was trading around par when yields were at *A,* would rise to *C*. At this point, if a new par bond is substituted for the original bond, which is now trading at a premium, the value of the index would not change. On the other hand, because the new par bond has a higher duration than the older premium bond, the sensitivity of the BBI to a change in bond yields is increased by the substitution. Now

EXHIBIT 5–5
Bond Substitution and Index Drift

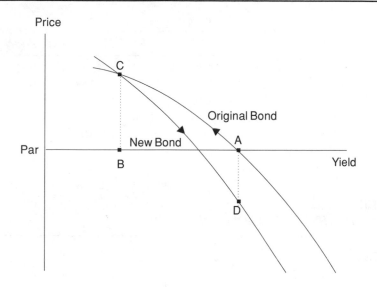

if yields return to point *A*, the value of the index would fall to *D*, which is lower than the initial value of the index.

To make this more concrete, we can trace out the behavior of the BBI and the coefficient used to calculate the BBI as yields rise and fall. The raw material for this exercise is provided in Exhibit 5–6, which shows the prices at various yields and the conversion factors of five hypothetical municipal bonds with coupons ranging from 3 to 7 percent.

Suppose at the outset that municipal bond yields are 5 percent, that the 5-percent bond in Exhibit 5–6 is the only bond in the index, and that the BBI coefficient is equal to 1.0000. Under these circumstances, the value of the BBI would be 129.18 [=(100.00/0.7741) × 1.0000], where 100.00 is the price of the bond and 0.7741 is its conversion factor.

Now suppose that municipal bond yields rise to 6 percent. The price of the 5 percent bond would fall to 86.16, and the value of the BBI would fall to 111.30. At this point, if a new par bond with a coupon of 6 percent is substituted for the older discount bond, the calculation of the index would require a new and lower coefficient. The price of the new par bond divided by its conversion factor of 0.8493 would be 117.74, which would have to be multiplied by 0.9453 to keep the index value at 111.30.

EXHIBIT 5–6
Yields, Prices, and Conversion Factors for Hypothetical Municipal Bonds

	Price at a Yield of:					Conversion
Coupon	3%	4%	5%	6%	7%	Factor
3%	100.00	86.62	69.09	58.49	50.11	0.6236
4%	110.02	100.00	84.55	72.32	62.58	0.6988
5%	118.65	109.46	100.00	86.16	75.06	0.7741
6%	127.24	117.70	108.94	100.00	87.53	0.8493
7%	135.82	125.87	116.81	108.47	100.00	0.9246

EXHIBIT 5–7
Index and Coefficient Drift in the BBI

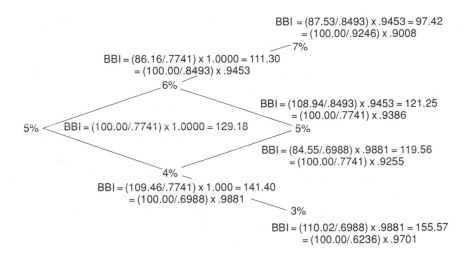

From here, suppose yields return to the original level of 5 percent. The BBI would increase to 121.25 [= (108.94/0.8493) × 0.9453], which is lower than the index value of 129.18 that we computed when yields were 5 percent in the first place (see Exhibit 5–7). It is apparent that the effect of yields rising and then falling would be a drop in the value of the index as well as in the coefficient. If a new 5 percent par bond is put back in the index in

EXHIBIT 5–8
The Bond Buyer *Index Coefficient Drift*

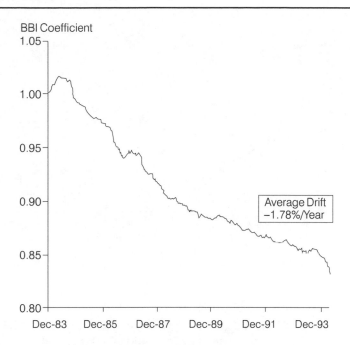

place of the 6 percent bond, the coefficient would now have to be 0.9386 rather than 1.0000.

Exhibit 5–7 also illustrates the tendency of the index and the coefficient to drift downward when yields fall and then rise. If yields were to fall to 4 percent and then return to 5 percent, the value of the BBI in this example would end up at 119.56, and the coefficient would be 0.9255. Note that neither the value of the index nor the value of the coefficient are the same as they were when yields first rose to 6 percent and then fell to 5 percent. This suggests that the value of the BBI at any given level of bond yields depends somewhat on the actual path that rates have followed to get to that yield.

It is not apparent from this example that the value of the BBI coefficient can rise as well as fall, but it can. Even so, increases in the coefficient tend to be smaller than decreases. As a result, the coefficient tends to fall over time as shown in Exhibit 5–8. Notice that the coefficient's path meanders both up and down, but on average the coefficient has fallen at a rate of about 1.78 percent per year.

EXHIBIT 5–9
Price Volatility and Coefficient Drift

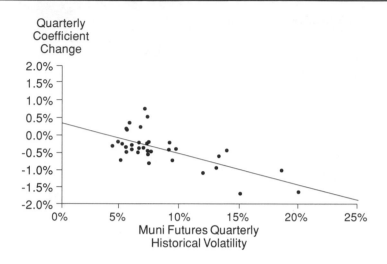

It is apparent from these examples that the size of any changes that must be made in the coefficient depends on how much and how often yields have risen or fallen. That is, the rate of drift should be related to the volatility of municipal bond prices. Exhibit 5–9 bears this out. Although other forces are at work on the coefficient, the rate of drift in the coefficient does seem to be accelerated by higher price volatility. On the basis of the evidence used to produce Exhibit 5–9, the estimated relationship between percent changes in the coefficient and 3-month volatility of municipal bond futures prices is:

$$\text{Quarterly percent change in BBI coefficient} = 0.36 - 0.0911 \times \frac{\text{Quarterly futures}}{\text{volatility}}$$

That is, a 1-percentage-point increase in three-month municipal bond futures price volatility increases the quarterly downward drift in the coefficient by 0.0911 percent of whatever the coefficient's value happens to be at that time. Because of the importance of index drift in determining the spread between the spot value of the BBI and the fair price of the futures contract, this means that a 1-percentage-point increase in bond price volatility is worth about 1.4 ticks (1.4/32nds) for the fair or expected value of the price of a municipal bond futures contract that has three months left to expiration.[1]

THE FAIR PRICE OF A MUNICIPAL BOND FUTURES CONTRACT

Now we can tackle the problem of what the fair value of a municipal bond futures contract should be. As illustrated in Exhibit 5–10, the spread between the spot value of the BBI and the fair value of the municipal bond futures contract should be split into two parts. The first is the spread between the spot and forward values of the bonds currently in the index, which can be thought of as carry. The second is the spread between the forward and futures values, which in the case of municipal bond futures is due to coefficient drift in the index.

The Fair Value of a Forward Position

In the taxable market, the problem of reckoning the forward value of a bond is simple because all gains and losses are taxed at the same rate. One need only calculate the difference between what one will earn in coupon income and what one must pay to finance the full purchase price of the bond, and then subtract that difference from the current spot price, to arrive at the forward price.

The problem in the municipal market is complicated in a number of ways. For example, the coupon income on the bond might be tax exempt, but the financing cost may or may not be deductible as a business expense. For another, one cannot short municipal bonds, but one can fail to deliver on a sale, which is almost the same thing except that there is no financing income to offset the liability generated by having to make good on the coupon income. As a result, any carry calculation seems to depend on the tax status of the trader, dealer, or portfolio manager, and whether the bond position is long or short.

Perhaps the most reliable fix on the relationship between the spot and forward prices of municipal bonds is obtained by considering two investments that should produce the same return: a real municipal bond and a

---

1 The tendency of the index to drift down over time apparently has been a nuisance to a number of market participants, and the Chicago Board of Trade has taken steps to check the trend. Subject to approval by the Commodity Futures Trading Commission, the CBOT plans to reset the coefficient to 1.0000 as of the June 30, 1995, BBI revision date so that the September 1995 futures will be the first settle to the new BBI. Also, to retard the rate of drift, *The Bond Buyer* will revise its criteria for the inclusion in the index to permit noncallable and discount bonds. Noncallable bonds would exhibit positive convexity, while discount bonds would exhibit either positive convexity or, at the very least, less negative convexity than par bonds.

EXHIBIT 5–10
Spot, Forward, and Futures Prices in the Municipal Bond Market

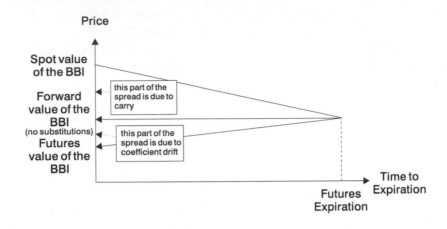

synthetic municipal bond. If the two investments have the same return, they should have the same price.

Synthetic Municipal Bonds

A synthetic municipal bond can be constructed by combining a position in tax-exempt money markets with a forward contract on a real bond. That is, whatever cash would otherwise be invested in a municipal bond is invested instead in tax-exempt money market instruments. Then, to capture any capital gains or losses, an appropriate position is taken in a forward contract. The return to such a synthetic municipal bond investment would be:

$$\begin{array}{l} \text{Synthetic} \\ \text{bond} \\ \text{return} \end{array} = \begin{array}{l} \text{Tax-exempt} \\ \text{money market} \\ \text{income} \end{array} + \begin{array}{l} \text{After-tax} \\ \text{forward gain} \end{array}$$

Tax-exempt money market income would be reckoned as the product of the real bond's full price, including accrued interest, the tax-exempt money market rate, and the number of days in the holding period, divided by 360. The forward contract gain or loss would be the difference between the contract's value at expiration or maturity and the original or today's contract value.

The real bond's return would be the sum of the coupon income on the bond plus any change in the bond's price:

$$\begin{array}{ccc} \text{Real} & \text{Tax-exempt} & \text{After-tax} \\ \text{bond} = & \text{coupon} \; + & \text{capital} \\ \text{return} & \text{income} & \text{gain} \end{array}$$

Because the bond's forward price equals its spot price at the expiration of the forward contract, we know that the gain or loss on the forward contract will be:

$$\frac{\text{After-tax}}{\text{forward gain}} = \left(\frac{\text{Expiration}}{\text{spot price}} - \frac{\text{Today's}}{\text{forward price}} \right) \times (1 - \text{Tax rate})$$

while the gain or loss on the bond will be:

$$\frac{\text{After-tax}}{\text{capital gain}} = \left(\frac{\text{Expiration}}{\text{spot price}} - \frac{\text{Today's}}{\text{spot price}} \right) \times (1 - \text{Tax rate})$$

If we substitute these expressions for gains or losses into the total return expressions and set the return on the synthetic bond equal to the return on the real bond, we find that today's value of the forward price should be:

$$\frac{\text{Forward}}{\text{price}} \approx \frac{\text{Spot}}{\text{price}} + \frac{\text{Money market income} - \text{Coupon income}}{1 - \text{Tax rate}}$$

where money market income and coupon income are both tax exempt. We use an "approximately equal" sign because there can be some ambiguity about what tax rate to use. But, if the marginal investor in the municipal market is an upper-bracket individual, the appropriate rate would seem to be the highest effective capital gains rate.

Except for the presence of the tax adjustment, this relationship between the spot and forward prices looks very much like a conventional carry relationship.

Coefficient Drift

The value of the BBI can be expected to drift down because of the combined effect of bond substitutions and downward drift in the coefficient, and one should make an allowance for this drift when determining the fair value of the futures price. Because the drift is produced by revisions to the index, we determine the effect of drift in the following way. *The Bond Buyer* revises the index twice a month, or 24 times a year. It is at these revisions that the coefficient ratchets either up or down. If the annual rate of drift is −1.78 percent per year, the expected downward effect of any one revision in the index would be −0.074 percent. To determine the expected effect of coefficient drift, we simply determine the number of revisions between today and the expiration of the futures contract, and multiply that number by our estimate of the effect of a single index revision on the value of the coefficient.

Rich/Cheap Analysis

On June 1, 1994, the spot value of the BBI was $91^{7}\!/_{32}$. The June 1994 futures price was $92^{5}\!/_{32}$, while the September 1994 futures price was $91^{11}\!/_{32}$. As shown in Exhibit 5–11, both of these futures prices appeared to be rich relative to the spot value of the index.

For the June contract, the effect of carry was worth 25/32nds if we use a marginal tax rate of 39.6 percent (15/32nds if we make no allowance for taxes). The effect of coefficient drift was worth 2/32nds. By our reckoning, the fair value of the futures price should have been somewhere between 17/32nds and 27/32nds below the spot value of the index. In other words, the theoretical value of the June 1994 municipal bond futures basis—the simple difference between the spot value of the BBI and the fair value of

EXHIBIT 5–11
Rich/Cheap Analysis (June 1, 1994)

				Cost of Carry	
Futures Contract Month	*BBI Index*	*Futures Price*	*Market Basis (a)*	*t = 39.6%*	*t = 0*
				(b)	
	(points and 32nds)				
Jun-94	91-07	92-05	–30	25	15
Sep-94	91-07	91-11	–4	139	84
		Theoretical Basis		*Net Basis*	
Futures Contract Month	*Index Drift (c)*	*t = 39.6%*	*t = 0*	*t = 39.6%*	*t = 0*
		(d = b + c)		(a – d)	
	(32nds)				
Jun-94	2	27	17	–57	–47
Sep-94	14	153	98	–157	–102

EXHIBIT 5–12
Futures Mispricing (Market Futures Price – Fair Value in 32nds)

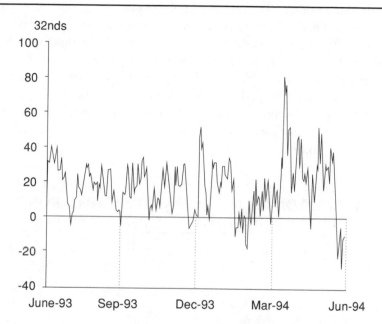

the futures price—should have been somewhere between 17/32nds and 27/32nds, or between 17 and 27 ticks. Instead, the market value of the basis was –30/32nds, which means that the actual futures price was 30/32nds above the spot value of the index. Altogether, then, the futures price was anywhere from 47 to 57 ticks above fair value.

With a market basis of –4 ticks, the September contract appeared to have been anywhere from 102 to 157 ticks above fair value.

The apparent richness or cheapness of a municipal bond futures contract can vary widely over the life of a contract. Exhibit 5–12 shows how the difference between the market price and the fair value of the lead municipal bond futures contract has behaved over the last four quarters, beginning the day after the expiration of the June 1993 contract and ending on the expiration of the June 1994 contract. As constructed, Exhibit 5–12 shows how the richness of the September 1993 contract behaved from June 1993 until its expiration in September. The exhibit then traces out the richness of the December 1993 contract until its expiration, the richness of the March 1994 contract until its expiration, and finally the richness of the June 1994 contract.

In all four instances, because the final settlement price of the expiring contract is set equal to the value of the BBI, the richness of the lead contract must eventually be zero on the last day of trading. The path that takes the futures price to fair value, however, cannot exactly be described as convergence. Rather, the path is erratic, and the swings in the contract's mispricings can be large and abrupt. In the last few days of the June 1994 contract's life, for example, the futures price went from 40 ticks above fair value to more than 20 ticks below fair value before finally arriving at fair value on the last day of trading.

DURATION OR *DV*01 OF A MUNICIPAL BOND FUTURES CONTRACT

We now have everything we need to produce a relationship between the fair value of municipal bond futures and the level of municipal bond yields. Examples of these relationships for the June and September 1994 futures contracts on June 1 are shown in Exhibits 5–13 and 5–14. To construct these relationships, we assumed that the yields on all of the bonds whose prices make up the BBI would rise or fall by the same number of basis points. In other words, we assumed parallel shifts in the yields of all the bonds in the BBI.

The result is a price/yield relationship that lies below the spot BBI by an amount equal to the sum of carry and anticipated index drift.

One of the most important applications of the price/yield relationships shown in Exhibits 5–13 and 5–14 is in the reckoning of an effective duration or *DV*01 for the futures contract that can be used for hedging and constructing spread trades. Consider the duration of the futures contract. The standard definition of effective or modified duration is the percent change in the instrument's price for a 100-basis-point change in the underlying yield. In this case, the underlying yield is the set of yields on the bonds in the BBI. If we consider a 100-basis-point increase and a 100-basis-point decrease in the level of underlying yields, the resulting duration calculation for the June 1994 futures contract on June 1, 1994, would be:

$$\text{Duration} = \frac{101.1545 - 79.604}{90.3635} \times \frac{1}{2}$$

EXHIBIT 5–13
Price/Yield Relationships

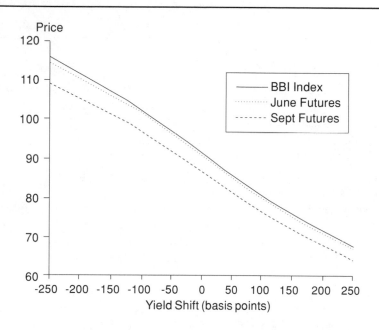

$$= \frac{21.3941}{90.3635} \times \frac{1}{2}$$

$$= 0.2368 \times \frac{1}{2}$$

$$= 0.1184 \text{ (or } 11.84\%)$$

If we consider instead a 1-basis-point increase and decrease in the yield, our duration calculation would produce:

$$\text{Duration} = \frac{90.4764 - 90.2507}{90.3635} \times \frac{100}{2}$$

$$= 0.1249 \text{ (or} 12.49\%)$$

The difference in the two calculations—one for a 100-basis-point change in either direction, and one for a 1-basis-point change in either direction—reflects the convexity of the price/yield relationship.

EXHIBIT 5–14
Price/Yield Relationship (decimal prices, June 1, 1994)

Yield Change (bps)	BBI Index		June Futures		Sept Futures	
	Price	Price Change	Price	Price Change	Price	Price Change
250	67.7626	–23.4509	67.1544	–23.2091	64.3524	–22.0780
200	71.6192	–19.5943	70.9726	–19.3909	67.9911	–18.4393
150	75.8491	–15.3644	75.1598	–15.2037	71.9784	–14.4520
100	80.4973	–10.7162	79.7604	–10.6031	76.3561	–10.0743
50	85.6153	–5.5982	84.8250	–5.5385	81.1712	–5.2592
25	88.3685	–2.8450	87.5491	–2.8144	83.7593	–2.6711
10	90.0719	–1.1416	89.2342	–1.1293	85.3593	–1.0711
5	90.6426	–0.5709	89.7988	–0.5647	85.8949	–0.5355
1	91.0995	–0.1140	90.2507	–0.1128	86.3235	–0.1069
0	91.2135	0.0000	90.3635	0.0000	86.4304	0.0000
–1	91.3277	0.1142	90.4764	0.1129	86.5375	0.1071
–5	91.7702	0.5567	90.9139	0.5504	86.9516	0.5212
–10	92.3194	1.1059	91.4568	1.0933	87.4653	1.0349
–25	93.9593	2.7458	93.0776	2.7141	88.9971	2.5667
–50	96.6786	5.4651	95.7642	5.4007	91.5309	5.1005
–100	102.1383	10.9248	101.1545	10.7910	96.5981	10.1677
–150	106.8249	15.6114	105.7705	15.4070	100.8861	14.4557
–200	111.1532	19.9397	110.0258	19.6623	104.8029	18.3725
–250	115.4833	24.2698	114.2789	23.9154	108.6991	22.2687

A *DV*01 for the contract can be calculated directly from the price/yield schedule as well. If we use a 1-basis-point increase and decrease in the yields of the underlying bonds, the DV01 would be calculated as:

$$DV01 = (90.4764 - 90.2507) \times \frac{1}{2}$$

$$= 0.1129 \,(\text{or } \$112.90 \text{ per futures contract})$$

which, given the $1,000 dollar value assigned to a one-point change in the futures price would translate into a *DV*01 per futures contract of $112.90.

EXHIBIT 5–15
Dollar Value of a Basis Point (DV01) (June 1, 1994)

Yield Change (bps)	BBI Index		June Futures		Sept. Futures	
	Price Change	Avg. DV01*	Price Change	Avg. DV01*	Price Change	Avg. DV01*
250	−23.4509	0.0938	−23.2091	0.0928	−22.0780	0.0883
200	−19.5943	0.0980	−19.3909	0.0970	−18.4393	0.0922
150	−15.3644	0.1024	−15.2037	0.1014	−14.4520	0.0963
100	−10.7162	0.1072	−10.6031	0.1060	−10.0743	0.1007
50	−5.5982	0.1120	−5.5385	0.1108	−5.2592	0.1052
25	−2.8450	0.1138	−2.8144	0.1126	−2.6711	0.1068
10	−1.1416	0.1142	−1.1293	0.1129	−1.0711	0.1071
5	−0.5709	0.1142	−0.5647	0.1129	−0.5355	0.1071
1	−0.1140	0.1140	−0.1128	0.1128	−0.1069	0.1069
0	0.0000	n/a	0.0000	n/a	0.0000	n/a
−1	0.1142	0.1142	0.1129	0.1129	0.1071	0.1071
−5	0.5567	0.1113	0.5504	0.1101	0.5212	0.1042
−10	1.1059	0.1106	1.0933	0.1093	1.0349	0.1035
−25	2.7458	0.1098	2.7141	0.1086	2.5667	0.1027
−50	5.4651	0.1093	5.4007	0.1080	5.1005	0.1020
−100	10.9248	0.1092	10.7910	0.1079	10.1677	0.1017
−150	15.6114	0.1041	15.4070	0.1027	14.4557	0.0964
−200	19.9397	0.0997	19.6623	0.0983	18.3725	0.0919
−250	24.2698	0.0971	23.9154	0.0957	22.2687	0.0891

* per $100 face amount

The importance of convexity in the pricing of municipal bonds suggests that some attention should be paid to the size and possibly to the direction of a change in municipal bond yields. As shown in Exhibit 5–15, for example, the average dollar value of a basis point (*DV*01) depends on both the size of the yield change and on the direction. Just how much the *DV*01 is influenced by convexity depends where on the price/yield relationship the BBI happens to be. In this instance, we can see the effects of positive convexity as yields rise. That is, the average *DV*01 is smaller for large yield changes than it is for small yield changes. Similarly, we can see that negative convexity also causes the average $DV01$ to be smaller for a large decrease in yields than for a small decrease.

These kinds of effects depend, of course, on whether the bonds that make up the BBI are trading mainly around par, at a premium to par, or at a discount from par. In this case, most of the bonds were trading at a discount.

Comparison with the Standard Services

The information on the duration or $DV01$ of municipal bond futures that is provided by standard financial services can be quite different. Exhibit 5–16 compares our results with those of two standard services — Municipal Market Data and Bloomberg. What we find is that our $DV01$ matches that of Municipal Market Data quite closely, although theirs is reported only for the index with a lag of one day. In contract, our durations are quite different. The reason for the difference is that Municipal Market Data reckons its duration as a Macaulay's duration, assuming the bonds are all priced to first call. In this case, hedge ratios calculated using their duration measure would be roughly 50 percent higher than those produced by their $DV01$.

Bloomberg approaches the problem simply by calculating the $DV01$ of a hypothetical proxy issue whose maturity is the average maturity of the bonds in the BBI rounded to the nearest year and whose coupon is the average coupon of the bonds in the BBI rounded to the nearest whole percent. On June 1, for example, their proxy issue was assigned a maturity of 26 years and a coupon of 6 percent. As shown in Exhibit 5–16, the $DV01$ for such a hypothetical bond was substantially higher than the $DV01$ we obtained through our yield scenario analysis, and their hedge ratios would have been substantially lower than ours.

TRADING THE MOB SPREAD

One of the most actively traded bond spreads at the CBOT is the MOB (i.e., munis over bonds). A history of this spread, which is quoted simply as the difference in 32nds between the municipal bond futures price and the long-term Treasury bond futures price, is shown in Exhibit 5–17. The effect of coefficient drift over the life of the muni contract on the value of the spread can be seen quite clearly. It is, in fact, this coefficient drift that causes

EXHIBIT 5–16
Comparison of Duration and DV01 Calculations (June 1, 1994)

	Dean Witter		Municipal Market Data		Bloomberg	
Contract	Duration	DV01*	Duration	DV01*	Duration	DV01*
Spot	12.51%	0.1141	8.50%	0.114	NA	NA
June 94	12.49%	0.1129	NA	NA	NA	0.1200
Sept. 94	12.38%	0.1070	NA	NA	NA	0.1184

* per $100 face amount

EXHIBIT 5–17
MOB (Munis over Bonds) Spread in 32nds

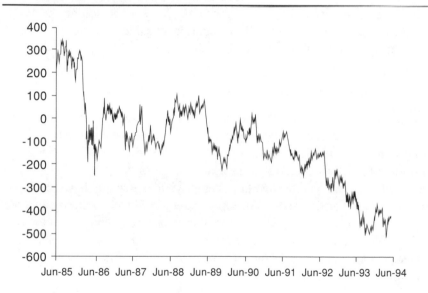

the MOB spread to reach new lows from time to time and that creates the appearance of spurious trading opportunities for those who are not steeped in the behavior of the municipal bond contract.

Evaluating a MOB Spread

The main reason for trading the MOB spread is to take advantage of expected changes in taxable Treasury yields relative to tax-exempt municipal bond yields. In particular, if you think tax-exempt yields are likely to fall relative to taxable Treasury yields, then you want to buy municipal bonds or municipal bond futures and to sell Treasuries or Treasury futures. Because you can trade the taxable/tax-exempt yield spread in both the cash and futures markets, a rich/cheap analysis helps to determine whether the spread in the futures market is fairly priced.

Exhibit 5–18 shows how the spread looked on June 1. In particular, both the Treasury bond and the 10-year Treasury note contracts appeared to have been more or less fairly priced. The municipal bond futures on the other hand appeared to be quite rich relative to the spot value of the index. The June contract price was trading 30 ticks over the spot value of the index rather than 27 ticks (the combined value of carry and drift) below. Thus, the June contract appeared to have been 57 ticks rich, which would argue in favor of buying the MOB spread in the cash market and selling the MOB spread in the futures market. Or you might consider selling the futures contract or the MOB futures spread outright.

Constructing the Trade Correctly

If your purpose in trading the MOB spread is to profit from an expected change in the spread between the prices of the two contracts, then a one-to-one spread ratio is appropriate. If, on the other hand, your purpose in trading the MOB spread is to take advantage of an expected change in the spread between taxable and tax-exempt yields, then you have to weight the trade other than one to one. An appropriately weighted yield spread trade is designed to give you equal but offsetting exposure to changes in the two yields. Given the dollar values of a basis point for the municipal and Treasury bond contracts on June 1, the correct ratio of municipal bond to Treasury futures would have been:

$$\text{Hedge ratio} = \frac{\text{Treasury futures } DV01}{\text{Muni futures } DV01}$$

$$0 = \frac{\$98.44}{\$112.9}$$

$$= 0.8719$$

EXHIBIT 5-18
Evaluating MOB and MUT Spreads (June 1, 1994)

June Futures Contract	Rich/Cheap Information					Futures Price/Price Change		
	Basis	Carry	Drift or Strategic Delivery Option Value	Theoretical basis	Adjusted Basis Net of Carry	Price	DV01	Duration
	(a)	(b)	(c)	(d = b + c)	(a − d)			
			(32nds)					
Municipal bonds	−30	23	2	25	−55	92-05	$112.90	12.65%
Long-term Treasury bonds	22	13	10	23	−1	104-09	$98.44	9.44%
10-year Treasury notes	16	8	9	17	−1	105-10	$60.77	5.77%

If you wanted to sell the MOB futures spread because you thought tax-exempt yields would rise relative to taxable yields, then you would sell 87 municipal bond futures against a long position of 100 Treasury futures.

Some traders prefer to trade the spread between Treasury note and municipal bond futures prices. The MUT (munis under 10-year Treasury note) spread is a popular alternative to the MOB spread. In this case, the appropriate hedge ratio for trading yield spreads would be 0.5383 [=$60.77/$112.90] or 54 municipal bond futures for every 100 ten-year Treasury note futures.

Managing a MOB Spread as Yields Rise or Fall

Your job isn't done when the trade is put on. Municipal bonds can exhibit a great deal of negative convexity because of the embedded call options, while Treasury bonds exhibit positive convexity. In practice, this means that the $DV01$ of a Treasury bond rises as yields fall, while the $DV01$ of a municipal bond falls. As a result, if you do the trade in the cash market, you will find it necessary to increase the ratio of municipal bonds to Treasuries as yields fall and to decrease the ratio as yields rise.

The situation is a little less clear in the futures market where the Treasury bond futures contract also exhibits negative convexity because of shifts in the cheapest to deliver. Even so, the convexities of the two contracts will generally not be the same, and your MOB trades will require reweighting as yields change. This is not as much trouble as it might seem. We provide our clients every day with the dollar values of a basis point for the municipal bond futures contract as well as for the Treasury bond and note contracts. As a result, correct hedge ratios are easy to calculate, and any rebalancing trades are straightforward and economical.

APPENDIX 5–A
The 40 Municipal Bonds in The Bond Buyer Index as of June 1, 1994

#	Description	Coupon	Final Maturity	Price	Yield to Maturity	Yield to 1st Call	Yield to Par Call	Yield to Worst	Conversion Factor	Dated Date	Date of Par Call	Date of 1st Call	1st Call Premium
1	NYC Govt Assist Corp ref rev Ser 93C	5.500	4/01/18	88.555	6.446	7.454	7.025	6.446	0.8143	7/01/93	4/01/05	4/01/03	102.0
2	NY State Power Auth gen purp Ser CC	5.250	1/01/18	86.531	6.360	7.582	7.079	6.360	0.7984	8/15/93	1/01/05	1/01/03	102.0
3	Salt River Proj AZ elec ref rev Ser 93C	5.000	1/01/16	84.688	6.308	7.406	6.945	6.308	0.7713	10/1/93	1/01/06	1/01/04	102.0
4	FL St Bd Ed pub ed cap outlay ref Ser 93D	5.125	6/01/22	84.502	6.311	7.615	7.339	6.311	0.8013	10/15/93	6/01/04	6/01/03	101.0
5	HI Dept Budg & Fin spec purp rev (Hawaiian Elec)	5.450	11/1/23	86.312	6.499	7.665	7.231	6.499	0.8117	11/1/93	11/1/05	11/1/03	102.0
6	MO Hlth & Ed Facs Auth rev (Barnes-Jewish)	5.250	5/15/21	84.393	6.482	7.868	7.348	6.482	0.7984	10/15/93	5/15/05	5/15/03	102.0
7	Orlando-Orange Co Expy Auth Fl jr lein rev Ser 93A	5.125	7/01/20	84.750	6.326	7.639	7.139	6.326	0.7864	11/1/93	7/01/05	7/01/03	102.0
8	Brazos River Auth TX coll rev Ser 93A (Houston L&P)	5.600	12/1/17	90.219	6.411	7.189	6.842	6.411	0.8211	12/1/93	12/1/05	12/1/03	102.0
9	FL Muni Pwr Agency rev Ser 93 (All-Req Pwr Supp Proj)	5.100	10/1/25	82.787	6.375	7.804	7.365	6.375	0.7835	12/1/93	10/1/05	10/1/03	101.0
10	Valdez AK marine term rev ref Ser 93C (BP Pipelines)	5.650	12/1/28	87.531	6.568	7.669	7.268	6.568	0.8211	12/1/93	12/1/05	12/1/03	102.0

Table continues

APPENDIX 5–A
continued

#	Description	Coupon	Final Maturity	Price	Yield to				Conversion Factor	Dated Date	Date of		1st Call Premium
					Maturity	1st Call	Par Call	Worst			Par Call	1st Call	
11	Reedy Creek Imprvmt Dist FL util ref rev Ser 94-1	5.000	10/1/14	85.742	6.247	7.111	6.769	6.247	0.7713	1/01/94	4/01/06	4/01/04	101.0
12	NYS Med Care Facil Fin Agncy mtg ref rev 94A (Pres Hsp)	5.250	8/15/14	87.844	6.323	7.153	6.769	6.323	0.7929	1/01/94	2/15/06	2/15/04	102.0
13	Salem Co Poll Control Auth NJ PCR Ser 94A (PS E&G) AMT	5.450	2/01/32	84.577	6.558	7.901	7.450	6.558	0.8117	2/01/94	2/01/06	2/01/04	102.0
14	San Antonio TX elec & gas sys ref rev Ser 94	5.000	2/01/14	84.739	6.371	7.380	6.927	6.371	0.7741	2/01/94	2/01/06	2/01/04	102.0
15	CA Hlth Facil Fin Auth Kaiser Perm Med Care Prog 85 REMKT	5.550	8/15/25	86.375	6.583	8.051	7.554	6.583	0.8328	11/19/85	2/15/04	2/15/02	101.0
16	NYS Dorm Auth Mt Sinai Sch of Medicine rev Ser 94A	5.000	7/01/21	82.913	6.326	7.590	7.133	6.326	0.7683	2/01/94	7/01/06	7/01/04	102.0
17	Triborough BR & Tunnel Auth NY gen purp re Ser 94A	5.000	1/01/24	81.323	6.417	7.925	7.432	6.417	0.7741	1/15/94	1/01/06	1/01/04	101.5
18	Lehigh Co Indust Dev Auth PA PCR ref Ser 94A (Penn P&L)	5.500	2/15/27	86.936	6.464	7.566	7.166	6.464	0.8117	2/15/94	2/15/06	2/15/04	102.0

Table continues

APPENDIX 5–A
continued

#	Description	Coupon	Final Maturity	Price	Yield to Maturity	Yield to 1st Call	Yield to Par Call	Worst	Conversion Factor	Dated Date	Date of Par Call	Date of 1st Call	1st Call Premium
19	San Francisco CA sewer ref rev Ser 94	5.375	10/1/22	87.188	6.355	7.657	7.148	6.355	0.8159	2/15/94	10/1/04	10/1/02	102.0
20	Fulton Co Sch Dist GA g.o. sch bonds Ser 93	5.625	1/01/21	92.031	6.243	6.926	6.620	6.243	0.8211	3/01/94	1/01/06	1/01/04	102.0
21	HI Housing Fin & Devlpmnt sing-fam mtge rev Ser 94A AMT	6.000	7/01/26	90.515	6.724	7.492	7.187	6.724	0.8455	3/01/94	7/01/06	7/01/04	102.0
22	NYC Muni Water Finance	5.500	6/15/23	89.250	6.312	7.121	6.823	6.312	0.8094	3/25/94	6/15/06	6/15/04	101.5
23	Anne Arundel Co MD PCR ref Ser 94 (Baltimore G&E)	6.000	4/01/24	93.141	6.524	7.124	6.854	6.524	0.8475	4/01/94	4/01/06	4/01/04	102.0
24	Harris Co TX toll rd unlim tax & sub lein rev Ser 94A	6.125	8/15/20	97.035	6.358	6.668	6.479	6.358	0.8571	4/01/94	8/15/06	8/15/04	102.0
25	NYS Envir Fac Corp wtr PCR 94A NYC Muni Wtr Fin 2nd Res	5.875	6/15/14	95.219	6.298	6.679	6.452	6.298	0.8380	3/15/94	6/15/06	6/15/04	102.0
26	Atlanta GA airport facs rev Ser 94B	6.000	1/01/21	94.844	6.406	6.894	6.644	6.406	0.8514	4/01/94	1/01/06	1/01/04	102.0
27	Kansas City KS util sys inprov ref rev Ser 94	6.375	9/01/23	100.188	6.360	6.488	6.351	6.351	0.8761	5/10/94	9/01/06	9/01/04	102.0

Table continues

#	Description	Coupon	Final Maturity	Price	Maturity	1st Call	Par Call	Worst	Conversion Factor	Dated Date	Par Call	1st Call	1st Call Premium
						Yield to					Date of		
28	Puerto Rico Electric Power Auth pwr rev Ser T	6.375	7/01/24	99.469	6.415	6.590	6.438	6.415	0.8761	4/01/94	7/01/06	7/01/04	102.0
29	Georgia Muni Elec Auth proj subordinated power rev 94A	6.500	1/01/26	100.625	6.453	6.563	6.422	6.422	0.8886	5/01/94	1/01/06	1/01/04	102.0
30	Illinois Regional Transportation Auth g.o. 94A	6.250	6/01/24	97.875	6.410	6.689	6.508	6.410	0.8681	5/01/94	6/01/06	6/01/04	102.0
31	Martin Co Indust Fac & PCR Fin Auth NC wst Wyrhausr AMT	6.800	5/01/24	99.875	6.809	6.960	6.815	6.809	0.9057	5/01/94	5/01/06	5/01/04	102.0
32	NYS Med Care Fac Fin Agncy mtg rev (St Vincent/SI Univ Hsp)	6.125	2/15/14	97.593	6.340	6.614	6.419	6.340	0.8607	4/01/94	2/15/06	2/15/04	102.0
33	Orange Co FL tourist development tax rev Ser 94B	6.000	10/1/24	97.094	6.213	6.528	6.342	6.213	0.8455	5/01/94	10/1/06	10/1/04	102.0
34	University of California Regents rev Ser D	6.375	9/01/24	99.719	6.395	6.604	6.411	6.395	0.8896	5/01/94	9/01/04	9/01/02	102.0
35	University of California Regents rev Ser D	6.375	9/01/19	99.750	6.394	6.599	6.407	6.394	0.8896	5/01/94	9/01/04	9/01/02	102.0
36	Humphreys Co IDB TN waste rev 94 (El duPont de Nemours)	6.700	5/01/24	99.766	6.718	6.876	6.728	6.718	0.9057	5/25/94	5/01/06	5/01/04	102.0

Table continues

APPENDIX 5-A
concluded

#	Description	Coupon	Final Maturity	Price	Yield to				Conver-sion Factor	Dated Date	Date of		1st Call Premium
					Maturity	1st Call	Par Call	Worst			Par Call	1st Call	
37	LA Co Pub Wks Fin Auth CA rev 94A (Park & Open Space Dist)	6.000	10/1/15	96.000	6.344	6.678	6.475	6.344	0.8455	5/01/94	10/1/06	10/1/04	102.0
38	NJ Econ Development Auth PCR Ser 94A (Pub Serv E&G) AMT	6.400	5/01/32	98.266	6.524	6.787	6.612	6.524	0.8775	5/01/94	5/01/06	5/01/04	102.0
39	Puerto Rico pub imprvmnt g.o. Ser 94	6.500	7/01/23	101.594	6.378	6.390	6.309	6.309	0.8856	5/01/94	7/01/06	7/01/04	101.5
40	Puerto Rico pub imprvmnt g.o. Ser 95	6.450	7/01/17	101.312	6.340	6.379	6.292	6.292	0.8856	5/01/94	7/01/06	7/01/04	101.5

Chapter Six

Introduction to Interest Rate Swaps

Ravi E. Dattatreya
Sumitomo Bank Capital Markets, Inc.

Raj E.S. Venkatesh
Infinity Financial Technology, Inc.

Vijaya Venkatesh
SolCom, Inc.

An interest rate swap is a contractual agreement between two parties to exchange a series of payments for a stated period of time. The nomenclature arises from the fact that typically the payments in a swap are similar to interest payments on a borrowing. When combined with an asset or a liability, a swap can change the risk characteristics of that asset or liability by changing the net cash flow. For example, a fixed-rate liability can be converted to a floating-rate liability using an interest rate swap.

Since its beginnings in the late 1970s, the interest rate swap has grown into an indispensable product and has proved to be a major advancement in the evolution of the world financial market. The annual size of the swap business is in excess of $3 trillion of notional amount (see Exhibit 6–1). Any market of this large size can be expected to exert significant influence on other markets. The influence of the swap market places the swap curve next in importance to the treasury yield curve.

The swap market has increased the interconnection between financial resources globally. It has changed, in a fundamental way, the manner in which institutions analyze funding decisions. This is a natural result of the fact that swaps provide new and efficient ways to manage assets and liabilities.

EXHIBIT 6–1a
Growth of Interest Rate Swap Market (Total Notional Principal)

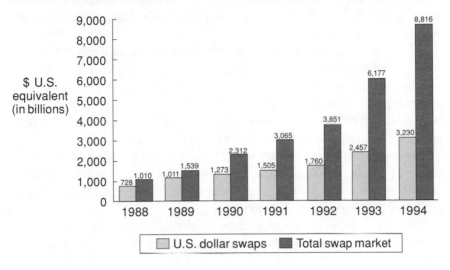

Source: ISDA, 1995.

EXHIBIT 6–1b
Growth of Cross-Currency Swap Market

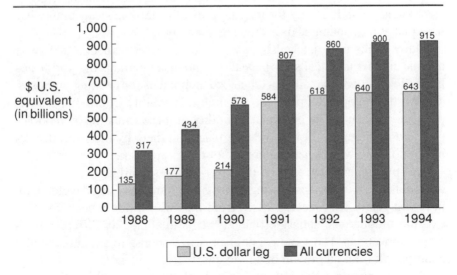

Source: ISDA, 1995.

The use of swaps is broad; it is no longer a specialized gadget limited to a select few. Swaps are used to reduce the cost of capital, manage risks, and exploit economies of scale. Worldwide, it has become an accepted financing technique to the extent that swap financing is considered routinely along with traditional alternatives.

Swaps are also used to arbitrage the different capital markets of the world. Borrowers and lenders access new markets using the swap technology by creating synthetic instruments. Several innovations, such as swap structures with optionlike features and derivatives such as caps and floors, have been developed. New users, notably insurance companies, and new uses emerge daily parallel with the increased use of swaps. The popularity of the swap has also brought several advantages to users, such as increased liquidity and standard documentation. The swap business is cooperatively promoted by the International Swap Dealers Association, Inc. (ISDA) which has nearly 150 members.

The capital markets have recently been characterized by unprecedented volatility. Institutional expectations naturally change in response to shifting market conditions. The swap provides an effective way for institutions to act on these changed expectations: They can lock in any gains or minimize higher potential losses. Available alternatives are either too expensive or have balance sheet implications (e.g., early retirement of debt). While hedging with the usual derivatives (e.g., futures and options) requires frequent monitoring and rebalancing, swap hedging requires no such constant attention and activity for long periods of time. The swap simply has no equal as a financing and risk management tool.

Many banks run matched books (i.e., they offset or hedge one swap against another identical swap). Dealers who make markets in swaps use a portfolio approach that applies advanced techniques for hedging purposes. The portfolio approach provides maximum flexibility in providing swap products to clients. The general availability of these valuation methodologies and the high level of confidence placed in them by the swap dealers has in no small way fueled the growth of the swap market.

The phenomenal success of the swap market justifies the prevailing sentiment that it is perhaps the single most important financing development in recent years. This success arises from the swap filling a need no other existing product can satisfy efficiently. It is qualitatively different from other innovations. The swap is not a specific response to a unique market condition. It is an outgrowth of a long unsatisfied demand.

The breadth and depth of the swap market; its enormous size, liquidity, and flexibility; and its significant influence on the world's capital markets

Exhibit 6–2
The Floating Asset/Fixed Liability Gap

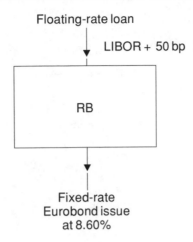

Floating-rate loan

↓ LIBOR + 50 bp

RB

↓

Fixed-rate
Eurobond issue
at 8.60%

mean that it is essential for every participant in these markets to obtain a thorough understanding of swaps.

A SIMPLE INTEREST RATE SWAP TRANSACTION

To understand how a swap works, let us look at a situation that can use a simple, so-called plain vanilla swap. Recall that a swap is an agreement between two parties, each called a *counterparty*.

Situation (A simple swap). RB is a regional bank. RB has just issued $100 million of a fixed-rate Eurobond of five-year maturity at a spread of 40 basis points over the five-year Treasury. The Treasury yield is at 8.20 percent; therefore, the coupon on the bond is 8.60 percent. RB is using the proceeds from the bond issue to fund a $100 million floating-rate loan. The loan is of five-year maturity and has a rate of three-month LIBOR plus 50 basis points.

In this case, RB has a floating-rate asset, the loan, but a fixed-rate liability, the bond (see Exhibit 6–2). This situation is known as an asset/liability *gap*. The gap is much more than an intellectual curiosity. It can have significant financial implications on RB in the following way. If rates fall, the cash flow from the loan will decrease but the cash flow due on the liability

Exhibit 6–3
A Simple Swap Transaction to Bridge the Asset/Liability Gap

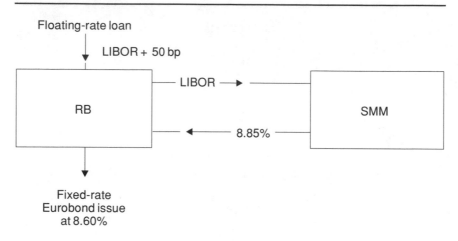

remains constant, resulting in a loss of the spread earned. Similarly, if the rates rise, the spread increases due to the higher level of cash flow from the asset. The spread that RB earns is thus subject to rate risk.

Situation. SMM is a swap market maker. SMM serves its clients by offering to enter into swap transactions of various kinds. SMM can help RB bridge the asset/liability gap and lock in the spread by providing an interest rate swap. Assuming that the swap spreads are at 65 basis points, RB can contract with SMM to pay, for a period of five years, three-month LIBOR on a notional principal amount of $100 million in return for fixed annual cash receipts from SMM of 8.85 percent (8.20 percent Treasury rate plus the 65 basis point swap spread) on the same notional amount. RB pays LIBOR to SMM out of the cash flow received from the loan, retaining the 50 basis point spread. The 8.60 percent interest payments due on the bond issue is covered by the 8.85 percent swap payments from SMM. Even here, RB retains the 25 basis point spread. Thus, RB earns a total of 75 basis points (50 basis point spread over LIBOR from the loan, 25 basis point spread over the bond coupon from the swap) from the combined transaction (see Exhibit 6–3).

More importantly, this spread is locked in. The earned spread is immune to interest rate changes. As the interest receipts from the loan change, the payments due on the swap change in lock-step, effectively insulating RB from rate volatility.

EXHIBIT 6–4
Cash Flow Profile of Swap

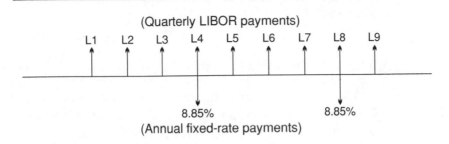

The swap transaction between RB and SMM is usually illustrated diagrammatically as in Exhibit 6–3 with each party in a box and cash flows represented by arrows. If more details are necessary or if the cash flows are more complex, a swap can be represented by means of a cash flow profile (see Exhibit 6–4).

Review of the Simple Swap Transaction

Several important characteristics of a swap can be illustrated using the simple transaction above. See the glossary at the end of the chapter for the meaning of terms used.

1. In an interest rate swap transaction, only payments resembling or corresponding to the interest payments on a notional (loan) amount are exchanged. The principal amount itself is not, which has important implications on the amount of credit risk in a swap transaction.

2. One party pays a floating rate, the other party pays a fixed rate. This is typical of most interest rate swap transactions even though both parties could pay floating or fixed.[1] Typical floating rate indexes used are LIBOR, commercial paper, Fed funds rate, prime rate, and T-bill rate. Most (about 75 percent) of the swaps in dollars are based on LIBOR.

3. The swap has a specific notional amount and maturity. The floating side has a specified index (e.g., three-month LIBOR).

---

1 If both parties pay fixed or floating, the payments would differ in one of more attributes, such as frequency or timing of payment, floating-rate index used, and compounding method.

4. The swap rate (i.e., the fixed rate) is quoted as a spread over the appropriate maturity current coupon Treasury. The payments on the floating side are usually made flat; that is, at the selected index rate without any spread.

EXAMPLES OF SWAP APPLICATIONS

There are countless ways of using interest rate swaps to manage cash flows. The actual objectives sought by swap users are also numerous. Generally, swaps are used by institutions for the following major purposes:

- To hedge, or to modify for risk management purposes, a genuine existing (or future expected) asset or liability. Hedging is the most straightforward and most common use of swaps.

- To sculpt an existing cash flow to a desired structure. This application is similar to hedging.

- To capture value in the market; for example, to decrease the effective interest cost on a borrowing or the realized yield on an investment. Value capture is usually achieved by arbitraging different market segments or by taking advantage of market anomalies. The swap market also offers interesting risk-reward trade-offs not easily available in the traditional debt markets. Borrowers and lenders who can tolerate these risks can achieve attractive financing or returns.

- To access synthetically markets otherwise not easily or efficiently accessible. Examples: (1) a U.S. corporation, not well known in Japan, borrows in yen by swapping its U.S. debt in U.S. dollars into yen liability; (2) a low-rated corporation with no access to long-term borrowing swaps its short-term floating-rate debt to fixed rate debt.[2]

- To improve the cosmetics of a transaction. In this application, optional characteristics are usually employed (e.g., to reduce the initial interest rate on a borrowing, an issuer might take the risk of a higher future coupon on the issue).

One of the attractions of swaps in financing applications is based on the concept of comparative advantage; that is, two institutions can achieve

---

2 The synthetic versions of the debt created are not exactly the same as the real thing. For example, even though the corporation can obtain fixed, long-term rates, it is still subject to funding risk from the short-term floating-rate debt.

mutual economic benefits by exchanging funds that are available to them at relatively cheaper costs. In many market conditions, the credit spread between higher- and lower-rated institutions for fixed-rate borrowings is wider than the corresponding spread for floating-rate borrowings. Obviously, the higher-rated borrower pays a lower rate in either market, but the lower-rated borrower pays a lesser credit spread in the floating-rate market. In other words, the lower-rated borrower has a *relative* or *comparative advantage* over the higher-rated borrower in the floating-rate market. Conversely, the higher-rated borrower has the relative advantage in the fixed-rate market.

If each borrower raises funds in the market in which it has the greater relative advantage, then the corresponding interest payments can be swapped to achieve cheaper funding rates for both. To illustrate this concept, consider the following situation:

Situation (Comparative advantage). HR, a high-rated borrower, can raise funds at 8.60 percent fixed or at LIBOR flat. LR, a low-rated institution, can borrow at 9.60 percent fixed or at LIBOR plus 0.50 percent. That is, the credit spread in the fixed-rate market is 100 basis points whereas it is just 50 basis points for floating rate borrowings. Suppose, HR borrows fixed at 8.60 percent and LR borrows floating at LIBOR plus 0.50 percent. HR and LR can then enter into a fixed/floating swap where HR pays LIBOR and receives 8.85 percent. The net interest payments are LIBOR minus 0.25 percent for HR and 9.35 percent fixed for LR. Thus, each borrower has achieved a saving on its own borrowing: HR saves 25 basis points relative to a straight floating-rate borrowing (LIBOR – 0.25 percent vs. LIBOR flat); LR also saves 25 basis points compared to a straight fixed-rate borrowing (9.35 percent vs. 9.60 percent). See Exhibit 6–5.

In many practical situations, comparative advantage may not always exist. When it does exist, the gross savings may not be enough to pay for expenses (e.g., the fee or the bid-asked spread required by the swap arranger or provider) or the net savings to each borrower may be too small to warrant the additional complexities of the transaction.

HR and LR could have used other derivative products such as exchange-traded futures and options for converting their risk profiles between fixed- and floating-rate exposure. However, in addition to achieving cheaper funding, effective interest rate risk management is also a common objective. Unlike the other derivative products, swaps can be used for interest rate hedging over long periods of time without any need

EXHIBIT 6–5

Using a Swap to Exploit Comparative Advantage

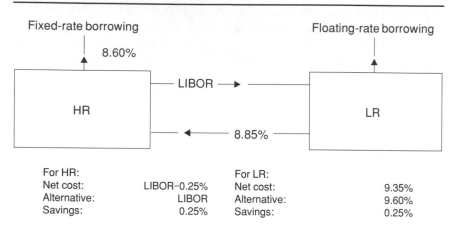

For HR:		For LR:	
Net cost:	LIBOR–0.25%	Net cost:	9.35%
Alternative:	LIBOR	Alternative:	9.60%
Savings:	0.25%	Savings:	0.25%

for frequent monitoring and rebalancing. Also, swaps do not have the inconvenience of daily margin cash flow. Swaps can achieve the conversion between fixed and floating rates with high predictability; transactions involving futures and options can have some inefficiency due to the divergence of the futures and cash markets.

The following additional examples illustrate the variety in swap usage.

Situation (Reduce fixed-rate cost). A Midwestern manufacturing company, MM, seeks fixed-rate funding for five years. It can borrow fixed for five years at 9.30 percent or floating at LIBOR plus $\frac{1}{8}$. Suppose that swap rates are 8.85 percent. The company can borrow floating and execute a swap transaction on which it would pay 8.85 percent and receive LIBOR. The net cost of funding using swaps is 8.975 percent (8.85 percent payment on the swap plus the $\frac{1}{8}$ spread over LIBOR paid on the loan), a 32.5 basis point saving relative to the straight 9.30 percent financing. See Exhibit 6–6.

Situation (Reduce floating-rate cost). A California retailer, CR, has traditionally borrowed at LIBOR plus $\frac{1}{8}$ from its banks. It discovers that five-year funding can be obtained from a private source at 8.80 percent or 0.60 percent above Treasuries. Swap rates are at 8.85 percent. The retailer

EXHIBIT 6–6
Using a Swap to Reduce the Fixed Rate

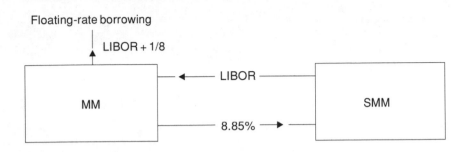

can borrow from the private source at fixed rate and enter into a swap paying LIBOR and receiving 8.85 percent. The combination of the bond and the swap results in a net funding cost of LIBOR minus 0.05 percent (LIBOR payment on the swap plus the 8.80 percent coupon on the bond less the 8.85 percent receipt on the swap), at a savings of 17.5 basis points relative to traditional borrowing. See Exhibit 6–7.

Situation (Convert to floating). A European automotive company, AC, borrowed fixed for 7 years at 11.25 percent three years ago (see Exhibit 6–8). Now, with the four-year Treasuries at 8.15 percent and swap spreads at 55 basis points, the treasurer feels that the average short rates will

EXHIBIT 6–7
Reducing Floating Rate Cost

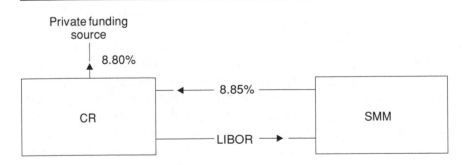

EXHIBIT 6–8
Converting to Floating Rate

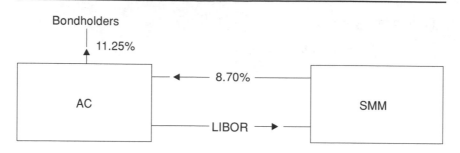

be considerably less that 11.25 percent for the remaining life of the debt. He therefore swaps into floating, receiving 8.70 percent and paying LIBOR. With six-month LIBOR at 8.06%, his net cost for the first six months is 10.61 percent (8.06 percent plus 11.25 percent on the bond issue less 8.70 percent received on the swap), a saving of 64 basis points (11.25 percent old coupon less 10.61 percent new initial coupon). He has potential for further savings in the future if his forecast of lower levels of interest rates holds good.

Situation (Obtain desired structure). A start-up company, SC, has access to floating-rate funds from its traditional banker, TB. SC, however, would like fixed-rate funding. In addition, it would like to keep its interest costs low in the initial years and is willing to pay a compensating higher rate in the later years. In this case, SC can enter into what is known as a step-up coupon swap (see Exhibit 6–9). This swap starts with a low interest rate coupon on the fixed side. After a few years, the rate will step up. Achieving the desired structure is perhaps more important to SC than squeezing the last basis point out of the market.

The swap participants in Exhibits 6–5 to 6–9 have different objectives. The swaps executed to meet these objectives are also different in overall structure. Yet, the attentive reader can observe that the needs of each party seem to mirror that of another and can be fulfilled by combining them appropriately in swap transactions. MM and CR can enter into a five-year fixed/LIBOR swap, where MM will pay fixed and CR will pay floating. Finally, AC can enter into a four-year fixed/LIBOR swap with a counterparty with the counterparty paying fixed, and AC paying floating.

EXHIBIT 6–9
Obtaining Desired Structure

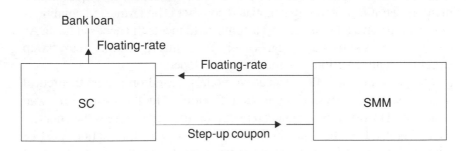

In the real world, however, the selection of counterparties is not as obvious, nor is their availability as easy, as is implied by these illustrative cases. The swap required by SC is a good example (see Exhibit 6–9). It is unlikely that SC would quickly find an appropriate counterparty wishing to pay floating and receive fixed on a step-up structure. In general, the situation is complicated by several factors such as:

1. The swapping needs of one party are not generally known to the other party.
2. Parties have very limited ability to evaluate and accept the credit risk of the counterparty.
3. The payment date and maturity requirements of one party may not match those of the counterparty.
4. Some parties may not be able to meet the cash buyout requirements of their counterparties.
5. The timing requirement of one party might differ from that of the counterparty.
6. There might be differences in funding sizes of the different parties.

Many of these problems can be solved by the intervention of a swap dealer. The dealer will be in contact with a number of swap users and will be aware of their specific needs. The dealer may perform a purely intermediary function or hold one of the swaps in inventory until another closely matching swap is available. The dealer typically will use liquid market securities, such as Treasuries and futures contracts, to hedge each swap completely during the inventory period and to hedge any residual mismatches after the offsetting swap has been executed.

SWAP STRUCTURES

One of the most striking features of a swap, which is a very liquid instrument, is that it is a privately negotiated contract. The terms and conditions of the swap contract thus can be customized to meets the needs at hand. As end users of swaps have aggressively used this flexibility, new swap structures with descriptive names have developed.

The prevalent cash flow valuation models, based on robust theoretical principles, have provided significant flexibility in the design of swap structures. However, when conceiving these structures there is the counterbalancing need for liquidity in the event that a swap transaction must be unwound. This need encourages swap structures to gravitate toward a select few formats. Market liquidity, aided by widely available sophisticated valuation models, also increases the ability of swap providers to hedge the swaps, resulting in a better price for the end user. Where liquidity is not a concern, from the view of both the end user and the provider, swaps can be engineered with almost limitless variety.

The Standard Interest Rate Swap

The standard interest rate swap consists of the exchange of a floating rate payment stream for a fixed rate payment stream. The agreement has a fixed maturity and the notional amount is held constant throughout the life of the swap.

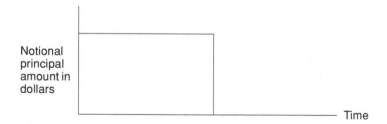

Situation (Achieving funding cost target). ESD, an electrical systems developer, is seeking $30 million of funding for 10 years on a fixed-rate basis. It finds that its interest rate cost of 8.10 percent for fixed-rate borrowing is slightly higher than its target rate of 7.90 percent. It can raise floating-rate dollar funds in the Eurobond market at LIBOR flat.

EXHIBIT 6–10
Achieving Funding Cost Target

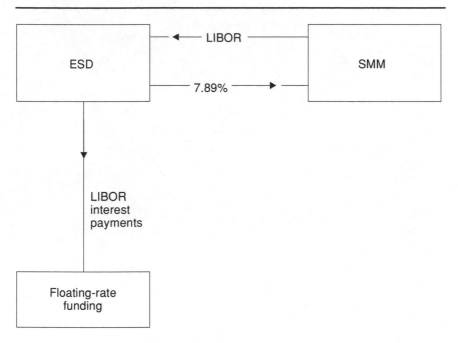

ESD can achieve its fixed-rate funding target by raising $30 million floating-rate funds in the Euromarket and swapping into a fixed rate. Under the swap, ESD pays interest at the fixed rate of 7.89 percent and receives LIBOR. Effectively, ESD will have a 10-year funding at a fixed rate of 7.89 percent on $30 million (see Exhibit 6–10).

Off-Market Swap

Interest rate swaps are usually initiated so that their initial value is zero; that is, the present value of the cash flows to be paid equals the present value of the cash flows to be received. Any change in the market rates, or simply the passage of time, can cause a deviation in the value of the swap. A swap with a nonzero value is called an *off-market swap*. If a new swap is off market, then a compensating up-front payment from one party to the other will be required to bring the net value to zero. The adjustment may also be made via a lower-than-market coupon.

EXHIBIT 6–11
Hedging an Ex-Warrant Bond

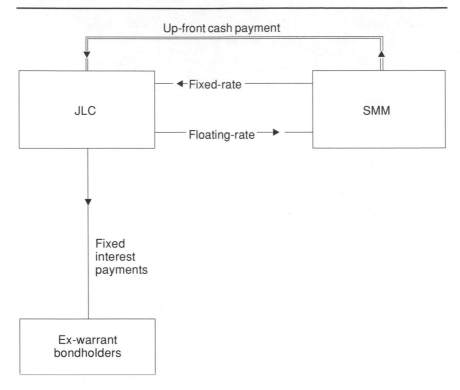

Situation (Hedging an ex-warrant bond). JLC is a Japanese leasing company which has just issued a fixed-rate, four-year, dollar-denominated bond in the Euromarket with attached equity warrants. JLC would like to hedge the bond issue alone, called the ex-warrant bond, by converting the bond cash flows into floating. The warrant exposure is left unhedged (see Exhibit 6–11).

The coupon on the bond is most likely to be below market, given that the bond has attached warrants. Therefore, JLC enters into an off-market interest rate swap. JLC receives cash up front from the swap provider or, more likely, enjoys a lower-than-market floating coupon.

Off-market swaps are used mostly to unwind or reverse out of older interest rate swaps when rates have moved since the inception of the swaps. They are also used where a given cash flow needs to be matched exactly

EXHIBIT 6–12
Reversing an Existing Interest Rate Swap

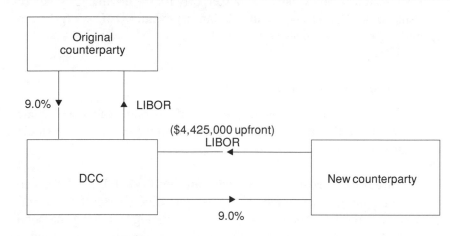

(see asset swaps) or to create discount or premium assets or liabilities in conjunction with a change in rate basis (fixed or floating), as in the discussion of zero-coupon swaps.

Situation (Reversing out of an old swap). DCC is a diversified chemical company that entered into a 10-year swap for $40 million, receiving fixed at 9 percent two years ago. The market has rallied, with prevailing eight-year swap rates at 7.20 percent. DCC now wishes to unwind the swap. DCC enters into an offsetting swap with another counterparty under which DCC pays 9 percent for eight years (i.e., 1.80 percent above the market rate) and receives LIBOR. The new counterparty makes an up-front adjustment payment of $4,250,000, reflecting the off-market status of the swap.[3] This payment is compensation to DCC for the above-market fixed-rate payments that it makes. See Exhibit 6–12.

The natural way to have unwound the swap would have been simply to terminate or cancel the swap. The original counterparty would have paid to DCC a settlement amount reflecting the difference between the 9 percent existing rate and the 7.20 percent market rate. DCC chose to enter into a

---

3 The market adjustment value of $4,250,000 is determined by using a swap pricing model.

new, offsetting swap. This situation arises when the settlement payment offered by the original counterparty for termination is less than the adjustment payment offered by the new counterparty for the off-market swap. In the former case DCC has no credit risk, but in the latter DCC is exposed to the credit risk of two counterparties.

Zero-Coupon Swap

A *zero-coupon swap* is an extreme case of an off-market swap in which one of the counterparties makes a lump sum payment instead of periodic payments over time.

Situation (Creating a zero-coupon liability). ETC, a European trading company, has just issued a floating-rate, five-year dollar-denominated bond in the Eurobond market. It is considering swapping the bond into a fixed-rate liability. However, it would like to conserve cash as much as possible for operational reasons, and would prefer zero-coupon funding.

ETC can achieve its goal by means of a zero-coupon interest rate swap. Under the swap, ETC will receive floating rate dollar cash flows for five years. These cash flows will exactly service interest payments on the outstanding Eurobond. As part of the swap contract, ETC will make a lump sum payment at maturity. This payment is the effective zero-coupon liability for ETC. See Exhibit 6–13.

Other variations of the zero-coupon swap are possible. The lump sum payment can occur at any time, up front, at maturity, or during the life of the swap.

Asset Swap: Synthetic Securities

Swaps are used not only for managing liabilities, but also for engineering the cash flows from assets into desired formats. For example, a floating-rate asset can be converted into a synthetic fixed rate asset using an interest rate swap.

Situation (Creating a synthetic fixed-rate asset). LIC, a life insurance company, has just acquired a floating-rate bond at an attractive yield. However, LIC's liabilities are typically long and fixed rate. Therefore, LIC would like to convert the bond into a fixed-rate asset (see Exhibit 6–14).

Exhibit 6–13
Creating a Zero-Coupon Liability

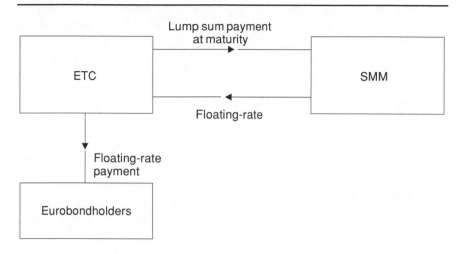

LIC can achieve its goal by entering into an asset swap. Under the swap contract, LIC will essentially pay all the floating cash flow received from the asset, except for the principal payment at maturity, to the swap counterparty. It will receive fixed-rate payments periodically. Note that the interest rate swap may be an off-market swap in order to match the exact cash flows from the floating-rate bond. Also, the swap counterparty might require that the bond be pledged as collateral, depending upon the credit rating of LIC.

Synthetic assets can provide attractive returns relative to conventional securities. Remember, however, that synthetic assets in general have lower liquidity and are appropriate only in those cases where they are expected to be held to maturity.

Situation (Hedging a fixed-rate asset). FI is a portfolio manager investing in fixed-income securities. He owns a fixed-rate bond that he considers a very attractive asset. However, he believes that interest rates will rise, resulting in the fall of the price of the asset owned. He can sell the fixed-rate bond and purchase floating-rate or shorter-term securities. Alternatively, he can continue to hold the attractive asset, but at the same time hedge his interest rate risk by entering into an asset swap. On the swap, he will pay fixed and receive floating. The payments made on the swap are offset by the coupon received on the bond. The receipts on

Exhibit 6–14
Creating a Fixed-Rate Asset

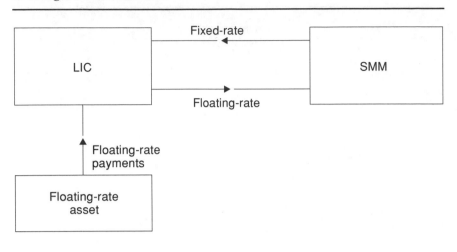

EXHIBIT 6–15
Hedging a Fixed-Rate Asset

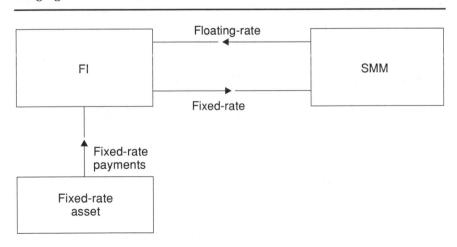

the swap effectively convert the fixed-rate bond into a floating-rate asset. See Exhibit 6–15.

Another way to view this asset swap is that the change in the value of the bond due to a rise (or fall) in interest rates will be matched by an equal and opposite change in the value of the swap. Thus, the swap effectively hedges the bond.

Forward Swap

A forward swap is one in which a significant delay occurs between the date on which the swap is traded or committed to and the settlement or effective date of the swap.

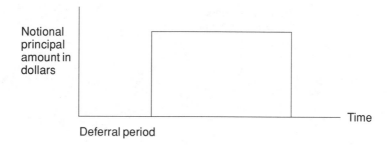

Situation (Hedging a future liability). MWCo is a Midwestern manufacturing company. In June, MWCo plans to raise fixed-rate funds for a future project. Funds would not be necessary until November. MWCo has determined that the optimal strategy would be to issue fixed-rate bonds in Europe in November. The risk to the company is the possibility that interest rates might rise between now and the future funding date.

MWCo can hedge this risk by entering into a forward interest rate swap immediately (see Exhibit 6–16). The swap will settle or become effective in November, coinciding with the planned bond issue. Under the swap, MWCo will pay a fixed rate (equal to, for example, X1 percent) and receive floating-rate payments. At the time of the Eurobond issue in November, MWCo will enter into another swap under which it will receive a fixed rate (equal to the market rate of, say, X2 percent) and pay floating. The coupon rate on the bond will also be X2 percent, reflecting the market levels.[4] The net cash flow from the forward swap, the coupon payments on the bond, and the second swap is simply the fixed payment on the forward swap. Thus, MWCo is hedged.

Forward swaps can be used similarly in conjunction with planned future asset acquisitions.

---

4 MWCo takes the risk that swap rates and its own bond rates might move by different amounts.

EXHIBIT 6–16
Hedging Future Bond Issue with a Forward Swap

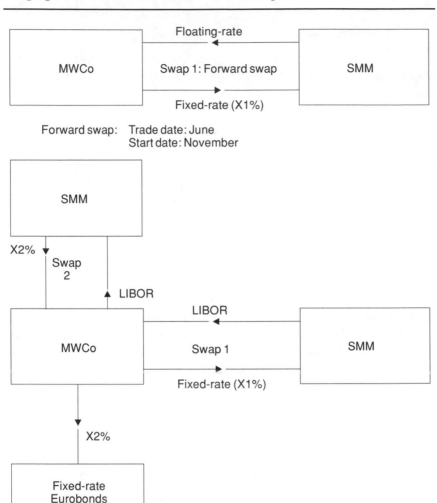

Variable Fixed-Rate Swaps

Sometimes, a swap on the fixed side has a series of fixed rates applied to time intervals that do not overlap. Thus, even though all the payments are known, they are not equal. Depending on the structure, these swaps are often called *step-up coupon* or *step-down coupon* swaps. They are mainly used to manage cash flow needs and constraints effectively.

EXHIBIT 6–17
Cash Flow Management with Step-Up Coupon Swap

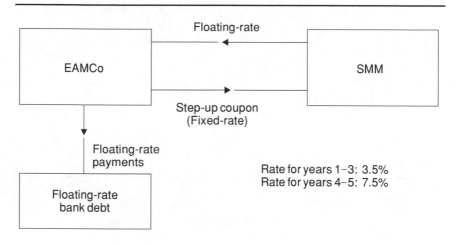

Situation (Cash flow management). EAMCo, an Eastern appli-
ance manufacturing company, would like to swap its floating-rate bank
loan into fixed rate for five years. However, its cash flows cannot comfortably service the market fixed rate. Therefore, it enters into a fixed-rate
swap with SMM under which SMM pays LIBOR in years 1–5. EAMCo
pays a low coupon rate of 3.5 percent for the first three years. To compensate SMM, it has to pay a significantly higher rate of 7.5 percent in the
last two years. EAMCo hopes that its cash flows will have improved by
then. See Exhibit 6–17.

Swaps with Variable Notional Amount

Usually, the notional or the principal amount of a swap is held constant
throughout the life of the swap. However, situations might arise in which
there is a need for varying the notional principal. The more common
varieties of variable notional principal swaps are discussed below.

In *amortizing swaps,* the notional principal starts at a high level and
gradually decreases. An amortizing swap is suitable when the asset or liability being hedged is itself amortizing. It is possible to analyze and price an
amortizing swap as a combination of smaller swaps of different maturities.

An *accreting swap* is one in which the notional principal starts low and
slowly increases over the life of the swap.

Amortizing Swap

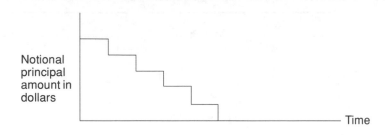

Accreting Swap

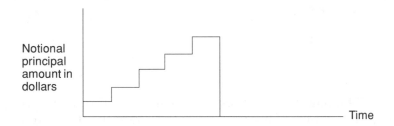

Situation (Hedging a construction loan—I). HEP is a construction company that develops hydroelectric projects. It has secured a floating-rate loan for a new energy project. It intends to draw down on the loan as the construction progresses. Also, it wishes to convert the liability into a fixed-rate loan now because it finds current interest rates attractive.

One alternative for HEP is to enter into a series of interest rate swaps, receiving floating and paying fixed, as and when the loan is drawn down (see Exhibit 6–18). In addition to the inconvenience of a potentially large number of small-sized transactions, this option also exposes HEP to changes in future interest rates. An acceptable alternative is to enter into an accreting interest rate swap with the notional principal increasing in step with the planned drawdown of the loan. The swap would be priced based on current market conditions, thus providing HEP protection from future changes in interest rates.

Two observations are notable in the context of Exhibit 6–18. First, HEP assumes the small risk that the actual drawdowns may not exactly match the planned drawdowns on which the swap is based. In most real-world

EXHIBIT 6–18
Hedging with an Accreting Swap

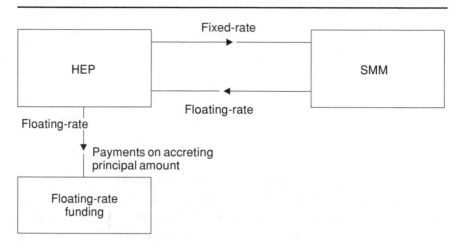

situations, it is best to retain this type of small, unquantifiable risk rather than hedge it out to the last penny by introducing optionlike features in the interest rate swap. The incremental cost of the optional features would probably not be justified in view of the small size of the risk. One reason for this is that any option incorporated into a swap is priced based on the potential movement of interest rates, whereas the drawdowns on the loan may not be so strongly correlated with interest rate levels. Thus, buying optional features for the risk could be an over-hedge. One simple principle to follow is to hedge *generic* risks in the market through derivatives, and retain *specific* risks. This way we apportion the task of hedging among different players optimally. In this example, HEP is far better equipped to handle the specific risk than any swap dealer. On the other hand, the swap dealer can easily hedge the market risk.

Second, notice that HEP could also achieve its goals by entering into a number of forward swaps, each corresponding to a planned drawdown. This illustrates the point that, conceptually, an accreting swap is simply a combination of forward swaps.

A *roller-coaster swap,* with its notional principal increasing and decreasing at different times, combines the properties of accreting and amortizing swaps. A roller-coaster swap is used to engineer, in detail, cash flows to a specific need. It is relatively less common in practice.

Roller-Coaster Swap

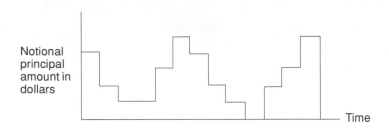

Situation (Hedging a construction loan—II). HEP is a construction company that develops hydroelectric projects. It has secured a floating-rate loan for a construction project. The terms of the loan require HEP to draw down the funds as the project progresses. The terms also require gradual repayment as soon as the project is completed and begins to produce income.

HEP can hedge the interest rate risk inherent in this project and its funding by means of a roller-coaster interest rate swap. The notional principal of the swap is set to increase in step with the projected draw-down schedule of the loan. Once the loan has been completely drawn down, the notional amount is set to decrease according to the projected cash flow to be received from the project.

As before, note that HEP retains the residual risk that the actual amounts drawn down and the actual cash flow from the project may not be exactly the same as the projected amounts used in the swap. It is not unreasonable on the part of HEP to accept this risk.

PARTICIPANTS IN THE SWAP MARKET

As in all financial markets, there are various types of participants in the swap business, each serving different functions.

An *end user* is the ultimate consumer of swaps. End users usually have some assets or liabilities that they wish to hedge using swaps. There are also those who enter into swap transactions seeking trading profits. In addition to outright swap positions, a popular trade is to match a short-term swap against a position in Eurodollar futures.

A *market maker,* as the name implies, provides liquidity by making two-way markets in swaps. In general, market makers are the major source of swaps for end users; that is, end users mostly execute swaps with market makers rather than with other end users.[5] Market makers usually hedge their swap positions with the more liquid instruments such as Treasuries and futures on an interim basis until an offsetting position can be executed in the swap market itself. They also actively seek offsetting swaps so as to reduce the size of their hedge positions and limit any risk not easily hedgeable with liquid market instruments.

An *intermediary* stands between two swap parties, shielding each from the other's credit risk. The major risk to the intermediary itself is the credit exposure to the two parties. The intermediary earns a fee as compensation for the credit risk. Intermediation is used when one party cannot take the credit risk of the other party or when other considerations (e.g., those related to tax and regulatory issues) apply.

These three types of players are principals in swap transactions, that is, they actually are the counterparties. On the other hand, *brokers* or *agents* do not enter into swaps themselves. For a fee, they find and bring together parties that can execute swap transactions. The cost to the end user is increased by the amount of the brokerage fee. Among brokers are many investment banks that do not have their own swap operations and brokers who provide information on available swaps through data screens.

SWAP PRICING BASICS

The maturity of the dollar interest rate swap market is indicated by the widely available bid and asked quotations on 1-to-10-year maturities. Swap rates are quoted as a spread over the bond yield of the on-the-run (i.e., the most liquid) Treasury of appropriate maturity.[6] Sometimes, the spread is

---

5 Among the reasons for this are that end users do not have access to or knowledge of other end users with matching swap needs, and they do not have the resources necessary to measure, monitor, and manage the resulting credit risk.

6 Usually, simultaneous execution of offsetting swaps by a swap dealer is uncommon. Therefore, it is likely that one or both parties to a swap will execute a Treasury trade to hedge the swap position. Swaps up to four to five years' maturity are usually hedged in the Eurodollar futures market. In general, the fixed-rate payer will base the rate on the asked price of the Treasury (or futures, as the case might be), and the receiver will base it on the bid side. Some end users control the bid-asked difference by actually selling or purchasing the appropriate Treasury from the dealer.

added to a rate interpolated from two on-the-run Treasuries whose maturities straddle that of the swap. For short maturities (up to four years), swap rates are often quoted using the money market practice (i.e., as an absolute level on an annual, actual/360 day basis).[7]

Example. On July 16, 1993, the two-year swap rate was quoted at 4.12 percent on an actual/360 basis. The five-year swap rate was quoted at 24 basis points over the five-year Treasury note, which in turn was quoted at a yield of 4.987 percent.

A swap is an exchange of two streams of cash flows. Therefore, a swap can be priced by determining the value of each stream of cash flows. The price of the swap is simply the difference between the values of the two cash flows. The value of each stream of cash flows is the net present value (NPV), that is, the sum of the discounted present values of each cash flow in the stream. If the cash flows are in different currencies, the present values are converted to one currency at the prevailing exchange rate before the difference is taken to price the swap.

For new swaps, this price has to be zero. In other words, if we are willing to exchange one stream of cash flows (the legs of the swap) for another, then the values of the two legs or streams of cash flows should be equal. In this context, pricing a swap means the determination of one or more parameters of the swap to make the values of the two streams equal. A common parameter that is computed in pricing a swap is the fixed rate on the fixed leg of a swap. That is, to price a new interest rate swap is to determine the *fixed rate* applied to the fixed leg of the swap. To price existing swaps, we compute *market value* of the swap, which is the difference between the net present values of the two legs.

The swap may be arbitrarily complex, and the market data that is used to determine the net present value of the legs may be large in number and may be obtained from different sources. Yet, the fundamental principle in pricing swaps remains the same: If two streams of cash flows are exchanged, then their values must be equal. If they are not, then one party to the swap must compensate the other for the difference. This adjustment payment is the price of the swap.

It helps to visualize the situation as a balance scale,[8] one side of which carries the present value of one leg while the other side carries the present

---

7 The reason for using money market convention is that short-dated swaps are priced off the Eurodollar futures.

value of the other leg. If the scale is not balanced or level (i.e., if the present values of the two legs are not equal), we have to add an adjustment weight to the lighter side. This adjustment, an up-front payment from one party to another, is the value of the swap. The balance scale analogy also illustrates another fact in swap pricing: The value of the swap to one party is equal and opposite to the value to the other parties; that is, if one party has a gain (one side of the balance goes up, swap value becomes positive) in the swap, the other party has a loss (the other side of the balance goes down, swap value becomes negative) of an exactly equal amount.

Other common financial evaluation techniques, such as the internal rate of return *(IRR),* are of little practical use in swap pricing. *IRRs* for different cash flows are not comparable in any way.[9] *NPV,* on the other hand, is in current dollars and has the attractive property of additivity and comparability.[10] Conceptually, the value of a swap can be easily computed by discounting the cash flows from each leg of the swap.

There are a few complications that need to be addressed before we can apply the discounting rules. First, we need an appropriate *discount function,* that is, a set of discount rates corresponding to the timing of each cash flow. The discounting function is popularly known as the *zero curve* or the *zero-coupon curve* because the rates correspond to yields on zero-coupon bonds compared with the *par curve,* which represents the yield on full-coupon bonds.[11] Often, it is represented in the form of *discount factors.* The discount factor for a given date is the present value of a $1 cash flow occurring on that date and is a number between 0 and 1.[12] In practice,

---

8 The balance scale analogy is courtesy of R. A. Beckstrom.

9 See the discussion of *IRRs* in the context of bond trading in Ravi E. Dattatreya and Frank Fabozzi, *Active Total Return Management of Fixed Income Portfolios* (Chicago: Probus Publishing, 1996).

10 Many weak measures, such as *IRR,* yield, and option-adjusted-spread (OAS), tend to get entrenched in capital market analyses. However, *NPV* is a more robust measure and will eventually prevail. More than any other group, practitioners in the swap and other derivative markets have contributed to the development of the correct line of thinking in this context.

11 The curve representing rates for plain vanilla or standard at-market swaps is also called the par curve. Rates from the par curve are not suitable for discounting. They represent a blend of various discount rates corresponding to each of the cash flows in a par bond. Compare this situation with the discussion of risk points in Chapter 24 where we show that the risk of a par bond is a combination of the risks in zero-coupon bonds corresponding to the coupon and principal cash flows.

12 In contrast with discount rates, discount factors do not have any attached conventions such as compounding frequency or day count method.

discount factors and zero rates are generated using a variety of market data, such as cash LIBOR deposit rates, the swap rates for plain vanilla structures, Eurodollar futures prices, and current Treasury yield levels. The goal in using all this data is to derive a curve that represents the rates that can be used for pricing swaps.[13] We discuss the derivation of zero rates and discount factors in more detail in the next section.

Second, unlike bonds or other investments, the swap has two-way cash flows. This problem can be handled simply by computing the values algebraically (i.e., by including the sign) or by splitting the incoming and outgoing cash flows and valuing them separately.

Third, the cash flows on the floating side are unknown, except perhaps for the first payment, which is set at the outset. The solution to this problem is to replace each of the unknown floating-rate cash flows by rates that can be locked in through hedging transactions in the capital markets. These rates are called *forward rates* and are discussed in detail in the next section. Forward rates are computed from the discount function or derived from the prices of Eurodollar futures.

Note that the zero curve or the discount function is used to serve two functions:

1. To determine the implied forward rates, which in turn fix, for valuation purposes, the future floating-rate cash flows.
2. To determine the appropriate discounting rate to use for cash flows occurring at various times on the fixed side as well as the floating side of the swap.

Normally, the zero curve derived represents LIBOR, given that the par curve is driven by swap rates and Eurodollar futures prices. However, if the floating-rate index used is not LIBOR, we need two zero curves: one to generate forward rates corresponding to the actual index and another (based on LIBOR) to discount all cash flows.[14]

---

13 Additional care is taken to ensure that the swap rates obtained are consistent with all liquid markets such as FRA (forward rate agreement), Eurodollar futures, etc. Otherwise, an arbitrage condition may exist between these markets and the swap market.

14 For example, in a T-bill-for-fixed swap, a Treasury curve is used to derive assumed cash flows corresponding to future T-bill rates, and the standard swap curve is used to derive the discount factors to present value the cash flows. Discounting "at LIBOR" has become a standard in the swap market. It assumes the willingness and ability to lend and borrow at LIBOR. However, if the swap structure implies significant net lending or borrowing (e.g., as in a zero-coupon swap), appropriate spreads are then added before discounting.

Thus, known forward rates are used to represent unknown future floating-rate cash flows. As far as swap valuation is concerned, we are indifferent between the unknown floating-rate cash flows or the known cash flows represented by forward rates.[15] Once the floating side has been so "fixed," its present value is computed by discounting each flow to the present.[16] The swap rate can then be determined by finding the fixed rate that will produce the same discounted present value as the floating side. Since the values of the two sides are equal, the swap is therefore said to have zero (net) value. The rate so derived is called the *midpoint* or the *break-even rate*. Bid-asked spreads are used to appropriately modify the swap rates derived as needed.

If market rates, and therefore zero-coupon rates and forward rates, have moved since the initial pricing of a swap, then the value of the fixed side of the swap will diverge from the value of the floating side. Even though the cash flows on the fixed side are fixed, its value will change because of the change in the zero-coupon rates, which are used for discounting. On the floating-rate side, the change in value results from changes in both the representative cash flows and the discounting rates. In this situation, the swap is said to be *off market;* that is, the present values of the floating side and the fixed side will not be equal due to changes in the forward rates.

The value of an off-market swap is not zero: It can be positive or negative with respect to a counterparty, depending on whether the receive or the pay side of the cash flow has greater value. This swap value is determined by:

1. Fixing the floating side, using the currently prevailing forward rates.
2. Computing the present values of each side by discounting, using the current discount function.
3. Finding the difference between the two present values.

---

15 Note however, that there is no assumption, implicit or explicit, that the interest rate in the future will actually be equal to the forward rate. We are willing to substitute known forward rates for unknown future rates for valuation purposes because we can, if we so desire, effectively lock in or fix the future cash flow at a level implied by the forward rates by using appropriate hedging techniques.

16 Appropriate day count conventions are used in computing the interest payments as well as in discounting. Payments on the fixed side are usually quoted on a 30/360-day basis. Floating payments are generally computed on an actual/360 basis. In addition, if there is any compounding involved, the correct forward rates based on the compounding calendar have to be used to compute the cash flows. Compounding usually is required when the reset frequency is greater than the payment frequency (e.g., LIBOR set monthly, paid semiannually).

Again, the value of the swap derived is the midpoint or break-even value. The actual price to the end user is obtained by modifying the breakeven value by the usual bid-asked spread.

The confidence and comfort in this simple and logical procedure has enabled swap dealers to price virtually arbitrary sets of cash flows. This has increased the availability of swap structures while providing greater liquidity, larger notional amounts, and narrower bid-asked spreads. In practice, however, several factors enter into the pricing of swaps, including the following:

Prevailing market conditions. The term structure of interest rates (e.g., the par curve or the Eurodollar futures prices). Market data represent the most visible and objective information in the pricing of swaps.

Structure of the swap. Maturity, floating index, and size. The structure of a swap is important because it influences the liquidity of the swap as well as the nature and amount of the hedge instruments required. The structure also determines the level of credit risk in the transaction (e.g., whether significant lending or borrowing is implied), which in turn can modify the discounting procedure.

The current position of the dealer. Normally, each dealer strives to balance the net swap positions; that is, to make equal the total receive-fixed position in each maturity to the total pay-fixed position. If this balance is achieved, the amount of liquid market securities used to hedge any net position is minimized, which in turn reduces the basis risk between the hedge and the swap position.

Ready availability of offsetting swaps. If transactions outside the swap market are required to hedge and manage a swap position, the dealer has to price in the resulting basis risk into the swap. If offsetting swaps are readily available, basis risk is minimized, improving the price to the end user.

Credit quality of the counterparty. In general, the swap market does not appear to price credit risk. It is not uncommon to quote the same rate for a AAA-rated counterparty and an A-rated party. Nonetheless, certain weak credits (e.g., construction projects) have to pay a higher rate.

If intermediaries are used for credit risk sharing or protection, the fee paid to the intermediary increases the swap cost.

Nature and level of competition. Pricing also depends on the level of competition. However, the savings, if any, resulting from increasing the number of dealers bidding are not significant. Many times, depending on the depth of the market, it is possible that increasing the number of bidders might actually move the market *adversely*.

Client relationship. Often, a transaction is awarded based on qualitative aspects of a relationship between the corporate end user and the dealer. In return, the dealer offers detailed analyses of the problem at hand, market information, innovative ideas, new techniques, and efficient solutions.

Regulatory constraints. Capital requirements and the required minimum return on capital. Under current rules, the capital required for a corporate counterparty is higher than that for a bank, and higher for currency swaps than for interest rate swaps.

The quantity and type of hedge instruments required. Since the dealer is subject to the bid-asked spread on the hedge instruments, the larger the hedge used, the larger the cost of hedging. This cost is reflected in the swap price.

The market maker considers all of these factors and others (e.g., desire for market share) in a quantitative as well as in a qualitative manner to determine the final swap price to the end user.

Exhibit 6–19 summarizes the pricing procedure: The par curve is generated using available market data. The zero curve is derived either from the par curve or in a more straightforward manner from Eurodollar futures. The *NPV* of the fixed leg is computed using these discount factors. On the floating side, assumed cash flows are first obtained from forward rates derived from the zero curve, and then discounted. The *NPV* of the floating leg is then compared with the *NPV* of the fixed leg to determine either the midpoint swap rate for new swaps or the midpoint swap price for existing swaps. The present value of the fixed leg is recomputed at a different fixed rate, if necessary, to obtain equality of the present values of the fixed and floating legs (dashed line in Exhibit 6–19). The various risk points are also computed. Finally, various other qualitative and quantitative factors (e.g.,

EXHIBIT 6–19
Summary of Swap Pricing Procedure

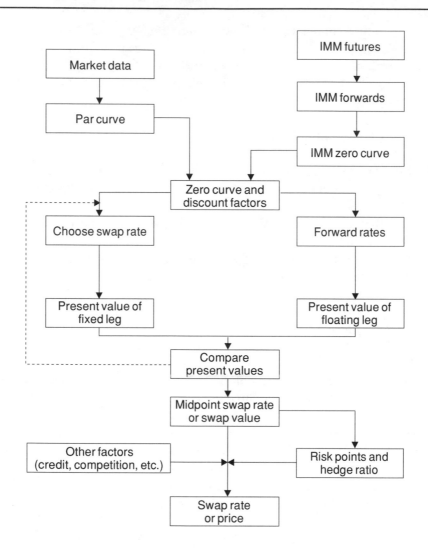

credit, required return on capital, competition) are used along with the risk points to determine the rate or price to the end user.

We illustrate the pricing methodology with an example. Some simplification is necessary to facilitate exposition.

EXHIBIT 6–20
The Generic Swap: Swap Parameters

Type	Generic Swap
Trade date	July 19, 1993
Effective date	July 21, 1993
Notional amount	$100,000,000
Maturity	5 years
Receive side	Fixed
	30/360 day count basis
	Semiannual payments
Pay side	Floating
	Cash curve
	Actual/360 day count basis
	Semiannual payments
Swap rate	5.2108%

Pricing a Generic Swap: Bootstrapping

LIBOR-based swaps can be conveniently priced using Eurodollar futures because they directly represent forward rates. From the forward rates, we can obtain the necessary zero rates and discount factors. This convenience is not available when other market data, such as swap rates, Treasury rates, and spreads, have to be used for computation. However, it is possible to derive zero rates from these data by means of a process called *bootstrapping*.

Consider the swap in Exhibit 6–20. This is a five-year, $100 million swap with semiannual payments. The floating side is based on six-month LIBOR and actual/360 day count. The fixed side is bond basis (i.e., semiannual 30/360 day count).

Exhibit 6–21 shows the market data used to price the generic swap. Column A shows the cash flow dates measured in number of years (semiannual periods) from the start date. Column D shows the yields of representative on-the-run Treasury instruments on a semiannual bond-equivalent basis. Column E shows the spreads over Treasuries for standard swaps.[17] The sum

---

17 For this purpose, we define a standard swap as semiannual pay, spot-start, 30/360 on the fixed side and actual/360 on the floating side, six-month LIBOR, and level notional amount.

EXHIBIT 6–21
The Generic Swap: Bootstrapping

Column	Year A	Date B	Day Count C	U.S. Treasury Yield (%) D	Swap Spread (bp) E	Swap Rate (%) F	Discount Factor G	Cumulative Sum H	Zero Rate (%) I	Forward Rate (%) J
1	0.0	07/21/93					1.00000000			3.43750000
2	0.5	01/21/94	184			3.4375	0.98273391	0.98273391	3.43750000	3.87358688
3	1.0	07/21/94	181			3.6875	0.96396027	1.94669418	3.68750000	4.21905780
4	1.5	01/23/95	186			3.9171	0.94339569	2.89008987	3.92260300	5.00109405
5	2.0	07/21/95	179	3.9706	20.17	4.1723	0.92050589	3.81059576	4.18477378	5.13872359
6	2.5	01/22/96	185			4.3836	0.89682318	4.70741894	4.40364249	5.67287826
7	3.0	07/22/96	182	4.2749	32.00	4.5949	0.87181978	5.5793872	4.62508648	5.79023504
8	3.5	01/21/97	183			4.7652	0.84689260	6.42613132	4.80484810	6.23309510
9	4.0	07/21/97	181	4.6254	31.00	4.9354	0.82115863	7.24728995	4.98713862	6.18930218
10	4.5	01/21/98	184			5.0731	0.79597847	8.04326842	5.13556397	6.61176520
11	5.0	07/21/98	181	4.9758	23.50	5.2108	0.77036948		5.28635750	

of the Treasury yields and the swap spreads gives the swap rates (column F). Any missing data in this column (e.g., 2.5 years) are interpolated.

For the bootstrapping process, Column F is assumed to represent the yield of semiannual coupon bonds priced at par except for the half-year and one-year points which represent LIBOR or money market equivalent rates. Now, the 0.5 year yield, 3.4375 percent, is a zero-coupon rate since a half-year bond has only one cash flow. Therefore, the discount factor using actual/360 convention is:

$$1/(1 + 0.034375 \times 184 / 360) = 0.983.$$

The discount factor at the one-year point is also computed similarly using the actual/360 convention.

The other discount factors can be determined through a process of induction as discussed earlier. Suppose the first n discount factors, $f_1, f_2, f_3,$ ... , f_n have been computed. Then the next factor $f(n+1)$ is related to the others as follows:

$$f(n+1) = \frac{[1 - c \times (f_1 + f_2 + \ldots f_n)]}{(1 + c)}$$

Column H contains the cumulative sum of the discount factors. The factors in column G are computed using column H sequentially. From the discount factors, we can compute the zero rates (column I), if needed.

The forward rates are derived from the discount factors as follows. If f_1 and f_2 are the discount factors for six months and one year, the forward rate, R, is related to f_1 and f_2 by the following equation:

$$1/f_2 = (1/f_1) \times (1 + R \times d/360)$$

where d is the number of days in the period. In this equation, the left-hand side, $(1/f_2)$, is the future value of a $1 investment at the end of one year. The right-hand side is the value of $1 invested for six months and reinvested for another six months at the forward rate of R. The equation simply means that an investor would be indifferent between a one-year investment on one hand and a six-month investment reinvested at the forward rate for another six months. The forward rate, then, is:

$$R = (f_1/f_2 - 1) \times 360/d$$

Forward rates for other periods (column J) are similarly derived.

Once the forward rates and discount functions have been obtained, the pricing of the swap becomes straightforward. In Exhibit 6–22, columns K and M show the assumed floating-rate cash flows and the fixed-rate cash flows. Columns L and N show the present values of these cash flows. The rate for the fixed leg has been selected (by an iterative procedure) to make the total present value of the fixed and floating legs equal. This fixed rate is 5.2108 percent.

We observe that the computed swap rate is exactly equal to the market rate for five-year swaps from Exhibit 6–21. Clearly, we expect this to be the case since the swap rate was derived from the market data. If the swap differed from the standard swap in any way (e.g., if it has quarterly payments), the swap rate would differ from the standard swap rate.

As before, we can also determine the risk points for this swap relative to the Treasury securities (see Exhibit 6–23). To do this, we change the yield on any give Treasury by 1 basis point and the risk point is the resulting change in the value of the swap. Interestingly, the risk point for this swap is zero for all maturities except at six months[18] and five years. This results from the dependence of the standard five-year swap rate on the five-year Treasury yield (plus the spread). It does not depend on any other rate. However, the total present values of the fixed and the floating legs do change when the yields on the other Treasuries change. However, the change in one leg is exactly matched by the change in the other leg. Thus, the value of the swap stays at zero.

To determine the hedge ratio, we need the dollar duration, or the price value of a basis point (*PVBP*) for each hedge security (Treasury), per million. The amount (in millions) of each Treasury for hedging is obtained by dividing the risk point by the *PVBP*. As expected, the par amount of five-year Treasuries required to hedge the swap is very close to the notional amount of the swap.[19]

---

18 The risk at the first cash flow is zero when Eurodollar futures are used (e.g., as in IMM swaps) and nonzero when the cash curve is used for pricing and hedging. The reason for this is subtle. Briefly, the difference arises from the fact that when futures are used, we assume that a change in the cash rate does not change the first forward rate (rate for the second period) as the latter depends solely on the futures price, not the cash rate. When the cash curve is used, a change in the rate for the first period automatically changes the forward rate for the second period. The forward rate depends on the cash rate for the first period.

19 The par amount of Treasuries is slightly larger because the actual maturity of the Treasury is slightly less than five years.

EXHIBIT 6–22
The Generic Swap: Cash Flows and Pricing

Column	Year A	Date B	Day Count C	Discount Factor G	Forward Rate (%) J	Floating Leg Cash Flow ($) K	Floating Leg Present Value ($) M	Fixed Leg Cash Flow ($) L	Fixed Leg Present Value ($) N
1	0.0	07/21/93		1.00000000	3.43750000				
2	0.5	01/21/94	184	0.98273391	3.97358688	1,756,944.44	1,726,608.89	2,605,400.00	2,560,414.93
3	1.0	07/21/94	181	2.96396027	4.21905780	1,947,533.40	1,877,364.10	2,605,400.00	2,511,502.09
4	1.5	01/23/95	186	0.94339569	5.00109405	2,179,846.53	2,056,457.83	2,605,400.00	2,457,923.14
5	2.0	07/21/95	179	0.92050589	5.13872359	2,486,655.10	2,288,980.65	2,605,400.00	2,398,286.03
6	2.5	01/22/96	185	0.89682318	5.67287826	2,640,732.96	2,368,270.53	2,605,400.00	2,336,583.11
7	3.0	07/22/96	182	0.87181978	5.79023504	2,867,955.12	2,500,340.00	2,605,400.00	2,271,439.25
8	3.5	01/21/97	183	0.84689260	6.23309510	2,943,369.48	2,492,717.84	2,605,400.00	2,206,493.98
9	4.0	07/21/97	181	0.82115863	6.18930218	3,133,861.70	2,573,397.57	2,605,400.00	2,139,446.68
10	4.5	01/21/98	184	0.79597847	6.51176520	3,163,421.11	2,518,015.11	2,605,400.00	2,073,842.32
11	5.0	07/21/98	181	0.77036948		3,324,248.61	2,560,899.67	2,605,400.00	2,605,400.00
	Swap rate: 5.2108%					26,444,588.46	22,963,052.18	26,054,000.00	22,963,052.08

EXHIBIT 6–23
The Generic Swap: Risk Points and Hedge Ratio

	Year	A	New NPV of Floating Leg ($) B	Change in NPV of Floating Leg ($) C	New NPV of Fixed Leg ($) D	Change in NPV of Fixed Leg ($) E	Risk Factor ($) F	PVBP ($/$ millions) G	Hedge Ratio ($ millions) H
Column									
1	0.5		$22,957,922.49	$(5,129.69)	$22,962,945.10	$ (107.08)	$(5,022.61)	49.16	102.18
2	1.0		22,962,691.96	(360.22)	22,962,691.96	(360.22)	0.00	97.29	0.00
3	2.0		22,962,211.33	(840.85)	22,962,211.33	(840.85)	0.00	185.81	0.00
4	3.0		22,961,763.58	(1,288.60)	22,961,763.58	(1,288.60)	0.00	263.05	0.00
5	4.0		22,961,299.34	(1,752.84)	22,961,299.34	(1,752.84)	0.00	150.41	0.00
6	5.0		23,005,500.40	42,448.22	22,961,435.31	(1,616.87)	44,065.09	435.25	(101.24)

Original NPV of fixed/floating leg: $22,963,052.18

TYPES OF RISKS IN SWAPS

Swaps are unlike most other financial instruments because they involve two-way payments and, correspondingly, two-way exposure to risk; that is, each party is exposed to the other in terms of credit risk. Usually, some type of offset is agreed upon, so that if one party defaults the other party is not obligated to continue to make the payments. It is useful to review the types of exposure in the swap markets. Credit risk in a swap, which has gained significant importance recently, is analyzed in more detail in a later section.

Interest rate risk or market risk. This is well understood but is clearly the leading concern of swap players. We have seen that the interest rate sensitivity or duration of a swap is similar to that of a bond. Therefore, when interest rates move, the value of the swap also moves. To the extent that the swap is used to match the gap between assets and liabilities, the variation in the value of the swap in response to market changes is not a concern. Swap dealers with unmatched swaps in their inventory are exposed to market risk, and hedge appropriately.

Mismatch risk. Normally, mismatch refers to the position of a swap dealer who has two offsetting swaps that hedge each other, but that are not exactly matched. They may differ in the timing and frequency of payments, maturity, floating-rate index used, and so forth. End users of swaps are also exposed to mismatch in certain circumstances.

Consider a situation in which an industrial corporation, IC, seeking fixed-rate funding, uses the commercial paper (CP) market to raise funds, and swaps into fixed. In this case, the corporation might be exposed to several mismatches. The floating payments on the CP/fixed swap are set to the A1/P1 commercial paper composite index. The actual rate paid on IC's commercial paper may be different from the index. In addition, the maturity and timing of the commercial paper actually issued may differ from the payment frequency and timing of the swap cash flows. The mechanism by which the index is set may be different from the way the borrowing rate is determined.

In general, however, the credit risk of the counterparty is the main concern to the end user. Since the swap market does not seem to differentiate finely between high- and low-quality credits, it is in the best interests of the end user to always deal with the highest-rated counterparty available at the desired rate. However, other considerations, such as diversification or offsetting exposures to the same counterparty, will determine the final decision.

CREDIT RISK IN SWAPS

Credit risk is an integral part of a swap transaction. In a generic interest rate swap, however, the perceived credit risk is small compared with that in an outright loan of the notional amount for two reasons. First, in interest rate swaps, only the interest payments are involved, not the principal amount. Since the principal amount represents a larger proportion of the value of a shorter-maturity loan, the shorter the maturity of the swap, the smaller is its credit risk relative to an outright loan. Second, there is usually an offset arrangement which, in the event of the default by one party, no longer requires the other to continue to make payments on the swap.[20]

However, in some special swap structures, the credit risk can be significant (e.g., zero-coupon swaps, where one party makes all payments before the other makes any). In such cases, it is best to examine the credit risk of the swap as if it were a loan or a combination of a loan and a swap. The swap spread used to price such transactions should also reflect this fact.

Measuring credit exposure accurately on swap transactions can be a difficult and complex exercise. However, it is important to allocate sufficient thought and resource in order to manage swap positions both from the point of view of a dealer and from that of an end user. For example, if a corporation raises funds through a fixed-rate bond issue, it is not exposed to any credit risk. If, on the other hand, it raises funds through a floating-rate borrowing and swaps into fixed, then it will be exposed to the credit risk of the swap counterparty. In the latter case, the corporation should determine if taking on the credit risk is prudent relative to other existing risks, determine if any savings in interest cost provides an adequate return for the additional risk taken, and consider if some loss reserves against swap counterparty default are necessary. Thus, there are three primary reasons for estimating credit exposure accurately:

1. To determine the maximum likely future exposure to a specific counterparty or industry for monitoring overall credit risk.

---

20 In general, the effective termination of a swap due to a default can suddenly increase the interest rate risk in a hedged position.

2. To determine the relative economic return on a transaction compared to an on-balance-sheet asset.

3. To determine the risk-asset size for capital adequacy and capital allocation purposes (where necessary).

The risk-capital requirements for swap transactions also provide a measure of the credit risk. The Bank for International Settlements (BIS) has proposed two procedures that compute the credit-risk equivalents as a function of the maturity of volatility of rates. These procedures resulted from Monte Carlo simulation of the movements in interest and currency exchange rates.

BIS requires that minimum capital standards be set for banks that are active internationally. The Basel Committee on Banking Regulations and Supervisory Practices issued a report called the Basel Accord of 1988, which governs the maintenance of capital and the calculation of risk-asset values. The Basel Accord is an agreement between the central banks and supervisory authorities of the G11 countries: Belgium, Canada, France, Germany, Italy, Japan, Netherlands, Sweden, Switzerland, the United Kingdom, and the United States. The Basel Accord describes two methods for deriving risk capital for off-balance-sheet transactions such as swaps.

SWAP DERIVATIVES

Whenever a product gains popularity, it is only natural that other derivative products will emerge to claim their rightful share of the market. The interest rate swap is no exception, and a cluster of its own derivatives with optionlike characteristics has developed.

In a *callable swap,* the fixed payer has the right, at his or her option, to terminate the swap on or before a scheduled maturity date.[21] The floating payer is compensated for this option either by an up-front premium or by an increase in the fixed rate received. A typical user for a callable swap is a fixed payer who expects the interest rates to fall. By terminating the swap at an opportune time, the fixed payer can enter into another one at a lower fixed rate.

---

21 When the swap is terminated under this optional right, no adjusting payment is required from either party. Therefore, the holder of the right will exercise it only when it is advantageous to do so.

A *putable swap* mirrors the callable swap. Here the floating payer has the termination right. The payment for this privilege is made either by reducing the fixed rate received or by making an up-front fee. A corporation that issues a fixed-rate callable bond and wishes to have floating-rate funding can use the putable swap. At the time the corporation calls the bond, it will also simultaneously exercise its right to terminate the swap.

Situation (Hedging contingent liabilities). CEC, a U.S. civil engineering company, is bidding on a construction project. Its own expenses on the project are to be funded by means of a floating-rate bank loan. The bidding process is expected to take about three months. CEC is bidding on a fixed-cost basis, but it is uncomfortable about the interest rate exposure inherent in the bid given the long processing time. CEC would like to fix the cost of its bid.

CEC can consider entering into an interest rate swap, converting its floating rate interest expense to fixed. However, if CEC does not win the bid, then it will have to unwind or terminate the swap contract at market levels then prevailing. Thus, a simple interest rate swap will still expose CEC to interest rate risk.

An acceptable alternative for CEC is to purchase an option on an interest rate swap. This option gives CEC the right to enter into a swap that pays a fixed rate and to receive the floating rate at prescribed terms. If CEC wins the bid, it will enter into the swap either at the market or through the exercise of the option, whichever gives it the lower dollar cost. If CEC does not win the bid, it will not enter into any swap. It will simply cash in the value, if any, of the option.

Swaps with option features are used to hedge risks of a contingent nature. In any such usage, we should remember not to overhedge; that is, not to hedge specific risk with a generic product. Always consider retaining part of the risk as long as it is prudent.

Situation (Hedging a callable bond). IC is an industrial concern that has issued a 10-year fixed-rate bond in the Euromarket. The bond is callable in seven years. IC is seeking to convert this bond into a floating-rate liability.

As far as IC is concerned, neither a 7-year nor a 10-year straight interest rate swap will achieve the full flexibility of the callable bond. It therefore enters into a callable 10-year interest rate swap with SMM, paying fixed and receiving floating. The swap can be terminated, at SMM's option, in years 7 through 10. If SMM exercises its option to terminate the swap, the IC plans to exercise its option to terminate the bond as well.

There is no requirement that IC exercise the call option on the bond when the option to terminate the swap is exercised by SMM. If the swap market and the bond market spreads diverge significantly, it might be advantageous for IC to terminate the one and not the other. IC, of course, retains the flexibility to profit from this advantage.

Extendible swaps are similar to callable and putable swaps. Here, one of the counterparties has the right to extend the swap beyond its stated maturity date according to an agreed upon schedule.

A *capped swap* is one in which a ceiling rate is set on the floating side. If the index rises above this ceiling, the floating-rate payer simply pays the ceiling rate. The floating-rate payer either pays an up-front premium or receives a fixed rate lower than the market in return for the protection provided by the ceiling or cap. Typical users of capped swaps are borrowers who wish to limit exposure to high short-term interest rates. Another example is an asset swap where the cash flow from a portfolio of capped adjustable-rate mortgages is converted to fixed.

Other variations such as the *floored swap* with a lower limit for the floating rate or the *collared swap* with both a cap and a floor are also available.

SWAPTIONS

Swaptions are options on swaps; that is, a swaption represents the right to enter into a swap (the underlying swap) that is described in the swaption agreement. For example, a *call swaption* gives the owner the right to enter into a swap where he or she receives fixed and pays floating.[22] A *put swaption,* on the other hand, represents the right to enter into a swap receiving floating and paying fixed. Callable and putable swaps can be viewed as combinations of regular swaps and swaptions. A callable swap, for example, is the same as short a plain swap (i.e., paying fixed) and long a call swaption. Swaptions have been used by corporations to monetize the call option owned by them in a callable bond issue.

---

22 The swaption terminology is designed to closely resemble option terminology in fixed income. Thus, a call swaption is roughly equivalent to a call option on a bond in terms of its response to interest rate movements. Correspondingly, a put swaption is similar to a put option on a bond.

Applications of Swaptions

Swaption applications can be divided into three areas: hedging applications, value capture applications, and cosmetic applications.

Hedging applications. A genuine asset or liability with option characteristics can be hedged with a swaption. Examples:

1. An issuer has an outstanding callable bond and wants to cash in the embedded option in the bond. It sells a swaption, which represents the embedded option.
2. A borrower has an anticipated but uncertain loan. To hedge against a rise in rates, he or she purchases a swaption. The swaption protects the borrower against an unexpected increase in rates.
3. A bank has issued a loan commitment. If rates drop, this commitment will not be used. If rates increase, the loan will be drawn down. The proper hedge for this type of optional commitment is the purchase of a swaption.
4. A floating-rate borrower purchases a swaption. If the rates should suddenly go up, he or she has the option to convert this loan to fixed by exercising the swaption and entering into the corresponding swap. In this instance, the swaption provides a protection similar to that provided by a cap.
5. A corporation is planning a future bond issue. It purchases a swaption to ensure a maximum interest rate on the bond issue.

Value capture applications. In value capture applications, the swaption is used entirely to arbitrage the rate differences between different market segments. Example:

Situation (Swaption arbitrage). A corporation, C, wishes to obtain seven-year fixed-rate debt. It issues a seven-year bond callable at par after four years. By doing so, C has implicitly purchased a call option from the bondholder, and paid for it in terms of the higher coupon on the bond relative to a noncall coupon. To monetize the call option it owns, C simultaneously sells a swaption giving the buyer the right to enter into a swap where C pays fixed. If the swaption is exercised, then C in turn will call its bond. Thus, it will pay a fixed rate for the full seven-year initial term of the bond issue to the bondholder until the bond is called and to the swap counterparty (swaption holder) after the swaption is exercised and the bond is called.

Arbitrage is the reason C prefers to enter into this type of financing rather than the more straightforward seven-year noncallable bond issue. The cost of the option, embedded in the callable bond issue, that it purchases from the bondholder is lower than the swaption that it sells. The profit thus generated effectively reduces C's funding cost on the fixed-rate financing.

Cosmetic applications. This is the most popular use of swaptions to date. Here swaptions are used mainly to make an asset or a liability "look" attractive. In most cases, there is always a party that is naked long or short a swaption. The other party hedges its swaption position with an offsetting transaction with a market maker. Examples:

1. A corporation issues a 10-year bond and sells a 5-year swaption. Effectively, the corporation pays a lower initial coupon for the first five years, in return for the uncertainty that in the second five years the coupon can be fixed or floating at the option of the buyer. The lower initial coupon is seen as a "saving" in borrowing cost.
2. A bank makes a loan which gives the borrower an option to set the interest rate according to a formula. The borrower pays a higher initial coupon in return for the option which is hedged by selling a swaption. The bank looks at the initial higher coupon as additional spread earned.

Other applications. There might be other applications where the premium paid or received for the swaption sold has some immediate accounting (or tax) advantages.

A *cap* is a contract that has a contingent periodic cash flow. Whenever the prevailing floating rate index is greater that an agreed-upon rate called the *cap rate,* the cash flow is equal to the difference between the cap rate and the prevailing interest rate applied to the notional amount. If the prevailing rate is lower than the cap rate, there is no cash flow. The lower the cap rate, the higher the price of a cap. A floating-rate borrower can cap or limit the interest expense in any period by purchasing a cap. A *capped swap* is simply a combination of a cap and a swap.

A floating rate lender who would like to be assured of a guaranteed minimum amount of interest income can purchase a *floor.* The cash flow from a floor is equal to the difference between the *floor rate* and the prevailing rate applied to the notional amount. This payment is made only when the interest rates are below the floor rate. Clearly, the higher the floor rate, the higher the price of the floor. A *floored swap* is a combination of a floor and a swap.

Often, floating rate borrowers who wish to limit their interest rate exposure purchase a cap and finance the purchase by simultaneously selling a floor. The effect of such a combination of a long position in a cap and a short position in a floor, called a *collar,* is that the interest expense to the borrower is always between the floor rate and the cap rate. Often, the floor rate and the cap rate are chosen, so that the cost of the cap is equal to the price of the floor. Such a combination is called a *zero-cost collar.*

The cap and the floor are also related to the swap in another way. If the cap rate and the floor rate are both set equal to the swap rate, the corresponding collar is simply an interest rate swap. This relationship is similar to the put-call parity condition in options analysis.

CONCLUSION

Since its inception several years ago, the swap market has grown into a multitrillion dollar global market. The swap market is so large that its influence can be seen in other areas, such as corporate debt issuance and interest rate futures. It therefore behooves us to obtain a basic understanding of how the market works and how swaps and swap products are evaluated.

The success of the swap as a product stems clearly from the fact that it serves a much needed function that cannot be satisfied by other existing derivative products. As a privately negotiated contract, it can be customized to fit the requirements of the situation at hand. Swap derivatives, such as swaptions, caps, and floors, are also beginning to make their presence felt in a significant way as legitimate financial products of today's capital markets. For most end users, the swap has no equal in efficient interest rate risk management.

GLOSSARY

at-market or at-the-money swap An interest rate swap in which no up-front payments by either party are necessary; that is, the value of the swap is zero. The corresponding swap rate is the at-market or at-the-money swap rate.

coupon The swap coupon refers to the fixed rate of interest in a swap; also known as swap price, swap rate, and swap strike.

counterparties The two principal parties involved in a swap transaction.

fixed-rate payer The party that pays the fixed rate in a swap transaction; also receives floating-rate flows and is said to be short the swap.

floating-rate payer The party that pays the floating rate in a swap; also receives fixed-rate cash flows and is said to be long the swap.

interest rate swap The contractual agreement to exchange specified cash flows between two parties.

intermediary A third party that stands between two principal parties in a swap transaction.

maturity date Interest stops accruing on this date; also referred to as the termination date. Generally, there is also an exchange of principal amount on this date in the case of a currency swap.

notional principal amount The amount used to determine the actual cash flows paid or received by applying the corresponding interest rates for the appropriate calendar periods.

off-market swap

    a. above-market The swap is above market if the rate is greater than the at-the-money swap rate. The value of the swap is positive. In this case, the fixed payer will receive an adjustment (e.g., up-front premium).

    b. below-market In a below-market swap, the fixed rate is less than the at-the-money swap rate. The swap value is negative. In this swap, the fixed receiver will receive an adjustment or premium.

reset date Date on which the floating rate is set. The rate set on this date is generally applicable for the subsequent period until the next reset date.

reset frequency Number of times reset dates occur in a year. Generally, reset frequency reflects the floating-rate index. This frequency is not necessarily the same as the number of payment dates in a year.

settlement date or effective date Date on which the coupon starts accruing. This is the first day of the swap term, and is usually two business days after the trade date.

term The period commencing from the first day of coupon accrual and ending on the maturity date.

trade date Date on which the counterparties enter into a swap transaction. The swap rate is also agreed upon on this date.

Chapter Seven

Indexed Amortizing Swaps[*]

Bjørn Pettersen
ABN Amro Bank

Vijay R. Raghavan
First National Bank of Chicago

An indexed amortizing swap (IAS) or note (IAN) is a synthetic mortgage product whose amortization characteristics are based primarily on the evolution of a specific interest rate index. The swap counterparty/investor typically receives a fixed rate on a varying notional amount. The latter is indexed to changes in the level of LIBOR or the yields of any of the constant maturity treasuries (CMTs). In return, on the outstanding notional amount, a floating rate is paid in the case of a swap. In the case of a note, the present value of the uncertain cash flows is paid as its initial price.

As a result, both indexed amortizing notes and swaps have return characteristics that replicate mortgage-backed securities (MBSs) such as collateralized mortgage obligations (CMOs). However, a note is an on-balance-sheet transaction that has credit exposure to the issuer, while a swap is an off-balance-sheet transaction with credit exposure to the swap counterparty. To avoid confusion, the remainder of the chapter focuses on IASs.

The first indexed amortizing structures were created in the late 1980s to compete with CMOs as alternative assets, held off balance sheet. The off-balance-sheet swaps gained popularity among banks as alternative assets to cash mortgage products. Since then, the use of indexed amortizing

[*] Reprinted from *Advanced Interest Rate and Currency Swaps,* ed. Ravi E. Dattatreya and Kensuke Hotta (Burr Ridge, IL: Irwin Professional Publishing, 1994), pp. 53–67.

swaps and notes has increased dramatically. The size of the market is presently estimated to be more than $200 billion in notional value. Other users interested in the product, either in the swap or note format, would primarily include investors in the mortgage market, such as insurance companies, mutual and hedge fund managers, and pension fund managers.

CHARACTERIZING AN INDEXED AMORTIZING SWAP

Before continuing further, four IAS-specific parameters—namely lockout period, base rate, amortization schedule, and cleanup call—are discussed.

The lockout period is the time interval during which there is no amortization. The lockout guarantees the counterparty a minimum duration. The lockout date must be less than the final maturity of the instrument. The choice of the lockout period affects the duration (or expected average life), but not the final maturity. Typically, an increase in the lockout period leads to an increase in the duration in a standard IAS structure.

The base rate is the specific value of the index that is chosen as a reference, which in turn determines the extent of the principal reduction at each reset date. The base rate has all the characteristics of a "strike" price in the terminology of options. The base rate in combination with the amortization schedule determines the expected amortization speed (or average life) at inception as well as the actual amortization during the life of the instrument, due to the evolution of the index. Typically, the actual rate of the index is compared to the base rate on a reset date. This difference (actual rate less base rate) determines, through the prespecified amortization schedule, the extent of the principal reduction. If the difference is a large negative number, the paydown is high, and if the difference is a large positive number, the paydown is usually zero.

Changing the base rate will change the characteristics of the indexed amortizing swap. In a plain indexed amortizing structure, a high base rate is usually associated with a greater amortization speed and a short duration. Usually the investor sets a base rate based on his or her view of future interest rates. The usual choice of indexes for the base rate are LIBOR and CMTs. The former has largely evolved out of the convenience it has offered swap dealers in hedging their portfolios on the supply side, and the latter have evolved from the demand side as they are the common benchmarks for fixed-income portfolio managers.

As mentioned, the amortization schedule combined with the set base rate determines how the product will amortize in the future. The prepayment schedule for an IAS is derived from the amortization table that is agreed upon prior to the trade. The table maps the deviations of the index from the base rate to the extent of principal reduction on any of the reset dates. Typically, large positive differences of the actual index value over the base rate at a reset date result in no paydown and large negative differences result in high paydown.

The paydown fractions on a reset date can be based on either remaining notional or original notional. An IAS based on remaining notional will amortize at a slower speed. The first IAS transactions were based on original notional. As the market for these transactions has mushroomed, paydowns closely mimicking mortgage transactions and based on remaining notional have emerged as the dominant format.

It is the amortization schedule that gives the security shortening and extension risk. The shortening risk is reduced by the lockout period, which protects the user against prepayment. All extension risk occurs between the lockout and the final maturity. The amortization schedule is chosen prior to the trade execution by the end user to satisfy his or her specific return or hedging needs. Usually the schedule is based on the investor's view of the level of interest rates in the futures. As an example, if the index is three-month LIBOR, the investor will pick an amortization schedule (in combination with the base rate) that fits his or her view of expected forward LIBOR rates. The current forward LIBOR curve can be observed in the Eurodollar futures market as traded on different futures exchanges worldwide (MERC, SIMEX, LIFFE).

It is common to include a cleanup call in the structure to avoid the nuisance of the notional amount decreasing to levels too low to administer. This feature will assure that the IAS will amortize to zero when the remaining notional is less than or equal to a prespecified percentage of original notional. It is common to have cleanup calls up to 20 percent. However, on occasion one may see them as high as 80 percent (embedded in some of the more recent "mega cleanup" call structures).

IASs have return characteristics similar to such MBSs as CMOs. Typically, the weighted average life of the structure (average maturity) shortens when the index rate drops and extends when the index rate rises relative to the base rate. The fixed-rate receiver is short volatility or convexity. Convexity is the change in the duration of the security due to a change in its yield. Duration is the weighted average term to maturity of a security's cash flow, and relates the change in the price of the security to a change in its yield. An option-free fixed-income coupon security usually has positive convexity. Because of the negative convexity of the indexed amortizing swap, the investor will receive an above-market coupon. The convexity of the IAS depends on the choice of the index and the amortization schedule. Under stable rate scenarios, the premiums inherent in negatively convex securities are realized as higher total returns to other comparable duration assets.

The differences between IASs and CMOs also have to be noted. While IASs are inherently tied to the LIBOR and swap market rates and volatilities, CMOs trade relative to mortgage rates and volatilities. In addition, the amortization schedules in CMOs depend on interest rate movements as well as a host of other special demographic and idiosyncratic factors inherent in specific mortgage pools. Conversely, IAS paydowns are purely determined by interest rate movements in reference to the chosen base rate. CMOs have uncertain maturities tied to unanticipated amortization. IASs, on the other hand, have relatively well-defined maturities. Most of the outstanding transactions at the present time were structured to have final maturities of under five years at inception. In addition, the advantageous lockout features in IASs mitigate prepayment risk by preserving the outstanding notional amounts with certainty until the lockout date. As a result, the maturity uncertainty on IASs is confined to a range between the lockout and final maturity dates.

INDEXED AMORTIZING SWAP STRUCTURE

The main advantage of an IAS is its flexibility in customization; it allows the users to design structures to meet their specific return needs and risk appetite. As an example, the term sheet for a typical IAS structure is shown in Exhibit 7–1.

IASs are usually traded with notional upwards of $25 million. Our example illustrates a spot settlement, but it is not uncommon to structure forward-starting IASs. The swap has a lockout period of two years and a final maturity of five years. The fixed coupon the investor receives is 6.25 percent semibond. In return, the investor will pay three-month LIBOR (floating). The IAS has quarterly resets, meaning that the floating payment is reset to LIBOR every three months. The amortization frequency decides how often the index is to be polled to set the current outstanding notional.

EXHIBIT 7–1
Indexed Amortizing Swap

Indicative Terms & Conditions

Principal amount:	$100 million
Settlement date:	March 11
Final maturity:	Five-year final maturity
Coupon rate:	6.25%
Index reset:	Quarterly
Payment frequency:	Quarterly
Amortization frequency:	Quarterly
Base rate (BR):	3.875% (3-month LIBOR)
Amortization schedule:	At the conclusion of the lockout period, the principal amount shall amortize quarterly based on the level of three-month $U.S. LIBOR. The amortization for each period shall equal the notional percentage reduction (NPR) and will be linearly interpolated between the points displayed in the table.

3M LIBOR	3M LIBOR – BR	Average Life	NPR
3.875%	+0 bp	2.00 years	100.00%
4.875	+100	3.00	17.28
5.875	+200	4.00	6.42
6.875	+300	5.00	0.00

The base rate is set at cash three-month LIBOR. The amortization schedule, in conjunction with the base rate, decides the expected amortization speed of the transaction and the actual amortization at each reset date in the future. To illustrate, if LIBOR is at or below 3.875 percent on March 9, 1996 (at the end of the lockout period), the notional will amortize by 100 percent and the IAS will mature. However, if LIBOR sets at 6.875 percent or higher, there will be no amortization of notional. For any LIBOR setting after the two-year lockout period where three-month LIBOR falls between the discrete rate points in the table, the swap will amortize based on the schedule using linear interpolation between the points. Changing any of the above parameters will change the duration and convexity features of the IAS and, hence, could lead to a change in the fixed coupon to be paid on the swap.

For the example discussed above, the structure gives a yield of 135 bp, 95 bp, and 45 bp over two-, three-, and five-year Treasuries respectively. On a comparable three-year PAC, the concurrent yield was about 60 bp over three-year Treasuries. It is therefore evident that the swap market may at times, depending on the existing volatility and rate structures, be able to give superior returns on synthetic securities over comparable securities in the mortgage market. At other times, when mortgage spreads and volatilities widen relative to the swap market, cash-based mortgage swaps may turn out to have potentially more attractive relative return characteristics.

THE NOTIONAL PERCENTAGE
REDUCTION SCHEDULE

Let us take a closer look at how one can design an amortization schedule based on the desired average life characteristics under specifically chosen rate scenarios. Average life represents the weighted-average (by notional outstanding) maturity (not to be confused with duration) on a particular rate path. Converting from average life to a notional percentage reduction *(NPR)* schedule is a fairly straightforward calculation. In the following example, the investor is interested in a two-year lockout, five-year final IAS, with quarterly amortization frequency. We want to match the following average life schedule to an appropriate *NPR* schedule for the following instantaneous LIBOR shifts. Assume a 15 percent cleanup call.

3M LIBOR – Base Rate	Desired Average Life
0bp	2.0 year
+100bp	3.0 year

Consider first the case of three-month LIBOR less base rate at 0 bp. The desired average life is 2.0 years. Assume that NPR = 100 percent. The transaction will have to amortize to zero at the two-year lockout date to result in an average life of two years as desired in this scenario.

3M LIBOR – base rate	Average life	*NPR*
0	2.0 year	100%

Consider now the case of (three-month LIBOR less base rate) at +100 bp. The desired average life is 3.0 years.

We illustrate by trial and error how to find the correct *NPR* that gives a 3.0 year average life. Try *NPR* equals 17.28 percent. The first column lists the time nodes and the second column shows the product of the following three items:

Notional remaining $(i) \times NPR(i) \times$ Time Period (i).

The net result is a time period weighted paydown in the second column.

Period i	Time Period Weighted Paydown
2.00 year node	$1.00 \times .1728 \times 2.00 = .345600$
2.25 year node	$.8272 \times .1728 \times 2.25 = .321615$
2.50 year node	$.684260 \times .1728 \times 2.50 = .295600$
2.75 year node	$.566020 \times .1728 \times 2.75 = .268973$
3.00 year node	$.468212 \times .1728 \times 3.00 = .242721$
3.25 year node	$.387305 \times .1728 \times 3.25 = .217510$
3.50 year node	$.320378 \times .1728 \times 3.50 = .193765$
3.75 year node	$.265017 \times .1728 \times 3.75 = .171731$
4.00 year node	$.219222 \times .1728 \times 4.0 = .151526$
4.25 year node	$.181340 \times .1728 \times 4.25 = .133176$
4.50 year node	$.150005 \times 4.50 = .675022$
4.75 year node	zero
5.00 year node	zero

Note that the 15 percent cleanup call terminates the deal at the 4.5 year node.

The sum of all the numbers in the second column gives an average life of approximately three years.

3M LIBOR – Base rate	Average life	NPR
0	2.0 year	100%
+100bp	3.0 year	17.28%

Therefore, by selecting an *NPR* of 17.28 percent we get an average life of 3.0 years for +100 bp as desired.

We can also calculate *NPR*s for 4.0 year average life (6.42 percent) and 5.0 year average life (0 percent) in the same way. The end result is an *NPR* schedule that matches the desired average life schedule the investor prefers for various assumed instantaneous movements of the chosen index.

PERFORMANCE CHARACTERISTICS OF INDEXED AMORTIZING SWAPS

In this section we examine the performance characteristics of the example previously discussed under three assumed future rate scenarios. We assume that rates evolve (1) at levels slower than the forward rates indicate (labeled

EXHIBIT 7–2
Interest Rate Scenarios (Implied Three-Month LIBOR Forward Rates)

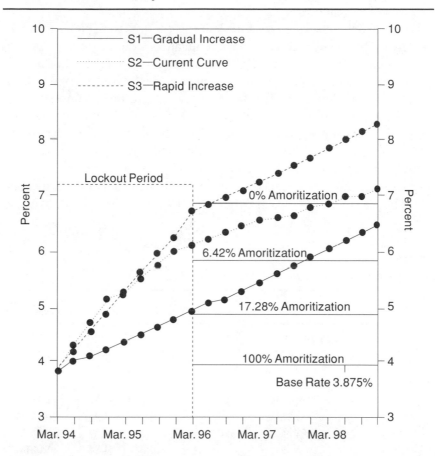

S1), (2) as indicated by the forward rate structure as of the transaction date (S2), and (3) at levels higher than those indicated by forward rates (S3). These assumptions are shown in Exhibit 7–2, which also indicates the levels of amortization expected at various LIBOR rate levels. Note that the higher the LIBOR realization, the lower the rate of amortization. The assumed rate paths for the three scenarios enter into decreasing levels of amortizations with time. From the term sheet, the base rate was set at 3.875 percent. The amortization schedule is marked on the graph with horizontal lines. We assume straight line interpolation between the amortization nodes.

If LIBOR follows the forward path as of today (S2), the structure will amortize by 4.815 percent at the lockout (two years from the start date) with a LIBOR set at that time at 6.125 percent. However, if LIBOR follows the slower rate increase path (S1), and sets at 4.875 percent, 17.28 percent of the notional will amortize.

For each of these scenarios we track the profits or losses (P&L) accumulated by the fixed-rate receiver. The accumulation is done by compounding the positions at the assumed LIBOR rates on a given path. The sensitivity of the swap P&L performance to various assumed based rates was also computed. Note, however, that the break-even fixed rates paid may vary slightly for these different base rates and, hence, the P&L numbers may not be strictly comparable. Nevertheless, it is useful to study the behavior of these swaps under the different rate scenarios. The same set of data was also compiled for a five-year final, three-year lockout structure (with a break-even fixed rate of 6.15 percent), to study the effect of extending the lockout date. These results are shown in Exhibit 7–3. Exhibit 7–4 shows the average

EXHIBIT 7–3
Comparative P&L Performance Details

	Slower than Forward		Forward Curve		Faster than Forward	
Base Rate	Average Life	Gain	Average Life	Gain	Average Life	Gain
5/2 Structure						
5.375	2.00	3.7MM	2.54	2.3MM	3.70	–1.3MM
4.875	2.00	3.9MM	3.52	2.1MM	4.23	–0.4MM
4.375	2.16	4.3MM	4.04	2.0MM	4.67	–0.8MM
4.125	2.74	5.4MM	4.31	2.2MM	4.84	–1.0MM
3.875	3.35	5.9MM	4.54	1.7MM	4.95	–1.2MM
3.625	3.58	6.1MM	4.76	1.5MM	5.00	–1.3MM
3.375	3.84	6.1MM	4.91	1.3MM	5.00	–1.4MM
5/3 Structure						
5.375	3.00	4.8MM	4.12	1.5MM	4.39	–1.1MM
4.875	3.15	5.2MM	4.19	1.4MM	4.39	–1.6MM
4.375	3.88	6.1MM	4.51	1.2MM	4.98	–1.9MM
4.125	3.88	6.1MM	4.70	1.1MM	5.00	–1.9MM
3.875	4.11	6.1MM	4.88	0.9MM	5.00	–1.9MM
3.625	4.26	6.1MM	4.98	0.7MM	5.00	–2.0MM
3.375	4.42	6.1MM	5.00	0.7MM	5.00	–2.0MM

EXHIBIT 7–4
Base Rate vs. Average Life

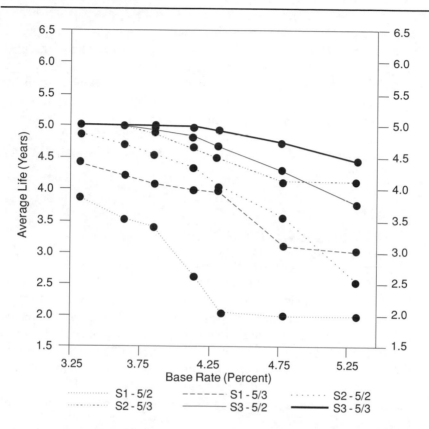

life variation with different base rates for the two structures under the different scenarios.

From Exhibit 7–4, the following observations can be made about average lives:

1. Increasing base rates decrease average lives because of increased amortization speeds.
2. Average lives tend to be higher for higher rate increases compared with lower rate increases, as should be expected.
3. Average lives increase with higher lockout periods.

Going back to Exhibit 7–3, the variation of the P&L over the different structures, scenarios, and base rates could now be easily explained through the linkage to average life behavior. As can be seen, profits tend to be higher with lower base rates (higher average lives) in scenarios with relatively slower rate increases. On the other hand, extension risk also contributes to higher losses in bearish scenarios with higher than expected rate increases. To summarize, if amortization is accelerated by either altering the amortization schedule or increasing the base rate, the average life and the break-even fixed rate decrease. The user will increase his or her yield pickup by increasing the option value embedded in the swap. This can be accomplished by an optimal choice of the base rate and by increasing the time period from lockout to final maturity (increasing duration risk). The optionality manifests itself in increased uncertainty of the duration of the swap.

PRICING AND HEDGING INDEXED AMORTIZING SWAPS

The indexed amortizing swap can be viewed as a callable swap, with the call structure predefined only to rate movements. However, while the exercise of the call (the notional paydown) is indexed to the short rate, the value of the paydown on a given interest rate path depends on the swap yield to the remaining term to maturity. The pricing of an IAS is therefore dependent on the entire yield curve movement over time. The models that are used to price IASs vary in the degree of the trade-offs between simplicity on the one hand and capturing the realities of term structure movements on the other.

In the former class, a variety of one-factor models have been developed, which assume that all yields along the term structure are completely correlated. These models have computational simplicity but may not be accurate in pricing the IASs because of the complete correlation assumption. Introducing a second factor in term structure models helps overcome this inaccuracy by incorporating an extra degree of freedom in term structure movements. However, utilization of the second factor is critically dependent upon having a source of liquid market pricing to calibrate the correlation between different parts of the yield curve. As the liquidity in the markets for instruments such as yield curve swaps, for example, is very low, calibrations to market are relatively meaningless. Often historical data are used to calibrate correlation parameters. It is well known that historical correlation data tend to be unstable and the noise introduced by inaccurate calibration may outweigh the advantages of incorporating a second factor. This is particularly true for the IAS market as it stands today because it is dominated by short average life structures (between two and three years) where the additional degree of freedom is of relatively low significance. On the other hand, if longer-dated structures become more popular, the need for a two-factor model becomes more imperative.

Regardless of the model used, the basic valuation principles dictate calibrating the model to the following observed market yields and volatilities:

1. The swap yield curve.
2. At-the-money cap volatilities.
3. At-the-money swaption volatilities.

Calibration to the above ensures that the model used is arbitrage-free in terms of observed market data. In general, because the IAS is a path-dependent option (the payoffs depend on the path of rate movements rather than on ending rate values as in a simple option such as a cap), Monte Carlo simulation procedures are used for pricing and hedging. Cleanup calls and IASs based on original notionals, in particular, make it difficult for simpler lattice-based transformations to be employed. The Monte Carlo procedure involves generating arbitrage-free rate paths consistent with given yield and volatility structures. Cash flows generated on these paths for a specified IAS structure are discounted backwards on both the fixed and floating rate payments. Pricing involves identifying the fixed rate that equates the present value of the floating rate payments.

The same procedures can also be used for hedging purposes. Perturbations of each of the individual rate and volatility inputs, holding everything else constant, alters the price of the structure. The same perturbations applied to the hedge instruments identify their respective sensitivities to the inputs. The objective is to find a set of hedge instruments at a given point in time (hence known as "dynamic" hedging) that match the sensitivities of the IAS to all of the input variables. It is also important to keep in mind that the relative stability of the hedges (for large perturbations) determines the level of transactions costs, especially in volatile conditions. The hedges are rebalanced on a dynamic basis. As the model is calibrated to the variables that are implicit in Eurodollar futures (or FRAs), swaps, at-the-money caps (and/or floors), and swaptions, these comprise the relevant hedge instrument universe.

VARIATIONS ON INDEXED AMORTIZING SWAPS AND USES

Alternative Indexes

In the discussion above, it was assumed that the indexing rate is three-month LIBOR. This index has the advantage of a high volatility and thus can be translated to higher coupons on the fixed side in lieu of the options sold. However, given that the market for IASs is intended to be an alternative to that for MBSs, it may be more pertinent to structure IASs that are tied to comparable indexes such as the five- or 10-year CMT rates.

The market has thus far been entirely one-sided in that the end users achieve yield enhancement on the fixed rate they receive in exchange for the underlying call options sold. It is, however, conceivable that with the yield curve bouncing upward and flattening considerably, the demand for IASs from end users may switch from using them as instruments for yield enhancement to hedges for their existing MBS portfolios. In other words, they may prefer to pay fixed (equivalent of shorting MBSs) rather than receive fixed. The hedges are likely to be more accurate if the index is the 10-year CMT rate. In addition, as the 10-year CMT rate is less volatile than three-month LIBOR, the cost of the options they purchase is likely to be lower. The constant maturity swap (CMS) rate is a likely alternative for a CMT rate.

The index could also be specified to be the difference between a long rate and a short rate, in which case the swap can be structured as a yield curve indexed amortizing swap. Alternatively, the index could be an exchange rate, with the swap enabling the sale of exchange rate volatility to enhance yields. It is obvious that the enormous flexibility available in the choice of the index could give rise to a variety of interesting structured products. However, the pricing and risk management of these swaps may be complicated by the additional correlation variable.

Alternative Amortizing Schedules

In the example discussed, the paydown schedule was constructed in such a way that the swap amortized when rates went down. Alternatively, if the swap accretes when rates fall and stays level when rates move upwards, the convexity of the IAS becomes completely positive. Such an instrument can provide a good prepayment hedge for the negative convexity of an existing

MBS portfolio when rates fall. Note that the investor buys call options on the swap in such a case. Alternatively, if the hedge is to be constructed for a rising rate scenario, the swap can pay down with rising rates and stay level under falling rates. Again, this accentuates the positive convexity of a regular swap, and the investor is buying put options.

Alternative Payoff Streams

In the previous examples, the idea of path-dependent amortization was applied to structure a swap. The same idea could be applied to the purchase of options such as caps and floors. For example, a corporation may be interested in limiting the costs of its floating-rate liabilities with the purchase of a cap. However, the cost of an outright purchase of an at-the-money cap may be perceived as too high. This cost can be lowered by purchasing caps at higher strike prices, out of the money, but the protection may be ineffective, particularly if rates hovered just below the strike level. Alternatively, we can think of buying down the price of an at-the-money cap by reducing the notional protected as rates fall. Such structures can be viewed as partial knockouts. The advantage of this structure is that the investor gets the protection when he or she needs it most. Similarly, floors can be subsidized by amortizing the notional as rates head upward. Such path-dependent caps and floors can be further customized in strike levels and amortizing schedules to suit the risk profiles needed in protection.

THE FUTURE FOR THE INDEXED AMORTIZING SWAP MARKET

The growth of the IAS market has largely evolved over a low interest rate, steep yield curve environment. As short-term LIBOR remained relatively stable over a fairly long period of time, investors gained substantially on their swaps. However, we are currently in a situation where the economy seems to be picking up steam and rates are headed upward. Further, as the expectation is that of a series of further Fed tightenings in the near future, the yield curve is likely to flatten as long as the inflation numbers remain fairly low. Investors extending out in maturity are likely to see a smaller carry in holding IASs, as assets, due to the yield curve component. The other factor that contributes to the yield pickup is volatility. As volatilities have been relatively low over the last year, the expectation is that they are likely to trend upward. Hence, this component is likely to contribute to a higher yield pickup over time. As mortgage originations and refinancings diminish, the supply in the mortgage market is likely to be constrained, making mortgage assets richer relative to IASs. On balance, IASs still have the potential for outperforming CMOs as alternative assets under the assumed scenarios.

However, in a bearish rate environment, the potential of IASs as hedge instruments for existing MBSs in portfolio has to receive greater emphasis. Investors could pay fixed on indexed amortizing swaps to utilize them as hedges in their portfolios. Alternatively, they could structure positively convex IASs to mitigate the effect of an increase in rates on the overall portfolio. Finally, the path-dependent cap as an alternative to other option products remains eminently attractive.

Chapter Eight

Applications of Index Amortization Swaps[*]

Ramine Rouhani
CDC Investment Management Company

Structured swaps emerged in early 1990 and since then have exploded in size and variety, providing the capital markets with a wealth of new products for investment, hedging, and speculation. Compared with plain vanilla swaps and swaptions, these new structures are much more flexible and can be more effectively customized to produce desired payoff patterns. With added flexibility comes additional complexity. Analytically, these structures are more demanding than traditional swaps and swaptions. Good intuition and experience in options are essential for understanding these products. However, intuition alone often fails to provide a comprehensive picture of the many risk/reward dimensions of these structures. These swaps are less liquid than their vanilla counterparts, and therefore it is often necessary to engineer hedges to limit their exposures to interest rates and volatility. To construct such hedges, one needs to evaluate the sensitivities of these instruments to changes in the level of rates, to the steepness of the yield curve and to interest rate volatility.

   The purpose of this chapter is to analyze the risk dimensions of the index amortization swap (IAS), known also as a principal amortization swap (PAS). There is a fairly large variety of these type of swaps. They are very

[*] Reprinted from *Advanced Interest Rate and Currency Swaps,* ed. Ravi E. Dattatreya and Kensuke Hotta (Burr Ridge, IL: Irwin Professional Publishing, 1994), pp. 381–396.

popular with investors, particularly banks. In 1992–1993, when yields were low and the yield curve was steep, these swaps were extremely effective off-balance-sheet vehicles for banks to enhance the yield on their portfolios. As we will see in the following sections, this yield enhancement is not a free lunch, but is accompanied by certain risks that are to be explicitly recognized and dealt with.

INDEX AMORTIZATION SWAPS

An index amortization swap (IAS) is a swap with a notional balance that depends on the random path of another index. The similarities with vanilla swaps are many: The client receives a fixed rate against a floating rate (LIBOR in most cases), there is a fixed maturity, and the two counterparties are exposed to each other's credit. The major difference is that the notional balance of an IAS may decline and may even converge to zero before the final maturity date of the swap. Furthermore the decline of the notional balance is nondeterministic and depends on the path of a short- or a long-term interest rate index, often referred to as "balance index." Three-month and six-month LIBOR have been the dominant balance indexes for index amortization swaps. Seven-year and 10-year constant maturity treasury (CMT) indexes also have been very popular. Index amortization swaps with notional balances linked to long-term rates have been used by portfolio managers as substitutes for mortgage products or as hedging vehicles for mortgage portfolios.

Here is an example of a 10-year CMT-linked index amortization swap as of September 17, 1993:

- Investor receives a fixed rate of 5.12 percent and pays three-month LIBOR.
- Payments are quarterly.
- The swap starts on September 17, 1993 and terminates on September 17, 1998.
- The notional balance of the swap is constant for the first year (September 17, 1993–September 17, 1994), that is, there is a "lockout" period of one year.
- After the lockout period, the notional amount changes at each reset time in accordance to the amortization table shown in Exhibit 8–1.

EXHIBIT 8–1
10-year CMT-Linked Index Amortization Swap

10-Year CMT Rate (basis points)	Average Life (years)	Amortization Rate (percent)
–150 bp	1.0 yr(s)	100.0%
–100	2.0	44.5
–50	2.5	30.5
Base (5.38%)	3.0	23.6
+50 bp	3.5	17.6
+100	4.0	11.8
+150	4.5	5.9
+200	5.0	0

The most important feature of an IAS is the amortization table. The table relates the amortization rate of the notional balance to the level of the 10-year CMT rates. On September 17, 1993, the 10-year yield was 5.38 percent. Exhibit 8–1 states that, after the lockout period, at each reset time the notional amount of the swap amortizes at a quarterly rate of 23.6 percent if the 10-year index is equal to 5.38 percent. However, if the 10-year CMT is 4.88 percent (i.e., 50 bp lower than the base rate of 5.38 percent), the amortization rate is 30.5 percent and, as the index's level drops to 4.38 percent and 3.88 percent respectively, the amortization rate grows to 44.5 percent and 100 percent respectively. Column 3 of Exhibit 8–1 shows the quarterly amortization rates that will apply to the remaining balances of the swap as a function of the 10-year rate at reset times. The CMT rates are expressed as offsets to the index level at origination (5.38 percent). At reset times, amortization rates are computed by linear interpolation between the two closest levels on the table. If the CMT index falls below 3.88 percent or increases above 7.38 percent, the closest amortization rate applies (100 percent and 0 percent respectively).

Clearly, as the balance index decreases, the amortization of the notional balance accelerates and the swap becomes shorter. On the other hand, as the CMT rate increases the amortization slows down and the swap lengthens. The second column of Exhibit 8–1 shows the average life of the swap for each amortization rate. It is important to comprehend the precise meaning of this column: If at the end of the lockout period, the 10-year CMT index were at 5.38 percent and remained there for the following four years, then the constant amortization rate to be applied every quarter would be 23.6 percent and the average life of the swap would be three years; similarly, if the CMT rate were to move to 6.38 percent at the end of the lockout period and were to stay there for the ensuing four years, the 11.8 percent constant amortization rate per quarter would result in an average life of four years.

This does not suggest that the average life of the swap is three years, nor does it mean that its expected average life is three years. There is no additional information in the Average Life column vis-a-vis the Amortization Rate column. However, describing the swaps in terms of average life rather than amortization rate is simpler, and investors often believe that they get a better picture of the transaction when it is described in terms of average life rather than amortization rate. While an average life description seems more intuitive, it also leaves more room for misinterpretation. A common misinterpretation is to tend to believe that the swap has "on average" three years of life, or that the "expected life" is three years. Another misinterpretation is to compare the fixed rate of the index amortization swap to the rate of a vanilla swap with maturity equal to that of the base average life (here three years) to assess the relative value of the structure. A simplistic way of assessing the IAS value has been based on comparing the fixed rate of the IAS to the swap rates with maturities corresponding to the shortest and to the longest average life (here one year and three years) to conclude that the swap is "cheap" if its fixed rate exceeds both swaps and "fairly" valued if it falls between the two rates. This type of analysis, while simple and attractive, does not necessarily lead to correct conclusions.

To the naked eye, the average life and the amortization table provide, at best, qualitative information: The buyer of such swaps is short volatility, short a series of call options (the swap is called as rates move down), and short a series of put options (the swap extends when rates move up). Everything else being equal (lockout, maturity, base rates, and offsets), the more steep the change of average life and amortization rate, the higher the volatility exposure of the structure. Beyond these and a few other qualitative assessments, it is very difficult to pursue the examination of the structure without using a model that mimics the behavior of the transaction under different interest rate and volatility scenarios.

PATH DEPENDENCY

At first glance, options embedded in IASs can be approximated by a series of calls and puts. In reality, however, these are more complex options. They differ from traditional fixed-income options in that they are path dependent and, from this perspective, similar to options embedded in mortgage securities and their derivatives. The payoff of a path-dependent structure depends not only on the state variables (here interest rates), but also on the path of these variables. A very common example of a path-dependent structure is a cap on the one-year average of three-month LIBOR: The payoff of such a cap depends not only on the final level of LIBOR, but more so on the path of LIBOR in the year preceding the maturity of the cap. To see how the path of the 10-year CMT rate affects the average life and the payoff of the structure, let us consider three scenarios. Exhibit 8–2 shows the CMT rates for each scenario at the end of the first, second, third, fourth, and fifth year. For example, in scenario 1 (path 1), the CMT rate moves from 5.38 percent to 4.88 percent at the end of the first year, then it declines to 3.88 percent at the end of the second year, and bounces back to 4.88

EXHIBIT 8–2
Path Dependency

Time	Path 1 (Balance)	Path 2 (Balance)	Path 3 (Balance)
0	5.38	5.38	5.38
	(100)	(100)	(100)
1	4.88	5.38	5.88
	(100)	(100)	(100)
2	3.88	6.38	6.38
	(55.6)	(88.24)	(88.24)
3	4.88	4.38	6.88
	0	(49.02)	(77.85)
4	5.88	6.38	7.38
	0	(43.26)	(68.69)
5	7.38	7.38	7.38
	0	(38.17)	(68.69)
Average Life	2.5	3.81	4.35

percent, 5.88 percent, and 7.38 percent at the end of the third, fourth, and fifth year respectively. Path 2 and path 3 of Exhibit 8–2 show two other scenarios for the balance index. The three paths start from the same level of 5.38 percent and end up at the same level of 7.38 percent at the end of the fifth year. The figures in parenthesis correspond to the notional balance of the swap. Because of the lock period of one year, the notional balance stays at its original level of 100 at the end of the first year in all scenarios. Following path 1, the notional balance declines to zero at the end of the third year and the resulting average life is 2.5 years. In the case of the second path, the interest rate moves up, comes down, and then increases steadily to 7.38 percent, resulting in a balance profile that declines from 100 to 38.17, and an average life of 3.81 years. Finally, the third path corresponds to a straight increase of the CMT rate from 5.38 percent to 7.38 percent, a slow decline of the notional balance from 100 to 68.69, and an average life of 4.35 years. Although the starting and the ending values of the CMT rates are the same for the three paths, the realized average lives are significantly different and so are the payoffs.

VALUATION

IASs are interest rate path-dependent options, the analysis of which requires contingent claim technologies similar to those used in pricing and valuation of mortgage-backed securities and their derivatives. The shape of the yield curve (the swap curve), the dynamics of the short-term rate (LIBOR) and of the long-term rate (10-year CMT), and their volatilities all affect the valuation of IASs. We use a two-factor arbitrage-free model of the yield curve where the state variables are the one-month rate and the 10-year CMT rate. We assume a volatility of 16 percent for the short-term rate and of 12 percent for the long-term rate. Since the optionality of the IASs are linked to the dynamic of the 10-year rate, we expect the volatility of this rate to have a major role in determining the value of these contracts. The valuation and analysis of these structures are based on Monte Carlo simulation. Hundreds of interest rate paths are generated, and for each path the cash flows of the IASs, as well as their present values, are estimated. The statistics of the present values are then used as the basis of valuation and analysis of the IASs.

Let us consider the IAS of the previous section, which we will refer to as IAS1. For purpose of comparison and discussion, we introduce a second

EXHIBIT 8–3
Swap Structure

Fixed Rate	5.12%	5.28%
	Swap 1 Average Life (years)	Swap 2 Average Life (years)
–150	1.0 yr(s).	1 yr(s).
–100	2.0	1
–50	2.5	2
Base (5.38%)	3.0	3
+50	3.5	4
+100	4.0	5
+150	4.5	5
+200	5.0	5

IAS (IAS2). The average life schedules of both swaps are shown on Exhibit 8–3. IAS1 receives a fixed rate of 5.12 percent and pays three-month LIBOR. IAS2 receives a fixed rate of 5.28 percent and pays three-month LIBOR. In the "base case" (i.e., when the 10-year CMT rate remains unchanged), both swaps have the same average life of three years. However IAS2 displays more average life variability: It shortens and lengthens more rapidly than IAS1. That is, IAS2 is "more callable" than IAS2, and at the same time it has a higher tendency to extend than IAS1. Compared to IAS1, IAS2 has a greater short position in options. However, IAS2 receives a higher fixed rate than IAS1 (5.28 percent compared with 5.12 percent). Is the rate differential of 16 basis points consistent with the excess option position that IAS2 is short?

Static Analysis

As of September 17, 1993 the three-year Treasury rate was 4.17 percent and the three-year swap rate was 4.42 percent. The fixed rates of IAS1 and IAS2 were 70 bp and 86 bp greater, respectively, than the three-year swap rate. To put these two rates in perspective and to be able to compare them, let us first assume that there are no interest rate uncertainties (volatilities are set to zero) and therefore future rates evolve as predicted by forward rates.

EXHIBIT 8–4
Treasury/LIBOR Yield Curve, September 17, 1993

Rate	3 mos.	6 mos.	1 yr.	2 yrs.	3 yrs.	4 yrs.	5 yrs.	7 yrs.	10 yrs.	30 yrs.
Treasury	3.000	3.150	3.390	3.860	4.170	4.455	4.740	4.930	5.380	6.040
LIBOR	3.125	3.313	3.500	4.020	4.420	4.695	4.970	5.290	5.720	6.380

Applying zero-volatility analysis to these structures we find that their average lives are 3.58 years for IAS1 and 4.08 years for IAS2. Exhibit 8–4 shows the yield curve and the swap curve as of September 17, 1993. The upward sloping yield curve suggests that forward CMT rates are greater than the current CMT rate, and therefore future CMT rates will be above the current CMT rate. The consequences are that both swaps will extend beyond three years, and the second swap extends further than the first one.

In a world with no interest rate uncertainty, the holder of IAS1 receives 5.12 percent for an average life of 3.58 years. Interpolating the swap curve between the three year and the four year, we get a swap rate of 4.58 percent for a bullet swap with a maturity of 3.58 years. The interpretation of this rate of 4.58 percent is similar to that of the "intrinsic value" of an option. The investor in ISA1 should receive 4.58 percent, since this is approximately[1] the swap rate corresponding to the expected average life under no uncertainty assumption. In reality, however, the volatility is not zero, and the investor should receive the "time value" of the option that is being sold through IAS1. Applying the same analysis to IAS2, we observe that the swap rate corresponding to the zero-volatility average life of 4.08 years is 4.72 percent, which is 14 bp in excess of the 4.58 percent of the first structure. Again this result suggests that the difference in value between the two structures should be at least 14 bp per year, which is the difference between the intrinsic values of the short option positions of the two structures. Note that the absolute difference between the fixed rates of the two structures is 5.28 percent less 5.12 percent, which equals 16 bp, of which 14 bp corresponds to the difference of the two intrinsic values.

---

1 Under zero-volatility assumption, the swap becomes an amortizing swap with deterministic notional balances, the average life of which is, for IAS1, equal to 3.58 years. The swap rate corresponding to such a swap is, at first approximation, equal to the swap rate of a bullet swap, with maturity equal to the average life of the amortizing swap.

OPTION-ADJUSTED SPREAD

We relax the zero-volatility assumption and examine the value of options that are embedded in these structures. The volatility of the long-term rate plays the dominant role in determining the option value of the structure because the average life variability is directly linked to the path of the 10-year CMT rate. We choose a volatility of 12 percent for the 10-year CMT rate.

Now let us examine the expected average lives of the above structures and compare them to the zero-volatility case. The expected average lives are shown on Exhibit 8–5 and are 3.37 and 3.27 years, respectively. Note that expected average lives of the swaps are shorter than their zero-volatility average lives. Volatility shortens the average life of IASs. Furthermore, we observe that the shortening of expected average life is more pronounced for the second structure than for the first one. The expected average life of the first structure is shortened by .21 years, and the average life of the second structure is .81 years. This result corroborates the intuition that the second structure is more extreme in its average-life variability than the first one.

To determine the value of the option embedded in these swaps, we determine their risk-neutral rates. An investor is risk neutral if he or she is indifferent between sets of different payoffs, as long as the expected value of the payoffs are the same. In the context of the current analysis, the risk-neutral investor is indifferent between a vanilla swap at market (the value of which is zero, abstracting from bid-ask spread) and an index-amortizing swap with a zero expected value. The risk-neutral rate is the fixed rate on the index amortizing swap that corresponds to a zero expected value for the swap. For the above two swaps, these risk-neutral rates are 4.80 percent and 4.96 percent respectively. The difference between these rates and the zero-volatility rates determined previously is the measure of the "time value" of the options. The values of the options embedded in the swaps, expressed in basis points per year, are as follows:

	*IAS*1	*IAS*2
Intrinsic value	458 bp	472 bp
Time value	22 bp	24 bp
Option value	480 bp	496 bp

The time value of the second swap is marginally greater than the time value of the first swap. This suggests that compared to the first swap, the short option position of the second swap is larger.

EXHIBIT 8–5
Expected Average Lives

Volatility = 12 %
E (avg. life) = 3.37 years   E (avg. life) = 3.27 years
Risk-neutral rate = 4.80%   Risk-neutral rate = 4.96%
"Time value" = 4.80 – 4.58 = 22 bp   4.96 – 4.72 = 24 bp
Option-adjusted spread
5.12 – 4.80 = 32 bp   5.28 – 4.96 = 32 bp

The option adjusted spread (OAS) on each swap is the difference between the fixed rate of the swap and the risk-neutral rate, that is:

OAS on IAS1 $5.12\% - 4.80\% = 32$ bp

OAS on IAS2 $5.28\% - 4.96\% = 32$ bp

A simple interpretation of these OASs is that the investor is expecting to receive 32 bp per year on these swaps net of all option costs. Therefore, it would seem that these spreads represent arbitrage opportunities. A more precise interpretation is the following: Assuming the markets are complete in interest rate domain, and volatility is known and constant, then an investor hedging the interest rate exposures of the swap will make about 32 bp per year. In this ideal situation, the OAS is not an expected spread, but an assured arbitrage. In such an idealized world, however, competitive pressure should eliminate this arbitrage opportunity and drive the OASs to zero. Furthermore, in the context of such markets, investors will use OASs as exclusive yardsticks of value. They should, at least in theory, prefer swaps with higher OASs to those with lower OASs. In particular, they should be entirely indifferent between the two swaps, IAS1 and IAS2, because they produce the same option-adjusted spreads.

In reality, however, markets are not frictionless and complete, and future volatility is not known. Hedging is bound to be imperfect, and the ex post realized spreads will be different from the ex ante OASs. OASs are imperfect measures of value; reducing the analysis of swaps to comparison of OASs may lead to very unpleasant surprises. Nevertheless, we contend that a full and comprehensive option-adjusted spread examination should remain an indispensable part and, in most cases, the starting point of the analysis. To see how such an analysis can shed light on different structures, let us again go back to our two examples.

EXHIBIT 8–6
Average Lives of Swaps

	Swap 1	Swap 2
	OAS = 32 bp	OAS = 32 bp
	Avg. life statistics	Avg. life statistics
E (avg. life)	3.37 years	3.27 years
STD	.82 years	1.38 years
Median	3.36 years	3.50 years
Skewness	−.01	−.35
95% percentile	4.73 years	5.00 years

Assume, for the moment, that volatility remains constant as 12 percent forever. Which of the two swaps is more attractive under the constant volatility assumption? Exhibit 8–6 shows the statistics of the average lives of the swaps. The average life of the second swap has a larger standard deviation and is more skewed than the average life of the first one. Exhibit 8–7 shows the average-life distributions of the two swaps. While the average life of the first swap has a bell-shaped distribution, the distribution of the average life of the second swap is more weighted on the two extremes. These statistics suggest that hedging the second swap is more difficult than hedging the first swap. To verify this intuition, we estimate the convexity of the swaps. The convexity of the first swap is equal to −1.3, and the convexity of the second swap is −2.0. The second swap is more negatively convex and therefore will be more difficult to hedge. In addition, since real-life hedging is not continuous and the swap market is not frictionless, discrete delta hedging will be more costly for the second swap than for the first. Because of the additional hedging complexity and costs, investors should demand a greater OAS on the second swap than on the first.

Now consider the effect of volatility uncertainty. As volatility increases, the swaps incur losses because it becomes more expensive to buy back the option positions that they are short. Hedging volatility exposure is usually more complex than hedging interest rate exposure. In volatility domain, markets are far from being complete, and market frictions are significant. As volatility increases, delta hedging of interest rate exposure becomes more expensive because of increased concavity (negative convexity) and because of the larger bid-ask spreads (liquidity decreases as volatility increases). Therefore, everything being equal, investors should demand a

EXHIBIT 8–7
Comparison of Weighted Average Lives

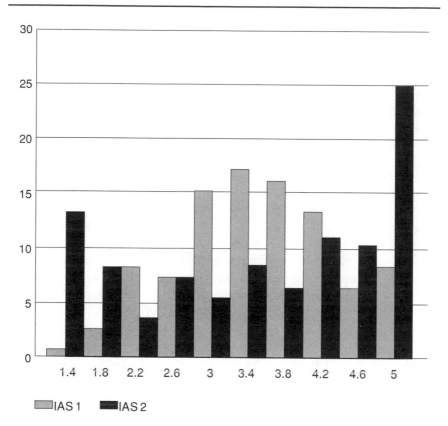

higher OAS for structures that are more sensitive to volatility. The premium that investors receive for volatility uncertainty should depend on the sensitivity of the swap to volatility changes. The higher the sensitivity to volatility, the higher the premium. Exhibit 8–8 shows the effect of volatility changes on the two swap values. The base case volatility is 12 percent. For lower volatilities (10 percent and 8 percent), both swaps increase in value. For higher volatilities (14 percent and 16 percent), the swaps experience losses. Clearly the sensitivity of the second swap to changes in volatility is greater than the sensitivity of the first swap. Therefore, the risk premium associated with uncertainty of future volatility should be higher for the second swap than for the first swap, that is, investors should demand a higher OAS on the second swap.

EXHIBIT 8–8
Sensitivity to Volatility

Volatility (percent)	Swap 1	Swap 2
8%	.30	.40
10%	+.15	.22
12%	0	0
14%	−.17	−.20
16%	−.35	−.38

Finally, investors should realize that index amortization swaps are illiquid contracts. Therefore, in addition to demanding premiums for market frictions and volatility uncertainty, investors should demand premium for illiquidity.

SENSITIVITY ANALYSIS

Now we turn our attention to sensitivity analysis and hedging. We will examine the sensitivities of the first swap to interest rate shifts and to volatility changes.

Exhibit 8–9 shows the change of the value of the first swap with respect to a parallel shift of the yield curve. The swap displays negative convexity. A parallel shift of the yield curve modifies the life of the swap as well as the discount rate of the cash flows. The table in Exhibit 8–9 shows how the duration and the convexity of the swap change as rates move. These duration and convexity numbers are normalized to the notional amount of the swap.

Exhibit 8–10 shows the value of the same swap with respect to changes in the short-term rate while the 10-year yield remains constant. The yield curve rotates around the 10-year yield, that is, the yield on the 10-year rate remains constant, and the three-month rate is moved by ±50 bp and by ±100 bp. Since the life of the swap does not depend on the short end of the curve, the duration and convexity numbers associated with Exhibit 8–10 are proxies for cash flow sensitivities of the swap. It is not surprising to see that the duration of the swap is fairly stable and that its convexity with respect to a move in the short end of the curve is slightly positive.

EXHIBIT 8–9
Sensitivity to Parallel Shift

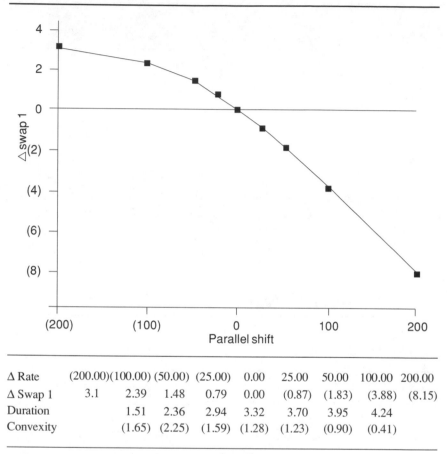

Δ Rate	(200.00)	(100.00)	(50.00)	(25.00)	0.00	25.00	50.00	100.00	200.00
Δ Swap 1	3.1	2.39	1.48	0.79	0.00	(0.87)	(1.83)	(3.88)	(8.15)
Duration		1.51	2.36	2.94	3.32	3.70	3.95	4.24	
Convexity		(1.65)	(2.25)	(1.59)	(1.28)	(1.23)	(0.90)	(0.41)	

Exhibit 8–11 shows the sensitivity of the swap to a move in the 10-year rate while maintaining the short-end constant. The curve rotates around the short end. The swap is negatively convex with respect to the 10-year rate. This result is consistent with the fact that the options embedded in the swap are linked to the 10-year rate, the movement of which is the prime determinant of the average life of the swap.

Sensitivities to volatility were shown in Exhibit 8–8. As volatility moves up, the swaps incur losses. Sensitivity to volatility is asymmetric. For the

EXHIBIT 8–10
Sensitivity to the Short End of the Curve

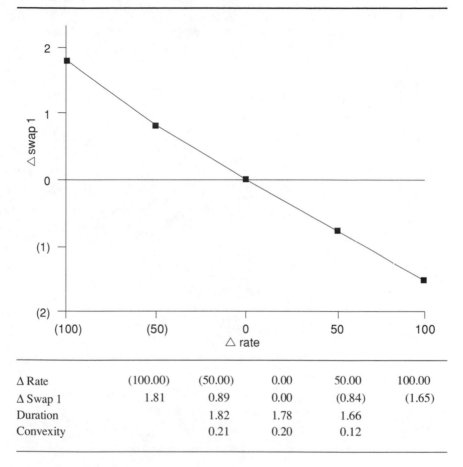

Δ Rate	(100.00)	(50.00)	0.00	50.00	100.00
Δ Swap 1	1.81	0.89	0.00	(0.84)	(1.65)
Duration		1.82	1.78	1.66	
Convexity		0.21	0.20	0.12	

same volatility increment in the first swap, losses are larger than gains (the swap is negatively convex with respect to volatility). The second swap displays positive convexity with respect to volatility.

To hedge the option components of the above structures, one has to use a combination of 10-year Treasuries (or futures contracts) and options on 10-year Treasuries (or on the associated futures contracts). To hedge the cash flow exposure, one can use a combination of Eurodollar contracts and short-term Treasury instruments.

EXHIBIT 8–11
Sensitivity to the 10-Year Rate

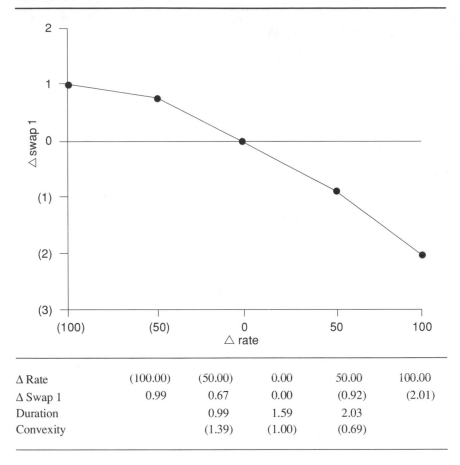

Δ Rate	(100.00)	(50.00)	0.00	50.00	100.00
Δ Swap 1	0.99	0.67	0.00	(0.92)	(2.01)
Duration		0.99	1.59	2.03	
Convexity		(1.39)	(1.00)	(0.69)	

COMPARISON WITH MORTGAGES

Index amortization swaps, or their cash-market equivalent, index amortization notes, are similar to mortgages. They are negatively convex, they extend as long-term rates increase, and they shorten as long-term rates decline. In the case of mortgages, the average life depends on the level of prepayment. The level of prepayment is strongly linked to the level of the long-term interest rate. As the long-term rate increases, refinancing declines and prepayment falls. But the relationship between prepayment and the level of the long-term rate is not deterministic. Therefore, the path of the long-term interest rate is not the only determinant of the average life of a mortgage security. In other terms, prepayment rates have a residual component that is not explained by the variation in the long-term rate. This component, the size of which is not insignificant, induces an additional level of uncertainty in the performance of mortgages. In contrast, index amortization structures are essentially interest rate products. A portfolio of mortgages can be hedged by taking a short position in an index amortization swap with appropriate characteristics. Such a hedging policy is much more effective than the short position in a vanilla swap or in Treasuries. While a significant portion of the duration and the convexity of a mortgage portfolio can be hedged with such amortizing swaps, the residual prepayment risks of mortgages cannot be covered. To mitigate residual prepayment exposures, mortgage portfolios have to use mortgage products. Pure rate products, such as index amortization swaps, are not substitutes for mortgage products.

Chapter Nine

How to Hedge Servicing and Other IO-Type Instruments

Laurie S. Goodman
Paine Webber

With the May 1995 Treasury market rally, many institutions owning mortgage servicing began to worry about hedging that servicing. There are a number of methods for hedging servicing, each of which has particular advantages and disadvantages. We discuss several alternatives in this chapter, focusing on the use of Super-POs, purchases of floors, and options as hedges. *Readers who don't own servicing, don't stop here.* It is important to realize that these techniques—and the analysis behind them—can be applied more broadly to hedge all IO-type cash flows. Moreover, these hedges can be adapted to hedge price compression in a mortgage investor's portfolio.

HOW SERVICING TRADES

Servicing is basically an IO strip. For example, assume a mortgage banker originates a new mortgage with a balance less than $203,150, a coupon of 8 percent, and documentation that conforms to agency standards. The mortgage will be sold into a pool of pass-through mortgage-backed securities, with a 7.5 percent coupon. The FNMA/FHLMC guaranty fees are approximately 25 basis points. The originator retains the remainder of the difference between the mortgage rate and pass-through rate, roughly 25 basis points, as servicing. (In GNMAs, the servicing averages about 44 basis points.) Out of this servicing strip, the originator must pay the fixed and variable costs of servicing the mortgages (collecting payments, sending out late notices, etc.). The originator has access to other sources of income as well, including escrow accounts for tax and insurance, which can be used as compensating balances to reduce borrowing costs (some states do not require originators to pay interest on escrow accounts), late fees, the cross-sale of other services (bank cards, etc.), and the sale of lists of borrowers' names to other commercial enterprises.

Servicing trades are a multiple of the servicing strip. In mid-May 1995, the multiple was 5.25 to 5.75 times the amount of the strip for a current-coupon conventional mortgage with a gross WAC near 8.0 percent. In other words, a 25-basis-points strip trades between 1.31 and 1.43 (0.25 × 5.25 = 1.31; 0.25 × 5.75 = 1.43). The multiple for a GNMA current coupon is typically a little lower—at that time, 4.50 to 5.00—because it is more costly to service GNMA mortgages. The multiple depends heavily on property location (the location determines whether interest must be paid on escrow accounts) and on the cost of servicing and delinquency foreclosure likelihood (it is very expensive for the servicer to go through foreclosure and liquidation).

During the first half of 1995, mortgage servicers became increasingly interested in hedging their servicing income, for a number of reasons. First, as originations trailed off in 1994, servicing became a greater percentage of net income. Recall that conventional agency pass-through production in the first quarter 1995 was down approximately 66 percent from 1993 levels. Second, the absolute size of servicing portfolios has grown, owing to continuing consolidation in the mortgage banking industry. This consolidation has resulted in some acquirers overseeing portfolios two to three times the size of those they had previously been accustomed to. Finally, even the most sophisticated servicers took significant write-downs on their servicing portfolios during the 1992–1993 refinancing boom and as a consequence have become determined to minimize their vulnerability going forward.

SELLING THE SERVICING

In evaluating hedging alternatives, it may be reasonable to consider the outright sale of the servicing. In mid-May, servicing was extremely rich relative to where IOs were trading. This simply reflects the fact that the IO market was quite efficient and had already incorporated expectations of faster prepayments going forward in current prices. By contrast, the market for servicing was not nearly as efficient and did not yet reflect the likelihood that prepayments would sharply accelerate in the new yield environment.

While it may strike some as totally unreasonable to sell off servicing, let's consider for a moment how rich it was at that time. Servicing for current-coupon conventional mortgages as of May 17, 1995, was selling at an average multiple of 5.25–5.75. At the beginning of the year, the average multiple was 5.5–6.0. Thus, the value of servicing had fallen only marginally. By contrast, the value of IOs had fallen sharply. Exhibit 9–1 compares Trust IO prices and multipliers on December 30, 1994 and May 17, 1995. The multiplier was computed simply as the price of the IO divided by the coupon of the IO. Thus, Trust 251, backed by FNMA 8s, had a price of 29:08. Since the coupon is 8 percent, the multiplier would be 3.66 (8/29.25). The multiplier for this at year-end 1994 was 4.73. Trust 254s, backed by 7.5s—the current-coupon collateral—in May had a multiplier of 4.19, down from 5.12 at the beginning of the year. Thus, the multiple for purchasing IOs backed by 7.5 percent collateral was considerably lower than the multiple for purchasing current coupon servicing (4.19 vs. 5.25–5.75). Moreover, as can be seen from Exhibit 9–1, the multipliers on virtually all IOs had fallen considerably since year- end. In contrast, servicing had not declined nearly as much. Indeed, the market for IOs proved much more efficient than the servicing market. Mortgage servicers thus have had a rare opportunity to sell at levels much higher than what they would probably be able to achieve within a few months.

AN OVERVIEW OF ALTERNATIVE HEDGING METHODS

Three approaches are commonly taken to hedge servicing: buying Super-POs, purchasing 10-year CMT floors, and using options. Each of these has its pluses and minuses. Before discussing each individually, Exhibit 9–2 presents a matrix of what I believe are useful conceptual categorizations. One crucial distinction is whether the hedge is linked to interest rates or prepayment rates. Obviously, the instrument to be hedged—the servicing or IO—is linked to prepayment rates. Another critical distinction is whether the hedge has premium risk or market risk. Let's examine each of these.

EXHIBIT 9–1
Multipliers on Trust IOs

				12/30/1994		5/17/1995	
Trust	*Cpn*	*WAC*	*WAM*	*Price*	*Mult*[*]	*Price*	*Mult*[*]
249	6.5	7.08	336	36:02	5.55	33.24	5.19
240	7.0	7.49	333	37:09	5.33	32:24	4.68
254	7.5	7.92	333	38:12	5.12	31:14	4.19
251	8.0	8.47	323	37:28	4.73	29:08	3.66
7	8.5	9.17	250	34:12	4.04	28:28	3.40
1	9.0	9.68	244	40:12	4.49	27:16	3.06
42	9.5	10.15	260	35:00	3.68	27:16	2.89
2	10.0	10.58	243	34:20	3.46	27:16	2.75

* Multiplier = Price/Coupon.

EXHIBIT 9–2
Protection Provided by Alternative Servicing Hedges

	Interest rate linked	Prepayment rate linked
Premium risk	10-yr. CMT floors, call options	Available only as very customized products
Market risk	Treasury securities	Super-POs POs

In an interest-rate-linked hedge, the payoff is linked to Treasury rates. For example, the payoff on 10-year CMT floors is based on the 10-year CMT rate over time. The payoff on the 10-year Treasury note or on options on the 10-year note is based on 10-year Treasury rates. Prepayment-linked products include mortgage securities as well as customized swaps tied to prepayment rates. Why does it matter if the hedge is tied to interest rates or prepayment rates? If there is a one-to-one link between the two, it clearly does not matter much which hedging vehicle is used. The problem is that the link is not necessarily one-to-one. Say, for example, you thought that the 10-year rate would be 6.10 percent forever. What would prepayments be? Most investors would feel comfortable giving a range but not an exact number. If the range is uniformly distributed around the median values currently being used, the impact on value is slight.

The issue that concerns us is that actual prepayments in a further rally may imply a prepayment curve steeper than historical prepayments—and prepayment models—would suggest. The steepness of the curve refers to the amount speeds are expected to accelerate as prepayment incentives (the difference between the underlying mortgage rates and the current mortgage rates) increase. The concern regarding the hedging of servicing with interest-rate linked instruments is that in a bull market, speeds will be considerably faster than the speeds built into most prepayment models. That is, if Treasury rates stay at existing levels, we could again expect to see short-term speeds faster than the Street consensus on higher coupon collateral (8 percent and higher coupons). If we are proved correct and we actually saw such speeds as 30 percent CPR on FNMA 9s at current rates, market participants would begin to trade bonds at levels more consistent with these short-term speeds than with their models' projections. This problem would accelerate if rates declined further. For example, the Street consensus speed on FNMA 8s under a scenario of rates dropping 50 basis points was 250 percent PSA. We believed this to be too slow; we think 400 percent to 500 percent PSA more reasonable. Hence, the value of the servicing could deteriorate without a commensurate drop in interest rates. Prepayment-linked hedges would protect against this eventuality, but interest-rate linked hedges would not.

The second distinction centers on whether the hedge has premium risk or market risk. That is, instruments with premium risk (options and optionlike instruments) involve the payment of an up-front premium. If the market goes against the position, the most that could be lost is the amount of the premium.

Ten-year CMT floors and call options on Treasury securities are two examples. By contrast, instruments with market risk include the outright purchase of Treasury securities and Super-POs. When a hedging instrument has premium risk, investors generally lose their premium over time if the market doesn't move. With a hedge that has market risk, most of the gains on the instrument to be hedged are traded away when there is a favorable market move to protect the position in case the market moves adversely.

EXHIBIT 9–3
Protection Provided by Alternative Servicing Hedges

	On-balance sheet	Off-balance sheet
High liquidity	Treasury securities	Call options
Moderate liquidity	Super-POs POs	10-year CMT floors

That is, most if not all of the potential price appreciation on the servicing will be traded away if the market sells off and one selects a hedge with market risk.

While distinguishing between interest-rate-linked and prepayment-linked hedges and between premium risk and market risk hedges are the most important tasks in selecting a strategy, mortgage servicers looking at hedges must also be concerned with balance sheet and liquidity issues. Exhibit 9–3 lays out the balance sheet and liquidity effects of different servicing hedges. It is important to note that servicing originated by the servicer is currently considered an off-balance-sheet item. However on May 12, 1995, FASB (Financial Accounting Standards Board) 122, an amendment to FASB 65, was approved, requiring original mortgage servicing to be moved on-balance sheet. This applies prospectively to fiscal years beginning after December 15, 1995. Earlier application is encouraged. Regardless of the balance sheet status of the servicing, servicers would prefer that the hedges be off-balance sheet to qualify for hedge accounting. Options and floors are both off-balance-sheet hedges, as are swaps. By contrast, securities used as hedges, such as Treasuries, Super-POs, and structured notes, are treated as on-balance-sheet hedges.

For many servicers, the liquidity of the hedge is also important. A liquid hedge can be unwound at a low cost (bid-ask spread) if the servicing is sold or if the hedge is no longer desired. Note that liquidity refers only to the bid-ask spread. If a servicer purchases a floor and interest rates rise, the value of the floor will decline. This is not a liquidity issue. Treasury securities, over-the-counter call options on Treasury securities, and exchange-traded options on bond and note futures have minimal transaction costs. By contrast, Super-POs have about a one-point bid-ask spread, while 10-year CMT floors have a bid-offer spread of around 15 basis points out to a maturity of five years, and 20 basis points thereafter. Thus the up-front fee for a 10-year CMT floor (with a 6.5 percent strike and a five-year term) may have an bid price of 1.73 and an offering price of 1.88.

In designing a hedging strategy, servicers must be explicit about what they are trying to hedge (e.g., changes in market value, changes in income over a specified time). The choice between option-type hedges with premium risk and hedges with market risk is also a matter of preference. We now look at some specific hedging alternatives.

SUPER-PO HEDGES

Super-PO hedges represent the best on-balance-sheet alternative. First, they are linked to prepayments instead of interest-rates; given our suspicion that the prepayment curve is actually much steeper than projected by most models, this is a very desirable characteristic. In addition, even if Wall Street prepayment curves are correct, Super-POs provide a degree of positive convexity that is not found in Treasury securities or in swaps. Servicing is negatively convex in the extreme. To see this, we fit a price curve on Trust 251 IOs, backed by FNMA 8s shown in Exhibit 9–4. Using these fitted results, Exhibit 9–5 shows the impact of instantaneous yield curve shifts on the price of $1,000,000 current face of IOs. It also shows the

EXHIBIT 9–4
A Simple Price Model for 8 Percent IOs

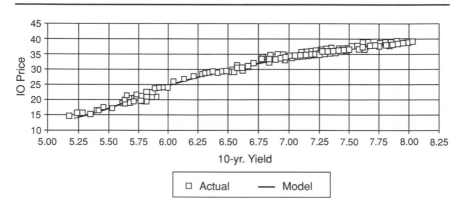

EXHIBIT 9–5
Hedging Servicing with 10-Year Note and Super-PO

	IO	10-Yr. Note	Super-PO
Initial Price	29:08	99:25	34:16
Face	1,000,000	1,288,998	874,992

Terminal Prices

Shift	Instant	1 yr.	Instant	1 yr.	Instant	1 yr.
150	37:25	37:14	89:20	90:11	22:03	23:15
100	36:25	36:11	92:27	93:11	25:21	27:04
50	33:26	33:09	96:08	96:16	29:26	31:11
unch	29:08	28:26	99:25	99:26	34:16	36:03
−50	23:18	23:23	103:16	103:07	41:00	42:22
−100	17:11	19:04	107:12	106:26	49:16	51:14
−150	11:12	14:24	111:14	110:17	60:00	62:04

Component P&L

Shift	Instant	1 yr.	Instant	1 yr.	Instant	1 yr.
150	85,185	128,127	−130,959	−111,725	−108,534	−114,613
100	75,322	116,287	−89,269	−72,733	−77,323	−82,689
50	45,649	85,257	−45,649	−32,090	−41,002	−45,793
unch	0	38,110	0	10,280	0	−4,174
−50	−56,875	−21,476	47,783	54,460	56,875	53,560
−100	−118,987	−89,042	97,811	100,535	131,249	129,998
−150	−178,647	−145,374	150,200	148,594	223,123	223,477

Combo P&L

Shift			IO+10-yr. Note		IO+Super-PO	
150			−45,774	16,402	−23,349	13,514
100			−13,947	43,555	−2,001	33,598
50			0	53,167	4,647	39,465
unch			0	48,391	0	33,937
−50			−9,091	32,984	0	32,085
−100			−21,176	11,493	12,261	40,956
−150			−28,447	3,221	44,476	78,104

effects over a one-year horizon. We do not use OAS-constant results; we know that IOs do not change in an OAS-constant manner.

Note from Exhibit 9–5 that IOs—our analytic proxy for servicing—have more downside than upside. If rates instantaneously rise 100 basis points, the value of the IO will appreciate by $75,322. If rates fall 100 basis points, the value of the IO will fall by $118,987. This analysis, then, captures the economic effects of an interest-rate shift on servicing.

We now compare hedging with the 10-year Treasury note and hedging with a Super-PO. A major disadvantage of hedging with a security that has market risk, such as the Treasury or the Super-PO, is that virtually all of the upside on the servicing will be eliminated. Assume that we buy enough 10-year notes so that the IO plus the 10-year note will have a zero profit or loss for a 50-basis-point instantaneous increase in rates. Thus, we would purchase 1.289 ten-year notes for each dollar current face of IO. When hedging with 10-year notes, it is clear that if the market trades off the IOs will not go up as much in price as the 10-year notes will go down. If, for example, we purchase $1,288,998 of 10-year notes, and interest rates rise by 150 basis points, the IO plus the 10-year note will decline in value by $45,774. Similarly, if the market rallies a great deal, the IO will fare much worse than the gain on the 10-year note. This can be seen in Exhibit 9–5; if the market rallies 100 basis points, the IO plus 10-year note combination will be down by $21,176. This is not a bad hedge, because the unhedged loss on the IO would have been $118,987.

Moreover, an instantaneous framework, such as that used here, makes the IO and the combination less attractive than it would be in a longer holding period. With a one-year horizon and unchanged rates, the IO will net $38,110, the effect of which is lost in an instantaneous horizon. In addition, in a one-year horizon, the 10-year note also generates positive carry. Thus, the base-case profit jumps from $38,110 to $48,391 with the IO–10-year combination. (We used a 5.5 percent financing rate on the 10-year note, reflecting that it is apt to be special at least part of the year.) Over a one-year horizon, with the IO–10-year hedge, the profile is positive everywhere. If rates rise, much of the gain is eliminated. If rates fall, all of the losses are turned into gains.

Now let us consider Super-POs as a hedge for mortgage servicing. The Super-PO used is FNR 93-216 E at a price of 34:16; we purchase 0.875 Super-POs for each dollar current face of IO. As can be seen in Exhibit 9–5, these results are considerably better than those obtained by hedging with 10-year notes. As rates rise in an instantaneous horizon, the Super-PO underperforms only marginally (the loss is $2,001 for a 100-basis-point increase in rates versus $13,947 for the 10-year note hedge). If rates fall, the positive convexity of the Super-PO more than offsets the negative convexity of the IO, actually producing gains as rates fall. If interest rates fall 100 basis points instantaneously, adding the Super-PO hedge changes a $118,987 loss into a $12,261 gain. If interest rates fall 150 basis points instantaneously, the gains are even more dramatic—a $178,647 loss is transformed into a $44,476 gain.

Over a longer horizon such as one year, the Super-PO hedge looks slightly less attractive. If rates are unchanged, the Super-PO costs a small amount to carry. Specifically, the yield on the instrument is less than the 6 percent financing rate, and the security costs about $4,174 to carry over the course of a year if rates are unchanged. If rates rise, the combination of the IO plus the Super-PO hedge shows a substantially positive profit and loss in a one-year horizon; the difference between the instantaneous case and the one-year horizon is attributable primarily to the carry on the IO. If interest rates decline, the combination of the servicing plus Super-PO hedge does extremely well. Note that both the Super-PO and the 10-year note provide substantial protection and produce a positive return profile regardless of the scenario.

While we have not explicitly discussed PO hedges, virtually everything that is said for Super-POs applies to Trust POs as well. In mid-May 1995 when this analysis was performed, Super-POs appeared to represent better relative value. Mortgage servicers can, of course, fine-tune the hedge ratio to produce a return pattern that fits their risk preferences.

TEN-YEAR CMT FLOORS

In the cap and floor market, LIBOR-based floors (London interbank-offered rate) are the most liquid. However, LIBOR floors are not well suited to hedge servicing because the largest determinant of servicing income is prepayments and prepayments are driven off the 10-year rate. Buying floors based off the 10-year CMT index solves this problem. Virtually all mortgage bankers who use floors to hedge have used 10-year CMT floors instead of LIBOR floors. The most the investor can lose hedging with 10-year CMT floors is the up-front premium. But this can be quite substantial. For example, the cost of purchasing a 10-year CMT floor struck at 6.5 percent for five years is 1.88 per $100 par. In determining how much of a floor hedge is required, it is necessary to decide the strike, the term, and whether to purchase bullet or amortizing floors. The advantage of an amortizing floor is that it can be designed to replicate the paydown pattern of a mortgage. The investor avoids paying up for unneeded protection. On the other hand, acquiring servicing is an ongoing business activity, and new servicing should replace what has run off, so that an amortizing floor may not be adequate.

Exhibit 9-6 shows the effect of hedging servicing, as proxied by IOs, with a 10-year CMT floor for an instantaneous horizon and for a one-year horizon. We use a five-year floor with a 6.5 percent strike, the initial up-front cost is 1.88. We assume that the change in rates is instantaneous. Note that the servicer must buy 3.5 ten-year CMT floors in to protect each current face dollar of IO. As these results show, the hedging power of the floors in an instantaneous horizon is great. However, this is not a fair comparison because the hedge loses no time value. A better comparison is to look at the hedge for a one-year horizon. As can be seen, the floors provide excellent protection against interest rate drops while preserving much of the gain on the servicing as interest rates rise; in a one-year horizon, if rates are unchanged, $1,000,000 current face of IOs will earn carry of $38,110. If a servicer buys 3.5 floors for each dollar current face value of the IO, the gain will drop to $21,310. That is, each floor purchased will drop from an initial value of 1.88 to 1.40. If rates rise, the value of the floor will erode more; however, the upside on the IO or servicing will offset this. If rates fall, the floor value will increase, cushioning the drop in the market value of the IO. Thus, the loss on the IO unhedged in a one-year horizon, if rates fall 150 basis points, would be $145,374. The 10-year CMT floor hedge would cut the loss to $3,480.

The most significant problem servicers face when hedging with floors is the whipsaw risk. That is, if rates fall and then rise very quickly, a substantial amount of prepayments could be generated on the servicing asset.Still, the floor payout is small, because rates were low for a very short time. A secondary problem is the interest rate link, not the prepayment link. It is possible the IO or servicing actually performs much worse than we are predicting if rates fall. If so, the floor or any other interest-rate-linked hedge will be unable to compensate.

CALL OPTIONS ON THE 10-YEAR NOTE

Another hedge for servicing is to buy call options. These can be traded on an exchange or over the counter. For illustrative purposes, we assume a servicer purchases a one-year over-the-counter call option on the 10-year note struck at-the-money forward; the premium would be 2:29. The profile in a one-year horizon from pursuing this strategy in combination with IOs is shown in Exhibit 9–6. The profile is similar to the 10-year CMT floors–IO combination; in the base case, the carry is cut roughly in half because of the lower cost of purchasing the options. Note that the servicer purchases 1.65 options per IO. That is, the number of options purchased is only 47 percent of the number of floors purchased. As with the 10-year note floors, the servicer does well if rates rise—he or she is able to preserve much of the upside on the servicing or IO position. If rates drop, the sizable loss on the unhedged IO has been cut to close to zero. In this case, for a rate drop of 150 basis points, a loss of $145,374 has been cut to $3,117.

Some servicers have objected to the up-front fee and prefer to hedge by purchasing at-the-money or slightly out-of-the-money call options and selling further out-of-the-money call options. This is termed a bull-call spread. (The logic of this name is simple; it is a call spread that does well in a bull market because the option purchased is more valuable than the option that has been sold.) Essentially, the fee on the low-cost option partially offsets the fee on the higher-cost option, limiting the up-front payment. This also limits the payout if rates drop substantially.

CONCLUSION

I have looked at various alternatives for hedging servicing. I have argued that in mid-May 1995, the best hedge was to sell because servicing had fared much better than IOs, its economic equivalent, as rates fell. A servicer wanting to keep the asset, however, could choose among three types of hedges commonly used: POs and Super-POs, 10-year CMT floors, and call options on the 10-year note. The choice of hedge is a matter of preference. From an economic point of view, the crucial decisions are whether the hedge is to be linked to interest rates or prepayment rates and whether the hedge has premium risk or market risk. I strongly believe that servicers who are willing to look at a nonoption hedge should use Super-POs. The servicing plus Super-PO combination is quite a lot more attractive than the servicing itself because the positive convexity of the Super-PO helps to offset the negative convexity of the IO or servicing position. The hedge has the further advantage of being prepayment linked. I believe this is an advantage because the econometric models heavily weighted with the experience of the 1980s underestimate the steepness of the prepayment curve and the

EXHIBIT 9–6
Hedging Servicing with Floors and Calls

	IO	10-Yr. CMT 6.5% Floor	1-yr. 10-yr. ATM Call[*]
Initial Price	29:08	188	2:29
Face	1,000,000	3,500,000	1,650,000

Terminal Prices

Shift	Instant	1 yr.	Instant	1 yr.	Instant	1 yr.
150	37:25	37:14	55	37	0:14	0:00
100	36:25	36:11	83	57	0:27	0:00
50	33:26	33:09	125	90	1:20	0:00
unch	29:08	28:26	188	140	2:29	0:26
−50	23:18	23:23	278	214	5:01	4:07
−100	17:11	19:14	399	314	8:00	7:26
−150	11:12	14:24	552	440	11:24	11:17

Component P&L

Shift	Instant	1 yr.	Instant	1 yr.	Instant	1 yr.
150	85,185	128,127	−46,550	−52,850	−40,734	−47,953
100	75,322	116,287	−36,750	−45,850	−34,031	−47,953
50	45,649	85,257	−22,050	−34,300	−21,141	−47,953
unch	0	38,110	0	−16,800	0	−34,794
−50	−56,875	−21,476	31,500	26,998	35,063	21,759
−100	−118,987	−89,042	73,850	79,895	84,047	80,738
−150	−178,647	−145,374	127,400	141,893	145,922	142,257

Combo P&L

Shift		IO+ Floor		IO+ Call	
150		38,635	75,277	44,450	80,174
100		38,572	70,437	41,291	68,334
50		23,599	50,957	24,509	37,304
unch		0	21,310	0	3,317
−50		−25,375	5,522	−21,812	283
−100		−45,137	−9,147	−34,941	−8,304
−150		−51,247	−3,480	−32,725	−3,117

[*] Strike = 99:00, Repo = 5.75, Vol = 16.50.

actual prepayments are more responsive to interest rates than prepayment projections suggest.

Servicers who want hedges with only premium risk should look at both 10-year CMT floors and call options on the 10-year note. Both instruments are off-balance sheet. Options are more liquid than 10-year CMT floors. However, 10-year CMT floors can be written for much longer periods. Exchange-traded options go out about nine months; over-the-counter options go out to a year, but liquidity diminishes sharply after six months. In 10-year CMT floors, the premium is much lower than the premiums obtained when buying and rolling an options position, but servicers who hold floors have the potential of being whipsawed. I believe this is a considerable risk.

Chapter Ten

A One-Factor Model of Interest Rates and Its Application to Treasury Bond Options*

Fischer Black
Goldman, Sachs & Co.

Emanuel Derman
Goldman, Sachs & Co.

William Toy
Goldman, Sachs & Co.

This chapter describes a model of interest rates that can be used to value any interest-rate sensitive security. To explain how it works, we concentrate on valuing options on Treasury bonds.

The model has three key features:

1. Its fundamental variable is the short rate—the annualized one-period interest rate r. The short rate is the one factor of the model; its changes drive all security prices.

2. It takes as inputs an array of long rates (yields on zero-coupon Treasury bonds) for various maturities and an array of yield volatilities for the same bonds. We call the first array the *yield curve* and the second array, the *volatility curve*. Together these curves form the *term structure*.

---

* This chapter first appeared in *Financial Analysts Journal* 46 (Jan./Feb. 1990).

3. It varies an array of means and an array of volatilities for the future short rate to match the inputs. As the future volatility changes, the future mean reversion changes.

We examine how the model works in an imaginary world in which changes in all bond yields are perfectly correlated; expected returns on all securities over one period are equal; short rates at any time are lognormally distributed; and there are no taxes or trading costs.

VALUING SECURITIES

Suppose we own an interest rate sensitive security worth S today. We assume that its price can move up to S_u or down to S_d with equal probability over the next time period. Exhibit 10–1 shows the possible changes in S for a one-year time step, starting from a state where the short rate is r.

The expected price of S one year from now is $1/2 \, (S_u + S_d)$. The expected return is $1/2 \, (S_u + S_d)/S$. Because we assume that all expected returns are equal, and because we can lend money at r, we deduce:

$$S = \frac{\frac{1}{2}S_u + \frac{1}{2}S_d}{1 + r} \tag{1}$$

where r is today's short rate.

EXHIBIT 10–1
A One-Step Tree

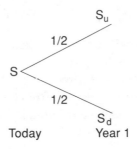

EXHIBIT 10–2
Two-Step Trees of Short Rates and Prices

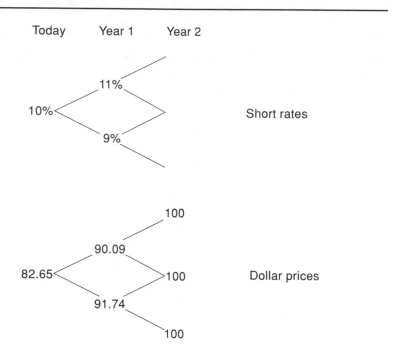

Today   Year 1   Year 2

11%

10%

9%

Short rates

100

90.09

82.65

100

91.74

100

Dollar prices

Getting Today's Prices from Future Prices

We can use the one-step tree to relate today's price to the prices one step away. Similarly, we can derive prices one step in the future from prices two steps in the future. In this way, we can relate today's prices to prices two steps away.

Exhibit 10–2 shows two-step trees for rates and prices. The short rate starts out at 10 percent. We expect it to rise to 11 percent or drop to 9 percent with equal probability.

The second tree shows prices for a two-year, zero-coupon Treasury. In two years, the zero's price will be $100. Its price one year from now may be $91.74 ($100 discounted by 9 percent) or $90.09 ($100 discounted by 11 percent). The expected price one year from now is the average of $90.09 and $91.74, or $90.92. Our valuation formula, Equation (1), finds today's price by discounting this average by 10 percent to give $82.65.

We can in this way value a zero of any maturity, provided our tree of future short rates goes out far enough. We simply start with the security's face value at maturity and find the price at each earlier node by discounting future prices using the valuation formula and the short rate at that node. Eventually we work back to the root of the tree and find the price today.

FINDING SHORT RATES FROM THE TERM STRUCTURE

The term structure of interest rates is quoted in yields, rather than prices. Today's annual yield, y, of the N-year zero in terms of its price, S, is given by finding the y that satisfies:

$$S = \frac{100}{(1 + y)^N} \tag{2}$$

Similarly, the yields y_u and y_d one year from now corresponding to prices S_u and S_d are given by:

$$S_{u,d} = \frac{100}{(1 + y_{u,d})^{N-1}} \tag{3}$$

We want to find the short rates that assure that the model's term structure matches today's market term structure. Exhibit 10–3 gives the assumed market term structure.

The price of a zero today is the expected price one period in the future discounted to today using the short rate. The short rate, r, is 10 percent. Using the price tree of Exhibit 10–4, we see that $S_u = S_d = 100$, and $S = 90.91$:

EXHIBIT 10–3
A Sample Term Structure

Maturity (in years)	Yield RB(in %)	Yield Volatility (in %)
1	10.0%	20%
2	11.0	19
3	12.0	18
4	12.5	17
5	13.0	16

EXHIBIT 10–4
Finding the Initial Short Rate Using a One-Year Zero

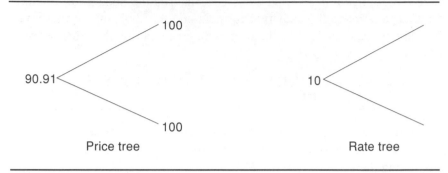

$$90.91 = \frac{\frac{1}{2} 100 + \frac{1}{2} 100}{1 + r} = \frac{100}{1 + r}$$

Short Rates One Period in the Future

We can now find the short rates one year from now by looking at the yield
and volatility for a two-year zero using the term structure of Exhibit 10–3.

Look at the two-year short rate tree in Exhibit 10–5. Let's call the
unknown future short rates r_u and r_d. We want their values to be such that
the price and volatility of the two-year zero match the price and volatility
in Exhibit 10–3.

We know today's short rate is 10 percent. Suppose we guess that $r_u =$
14.32 percent and $r_d = 9.79$ percent.

Now look at the price and yield trees in Exhibit 10–5. A two-year zero
has a price of $100 at all nodes at the end of the second period, no matter
what short rate prevails. Using the valuation formula in Equation (1), we
can find the one-year prices by discounting the expected two-year prices by
r_u and r_d; we get prices of $87.47 and $91.08. Using Equation (3), we find
that yields of 14.32 percent and 9.79 percent correspond to these prices.
These are shown on the yield tree in Exhibit 10–5.

Now that we have the two-year prices and yields one year out, we can
use the valuation formula to get today's price and yield for the two-year
zero. Today's price is given by Equation (1) by discounting the expected
one-year-out price by today's short rate:

EXHIBIT 10–5
Finding the One-Year Short Rates Using a Two-Year Zero

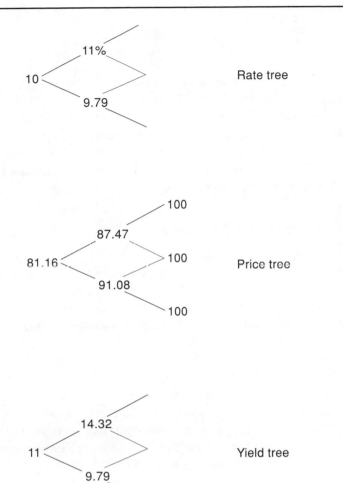

$$\frac{\frac{1}{2}(87.47) + \frac{1}{2}(91.08)}{1.1} = 81.16$$

We can get today's yield for the two-year zero, y_2, by using Equation (2) with today's price as S. As the yield tree in Exhibit 10–5 shows, y_2 is 11 percent.

The volatility of this two-year yield is defined as the natural logarithm of the ratio of the one-year yields:

$$\sigma_2 = \frac{\ln \dfrac{14.33}{9.79}}{2} = 19\%$$

With the one-year short rates we have chosen, the two-year zero's yield and yield volatility match those in the term structure of Exhibit 10–3. This means that our guesses for r_u and r_d were right. Had they been wrong, we would have found the correct ones by trial and error.

So an initial short rate of 10 percent followed by equally probable one-year short rates of 14.32 percent and 9.79 percent guarantee that our model matches the first two years of the term structure.

More Distant Short Rates

We found today's single short rate by matching the one-year yield. We found the two one-year short rates by matching the two-year yield and volatility. Now we find the short rates two years out.

Exhibit 10–6 shows the short rates out to two years. We already know the short rates out to one year. The three unknown short rates at the end of the second year are r_{uu}, r_{ud} and r_{dd}.

The values for these three short rates should let our model match the yield and yield volatility of a three-year zero. We must therefore match two quantities by guessing at three short rates. This contrasts with finding the one-year short rates, where we had to match two quantities with two short rates. As a rule, matching two quantities with two short rates is unique; there is only one set of values for the short rates that produces the right match. Matching two quantities with three short rates is not unique; many sets of three short rates produce the correct yield and volatility.

Remember, however, that our model assumes that the short rate is lognormal with a volatility (of the log of the short rate) that depends only on time. One year in the future, when the short rate is 14.32 percent, the volatility is $1/2 \ln(r_{uu}/r_{ud})$; when the short rate is 9.79 percent, the volatility is $1/2 \ln(r_{ud}/r_{dd})$. Because these volatilities must be the same, we know that $r_{uu}/r_{ud} = r_{ud}/r_{dd}$, or $r_{ud}^2 = r_{uu}r_{dd}$.

So we don't really make three independent guesses for the rates; the middle one, r_{ud}, can be found from the other two. This means we have to match only two short rates—r_{uu} and r_{dd}—with two quantities, the three-year yield and volatility in the model. This typically has a unique solution.

EXHIBIT 10–6
Finding the Two-Year Short Rates

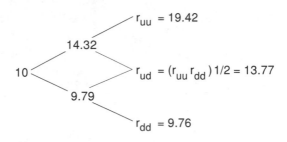

In this case, Exhibit 10–6 shows that values for r_{uu}, r_{dd} and r_{ud} of 19.42, 9.76, and 13.77 percent, respectively, produce a three-year yield of 12 percent and volatility of 18 percent, as Exhibit 10–3 calls for.

We now know the short rates for one and two years in the future. Using a similar process, we can find the short rates on tree nodes farther in the future. Exhibit 10–7 displays the full tree of short rates at one-year intervals that matches the term structure of Exhibit 10–3.

VALUING OPTIONS ON TREASURY BONDS

Given the term structure of Exhibit 10–3 and the resulting tree of short rates shown in Exhibit 10–7, we can use the model to value a bond option.

Coupon Bonds as Collections of Zeroes

Before we can value Treasury bond options, we need to find the future prices of a Treasury bond at various nodes on the tree.

Consider a Treasury with a 10 percent coupon, a face value of $100, and three years left to maturity. For convenience, consider this 10 percent Treasury as a portfolio of three zero-coupon bonds: a one-year zero with a $10 face value, a two-year zero with a $10 face value, and a three-year zero with a $110 face value.

This portfolio has exactly the same annual payoffs as the 10 percent Treasury with three years to maturity. So the portfolio and the Treasury should have the same value. The tree in Exhibit 10–7 was built to value all zeroes according to today's yield curve; hence we can use it to value the three zeroes in the portfolio above.

EXHIBIT 10–7
Short Rates That Match the Term Structure of Exhibit 10–3

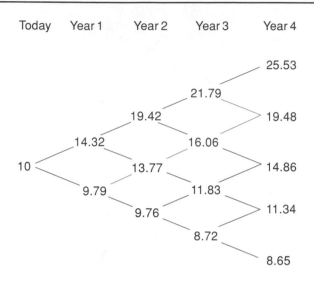

Panel (*e*) of Exhibit 10–8 shows the price of the 10 percent Treasury as the sum of the present values of the zeroes: $95.51. The tree in panel (*f*) gives the three-year Treasury prices obtained after subtracting $10 of accrued interest on each coupon date.

Puts and Calls on Treasuries

We found a price of $95.51 for a three-year, 10 percent Treasury. The security is below par today; it has a 10 percent coupon and yields in today's yield curve are generally higher than 10 percent.

We want to value options on this security—a two-year European call and a two-year European put, both struck at $95. From Exhibit 10–8 (*e*), we see that in two years the three-year Treasury bond may have one of three prices: $110.22, $106.69, or $102.11. The corresponding prices without accrued interest are $100.22, $96.69, and $92.11.

At expiration, the $95.00 call is in the money if the bond is worth either $100.22 or $96.69. The call's value will be the difference between the bond's price and the strike price. The $95.00 call will be worth $5.22 if the bond is trading at $100.22 at expiration and $1.69 if the bond is trading

EXHIBIT 10–8
Three-Year Treasury Values Obtained by Valuing an Equivalent Portfolio of Zeroes

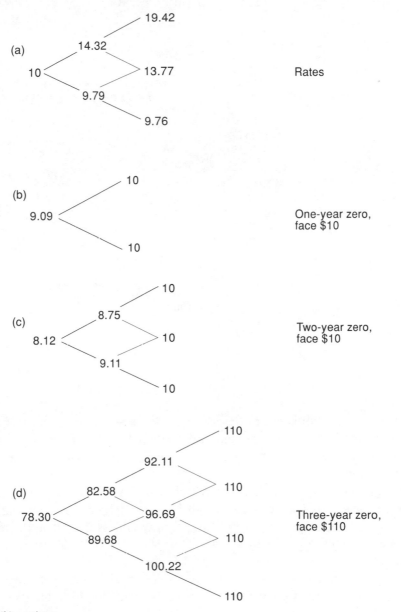

Exhibit continues

EXHIBIT 10–8
(*continued*)

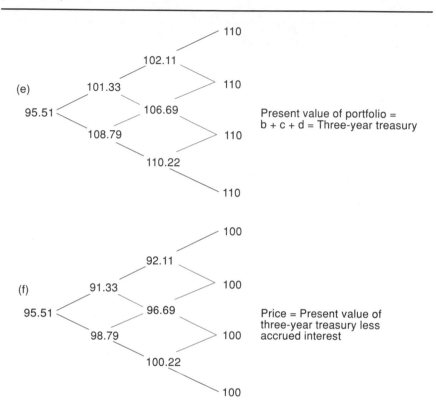

(e)

Present value of portfolio =
b + c + d = Three-year treasury

(f)

Price = Present value of
three-year treasury less
accrued interest

at $96.69. The call is out of the money, and therefore worth zero, if the
bond is trading at $92.11 at expiration. Exhibit 10–9 is the short-rate tree
over two years, as well as possible call values at expiration of the option
in two years.

At expiration the put is in the money if the bond is worth $92.11 (without
accrued interest). The put's value will be the difference between $92.11
and the $95 strike price—$2.89. The put is worthless if the bond's price
is one of the two higher values, $100.22 or $96.69. Exhibit 10–9 gives the
put values.

   Knowing the call values at expiration, we can find the possible values of
the call one year before expiration, using the valuation formula given in
Equation (1).

EXHIBIT 10–9
Two-Year Options on a Three-Year Treasury

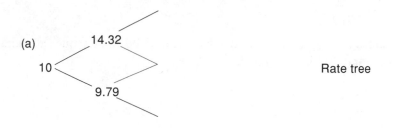

(a) 14.32

10

9.79

Rate tree

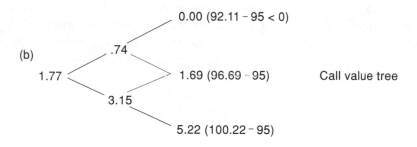

(b)

0.00 (92.11 − 95 < 0)

.74

1.77

1.69 (96.69 − 95)

3.15

5.22 (100.22 − 95)

Call value tree

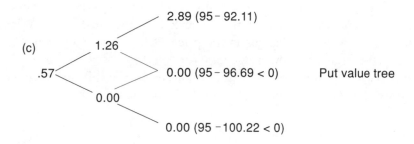

(c)

2.89 (95 − 92.11)

1.26

.57

0.00 (95 − 96.69 < 0)

0.00

0.00 (95 − 100.22 < 0)

Put value tree

If the short rate is 14.32 percent one year from today, the call's value one year before expiration will be:

$$\frac{\frac{1}{2}(0.00) + \frac{1}{2}(1.69)}{1.1432} = 0.74$$

If the short rate is 9.79 percent one year from today, the call's value will be:

$$\frac{\frac{1}{2}(1.69) + \frac{1}{2}(5.22)}{1.0979} = 3.15$$

Given the call values one year out, we can find the value of the call today when the short rate is 10 percent:

$$\frac{\frac{1}{2}(0.74) + \frac{1}{2}(3.15)}{1.1} = 1.77$$

Put values are derived in a similar manner. Exhibit 10–9 shows the full trees of call and put values.

We have priced European-style options by finding their values at any node as the discounted expected value one step in the future. American-style options can be valued with little extra effort. Because an American option may be exercised at any time, its value at any node is the greater of its value if held or its value if exercised. We obtain its value if held by using the valuation formula to get any node's value in terms of values one step in the future. Its value if exercised is the difference between the bond price at the node and the strike price.

Option Hedge Ratios

When interest rates change, so do the prices of bonds and bond options. Bond option investors are naturally interested in how much option prices change in response to changes in the price of the underlying bond. We measure this relation by the hedge ratio (or delta).

Exhibit 10–10 shows one-step trees for a Treasury, a call, and a put. For a call worth C on a Treasury with price T, the hedge ratio is:

$$\Delta_{call} = \frac{C_u - C_d}{T_u - T_d} \tag{4}$$

where C_u and C_d are the values of the call one period from today in the tree corresponding to possible short rates r_u and r_d. A similar formula holds for a put, P, on a Treasury; we simply replace C with P in Equation (4).

For the two-year put and call on the three-year Treasury considered above, start by finding the differences between possible prices one year from today. Given the Treasury prices shown in Exhibit 10–8 and the option prices from Exhibit 10–9:

EXHIBIT 10-10
Hedge Ratios for a Call and a Put on a Treasury

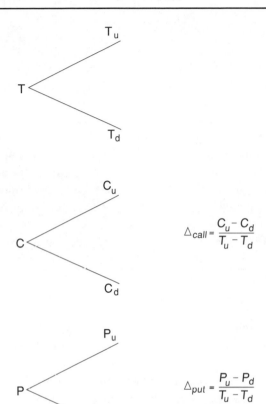

$$T_u - T_d = 91.33 - 98.79$$

$$= -7.46$$

$$C_u - C_d = 0.74 - 3.15$$

$$= -2.41$$

$$P_u - P_d = 1.26 - 0.00$$

$$= 1.26$$

We can now derive the hedge ratios, using Equation (4):

$$\Delta_{call} = \frac{(-2.41)}{(-7.46)}$$

$$= 0.32$$

$$= \frac{(1.26)}{(-7.46)}$$

$$= -0.17$$

These hedge ratios give us the option's sensitivity to changes in the underlying Treasury price by describing the change in the option's price per dollar change in the Treasury's price. They therefore tell us how to hedge the Treasury with the option, and vice versa. The call hedge ratio is positive because the call prices increase when the Treasury price increases. In contrast, the put hedge ratio is negative because put prices decrease as the Treasury price increases.

We compute these ratios much more accurately by using finely spaced trees.

Reducing the Interval Size

In the previous examples, the short-rate tree had coarse one-year steps, Treasuries paid annual coupons, and options could only be exercised once a year.

To get accurate solutions for option values, we need a tree with finely spaced steps between today and the option's expiration. Ideally we would like a tree with one-day steps and a 30-year horizon, so that coupon payments and option exercise dates would always fall exactly on a node. We would also like to have many steps to expiration, even for options on the verge of expiring.

In practice, our computer doesn't have enough memory to build a 30-year tree with daily steps. Even if it did, it would take us hours to value a security. Instead, we can build a sequence of short-rate trees, each with the same number of steps but compressed into shorter and shorter horizons. Thus each tree has finer spacing than the one before it. For example, we might use today's term structure to build short-rate trees that extend over 30 years, 15 years, 7 1/2 years, and so on. In this way, no matter when the option expires, we will always have one tree with enough steps to value the option accurately.

To value an option on any Treasury, we use two trees: a coarse one with enough steps to value the Treasury accurately from its maturity back to today, and a fine one with enough steps to value the option accurately from its expiration until today. We find the Treasury values on the coarse tree by using the model's valuation formula from maturity to today. Then we interpolate these Treasury values onto the fine tree, which may often have as many as 60 periods. Maturity, expiration, and coupon dates that fall between nodes are carefully interpolated to the nearest node in time. In this way, the option can be accurately valued.

Interpolating across trees gives us accurate, yet rapid, results. Once model values have been found to match the term structure, we can value options in a few seconds.

IMPROVING THE MODEL

We considered more complex models that use more than one factor to describe shifts in the yield curve. Increasing the number of factors improves the model's results. The more factors we use, the better the model. But a multifactor model is much harder to think about and work with than a single-factor model. It also takes much more computer time. Therefore, we think it pays to work with different single-factor models before moving on to a multifactor model.

Along these lines, we examined the effects on our model of letting forward mean reversion and forward short-rate volatility vary independently. (They are tied together in the current model only by the geometry of a tree with equal time spacing throughout.) We found that varying forward mean reversion and varying forward short-rate volatility give very different results. We can use one or the other alone, or a mixture of both, in matching the term structure.

Chapter Eleven

Bond and Option Pricing When Short Rates Are Lognormal

Fischer Black
Goldman, Sachs & Co.

Piotr Karasinski
Chemical Bank

This chapter presents a one-factor model of bond prices, bond yields, and related options. The single factor that is the source of all uncertainty is the short-term interest rate. We assume no taxes or transaction costs, no default risk, and no extra costs for borrowing bonds. We also assume that all security prices are perfectly correlated in continuous time.

We can choose from among a number of models of the local process for the short-term interest rate—a normal process, a lognormal process, a "square-root" process or others.[1] The nominal interest rate cannot fall below zero as long as people can hold cash; it can become stuck at zero for long periods, however, as when prices fall persistently and substantially. None of the models we have to choose from allows for both these features.

---

1 For a normal process, see O. Vasicek, "An Equilibrium Characterization of the Term Structure," *Journal of Financial Economics*, November 1977, and F. Jamshidian, "An Exact Bond Option Formula," *Journal of Finance*, March 1989. For a lognormal process, see U. L. Dothan, "On the Term Structure of Interest Rates," *Journal of Financial Economics*, March 1978. For a square-root process, see J. C. Cox, J. E. Ingersoll, Jr., and S. A. Ross, "A Theory of the Term Structure of Interest Rates," *Econometrica*, March 1985; G. M. Constantinides, "Theory of the Term Structure of Interest Rates: The Squared Autoregressive Instruments Nominal Term Structure (SAINTS) Model" (Working paper,

Lognormal models keep the rate away from zero entirely, while some square-root models make zero into a "reflecting barrier."

The lognormal model we use is more general than others, because we allow the local process to change over time. So long as the process for log r is linear in log r at each time, we will have a lognormal distribution for the possible values of the short rate at a given future time. In contrast, the square-root process does not give a square-root distribution at a given future time.

A LOGNORMAL MODEL

A lognormal distribution has a mean and a variance. Assuming a different lognormal short-rate distribution for each future time allows both mean and variance to depend on time.

As Hull and White point out, however, a normal (or lognormal) model with mean reversion can depend on time in three ways, not just two ways.[2] In their notation, the continuous-time limit of the Black-Derman-Toy one-factor model is:[3]

$$d(\log r) = [\theta(t) - \varphi(t) \log r]dt + \sigma(t)dz \tag{1}$$

where r is the local interest rate and $\sigma(t)$ depends on $\varphi(t)$.

To create a lognormal model that depends on time in three ways, we can simply drop the tie between $\sigma(t)$ and $\theta(t)$. Hull and White do this for a general model.[4] Our model is a special case of theirs.

September 1990); F. Longstaff, "The Valuation of Options on Yields" (Working paper, February 1990); and F. Longstaff, "The Valuation of Options on Coupon Bonds" (Working paper, January 1990). Other processes are given in T. S. Y. Ho and S-B Lee, "Term Structure Movements and Pricing Interest Rate Contingent Claims," *Journal of Finance*, December 1986; D. Heath, R. Jarrow, and A. Morton, "Bond Pricing and the Term Structure of Interest Rates: A New Methodology for Contingent Claims Valuation" (Working papers, October 1990); D. Heath, R. Jarrow, and A. Morton, "Contingent Claim Valuation with a Random Evolution of Interest Rates," *Review of Futures Markets*, forthcoming; J. Hull and A. White, "New Ways with the Yield Curve," *Risk*, October 1990; and F. Black, E. Derman, and W. Toy, "A One-Factor Model of Interest Rates and its Application to Treasury Bond Options," *Financial Analysts Journal*, January/February 1990. Some of these models of short-rate behavior are tested in K. C. Chan, G. A. Karolyi, F. A. Longstaff, and A. B. Sanders, "Alternative Models of the Term Structure: An Empirical Comparison" (Working paper, October 1990).

2 J. Hull and A. White, "Pricing Interest Rate Derivative Securities," *Review of Financial Studies* 3 (1990), pp. 573–92.

3 See Black, Derman, and Toy, "A One-Factor Model."

4 Hull and White, "New Ways with the Yield Curve."

We make one change in the way Hull and White write their model. We write $\mu(t)$ for the "target interest rate." When $\log r$ is above $\log \mu(t)$, it tends to fall, and when it is below $\log \mu(t)$, it tends to rise. Thus we rewrite equation (1) as:

$$d(\log r) = \varphi(t)[\log \mu(t) - \log r]dt + \sigma(t)dz. \qquad (2)$$

We take $\mu(t)$ as the target rate, $\theta(t)$ as mean reversion, and $\sigma(t)$ as local volatility in the expression for the local change in $\log r$. We choose these three functions (inputs) to match three features of the world (outputs).

For their outputs, Hull and White choose:

- The yield curve.
- The volatility curve.
- The future local volatilities $\sigma(t)$.

The yield curve gives for each maturity the current yield on a zero-coupon bond. The volatility curve gives for each maturity the current yield volatility on a zero-coupon bond. The future local volatilities output is the same as the corresponding input.

For our outputs, we choose:

- The yield curve.
- The volatility curve.
- The cap curve.

Our first two outputs are the same as Hull and White's. The cap curve gives, for each maturity, the price of an at-the-money differential cap. A differential cap pays at a rate equal to the difference (if positive) between the short rate and the strike price. For any maturity, an at-the-money cap has a strike equal to the forward rate for that maturity. A full cap is the integral of differential caps over all future horizons up to the full cap's maturity.

An advantage of these outputs over Hull and White's is that all of them are (in principle) observable. They all correspond to market prices.

We do not claim that our inputs imply a reasonable process for the short rate, except as a rough approximation. We choose inputs that give reasonable outputs, though they may be somewhat unreasonable themselves.[5] We

---

5 Cox, Ingersoll, and Ross, "A Theory of the Term Structure," and Constantinides, "Theory of the Term Structure," imagine they are choosing a sensible process for the short rate and look at the

are following in the footsteps of Cox, Ross, and Rubinstein, who value options by generating a "risk-neutral" distribution of future stock prices.[6] This is not a true distribution, but it nonetheless gives correct option prices.

Input and Output Volatilities

We were surprised at the relation we found between input and output volatilities. The input volatilities are the local volatilities for the short rate at all horizons. The output volatilities are the current yield volatilities for zero-coupon bonds at all maturities.

Imagine that we hold the local short-rate volatilities fixed out to a certain time, but raise the local volatilities after that time. We hold all other inputs fixed. For our lognormal model, raising the future input volatilities will, if anything, *lower* the output yield volatilities.

One way to raise the output volatilities, then, is to lower the future input volatilities. Another way is to reduce the amount of mean reversion. To arrive at very high output volatilities, we can even turn to negative mean reversion.

When all the inputs are constant in a lognormal model, the volatility curve will decline. The higher the local short-rate volatility, and the greater the mean reversion, the faster it will decline. A declining volatility curve is a persistent feature of the world. We can model this feature in a lognormal model without using the time-dependence of our inputs.

BUILDING A TREE

Black, Derman, and Toy show how to build a binomial tree for some lognormal models.[7] They use the location and spacing of the nodes for each future time to vary the inputs. They are able to match two of the outputs (yield curve and volatility curve), but not the third (cap curve).

---

resulting outputs, including option prices. Ho and Lee, "Term Structure Movements," on the other hand, believe their outputs are reasonable but do not claim that their inputs are reasonable. In fact, their inputs are quite unreasonable, as shown by P. H. Dybvig, "Bond and Bond Option Pricing Based on the Current Term Structure" (Working paper, February 1989).

6 J. C. Cox, S. A. Ross, and M. Rubinstein, "Option Pricing: A Simplified Approach," *Journal of Financial Economics*, September 1979.

7 Black, Derman , and Toy, "A One-Factor Model."

With their models, choosing a yield curve and volatility curve implies choosing a cap curve. They cannot vary the target rate, local volatility, and mean reversion separately.

Hull and White solve this problem by using a trinomial tree instead of a binomial tree.[8] From each node of a trinomial tree, you can move to one of three adjacent nodes one period later. What those three nodes are depends on the problem at hand. So do the probabilities associated with the three nodes.

We solve the problem by varying the spacing in the tree. This gives us another degree of freedom, so we can vary all three inputs within a simple binary tree. We can continue to assume that the probabilities of up and down moves are identical and both equal to 0.5. This helps make our use of the tree efficient. We preserve the topology of the simple binary-tree method.

When mean reversion is positive, this method has a problem of its own:

The spacing declines over time. For a reasonable number of nodes, the time separation of the early branches can be so large that we don't have the detail we want for applications such as valuing short-term options on long-term bonds.

We may thus need to prune the tree as we build it. We build it out to a certain point and then chop off half the nodes. When we are working back in the tree, we interpolate and extrapolate when we come to a place where the number of nodes doubles.

Possible Outputs

We can't use our process to match any output curves we might write down. For example, we can't match a yield curve that implies negative forward rates, or a discontinuous volatility curve.

We thus need to use smooth output curves. If we see bumpy curves in the world, we may be seeing swap or arbitrage opportunities, or we may be seeing data errors. In either case, we need to smooth if we hope to match successfully.

A "normal" model that allows negative interest rates may be easier to match. But we prefer our lognormal models, because curves we can match only with a "normal" model present profit opportunities.

---

8 Hull and White, "New Ways with the Yield Curve," and J. Hull and A. White, "One Factor Interest-Rate Models and the Valuation of Interest-Rate Derivative Securities" (Working paper, June 1990).

With Known Inputs

Suppose we know the functions $\mu(t)$, $\theta(t)$, and $\sigma(t)$ (the target rate, mean reversion, and local volatility). How can we build a tree to fit these functions?

Given the values of log r, the tree will be rectilinear. For a given time, it will have equal spacing, though the time spacing will vary. The spacing for a given time will fit local volatility. The drift of the points from one time to the next will fit the target rate. And the time spacing will fit mean reversion.

Write τ_n for $t_{n+1} - t_n$, φ_n for $\varphi(t_n)$, and σ_n for $\sigma(t_n)$. Then the formula for mean reversion is:

$$\varphi_n = \frac{1}{\tau_n}\left(1 - \frac{\sigma_n \sqrt{\tau_n}}{\sigma_{n-1}\sqrt{\tau_{n-1}}}\right) \tag{3}$$

Solving this formula for τ_n, we have:

$$\tau_n = \tau_{n-1} \frac{4\left(\dfrac{\sigma_{n-1}}{\sigma_n}\right)^2}{\left(1 + \sqrt{1 + 4\varphi_n \left(\dfrac{\sigma_{n-1}}{\sigma_n}\right)^2 \tau_{n-1}}\right)^2} \tag{4}$$

We can choose τ_0 as we wish. The smaller it is, the finer the tree and the more accurate the answers. We have σ_0 from $\sigma(0)$, σ_1 from $\sigma(t_0)$, and φ_1 from $\varphi(t_0)$. We can use equation (4) to find τ_1 and then repeat. We will

EXHIBIT 11–1
Time Spacing

n/N	t_n
0	0.0
1/5	4.1
2/5	6.3
3/5	7.9
4/5	9.0
1	10.0

gradually build up the full tree. At each time, we will use $\mu(t)$ to help locate the first point.

Suppose, for example, that mean reversion is constant at 0.1, that local volatility is a constant annual 0.20, and that we divide a 10-year period into $N = 160$ subperiods. Exhibit 11–1 gives the resulting time spacing.

Recall that t_n is years until time interval n. Note how the spacing declines over time with positive mean reversion. The level of mean reversion in the table is high (0.1) to exaggerate its effect on time spacing.

With Known Outputs

Suppose we want to choose the inputs [$\mu(t)$, $\varphi(t)$, and $\sigma(t)$] to match known outputs (yield curve, volatility curve, and cap curve). How can we do it?

We divide time into segments and each segment into many time intervals. We choose μ, φ, and σ to match the outputs at the end of the first segment. Then we choose μ, φ, and σ from the start to the end of the second segment to match the output at the end of the second segment, and so on.

We might call the resulting inputs "implied target rate," "implied mean reversion," and "implied local volatility." We do not say that the short rate follows a process with these features. We do say that securities behave *as if* we lived in a one-factor world and the short rate followed this process.

After a time, we can estimate the model again and get a new process. The implied process changes each time security prices and volatilities change.

We go through similar steps when we figure implied volatility: When the option price changes, the implied volatility changes. When we value the option, we are assuming that its volatility is known and constant. But a minute later, we start using a new volatility. Similarly, we can value fixed-income securities by assuming we know the one-factor short-rate process. A minute later, we start using a new process that is not consistent with the old one.

Another approach is to search for an interest rate process general enough that we can assume it is true and unchanging. It will have many variables and constants. We estimate the constants and hope that when we repeat the estimation, the variables change, but not the constants. While we may reach this goal, we don't know enough to use this approach today. For now, we must continue to reestimate simple models.

Auto-Correlation

Because the distribution of short rates at any horizon is lognormal, we need only a mean and a variance to describe it. Yet we need a target rate, mean reversion, and local volatility to describe the short-rate process in our model. For a given distribution of short rates for every horizon, our model has a whole family of possible process. How can this be?

It turns out that processes differ in the auto-correlations they imply for future short rates. When mean reversion is strong, a rise in the short rate above the target will probably be largely reversed before long. When it is weak, we won't see this.

If we have a narrow distribution of possible short rates in the future, we can infer that either mean reversion is strong or local volatility is low between now and then.

EXAMPLES

To see the relation between inputs and outputs, consider what happens when we keep all the inputs [target rate $\mu(t)$, mean reversion $\varphi(t)$, and local volatility $\sigma(t)$] constant.

Exhibit 11–2 shows the yield curve for three cases. In each curve, mean reversion is constant at 0.02, local volatility is constant at 12 percent, and the current short rate is 10 percent.

For the middle curve, the target rate is the same as the current rate. Note that the curve rises slightly up to about seven years and then falls off. This is a typical pattern when the target rate is constant and equal to the current rate. Note that the curvature eventually reverses from concave down to concave up. This is typical too.

The top curve shows what happens when the current rate is 10 percent and the target rate 15 percent. The bottom curve shows a current rate of 10 percent and a target rate of 5 percent. Even when the target rate is 15 percent, the yield curve never approaches 15 percent. For the case we show, it never goes above 11 percent. We don't know how to create a model that shows a consistently rising yield curve with reasonable assumptions—even by adding features that our model doesn't have.

Exhibit 11–3 shows the volatility curve for three cases. In each case, the current rate is 10 percent, the target rate is constant at 10 percent, and mean

EXHIBIT 11–2
Zero-Coupon Yield (Initial Rate = 10%; Rate Volatility = 12%; Mean Reversion = 0.02)

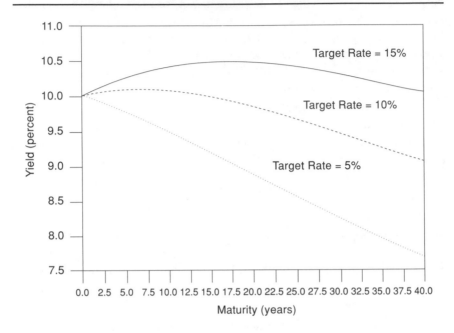

reversion is constant at 0.02. The three curves show (from the top down) constant local volatilities of 16, 12, and 8 percent.

The volatility curve starts at the local volatility and declines. The higher the volatility, the faster it declines. This is also a typical pattern in real-world volatility curves: Yield volatilities for shorter-term bonds tend to be higher than yield volatilities for longer-term bonds.

Exhibit 11–4 shows that mean reversion affects the slope of the volatility curve. The higher the mean reversion, the more negative the slope. But the curve slopes down even when mean reversion is zero. Actually, the slope of the curve at zero maturity is proportional to the negative of the mean reversion.

Comparing Exhibits 11–3 and 11–4, we see that we can match both the short end and the long end of the volatility curve even with constant inputs. We choose local volatility to match the short end and mean reversion to match the long end.

EXHIBIT 11–3
Zero-Coupon Yield Volatility (Initial and Target Rates = 10%; Mean Reversion = 0.02)

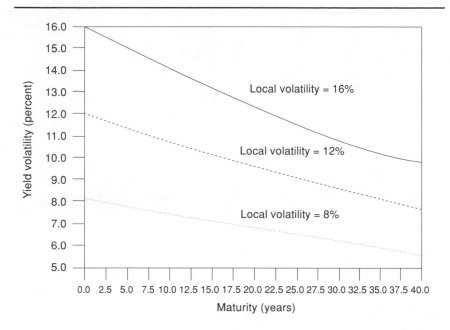

Exhibit 11–5 shows the differential cap curves for different levels of local volatility. For each curve, we hold all the inputs fixed and have the current rate equal to the target rate. Note that doubling the local volatility roughly doubles the cap values at every maturity.

For every level of local volatility, the differential cap curve rises sharply to a maximum and then falls sharply. The rise is due to a gain in the effect of volatility as we increase maturity. But two other factors overpower this—an increase in the discount factor and a fall in the forward rate, which is the cap's strike price.

Exhibits 11–6 and 11–7 analyze this. In Exhibit 11–6, we divide the differential cap value by the discount factor (the value of a zero-coupon bond with corresponding maturity and unit face value). In Exhibit 11–7, we divide by the strike price as well. The resulting curves rise smoothly with maturity, reflecting the impact of volatility.[9]

---

9 We thank Emanuel Derman and Francis Longstaff for their helpful comments.

EXHIBIT 11–4

Zero-Coupon Yield Volatility *(Initial and Target Rates = 10%; Rate Volatility = 12%)*

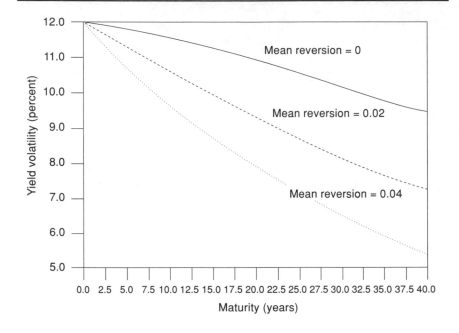

EXHIBIT 11–5
Differential At-the-Money Cap (Initial and Target Rates = 10%; Mean Reversion = 0.02)

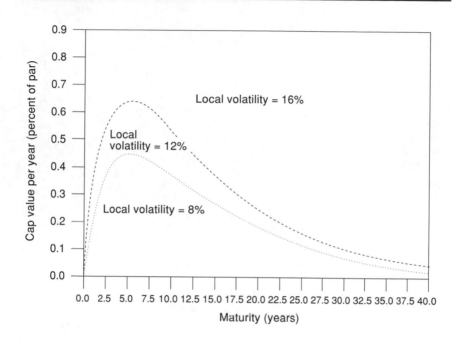

EXHIBIT 11–6
Differential At-the-Money Cap Divided by Discount
(Initial and Target Rates = 10%; Mean Reversion = 0.02)

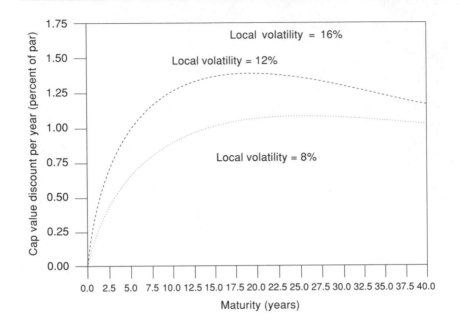

EXHIBIT 11–7

Differential At-the-Money Cap Divided by Discount and Strike
(Initial and Target Rates = 10%; Mean Reversion = 0.02)

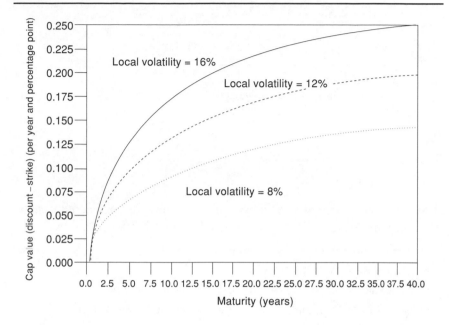

Chapter Twelve

Range Floaters[*]

Satyajit Das
Financial Services & Risk Management

The market environment in a number of currencies has spawned a variety of product innovations. This environment has been characterized by:

- Low nominal interest rate levels.
- Positive and often steep yield curves.
- Significant volatility in the interest rate term structure.
- A number of financial variables that appear to be locked in particular trading ranges.

Against this background, a number of investors, primarily money market portfolio managers, have experienced unprecedented pressures on their return levels. This historically low level of portfolio returns has prompted the demand for a number of yield-enhancing products designed to allow these portfolio managers to capture higher returns in this particular market environment. Products of this type include reverse or inverse floating rate notes (FRNs); collared, floored, or capped FRNs; deleveraged FRNs, or step-up recovery FRNs (SURFs). The driving force behind these product innovations has been the willingness of investors to embed a derivative (a forward or an option) element into a debt security in order to enhance yield on their investments.

Over the last year, a popular product called the range FRN has emerged in the marketplace. This chapter examines the range FRN, which is also

---

* Copyright © Satyajit Das, 1995.

known as a corridor or a fairway note, in terms of its concept, pricing, and hedging considerations. Product variations are also briefly discussed.

CONCEPT

Description

A range FRN basically embodies the following concepts:

1. It is a floating rate security that pays a return relative to the normal money market index (e.g., US$ LIBOR—London interbank-offered rate).
2. The range FRN typically pays an above-market or richer coupon than a conventional FRN.
3. The coupon payment on the FRN is conditional on a specific financial market variable fixing within a set range at specified points in time.

The second and third concepts presented above require additional explanation. Traditionally, interest rates have been the only financial market variable to be utilized in the range FRNs (see the section in this chapter on product variations). Under this arrangement, the range FRNs would only pay above-market coupons, relative to LIBOR, each day the LIBOR fixes within a set range. Although the timing and the denomination of the range may vary between transactions, the following is true for almost all transactions.

- The LIBOR range is typically set at the outset of the issue, although there are variations on this.
- The actual date on which LIBOR fixes must be within a set range that varies according to the following two general formulas:

Periodic set. Where the relevant financial market variable, say LIBOR, must set within the specified range at the start of each reset period. This must coincide with the interest period on the FRN, which may be three or six months.

Daily set. Where the financial market variable fixes are on a daily basis. On each day that the financial market variable sets outside the range, the coupon on the range FRN is 0 percent per annum. In contrast, when the financial market variable sets within the range on any relevant day, the range FRN pays the normal above market coupon relative to LIBOR.

EXHIBIT 12–1
Example of a Range FRN

Issuer	AA or AAA borrower
Amount	U.S. $100 million
Term	2 years
Issue price	$100
Redemption price	$100
Coupon	3-month US$ LIBOR + [percent p.a. accruing daily]
Coupon payments	Coupons are payable only if US$ LIBOR falls within the following range on the relevant business day.

Period	Maximum Rate (% p.a.)	Minimum Rate (% p.a.)
0–6 months	4.00	3.00
6–12 months	4.75	3.00
12–18 months	5.50	3.00
18–24 months	6.00	3.00

The terms of a typical transaction are set out in Exhibit 12–1.

Any counterparty wishing to gain the cash flow and return profile of a range FRN without necessarily purchasing the underlying security can do so using an *accrual swap*. Under this structure, a swap trader would pay the counterparty a floating rate (say, LIBOR) plus a margin in return for a fixed or floating rate when the nominated financial market variable sets within a specified range. This would enable an existing counterparty to swap either a fixed or floating rate asset into a range FRN structure. Alternatively, a liability manager could structure a swap where his or her LIBOR receipts under a fixed-floating interest rate swap would have a payoff profile matching that of a range FRN. This in effect would lower the fixed cost of paying under an interest rate swap that seeks to manage the cost of the organization's debt portfolio.

Reverse Engineering

By reverse engineering the transaction, the components of a range FRN can be easily discerned to be (1) a conventional FRN and (2) a sold digital option on the relevant financial market variable (in the example, US$ LIBOR rates). In effect, the investor sells a series of periodic or daily digital options to obtain an above-market coupon that effectively equates to the premiums captured from the sale. The loss of coupon on days when the relevant financial market variable is outside the nominated range represents a fixed or digitized payout, which is owed by the investor to the purchaser of the digital option.

Issuer and Investor

Objectives. The objectives of both issuers and investors are relatively clear. The issuer will typically seek to be insulated, usually through the arranger or another derivatives dealer, from the exposure under the digital option. This will require the issuer to sell the digital option and capture a premium from the sale. The proceeds received from the sale will bring the issuer's borrowing cost below its targeted level. The insulation of the issuer from the derivative elements in the security structure ensures its appeal to arbitrage funders.

From the perspective of the investor, the major attraction of a range FRN is its higher coupon, which is designed to increase portfolio earnings using the premium captured from the sale of the digital options. The economic logic behind the investment in a range FRN stems from the assumption that rates will continue to move in a relatively narrow range— biologists refer to this as homeostasis, a state in which organisms regulate their activities so that their temperatures do not fluctuate wildly.[1] Investors derive their enhanced return by creating digital options which reflect this underlying economic view.

The second economic reason for the investment is that the value in a digital option is derived from the pattern of forward rates implied from the yield curve. If the investor believes that the current implied forward rates (also called market expectations) are likely to be higher than the short-term rates that will be realized in the future (also called realized rates), the value transferred as a result of the sale of the digital option will be greater than that realized by the option. Under this approach, investors who believe that market expectations are higher than the realized rates can indeed structure range FRNs to capture the spread arising from a difference in views.

---

1 "Fashion and Homeostasis," *IFR Swaps Weekly,* no. 58 (March 2, 1994).

PRICING AND HEDGING

Approach

The pricing and hedging of a range FRN revolves around the decomposition of the structure into its components. The pricing process, for example, requires the following two-stage approach:

1. The conversion of the FRN component into a fixed rate instrument either by swapping the floating rate payments for fixed payments or, alternatively, by utilizing FRAs/futures to convert the future payments to fixed payments.
2. The valuation of the digital option itself.

The conversion of a floating rate payment into a fixed rate dollar equivalent is needed to create a net uniform series (NUS) of cash flows (i.e., the dollar amount of the FRN payments as implied by the current yield curve are calculated). This is necessary because only through the NUS process can we arrive at the exact payout of a digital option.

In a number of other issues, the corridor structure also entails a fixed rate bond, in which the payments are known in dollar amounts, thus eliminating the need for this step in the pricing.

Pricing Digital Options

The pricing of a digital option (more commonly known as a binary or a bet option) is more complex because the premium is predicated on:

- The tendency of the payoff of the digital option to be switched completely one way or the other, depending on the satisfaction of that condition by the underlying asset price.
- The payoff of the option, provided it is in the money, is a constant amount independent of how much the option is in the money. This contrasts with the in-the-money payoff profile of a normal option, which is a linear function of the in-the-moneyness of the option.[2]
- The value of the option which is derived from the probability that the option will expire in the money.

---

2 The interested reader is referred to K. Ravindran, *Exotic Options* (1995), for an in-depth discussion of digital options.

It is possible to utilize a variation of the Black-Scholes formula to value a digital option, assuming that:

- The return on the underlying asset follows a log normal random walk.
- Arbitrage arguments allow a risk-neutral valuation approach whereby the expected payoff of the option at expiration is discounted by the riskless interest rate, and the underlying asset price is expected to appreciate at the same riskless rate, less the payouts.

Along with the other set of assumptions used to derive the classic Black-Scholes formula, Rubinstein and Reiner state the Black-Scholes formula for a standard option to be:

$$C = \varphi S_0 d^{-t} N(\varphi x) - \varphi K r^{-t} N(\varphi x - \varphi \sigma \sqrt{t})$$

where

$$x = \frac{\ln\left(\dfrac{S_0 d^{-t}}{K r^{-t}}\right)}{\sigma\sqrt{t}} + \frac{\sigma\sqrt{t}}{2}$$

S_0 = present value of the underlying asset
K = strike price
r = 1 plus rate of interest
d = 1 plus payout rate of the underlying asset
t = time to option expiration
σ = volatility of the underlying asset
$N(\ )$ = standard normal distribution function
φ = the binary variable (+1 for a call; −1 for a put).

Given that the value of a standard European option depends only on the price of the underlying asset at expiration, it is possible to let r, d, and σ be known functions of time, although Rubinstein and Reiner assumed these variables to be constants in derivation. Under their framework, the approach to valuing the digital options of the type embedded in a range FRN would be based on the additional assumption that all the digital options are independent of each other. This means that each digital call (put) would pay nothing if the underlying asset price finishes below (above) the strike price and a predetermined constant amount, B, if the underlying asset price finishes above (below) the strike price. Mathematically, this can be stated as:

Call: O if $S* \leq K$ or B if $S* > K$

Put: O if $S* \geq K$ or B if $S* < K$

where

$S*$ = underlying asset price at maturity of the option.

This type of option, referred to as a cash-or-nothing call/put option, is valued by decomposing the Black-Scholes formula into two terms:

1. The unprotected present value of the underlying asset price conditional upon exercising the option ($S_0 d^{-t} N(\varphi x)$).
2. The present value of the strike price (Kr^{-t}) times the risk neutral probability of exercising the option ($N(\varphi x - \sigma \sqrt{t})$).

If the predetermined payoff of the cash-or-nothing call (B) were equal to the strike price (K), then a cash-or-nothing call would be like a standard written call except that, although the writer receives the strike price, he or she is obligated to deliver a cash value of $2K$. Such a call would then be worth $(2K-K)r^{-t}N(x - \sigma\sqrt{t}) = Kr^{-t}N(x - \sigma\sqrt{t})$ to the writer. When $B \neq K$, the value of a cash-or-nothing call (put) would be $Br^{-t}N(\varphi x - \varphi\sigma\sqrt{t})$ with $\varphi = 1$ ($\varphi = -1$).

Pricing Dynamics

The dynamics of a digital option premium depends on the interaction of the following variables:

1. The digitized payout, which is a function of the coupon on the debt security (as the payout cannot be larger than this amount).
2. The premium of the digital option, which is a function of:
   - The nominated range.
   - The volatility of the underlying asset (in the example, interest rates).
   - The pattern of the forward asset prices (in the case of interest rates, the shape of the forward yield curve as implied by the current interest rate term structure). This reflects the option value insofar as the options may be further in or out of the money.

PRODUCT VARIATIONS

Range FRNs originally emerged in the second half of 1993 with the majority of the transactions being undertaken in U.S. dollars. In early 1994, with U.S. short-term interest rates moving up, the formula of a range FRN that was traditionally linked to US$ LIBOR rates became increasingly unattractive. As such, the need for higher yielding returns continued to be satisfied by product innovations on the floating rate investments. These innovations included adjustments to the traditional range FRN structure as well as extensions to the basic concept, incorporating cross-market linkages.

The first variation reflected investors' concern that they were significantly exposed under the range FRN pricing formula to LIBOR resets on specific days. This concern led to the evolution of the daily accrual formula with the LIBOR fixes being taken daily to allow the investors to reduce their exposure to specific fixing dates. However, the fixing-date adjustment did not address the difficulties of the investors of this type of instrument in an increasing interest rate environment. As the market for U.S. dollar interest rates experienced greater volatility, additional variations included:

- Range FRN structures linked to term interest rates, typically 5- or 10-year CMTs.
- Constant spread range structures where the linkage to longer-term rates was motivated by the expectation that the yield curve would flatten with an interest rate increase and the view that volatility would be concentrated on the shorter end of the yield curve.

The *constant spread structure* embodied a changing range spread to provide additional protection for the investor in a higher volatility environment. This structure, also known as the *constant spread range index bonds* (CS-RIBS), was offered by J.P. Morgan and operated as follows:

The investor nominated a range of parameters:

- The reference rate, the range, the observation frequency (daily, weekly, monthly or quarterly).
- The form (the product was available as both a debt security and a swap).
- The coupon frequency—the reset frequency.
- The minimum coupon.

The return was determined by the frequency of the observed financial market variable (interest rate) falling within the nominated range. For example, if the target rate was the three-month LIBOR and every observation fell within the range, then the return was the three-month LIBOR plus 1.00 percent per annum. However, if only 90 percent of the observations fell within the range, the return is (90% × the base rate), or equivalently:

90% × (three-month LIBOR + 1.00% per annum)

The major feature of the constant spread range structure was that the target range was adjusted at the beginning of each interest period to a maximum set according to the nominated range. In effect, the target range floated together with the reference rate in contrast with a traditional range FRN where the target range for each period was preset at the commencement of the transaction. As such, the additional return generated from a constant spread range structure was lower than that due a traditional range FRN, reflecting lower values of the digital options or equivalently lower risk to the investor of this structure.

The constant spread range structures that were undertaken were typically relative to the three or six-month LIBOR and the two-year CMT, with a typical chosen range of 50 basis points above and 25 basis points below the reference rate. Although in certain transactions the constant spread option was applied to only part of a security's life, typical transactions tended to be for shorter maturities, particularly one to three years.

Increasingly, the range FRN concept has also been applied to cross-market variations. Two such variations include:

Quanto-range FRNs. These occur when the range FRN is hedged through a quanto option into a third currency. An example of this transaction was undertaken by Creditanstalt for the Austrian Postal Savings Bank. The transaction was based on the three-month Italian Lira interest rate range with the currency risk hedged through the quanto option into U.S. dollars. The one-year transaction paid a coupon of 4.5 percent in U.S. dollars and the nominated range was 7.5 percent to 9.0 percent for the first six months and 6.5 percent to 8.5 percent for the second six months.

Cross-market range FRN. This type of FRN may occur when the relevant range financial variable is a currency. A number of transactions have been undertaken for periods of one year where the coupon (usually LIBOR plus 1.00 percent per annum accruing daily) was only payable if the U.S. dollar/Japanese yen (US$/JPY) exchange rate fell within the nominated range on that particular date. This nominated range was based on the recent historical US$/JPY trading range of 100/101 – 108/115 JPY/US$. Although the underlying financial variable was a currency instead of an interest rate, the cross-currency based range FRN was similar in spirit to that of a standard range FRN.

Range FRNs and product variations utilizing the concept represent intriguing variations on credit-embedded securities that allow investors to capture values from specific expectations regarding the anticipated trading behavior of a nominated financial market variable.

REFERENCES

Ravindran, K. "Exotic Options: The Basic Building Blocks and Their Applications." *Handbook of Derivative Instruments,* 2nd ed. Chicago, IL: Irwin Professional Publishing, 1995.

Rubinstein, M., and E. Reiner. "Unscrambling The Binary Code." *Risk,* October 1991.

II

EQUITY DERIVATIVES

Chapter Thirteen

Stock Index Futures, Options, and Trading Strategies

Satish Swamy
Lincoln Investment Management

The S&P 500 Index is perhaps the most widely used benchmark in the investment business. More often than not, the performance of equity portfolio managers is judged by comparing the portfolio's returns to the index. Stock index futures and options on futures are effective trading and risk management tools used by a variety of market participants. Because these equity index products are able to replicate the price movement of an underlying stock portfolio, they hold great appeal for both hedgers and traders. Stock index futures and options are powerful and versatile instruments, whether the intention is to risk personal capital for investment reward or to insulate investment capital from risk. In 1982, the Chicago Mercantile Exchange (CME) introduced the S&P 500 stock index futures contract and in 1983 the same exchange established options on S&P 500 futures.

The Standard & Poor Corporation designed and maintains the index to be an accurate proxy for a diversified equity portfolio. The S&P 500 Index is based on the stock prices of 500 large capitalized companies. The market value of the 500 firms is equal to approximately 80 percent of the value of all stocks listed on the New York Stock Exchange. The S&P 500 is a capitalization-weighted index representing the market value of all outstanding common shares of the firms listed (share price times shares outstanding). This means that a change in the price of any one stock influences the index in proportion to the relative market value of that firm's outstanding shares.

Stock index derivatives afford unique advantages by allowing investors to:

1. Participate in broad market moves with one trading decision and without having to select individual issues. The additional advantage is having no uptick requirement for selling short ("uptick rule").

2. Protect the value of a portfolio during bear markets without incurring high transaction fees and without adding to downward selling pressure on individual issues.

3. Speculate on short-term market moves.

4. Benefit from a bull market move even before funds become available to purchase stocks.

This chapter will offer detailed explanations of the intricacies of trading stock index futures and options and trading strategies. It will also briefly discuss program trading and its ramifications on the market.

ESTABLISHING A TRADING ACCOUNT

A trading account must be established prior to buying or selling a futures contract. This entails depositing a performance bond, usually in the form of a cash deposit or some other acceptable form of collateral, with a broker. This performance bond serves as a good faith deposit, guaranteeing fulfillment of any financial obligations (i.e., the daily cash margin adjustments) that can arise from maintaining a futures position.

After initiating a buy or sell transaction, the executed price becomes the entry price. At the end of trading on that day, the contract value is marked to market. The marked-to-market (MTM) procedure is the adjustment to the account for daily profit or loss, based on the difference between the entry price and the settlement or closing price with the CME Clearing House standing between every buyer and seller, and acting as the third-party guarantor to each trade. This procedure is repeated every day until the position is liquidated, offset, or the contract expires. Daily profits that bring the account above the initial level can be withdrawn, but if losses cause the trading account to fall below a certain level, the balances will have to be brought back to the initial requirement.

STOCK INDEX FUTURES

The Fundamentals

The S&P 500 futures contract that trades on the CME has a multiplier of 500. A price move from 560 to 562.5 would represent a gain of $1,250 (2.5 × 500) to the long (buying) position and a loss of $1,250 to the short (selling) position. The minimum price change, or "tick" size, for the S&P 500 futures contract is .05 index points, valued at $25 per contract (.05 × 500). The S&P 500 futures contract expires quarterly (March, June, September, and December). No physical delivery takes place. Instead, the contracts are said to be cash settled, with a final debit or credit in the trading account that reflects the final settlement prices at expiration. The S&P 500 futures settlement price is the special opening quotation of the S&P 500 Index the morning following the last trading day. For the contract specifications and other details of the contract, see Appendix 13–A and 13–B.

Participants in the stock index futures market can be either long or short the market. When an investor goes long (buys) a contract, the expectation is that the market is likely to go higher, resulting in a profit when the contract is sold back prior to or before termination. Similarly, when one shorts (sells) a contract, the perception is that the market is likely to come down and a profit can be realized by buying back the contract at a price lower than the initial purchase.

Stock index futures can be used either as trading vehicles or hedging instruments. The practice of hedging is the use of futures with an existing or planned stock market position to offset the change in value of the position by the performance of the futures contracts. For example, a short S&P 500 futures position can protect a stock market investor currently holding a diversified portfolio of large-capitalization equities during market corrections or bear markets. At such times, the value of the stocks will fall, but the change in net worth will be offset by the gains generated by the short futures position.

STRATEGIES FOR SPECULATION WITH FUTURES

Case 1: The "long" and the "short" investor. Speculating with stock index futures contracts is very similar to speculating with any other futures contracts. In this trading strategy, the speculator is simply betting

EXHIBIT 13–1
"Long" Strategy

Trade Date	Trade
July 31	Buy 1 Dec S&P 500 futures contract at 570.00
Sept 15	Sell 1 Dec S&P 500 futures contract at 590.00
Total Profit (Loss) = (590.00 – 570.00) × 500 = $10,000.00	

on the direction of the market. The "long" (buy) investor is hoping for a price increase in the futures contracts as the market rallies and the "short" (sell) investor is expecting the price of the futures contracts to come down as the market falls.

Let's assume that on July 31, a long investor buys one December S&P 500 futures contract at 570.00 (see Exhibit 13–1). It should be pointed out that for every "long" investor who buys a contract, there is a "short" investor who happens to have an opposing view of the market and hence "sells" a contract. If, on September 15 the same December futures contract is trading at 590.00, then the long investor has made a profit of $10,000 ((590 – 570) × 500) and the short position has a loss for the same amount.

Case 2: A "spread" position. Sometimes, an investor bullish on the market expects long dated futures to move substantially compared with the short dated futures contracts. In this situation, assume that on July 31, 1995 an investor buys one March 96 contract at 572.85 and subsequently sells one September 1995 contract at 564.30 (see Exhibit 13–2). Assuming that his perception about the market is correct, suppose that on September 1, the March 96 has moved up to 586.92 and the September contract has moved up to 569.89.

To close the trade, the investor sells one March 96 and buys one September S&P 500 futures contract to make a profit as shown in Exhibit 13–2.

HEDGING AND RISK MANAGEMENT STRATEGIES

Hedging stock index futures applies directly to the management of equity portfolios. The usefulness of stock index futures in portfolio management stems from the fact that they directly represent a market portfolio. Before

EXHIBIT 13–2
"Spread" Strategy

Trade Date	Trade
July 31, 1995	Sell 1 Sept. S&P 500 futures contract at 564.30
	Buy 1 March 96 S&P 500 futures contract at 572.85
Sept. 1, 1995	Buy 1 Sept. S&P 500 futures contract at 569.89
	Sell 1 March 96 S&P 500 futures contract at 586.92

Profit for the Mar96 contract = (586.92 − 572.85) × 500 = $7,035
Loss for the Sep contract = (564.30 − 569.89) × 500 = ($2,795)
Total Profit = $7,035 − $2,795 = $4,240

stock index futures began trading, there was no comparable way of trading an instrument that provided price performance so closely tied to a broad market index. Further, stock index futures have great potential in portfolio management due to their low transaction costs. The following describe some of the hedging strategies that can be used.

Diversifiable vs. Market Risk

The stock price of an individual firm is influenced by events and factors unique to that firm: an unexpectedly poor or strong earnings report, a union walkout, and so forth. The desire of investors to minimize firm-specific risk was a prime factor in the development of mutual funds.

In a diversified portfolio, unexpected increases in the prices of some stocks are likely to offset unexpected decreases in the prices of others, with the portfolio value as a whole remaining fairly constant. Diversifiable risk declines rapidly as the number of issues in the portfolio increases, but it is never completely eliminated. Even though portfolio risk is inversely related to the number of issues in the portfolio, there is a limit to the risk-reduction potential of portfolio diversification.

Some events have an impact on the economic well-being of the entire market; for example, a change in U.S. monetary policy. This type of price variability is called market or systematic risk, and it is a major risk facing holders of diversified portfolios of stock.

Stock index futures and options contracts can adjust the impact of market risk on the portfolio. By holding an appropriate number of futures or option contracts, investors can insulate their portfolio value from market risk. Gains in the futures or options positions offset losses suffered by the stock portfolio. This approach to risk management is called "hedging." The practice of hedging simply integrates the use of futures or options with the preexisting or planned stock market investment to offset the change in value of the equity position with the performance of the futures or options positions.

Case 1: Stock portfolio—The long hedge. Suppose on July 31 an equity portfolio manager finds out that she will be getting $10 million to invest in the stock market on August 15. The portfolio manager's view on the market is bullish as she expects the market to go up substantially between July 31 and August 15. Instead of waiting to receive the $10 million, she decides to invest in S&P 500 futures contracts to participate in the market rally.

On July 31, the manager "buys to open" 36 (36 = 10,000,000 / (564.30 × 500)) Sep S&P 500 futures contracts at 564.30. On August 15, the market has moved up substantially and the September contract has moved up to 569.85. The manager "sells to close" 36 contracts and locks in a profit of $99,900 ((569.85 − 564.30) × 36 × 500).

Case 2: Stock portfolio—The short hedge. Consider a portfolio manager who is currently managing $100 million in equities. The portfolio beta is 1.21, implying that a 1 percent move in the market index would be expected to induce a change of 1.21 percent in the total value of the stock portfolio. Going forward, the manager is of the opinion that a market correction is imminent and he is expecting his stock portfolio to come down in value. One hedge possibility is that he liquidates the portfolio and invests the proceeds in a money market or some fixed-income instrument. However, the transaction costs associated with this kind of strategy are very high. Furthermore, if the manager is holding sizeable amounts of individual stocks, then he could drive down the stock price by liquidating. This would prevent the portfolio manager from liquidating the portfolio at prices currently quoted for individual stocks.

An obvious alternative to liquidating the portfolio is selling the S&P 500 stock index futures contract. By selling futures, the manager should be able to offset the effect of a bear market on the portfolio by generating gains in the futures market. One kind of strategy, though not correct, would be to sell an equivalent number of futures contract to hedge against market declines. If the futures contract stands at 565.00, the manager would need to sell 354 contracts (100,000,000 / (565 × 500)). However, the beta of the portfolio is 1.21 and the manager, to be completely hedged, would need to sell 429 (354 × 1.21) contracts.

If the market does fall by an amount equal to 4 percent, then the stock portfolio would have lost 4.84 percent (4 percent × 1.21). The stock portfolio would be reduced in value to $95,160,000 (a loss of 4.84 percent) and the futures would have been reduced to 542.4 (a loss of 4 percent). The closing positions then on the trade would be as follows:

Actual portfolio: loss of $4,840,000

Futures: gain of $4,847,700 ((565.00 − 542.4) × 429 × 500)

Net profit: $7,700.00

Caveat for Case 2. The above results depend on two hypothetical assumptions made about the markets. First, it is possible to achieve such results only if the movement of the stock portfolio during the hedge period exactly corresponds to the volatility implied by its beta. Second, the formula used to compute the number of contracts for the hedge uses the beta of the stock portfolio as measured against the index itself. This assumes that the futures contract moves along with the spot index. This assumption is violated by recent market experience because the futures contracts for all of the indexes are more volatile than the index themselves. This is reflected by the fact that the futures contracts generally have betas above 1.0 when they are measured relative to the stock index itself. The methodology of computing the number of contracts does not take this into account, since it implicitly assumes the index and the futures contracts to have the same price movements, which would imply equal betas.

OPTIONS ON STOCK INDEX FUTURES

The Fundamentals

Options on stock index futures add further variety to the broad market coverage offered by futures—limited risk. The buyer of a call or put option has the unlimited profit potential with the risk limited to the price (called the "option premium") paid for the option. The option seller, on the other hand, accepts potentially unlimited risk in return for the option premium at the time of the sale. For instance, an S&P 500 call option gives the buyer the right, but not the obligation, to buy one S&P 500 futures contract (at a specific price less the strike or exercise price). An S&P 500 put option gives the buyer the right, but not the obligation, to sell one S&P futures contract (at a specific price less the strike or exercise price). These rights can be exercised at the discretion of the option buyer at any time before expiration (if American style). Alternatively, the option itself can be resold (offset) on the exchange. To offset a call purchase, you would sell the same call (i.e., same expiration, same strike price); to offset a put purchase, you would sell the same put.

The key phrase for the option buyer is *right,* not obligation. The option writer or seller, on the other hand, is obligated to perform if the buyer chooses to exercise the option. When a holder exercises, a writer of the same option is randomly selected from all those who currently hold open short option positions. That assigned writer receives a futures position (short for a call, long for a put) at the same strike price. The seller accepts the unlimited risk of being assigned an adverse futures position if and when the buyer exercises. At expiration, open option positions may be automatically exercised and assigned if the options are in the money or if they have intrinsic value. The availability of options with differing expiration dates and strike prices provides option buyers and sellers alike with a wide range of trading and hedging position alternatives. For example, options may be used independently, in conjunction with cash market portfolios, or in combination with other futures and options positions.

OPTIONS STRATEGIES

Options are attractive because many of their uses involve known and limited risk. But another attraction is flexibility: They can be employed in expectations of rising or falling markets, of stable or volatile markets. The examples below show some ways to use S&P 500 options. However, all of the examples ignore transaction costs and taxes and the impact of these factors could be significant.

Buying Call Options

Profiting from a rising market. Consider that on July 31, 1995, the S&P 500 closed at 560.00. If a stock market advance is perceived, we can buy the Sep 560 call at a premium of 8.80 or $4,400. The profit potential on the purchase of the call option is limited only by the increase in the underlying S&P futures contract. The higher the S&P futures contract moves, the more profit realized when the call is sold.

Assume that the price of the futures contract declines and the option moves out of the money. An investor still can recapture a part of the premium by reselling the option sometime before its expiration for any value it may retain. However, in no circumstances does the loss exceed $4,400 (the "premium" paid for the option). Exhibits 13–3a and 13–3b show the profit profile for an array of possible futures prices at expiration. Option profit or loss is calculated by subtracting the premium of the option from the value of the option at expiration. The value of the call at expiration, if any, is the amount by which the futures prices exceeds the exercise price of the option—560.00.

The example assumes the purchase of an at the money option with less than two months to expiration. But there are several call options available for purchase at any time: some with a very short time to expiration and some with longer periods of time; some with exercise prices approximately equal to or below the underlying futures price and some with exercise prices above the underlying futures price. How is the right call option selected?

As noted, an option with a longer time until expiration generally costs more than one with a shorter time until expiration. More time until expiration means more time to be correct in forecasting market direction and, hence, more time for the option to become profitable. The pricing of options is such that the time gained through the purchase of a longer-term option is proportionately less costly than that of a shorter-term option.

So, decide whether to purchase an in- or at-the-money option as opposed to an out-of-the-money option. For the same move in the futures price, the dollar amount of profit earned on, for example, an at-the-money option is greater than that from an out-of-the-money option. But an out-of-the-money option costs less, so any loss is less and, should the market move substantially, the rate of return on the out-of-the-money option will be greater than that on an in- or at-the-money option.

Consider the same situation: with the September S&P 500 futures price at 560.00, buy an at-the-money Sep S&P 500 560 call at 8.80 (4,400) or an out-of-the-money Sep S&P 570 call at 4.20 ($2,100). If the closing price for the S&P 500 Index on the option's expiration date is below 560.00, the entire premium is lost in either case. The loss is less for the out-of-the-money call than for the at-the-money call. However, in a rising stock market climate reflected in rising futures prices, the at-the-money call reaches the break-even point sooner and enjoys a greater dollar profit (but not rate of return) as the futures price increases.

EXHIBIT 13-3a
Long Call: Profit Profile at Expiration

Profit or Loss at Expiration

Sep Futures Price	Profit (or Loss)
560 or below	8.80-point (4,400) loss
565	3.80-point (1,900) loss
568.8	breakeven
570	1.20-point $600 profit
580	11.20-point $5,600 profit
590	21.2-point $10,600 profit

EXHIBIT 13–3b
Profit/Loss Profile and S&P 500 Futures Prices

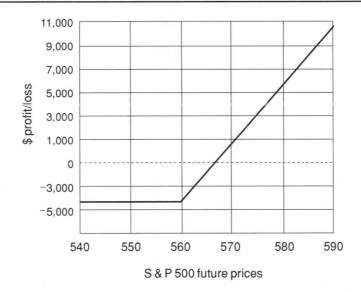

S & P 500 future prices

Exhibit 13–4 locates the break-even points of the two options if held to expiration. (The last column shows the profit/loss for the purchase of two 570 calls, which cost about the same as one 560 call. The out-of-the-money calls provide greater leverage, but the futures have to move further before

EXHIBIT 13–4

Profit or Loss Resulting from Purchase of Different Call Options

Closing Price of the S&P 500 Index at Expiration	Sep 560 Call	Sep 570 Call	Two Sep 570 Calls
560 or below	$4,400 loss	$2,100 loss	$4,200 loss
565	$1,900 loss	$2,100 loss	$4,200 loss
568.8	breakeven	$2,100 loss	$4,200 loss
570	$600 profit	$2,100 loss	$4,200 loss
574.2	$2,700 profit	breakeven	breakeven
580	$5,600 profit	$2,900 profit	$5,800 profit
590	$10,600 profit	$7,900 profit	$15,800 profit

they become profitable.) It is evident that the decision concerning which strike price to use has much to do with the investor's opinion about the magnitude of the expected stock market advance.

Using call options with a short S&P futures position. Call options can be purchased either to lock in the profit or limit the loss on a short futures position. Suppose a September S&P 500 futures contract is sold in anticipation of a drop in the market. By mid-August, the futures indeed has fallen from 565 to 550, and shows a 15-point or $7,500 (15 × 500) profit. Further decline after an upward price correction is expected. To realize profit, instead of buying in the short futures, consider buying a Sep 550 call for 4.20 ($2,100).

Original position: short Sep S&P 500 futures at 565

Current September futures price: 550

Transaction: buy a Sep 550 call for 4.20 ($2,100)

The investor is assured a profit of at least $5,400 at expiration and still can benefit from a further downward price movement. The call serves as insurance against an upside move. In a similar fashion, a long call can be used to limit the loss on a newly placed short futures position. For either a new or already profitable short futures position with the call having the same expiration as the futures, the minimum profit (or the maximum loss) is defined as: short futures entry price less call strike price less call premium.

Buying Put Options

Profiting from a falling market. In May, the investor believes the stock market will fall. With the June S&P 500 futures price at 562.00, he purchases a Jun S&P 560.00 put at a premium of 3.60 or $1,800, and in two weeks the same contract declines to 554. Reflecting a decrease in the underlying futures price, the put option increases to $8.00, or $4,000. He may sell the put option and realize a profit of $2,200 (4,000 – 1,800). Or he may hold the put option, hoping for an even greater increase in premium, while recognizing that the time value of the option diminishes as the time to expiration approaches.

Using put options with a long S&P 500 futures position. Buying put options in conjunction with a long futures position can set limits to the potential loss or lock in profits from an already profitable futures position. The purchase of the put guarantees, in effect, a selling price for the long S&P 500 futures position. The long put position provides insurance against a drop in the stock market and lower S&P futures price, thereby placing limits on the loss that might occur from the long futures position alone. The decision concerning which put option to buy depends on investor risk tolerance.

Writing Call and Put Options

Profiting from a stable or declining market. The writer (or seller) of an S&P call option receives payment (the premium) from the buyer of the option in return for the obligation of taking a short position in the futures contract at the exercise price if the option is exercised. The call writer's risk is unlimited while that of the call buyer is limited; and the call writer's profits are limited while those of the call buyer are unlimited. Note that an option writer can buy in the contract at any time before expiration or assignment to liquidate the obligation. Be sure to understand and have the ability to bear the risk involved in writing uncovered call options.

The principal reason to write call options is to earn the premium. In periods of stable or declining markets, call writing can mean an attractive cash flow from a relatively small capital investment. It is hoped that, at expiration, the settlement price of the futures contract is at or below the exercise price of the option. The option then expires worthless and the entire premium can be kept.

Suppose a decline in the stock market is expected and an investor sells an S&P Jun 565 call for 5.15, or $2,575. At expiration in June, the S&P 500 Index is quoted at 550. The S&P Jun 565 call expires worthless; he retains the entire premium of $2,575.

On the other hand, if he holds the short call option position and the futures price at expiration is above the exercise price, he forfeits the in-the-money amount. This results in the loss of at least a portion of the premium, possibly more. The writer of a call option should keep in mind that he or she may be assigned at any time during the life of the option. Exercise becomes more likely if an option has a large intrinsic value and little time value. If a call has gone deeply in the money and if the writer does not wish to take a futures position, he or she should consider buying back the call.

Profiting from a stable or rising market. The primary motivation for writing put options is, again, to earn the premium. Like the call writer, the put writer is subject to substantial risk in return for earning the premium.

The writer of an S&P put option is obligated to take a long S&P 500 futures position if he or she is assigned for exercise. The put writer hopes that the futures price is at or above the put's exercise price at expiration. The put option then expires worthless, and the writer keeps the entire premium received for the sale of the put option.

Again, a put writer should understand that the option may be exercised by the put holder at any time during the life of the option. Monitor in-the-money puts carefully so as not to take a long futures position.

Income and limited protection. Writing a call option against a long futures position is a strategy that can produce an attractive return over the margin required if the stock market stabilizes or rises only slowly. The long futures protects the short call in a rising market to assure that the writer keeps the premium received (less intrinsic value if the call is sold in the money). If an out-of-the-money call is sold and the futures price rises, but not through the strike, the premium plus the futures gain both are profit at expiration.

The premium also gives limited protection against a drop in the futures price. The risk is that the futures price might decline by more than the premium received, and the investor may experience a net loss. Similarly, a strategy of writing a put against a short S&P 500 futures position can suit the expectation of a stable or slowly declining market. The risk in the combination of short S&P put, short S&P futures is that the futures price may rise by an amount greater than the premium received, causing a loss equal to that of having a short futures position less the premium.

PROGRAM TRADING

Large-sized institutional investors use computers to rapidly execute stock trades. When an arbitrage opportunity is imminent, a large-sized money manager can execute a computer order to buy each and every stock represented in the S&P 500. Simultaneously, the institution would sell the S&P 500 futures contract. The use of computers to execute large and complicated stock market orders is called *program trading*. While computers are used for other kinds of stock market transactions, index arbitrage is the main application of program trading. The words *program trading* and *index arbitrage* are often used interchangeably.

Whenever the actual futures price falls outside the no-arbitrage band, there is an opportunity for profit. This is why parity relationships are so important. Far from being theoretical academic constructs, they are, in fact, a guide to trading rules that can generate large profits. Index arbitrage is an investment strategy that exploits divergences between the actual futures price and its theoretically correct parity value.

The index arbitrage strategy is quite simple. If the futures price is too high, short the futures contract and buy the stocks in the index. If it is too low, go long in futures and short the stocks. You can perfectly hedge your position and should earn arbitrage profits equal to the mispricing of the contract. To accomplish this, arbitrageurs need to trade an entire portfolio of stocks quickly and simultaneously if they hope to exploit disparities between the futures price and its corresponding index. For this they need a coordinated trading program; hence, the term program trading, which actually refers to coordinated purchases or sales of entire portfolios of stocks. The response has been the designated order turnaround (DOT) system, which enables traders to send coordinated buy or sell programs to the floor of the exchange via computer.

Every year, there are four maturing S&P 500 futures contracts. On these four Fridays, which occur simultaneously with the expiration of S&P index options and options on some individual stocks, the market has tended to exhibit above average volatility. These dates have been dubbed the *Triple Witching Hour* because of the volatility associated with the expirations in the three types of contracts, although it appears that only the futures contract expiration actually affects the market. The *Double Witching Hour* refers to the simultaneous expiration of the S&P 500 stock index option and the Major Market Index (discussed in the next section) futures and options contracts.

Expiration day volatility can be explained by program trading to exploit arbitrage opportunities. Suppose that some time before a stock index futures contract matures, the futures price is little above its parity value. Arbitrageurs will attempt to lock in superior profits by buying the stocks in the index (the program trading buy order) and taking an offsetting short futures position. If and when the pricing disparity reverses, the position can be unwound at a profit. Alternatively, arbitrageurs can wait until contract maturity day and realize a profit by simultaneously closing out the offsetting stock futures position. By waiting until contract maturity, arbitrageurs can be assured that the futures price and stock index price will be aligned—they rely on the convergence property.

Obviously, when many program traders follow such a strategy at contract expiration, a wave of program selling passes over the market and, as a result, stock prices go down. This is the expiration day effect. If execution of the arbitrage strategy calls for an initial sale (or short sale) of stocks, unwinding on expiration day requires repurchase of stocks, with the opposite effect, and prices will increase.

The success of these arbitrage positions and associated program trades depends on only two things: the relative levels of spot and futures prices and synchronized trading in the two markets. Because arbitraguers exploit disparities in futures and spot prices, absolute price levels are unimportant. This means that large buy or sell programs can hit the floor even if stock prices are at "fair" levels, that is, at levels consistent with fundamental information. The markets in individual stocks may not be sufficiently deep to absorb the arbitrage-based program trades without significant price movements despite the fact that those trades are not informationally motivated.

OTHER EQUITY INDEX PRODUCTS AT THE CME

Currently, the CME offers futures and options on futures on U.S. and non-U.S. equities:

- S&P MidCap 400 Index

- Major Market Index (MMI)
- Russell 2000 Index
- Nikkei 225 Stock Average
- FT-SE 100 Share Index

The following offers a brief description of these indexes:

The S&P MidCap 400. Like the S&P 500, the S&P MidCap 400 Index is capitalization weighted. However, while the S&P 500 is a large-capitalization index, the S&P MidCap 400 tracks the market performance of medium-capitalization stocks. The index comprises 400 U.S. companies, including such familiar names as Dole Foods, Fruit-of-the-Loom, and Storage Technology. Again, like the S&P 500 Index, the MidCap 400 is not static. Standard & Poor's can add and delete stocks as conditions change, but under no circumstances will a given stock be included in both the S&P 500 and the S&P MidCap 400 indexes.

The Russell 2000. The Russell 2000 index, based on 2,000 stocks, is the most widely recognized small-capitalization U.S. benchmark. The S&P 500, the S&P MidCap 400, and the Russell 2000 represent close to 92 percent of total U.S. equity market capitalization.

Like the S&P 500 and S&P MidCap 400, the Russell 2000 is capitalization weighted. It is rebalanced every June 30 to reflect changes in the marketplace. The number of firms represented may vary during the year because securities that are deleted from the index because of a merger, acquisition, or bankruptcy are replaced only when the index is rebalanced.

The Major Market Index. The Major Market Index (MMI) was developed by the American Stock Exchange (AMEX) in 1983. Commonly known either by its acronym or by XMI, the ticker symbol for the underlying cash index, the MMI is designed to measure the performance of the blue-chip sector of the U.S. stock market. The index is based on 20 large-capitalization, well-known U.S. companies such as American Express, McDonald's, Eastman Kodak, and Walt Disney.

Unlike the S&P 500 Index, the S&P MidCap 400, and the Russell 2000, the MMI is price weighted; that is, the index is calculated by adding the prices of the 20 stocks and dividing the sum by the divisor. Thus, a given price change in any of the included stocks would have an identical impact on the index, regardless of market capitalization.

EXHIBIT 13–6
Total Value of Four Major Indexes

	S&P 500	*Statistics of Selected Indexes (Millions of Dollars)*		
		S&P MidCap400	*Russell 2000*	*MMI*
Total market value	$3,310,611	$456,543	$590,600	$726,997
Average stock	6,621	1,141	255	36,349
Median stock	3,566	901	203	35,973
Largest stock	86,160	9,102	1,000	86,160
Smallest stock		51	25	9,029

EXHIBIT 13–7
Price Moves on Five Major Indexes

	S&P 500	Dow Jones Industrial Averages	S&P MidCap 400	Russell 2000	MMI
2% Price Move	9.30	77.0	3.50	5.0	7.8
5% Price Move	23.25	192.5	8.75	12.5	19.5

Exhibits 13–6 and 13–7 compare the size and price moves of the underlying indexes. Statistics are as of July 29, 1994.

International Equity Index Products

With an expanding volume of financial trading across borders, the growing demand for international equity index products was a natural evolution. The CME responded to that demand by introducing futures and options products on the leading Japanese stock index, the Nikkei 225 Stock Average, and on the United Kingdom's Financial Times Share Index (FT-SE 100 Share Index).

The Nikkei 225 Stock Average. The Nikkei 225 Stock Average is Japan's most widely followed and most frequently quoted equity index.

Like the MMI, the Nikkei is price weighted. It comprises 225 top-tiered (the "bluest" chip) Japanese companies listed in the First Section of the Tokyo Stock Exchange (TSE). The Nikkei lists some of the most widely known companies in the world: Sony, Fuji Photo Film, Honda, Toyota, Yamaha, NEC, Citizen Watch, and Nippon Telephone & Telegraph (NTT).

The FT-SE 100 Share Index. The FT-SE 100 Share Index was created by the London Stock Exchange (LSE) as the benchmark for the U.K. equity market. The index is capitalization weighted, based on the 100 largest U.K. stocks traded on the LSE. The FT-SE 100 represents about 72 percent of the total market capitalization of U.K. stocks, making it an effective and very recognizable proxy for equity trading in the United Kingdom.

CONCLUSION

Stock index futures and options on the CME provide hedgers and traders with a myriad of risk-management techniques and profit opportunities. Trading the S&P 500 futures and options not only provides the diversification of an entire market, but also establishes a large liquid position, with economy of execution time and transaction costs. Stock index contracts give speculative traders an opportunity to trade in markets that react to the most basic economic and political factors. Furthermore, investors can also increase equity investment and hold it through market down cycles by using S&P stock index futures and options as a control for market risk. These contracts provide staying power to help achieve the capital gains of productive investment.

Appendix 13–A
Contract Specs

EXHIBIT 13–A1
Chicago Mercantile Exchange Equity Index Futures and Options Contract Highlights[1] *(CME Equity Index Futures (U.S.))*

	S&P 500 Stock Index Futures	S&P MidCap 400 Index Futures	Russell 2000® Index Futures	Major Market Index (MMI) Futures
Ticker symbols	SP	Md	RL	BC
Contract size	$500 × S&P 500 Stock Index	$500 × S&P MidCap 400 Index	$500 × Russell 2000 Index	$500 × MMI
Minimum price fluctuation (tick)	.05 index points = $25.00 per contract	.05 index points = $25.00 per contract	.05 index points = $25.00 per contract	.05 index points = $25.00 per contract
Trading hours (Chicago time)		8:30 A.M. – 3:15 P.M.		8:15 A.M. – 3:15 P.M.
Contract months	March, June, September, December	March, June, September, December	March, June, September, December	The first 3 consecutive months and the next 3 months in the Mar, Jun, Sep, and Dec cycle
Last day of trading	The business day immediately preceding the day of determination of the Final Settlement Price (normally, the Thursday prior to the 3rd Friday of the contract month)			Usually, the 3rd Friday of the contract month

Quarterly Futures & Options Settlement Procedures, S&P and Russell Cash settlement. All open positions at the close of the final trading day are settled in cash to the Special Opening Quotation on Friday morning of the S&P 500 Stock Index, the S&P MidCap 400 Index, or the Russell 2000 Index.

MMI Monthly Futures & Options Settlement Procedures: Cash settlement. All open positions are settled in cash to the closing value of the American Stock Exchange's Major Market Index on the last day of trading.

[1] Contract specifications are subject to change without notice. Check with your broker to confirm this information.

EXHIBIT 13–A2
CME Equity Index Futures (U.S.)

	Options on S&P 500 Futures	Options on S&P MidCap 400 Futures	Options on Russell 2000® Futures	Options on MMI Futures
Ticker symbols	Calls: CS Puts: PS	Calls: MD Puts: MD	Calls: RL Puts: RL	Calls: BC Puts: BC
Contract size	One S&P500 futures contract	One S&P MidCap 400 futures contract	One Russell 200 futures contract	One MMI futures contract
Strike prices	See note[1]	See note[1]	See note[1]	5 point intervals
Minimum price fluctuation (tick)	.05 index points = $25.00 per contract[2]	.05 index points = $25.00 per contract[2]	.05 index points = $25.00 per contract[2]	.05 index points = $25.00 per contract[2]
Trading hours (Chicago time)		8:30 A.M.–3:15 P.M.		8:15 A.M.–3:15 P.M.
Contract months	All 12 calendar months (The underlying instrument for the 3 monthly option expirations within a quarter is the quarter-end futures contract.)			The first 3 consecutive months and the next 3 months in the Mar, Jun, Sep, and Dec cycle
Last day of trading	March, June, September, December: same date as underlying futures contract. Other 8 months: the 3rd Friday of the contract month			Usually, the 3rd Friday of the contract month

[1] Strike price increments vary per contract month. Refer to contract specifications for specific requirements.

[2] A trade may occur at a nominal price—cabinet—whether or not such trades result in the liquidation of positions for both parties to the trade.

EXHIBIT 13–A–3
CME International Equity Index Futures and Options

	Nikkei 225 Stock Average Futures	Options on Nikkei 225 Futures	FT-SE 100 Index Futures	Options on FT-SE 100 Futures
Ticker symbols	NK	Calls: KN Puts: JN	FI	Calls: FI Puts: FI
Contract size	$5 × The Nikkei stock average	1 Nikkei 225 futures contract	$50 × FT-SE 100 share index	1 FT-SE 100 share index futures contract
Strike price	N/A	500 point intervals	N/A	See note[1]
Minimum price fluctuation (tick)	5 index points = $25.00 per contract	5 index points = $25.00 per contract[2]	.5 index points = $25.00 per contract	.5 index points = $25.00 per contract[2]
Trading hours (Chicago time)	8:00 A.M.–3:15 P.M.	8:00 A.M.–3:15 P.M.	8:30 A.M.–3:15 P.M.	
Contract months	Mar, Jun, Sep, Dec	All 12 calendar months[3]	Mar, Jun, Sep, Dec	All 12 calendar months[3]
Last day of trading	The business day preceding the determination of the Final Settlement price, usually the business day preceding the 2nd Friday of the contract month[4]	March, June, September, December: Same date and time as underlying futures contract; other 8 months: the 3rd Friday of the contract month[4]	The business day preceding the determination of the Final Settlement price, normally the Thursday prior to the 3rd Friday of the contract month[4]	March, June, September, December: Same date and time as underlying futures contract; serial months: the 3rd Friday of the contract month[4]

Futures Settlement Procedures, Nikkei: The final settlement price shall be the special opening quotation of the Nikkei Stock Average, used to settle the Nikkei Stock Average futures at the Osaka Securities Exchange, rounded to the nearest 1/10th of an index point. **FT-SE:** Cash settlement in U.S. dollars. The final settlement price shall be the EDSP (Exchange Delivery Settlement Price) used to settle the FT-SE 100 Share Index futures at the LIFFE.

Options Settlement Procedures, Nikkei: Options in the quarterly cycle will be settled in U.S. dollars to the special opening quotation used to settle the Nikkei Stock Average futures at the Osaka Securities Exchange. Settlement for serial month options results in a position in the underlying quarterly futures contract. **FT-SE:** Options in the quarterly cycle will be settled in U.S. dollars to the EDSP of the FT-SE 100 Share Index at the LIFFE. Settlement for serial month options results in a position in the underlying quarterly futures contract.

[1] Strike price increments vary per contract month. Refer to contract specifications for specific requirements.

[2] The underlying instrument for the 3 monthly option expirations within a quarter is the quarter-end futures contract.

[3] A trade may occur at a nominal price—cabinet—whether or not such trades result in the liquidation of positions for both parties to the trade.

[4] See current CME rules for holiday exceptions.

Appendix 13–B
Monitoring Trading Activity

Futures

1. Prices represent the open, high, low, and settlement (for closing) price for the previous day.
2. Contract delivery months that are currently traded.
3. The number of contracts traded in the previous two trading sessions.
4. One day's change in the settlement price.
5. The actual index high: low, close, and change.
6. High and low prices over the life of the contract.
7. The number of contracts still in effect at the end of the previous day's trading session. Each unit represents a buyer and a seller who still have a contract problem.
8. The total of the right column and the change from the previous trading day.

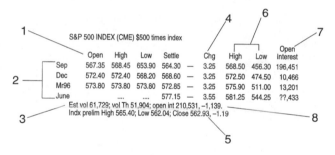

The Wall Street Journal, July 31, 1995

Futures Options

1. Expiration months.
2. Most active strike prices.
3. Volume of options traded in the previous two trading sessions.
4. Closing prices in each option.
5. The number of options (each unit represents both the holder and the writer) still open at the end of the previous day's trading session.

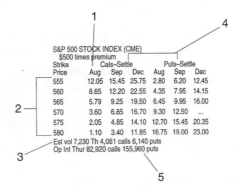

GLOSSARY

arbitrage The simultaneous purchase and sale of equivalent securities and futures in order to benefit from an anticipated change in their price relationship.

ask The price at which a party is willing to sell; also called the "offer."

at-the-money An option with an exercise price equal or near to the current underlying futures price.

basis The difference between the futures price and the current index value.

basis point One-hundredth (.01) of a full index point, worth $5.

bear spread A spread that is put on with the expectation that the futures price will decline.

beta The relationship between the movement of an individual stock or a portfolio and that of the overall stock market.

bid The price at which a party is willing to buy.

bull spread A spread position taken with the expectation that the futures price will rise.

call option An option that gives the holder the right to enter a long futures position at a specific price, and obligates the seller to enter a short futures position at a specific price if the seller is assigned for exercise.

cash settlement Applies to the expiration of quarterly index options and futures contracts. There is no delivery of securities, and the full value of the contract is not transferred. Final settlement occurs on the morning following the last day of trading when all open positions will be marked to a special opening quotation based on the component stocks in the S&P 500 Index. Expiring options which are in the money based on the special opening quotation are automatically exercised. This results, in effect, in cash settlement for the in-the-money amount.

CFTC The Commodity Futures Trading Commission is the independent federal agency created by Congress in 1974 to regulate futures and options trading.

Clearing House An adjunct of the Chicago Mercantile Exchange through which all CME futures and options on futures transactions are made, and through which all financial settlements against those contracts are made.

covered writing The sale of an option against an underlying position.

credit spread A spread in which the value of the option sold exceeds the value of the option purchased.

debit spread A spread in which the value of the option exceeds the value of the option sold.

delivery The process by which funds and the physical commodity change hands on expiration of a futures contract.

delta A measure of the price-change relationship between an option and the underlying futures.

exercise notice The price at which futures positions are established upon exercise of an option. This is also called the "Strike Price."

expiration date The last day that an option may be exercised.

futures contract A standardized, transferable legal agreement to make or take delivery of a certain commodity at a specific time in the future. The price is determined by open outcry auction, and is adjusted daily to the current market (see also "mark to market").

hedge To take a position in a futures market opposite to a position held in the cash market to minimize the risk of financial loss from an adverse price change.

in-the-money A situation in which the market price of a futures contract is higher than the exercise price of a call, or lower than the exercise price of a put.

intrinsic value That portion of an option's premium that represents the amount an option is in the money.

last trading day For the S&P 500 futures and for the quarter-end options, this is the Thursday prior to the third Friday of the contract month. For the eight interim-month expiration options, this is the third Friday of the contract month. If that day is a holiday, it is the preceding business day.

limit order An order in which a customer specifies a price; the order can be executed only if the market reaches or betters that price.

long position Indicates ownership. In futures, the long has purchased the commodity or security for future delivery. In options, the long has purchased the call or the put option.

maintenance margin A sum usually smaller than but part of the original margin. If a customer's account with his or her broker drops below the maintenance margin level, the broker must issue a "margin call" for the amount of money required to restore the customer's balance in the account to the initial margin requirement.

margin Funds that must be deposited with the broker for each futures or written option contract as a guarantee of fulfillment of the contract. Also called "security deposit."

mark to market Daily, the CME Clearing House adjusts to all open futures and options positions to reflect changes in the settlement price of the contract. Each position is credited with profit or charged with loss.

market order An order to buy or sell at the best price available at that time.

offset Any transaction that liquidates or closes out an open contract position.

open interest The number of contracts that have been opened and have not been offset, delivered, or exercised. Equal to half of the summed long and short positions.

out of the money A situation in which the market price of a futures contract is below the exercise price of a call or above the exercise price of a put.

premium The price of an option agreed upon by the buyer and seller in open, competitive trading on the exchange trading floor.

put option An option that gives the holder the right to enter a short futures position and obligates the seller to enter a long futures position at a specific price if the seller is assigned for exercise.

settlement price The end-of-day price used to calculate gains and losses in futures market accounts.

short position In futures, the short has sold the commodity or security for future delivery. In options, the short has sold the call or the put and is obligated to take a futures position if the short is assigned for exercise.

spot price The current market price of the actual stock index. Also called "cash price."

spread Holding a long and a short position in two related contracts to capture a profit from a changing price relationship. The term also refers to the price difference between the contracts.

stop order A contingent order to buy futures (buy stop) only if some higher price (the stop price) is reached; or a contingent order to sell futures (sell stop) only if some lower price (the stop price) is reached.

straddle The purchase or sale of both a put and a call having the same exercise price and expiration date.

time value That portion of an option's premium that represents the amount in excess of the intrinsic value.

uncovered sale The sale of an option without an underlying futures position.

volume The number of transactions in a contract during a specified time period.

writer The seller of an option.

REFERENCES

Chicago Mercantile Exchange. "Using Stock Index Futures and Options." Chapter 9 in *The Handbook of Derivative Instruments: Investments Research, Analysis and Portfolio Applications*. A. Konishi and R. Dattatreya, eds. Chicago: Probus Publishing, 1991.

Collins, B., and F. Fabozzi. "Mechanics of Trading Stock Index Futures." Chapter 5 in *The Handbook of Stock Index Futures and Options*. F. Fabozzi and G. Kipnis, eds. Homewood, IL: Dow Jones-Irwin, 1989.

Fabozzi, F., and E. Peters. "Hedging with Stock Index Futures." Chapter 13 in *The Handbook of Stock Index Futures and Options*. F. Fabozzi and G. Kipnis, eds. Homewood, IL: Dow Jones-Irwin, 1989.

Hull, John C. *Options, Futures and Other Derivative Securities,* 2nd. ed. Englewood Cliffs, NJ: Prentice Hall, 1993.

## Chapter Fourteen

Managing Cash Flow Risk in Stock Index Futures: The Tail Hedge

Ira G. Kawaller
Chicago Mercantile Exchange

Timothy W. Koch
University of South Carolina

This chapter examines the use of the tail hedge as a means of managing cash flow risk associated with variation margin calls. A tail hedge takes a secondary position in the futures market to offset some of the original futures position. Traders take the opposite futures position with tails, expecting to generate gains that offset the financing costs of variation margin calls. Conversely, potential gains from cash inflows of variation margin offset losses on the tail.[1]

BACKGROUND

Stock index futures have existed only since 1981, yet the growth in their trading volume has been dramatic. The value of index futures trading often exceeds the corresponding dollar value of traditional equity trading.

---

1 When futures prices change favorably, traders can withdraw and invest the excess variation margin. The use of a tail hedge eliminates this potential benefit. Firms that establish separate liquidity reserves gain directly from cash inflows associated with their variation margin position.

Speculators, hedgers, and arbitrageurs may follow different trading strategies, but all futures market participants face the same practical problem of uncertain cash flow obligations. Specifically, all bear the risk of intermittent cash outflows resulting from variation margin payments required because of adverse price movements of the futures position. At the very least, the cost of financing these dollar flows detracts from the profitability of the futures position. At worst, the cash flow obligation can force premature liquidation and seriously disrupt a well-considered hedging or trading strategy.

B. Fielitz and G. Gay developed a model that portfolio managers can use to establish liquidity reserves against such potential cash outflows. The model determines the amount of funds to be held in reserve given the portfolio's size, its systematic risk (beta), the investment term, and management's assessment of an acceptable probability of exhausting the liquidity reserve.[2]

One problem with this approach, however, is that the liquidity reserve is potentially large. In one example, the target reserve equaled 13.8 percent of the total portfolio to provide a 99 percent probability that the fund could handle margin calls over a 20-day period. If the investment term doubled to 40 days, say, the required liquidity reserve increases to 19.6 percent, which amounts to $9.8 million for a $50 million equity portfolio.

Such a liquidity reserve effectively increases the capital requirements for transacting in futures by a nontrivial amount. Moreover, because the reserve likely consists of highly marketable securities such as federal funds and Treasury bills, investment in qualifying instruments may alter a firm's desired portfolio risk and return profile. The tail hedge is an alternative means of dealing with this reserve problem.

THE INSTITUTIONAL MECHANICS OF TAIL HEDGES

Futures transactions entail cash flow risk associated with variation margin requirements. Whenever futures prices move against the initial futures position, a trader or hedger must pay cash equal to the change in value of

---

2 B. Fielitz and G. Gay, "Managing Cash Flow Risks in Stock Index Futures," *Journal of Portfolio Management*, Winter 1986, pp. 74–78.

the position to cover the loss.[3] However the payment is financed, the margin requirement imposes both explicit costs that reduce the effective return and implicit costs that the increased monitoring entails. Establishing a liquidity reserve is one approach to handling margin calls, as Fielitz and Gay recommend.

An alternative method of managing this risk is to establish a tail, or underhedge position. The tail is a smaller futures position that offsets a small fraction of the initial futures trade. For example, a trader long 200 contracts without tailing might take a coincident short position in five of the same futures contracts. Ideally, the interest cost of variation margin financing on the long position, should the futures price decline, is offset by gains on the tail. If a trader is short futures initially, a tail calls for a smaller, long offset.

Operationally, the cash flow requirements can be satisfied by establishing a trilateral arrangement betwen the customer (trader), the futures broker, and the bank that handles the cash flows. The arrangement consists of an open line of credit, allowing the customer to take down funds as required, and a companion interest-bearing deposit account. The bank lends the customer funds when margin calls require cash infusions and invests excess margin balances when they occur.[4]

Loans of this type generally require a demand note that stipulates the maximum amount of available funds, a security agreement that establishes a lender's lien on assets used as collateral, and the assignment of a hedge account that attaches funds in the brokerage account as collateral. Within this framework, the broker contacts the bank directly when additional margin financing is needed and the bank increases the customer's loan. When prices move favorably and excess margin exists, the bank withdraws the excess to pay down the loan or deposits it in an interest-bearing account. Such an arrangement satisfies liquidity concerns but does not alleviate the risk associated with unknown financing costs.

---

3 The mechanics and institutional requirements underlying variation margin rules are described in B. Collins and F. Fabozzi, "Mechanics of Trading Stock Index Futures," in *The Handbook of Stock Index Futures and Options,* F. Fabozzi and G. Kipnis, eds. (Homewood, IL.: Dow Jones-Irwin, 1989), chap. 5.

4 Such lending arrangements are common in the case of agriculture hedge loans to finance initial margin, maintenance margin, and brokerage commissions arising from trading futures contracts. See "Risk Management Guide for Ag Lenders" (Chicago: Chicago Mercantile Exchange, 1985.)

DETERMINING THE SIZE OF THE TAIL HEDGE

The purpose of a tail hedge is to offset the interest cost associated with financing the line of credit in support of margin calls. The tail should be constructed so that the change in value of financing the original futures variation margin is exactly offset by the change in value of the tail position:

$$(i)\ (d/360)\ (FP)\ N = -(FP)n, \tag{1}$$

where:

i = the assumed annual interest rate applied to the variation margin payment or receipt

d = the number of days remaining until settlement of the variation margin financing or investment

FP = change in value of a single futures contract

N = the number of contracts in the initial futures position

n = the number of contracts in the tail position

The negative sign indicates that the tail position is opposite in form (short versus long) to the initial futures position. The size of the tail implied by Equation (1) reduces to:

$$n = -(i)\ (d/360)\ N \tag{2}$$

Equation (2) shows that, when multiplied by the change in the value of a single futures contract, the term on the left equals the expected profit (loss) on the tail, and the term on the right equals the expected interest payment (return) on the variation margin financing (investment). In other words, the tail hedge tries to equate the present value of interest flows on variation margin activity with the present value of gains or losses on the tail. A liquidity reserve, in contrast, imposes an up-front cost that far exceeds the present value cost of variation margin payments.

One difficulty in applying Equation (2) arises from the uncertainty regarding the relevant interest rate and the natural drift in d as the expiration of the futures contract approaches. Two factors complicate the choice of interest rate. First, financing rates applicable when the margin is deficient typically exceed investment yields when surplus margin exists. Because the tail hedger does not know the direction of futures prices over the hedge period, neither rate is better ex ante. Second, variation margin requirements normally are handled daily; so a different interest rate applies each successive day unless the yield curve remains flat throughout the holding period and the futures price moves consistently for or against the hedger.[5]

Finally, even if managers knew which interest rate applied, expected interest payments decrease toward expiration date as d approaches zero. Appropriate risk management thus requires that portfolio managers periodically recalculate the size of the tail to ensure that it offsets the interest obligation from variation margin. Because these problems cannot be eliminated, the final tail results only approximately offset the costs or benefits of variation margin flows.

AN ILLUSTRATION

Consider the problems faced by an equity portfolio manager who decides to hedge $25 million in equities. The equities exhibit a beta equal to 1.0. The manager is concerned that stock prices will decline over the next six months and so decides to use the S&P 500 futures contract to hedge.[6] At the time of the decision, the S&P 500 futures contract is priced at 205 with 150 days remaining to expiration, and the S&P 500 Index is trading at 200. In this instance, the correct base hedge requires selling 250 futures contracts ($25 million/(200)(500) = 250).

If the hedge is maintained until the futures expiration date, the manager can expect to earn an amount equal to the reinvested value of the dividends paid on the equities over the next 150 days plus the basis adjustment.[7] The dollar value of the basis adjustment equals the product of the basis (the futures price minus the spot index value), the number of contracts in the hedge, and the multiplier of 500. In this case, the dollar amount is $625,000 [($205 − $200)(250)(500)].

---

5 It is possible that changes in the level of rates can be offset exactly by changes in rates associated with movements along the yield curve.

6 A beta of 1.0 indicates that changes in the value of the firm's equity portfolio exactly match percentage movements on the S&P 500 Index. A portfolio beta different from 1.0 affects the number of contracts that should be used to hedge the initial equity exposure. See F. Fabozzi and E. Peters, "Hedging with Stock Index Futures," in *The Handbook of Stock Index Futures and Options*, F. Fabozzi and G. Kipnis, eds. (Homewood, IL.: Dow-Jones-Irwin, 1989), chap 13.

7 The target earnings need to be adjusted whenever the projected hedge period ends prior to expiration of the futures contract. The incomplete basis adjustment reduces target earnings by a factor equal to the theoretical basis anticipated at the end of the hedge period.

Before establishing a tail hedge, the manager must determine the term to settlement day for all variation financing or investing, and the relevant interest rate. Typically, the term of the hedge is set equal to the number of days until the original futures position is expected to be closed, but any subsequent day can be used. Similarly, the interest rate is set at the term rate available over the same interval, assuming that the yield curve remains flat during the holding period.

A 10 percent interest rate in this example, with a term of 150 days, requires a tail hedge of 10 contracts:

$$n = 250 \, (0.10) \, (150/360) = -10.4$$

If the base hedge is 250 short contracts, the tail requires 10 long contracts because contracts are traded only in unit increments. The net position, therefore, is 240 short contracts.

Exhibit 14–1 demonstrates the recalculation of the tail every 15 days. It assumes that even though the period for financing or investing decreases every day, the appropriate financing rate remains at 10 percent. Exhibit 14–2 shows the resulting variation margin changes on the base positions and

EXHIBIT 14–1
Calculating the Tail

Days Remaining in Hedge Period (d)	Tail Calculation $[n = -250(0.1)(d/360)]$
150	$10.4 \approx 10$
135	$9.4 \approx 9$
120	$8.3 \approx 8$
105	$7.3 \approx 7$
90	$6.3 \approx 6$
75	$5.2 \approx 5$
60	$4.2 \approx 4$
45	$3.1 \approx 3$
30	$2.1 \approx 2$
15	$1.0 \approx 1$
0	$0 \approx 0$

EXHIBIT 14–2
Simulation

Days Remaining in Hedge	S&P Futures Price	Variation Margin	Interest on Variation Margin[a]	Number of Contracts in Tail[b]	Tail Profit[c]
150	207.50	$312,500	$13,021	10	$12,500
135	210.00	312,500	11,719	9	11,250
120	212.50	312,500	10,417	8	10,000
105	215.00	312,500	9,115	7	8,750
90	217.50	312,500	7,813	6	7,500
75	220.00	312,500	6,510	5	6,250
60	222.50	312,500	5,208	4	5,000
45	225.00	312,500	3,906	3	3,750
30	227.50	312,500	2,604	2	2,500
15	230.00	312,500	1,302	1	1,250
0	232.50	312,500	0	0	0
Cumulative Results		$3,437,500	$71,615		$68,750

[a] [0.10 (days remaining in hedge)/306] (variation margin).
[b] 250 [0.10 (days remaining in hedge)/360]; rounded to nearest integer.
[c] $500 (2.50) (number of contracts in the tail position).

corresponding offsets generated by the tail under a scenario assuming a rising futures price. The exhibit also assumes that futures prices increase by 250 basis points (2.50 index points) immediately following the adjustment to the tail.[8] Note that the actual tail reflects a rounding of the calculated value for *n* because contracts must be bought or sold in whole units. In this example, the rounding consistently caused a somewhat smaller tail than that stipulated by the equation.

At the outset, the objective was to earn the dividends from owning the stocks plus the basis adjustment, where this latter component equals five index points per contract ($625,000) for the base hedge. In this example, the expected outcome is not achieved precisely. In the scenario presented, the original equities appreciate by $4,062,500, reflecting an 18.75 percent increase in the S&P 500 Index. The hedge, however, produces a consoli-

---

8 This is the worst possible timing sequence of price changes.

dated loss of $3,440,365 made up of (1) the base variation margin ($3,437,500); (2) its associated finance charges, $71,615; and (3) the tail profits, $68,750, which serve to reduce overall hedge losses.

The net result is that the hedger earns $622,135 plus dividends. The tailed hedge position actually earns $2,865 less than the target established when the hedge was initiated. This is a mismatch of less than 0.5 percent of the expected basis adjustment. What is most important, however, is that the earnings would have been $71,615 less, or a mismatch of over 11 percent of that target, without the tail.

Suppose instead that the S&P 500 futures price decreases by 250 basis points every 15 days. Interest on variation margin then represents income exactly equal to the amount in Exhibit 14–2 and the tail position produces losses. In this case, the spot index and futures prices settle at $177.50, and the loss in equity value equals $2,812,500. The original hedge position produces a gain of $3,440,365 net of the tail, for aggregate earnings of $627,865, or $2,865 above the target.

As is true for most hedges, it is difficult to execute the tail hedge with the precision demonstrated in Exhibit 14–2. The biggest challenge is to match the correct number of base futures contracts with the underlying equities. Any discrepancy, or any missed estimate of n, affects the tail hedge results. Still, the tail hedge clearly reduces the variance of expected returns around the target.

CONCLUSION

Variation margin requirements on stock index futures transactions increase the cash flow risk that portfolio managers face. Rather than establish a liquidity reserve from which funds can be withdrawn to meet payment obligations, the manager may want to follow an alternative procedure that uses tail hedges. The tail hedge requires a smaller up-front investment and does not alter a firm's risk and return profile.

REFERENCES

1. Collins, B., and F. Fabozzi. "Mechanics of Trading Stock Index Futures." Chapter 5 in *The Handbook of Stock Index Futures and Options*, F. Fabozzi and G. Kipnis, eds. Homewood, IL.: Dow Jones-Irwin, 1989.

2. Fabozzi, F., and E. Peters. "Hedging with Stock Index Futures." Chapter 13 in *The Handbook of Stock Index Futures and Options,* F. Fabozzi and G. Kipnis, eds. Homewood, IL.: Dow Jones-Irwin, 1989.

3. Fielitz, B., and G. Gay. "Managing Cash Flow Risks in Stock Index Futures." *Journal of Portfolio Management,* Winter 1986, pp. 74–78.

4. Kawaller, I. "Going the Extra Mile." *Journal of Cash Management,* July/Aug. 1986.

5. *Risk Management Guide for Ag Lenders.* Chicago: Chicago Mercantile Exchange, 1985.

Chapter Fifteen

Introduction to Stock Options[*]

Richard M. Bookstaber
Salomon Bros., Inc.

Every security and financial market has its own definitions. Because of its unique characteristics, the option market probably has more than its share. This chapter covers the basic definitions that characterize call and put option contracts. It presents in a brief, conceptual form the options features that have led to their pivotal role in the financial market. It also describes the role options serve and the nature of option pricing and trading.

DEFINITIONS OF CALL AND PUT OPTIONS

Call Options

A call option is the right to buy a given amount of a security at a given price on or before a specific date. A particular call option is characterized by four features: (1) the security to which the option refers, (2) the amount of the security that the option holder has the right to buy, (3) the price at which the security can be bought, and (4) the time at which the option expires.

The security involved in the option contract is called the underlying security. The price at which the security may be bought is called the exercise price or the striking price. The last date on which the option may be

---

[*]Adapted from Chapter 3, *Option Pricing & Investment Strategies, Third Edition*, by Richard Bookstaber (Chicago, IL: Probus Publishing Company, 1991).

exercised is called the expiration date or the maturity date. The amount of the security controlled by the option contract is standardized on the various option exchanges.

For example, a Polaroid July 40 option gives the holder of the option the right to purchase 100 shares of Polaroid stock at the price of $40 per share on or before the expiration date in July. If the option is exercised, the option holder pays $4,000 in exchange for 100 shares of Polaroid stock.

The word *right* in the definition of the call option deserves some emphasis. It is the use of right rather than obligation that makes the option market so interesting. Because a buyer has the right but not the obligation to exercise an option, the buyer only exercises the option when it is profitable to do so. If the stock never rises above $40 a share, the buyer obviously does not exercise the option because the stock can be purchased at a lower price in the market. The cost of the option contract is lost. On the other hand if the stock price rises above $40, then the buyer profits from exercising the option. The $40 per share stock can be sold at the higher market price. If the market price goes to $45, the buyer can sell it for $4,500, making $500 less the cost of the option. So an option gives the buyer the potential for large gains, while limiting losses to the cost of the option contract itself.

The profit profile for the option buyer is illustrated in Exhibit 15–1. The option giving the holder the right to buy 100 shares of stock is assumed to cost $600. The profit is expressed in per share terms. If the stock price is below the exercise price of $40 on the expiration date, the option expires worthless; the investor loses the initial investment in the option, which comes out to $6 per share of stock. If the stock price is above $40 per share, the investor gains the difference between the cost of buying the stock and the higher market price at which the stock can be sold. The buyer's profit is equal to the final stock price minus the $40 exercise price less the initial cost of the option. So, if the stock rises to $50, the investor's net profit is $50 – $40 – $6 = $4 per share of stock, for a total profit of $400.

Call option writing. An option agreement is initiated between two parties. When an investor buys an option contract, someone on the other side of the contract agrees to sell the buyer the security at the exercise price. This person is called the option writer.

If the security rises above the exercise price, the option is exercised, and the writer does not make any gain above that price. If the writer owns the Polaroid stock and writes the Polaroid July 40, he or she needs to part with the stock at $40 per share even though the stock is going for more than that

EXHIBIT 15–1
Payoff of a Call Option

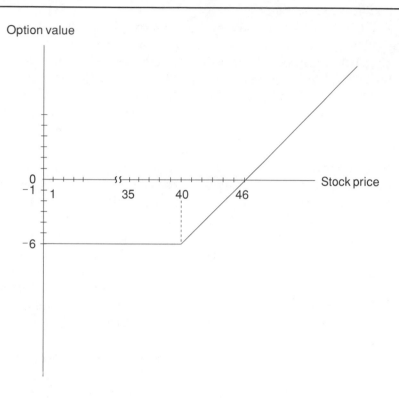

Option value

in the market. On the other hand if the stock drops in price, the option writer is left holding the bag—the option buyer walks away without exercising and the writer absorbs all of the loss: The writer has all of the potential loss from the stock, but has given all of the gain above the exercise price to the option buyer.

The writer may want to issue the option contract without holding the underlying stock. In this case, the writer is said to write a naked option, which means the writer does not have the stock that he or she has agreed to sell to the buyer. Unlike the covered option writer who holds the stock on the option written, the writer of a naked option does not lose if the stock drops in price. However, there is considerable risk if the stock increases in value. For example, if Polaroid goes up to $45, the writer has to buy the stock at $45 a share and then sell it to the option buyer at the exercise price

EXHIBIT 15–2
Payoff of a Call Option Writer

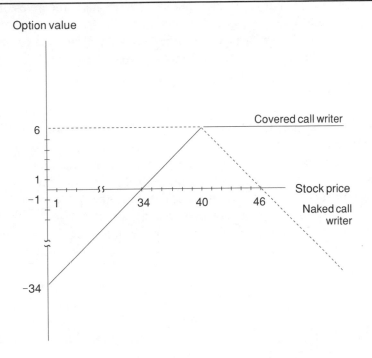

of $40 a share: The writer realizes a loss of $5 a share, for a total loss on the 100-share contract of $500.

The writer receives the option premium at the time the option is issued. If the going price for the Polaroid July 40 is $600 for an option contract of 100 shares, the writer gets $600 at the time that the contract is issued.

The profit profile for the writer of the Polaroid July 40 is shown in Exhibit 15–2, which indicates the return for both the covered (solid line) and naked (dotted line) option writer.

Put Options

A put option is the right to sell a given amount of a security at a given price on or before a specific date.

The put option differs from the call option only by replacing the word *buy* with *sell*. If the investor buys a Polaroid July 40 put option and the stock drops to $35, the investor can buy 100 shares of the stock in the market for $3500, and then turn around and sell it to the writer at $40 per share, for a net gain of $400. But if the stock is above $40 per share, the investor does not exercise the option because the stock can be sold in the market for a higher price than it can through the option contract. While the call option increases in value as the security increases in price, the put option increases in value as the security decreases in price.

Once again, the use of the word *right* is important. If the contract involved the obligation rather than the right to sell the stock, it would be the same as selling the stock short at $40. (A short sale involves selling stock the investor does not currently own, with the anticipation of covering the sale by buying the stock later at a lower price.) If the stock drops in value, the short sale yields a profit; but if the stock goes above $40, the short sale involves a loss because the investor has to buy the stock at the higher price and sell at the lower price. With the option, however, the investor does not face the same potential for loss from the stock rising in price; the stock does not have to be sold at the exercise price. The investor does so only if it is profitable. The maximum loss is the cost of buying the option.

The profit profile for the put option buyer is shown in Exhibit 15–3. If the stock price is above $40, the option is not exercised and the buyer does lose the initial cost of the option. If the stock is below the exercise price, the investor's profit is $40 minus the stock price minus the option price. Assuming the Polaroid July 40 put option is bought for $500, if the stock price drops to $35 a share, the investor breaks even, with the proceeds of the option equaling the $5 per share cost of the option contract.

Put option writing. Like the call option, every put option bought has an investor on the other side of the transaction who has written the contract. If the put option is exercised, the option writer buys the stock at the $40 exercise price, even though the going market price is lower. In return for this unfavorable possibility, the writer receives a premium from the buyer for issuing the put option.

THE ROLE OF OPTIONS

Individual investors and market traders dominated the option markets in the first decade of its existence. These traders use options to make plays on the underlying securities or form arbitrage strategies on the options themselves. Over the past few years, a second role of options has become increasingly

EXHIBIT 15–3
Payoff of a Put Option

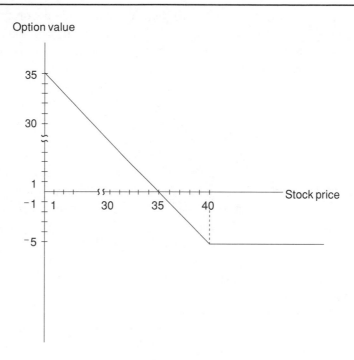

prominent: This is the use of options to mold return distributions to form a more complete market that can better match the investment objectives of portfolio managers, pension plan sponsors, and financial institutions with asset/liability needs. This second role, while slower in unfolding, is the more important of the two. The principal justification for options and for the application of option theory is to create payoffs and returns that meet the needs of the market.

Two key propositions provide the statement of the role options and option theory play in the financial markets:

Proposition 1. Any feasible payoff can be created with the appropriate set of options.

Proposition 2. Any option can be created through the appropriate trading strategy.

Using Options to Create Payoffs to Meet Investment Objectives

A stock option may appear to be nothing more than a side bet on the price of the underlying security. Certainly a company on which an option is listed receives no income from the option contract. The two parties that enter into the option agreement appear to be in a zero sum game—the "winner" gains at the expense of the "loser." Are options just an instrument for the speculators and gamblers, or does having this derivative claim on the stock serve a useful function? To answer this question, take a closer look at the motivation for making investments.

The process of investing takes place in two stages. First, the investor makes an appraisal of the most likely course of events and then chooses investments that will pay off if those events occur. An investor may make an analysis of General Motors (GM) and come to the conclusion that GM will be very profitable over the next year. To take advantage of this assessment, the investor buys a security that will appreciate should GM be profitable. In the ideal financial market, there is a range of securities available to give the investor flexibility in making investments that precisely follow this assessment, as well as the flexibility to take advantage of the events that the investor perceives will most likely occur.

If GM stock is the only security available for trading on the investor's perceptions of GM, the investor is limited in the range of events that can be met with a market position. The investor can buy the stock in the belief that the company will do well and can sell the stock in the belief that it will do poorly. But what if the investor's analysis is more precise than this? What if the investor is convinced GM will go up between 20 percent and 50 percent? This is a more precise appraisal than simply saying the stock will go up, but the only way the investor can take advantage of this analysis is to buy the stock. The individual is forced to follow a diluted appraisal, taking a position that the stock might go up 5 percent or 80 percent along with his or her actual belief that the stock appreciation will be in the 20 percent to 50 percent range. The nature of the stock itself limits the precision with which perceptions can be acted on in the market. Faced with the inability to match personal beliefs exactly through a market transaction, the investor is forced into a suboptimal investment strategy, and so may fail to invest as much as if a tailor-made security existed.

The ideal market has a range of financial instruments available to enable investors to meet their investment objectives exactly. There is a security that gives a payoff if the stock appreciates between 20 percent and 50

EXHIBIT 15–4
An Option Strategy Payoff (Strategy Cost = $.50)

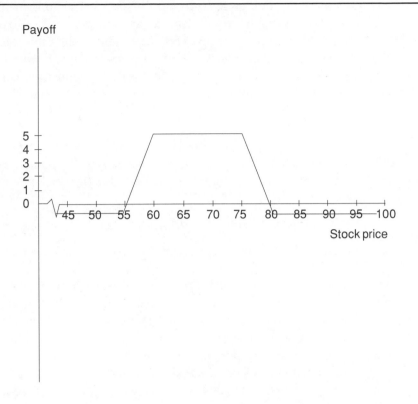

percent and gives no payoff if any other return is realized. The ideal market permits the investor to cover any contingency in the market, to fine-tune a portfolio to meet personal investment objectives and perceptions exactly. Options create such a market.

To see how such a payoff can be created, suppose an investor buys a call option with an exercise price of 55, writes an option with an exercise price of 60, writes another option with an exercise price of 75, and then buys yet another call option with an exercise price of 80. The result of this strategy is shown in Exhibit 15–4. The payoff (exclusive of the options' cost) is $5 for prices between 60 and 75, and tapers off quickly to no payoff for prices outside of that range. Therefore, it represents a close-to-ideal strategy for this investor. (To see how this combination of options leads to the payoff depicted in Exhibit 15–4, note that as the stock price moves from 55 to 60, the option with the 55 exercise price gains $5. At 60, the second option written offsets further gains in the first option. For prices above 60, the combination of these two options leads to a payoff of $5. The option with the 75 exercise price loses dollar for dollar with an increase in the price of GM above 75; by the time GM gets up to 80, the combination of this third option with the other two leads to a net payoff of zero. The option with the exercise price of 80 then nets out the impact of this third option, leading to no payoff for any stock price above 80. The payoff can be brought down to zero more quickly by using endpoint options with exercise prices closer to 60 and 75.)

This example shows that options expand the set of alternatives that can be met through investment strategies, and options expand the number of contingencies that can be met through investments in the financial market.

Creating Options through Trading Strategies

In the extreme case where options are available with exercise prices equal to every possible stock price, every possible investment contingency can be covered. Of course, the complete set of options also needs to be available for a range of securities that cover every variable of concern to the investor; not just GM stock, but IBM stock and AT&T stock; and not only stocks, but foreign exchange rate, interest rates, and the overall market. In addition, the time to expiration of the options needs to be consistent with the investment horizon of the investor. The reality is that options are available with some exercise prices, with some times to expiration and on some financial assets. So while the option market increases the flexibility of the market in meeting the needs of the investor, it does not cover all possible contingencies.

However, investors are not limited by the availability of options in the marketplace. It is possible to construct options through trading strategies in other instruments. If an instrument can be easily and liquidly traded, it is possible to make a tailored option with the desired time to expiration and exercise price. If investors cannot buy it in the market, they can build it using the security underlying the option as the raw material. The procedure for doing this is the foundation of option pricing and strategies.

To illustrate how a trading strategy can replicate an option payoff, suppose an investor wants to create an option on 100 shares of GM with one year to expiration and an exercise price of 60. To create the option, ask the question at every point in time, "If this option were trading efficiently in the market, how much would its price change with a change in the underlying value of GM?" As is explained later in the chapter, this is a question that is answered through the use of option pricing models.

Suppose that at the current stock price of $60 a share, the option changes in value by $.50 with every $1.00 change in the price of GM. To create a payoff that matches that of the option, then, the investor needs to buy 50 shares of stock. Having done this, if GM stock changes by a quarter of a point, the position changes by an eighth of a point. An observer looking at the price behavior of this position is unable to differentiate its performance from the price performance the investor would have had if he or she actually had purchased the option in the marketplace rather than had created it.

The exposure to the stock required to replicate the option changes over time and with changes in the price of the stock. For example, if the stock moves up to $80 a share, the call option is far in the money, and moves nearly dollar for dollar with the stock. To replicate the price movement of the option may then require an increase in stock exposure to 95 shares. The replication process, therefore, is dynamic in nature. If day by day the investor continues to mirror the price movements of the option he or she is seeking to replicate, at the time of expiration that investor also replicates the payoff of the option.

The dynamic trading technique not only can be used to create options to meet investment objectives, it also can be used to arbitrage options that are available in the marketplace when these options are incorrectly priced.

Suppose an investor finds a listed option on GM selling for $7 and, working through an option pricing model, finds that same option payoff can be created for only $5. By writing the market option for a cash inflow of $7 and then spending the $5 to create the same payoff using the dynamic trading methods, the investor will find that at the time of expiration the payoff of the replicated option matches the payoff of the option written by the investor, and it leaves no net obligation. However, the investor has pocketed $2 at the outset because of the mispricing of the listed option. The investor has created an option for one price and sold it in the marketplace for another.

This type of a strategy is called an arbitrage strategy, because it leads to a profit for no net investment and no risk. Obviously, the notion of no risk is not quite correct, because the replication may be imperfect; but generally such strategies can be performed with low enough risk to make this a widespread, though sophisticated, investment strategy, but there are a number of sophisticated trading firms that specialize in such arbitrage strategies.

PRICING OPTIONS

The most important breakthrough in option analysis has been the development of option pricing models. These models give the price of an option as a function of observable variables, such as the security price and security price volatility, the exercise price, the time-to-maturity of the option, and interest rates. Option models are one of the most powerful tools in finance. The analytical method they use can be applied to virtually any financial security, opening up a new era in understanding and pricing financial instruments.

Because the variables used in the models are observable, the use of the option pricing models has been of practical value to the investment profession at large. However, the number of people who use these models exceeds the number who understand them. The models were derived originally from advanced mathematical methods that obscured the intuition behind the formula. The practical implications of the models for profiting from mispriced options and for deriving hedges in more complex strategies has remained unexplored until recently.

This is an explanation of the methodology behind the option pricing models and shows how to exploit profit opportunities if the market price of the option differs from the option model price. Appendix A presents a derivation of the option pricing formula that uses only elementary algebra, progressing from the simple one-period formula to a many-period formula. Later sections use option pricing techniques to describe trading strategies.

A One-Period Example

Suppose a stock is priced currently at $100 a share, and in one period it will be worth either $95 or $110. There is a call option available on the stock with an exercise price of $100 and one period to expiration. The current price of the option is $800. (See Exhibit 15–5.) The riskless interest rate for both borrowing and lending is 5 percent over the one time period.

Consider the following portfolio strategy. The investor writes three call options, receiving an income of $2,400, and buys 200 shares of the stock at $100 per share. The net initial position is $17,600. Assume the investor can then borrow at the 5 percent rate to cover the position, so that the net initial investment is zero (the stock is being purchased entirely from the proceeds of the option sale and the borrowed funds). What will the investor's return be at the end of the period?

EXHIBIT 15–5
A Call Option with One Period to Expiration

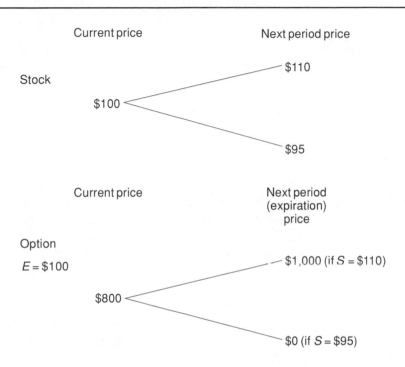

If the stock drops to $95 by the next period, the option expires worthless. The investor then needs to repay $18,480 (the $17,600 plus 5 percent interest to the bank), and holds $19,000 worth of stock. The net position is $19,000 − $18,840 = $520. Because the initial investment is zero, the investor makes a profit if the stock drops.

If the stock increases to $110 in value, $3,000 is needed to cover the option position, and the stock is worth $22,000. With the cost of the borrowed funds, the investor's net position is $22,000 − $3000 − $18,480 = $520. Once again the strategy nets a profit. This strategy is illustrated in Exhibit 15–6.

This transaction is remarkable because not only is a profit made in either case, but the profit is riskless—it is exactly the same no matter which way the stock moves. Also, the profit is made for no net investment. A profit that is obtained at no risk and for no initial investment is called an arbitrage profit. If any amount of arbitrage profit is possible, then an investor can

EXHIBIT 15–6
Trading Strategy When the Option Price is $800

Current Position		End-of-Period Position	
		$S = 95$	$S = 110$
Write 3 call options	2,400	0	(3,000)
Buy 200 shares	(20,000)	19,000	22,000
Borrow at 5 percent	17,600	(18,480)	(18,480)
Net profit	0	520	520

make unlimited profits. Given a chance to make a certain profit of $520 with no investment, the investor's position needs only to increase by x times and make x times as great a profit risklessly and with no initial investment.

There is only one price for the option that eliminates this profit opportunity. As Exhibit 15–7 shows, if this strategy is followed when the option is priced at $635, there is no arbitrage profit. If the price is below $635, the reverse strategy of buying three options, selling short 200 shares of stock, and placing the proceeds of the transaction into the riskless asset yields an arbitrage profit. The results of this strategy are illustrated in Exhibit 15–8 for an option price of $500.

In this simple example, the option price of $635 is the correct option price. If the option is at this price in the market, there is no arbitrage opportunity. If it is mispriced, there is the possibility of obtaining large profits for no risk. The option pricing formula in the next section gives this correct option price under far more realistic assumptions than those used in this example. There is no law that requires the market price to equal this correct option price. But if it does not, then the knowledgeable investor can make large profits for little or no risk by taking the appropriate position in this mispriced option and the underlying stock.

The existence of an arbitrage profit puts a mechanism into action that drives the option price to the value that eliminates the profit opportunity. For example, if the option is initially priced at $800 and more investors follow the arbitrage strategy by selling options, the option price needs to drop to entice others to buy the increased supply of options. If the option price is below the correct value, the option price is driven up as investors try to buy more options. The pressure on the option price continues in either case until the option is priced at $635.

EXHIBIT 15–7
Trading Strategy When the Option Price is $635

Current Position		End-of-Period Position	
		$S = 95$	$S = 110$
Write 3 call options	(1,905)	0	(3,000)
Buy 200 shares	(20,000)	19,000	22,000
Borrow at 5 percent	18,095	19,000	19,000)
Net profit	0	0	0

EXHIBIT 15–8
Trading Strategy When the Option Price is $500

Current Position		End-of-Period Position	
		$S = 95$	$S = 110$
Buy 3 call options	(1,500)	0	3,000
Sell short 200 shares	20,000	(19,000)	(22,000)
Lend at 5 percent	(18,500)	19,425	19,425)
Net profit	0	425	425

Note that any of the three securities—the stock, the option, or the interest rate—can adjust to eliminate the profit opportunity. Just as the arbitrage strategy puts pressure on the option price, it also tends to move the other securities in the direction that eliminates the arbitrage profit. As investors follow the arbitrage strategy to take advantage of an overpriced option, they buy stock, raising the price of the stock, and they borrow more funds, putting upward pressure on the riskless rate of interest. So the option price is set by relative, not absolute, prices.

If an arbitrage profit is possible, the option is no more mispriced than the underlying security or the interest rate. Given any values for two of the securities, there is a unique price for the third security that eliminates the profit opportunity. Because the option market usually is thinner and more elastic than the other markets, it adjusts to a relative price discrepancy before the underlying security or the riskless asset does. So, for convenience, the option is said to be mispriced.

Anatomy of an Arbitrage: Making $1.5 Million at the State Fair

To understand how arbitrage works, take a more down-to-earth example. Imagine a refreshment stand at the state fair. There are three other stands there, one selling hot dogs for 50 cents each, one selling nine-ounce cups of cola for 30 cents, and another selling hot dogs with a six-ounce cup of cola for 75 cents.

It is apparent that a buyer can package the hot dogs and six-ounce cola for less than the going price of 75 cents. He purchases hot dogs from the one stand and cola from the other in the proportions of two colas for every three hot dogs, and repackages the two to match the product of the third stand.

If the market is competitive, he can sell all the servings of hot dogs and six-ounce colas at 75 cents. The cost of the package is only 70 cents; so by buying the parts and packaging them as the whole, he makes a sure profit. If the pricing went the other way so that the hot dog–cola combination costs only 60 cents, he buys the package and resells it separately. The relationships are shown in Exhibit 15–9.

That two items can replicate the third indicates that the two must be priced in a certain proportion relative to the third. To eliminate this profit opportunity, three hot dogs and two of the nine-ounce colas must sell for the same price as two of the hot dog–cola combinations.

The pricing of the options relative to the stock and the riskless asset is determined in the same way. The combination of the short position in the call option and the long position in the stock replicates the riskless asset, in that the return from the position is riskless. Because the option and stock can be packaged in a particular proportion that replicates the riskless asset, it must be that the portfolio of the two sells for the same amount as the riskless asset. If it does not, then construct a "homemade" riskless asset by taking the appropriate position in the option and the stock, with the homemade riskless asset costing less to produce than the going market price for the riskless asset.

Or, combine the stock and the riskless asset in a proportion that yields the same payoff as the option at the time of expiration. Still another possibility is to combine the option with the riskless asset to ensure a return that is the same as the return to the stock at the end of the period.

EXHIBIT 15–9
How to Make $1.5 Million at the State Fair

1. *Buy*	*Going price*	
3 hot dogs	$.50 each =	$1.50
2 nine-ounce colas	.30 each =	.60
Total		$2.10
2. *Repackage and sell*	*Going price*	
3 hot dog-six-ounce cola combos	$.75 each =	$2.25
Profit		$ .15
3. *Repeat 10 million times*		

For example, if the investor combines a long position in three options with $18,095 in the riskless asset, the return is the same as if 200 shares of the stock are held. If the stock drops to $95 a share, the investor receives $18,095 (1.05) = $19,000; if the stock goes up to $110 a share, the investor receives $19,000 from the riskless asset and $3,000 from the option, for a return of $22,000. Because the portfolio of the options and the riskless asset exactly replicates the payoff of the stock at the end of the period, it must be that the portfolio of the two is priced so that it equals the stock price at the start of the period. Otherwise, profit opportunities are possible by taking a long or a short position in the portfolio.

The key to the arbitrage opportunity occurs when any two of the assets can be combined to produce a portfolio with the same payoff as the third. If the relative price of the three is such that the replicating portfolio for any of the assets has a different price than the price of the asset itself, then an arbitrage opportunity exists. By simultaneously buying at the lower price and selling the asset at the higher price, it is possible to get a positive return for no net investment.

The example shown here obviously is simplified to deal with one time period to expiration and with stock price movements that are unrealistic. However, this example does provide the basis for option pricing in the more realistic setting. The extension of this example to a more realistic setting is treated in Appendix A to the chapter. The formation of the riskless hedge and the possibility for arbitrage profits are the motivating principles for option pricing in the more complex setting.

THE OPTION PRICING MODEL

The option example used in the previous section is unrealistic. A security can take on any number of values, not just one of two values as assumed. Nor is trading done on a period-by-period basis. Markets operate continuously during trading hours.

However, a more realistic approach can be developed by extending the example. If the example is extended to many periods instead of one and the length of each time period becomes small (e.g., 180 periods of one-day duration rather than two periods of three-month duration each), then trading conditions are more realistic. If it is further assumed that the security price can take on any number of values in a given period of time, then the objection of the two-state security price movement is removed as well.

These assumptions are far less restrictive, and it is possible to fashion an example such as the one used in the previous section with these assumptions. There is still a correct option price, and it still is the case that an arbitrage profit is possible if the option price differs from the correct price. The extension of the illustration to the many-period case and the derivation of the option pricing formula is described in Appendix A.

The correct option price in this more realistic case is due to Black, Scholes, and Merton, and it is called the Black-Scholes formula. The formula determines the option price that is necessary to eliminate the possibility of profit opportunities. As in the one-period example, if the option price does not conform to this price, there is the opportunity to make large profits by using the correct hedging strategy with the option and the stock. Unlike the example, the Black-Scholes formula finds the correct price under assumptions that more closely resemble the actual trading price.

The Black-Scholes formula is:

$$C = SN(d_1) - Ee^{-rT}N(d_2)$$

where

$$d_1 = ((lnS/E) + (r + \tfrac{1}{2}\sigma^2)T)/\sigma\sqrt{T}$$

and

$$d_2 = d_1 - \sigma\sqrt{T}.$$

In this formula, ln is the natural logarithm, e is the exponential ($e = 2.718$), and σ^2 is the instantaneous variance of the security price, which is the measure of security return volatility in the formula (so σ is the standard deviation of the returns). $N(\cdot)$ is the normal distribution function, which is tabulated in most probability and statistics texts. The other variables are defined as before.

Computing the Correct Option Price

The use of the formula requires the input of five variables: the price of the underlying security, the exercise price, the time of maturity, the interest rate, and the volatility of the security price. To illustrate the use of the formula, particular values for these variables are specified to calculate the value of an S&P 100 (OEX) option that has 90 days to expiration:

$S = 236$
$E = 235$
$T = 90/365 = .247$ years
$r = 6$ percent per annum
$\sigma = 18$ percent

The first three variables are easily observable from the option quotation. The time to maturity is obtained by counting the number of calendar days until the time of maturity, and then dividing it by 365 to get the time to maturity in annual terms. The method for estimating the volatility is described in Appendix B of this chapter. $T, r,$ and σ all are expressed in annual terms. Recalling the formula and substituting the appropriate variables, the option price is:

$$d_1 = \frac{ln(236 / 235) + (.06 + .18^2 / 2) .247}{.18\sqrt{.247}}$$

$$= .023 / .089 = .258$$

$$d_2 = .258 - .18\sqrt{.247} = .168$$

Using the normal distribution tables, it is found that:

$N(d_1) = N(.258) = .60169$
$N(d_2) = N(.168) = .56684$

The values for $N(.258)$ and $N(.168)$ are tabulated in most elementary probability and statistics texts, and are found also in mathematical handbooks. Using these values, we obtain the call option price

$$C = 236 \times .60169 - 235 \times e^{-.01479} \times .56684 = 10.75.$$

The option formula gives the correct option price in the sense that if the option price differs substantially from this price, there are arbitrage profit opportunities.

The correct option price as given by the formula depends on the security price, the exercise price, the time to expiration, the riskless interest rate, and the volatility of the security. In terms of practical usefulness, what the formula does not depend on is almost as important as what it does depend on. In particular, the formula is not contingent on any assessment of the future or expected security price. Also, it does not depend on investor attitudes toward risk. Because these are not observable, any formula that requires them as inputs is of little practical value. The fact that the option formula is independent of expectations and other subjective measures bodes well for its applicability.

Options on Dividend-Paying Stock

A stock dividend can be used to finance partially the borrowing cost for the option strategy, leading to a lower cost for the option. To see this, modify the option strategy presented at the start of the chapter to have the stock pay out a 3 percent dividend. While the premium from writing the option still can be invested at the market interest rate of 5 percent, the effective borrowing rate for the stock drops to 2 percent, because the dividend payout compensates for 3 percent of the borrowing cost. As shown in Exhibit 15–10, the option is less expensive than the $635 of the example presented in Exhibit 15–6 because the implied borrowing cost for the option is lower.

THE HEDGE RATIO

Going back to the initial example, the detection of the mispriced option is just the start of the arbitrage strategy. A position not only was taken in the option, but also in the security. This position gave the investor a hedge against unfavorable security price movements; no matter which way the security price moved, the value of the investor's position and the profit were unchanged.

As this suggests, a successful option strategy not only involves taking the appropriate position in a mispriced option, but also involves the second step of taking the appropriate hedge position in the underlying security. The option position allows the investor to profit from the mispriced option, and

EXHIBIT 15–10

Trading Strategy for an Option on a Stock with a 3 Percent Dividend

Current Position		End-of-Period Position	
		S = 95	S = 110
Write 3 call options	1,333	0	(3,000)
Buy 200 shares	(20,000)	19,000	22,000
Borrow at 2% effective rate	20,000	(20,400)	(20,400)
Lend at 5%	(1,333)	1,400	1,400
Net profit	0	0	0

the hedge position in the security allows the profit to be obtained risklessly, unaffected by shifts in the security price.

This hedge is of critical importance later on in the chapter. Because the calculation of the proper hedge is related to the option formula, it is introduced now.

Suppose an investor feels that a particular option currently selling at 7 is overpriced in the market. If it is overpriced, the investor gets a premium for writing it above the fair premium. But once the option is written, the investor is subject to the risks of later changes in the security price. The option may be overpriced now, but if the underlying security increases a few points, the option rises in price. If the investor's position in the option is not covered, a substantial amount is lost because of the change in the security price, even if the investor initially was correct about the mispricing.

Suppose the option price changes by half as much as any change in the security price. If the security rises by one point, the option rises by half a point. A one-point rise in the security means the value of the investor's short option position drops. To cover the position after the security rise, the option that the investor originally sold for only $700 needs to be bought back for $750. The .5 point rise in the option, therefore, means a loss of $50.

The investor can guard against this possible loss by taking a hedge position in the security. By buying 50 shares of security, the investor is hedged against a shift in the security price; if the security rises (or drops), the total position is unaffected. If the security rises by one point, the option position drops by $50; but the security position increases in value by $50—the $1 increase in the security price multiplied by the 50 shares of security held long.

If the security drops a point, then the option position increases in value by $50 because the option sold for $700 can now be bought back for $650. However, the security position drops by $50 from the one-point decline in the security price. In either case, the net position is unchanged—the investor has been insulated from movements in the security price.

If the investor is buying the option rather than writing it, the position in the option is hedged by selling the security short rather than buying it. So the hedge position in the security is always the opposite direction of the position in the call option. If long in the call option, the investor is short in the security. If short in the call option (i.e., if the investor writes the option), then a long position should be taken in the security to hedge.

The position is always opposite for a call option because the call option moves in the same direction as the security price; in a hedge, the option and security position must move in opposite directions. If the security and the option are held in the right proportions, the movements exactly counterbalance each other, so that the investor's total position is unchanged. On the other hand because a put option moves in the opposite direction of the underlying security, the proper hedge for a long put option is a long position in the security. Thus, the hedge position in the security is always the same direction as the position in the put.

The change in the price of an option with a dollar change in the price of the underlying is called the delta of the option, denoted by Δ. (In the example given, the delta of the call option is .5.) If the hedge ratio is set according to the value of delta so that Δ times as much security is held in a position opposite to the position of the call option (i.e., with the security held long if the call option is written, and with the security sold short if the call option is bought or Δ times as much of the security is held in a position the same as the put option), then the movement in the option position exactly counteracts any movement induced by shifts in the security price and the value of the investor's position is unchanged on net.

In summary, the ideal hedge ratio from the standpoint of eliminating the investor's exposure to the risk of the security is to hold $-\Delta$ shares of security for every option. In the Black-Scholes model, the value of Δ for a call can be computed using the first term of the formula:

$$\Delta = N(d_1)$$

When $N(\cdot)$ is the cumulative normal distribution function, and when d_1 is defined as in the Black-Scholes formula. For the generalized option model, the delta of a call option is:

$$\Delta = e^{-\delta T} N(d_1)$$

Using the S&P 100 option from the example of the Black-Scholes model in the previous section, compute the delta for that option as:

$$\Delta = N(.258) = .602$$

This delta means that if the S&P 500 Index changes in value by one point, the value of the call option changes by slightly over .6 points. If the index goes from 236 to 237, the option goes from 10.75 to 11.35. So if .6 units of the index are used to hedge each call, the change in the index value counterbalances any change in the option price and the investor's position is unaffected by the movement in the index (see Exhibit 15–11).

Using the put-call parity relationship, the delta of a put option in the Black-Scholes model and the generalized option model, is, respectively:

$$\Delta = N(d_1) - 1$$

and

$$\Delta = e^{-\delta T} N(d_1) - e^{-\delta} T$$

EXHIBIT 15–11
Effect of Security Price Change on Hedge Position

Current Price	
S&P 100 Index	236
S&P 235 call option	10.75
New Price	
S&P 100 Index	237
S&P 235 call option	11.35
Initial Delta	.60
Strategy	
Buy one 235 call	
Sell short .60 units of the S&P 100	
Effect of Price Change on Position	
Profit on option position	$11.35 - 10.75 = .60$
Profit on index position	$-.60\,(237 - 236) = -.60$
Net Change in Position	0

Once a mispriced option is discovered, the investor can form a riskless hedge by buying Δ shares of security for each option written (if the option is above its correct price) or by selling short Δ shares of security for each option bought (if the option is below the correct price).

The hedge position for the option changes as the underlying security price changes. It also changes as the time to expiration changes. So the hedging strategy involves a dynamic hedge. The ratio must be reevaluated frequently and the riskless hedge adjusted whenever the security price changes significantly, and as the time to expiration declines. Also, the delta is a local measure. That is, it represents a riskless hedge only if the security price moves by small amounts. If the security price suddenly jumps 5 or 10 points, the ratio does not ensure that the riskless hedge is maintained. This means that the possibility of jumps in the security price that cannot be covered by adjusting the hedge affects the riskiness of the hedging strategy.

APPENDIX A
THE DERIVATION OF THE OPTION PRICING FORMULA

While this chapter permits some intuition about the option formula, this appendix presents a more detailed look at the derivation of the formula. First, a one-period option formula is derived and then extended to a many-period formula. The resulting option pricing model, known as the binomial model, is not only easy to derive and intuitively appealing, it is also the most widely used model among professional option strategists.

The binomial model also provides a basis for understanding the derivation of the continuous-time formula. Indeed, the continuous-time formula is simply an extension of the binomial model to the case when the length of the time periods used is very small.

The Option Pricing Formula: A Simplified Case

As an introduction to the development of the option model, the example presented is expanded in the first section of the chapter.

Consider a security with a current price of S that changes by either a factor u or d by the next period. In the example of the first section of the chapter, $S = 100$, $u = 1.1$, and $d = .95$. By the next period, when the option reaches its expiration date, the security either increases to uS or decreases to dS. The option price on expiration is uniquely related to the value of the security at expiration, being worth $C_u = \text{MAX}(0, uS - E)$ if the security rises by a factor of u percent or $C_d = \text{Max}(0, dS - E)$ if the security drops by a factor d of its initial price.

The values for the security and the related values for the option are presented in Exhibit 15–12. This exhibit is the same as Exhibit 15–1, with the numbers replaced by symbols.

Using this specification for the behavior of the security price, the option price with one period to expiration is given by:

$$C = (pC_u + (1 - p)C_d) / r \qquad (1)$$

where

r = one plus the riskless interest rate and

p = $(r - d) / (u - d)$

The associated delta is:

$$\Delta = \frac{C_u - C_d}{(u - d)S} \qquad (2)$$

This formula was used in constructing the example in the preceding chapter. The delta for that example can be derived directly from Equation (2); the option price can be determined from Equation (1). Using that example to illustrate the formula:

$u = 1.1, d = .95, S = 100, r = 1.05$

$C_u = \text{Max}(0, (1.1 \times 100) - 100) = 10$

$C_d = \text{Max}(0, (.95 \times 100) - 100) = 0$

The delta is computed as:

$$\Delta = \frac{C_u - C_d}{u - d)S} = \frac{10 - 0}{(1.1 - .95)\,100} = \frac{2}{3}$$

Thus, the proper hedge ratio is to write calls against the security in a ratio of 3 to 2.

To compute the correct option price, use Equation (1), with:

$$p = \frac{1.05 - .95}{1.1 - .95} = \frac{2}{3}$$

Therefore:

$$C = \left(\frac{2}{3} \times 10 + \frac{1}{3} \times 0\right)\frac{1}{1.05} = 6.35$$

EXHIBIT 15–12
One-Period Option Pricing

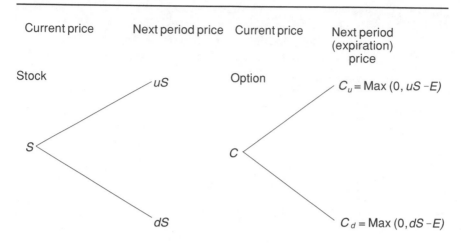

If the option is not priced according to the pricing formula given in Equation (1), then an arbitrage profit is possible. If the option price is higher than the formula states, then the investor makes arbitrage profits by following the strategy of writing calls and buying the security in the ratio Δ and financing the difference between the option premium and the price of the security through borrowing at the riskless rate. If the market price for the call is below the price given by the equation, then the investor uses the reverse strategy of buying calls and selling the security short in the proportions dictated by the delta and putting the proceeds into the riskless asset to yield an arbitrage profit.

The delta-neutral hedge. The first step in constructing the option model is creating a delta-neutral hedge—a position that guarantees the same return no matter what the security price is at the end of the period. This position is formed by writing one call option against Δ units of the security. With this position, the initial cost is the cost of the shares, Δ S, minus the income from the option, or Δ S − C. At the end of the period, the position is worth either $\Delta uS - C_u$ or $\Delta dS - C_d$, depending on whether the security rises or falls in value.

What determines the size of the hedge? To get a riskless position, choose a hedge that ensures that the position is the same no matter which way the security moves. That is, choose a Δ so that:

$$\Delta uS - C_u = \Delta dS - C_d \tag{3}$$

Solving for Δ, this implies that the delta should be

$$\Delta = \frac{C_u - C_d}{(u - d)S} \tag{4}$$

The one-period option formula. With this ratio of the security held to options written, there is a return that is certain no matter which way the security moves. This portfolio, therefore, replicates the riskless asset. Because the return is riskless, it must be that it yields the riskless rate of interest. That is, the value of the security-option position at the end of the period must equal the initial investment in the position brought forward by one period's interest, or:

$$\Delta = uS - C_u = r(S\Delta - C) \tag{5}$$

In this equation, r equals one plus the riskless rate. Rewriting this equation and substituting for Δ from Equation (4):

$$C = \left(\frac{(r - d)}{u - d} C_u + \frac{(u - r)}{u - d} C_d \right) / r \tag{6}$$

Defining $p = (r - d) / (u - d)$, rewrite Equation (6) in the simpler form:

$$C = (pC_u + (1 - p)C_d) / r. \tag{7}$$

This is the equation for the price of a call option with one period to maturity.

There is valuable insight into the option pricing formula by thinking of the variable p as a probability. If p is the probability that the security will go up and $(1-p)$ is the probability the security will go down, the current option price in Equation (7) simply equals the expected future option price discounted by the riskless interest rate. Keep in mind that the value of p is not obtained as a probability of the security price going up or down. As already noted, one of the attractive features of the option pricing formula is that the probability of the security price moving up or down is not needed as an input. But it turns out that p is the probability of the security going up if the expected return to the security is set equal to the risk-free rate. That is, if p equals the probability of the security going up to uS and if the expected return of the security is set equal to the risk-free return, then:

$$p(uS) + (1 - p)(dS) = rS$$

Solving for p in this equation, $p = (r - d) / (u - d)$. For the purpose of option pricing, the riskless hedging argument indicates that the expected return of the security equals the riskless rate of return because the hedge eliminates any risk from the security price. The option pricing problem thus can be approached from a risk-neutral perspective. This means that when a riskless hedge exists, the price of an option can be calculated as the present value of its expected return, assuming the expected return to the security equals the risk-free rate.

Note that the call option price is a function of the price of the security, the exercise price, the riskless interest rate, and the range of the future security price as represented by u and d. These are the same variables that determine the option value in the Black-Scholes formula. In this case, the parameters u and d provide a measure of volatility.

Put options are priced in the same way as calls; the only difference is in the specification of the end-of-period payoff. While $C_u = \text{Max} (0, uS - E)$ and $C_d = \text{Max} (0, dS - E)$ for a call option, we have $P_u = \text{Max} (0, E - uS)$ and $P_d = \text{Max} (0, E - dS)$ for a put option. Indeed, in addition to calls and puts, a wide set of contingent claims can be priced by this arbitrage relationship by specifying the terminal value of the claim as a function of the underlying asset.

The two-period option formula. The one-period case is unrealistic because the security price may move many times between a given date and the time the option expires. However as previously described, the same arbitrage principle can be applied in the many-period case, although the computations become more tedious. To obtain the pricing formula for many periods, first extend the technique to the two-period case. Go back one period from the formula derived and see what the pricing formula is when there are two periods before the option expires.

Let the price of the security two periods before the expiration be S. With one period to expiration, the security is worth either uS or dS dollars, assuming that the security follows the same binomial process for price changes each period. At the time of maturity of the option, the security again goes up by u or down by d. At the time of maturity, then, its price is uuS (if it goes up by u both times), udS (if it goes up one time and down one time) or ddS (if it drops by d percent both times). Note that $udS = duS$, so that the price of the security at expiration is the same regardless of which period it goes up and which period it goes down.

The price of the option when there are two periods to expiration can be denumerated in a similar way. If the price of the option with two periods to expiration is C, then by the next period it will have a price of C_u or C_d depending on whether the security goes up or down. On expiration its price is $C_{uu} = \text{Max} (0, u^2 S - E)$ if the security rises both periods, $C_{ud} = \text{Max} (0, udS - E)$ if the security goes up one period and down the other, and $C_{dd} = \text{Max} (0, d^2 S - E)$ if the security drops in both periods. The possible movement of the security price and the related movement of the option price are illustated in Exhibit 15–13.

The value of the options with one period left can be derived by the same methods that are used in the one-period case. If the value of the option with one period left is C_u, then it is worth either C_{uu} or C_{ud} at maturity, depending on whether the security is worth $u^2 S$ or udS at maturity. Relating back to Equation (7), it is apparent that if the security price with one period left is uS, the option price is:

$$C_u = (pC_{uu} + (1 - p)C_{ud}) / r \qquad (8)$$

and if the security price is dS, the call option is worth:

$$C_d = (pC_{du} + (1-p)C_{dd}) / r \qquad (9)$$

Moving two periods back from the time of expiration, the same reasoning is applied again. With two periods left, the security price is S and the security price the next period is either uS or dS. The related options prices are C_u and C_d. The option then is priced with two periods left to expiration according to Equation (7):

$$C = (pC_u + (1-p)C_d) / r \qquad (10)$$

When C_u and C_d already have been determined given by the application of Equations (8) and (9).

This recursive solution method permits pricing a two-period option by repeated application of the one-period formula. As with option pricing in the one-period setting, the price here is expressed in terms of known parameters, $S, E, r, u,$ and d. Because the possible values of the option at maturity are known, the two-period value can be determined exactly.

The use of the two-period case can be illustrated by extending the one-period example.

Profiting from Mispriced Options: A Two-Period Example

If the security is at \$100 with two periods to go, its values with one period left is 95 or 110, and at expiration the security is worth either $uuS = (1.1)(1.1)100 = 121$, $udS = (1.1)(.95)100 = 104.50$, or $ddS = (.95)(.95)100 = 90.25$. The option at maturity is worth either zero or the final security value at expiration minus the exercise price of \$100, $C_{uu} = 21$, $C_{ud} = 4.5$, or $C_{dd} = 0$. Working back to one period before expiration, the option price can be obtained by using the one-period option formula. If the security is at 110 with one period left, then $C_u = 21$ and $C_d = 4.5$, so that:

$$C = (\frac{2}{3} \times 21 + \frac{1}{3} \times 4.5) / 1.05 = 14.76$$

If the security is at 95 with one period remaining, the option price can be computed as:

$$C = (\frac{2}{3} \times 4.5 + \frac{1}{3} \times 05) / 1.05 = 2.86$$

The price of the option with two periods remaining now can be obtained by again applying the one-period formula, with the values for C_u and C_d being 14.76 and 2.86, respectively. The resulting value is:

$$C = (\frac{2}{3} \times 14.76 + \frac{1}{3} \times 2.86)/1.05 = 10.28$$

EXHIBIT 15–13

An Example of Security Price Movement and Two-Period Option Pricing

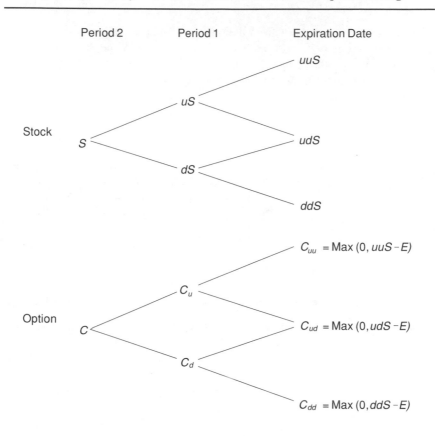

The security prices and the related option prices are shown in Exhibit 15–14. The delta is placed in parentheses below the option prices in that exhibit. The delta is calculated using Equation (2).

Depending on the market price of the option, the delta dictates either buying Δ shares of a security for each option written or selling short h shares of security for each option bought. Denoting the market price of the option C_m, trading strategies are:

Period 1

If $C_m > C$, buy 79.3 shares for each 100 call options written.

If $C_m < C$, sell 79.3 shares for each 100 call options bought.

Period 2

$S = 110$

If $C_m > C_u$, buy 100 shares for each 100 call option written.

If $C_m < C_u$, sell 100 shares for each 100 call options bought.

$S = 95$

If $C_m > C_d$, buy 31.6 shares for each 100 call options written.

If $C_m < C_d$, sell 31.6 shares for each 100 call options bought.

To illustrate the strategy, take a particular path for the security price. Suppose the security goes from 100 to 110, and that the option price in the market, C_m is $11.

The period-by-period steps in the strategy are:

Period 1

S = $100, C = 10.28, \Delta = .793$

Write 100 options at 11	1,100
Buy 79.3 shares of security at 100	(7,930)
Borrow (7,930 – 1,100) at 5 percent	6,830
Net position	0

By the next period, the security is at $110. Say that the option goes to $16. It therefore remains overpriced. The investor maintains a short position in the option, but with a delta of 1. By buying 20.7 more shares of security in period 2, revise the delta to the prescribed 100 shares of security per 100 options.

Period 2

S = $100, C = 14.76, \Delta = 1.0$

Buy 20.7 shares of security 110	(2,277)
Borrow 2,277 at 5 percent	2,277
Net position	0

Following this strategy through to expiration date, the final profit is $79 no matter which direction the security moves on the expiration date:

Expiration date

S = $121, C = 21$

Sell 100 shares of security at 121	12,100
Buy 100 options at 21	(2,100)
Repay loan of 6,830 $(1.05)^2$	(7,530)
Repay loan of 2,277 (1.05)	(2,391)
Net Profit	79

EXHIBIT 15–14
An Example of Two-Period Option Pricing

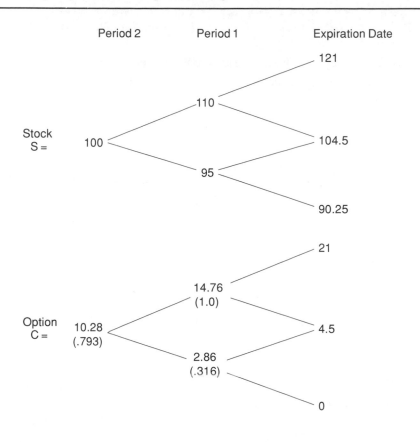

$S = 104.5, C = 4.5$

Sell 100 shares of security at 104.5		10,450
Buy 100 options at 4.5		(450)
Repay loan of 6,830 $(1.05)^2$		(7,530)
Repay loan of 2,277 (1.05		(2,391)
Net profit		79

The delta changes from period to period, requiring constant updating of the portfolio position. Over the two periods, the delta moved from .793 to 1.0. Because of the constant updating of the hedge position, this strategy is called a dynamic hedging strategy. To maintain the riskless position, the ratio of options to security must change as the time to expiration gets closer and as the security price changes. If the delta is not adjusted, the once riskless position becomes risky, and the opportunity for an arbitrage profit is lost.

Option Pricing with Early Exercise

Most listed options are American options, options that can be exercised any time on or before the expiration date. For call options that do not have discrete cash flows it turns out that the value of an American call option is the same as that of a European call option. However for call options with dividends or other cash flows and for put options in general, it may be optimal to exercise early. The American option then has a greater value than its European counterpart.

The possibility of early exercise adds substantial complexity to option pricing. Rather than evaluating the exercise value of the option only at expiration, a check now must be made at every time period to see if the option is worth more exercised than not, and the option price must take on the greater of these two values. Fortunately, the numerical procedure of the binomial pricing method provides a natural way for making this check because the solution already involves a pricing calculation at every time period. When the one-period option pricing formula is applied at every time period, include a second check to compare the resulting option price with the value the option will have if it is exercised, and then use the greater of these values as the option price.

For American options, evaluate each period whether the option is worth more dead than it is alive. The value of the option dead is simply its intrinsic value: the maximum of 0 or $S - E$ for a call option, the maximum of 0 or $E - S$ for a put option. The value of the option alive is the value brought back by the recursive pricing methodology described earlier:

$$C = [p\,C_u + (1 - p)\,C_d] \,/\, r$$

At each node in the option model, instead of solving recursively for the option value as shown in Exhibit 15–13, take the greater of the value of the option dead or alive. For an American call option, then, the value at each node is:

$$C = \text{Max}(C_{\text{dead}}, C_{\text{alive}})$$
$$= \text{Max}\,(S - E, [p\,C_u + (1 - p)\,C_d] \,/\, r)$$

The Black-Scholes Model as a Limiting Case of the Binomial Model

The binomial formula approximates reality better as more time periods are used; that is, rather than splitting six months into six periods of one month each, split six months into 26 periods of one week each. The objections to having the security

EXHIBIT 15–15
Comparison of the Binomial and Black-Scholes Models

(Stock price = 50; Risk-free interest rate = 10%)

Model	Days to Expiration	$\sigma = .2$ Exercise Price			$\sigma = .4$ Exercise Price		
		45	50	55	45	50	55
Binomial	30	5.38	1.40	.07	5.87	2.60	.83
with	120	6.74	3.21	1.12	8.03	5.53	3.06
$N = 5$	210	7.95	4.59	2.14	10.00	7.58	5.15
Binomial	30	5.37	1.36	.08	5.82	2.50	.78
with	120	6.70	3.13	1.08	8.23	5.35	3.29
$N = 25$	210	7.93	4.49	2.14	10.07	7.35	5.21
Black-Scholes	30	5.39	1.36	.08	5.83	2.49	.77
(Binomial	120	6.75	3.15	1.09	8.25	5.35	3.27
with							
$N = \infty$)	210	8.02	4.54	2.21	10.11	7.36	5.22

follow a simplistic binomial price change are reduced with further time periods because over those time periods the security can take on a wide range of values. The most important question for application then is how many time periods are necessary to get a good approximation of reality. Exhibit 15–15 answers this by comparing the binomial model for various volatilities, times to expiration, and exercise prices. It also compares the price from the binomial formula with the price of its continuous time counterpart, the Black-Scholes formula. The table looks at the binomial approximation with only five periods and with 25 periods.

As each time period becomes smaller and smaller and the number of time periods used in the binomial formula approaches infinity, the binomial formula approaches the Black-Scholes formula. (The Black-Scholes formula has the drawback, however, of not being able to consider the possibility of early exercise.) It is clear from Exhibit 15–15, however, that the number of time periods does not need to get too large for the formula values to coincide closely. For 25 periods, the two formulas are often within a few pennies of each other. For practical purposes, as few as 25 periods may be sufficient.

APPENDIX B
VOLATILITY ESTIMATION

The five principal inputs into the option pricing formula are the price of the underlying security, the exercise price of the option, the time to expiration of the option, the risk-free interest rate, and the security's price volatility. The first three are determined immediately by the terms of the option contract; the risk-free interest rate can be proxied by the Treasury bill rate or the certificate of deposit rate prevailing until the expiration of the option. The critical input that remains for the successful use of the option pricing formula is volatility.

In theory, there is little problem in getting an adequate volatility estimate. Unlike attempts to estimate the direction of the security price, the estimation of price volatility does not require any divination into the future course of the price or into the mind-set of other investors in the market. Volatility estimators are simply a reflection of how variable price movement is expected to be. The direction of the security movement does not matter. A security can be just as volatile going up 20 percent in value as it can when it is trading up and down in a 10 percent trading range.

In practice, volatility estimation is complicated by a number of factors. The most significant problem is the instability of volatility over time. Exhibit 15–16 traces the volatility for the S&P 500 over a nine-year period. Each of the estimates in this exhibit was made using data over 60 trading days. The volatility has a mean of approximately 15 percent, but there are times when the market heats up and volatility takes sudden jumps—at two points, the volatility went to nearly 24 percent, over one and one-half times the average volatility. This instability exacerbates volatility estimation methods that rely on past data. If volatility shifts about erratically, there is no reason to expect volatility estimated over the past to reflect current volatility.

Volatility Estimation Using Past Prices

Because volatility is a measure of the standard deviation of security returns, the estimators for volatility are essentially variance estimators. Indeed, the most straightforward volatility estimator, which uses closing stock prices, is simply the maximum likelihood variance estimator from elementary statistics. But estimating volatility with only closing prices ignores other valuable information in the price summary data. The high and low prices also contain information about the variability of prices, and after the close-to-close estimator is described, a more powerful volatility estimator that uses high and low prices is outlined.

EXHIBIT 15–16
S&P 500 60-Day Volatility

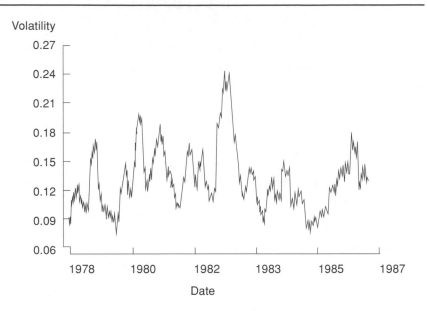

Estimation Using Close-to-Close Price Changes

Letting CDD_t be the closing price of the security for period t, the security return RDD_t is defined as the price relative between period t – 1 and period t, $R_t = C_t / C_{t-1}$. To approximate the continuously compounded returns, use the natural log of R_t in the computations. Denoting the mean return over n time periods by m:

$$m = \frac{1}{n} \sum_{t=1}^{n} (ln\ R_t)$$

The variance can be computed using the standard maximum likelihood variance estimator:

$$\sigma^2 = \frac{1}{n-1} \sum_{t=1}^{n} (ln\ R_t - m)^2$$

Volatility is obtained as the square root of σ^2. Note that the sum is divided by $(n-1)$ rather than n. This is necessary to obtain an unbiased estimate of the variance.

From this, volatility is seen simply as the square root of the variance of returns. Volatility should be adjusted to give an annualized value. If weekly closing prices are used in the variance calculation, then resulting volatility is multiplied by the square root of 52. If daily closing prices are used, daily volatility must be multiplied by the square root of the number of trading days in the year. While this varies from year to year, it is approximately 250 days.

A precise estimate of the volatility over any time period is possible with only a moderate number of observations. The accuracy of the estimate of past volatility is not the critical problem. Since market volatility may vary substantially over short time periods, the critical problem is whether that volatility estimate, based as it is on past prices, reflects the current volatility.

Volatility Estimation Using the Volatilities Implied in Option Prices

For investors who have a high regard for the wisdom of the market, the ideal estimate of volatility comes from polling those who are trading in the market. The volatility estimates of the traders might be averaged together, perhaps with more weight given to the larger and presumably better-informed traders. Unfortunately, no such poll is taken and, in any event, the more successful traders probably would not be forthcoming with their estimates. But the result of the poll—the weighted average of the volatility estimates held by those in the market—is readily available; it is embedded in the market price of every option.

It is already known that fair option value is a function of the security price, the time to expiration and exercise price of the option, the riskless interest rate, and the security's price volatility. Given the values of the other parameters and the market price of the option, a unique volatility can be solved that leads to that market option price. If the market price of the option is taken to be the correct price, the volatility backed out of the formula is the best estimate of the correct volatility. Put another way, the volatility implied by the market price is the market's opinion of what the volatility should be because in the aggregate the market takes the market price to be correct.

This volatility estimate is called implied volatility, which can be derived using an option formula. If the option formula $C\ (S,T,\ E,\ r,\ \sigma)$ is known as well as the current market price, denoted by C_m, then the implied volatility is that volatility σ that sets the formula value equal to the market value; the implied volatility is the value σ^* that solves the equation:

$$C_m = C\ (S,\ T,\ E,\ r,\ \sigma^*)$$

The resulting implied volatility obviously depends on the option model used.

The implied volatility is an attractive shortcut to volatility estimation. It lets the market do the work, leaving the final calculation to depend only on the current stock and option quotes, and the choice of the model. But there are obvious problems in using the implied volatility as presented here for finding mispriced options. Putting implied volatility into the option pricing formula always shows the option to be correctly priced, because implied volatility comes from setting the formula price equal to the market price in the first place. This identity between the market option price and the formula price can be avoided by using the average of the implied volatilities of a number of options on the same stock. Also, implied volatility can be used directly in pinpointing mispriced options without reentering implied volatility into the option pricing formula.

Implied Volatility Provides a Method for Finding Mispriced Options

There is only one volatility for each security. If implied volatility for one option on a particular security is 24.8 percent and the implied volatility for another option is 21.5 percent, both volatilities cannot be correct. There is no way to know which of the two volatilities is closest to the truth without further investigation; but for some option trading strategies, it is enough to know that the two volatilities differ significantly. Because a higher option price leads to a higher implied volatility, it is clear that the option with 24.8 percent volatility is overpriced relative to the option with 21.5 percent volatility; a profitable spread may be executed by buying the underpriced option and writing the overpriced option against it.

The implied volatility already has all the information necessary to find relatively mispriced options. If two options have a wide spread in implied volatilities, a profit opportunity may exist. If the implied volatility on one option is far out of line with the implied volatilities on the other options, that alone may be enough to indicate a mispricing. It must be kept in mind that implied volatility is only as correct as the option formula that was used to find it. If the option formula does not allow for early exercise or does not include dividends, implied volatility reflects that misspecification. In some cases, however, misspecifications affect all of the option prices in the same way and the variations in implied volatilities of the options still may reflect relative mispricing. If the magnitude of the specification errors does not vary greatly from option to option, the spreads in the implied volatilities can still lead to the discovery of profit opportunities.

Chapter Sixteen

Analyzing the Equity-Linked Note

James J. Crawford, M.S.

Investors who want equity exposure with guaranteed return of principal can get it by purchasing an equity-linked note (ELN). ELNs are typically medium-term structured notes that provide equity index participation with downside protection. They can be linked to any equity index with a guaranteed minimum return in the investor's home currency. The guarantee makes ELNs a safe way to participate in any equity market or customized equity basket, but the downside protection comes at a price. The expected return of an ELN is lower than an outright equity position.

ELNs are a cross between a fixed-income security and an equity index. Not surprisingly, the risk and return lie between that of fixed income and equity. When interest rates are high and expected to fall, ELNs are particularly attractive because of the fixed-income portion of the note. Also, equity markets tend to perform well in declining-rate environments.

ELNs have variable structures and investors can set the terms to match their portfolio objectives. For instance, to increase the equity participation of the note, lengthen the maturity and lower the minimum return guarantee. These adjustments increase risk as well. Extending the maturity increases credit risk while lowering the minimum return incurs more downside risk.

U.S. insurance companies hold a significant portion of the ELN market. In 1993, the National Association of Insurance Commissioners (NAIC) made risk-based capital (RBC) requirements significantly higher for common stock. Fortunately, the capital requirements for ELNs are insignificant.

Because ELNs have equity exposure, insurance companies could invest in equity-based securities with favorable regulatory treatment. Although the returns from ELNs are not as high as those from equities, they provide higher returns on average than fixed-income securities.

ELNs contain several costs. Highly rated issuers of ELNs are usually given funding concessions, typically between 25 to 60 basis points. Because ELNs contain embedded options, dealers usually get a 25 to 35 basis point commission for deal structuring. Complicated deals can have up to 100 basis point commissions. By canvassing many dealers, I find that nominal levels for both concessions and commissions are between 25 and 30 basis points for ELNs.

The remainder of this chapter explains the technical details of pricing an ELN from the investor perspective. The first section will show that an ELN is best viewed as a combined position in a zero-coupon corporate bond and a call option on an equity index. Insurance company demand for ELNs is briefly explained, focusing on the regulatory changes which give favorable accounting treatment to ELNs versus equity. Finally, I cover the pricing model, using a stochastic simulation approach.

ELN = INDEX CALL OPTION + ZERO-COUPON CORPORATE BOND

Equity-linked notes are designed to give investors exposure to an equity index with a guaranteed minimum return. There are many types of ELNs, but they usually have the same basic structure—a combined position in a zero-coupon bond and a long-dated call option on an equity index or basket of equities. There is no real standardization in the structured note market; for instance, the ELNs we discuss can have completely different indicative pricing sheets and payoff formulas and yet be mathematically equivalent or at least very similar. It is up to the analyst to check all payoff formulas presented by different offerings. Better yet, investors should become comfortable with a particular structure and format and then have dealers conform to it.

The payoff of an ELN is option-like because the ELN participates at a multiple of the index if the average level of the equity index goes above a certain value. Otherwise the ELN returns a preset minimum. For this analysis, we will price an ELN on the S&P 500 index. The approach taken will work for any zero-coupon domestic ELN. Our aim is to decompose the structure and price each piece separately, keeping an eye out for credit risk, funding costs, LIBOR financing, and option pricing.

The option embedded is usually an arithmetic average rate (Asian) option. This option pays off if the average return of the underlying equity index is above a preset return level. The averaging feature lowers the cost of the option relative to a standard call option. Because the maturity of ELNs is usually greater than exchange-traded options, the option must be synthesized by means of dynamic hedging by the dealer. Dynamic hedging is a trading strategy that replicates the payoff of an option. The cost of this strategy, plus fees, is the cost of the option. As markets become more volatile, the cost of dynamic hedging increases. In other words, the option is more expensive. The Asian option is less sensitive to volatility than plain calls and is subsequently cheaper to hedge. As a result, the dealer can pass the cost savings on to the investor. The Asian option is also less sensitive to one specific date, when a temporary market crisis could severely hinder returns.

Virtually any type of equity index call option can be embedded within an ELN; for instance, an up-and-in barrier call would not be an unusual substitute for the Asian call. As with any structured note, the nature of the future return distribution can be significantly skewed or even bimodal. The main task of the analyst is to price the security correctly while understanding the potential returns from the security. Risk is no longer defined as just the standard deviation of the return distribution. The shape of the distribution is ultimately what is being purchased and the investor must assess his or her utility for it. We will investigate ELNs with an embedded Asian call, but the analysis works for any ELN provided that one has and understands the correct option pricing model. Exotic option pricing models are readily available from off-the-shelf financial software firms.

INSURANCE COMPANY ELN DEMAND

Risk-based capital (RBC) is a regulatory accounting measure for setting a minimum capital level for a financial institution. It is a short-term solvency measure. The amount of capital required is determined by the risk classification set forth by the regulators. RBC is now a fact of life for insurance companies, and regulators are monitoring the RBC ratio, which is the adjusted capital divided by total RBC. The RBC factor is the capital charge

EXHIBIT 16–1
NAIC Risk-Based Capital Factors

Asset Class	Capital Requirement (Percent)
U.S. Treasuries	0.0%
AAA–A corporate bonds	0.3
BBB corporate bonds	1.0
BB corporate bonds	4.0
B corporate bonds	9.0
Common stock	30.0

for a specific asset class; that is, a 30 percent RBC factor for common stock means that 30 percent of the common stock value held must be applied to the total RBC calculation. In simple terms, if common stocks are held, 30 percent of the value must be set aside in a reserve (see Exhibit 16–1).

The RBC charge for equities is significantly greater than that for investment grade bonds. Equity exposure has become "expensive" in terms of RBC. If an insurance company buys an ELN from a AAA–A credit, the RBC charge is only 0.3 percent—100 times less than the RBC for equity. The RBC factor for ELNs is the same as fixed income because of the guaranteed minimum return. The return from an ELN is not as high as equities but is higher on average than comparable fixed income. The equity component raises the return relative to fixed income. There is also more risk. If the equities do not increase by a certain amount within the life of the ELN, the ELN return will be less than comparable fixed income.

BASIC STRUCTURE OF THE ELN

There are typically three participants in an ELN structure: the investor, issuer, and dealer. In our example, the investor is an insurance company that finds ELNs attractive because of RBC cost savings. The issuer who traditionally funds at LIBOR would be interested in borrowing through an ELN if a funding target of LIBOR—30 basis points—could be achieved. The dealer provides the service of structuring the note, using the resources of equity derivatives for the options, structured notes for the packaging, and fixed income for the funding arrangement. The main contribution of the dealer is to provide the dynamic hedging operations that make it possible to structure the cash flows according to the wishes of the issuer and investor. In return, the dealer profits from option mispricings and commissions. In the case of the ELN, the dealer is selling an option above the cost of producing that option for the customer. The option is created through a trading strategy using futures, which replicates the payoffs of the option. It is important for the investor to understand and quantify the embedded fees and concessions built into the deal.

Typically, investors do not have a thorough grasp of the principles and practices of options pricing, which causes them to rely solely on dealers for the correct analysis and pricing of the deals. Unless the investor's model prices the ELN cheaper, the investor may accept an expensive offer. Option pricing has many factors, particularly in longer-dated OTC markets where traditional option models may not be suitable for pricing without some adjustments. As longer-dated markets are thin, relative value comparisons become difficult or impossible, increasing dependence on models. We focus on the specifics of pricing and adjustments of option models in a later section.

For this analysis, we consider a six-year ELN linked to the S&P 500 with a minimum return of 120 percent of par (see Box 16–1).

This ELN returns the greater of 120 percent of par or 1.28 times the average return of the S&P 500. There are three averaging points. They occur at years 4, 5, and 6. The 1.28 is called the participation factor and is stated in units of percentage points. We call this issue a six-year ELN on the S&P 500 with a 128 percent participation and a minimum return of 3.062 percent (BEY) with three discrete averaging points in years 4, 5, and 6.

CASH FLOWS

Not surprisingly, many structured notes with indicative pricing sheets that appear fairly simple have complicated cash flow exchanges behind them. The cash flow arrangement behind an ELN is simple compared with that of many other structured notes. First, the investor lends the money to the issuer. The issuer then enters a swap with the dealer. The issuer pays a fixed coupon to the dealer in exchange for the ELN payment at maturity. At maturity, the issuer passes on the ELN payment to the investor. The result is that the investor gets an ELN, the issuer gets a fixed rate loan at an attractive rate,

---

Box 16–1

Six-Year ELN

Maturity: 6 Years
Price: 100 (percent of par)
Settlement date: 1/15/95
Maturity date: 1/15/01
Payment at maturity:
The maximum of

$$100 + 1.28 \times (S4 + S5 + S6)/3$$

or

$$120$$

where S4, S5, and S6 are the percentage returns from the settlement date
to the following dates:

S4 date: 1/15/99 (four years from settlement)

S5 date: 1/15/00 (five years from settlement)

S6 date: 1/15/01 (Maturity date – 6-year maturity)

The percentage returns are in units of percentage points (i.e., if the S&P
500 went up by 10 percent from the settlement date to the S4 date, then S4
is equal to 10).

---

and the dealer receives a fee for providing the resources. The investor is
exposed only to the credit of the obligor (see Exhibit 16–2).

Because the ELN is actually a combined position in an average rate call
option and a zero-coupon bond, the coupon payments made by the issuer to
the dealer are composed of the amortized cost of the call option plus interest
payments. The option produces the equity participation feature of the note.
The dealer can structure the deal in many ways according to the preferences
of the investor and issuer. For instance, the participation factor and guaranteed minimum can be set by the investor (unless the ELN is a prespecified
offering). The issuer in our example pays a fixed-rate loan but this can also
be floating or amortizing.

EXHIBIT 16–2
ELN Cash Flow Pattern

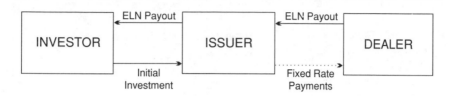

PRICING METHODOLOGY

For this example, all cash flows received from the ELN will occur in six years. To price the cash flows correctly, we need to use the right set of discount rates. Because no coupons are received, we only need to get the zero-coupon cost of funds rate for the issuer. Since the issuer funds at LIBOR, we must use the zero coupon swap rates based on LIBOR. Zero-coupon swap rates are derived from the swap par curve by a well-known bootstrapping algorithm.[1] On the Bloomberg, the function BCSW provides a set of zero-coupon swap rates. These rates can be thought of as the LIBOR spot rates.

In this example, we make the following assumptions (see Box 16–2). In six years, the ELN will pay the greater of 1.28 times the average return of the S&P 500, averaging points in years 4, 5, and 6, or 120 percent of par.

PAYOFF FUNCTION

To price this ELN, we must write out the payoff function so that the option and the fixed-income side are separate terms. The general formula is:

$$ELNPayoff = \frac{PF}{S_0}\max(\overline{S} - K, 0) + MR$$

where

---

1 John C. Hull, *Options, Futures, and other Derivative Securities*, 2nd ed. (Englewood Cliffs, NJ: Prentice Hall, 1993).

Box 16–2

Pricing Inputs

6-Year LIBOR (zero-coupon swap rate in BEY): 6.3%
Concession: 30 basis points
Maturity: 6 years
Minimum return: 120%
Participation factor: 128%
Dividend yield: 2.85% (annualized)
6-Year S&P 500 volatility: 15%

PF = Participation factor in decimal
S_0 = Starting value of the index
$\overline{S}$ = Average value of the index at specified points (at years 4, 5, and 6 for our case)
MR = Minimum return payoff in decimal

and

$$K = \frac{S_0}{PF}(MR + PF - 1) \qquad K \text{ is the strike price of the Asian option.}$$

The strike price or average index level that must be reached to receive equity participation for our example is (assume current index is at 451):

$$\frac{451}{1.28}(1.2 + 1.28 - 1) = 521.47$$

In other words, the index must increase by over 15.625 percent in six years or the investor gets the minimum return of 20 percent over par (120), which is equivalent to a bond yield of 3.062 percent.

The minimum return (MR) is simply the fixed-income portion of the note. In this case, it is 1.2. To price this piece, we discount 1.2 at the six-year LIBOR rate (6.3 percent) minus the concession (30 basis points):

$$\frac{1.2}{(1 + 0.06/2)^{12}} = 0.84166$$

The value of the fixed-income side is 84.166 in percentage par. Since the note is priced to par (100 percent), the remaining 15.834 (100 − 84.166) should be the value of the option.

To price the option, we need a model. For now, we will use a simple extension of the Black-Scholes option model for pricing options on an index with a known and constant dividend yield. This model has a closed-formula solution for European-style options and it assumes that prices are lognormally distributed.

Unfortunately, we need to price a European-style Asian call on an index. There are no exact closed-formula solutions for this type of option because of the nature of the arithmetic averaging on a lognormal price distribution.[2] A simple way to approximate the Black-Scholes formula while admitting the averaging feature is to use stochastic simulation methods, also called Monte Carlo simulation. The value of an option is the present value of the average option payoff, over all scenarios of the underlying security, in a risk-neutral economy. In a risk-neutral economy, we can assume that all assets grow at the risk-free rate and therefore can be discounted back at the risk-free rate. These arguments are based on the fundamentals of contingent-claims analysis, which is the cornerstone of all options pricing. It is well worth understanding the basics of this analysis because all option pricing models are based on fairly restrictive assumptions, which must be relaxed in order to use the models in practice. A good experience with the models permits users to "stretch" them for a particular situation while understanding the implications for the deal pricing. We present a small bit of experience here to shed some light on the problems investors should address when pricing an ELN.

RISK-NEUTRAL SIMULATION OF THE UNDERLYING INDEX

To price the option, we need to generate the paths of the underlying asset. To do this, we need a random number generator that produces normally distributed deviates (numbers) with zero mean and unit variance. These are

---

2 The details of this problem are beyond the scope of this paper. A good discussion of the Black-Scholes formula, its extensions, and Asian options can be found in Hull, *Options, Futures, and Other Derivative Securities*.

easy to come by as most of the popular spreadsheets have them built in. Next, we need the correct equation, which takes as input

S_t = Value of the underlying at time t
δ = Dividend yield
σ = Volatility
r = Risk-free rate
Δt = Time step size
ε_t = Random number generated at time t from a normal distribution with zero mean and variance of one.

and produces

S_{t+1} = Value of the underlying at time $t+1$.

t is in the units of the step size Δt. If Δt is 1/250, then t is in the units of one, two hundred, and fiftieths of a year (approximately one trading day). For instance, S_{1000}, S_{1250}, and S_{1500} are the values of the index at years 4, 5, and 6, respectively.

For now, δ, σ, r, and Δt remain constant throughout the simulation. The equation that generates S_{t+1} is

$$S_{t+1} = S_t \exp\left\{ (r - \delta - \sigma^2 / 2)\Delta t + \sigma_{\varepsilon_t} \sqrt{\Delta t} \right\}$$

Epsilon is normally distributed with zero mean and unit variance. This equation can be used to generate paths for the underlying index with a known dividend yield. It is the correct formula for generating lognormally distributed prices. It is based on fundamental arguments from stochastic calculus, which are beyond the scope of this chapter, but can be found in many textbooks.

In our example

σ = 0.15
r = $2\ln(1 + 0.063/2)$
δ = $\ln(1 + 0.0285)$
Δt = $1/250$

Note that r and δ are both converted to continuously compounded rates. This is a requirement since the simulation is mimicking a continuous time function.

Our first goal is to use the simulation to approximate the Black-Scholes exact solution. This is a good test of the simulation because we have the exact solution and can quantify the error of the approximation. After passing that test, we add the averaging feature, which is a trivial addition to the simulation. Since there is no exact solution for the Asian option, we must be meticulous when incorporating the averaging. The test against the straight Black-Scholes solution gives us confidence in the correctness of the final result, but it does not prove its correctness.

Δt must be small enough to give results close enough to the exact solution. A good method for choosing Δt is to start with an arbitrary value for it, run the simulation checking the result (option value), and then cut Δt in half, rerunning the simulation to see if the result improves. If it does (improve), cut Δt in half again and recheck the result. Continue cutting Δt in half until the final result no longer improves. If Δt is too small, computer rounded errors will dominate and corrupt the solution, so when choosing the initial Δt make sure it is not too small; try a quarter year first (0.25).

THE RISK-FREE RATE PROBLEM

According to option pricing theory, r is supposed to be the risk-free rate, more precisely, the zero-coupon Treasury rate (called the Treasury spot rate) with the same maturity as the option. But we are actually using the six-year LIBOR spot rate (alternatively called zero-coupon swap rate), which is more like a zero-coupon single-A financing rate.

Call options are effectively replicated by purchasing more equity when the market increases, by borrowing, and by selling equity as the market declines and lending the proceeds. The risk-free rate in the option model corresponds to this borrowing and lending rate. Clearly, dealers cannot borrow at the risk-free rate. LIBOR is used in practice because the dealers cannot replicate (hedge) the option that they are shorting by borrowing at the risk-free Treasury rate. The higher this rate, the more expensive the call option is to the investor, and LIBOR is typically higher than Treasuries. This hedge accounting is a particularly sensitive topic for longer-dated equity options, where the correlation between interest rates and stock prices lowers the dealer's hedging costs. To see this, we must realize that call options are replicated by purchasing more equity when the market increases and selling equity as the market declines. Because interest rates are negatively correlated to stocks, when the option replication strategy requires more equity (stock market increasing), rates tend to go down, making the financing of the equity cheaper and thereby lowering the cost of the option. When the stock market declines and the option replication dictates selling equity, the proceeds from the sales are put into the bond market. Since high rates and bear markets *tend* to go together, the option hedger (dealer) gets to park the money in higher-yielding bonds. This correlation issue suggests the use of a different model for the much longer-dated options (over 10 years) where correlation has more impact. We address alternative models in a later section.

SIMULATING THE INDEX TO GET BLACK-SCHOLES APPROXIMATION

By setting S_0 to the starting value of the index, one can calculate the value of the index at time $1, S_1$. In years, this would be the index value at time $1/250$. After that, plug in S_1 to get S_2 and then S_2 to get S_3 and so on, until six years of time has elapsed (because this ELN maturity is six years). To generate another path, repeat the process using a different set of values from the random number generator. If one generated one million paths in this fashion, one million future values for the stock index would result. Plugging these values into the standard European-style option payoff of $\max(S - K, 0)$ would give one million values, some of which would be $S - K$ and others which would be zero. By taking an average of these values and discounting at r, one should arrive at a very close approximation to the Black-Scholes closed formula for an index with a known dividend yield. This is done as follows:

$$OptionValue* = \exp(-rT)\overline{\max(S - K, 0)}$$

where

$OptionValue*$ = Approximated Black-Scholes for European call

r = Effective risk-free rate (continuously compounded)

T = Expiration time in years

$\overline{\max(S - K, 0)}$ = The average value of the payoff function at maturity

Once the simulated value approximates the Black-Scholes equation within an acceptable range, the averaging feature can be added.

For the straight Black-Scholes simulation, we get a set of values for the index at year 6. What we want for the Asian option is the set of average index values at year 6. For the six-year ELN with averaging in years 4, 5, and 6, simulate a path, saving the index values at years 4, 5, and 6 in simulated time, then take the average of these three numbers. Doing this for each path gives the set of average index values at year 6.

$$ELN\_Payoff\_for\_path\_i = \frac{PF}{S_0} \max(\bar{S}_i - K, 0) + MR$$

where

$$\bar{S}_i = \frac{S_{1000} + S_{1250} + S_{1500}}{3}$$

(This is the average value of the index for path i.)

and

$$K = \frac{S_0}{PF}(MR + PF - 1)$$

After generating the $\bar{S}_t$'s, calculate the following:

$$\ddot{S} = \frac{1}{N} \sum_{i=1}^{N} \max(\bar{S}_i - K, 0)$$

where

N = total number of paths generated

The future expected value of the ELN is

$$\frac{PF}{S_0}\ddot{S} + MR$$

The left hand side of this expression is the expected future value of the Asian option (risk-neutral). The right side is the future value of the guaranteed minimum return. The present value is calculated by discounting $\frac{PF}{S_0}\ddot{S}$ at the zero-coupon swap rate and discounting MR at the target funding rate, which in this case is LIBOR minus 30 basis points.

$$(1 + LIBOR)^{-12} \frac{PF}{S_0}\ddot{S} + (1 + LIBOR - concession)^{-12} MR$$

where

> LIBOR and *concession* are in decimal; that is, 6.3 percent is 0.063 and 30 basis points is 0.003.

Using the pricing inputs stated earlier, we calculate the value of the ELN to be 98.72. Since the note is priced to par, this ELN is selling for 100; the note is overpriced. By changing the participation factor from 128 to 136, the value of the note is 100. When pricing an ELN, the participation factor typically is adjusted until the issuer funding target is reached *and* the investor perceives fair value. Note that this fair value is based on a model that assumes constant and flat term structure of interest rates, with a constant dividend yield and constant volatility. In reality, all these factors change over time; the longer the maturity, the less reliable the model.

ALTERNATIVE MODELS

The simulation approach we have used is very flexible. The main restrictive assumptions of the model we used are:

- Flat term structure of interest rates
- Constant dividend yield
- Constant volatility
- Deterministic interest rates

We briefly explain possible extensions of the model.

Flat Term Structure

The Asian option in our example had three points, at years 4, 5, and 6, where the value of the index was needed in the simulation. Because of risk neutrality, we should use the effective risk-free rate as the index growth rate to obtain the correct forward index levels. In our model, we used the single rate corresponding to the maturity of the note. This gives the correct forward price at year 6, but not at years 4 and 5. If the yield curve is upward sloping, the forward prices will be lower at years 4 and 5. This will *lower* the value of the option. To extend the simulation model, the constant r should be replaced by $r(t)$, where r is a function of time. A simple way to do this for our case is to have $r(t)$ follow the following rules:

$r(t)$: Effective four-year risk-free rate if t ≤ 4

$r(t)$: Linearly interpolated risk-free rate between the five- and four-year rates if 4 < t ≤ 5

$r(t)$: Linearly interpolated risk-free rate between the six- and five-year rates if 5 < t ≤ 6

While simulating the index, $r(t)$ is now a function of time, which will give the correct values for the forward levels of the index at years 4, 5, and 6. This form of the model should be used for actual pricing because the term structure of interest rates is readily available from the market.

Constant Dividend Yield

Since future dividend yields cannot be determined at the time of pricing, they must be forecast. With the call option, the higher the input dividend yield, the *lower* the price of the option. Dealers tend to input the average of the past two or three years' index dividend yield. To circumvent this problem, an ELN that pays off the total return of the index can be structured. This will eliminate the dividend yield as an input to pricing from the investor's perspective. Dealers will usually charge more for total return structures because of increased hedging costs. Typically, index futures are used to hedge the option. The index futures do not include dividends so hedgers must devise hedging schemes to track the dividends. A costly way of doing this would be to buy either the actual securities in the index or an index-tracking basket of securities that produced the total return of the index.

Constant Volatility

Volatility is not constant over time. A quick-and-dirty way to see this is to compute historical volatility for different time periods. For the six-year option, one would view a six-year rolling historical volatility using daily data. This time series of historical volatility will fluctuate over time. Some dealers incorporate this uncertainty into the simple model (constant volatility) by calculating the standard deviation of the rolling historical volatility time series and adding one to two times this number to the current historical volatility. The current historical volatility for a six-year expiration would be the historical volatility over the past six years.

Implied volatility for equities is usually above the historical volatility because of the uncertainty of volatility estimates. Option models are constructed assuming a particular probability distribution for price or rate movements. The assumed distribution will always fail to capture actual movements all the time because the markets are continually evolving. We can never achieve certainty in financial markets; even in the case of probability.

Deterministic Interest Rates

The interest rates in our model are not random. In markets, interest rates vary over time and the changes are negatively correlated to price changes of equities. To capture this effect, one would implement a two-factor stochastic simulation where the factors are the interest rates and the equity index. The correlation between the index and the interest rates would have to be estimated. This type of model would be required to investigate the pricing of longer-dated options since the variable interest rates will have more influence. The two-factor model can be implemented by generating two random numbers with zero mean and unit variance with the specified correlation. This can be done as follows:

1. Generate two random numbers, x_1 and x_2, from N(0,1).
2. Transform them into two new random numbers, ε_1 and ε_2, from N(0,1) by the following equations:

$$\varepsilon_1 = x_1$$
$$\varepsilon_2 = \rho x_1 + x_2 \sqrt{1 - \rho^2}$$

   At each step of the simulation, generate new epsilons, one for the index and one for the rates.
3. Plug the two random numbers into:

$$r_{t+1} = r_t \lambda_t \exp\left\{\sigma_r \varepsilon_1 \sqrt{\Delta t}\right\}$$
$$S_{t+1} = S_t \exp\left\{(r_t - \delta - \sigma^2/2)\Delta t + \sigma_t \varepsilon_2 \sqrt{\Delta t}\right\}$$

   where the new terms are:

   σ_r = Volatility of short-term interest rate
   σ_I = Volatility of the index
   λ_t = Risk-neutral adjustment for interest rate process

The risk-neutral adjustments must be solved for numerically so that the short-rate paths correctly price the zero-coupon term structure (spot curve). The implementation must handle this calibration process before the index values can be generated.

Because the correlation between the index and the short-term interest rates is not directly observable, it must be estimated. Methods for doing this are sophisticated. Historical correlation can be used as a guide by trying a range of correlations centered on the sample value. It is clear that longer-dated options become much more difficult to analyze and each new addition to the model can introduce more error.

PAYOFF DIAGRAMS AND RETURN DISTRIBUTIONS

To understand the market risks of any investment, one must look at the payoff diagrams and return distributions at all relevant future times. Payoff diagrams show the gain or loss at a particular time relative to underlying values. Payoff diagrams represent the potential outcomes for the investment. In the case of an equity or a zero-coupon bond held to maturity, the payoff functions are linear. A zero-coupon bond sold before maturity has a nonlinear payoff, but it is well approximated at any point by a line plus a parabola corresponding to the duration and convexity of the bond. A range note pays a high coupon as long as rates are between a specified range. No coupon is received outside that range, but principal is returned. Payoffs for a call option and an ELN have the characteristic "hockey stick" profile.

Return distributions show the range of returns along with probabilities of occurrence. The distributions must be assumed or based on history since no one can know the exact future distribution. The standard assumption for stocks is to use the normal distribution for returns.

With combined linear payoffs and normally distributed returns, the capital asset pricing model (CAPM) provides a framework for understanding risk and return. Risk is defined as the standard deviation and return is the mean. Many investors now embrace the notion that risk and return tend to go together. But this is based on a linear and normally distributed world. Structured notes need more than standard deviation of returns to identify risk.

Investors must examine potential return distributions of investments before including them in a portfolio. Once the investments are in the portfolio, investors must not make the mistake of applying CAPM without extending the definition of risk to incorporate skewness and downside risk measures.

HISTORICAL ANALYSIS

To compare the performance of ELNs to the S&P 500, we test how the ELN performed relative to the S&P using Ibbotson data from 1926 to the present. Exhibit 16–3 shows how a six-year ELN with 126 percent participation and 120 percent of par minimum performed relative to the total return of the S&P 500. The upward sloping diagonal line indicates where the ELN and S&P 500 total return break even. Each point of the graph is an outcome of the ELN. Points below the break-even line show where the ELN underperformed the S&P. As one can see, the ELN rarely outperforms the S&P on the upside.

To see the impact of lowering the minimum return of the ELN, we plot the same type of graph for a fairly priced ELN with a minimum return of

EXHIBIT 16–3
Six-Year ELN (126 Percent Participation; 120 Percent Par Minimum)

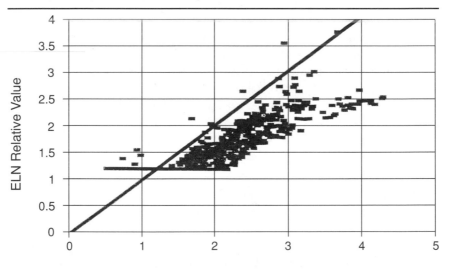

S&P 500 Relative Value

EXHIBIT 16–4

Six-Year ELN *(189 Percent Participation; 90 Percent Par Minimum)*

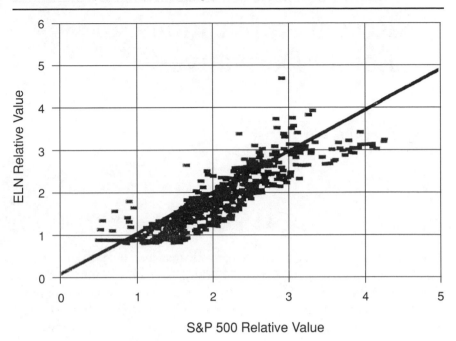

S&P 500 Relative Value

90 percent par (see Exhibit 16–4). In other words, 10 percent of principal is at risk. The cluster of returns is closer to breakeven as the minimum return drops.

Chapter Seventeen

Recent Applications for Equity Derivatives

Ronald T. Slivka

ING Baring (U.S.) Securities, Inc.

Applications of equity derivatives to portfolio management fall comfortably into three general categories: asset hedging, asset substitution, and asset allocation. Within each category are traditional strategies and new or more recent applications. Most of the historical applications have been covered well in survey articles, texts, and research papers over the past few years. [1] While they deserve reference, little time will be spent here reviewing such strategies. Instead, the focus will be on new or emerging applications.

ASSET HEDGING

Asset hedging involves pairing a derivative with an asset to modify its total exposure to price fluctuations. Historical activities in this category include:

Index arbitrage in which a stock basket is purchased and futures sold to form a market neutral combination having an above average rate of return.

Portfolio insurance in which index puts are purchased systematically to protect an investment portfolio against market declines.

Covered call writing in which calls covering the shares of a single stock or stock basket are sold to raise premium income and reduce downside risk.

---

1 See, for example, *The Equity Derivatives Handbook,* John Watson, ed. (Euromoney, 1993).

Covered swaps in which a swap paying the return on shares held of a stock or stock basket is negotiated in exchange for a floating rate payment.

While these activities continue to be pursued by a number of managers on behalf of their clients, a demand is emerging for more sophisticated hedge designs to suit less standard investment circumstances or to better suit existing ones. Many investment problems have yielded to the application of options with special features. Two examples follow.

Short Sales

An investor is short a single stock and wants protection against a substantial rise that would result in large losses. Ideally, the stock position should be liquidated if the price rises above a targeted maximum risk level. Assuming, for example, that this level is 10 percent above the current market price, at least three alternatives are available:

1. Place a stop loss order at 10 percent above the current stock price.
2. Buy a European call struck 10 percent out of the money.
3. Buy an at-the-money knockout call with rebate and with a barrier 10 percent in the money. Arrange for physical delivery at the barrier price once the barrier is reached.

A stop loss order will result in the purchase of stock but at an uncertain price. The investor risks purchase at a price potentially well above the 10 percent level as this type of order becomes a market order once the stop loss level is touched. This is especially true if the barrier is penetrated in a sharply rising market. Such an order also must be refreshed daily, thereby placing an additional administrative burden on the investor. Finally the broker must attend to this order in the course of a busy day. Because of the careful scrutiny they must receive throughout the day, such orders have a high nuisance value and accordingly are less effective in practice than in theory.

The second solution also has certain disadvantages. A Eurocall cannot be exercised prior to its expiration, thereby forcing the investor either to sell it and buy stock at the market, or to hold the position to the maturity of the call, thereby tying up capital in a possibly undesirable position. If the call were American, the premium price would have been higher than the Eurocall and any remaining time premium would be forfeited upon premature exercise. None of these shortcomings need exist with barrier options. Finally, use of American calls and Eurocalls severely restricts the universe of stocks for short sales, whereas customized barrier calls can be constructed on most single stocks that trade.

By electing to use the barrier call, these shortcomings are avoided. When the stock price reaches the barrier, a rebate is received equal to the in-the-money call amount and stock is called in at the barrier price for delivery against the short position. This customized call enjoys several advantages over the prior two solutions. The barrier, when touched, automatically extinguishes the call. No separate sale is required. The rebate, equal to intrinsic value (in-the-money amount), offsets the then current stock loss on the short position. The separately negotiated physical delivery of stock to the investor at the barrier price allows the short position to be extinguished with no further uncertainty of capital losses. Here, then, is a hedging application that fits with a commonly pursued bearish strategy.

Alternatives two and three are not designed to be truly equivalent in their end results. Because the Eurocall is struck out of the money, it will be cheaper than the knockout call which protects fully against losses, much as an at-the-money Eurocall might. A sense of relative value for at the money knockout and Eurocalls is portrayed in Exhibit 17–1. You can see that the knockout with rebate is cheaper than the Eurocall and becomes increasingly

EXHIBIT 17–1
In-the-Money Knockout Call Option versus a Standard European Call

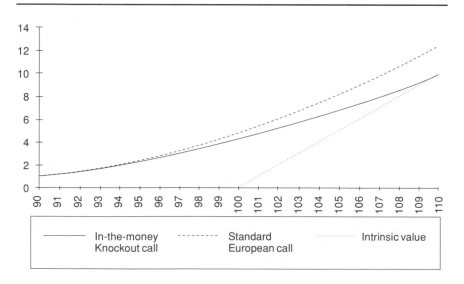

so as the barrier is approached. With this knowledge and a known level of risk tolerance, a short seller can design the proper knockout features to work in an investment portfolio.

Portfolio Insurance

A portfolio manager pursues a strategy of systematically hedging a diversified investment portfolio by purchase of listed index puts struck 10 percent out of the money. As the stock market rises (falls), the current puts are replaced by new ones with a higher (lower) strike price. The costs involved include the commissions to sell and buy puts whenever market price movement calls for put replacement and the bid-ask spread on puts at every replacement point. Administrative burdens include the time spent to monitor daily market levels that dictate a need for put replacement and time spent to devise, place, and verify that option orders were executed properly and effectively. If orders are sizable or the market volatile, multiple strike prices from executions will make the resulting effective strike price for the hedge uncertain. In addition, if listed puts are employed with strike prices fixed at set intervals, the available strike prices will rarely correspond to the desirable strategy's 10 percent out-of-the-money target. Finally, as liquidity in the listed markets is often confined to short-term contracts with one- to three-month maturities, the annual premium costs for implementing this strategy can be two to four times more expensive than that for a single one-year put, if it were available.

Solutions to these burdens include the use of strike reset puts or ladder puts.

Strike reset puts. A strike reset put allows the strike price to rise according to an agreed upon schedule as the market rallies. This feature prevents the put's protection features from diminishing as the underlying market rallies. Consider a strike reset put struck at 90 with the market at 100. In our example strategy of buying 10 percent out-of-the-money puts, the strike reset could be at 99 or 10 percent below the market when it reaches 110. Should the market rally to 110, the strike automatically resets to 99. This reset feature makes the put behavior equivalent to a manager selling a Europut struck at 90 and purchasing a new Europut struck at 99. However, the strike reset feature makes this administrative task simple. In addition, due to the way in which the strike reset feature is priced analytically, its purchase cost is less than that of the separate Europuts, especially when bid/ask spreads, commissions, and market price uncertainty are considered.

Ladder puts. If significant downside market movement is antici-pated, a ladder put might be purchased as part of the protection program. The ladder feature enables downside price movement to be captured or locked in as the market falls past values preset by the manager and called *rungs*. At a minimum, the payoff at maturity is the difference between the put strike and the lowest rung touched. For example, the rungs might be set at 85 and 80. If the put expired with the market at 91—having touched 85 (but not 80) during the put's lifetime—the payoff locked in will be 5 (90–85). It is easy to see that this feature prevents a subsequent market rally from eroding the protection value achieved by the put. In our example, a standard Europut would have expired worthless.

Combining these features into a mixed put strategy, the portfolio insur-ance manager can obtain useful investment features at a reasonable cost. Downside movement is realized as rungs of a ladder put are touched while the strike reset feature enables nearly automatic tracking of the desired 10 percent out-of-the-money protection program during market rallies.

ASSET SUBSTITUTION

Asset substitution involves creating a derivative instrument position that replicates the economic payoff of another investment position without a derivative. These asset substitution positions generally provide some com-bination of cost savings, return enhancements, or administrative simplicity. Examples include:

1. *Synthetic index funds* in which a cash position is paired with a long futures or swap contract to provide the equivalent payoff of a position in the stocks.
2. *Equity-linked bull notes* in which a call option or swap is embedded in a low or zero coupon note to provide an instrument whose return is linked to the performance of the equity.

Investors and investment managers continue to pursue these applications extensively. Two examples illustrate these applications.

Synthetic DAX Fund

A manager wishes to obtain one-year exposure to the German stock market as represented by the local DAX index. While a direct investment in stocks is possible, a synthetic index fund alternative is available. To create the

EXHIBIT 17–2

Synthetic DAX Index Fund

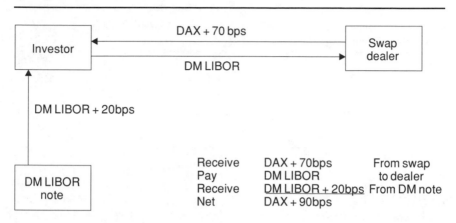

synthetic DAX index fund, a local currency floating rate note is purchased that yields DM (deutsche mark) LIBOR + 20 basis points (bps) semiannually. The manager next executes an equity swap in which DM LIBOR is paid semiannually as it is received from the note. The market quote on this swap indicates that in return for the DM LIBOR payment, the investor receives the DAX return plus 70bps. The combination of these two investment instruments now gives the manager the equivalent of an index fund enhanced by 90bps (70bps from the swap plus 20bps from the note). The manager's investment position is outlined in Exhibit 17–2.

The DAX enhancement of 70bps from the swap has its origins primarily in certain tax advantages held by a local swap provider. These are not generally available to a nonresident investor. Swaps on the German stock market provide a particularly dramatic illustration of the pricing advantages of synthetic over stock index funds. Enhancements available from swaps on other world equity markets are generally far smaller, so the attraction of synthetic index funds must come to rely as well on a second advantage they have, namely, a lower cost of implementation.

The annual round-trip costs encountered in running index funds with stock investments include commissions, stamp taxes, custody charges, withholding taxes, and rebalance costs. These costs range from about 80 to 150bps depending on the country (see Exhibit 17–3).

A fuller comparison of a DAX stock index fund with its synthetic equivalent in Exhibit 17–4 shows the cost advantage of the synthetic. For

EXHIBIT 17-3
Stock Index Fund Estimated Costs (in Basis Points)

Country	Commissions Round-Trip	Stamp Tax	Custody Cost	Withholding Tax	Rebalance Cost	Total Cost
Japan	20	30	20	8	9	87
UK	20	50	20	54	9	153
Germany	30	0	20	40	9	99
France	30	0	20	30	9	89
Switzerland	20	0	20	34	9	83

EXHIBIT 17–4
DAX Index Fund Estimated Costs[*]

Cost Category	Stock Costs	Swap Costs
Commissions	30	—
Bid/ask spread	25	—
Custody charges	20	—
Rebalance costs	9	—
Stock loan	−50	—
Withholding tax	40	—
Net costs	74	—
Enhancements	0	70
Net results	DAX − 74	DAX + 70

[*] All costs in basis points for a one-year investment, round trip.

the purposes of this analysis, a benefit has been provided to the stock fund for stock loan proceeds, but the costs of the bid/ask spread also have been charged. As long as such economic advantages of synthetic over stock index funds persist, it is reasonable to expect their continued growth.

Futures contracts that exist on the DAX index also could be used to construct a synthetic index fund. U.S. investors, who currently are not permitted to use this contract according to their own rules, will choose the swap as the preferred form of derivative. Synthetic index funds on other contracts that are permitted are possible and invite comparison. For the most part, swaps are more economical at maturities greater than six months and in larger instead of smaller sizes. In addition, swaps are available to cover more countries and can have special features available not present in standardized futures contracts. These and other factors need to be considered in the choice of instruments with which to assemble these funds.

Average Price Equity Bull Note

An investor seeking longer-term U.S. stock market returns with protection against market declines chooses to purchase a three-year bull note with an embedded average price call. A termsheet for such a bull note appears in Exhibit 17–5.

EXHIBIT 17–5
Equity-Linked S&P 500 Bull Note with Average Price Option

Indicative Summary of Terms
March 8, 1995

Issuer	A-rated corporation
Buyer	U.S. pension fund
Principal amount	$25 million
Fees	None
Trade date	March 8, 1995
Settlement (issue) date	March 15, 1995
Valuation date	March 6, 1998
Maturity date	March 8, 1998
Coupon	0%
Issue price	100
Redemption	Principal amount plus Index payment
Index payment	On Maturity date the Issuer will pay to the Buyer, if positive, a dollar amount equal to the following value: $R \times \text{Principal} \times \{ Sa/St - 1 \}$ where R = Participation rate of 202% St = S&P 500 Index on Trade date Sa = On Valuation date the monthly average S&P 500 Index price measured over the lifetime of the note.

EXHIBIT 17–6
Parties to a Bull Note Issue

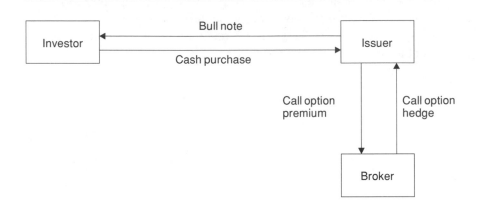

There are three parties to this transaction: the investor, the broker/dealer, and the issuer (see Exhibit 17–6). The investor specifies the acceptable credit of the issuer, size of the note, coupon, maturity, and the equity index to which the redemption is tied. The investor receives the note from the issuer and has the normal credit exposure that accompanies such a purchase. The issuer, to cover its exposure on the embedded call, looks to the broker/dealer for its hedge. As long as the issuer's all in cost of financing is met, the transaction is economical and attractive.

Referring to the termsheet, we see that at maturity the buyer will receive back the principal, plus an index payment equal to 202 percent of the percentage rise, if any, of the daily average S&P 500 Index price experienced over the period. While this may seem a generous return, it is fairly calculated and based on the following considerations.

First, the investor receives no coupon over the life of the note, only the index payment at maturity. This zero-coupon feature of the note means that the present value of the fixed-income portion is less than par, say 84.81 percent. As the investor pays par for the note upon purchase, the difference (100 percent–84.81 percent) can be used to purchase the average price call option whose fair premium is 7.52 percent. Thus 2.02 options can be purchased with the difference between par and the zero-coupon value.

The average pricing feature of the call option is helpful to the investor in several ways. To begin with, event risk at maturity is mitigated. A standard

Eurocall, in-the-money at maturity, could lose all or a substantial portion of its premium due to a market drop on the final day. Such an event for an average price option constitutes only one of hundreds experienced over the three-year lifetime of the average price call. Accordingly the period-end risk to premium erosion is minimal. A second investor advantage of the average price option is its lower premium cost. This feature arises directly from the fact that the volatility of an average price is less than simple price volatility. Lower volatility translates directly into lower call option premium, typically 30 percent lower for average price call options than for standard Eurocalls. Accordingly, the participation rate (202 percent) in upside movement is raised above that for a Eurocall.

Such notes have been issued in considerable size over the past three years and have been linked to equity markets in emerging as well as developed countries. Institutional investors cite at lease four separate features motivating the purchase of such notes for their portfolios:

1. Ability to control risk.
2. Administrative simplicity.
3. Ease in portfolio diversification.
4. Flexibility in design.

Ability to control risk. Bull bonds are particularly appropriate for investors concerned with eliminating or reducing downside market movement. A pension fund wishing to increase its exposure to the Japanese stock market but fearful of further losses from the current price level might consider purchase of a bond with an embedded call. Investors who are confident of a further fall and who wish to protect their investments could consider a bear bond purchase instead.

Administrative simplicity. There is also the attractive feature of administrative simplicity. If a bond is constructed by two separate purchases of the zero-coupon portion and the option, separate documentation and negotiations must take place for each portion. Some investors are willing to undertake this task themselves and potentially realize cost savings. Many, however, prefer the simplicity of a single note containing the desired features. For such investors, simplicity translates into a cost savings realized in the reduced management time allocated to acquire the investment exposure.

Ease in diversification. A convertible bond manager desiring exposure to market sectors where no convertibles exist could request the design of a bull bond to fill the portfolio void. Similarly, a mix of country/currency exposures could be designed to complement an asset allocation plan. The resulting bonds are valuable for their return characteristics and the portfolio diversification they provide.

Flexibility in design. Institutional investors unwilling to use options directly to hedge positions sometimes may find it easier to make implicit use of them through the purchase of securities with the option features embedded. Provided these bonds are suitable, these investors thereby are able to make use of the benefits that option patterns provide. The reach of design can be limited to a single stock or expanded to include most major global equity markets.

The successful use of bull bonds depends on the evaluation by the investor of three concerns:

1. Liquidity
2. Credit
3. Pricing

Liquidity. Because of their special design features, bull and bear bonds generally are not highly liquid securities. Nevertheless, secondary markets exist wherein bonds are purchased, sold, and restructured. Prices of these bonds reflect the costs of assembling and disassembling the constituent components. Investors wishing to avoid bid/offer spreads should purchase these bonds and hold to maturity.

Credit. The credit of the issuer is a proper concern of any investor. The normal evaluation methods used for debt securities should be employed to evaluate the intended issuer's creditworthiness. If sufficiently large sums are intended for bull or bear bond purchases, credit risk can be diversified by spreading purchases across several issuers.

Pricing. Investors realistically can expect bull and bear bonds to cost a bit more than the separately purchased components because, as noted, issuers require an incentive to enter into such customized transactions. A cost of funding, lowered by a few basis points, is generally sufficient. After evaluating liquidity, credit, and pricing, if such investments are considered attractive and suitable, the investor can pursue and implement a successful final design.

With their attractive features of risk/return control, simplicity, global reach, and design flexibility, such notes have come to occupy a place of growing importance among institutional investors. This new form of investment represents a creative and successful response of the equity derivative markets to the growing needs of both issuers and investors.

ASSET ALLOCATION

Asset allocation involves shifting economic exposure from one asset to another. For large investors, these shifts typically take place between stocks, bonds, and cash. Implementation has traditionally taken place in the physical securities markets or in the futures markets. The cost advantages, speed, and simplicity of using futures contracts has made them the instruments of choice for much of this now global activity. Swaps are newer and thus less frequently used.

A simple swap example is illustrated in Exhibit 17–7 where an investor with an S&P 500 Index fund exchanges the equity exposure for long-term bond exposure. The swap employed requires the investor to pay the total rate of return on the S&P 500 index for which the total return on the U.S.

EXHIBIT 17–7
Asset Allocation Swap

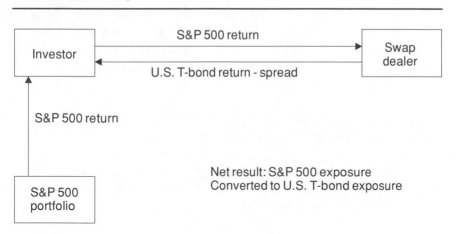

EXHIBIT 17–8
Cross Currency Equity Swap

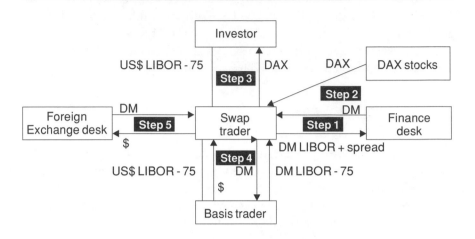

30-year Treasury bond is paid. The combination of the index fund and the equity leg of the swap creates a position which is neutral in exposure to the S&P 500. The second leg of the swap exposes the same asset base to the U.S. long bond. The spread identified in the figure reflects the costs to the swap provider of constructing and hedging this offering.

A second and challenging example is that of a U.S. investor preferring to retain dollar assets and acquire non-U.S. equity exposure by means of a cross-currency equity swap. Suppose the dollar assets of $23MM are in a short-term fixed income fund yielding the equivalent of LIBOR + 30bps. To transform this cash into equity exposure in the German stock market the investor simply pays a quoted floating rate, say U.S. dollar LIBOR – 75bps, to a swap provider and receives a DAX payment which mimics a full investment of principal in the stocks. From the point of view of the investor, this swap and its terms seem simple. To provide this swap, however, the investor's counterparty must take several steps as diagramed in Exhibit 17–8.

Step 1. The swap trader must first borrow DM from the firm's finance desk versus paying DM LIBOR plus a spread.

Step 2. Proceeds from this borrowing are invested in a DAX hedge, say, stocks for simplicity of understanding. This investment enables the full DAX return to be paid as agreed to the investor.

Step 3. The investor pays U.S. dollar LIBOR to the swap provider, who must transform this dollar flow into a DM LIBOR flow to match the local currency of the German trading book.

Step 4. This can be accomplished by executing a cross-currency swap in which another trader (basis desk trader) receives the U.S. dollar LIBOR flow and pays a DM LIBOR flow in return. An initial exchange of principal at the start of the swap at the spot rate assures, when reversed, that the full swap notional amount of $23MM is properly exposed to DM currency moves as desired.

Step 5. This exchange is accompanied by a spot currency trade to meet the basis desk requirement for deutsche marks in the initial principal exchange.

This example illustrates both the simplicity for the investor of arranging for asset exposures to be transformed, and the complexity for a provider to construct and offer such swaps. Without a substantial commitment to equity swaps, basis swaps, foreign exchange, and financing desks, the offering of such products efficiently and at reasonable costs is prohibitive.

At this point, the transformation of other assets to acquire the correct asset mix is easy to imagine from the investor's perspective. For example, the investor could have elected to pay the U.S. Treasury bond return and to receive the return on any major world equity or bond market. By choosing to receive on a weighted combination of world equity markets, for example, a global equity swap could be constructed.

It might at first be thought that simple futures executions could accomplish the same asset allocation shifts as swaps. Upon reflection, however, it becomes clear that more is required. For example, the DAX swap shown in Exhibit 17–8 could not be mimicked by DAX futures alone. If the investor's full principal is to be exposed to deutsche marks, then a currency forward also must be executed to fulfill this need. If the DAX were replaced by the KOSPI index for Korea, no futures execution would be possible because Korea lacks a futures market. Thus, swaps can add administrative simplicity to investing and extend the reach beyond futures markets for global asset allocation.

Futures are usually the best choice for tactical asset allocation where an investor seeks to take advantage of shifts in relative value between various asset classes over a brief period of time. Futures, when available, are generally liquid, have low commission costs, and have small face values to allow

EXHIBIT 17–9
Characteristics of Equity Index Futures and Equity Swaps

Feature	Equity Index Futures	Equity Swaps
Primary users	Retail and institutional	Institutional
Flexibility		
Availability	In most major capital markets	In major and minor capital markets on single stocks, stock baskets, and indexes
Special features available	None—standardized contracts	Currency hedging, averaging, etc.
Liquidity	High for small sizes and maturities 1–3 months	Moderate in most markets
Maturity	Fixed dates up to 1 year	6 months–5 years
Settlement	Normally 1 day	Negotiated
Costs		
Commissions	Negotiated	None—all costs priced at inception
Margin	Initial + variation	NA
Risks		
Basis risk	Mostly for shorter-term strategies	NA
Roll risk	Mostly for longer-term strategies	NA
Credit risk	To broker	To counterparty

for shifts of small size. Swaps are not normally offered in very small sizes and short maturities, making them less suitable for short-term asset allocation decisions. A more complete comparison of futures and swaps appears in Exhibit 17–9, which is organized around flexibility, costs, and risks.

Flexibility

Availability

Futures. Index futures contracts are available on most indexes in most major and many minor capital markets globally, although the Commodity Futures Trading Commission (CFTC) limits certain uses by U.S. citizens.

Swaps. Swaps are available in almost all developed and emerging markets on any underlying issue for which there is sufficient liquidity, including most equity indexes, custom baskets, and single stocks.

Special Features Available

Futures. Listed futures carry only standardized features.

Swaps. All swap terms can be customized, allowing for currency hedging and other special features.

Liquidity

Futures. In most major markets, the liquidity of futures is moderate to high in the shortest maturity contracts and much lower in longer-term contracts. The bid/ask spread, a common measure of liquidity, can be quite narrow for contracts like the S&P 500 futures; however, market impact, another measure of liquidity, can be substantial, indicating that large orders need to be worked carefully into the futures markets.

Swaps. Equity swaps generally have moderate liquidity. However, a price can be set for large sizes at the time of the transaction. This price may reflect a liquidity premium that depends on the state of the swap dealer's trading position. The swap dealer assumes all market impact risk.

Maturity

Futures. Futures contracts are offered with fixed-date maturities of up to a year or more, with the short maturity contracts (typically one to three months) having the most liquidity.

Swaps. Swaps maturity dates are customized. Swap counterparties with a strong commitment to the swap and OTC markets will generally offer maturities ranging from six months to five years, with longer maturities available.

Settlement

Futures. Settlement terms for futures are standard and set by the exchange on which the contract is listed. The actual settlement normally takes place within one day of maturity.

Swaps. Swaps are settled according to terms negotiated between the counterparties. These terms are set at initiation of the swap.

Cost Aspects

Commissions

Futures. Commissions on futures are negotiated between executing brokers and customers and range from approximately 3 to 8 basis points per year in the U.S., 5 to 30 basis point in non-U.S. countries with liquid futures markets and quarterly rolls, and up to 300 basis points in other countries.

Swaps. No commissions are charged. All costs are priced into the contract at initiation.

Margin

Futures. Futures require an initial margin by the investor, which acts as a good faith deposit to ensure performance. The variation margin on futures corresponds to a daily flow of funds between the investor and the clearing broker, settling the daily change in value of the contracts.

Swaps. Neither initial nor variation margin is generally required for swap contracts. Swaps may be marked to market periodically and cash differences exchanged between the two counterparties. A final exchange takes place at maturity.

Risks

Basis Risk

Futures. The difference between the futures prices and the price of the underlying is known as the basis. The basis may deviate from its theoretical fair value depending on market conditions, thus subjecting holders who liquidate positions before contract maturity to basis risk.

Swaps. Swaps counterparties are subject to basis risk only if the contract is unwound before maturity. Since the maturity of a swap can be customized, this risk can be mitigated.

Roll Risk

Futures. Investors with horizons longer than the maturity of the current, liquid futures contract need to roll futures near expiration by replacing the existing position with a new position in the next liquid contract. The price paid to roll, which includes commissions and the futures basis, can very widely with changes in the basis, exposing futures users to roll risk.

Swaps. Swaps have customized maturities; hence, they need not be rolled.

Credit Risk

Futures. Buyers and sellers of futures look first to their brokers for credit satisfaction and ultimately to the clearinghouse for that contract. The credit of the clearinghouse is based on the particular arrangements made between the clearinghouse and its members. Clearinghouses generally do not carry credit ratings by independent rating agencies.

Swaps. Swap counterparties have exposure to each other's credit, hence credit quality is an important input into the choice of counterparty, especially for long maturity swaps.

The decision between the use of equity futures and equity swaps can be made only in the context of the investment strategy employed. For a given strategy, investors need to determine the relative importance of flexibility, implicit and explicit costs, and risks. The framework provided here allows the investor to choose between futures and swaps and to see when futures and swaps can be employed together to further an investor's objectives.

Chapter Eighteen

Universal Hedging
Optimizing Currency Risk and Reward in International Equity Portfolios

Fischer Black
Goldman, Sachs & Co.

In a world where everyone can hedge against changes in the value of real exchange rates (the relative values of domestic and foreign goods), and where no barriers limit international investment, there is a universal constant that gives the optimal hedge ratio—the fraction of your foreign investments you should hedge. The formula for this optimal hedge ratio depends on just three inputs:

- The expected return on the world market portfolio.
- The volatility of the world market portfolio.
- Average exchange rate volatility.

The formula in turn yields three rules.

- Hedge your foreign equities.
- Hedge equities equally for all countries.
- Don't hedge 100 percent of your foreign equities.

This formula applies to every investor who holds foreign securities. It applies equally to a U.S. investor holding Japanese assets, a Japanese investor holding British assets, and a British investor holding U.S. assets. That's why we call this method "universal hedging."

WHY HEDGE AT ALL?

You may consider hedging a "zero-sum game." After all, if U.S. investors hedge their Japanese investments, and Japanese investors hedge their U.S. investments, then when U.S. investors gain on their hedges, Japanese investors lose, and vice versa. But even though one side always wins and the other side always loses, hedging *reduces risk* for both sides.

More often than not, when performance is measured in local currency, U.S. investors gain on their hedging when their portfolios do badly, and Japanese investors gain on their hedging when their portfolios do badly. The gains from hedging are similar to the gains from international diversification. Because it reduces risk for both sides, currency hedging provides a "free lunch."

WHY NOT HEDGE *ALL*?

If investors in all countries can reduce risk through currency hedging, why shouldn't they hedge 100 percent of their foreign investments? Why hedge less?

The answer contains our most interesting finding. When they have different consumption baskets, investors in different countries can all add to their expected returns by taking some currency risk in their portfolios.

To see how this can be, imagine an extremely simple case, where the exchange rate between two countries is now 1:1 but will change over the next year to either 2:1 or 1:2 with equal probability. Call the consumption goods in one country "apples" and those in the other "oranges."

Imagine that the world market portfolio contains equal amounts of apples and oranges. To the apple consumer, holding oranges is risky. To the orange consumer, holding apples is risky. The apple consumer could choose to hold only apples, and thus bear no risk at all. Likewise, the orange consumer could decide to hold only oranges. Surprisingly, each will gain in expected return by trading an apple and an orange. At year-end, an orange will be worth either two apples or 0.5 apples. Its expected value is 1.25 apples.

EXHIBIT 18–1
Siegel's Paradox

	Start-of-Quarter Exchange Rates		Percentage Changes in Exchange Rates	
	Mark	*Dollar*	*Mark*	*Dollar*
Quarter	*Dollar*	*Mark*	*Dollar*	*Mark*
1Q84	2.75	.362	−5.58	5.90
2Q84	2.60	.384	7.18	−6.69
3Q84	2.79	.358	9.64	−8.79
4Q84	3.06	.326	3.66	−3.52
1Q85	3.17	.315	−1.83	1.84
2Q85	3.11	.321	−2.25	2.30
3Q85	3.04	.328	−13.04	15.01
4Q85	2.64	.377	−7.59	8.21
1Q86	2.44	.408	−4.46	4.67
2Q86	2.33	.427	−6.80	7.29
3Q86	2.17	.459	−7.16	7.73
4Q86	2.02	.494	−5.19	5.46
1Q87	1.91	.521	−5.11	5.41
2Q87	1.81	.549	0.49	−0.49
3Q87	1.82	.547	1.09	−1.08
4Q87	1.84	.541	−14.00	16.28
1Q88	1.58	.629	4.29	−4.12
2Q88	1.65	.603	9.83	−8.95
3Q88	1.82	.549	2.27	−2.22
4Q88	1.86	.537	−4.88	5.12
Average			−1.97	2.47

Similarly, an apple will have an expected value of 1.25 oranges. So each consumer will gain from the swap.

This is not a mathematical trick; It's real, and it is sometimes called "Siegel's paradox."[1] It means that investors generally want to hedge less than 100 percent of their foreign investments.

---

1 J. J. Siegel, "Risk, Interest Rates, and the Forward Exchange," *Quarterly Journal of Economics,* May 1972.

To understand Siegel's paradox, consider historical exchange rate data for deutsche marks and U.S. dollars. Exhibit 18–1 shows the quarterly percentage changes in the exchange rates and their averages. Note that in each period and for the average, the gain for one currency exceeds the loss for the other.

WHY *UNIVERSAL* HEDGING?

Why is the optimal hedge ratio identical for investors everywhere? The answer lies in how exchange rates reach equilibrium.

Models of international equilibrium generally assume that the typical investor in any country consumes a single good or basket of goods.[2] The investor wants to maximize expected return and minimize risk, measuring expected return and risk in terms of his or her own consumption good.

Given the risk-reducing and return-enhancing properties of international diversification, an investor will want to hold an internationally diversified portfolio of equities. Given no barriers to international investment, every investor will hold a share of a fully diversified portfolio of world equities. In the absence of government participation, some investor must lend when another investor borrows, and some investor must go long a currency when another goes short.

Whatever the given levels of market volatility, exchange rate volatilities, correlations between exchange rates, and correlations between exchange rates and stock, in equilibrium prices will adjust until everyone is willing to hold all stocks and until someone is willing to take the other side of every exchange rate contract.

Suppose, for example, that we know the return on a portfolio in one currency, and we know the change in the exchange rate between that currency and another currency. We can thus derive the portfolio return in the other currency. We can write down an equation relating expected returns and exchange rate volatilities from the points of view of two investors in the two different currencies.

---

2 See, for example, B. H. Solnik, "An Equilibrium Model of the International Capital Market," *Journal of Economic Theory,* August 1974; F. L. A. Grauer, R. H. Litzenberger, and R. E. Stehle, "Sharing Rules and Equilibrium in an International Capital Market Under Uncertainty," *Journal of Financial Economics,* June 1976; P. Sercu, "A Generalization of the International Asset Pricing Model," *Revue de l'Association Française de Finance,* June 1980; and R. Stulz, "A Model of International Asset Pricing," *Journal of Financial Economics,* December 1981.

Suppose that Investor A finds a high correlation between the returns on his stocks in another country and the corresponding exchange rate change. He will probably want to hedge in order to reduce his portfolio risk. But suppose Investor B in that other country would increase her own portfolio's risk by taking the other side of A's hedge. Investor A may be so anxious to hedge that he will be willing to pay B to take the other side. As a result, the exchange rate contract will be priced so that the hedge reduces A's expected return but increases B's.

In equilibrium, both investors will hedge. Investor A will hedge to reduce risk, while Investor B will hedge to increase expected return. But they will hedge equally, in proportion to their stock holdings.

THE UNIVERSAL HEDGING FORMULA

By extending the above analysis to investors in all possible pairs of countries, we find that the proportion that each investor wants to hedge depends on three averages: (1) the average across countries of the expected excess return on the world market portfolio; (2) the average across countries of the volatility of the world market portfolio; and (3) the average across all pairs of countries of exchange rate volatility. These averages become inputs for the universal hedging formula:[3]

$$\frac{\mu_m - \sigma_m^2}{\mu_m - \frac{1}{2}\sigma_e^2}$$

where

μ_m = the average across investors of the expected excess return (return above each investor's riskless rate) on the world market portfolio (which contains stocks from all major countries in proportion to each country's market value)

σ_m = the average across investors of the volatility of the world market portfolio (where variances, rather than standard deviation, are averaged)

σ_e = the average exchange rate volatility (averaged variances) across all pairs of countries

---

3 The derivation of the formula is described in detail in F. Black, "Equilibrium Exchange Rate Hedging," National Bureau of Economic Research Working Paper No. 2947, April 1989.

Neither expected changes in exchange rates nor correlations between exchange rate changes and stock returns or other exchange rate changes affect optimal hedge ratios. In equilibrium, the expected changes and the correlations cancel one another, so they do not appear in the universal hedging formula.

In the same way, the Black-Scholes option formula includes neither the underlying stock's expected return nor its beta. In equilibrium, they cancel one another.

The Capital Asset Pricing Model is similar. The optimal portfolio for any one investor could depend on the expected returns and volatilities of all available assets. In equilibrium, however, the optimal portfolio for any investor is a mix of the market portfolio with borrowing or lending. The expected returns and volatilities cancel one another (except for the market as a whole), so they do not affect the investor's optimal holdings.

INPUTS FOR THE FORMULA

Historical data and judgment are used to create inputs for the formula. Exhibits 18–2 through 18–8 give some helpful historical data.

Exhibit 18–2 lists weights that can be applied to different countries in estimating the three averages. Japan, the United States, and the United Kingdom carry the most weight.

Exhibits 18–3 to Exhibit 18–5 contain statistics for 1986–1988 and Exhibits 18–6 to 18–8 contain statistics for 1981–1985. These subperiods give an indication of how statistics change from one sample period to another.

When averaging exchange rate volatilities over pairs of countries, we include the volatility of a country's exchange rate with itself. Those volatilities are always zero; they run diagonally through Exhibits 18–3 and 18–6. This means that the average exchange rate volatilities shown in Exhibits 18–5 and 18–8 are lower than the averages of the positive numbers in Exhibits 18–3 and 18–6.

The excess returns in Exhibits 18–4 and 18–6 are averages for the world market return in each country's currency, minus that country's riskless interest rate. The average excess returns differ between countries because of differences in exchange rate movements.

The excess returns are *not* national market returns. For example, the Japanese market did better than the U.S. market in 1987, but the world market portfolio did better relative to interest rates in the United States than in Japan.

EXHIBIT 18–2
Capitalizations and Capitalization Weights

	Domestic Companies Listed on the Major Stock Exchanges as of December 31, 1987[*]		Companies in the FT-Actuaries World Indices[TM] as of December 31, 1987†	
	Capitalization (U.S. $ billions)	Weight (%)	Capitalization (U.S. $ billions)	Weight (%)
Japan	$2,700.0	40.00%	$2,100.0	41.00%
U.S.	2,100.0	31.00	1,800.0	34.00
U.K.	680.0	10.00	560.0	11.00
Canada	220.0	3.20	110.0	2.10
Germany	220.0	3.20	160.0	3.10
France	160.0	2.30	100.0	2.00
Australia	140.0	2.00	64.0	1.20
Switzerland	130.0	1.90	58.0	1.10
Italy	120.0	1.80	85.0	1.60
Netherlands	87.0	1.30	66.0	1.30
Sweden	70.0	1.00	17.0	0.32
Hong Kong	54.0	0.79	38.0	0.72
Belgium	42.0	0.61	29.0	0.56
Denmark	20.0	0.30	11.0	0.20
Singapore	18.0	0.26	6.2	0.12
New Zealand	16.0	0.23	7.4	0.14
Norway	12.0	0.17	2.2	0.04
Austria	7.9	0.12	3.9	0.07
Total	$6,800.0	100.00%	5,300.0	100.00%

[*] From "Activities and Statistics 1987 Report" by Federation Internationale des Bourses de Valeurs (page 16).

† The FT-Actuaries World Indices[TM] are jointly compiled by The Financial Times Limited, Goldman, Sachs & Co., and County NatWest/Wood Mackenzie in conjunction with the Institute of Actuaries and the Faculty of Actuaries. This table excludes Finland, Ireland, Malaysia, Mexico, South Africa, and Spain.

Because exchange rate volatility contributes to average stock market volatility, σ_m^2 should be greater than $\frac{1}{2}\sigma_e^2$. Exchange rate volatility also contributes to the average return on the world market, so μ_m should be greater than $\frac{1}{2}\sigma_e^2$ too.

EXHIBIT 18–3
Exchange Rate Volatilities, 1986–1988

	Japan	U.S.	U.K.	Canada	Ger-many	France	Aust-ralia	Switzer-land	Italy
Japan	0	11	9	12	7	7	14	7	8
U.S.	11	0	11	5	11	11	11	12	10
U.K.	9	10	0	11	8	8	14	9	8
Canada	12	5	11	0	12	11	12	13	11
Germany	7	11	8	12	0	3	15	4	3
France	7	11	8	11	2	0	14	5	3
Australia	14	11	14	12	14	14	0	15	14
Switzerland	7	12	9	13	4	5	15	0	5
Italy	8	10	8	11	3	3	14	5	0
Netherlands	7	11	8	11	2	3	14	5	3
Sweden	7	8	7	9	5	5	12	7	5
Hong Kong	11	4	11	6	11	11	11	12	10
Belgium	9	11	9	12	6	6	14	8	6
Denmark	8	11	8	11	4	4	14	6	4
Singapore	10	6	10	8	10	10	12	11	10
New Zealand	17	15	16	15	17	17	14	18	17
Norway	9	10	9	10	7	7	13	9	7
Austria	8	11	9	12	5	5	15	7	5

	Nether-lands	Sweden	Hong Kong	Belgium	Den-mark	Singa-pore	New Zealand	Nor-way	Austria
Japan	7	7	11	9	8	10	17	9	8
U.S.	11	8	4	11	11	6	15	10	11
U.K.	8	7	11	9	8	10	16	9	9
Canada	11	9	6	12	11	8	15	10	12
Germany	2	5	11	6	4	10	17	8	5
France	3	5	11	6	4	10	17	7	5
Australia	14	12	11	14	14	12	14	14	14
Switzerland	5	7	12	8	6	11	18	9	7
Italy	3	5	11	6	4	10	17	7	5
Netherlands	0	5	11	6	4	10	17	7	5
Sweden	5	0	8	6	4	8	16	6	5
Hong Kong	11	8	0	11	11	5	14	10	11
Belgium	6	6	11	0	6	10	17	8	6
Denmark	4	4	11	6	0	10	17	7	5
Singapore	10	8	5	10	10	0	15	10	10
New Zealand	17	15	14	17	17	15	0	16	17
Norway	7	5	10	8	7	10	16	0	7
Austria	5	5	11	6	5	10	17	8	0

EXHIBIT 18–4
World Market Excess Returns and Return Volatilities in Different Currencies,
1986–1988

	Excess Return			Return Volatility		
Currency	1986	1987	1988	1986	1987	1988
Japan	8	−12	21	14	26	15
U.S.	29	12	14	13	25	11
U.K.	23	−14	16	14	26	15
Canada	26	4	5	14	24	11
Germany	8	−5	30	15	27	14
France	11	−7	27	14	26	14
Australia	23	−2	−6	19	25	14
Switzerland	8	−8	36	15	27	15
Italy	2	−6	23	15	27	14
Netherlands	8	−7	30	15	27	14
Sweden	16	−6	19	13	25	13
Hong Kong	30	13	17	13	25	11
Belgium	7	−8	28	15	27	14
Denmark	8	−10	26	15	27	14
Singapore	36	6	16	12	25	12
New Zealand	15	−22	13	20	29	14
Norway	19	−11	15	14	26	12
Austria	7	−6	30	15	27	14

Source: FT-Actuaries/World Indices[TM] database.

AN EXAMPLE

Exhibits 18–5 and 18–8 suggest one way to create inputs for the formula.
The average excess return on the world market was 3 percent in the earlier
period and 11 percent in the later period. We may thus estimate a future
excess return of 8 percent.

The volatility of the world market was higher in the later period, but that
included the 1987 crash, so we may want to use the 15 percent volatility
from the earlier period. The average exchange rate volatility of 10 percent
in the earlier period may also be a better estimate of the future than the 8
percent in the 1986–1988 period.

This reasoning leads to the following possible values for the inputs:

EXHIBIT 18–5
World Average Values, 1986–1988

	Excess Return	Return Volatility	Exchange Rate Volatility
1986	17	14	9
1987	−3	26	8
1988	18	13	8
1986–88	11	18	8

EXHIBIT 18–6
Exchange Rate Volatilities, 1981–1985

	Japan	U.S.	U.K.	Canada	Germany
Japan	0	12	13	11	10
U.S.	11	0	12	4	12
U.K.	12	13	0	12	10
Canada	11	4	11	0	11
Germany	10	12	10	12	0
France	10	13	11	12	4
Australia	12	10	13	10	12
Switzerland	11	14	12	13	7
Italy	9	10	11	10	5
Netherlands	10	12	10	11	2

	France	Australia	Switzerland	Italy	Netherlands
Japan	10	12	11	9	10
U.S.	13	11	13	10	12
U.K.	11	14	12	11	10
Canada	12	10	12	10	11
Germany	5	13	7	5	2
France	0	12	8	5	5
Australia	12	0	13	11	12
Switzerland	8	14	0	8	7
Italy	5	12	8	0	5
Netherlands	5	12	7	5	0

EXHIBIT 18–7
World Market Excess Returns and Return Volatilities in Different Currencies,
1981–1985

Currency	Excess Return	Return Volatility
Japan	3	17
U.S.	−1	13
U.K.	10	16
Canada	2	13
Germany	8	15
France	7	16
Australia	7	18
Switzerland	9	16
Italy	4	15
Netherlands	8	15

EXHIBIT 18–8
World Average Values, 1981–1985

Excess Return	Return Volatility	Exchange Rate Volatility
3	15	10

$$\mu_m = 8 \text{ percent}$$
$$\sigma_m = 15 \text{ percent}$$
$$\sigma_e = 10 \text{ percent}$$

Given these inputs, the formula tells us that 77 percent of holdings should be hedged:

$$\frac{0.08 - 0.15^2}{0.08 - \frac{1}{2}(0.10)^2} = 0.77$$

To compare the results of using different inputs, we can use the historical averages from both the earlier and later periods:

$$\mu_m = 3 \text{ percent or 11 percent}$$
$$\sigma_m = 15 \text{ percent or 18 percent}$$

σ_e = 10 percent or 8 percent

With the historical averages from the earlier period as inputs, the fraction hedged comes to 30 percent:

$$\frac{0.03 - 0.15^2}{0.03 - \frac{1}{2}(0.10)^2} = 0.30$$

Using averages from the later period gives a fraction hedged of 73 percent:

$$\frac{0.11 - 0.18^2}{0.11 - \frac{1}{2}(0.08)^2} = 0.73$$

Generally, straight historical averages vary too much to serve as useful inputs for the formula. Estimates of long-run average values are better.

OPTIMIZATION

The universal hedging formula assumes that you put into the formula your opinions about what investors around the world expect for the future. If your own views on stock markets and on exchange rates are the same as those you attribute to investors generally, then you can use the formula as it is.

If your views differ from those of the consensus, you may want to incorporate them using optimization methods. Starting with expected returns and covariances for the stock markets and exchange rates, you would find the mix that maximizes the expected portfolio return for a given level of volatility.

The optimization approach is fully consistent with the universal hedging approach. When you put the expectations of investors around the world into the optimization approach, you will find that the optimal currency hedge for any foreign investment will be given by the universal hedging formula.

A NOTE ON THE CURRENCY HEDGE

The formula assumes that investors hedge real (inflation-adjusted) exchange rate changes, not changes due to inflation differentials between countries. To the extent that currency changes are the result of changes in inflation, the formula is only an approximation.

In other words, currency hedging only approximates real exchange rate hedging. But most changes in currency values, at least in countries with moderate inflation rates, are due to changes in real exchange rates. Thus currency hedging will normally be a good approximation to real exchange rate hedging.

In constructing a hedging basket, it may be desirable to substitute highly liquid currencies for less liquid ones. This can best be done by building a currency hedge basket that closely tracks the basket based on the universal hedging formula. When there is tracking error, the fraction hedged should be reduced.

In practice, hedging may be done using a basket of a few of the most liquid currencies and using a fraction somewhat smaller than the one the formula suggests.

The formula also assumes that the real exchange rate between two countries is defined as the relative value of domestic and foreign goods. Domestic goods are those consumed at home, not those produced at home. Imports thus count as domestic goods. Foreign goods are those goods consumed abroad, not those produced abroad.

Currency changes should be examined to see if they track real exchange rate changes so defined. When the currency rate changes between two countries differ from *real* exchange rate changes, the hedging done in that currency can be modified or omitted.

If everyone in the world eventually consumes the same mix of goods and services, and prices of goods and services are the same everywhere, hedging will no longer help.

APPLYING THE FORMULA TO OTHER TYPES OF PORTFOLIOS

How can you use the formula if you don't have a fully diversified international portfolio, or if foreign equities are only a small part of your portfolio? The answer depends on why you have a small amount in foreign equities. You may be:

1. Wary of foreign exchange risk.
2. Wary of foreign equity risk, even if it is optimally hedged.
3. Wary of foreign exchange risk and foreign equity risk, in equal measure.

In case (1), you should hedge more than the formula suggests. In case (2), you should hedge less than the formula suggests. In case (3), it probably makes sense to apply the formula as given to the foreign equities you hold.

If the barriers to foreign investment are small, you should gain by investing more abroad and by continuing to hedge the optimal fraction of your foreign equities.

FOREIGN BONDS

What if your portfolio contains foreign bonds as well as foreign stocks?

The approach that led to the universal hedging formula for stocks suggests 100 percent hedging for foreign bonds. A portfolio of foreign bonds hedged with short-term forward contracts still has foreign interest rate risk as well as the expected return that goes with that risk.

Any foreign bonds you hold unhedged can be counted as part of your total exposure to foreign currency risk. The less you hedge your foreign bonds, the more you will want to hedge your foreign stocks.

At times, you may want to hold unhedged foreign bonds because you believe that the exchange rate will move in your favor in the near future. In the long run, though, you will want to hedge your foreign bonds even more than your foreign equities.

CONCLUSION

The formula's results may be thought of as a base case. When you have special views on the prospects for a certain currency, or when a currency's forward market is illiquid, you can adjust the hedging positions that the formula suggests.

When you deviate from the formula because you think a particular currency is overpriced or underpriced, you can plan to bring your position back to normal as the currency returns to normal. You may even want to use options so that your effective hedge changes automatically as the currency price changes.

## Chapter Nineteen

Convertible Bond Basics

Dan Rissin
TrueRisk Inc.

A convertible bond is a bond that can be converted into shares at the option of the bondholder. The issuer is committed to paying a periodic coupon on the bond and repaying the principal at maturity, like any other bond. However, under specified conditions, the holder may elect to have the bond exchanged for a fixed number of shares of the issuer. This gives the holder an option to acquire the shares for the value of the bond at that time.

Convertibles combine the characteristics of straight bonds and equity derivatives: convertibles may include call, put, and conversion options. The value of a convertible is influenced by those economic factors that affect straight bonds (interest rate risk, credit risk of the issuer, foreign exchange risk). However, convertibles are also strongly affected by the volatility of the underlying stock and news pertaining to the performance of the issuing company.

Convertibles may be regarded as bonds with an equity option added to make them more attractive. Holders will accept the lower coupon rate because of the potential profit if the stock price increases, and issuers potentially give up some equity in exchange for a lower funding cost. Alternatively, convertibles may be viewed as stock substitutes. The bond allows the holder to acquire the stock for a set amount, but it provides protection should the stock price perform poorly. Also, up to conversion the holder receives the coupon instead of the stock dividend. Since the coupon is typically higher than the dividend, this makes the convertible bond attractive. If the stock price increases quickly and the bonds are converted, the issuer will receive more for the shares than if the shares had been issued directly.

Many convertible bonds have several additional features. A common feature is to permit the issuer to redeem the bonds at a fixed price over some future period. This is a call feature. In addition, sometimes the bondholders have a put feature, which allows them to choose to have the bonds redeemed at a certain price at a certain time in the future.

BASIC FEATURES AND BEHAVIOR

The value of a convertible bond is affected most by the price of the underlying stock, together with timing and features of the conversion and issuer call options. The value of the convertible increases as the price of the underlying stock increases, due to the conversion feature.

Call provisions can allow the issuer to force conversion of the bond into shares. The bond is called with several weeks advance notice, during which time the bondholder may decide to convert. If the value of stocks receivable on conversion is higher than the call redemption amount, it makes sense to convert rather than to have the bond redeemed.

The conversion price is the amount of face value of the bond that must be surrendered for each share received on conversion. For example, if a $1,000 face value bond is convertible into 20 shares, the conversion price is $50 per share. If the bond price is 100 percent of face value, the conversion price is the strike price of the conversion option of the bondholder; that is, what the holder will have to pay on exercise to receive the stock. As shown in Exhibit 19–1, the conversion and call features imply different behaviors for the convertible bond as the price of the stock changes.

Conversion Features

The conversion ratio is the number of shares of the underlying stock that can be exchanged for one bond. This is set when the bond is issued. The conversion price is the face value divided by the conversion ratio. Conversion may be allowed only at maturity, at any time after issue, or between specific dates. Restrictions on convertibility reduce the value of the bond.

Conversion value or equity value or parity is the current market value of shares per bond received on conversion, that is, the conversion ratio times the current share price. At any time during which the security can be converted into shares, the market value of the security should be at least

EXHIBIT 19–1
Convertible Bond Value

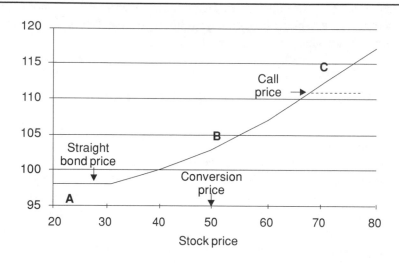

A.   When the stock price is far below the conversion price, the convertible bond
     behaves similarly to a straight bond, with its value determined primarily by
     interest rates.

B.   When the stock price approaches the conversion price, the price of the convertible
     includes the value of the option to convert the bond into shares. The value of this
     option increases with an increasing stock price and stock volatility. The
     convertible behaves most like a portfolio of a straight bond and a stock option.

C.   When the stock price is above the equivalent call price, the convertible trades for
     its equity value. If the issuer calls the bond, the bondholder will exercise the
     conversion option. The convertible behaves like an in-the-money stock option.

equal to its conversion value. At maturity, a typical convertible security is
worth the greater of the conversion value or the redemption value. A high
conversion ratio gives the convertible bond greater sensitivity to stock price
changes (see Exhibit 19–2).

Call Provisions

A call provision gives the issuer the right to buy the bond back from the
investor at the call price. In essence, the bondholder has sold the call option
to the issuer. The call schedule is a list of dates over which the call may be

EXHIBIT 19–2
Effect of Conversion Ratios on Convertible Bond Price

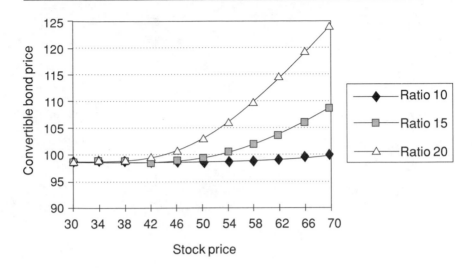

Stock price

exercised, with associated call prices for each range of dates. Call provisions reduce the value of the convertible because a call forces the investor to give up the potential remaining value of the convertible (see Exhibit 19–3).

Many convertibles with call provisions have a call protection period during the first two or three years of the bond, during which the issuer cannot call the bond. This is absolute call protection. Provisional call (also called soft call) protection allows the issuer to call the bond only if the underlying stock reaches a given price level. For example, the stock may have to trade at a level at least 130 percent of the conversion price for 20 out of 30 days before the convertible can be called. Call protection tends to increase the value of the convertible.

If the bond is called by the issuer, the holder can decide to convert the bond or receive the redemption amount. The issuer usually prefers to have the bond converted rather than redeemed, because delivery of shares is preferable to a cash outlay. Further, the issuer would prefer the bonds to be converted sooner rather than later to reduce coupon payments and to avoid a potential cash redemption if the stock price declines. It is therefore in the interest of the issuer to call the bond if the conversion value is significantly above the call price, and conversion will be forced.

EXHIBIT 19–3
Effect of Call Provisions on Convertible Bond Price

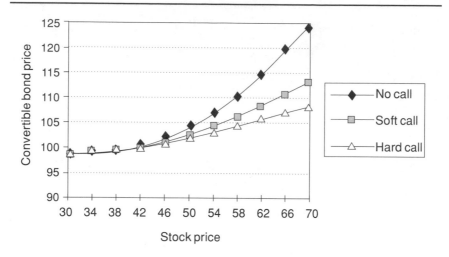

Put Provisions

A put provision or retraction feature allows the holder of a convertible bond to put or sell the bond to the issuer on certain dates and at certain put prices, as provided in the put schedule. The put provision increases the value of a convertible bond because it provides the bondholder with downside protection against poor performance of the underlying equity, and subsequent low conversion value (see Exhibit 19–4). The put strike price is usually higher than the face value, and the first put date does not occur until at least three years from the issue date.

Accrued Interest

The call and put prices are usually specified clean; that is, the bondholder will receive the call or put price plus the interest accrued since the last coupon payment. However, if the holder converts, only shares will be received, without any compensation for accrued interest. It is therefore to the holders advantage to convert after a coupon payment, not before. Some convertibles have a clause that prevents the bondholder from receiving a coupon before converting.

EXHIBIT 19–4
Effect of Put Provisions on Convertible Bond Price

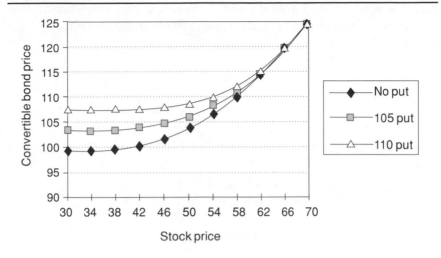

International Convertibles

A domestic convertible is issued in the country in which the issuers' stock trades. International convertibles can be sold in markets other than the issuers' domestic market. They can be denominated in any currency: Japanese yen, U.S. or Canadian dollars, and EC currencies. International bonds are issued to attract a wider range of investors or to take advantage of international market conditions. Where the underlying stock is in a different currency from the bond, the holder also assumes some exchange rate risk. The value of the stock received on conversion depends on the share price in the domestic currency and the exchange rate. Since the number of shares per bond is fixed, the conversion price (expressed in the bond currency) is usually set based on a fixed foreign exchange rate.

Convertible Preferred Shares

Convertible preferred shares and convertible bonds have similar characteristics. Preferreds are stocks that pay a regular dividend in perpetuity. As such, they behave similarly to a perpetual bond . They are junior to bonds in terms of claims against the issuer, and therefore carry a higher credit risk.

Preferreds convey no tax benefit to the issuer, but the stockholder may benefit from partial tax exemption. Preferreds increase in price with any increase in the issuer's equity value. Convertible preferreds can be converted into common stock according to specified conditions similar to those of convertible bonds.

CONVERTIBLE BOND ANALYSIS

The best way to analyze a convertible depends on the investment objective and the particular bond. Two of the simpler approaches involve valuing the convertible as a stock substitute or as a bond with a warrant. A more sophisticated approach entails using a specialized option pricing model to price the convertible as a composite derivative security.

Convertibles as Stock Substitutes

Where the convertible is regarded as a substitute for holding the underlying equity, it can be analyzed by comparing it to the conversion value.

Premium over conversion value. The conversion value is the conversion ratio times the current market price of the stock. Usually a convertible bond trades at a price somewhat higher than the conversion value. This is because the convertible provides a higher yield than the stock, and the convertible's value will not decline as much as the stock price. The premium over conversion value can be expressed as a percentage of the equity value:

$$Premium = \frac{Convertible\ price - Conversion\ value}{Conversion\ value} \times 100$$

This premium will be expected to increase if the stock price falls, or if the stock price volatility increases. Likewise, it will decline if the stock price increases or volatility drops.

Yield advantage. The annual coupon income offered by the convertible bond can be compared to the annual dividend income of the underlying equity:

$$Yield\ advantage = \frac{Ann.\ coupon - (Con.\ ratio \times Ann.\ dividend)}{Face\ value} \times 100$$

This represents the yield advantage from holding the convertible bond instead of converting it into stock.

Break-even period. The convertible bondholder pays a premium over the underlying equity value and in return receives some downside protection and the yield advantage. It is of interest to calculate approximately how long it would take for the yield advantage to fully compensate for the premium paid. This is called the break-even period:

$$Break\ even = \frac{Convertible\ price - Conversion\ value}{Ann.\ coupon - (Con.\ ratio \times Ann.\ dividend)}$$

At the end of the break-even period, the holder would have recouped the premium paid over the equity value. If the bond were converted at the break-even point, the shares would have cost the same as if the holder had purchased the shares outright instead of buying the convertible. If the bond was converted before the break-even point, it would have been less expensive (although probably more risky) to have bought the shares outright. The break-even period does not reflect the downside protection afforded by the convertible. However, it is a useful measure if the stock is performing well and is in danger of being called before the breakeven.

Expected cash flow. This analysis is similar to the break-even method. Coupon and dividend payments are projected to the date of expected conversion of the bond (e.g., the first call date). The expected cash flow value of the convertible can then be calculated by determining the present value of these cash flows.

Cash flow value = Con. value + PV of coupons – PV of dividends

This analysis is sophisticated, taking into account dividend growth and different possible conversion dates. However, it is of little use if there is a significant probability that the bond will be held to maturity and redeemed.

Convertibles as Bonds with Equity Options

Where the equity value of the convertible is low and conversion is less likely, the bond cannot be regarded as a stock substitute. It is sometimes then treated as a straight corporate bond with a stock call option.

Premium over investment value. Because of the option, the convertible bond will have a higher price than an equivalent straight bond of the same issuer. The price of the equivalent straight bond (called the investment value) can be calculated using a standard bond pricing formula. The premium can be expressed as a percentage of the investment value:

$$Premium = \frac{Convertible\ price - Investment\ value}{Investment\ value} \times 100$$

This premium represents the amount paid for the equity option. If the price of the underlying stock goes up or the stock volatility increases, the premium should increase. If the conversion value never increases above the investment value, the premium will decline over time until it is zero at maturity. Calculating the investment value can sometimes be difficult because the appropriate yield depends on the credit quality of the issuer as well as the time to maturity. If the particular issuer does not have similar straight debt, it may not be possible to determine the yield accurately.

Bond plus warrant. The convertible value can be estimated by calculating the value of the conversion option using a standard stock option or warrant pricing model. The face value of the bond is used as the strike price of the option. The value of the convertible bond is then the sum of the investment value and the stock option value. This method has merit in that it incorporates the volatility of the stock. However, it ignores two important factors: call features and changes in the investment value. The value of the conversion option is significantly reduced by any issuer's call features. Also, the bond and the conversion option are not separate securities bundled together. The bond must be sacrificed to exercise the option. Therefore the value of the option depends on the value of the straight bond (the investment value) at all potential exercise dates. This investment value changes as the bond approaches maturity (decreases for premium bonds and increases for discount bonds) and fluctuates with each coupon payment. Because of these problems, simple bond plus warrant approaches have very limited use.

Convertibles as Composite Derivative Securities

While the analytic approaches described are useful for understanding the pricing and behavior of convertible bonds under certain circumstances, none can be universally applied to most convertible bonds under all market conditions. The only generally applicable approach to analyzing convertible bonds is with a sophisticated special-purpose lattice-based model. This treats the convertible as a single derivative security, but one with many related cash flows and embedded options. The calculation of a theoretical price for the convertible is based on the various conversion, call, and put features and market parameters (e.g., stock price, volatility, yields).

An accurate model would ideally have these features:

1. The convertible bond is treated as a single security throughout the model.
2. The underlying stock price is treated as uncertain, with specified volatility.
3. Interest rates are uncertain, with specified volatility.
4. Individual coupon and dividend payments are included in all calculations.
5. The conversion, call, put, and other features of the convertible bond are incorporated.
6. The model should be able to incorporate some estimate of how the issuer will behave with respect to calling the bonds.

Convertible Valuation Model Inputs

The inputs to a convertible bond theoretical model fall into three distinct groups: the terms of the convertible, observable market data, and estimates. The first group, the terms of the convertible, can be obtained from the indentures of the bond or from other sources of bond data. These inputs include the bond maturity, coupon rate, conversion terms, call prices, dates, and other provisions. The observable market data include the underlying stock price and government bond yields. The most problematic inputs are in the third category, the estimates. The stock volatility over the life of the convertible must be forecast. Historic stock volatility and implied volatility of traded options on the stock can be used as a guide. The appropriate yield spread to reflect the credit of the issuer must also be estimated. Yields on any other bonds of the issuer can be measured, as well as yields on bonds with a similar credit rating. These estimates are somewhat subjective, but they can have a significant influence on the value of the bond. It is important to understand which factors influence the value of the bond and how best to estimate them.

A CONVERTIBLE BOND THEORETICAL PRICING MODEL

The option characteristics of a convertible bond can be modeled by using a tree to represent the uncertainty in future market variables. Such a model can incorporate the uncertainty in future stock prices, interest rates, or both. In the case of only stock price volatility, a binomial tree is used. In a binomial tree each node in the tree branches into two other nodes. This represents possible up or down movements of the underlying variable over some time interval. Where both underlying stock prices and interest rates are uncertain, a quadrinomial tree is used. In a quadrinomial tree, each node branches into four other nodes. This represents increases or decreases in both variables.

The Stock Process

Stock price uncertainty is modeled using a tree of stock prices (S) representing the probable development of the underlying stock price in a risk-neutral world (see Exhibit 19–5).

The first node of the tree is today's stock price (S). The tree goes forward in time branching into up and down moves (Su and Sd) at regular time intervals (Δt). The size of the up and down moves depends on the time interval, the default-free interest rate (r), and the volatility of the stock price (σ):

$$u = e^{r\Delta t + \sigma\sqrt{\Delta t}}$$
$$d = e^{r\Delta t - \sigma\sqrt{\Delta t}}$$

The probability (p) of an up move at any node is:

$$p = \frac{e^{r\Delta t} - d}{u - d}$$

There are numerous different formulations of binomial stock trees which reproduce the same process. This particular formulation was chosen because it is quite efficient and works well at low volatilities.

The Interest Rate Process

Interest rate uncertainty can also be modeled with a binomial tree (see Exhibit 19–6). The first node is today's short term default-free interest rate. The branches represent increases and decreases of the rate over the time

EXHIBIT 19–5
Binomial Tree of Stock Prices

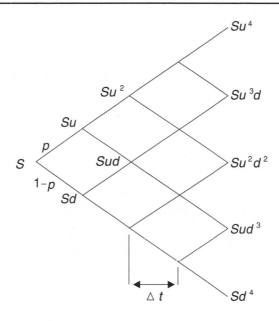

interval. However, in the interest rate tree the up and down moves need to be adjusted so that the tree conforms to the current term structure of interest rates. This is required so that theoretical prices for bonds calculated using the tree will be the same as the prices calculated using the yield curve.

The relationship between the rates at adjacent up and down nodes is determined by the volatility of interest rates and the time interval between nodes:

$$Ru = Rd \times e^{2\sigma\sqrt{\Delta t}}$$

and the probability of an up move is the same as the probability of a down move:

$$p = 0.5$$

The tree constructed in this manner is consistent with the interest rate volatility estimate and the term structure of interest rates.

EXHIBIT 19–6
Binomial Tree of Interest Rates

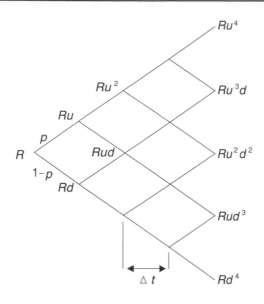

Traversing the Tree

The two factor version of the model uses a quadrinomial tree incorporating the stock and interest rate processes described above. From each node in the quadrinomial tree there are four branches representing up and down stock and interest rate movements (see Exhibit 19–7).

Irrespective of which tree is used, the process of traversing the tree to determine the convertible bond price is the same. At each node, the stock price and interest rate is known. We start at the end of the tree, which represents the maturity of the bond. At maturity, the convertible bond price is the maximum of the conversion value or the redemption value (let us assume that the bond is convertible from today to maturity). We calculate this for each node at maturity. At a node one period before maturity, we define the continuation value as the expected present value of the bond if it is not converted, called, or put at that node. The continuation value is therefore the sum of the values at each of the following branches, multiplied by their respective probabilities, and present valued at the interest rate for the node. If the bond is convertible at this node, the value is the higher of

EXHIBIT 19–7
Quadrinomial Tree of Stock Prices and Interest Rates

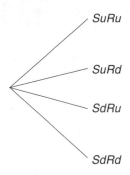

the conversion value and the continuation value. If it is also callable, the value is the higher of the conversion value and the lower of the continuation value and the call value because the bond would be called if the continuation value were higher than the call value (including any accrued), and conversion would be forced if the conversion value were higher than the call value. We then work backward through the rest of the tree node by node. The final result is the convertible bond value at the first node, that is, today. This value incorporates the uncertainty in the underlying variables represented in the tree, and takes into account the effects of calls and conversions between today and maturity.

This is of course a simplified explanation of the model. The model must also take into account the payments of stock dividends and bond coupons, any put options, and numerous other specific bond and model features.

REFERENCES

Figlewski, Stephen, William L. Silber, and Marti G. Subrahmanyam. *Financial Options: From Theory to Practice*. Homewood, IL: Business One Irwin, 1990.

Kalotay, Andrew J., George O. Williams, and Frank J. Fabozzi. "A Model for Valuing Bonds and Embedded Options." *Financial Analysts Journal*, May/June 1993.

Chapter Twenty

Pricing Convertible Bonds

Thomas Ho
G.A.T.

The convertible bond market is an important part of the fixed-income sector. The convertible bond offers the holder the option to convert a corporate bond into a specified number of shares of the firm, usually any time up to the maturity of the bond. Other features include:

- The call provision that allows the firm to buy back the bonds at prespecified prices.
- The sinking fund requirement that obligates the firm to redeem the bonds over a period of time.
- The put option that gives the investor the right to sell the bond back to the firm at a predetermined price.

These features often dramatically affect the bond's behavior and value. Although similar to nonconvertible corporate bonds, convertible bonds represent a spectrum of vastly different securities. Because convertibles are hybrids of bonds and stocks, they must inherit all the complexities of the underlying instruments and behave in an often complicated fashion as a mix of two securities. While convertible securities offer many opportunities for investing and for formulating portfolio strategies, they are also relatively complicated to analyze. This chapter provides a basic framework for analyzing these securities given their diverse characteristics. It offers an analytical framework that enables bond issuers and investors to deal with these difficulties in a systematic fashion.

The description shows how the complex structure of a convertible may be broken down into five basic components: the underlying bond, the latent warrant, the latent call option, the sinking fund option, and the put option. Each component is analyzed separately, including the value and behavior of each part and how it affects the convertible bond. The analytical approach provides valuable insights into the convertible bond's behavior and demonstrates how the analysis yields fair value of a convertible bond.

THE BASIC FRAMEWORK

A description of the basic assumptions of the model uses the standard framework for studying securities pricing to derive the fair value of a convertible bond, so the determining factors of the bond price must be considered in a specific way using perfect capital market assumptions.

The framework ignores all types of transaction costs: the commissions, the bid/ask spreads, the issuance costs, and all the explicit costs involved in a transaction. The reason is that the price at which an investor can buy or sell a bond is not relevant; what is relevant is the price at which the bond should be sold at equilibrium in order to determine the bond price if the market is functioning perfectly (i.e., at fair value).

These assumptions focus on the options aspect of the pricing problem, ignoring topics such as tax implications of the convertible, marketability of the issues, and corporate strategies. Although these issues are important to the bond pricing, they are beyond the scope of this chapter.

The question is, given the stock price and the investment value, how should a convertible bond be priced in a perfectly functioning market?

An Illustrative Example

There are many terminologies and notations used to describe a convertible bond. An example is Corroon and Black (CBL), 7.5, June 1, 2005. The bondholder can convert each $100 face value bond into 3.5714 Corroon and Black shares any time up to the maturity. (For this chapter, $100 face amount denominations and the associated conversion values are used instead of the commonly used $1,000 denomination.) The issuer can call back the bond at 107.5 percent of par in year 1985. The call schedule then decreases linearly to 100 percent in 1994 and remains on that level until maturity. However, the firm cannot call the bonds before June 1, 1987, unless the common stock trades above 140 percent (the call trigger) of the conversion price at the time of call. The bond also has a sinking fund. The firm is obligated to retire 7.5 percent of the amount issued each year from 1995 through 2004.

On November 15, 1986, the stock was traded at $35 per share and the bond was $131. The stock at that time was paying $0.65 dividend per share. The credit risk of the bond is given by the Moody's rating of A2. The information below is summarized with the notations of each item given in the first column:

Corroon and Black (CBL)

T =	the bond maturity	6/1/2005
c =	the bond coupon rate	7.5%
k =	the conversion ratio	3.5714
t =	the call trigger	140%
B =	the market bond price	$131
S =	the market stock price	$35
d =	the dividend	$0.65
R =	the rating	Moody's A2

Given this information, some other parameters can be calculated.

P = parity (conversion value)

The parity, or conversion value, is the value of the bond if the holder decides to convert. It is therefore the equity worth of the convertible bond; the share price is not important. More important is the parity, the product of the conversion ratio and the share price:

$$P = kS \text{ or } (3.5714 \times 35) = \$124.99$$

The conversion price, Cp, is the price of a share that creates parity value of $100. That is,

$$100 = kCp$$

In this case, Cp equals $28 per share.

The investment value (I) is the value of the bond, ignoring the possibility of converting the bond to equity. The investment value is therefore the underlying bond value given by the present value of the bond cash flow (coupons and principal) adjusted for the credit risk, the sinking fund provision, and other bond-related features.

Basics of the Convertible Bond

The convertible offers the investor the upside return when the common stock value increases. This is possible because, when the stock value becomes high, the investor can convert the bond to equity. But that does not mean that the investor must convert to capture the price appreciation of the equity. When the parity value is high, the convertible trades like equity, and the convertible bond value appreciates in step with the stock price. If the stock value drops, the investor, at worst, still receives the coupons and principal; that is, the investor still holds the bond or has the investment value. As a result, the downside risk of the investment is protected.

In short, the convertible offers the upside return and protects the investor from the downside risk. The investor, in essence, is holding a straight bond and a warrant. A warrant is an instrument that provides the holder with the right to purchase a prespecified number of shares of stock at a specific price. Although this is a useful way of thinking about a convertible, it does not describe accurately most of the convertible bonds traded in the U.S. market.

With most bonds, investors are expected to be forced to convert to stocks in a relatively short time period. For this reason, it is more appropriate to think of the convertible bond as the parity value (the equity value) plus the present value of the coupons net of the present value of the dividends that the investor can receive before being forced to convert. This alternative way of viewing a convertible bond can affect the analysis of the bonds significantly.

However, this description of a convertible bond is incomplete because the estimate of the inflow of coupons net of dividends is inadequate to describe the optionlike feature of the bond. The firm, at its option, can force the bondholders to convert the bond to equity, and such an option must be priced. Below is a formal analysis of this and other option aspects of the problem.

CONVERTIBLE BOND MODELS

The simplest possible convertible bond model captures the essential features of the convertible; gradually, other features of the bond are incorporated to create a model that can describe adequately total bond behavior.

The Latent Warrant

First is the simplified version of the Corroon and Black (CBL) bond. To determine the fair value of the bond, assume that the bond has no call or sinking fund provisions and no credit risk. For the time being, assume that the bond pays no coupon and the stock gives no dividends.

The important observation here is that, although the bondholder can convert the bond to stocks any time up to maturity, there are no economic incentives to do so. The argument is quite simple. If the investor converts the bond, then at maturity the investor has the prevailing value of the parity value. On the other hand if the investor holds the bond to maturity, the bond can be converted whenever it is beneficial to do so. Indeed, when the parity value is above the bond value, the bondholder would convert. That is, the bondholder not only has the stock return, but also is guaranteed the minimum value of the bond par value (investment value). For this reason, it is always advantageous to hold the bond to maturity because there is value in retaining the option to convert. Even if the parity value is high and the convertible bond is traded like equity, the convertible bond still offers the protection of the downside risk. Once the conversion is effected, the downside protection is eliminated.

Recognizing that there is no value to the early exercise, focus now on what the investor optimally should do at maturity. When the parity is above par, the investor gives up the principal and receive the shares, but that is precisely the same as receiving the principal and using the amount to exercise a warrant. In sum, the convertible bond is the same as the basic bond plus a warrant when the exercise price of the bond is par value and the expiration date is the bond's maturity. This warrant is called the *latent warrant*.

To illustrate the latent warrant, refer to the CBL bond. It has a warrant that gives the holder the right, but not the obligation, to buy 3.5714 shares on June 1, 2005, for $100. Therefore, the latent warrant is a long-term American option.

Coupons and Dividends

So far, the analysis assumes that there are no coupons and dividends, but that assumption is made for the clarity of exposition, and relaxing the assumption affects little of the analysis. The crux of the argument is to recognize whether the warrant would be exercised early. When the bond pays coupons, there is even less incentive to exercise early because, by holding onto the bond, the investor receives all the coupons in addition to retaining the option to the last minute. This ignores the dividends on the stock because, if the investor converts the bond to equity, he or she receives the stock dividend. However, it is clear that as long as the coupon payments are higher than the dividends, the warrant would not be exercised early. Luckily, most convertible bonds pay coupons that yield significantly more than the dividends on the stock. For this reason, the arguments apply for nearly all convertible bonds. In the example of CBL, the annual dividend on the parity is given by the product of the conversion ratio and the dividends ($0.65 × 3.5714 = $2.3214). It is significantly less than the $7.50 earned on each $100 par bond. Note that this ignores the growth rate of the dividend per share for illustrative reasons.

As the investor holds the bond until maturity, the convertible bond value should be equal to the consolidated investment value of the underlying bond plus the latent warrant. The latent warrant is denoted by W in a simple formula:

$$B = I + W \tag{1}$$

It is instructive to represent the convertible bond value diagrammatically; the diagram is called the value diagram.

The Value Diagram

The value diagram is a graphic representation of the security's value as a function of the parity value at any time before the bond's maturity. This shows how the underlying bond value, latent warrant, the convertible bond, and other related instruments change values as parity value varies.

On the value diagram, the y-axis is the value of any instrument and the unit of measure is in dollars. The x-axis is the parity value, also in dollars. The underlying bond curve is the investment value of the bond. When the parity is high (i.e., the stock value is high), the bond presumably has little credit risk; for this reason, the curve should be flat, taking the value of the present value of the coupons and principal.

However, when the parity is low, the share value has dropped, reflecting a drop in the firm value. In this case, the bond credit risk increases and the bond value drops. The bond curve in Exhibit 20–1 depicts the behavior of this bond. The 45-degree line through the origin is called the parity line. It represents the convertible bond value at the instant the bond is converted to equity (conversion value).

EXHIBIT 20–1
Bond Curve and Parity Line

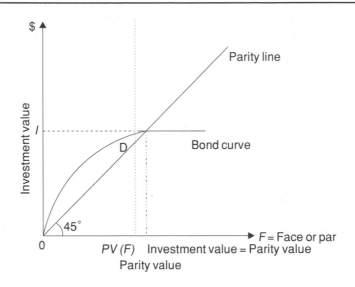

Note that the investor always converts when it is advantageous to do so. Because it is never advantageous for bondholders to convert the bond early, the convertible bond fair value must lie above both the underlying investment value and the parity value. For this reason, the curve that is the higher of the bond curve and the parity line represents the formula prices. The formula prices are the lower bound of the values of the convertible bond. Turning to the latent warrant, the formula value of the warrant is the higher of the following two lines: the 45-degree line starting from the exercise price (par value) and the horizontal line on the x-axis from the origin to the par value. The formula price curve represents the minimum value of the warrant.

Standard option theory shows that the minimum warrant value is in fact the 45-degree line that intersects the x-axis at the present value of the exercise price, or the present value of the par value, in this case. Given this argument, the warrant curve in Exhibit 20–2 can be sketched.

So the convertible bond is the sum of the bond curve and the warrant curve. It is represented in Exhibit 20–3, where the curve XY represents the convertible bond value. Exhibit 20–3 also depicts the composition of the convertible bond value. The line OA is the parity line. However, when the

EXHIBIT 20–2
Warrant Curve

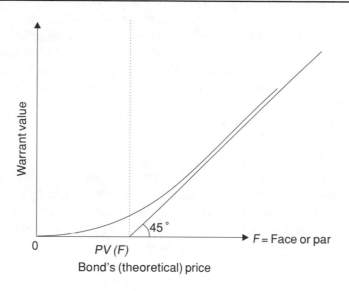

EXHIBIT 20–3
Composition of the Convertible Bond Value

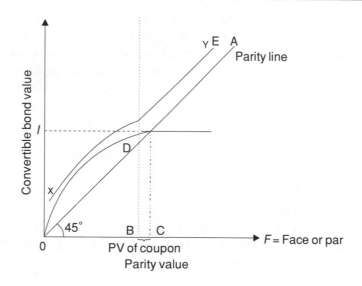

parity value is high, the convertible bond value does not converge to the parity line; it converges instead to the parallel line of DE. The distance of point D from the y-axis (the distance is the same as OB) is the present value of the face value of the bond. Because the bond value, or investment value, is the sum of the present value of the face value and the coupon value, it follows that the distance between the parity value and line DE is the present value of the coupon. Therefore, the convertible bond value must exceed the higher of the investment value, or the sum of the parity value and the present value of the coupons. The level of excess is the term premium of the intent warrant. This excess is the cost to the convertible bondholder for having a position that participates on any upside return of the stock and is limited on the downside to the investment value of the bond.

Because the latent warrant is a long-term stock option, this excess value is very sensitive to the estimate of the stock return volatility. Unfortunately, the stock return volatility is not observable (as a price is observable). As a result, the market has to determine the precise value of the term premium, and convertible bond models can prove only relatively rough estimates of fair value.

If there is any dividend on the stock, the description can be altered by considering the present value of the coupon net of the dividends, instead of only the coupon. Many analyses of convertible bonds tend to focus on the latent warrant value. Unfortunately, this analysis is far from complete. As in the case of straight corporate bonds, the call provision must be taken into account in analyzing the convertible bond value.

First, the minimal value of the warrant is estimated by assuming that there is no early exercise of the dividend-paying stock. Then the option value is greater than the stock value (parity) net of both the present value of the stock dividends that the option holder will not receive and the present value of the strike price. In the case of the convertible bond in the earlier example with a 7 percent discount rate, the present value of the strike price over 19 years is $27.65. Assuming constant dividends (a conservative estimate) of $2.3214 per year, the present value of all the dividends in the next 19 years is the product of $2.3214 and the present value annuity factor at 7 percent for 19 years. The value is $26.3144. Therefore, the warrant value should exceed $71.025 ($124.99 – $27.65 – $26.3144).

Now the investment value of the bond can be estimated. It is shown that the investment value of the bond cannot be greater than the convertible bond traded price net of the lower bound value of the warrant. So the investment value cannot exceed $59.975 ($131 – $71.025).

The Call Feature

The call provisions on convertible bonds are homogeneous and similar in many ways to the call provisions of industrial corporate bonds. The call provision allows the issuer to call back the bonds in part or in whole at the prespecified price, or the call price. The call schedule tends to decline linearly, reaching the lowest call price, or the par value, some time before maturity. But the similarities between the call provisions in the convertibles and the corporates end here.

Although the convertible bond call provision also has a call protection period, it is implemented differently. Most convertible bonds issued after 1985 have a call trigger price stated typically in percentages (140 percent, as in the case of CBL). In these cases, the firm cannot call the bond unless the common stock is traded above the product of the call trigger price and the conversion price. This restriction of calling the bonds applies only for a period of time, typically two to three years. After this call protection period, the firm can call the bonds whenever it is advantageous to the issuer. But that does not mean that the firm would call the bonds when they are traded slightly above the call price. Instead, a firm usually calls the bonds with a coupon rate similar to those of the current new issues only when the bonds are traded 20 to 25 percent above the call price. There are many arguments to explain this observation. For example when the bond is called, the investor has one month to decide whether to convert the bond into stock or surrender it for cash based on the call price.

If it cannot be sure whether the investors will decide on cash or shares, the firm must prepare to issue the shares as well as to pay cash. This scenario may create administrative complications. However, if the firm waits until the market price of the stock reaches a level that makes it obviously more advantageous to convert rather than to accept cash, then the firm calls its bonds. In line with this reasoning, the firm would have to decide that, over the one-month period, there would be a small probability that the stock price would drop to a level causing investors to change their minds and select cash.

Notice that calling the bond is motivated by the rise in the parity value. There is also another reason: It may be an optimal call period. When market interest rates have fallen significantly, the firm may call the bond to refinance the issue at a lower interest cost. In this case, there is no need to consider the complexities involved in forced conversion. The firm may call the bond because it is economically optimal.

Without dwelling on this issue, note that convertible bonds usually are called when the bonds are traded significantly above the call price for whatever reason.

When the bond is called, the parity value must be high or the bond would not be traded at such a high premium. For this reason, investors always prefer to convert into equity than to receive that call price. This calling of bonds is called *forced conversion* and is the most important aspect of the call provision of the convertibles. The provision is used by the firm to force the bondholders to convert the bond into equity.

The forced conversion feature significantly affects the pricing of the convertible. Suppose there is a market consensus that when the convertible bond trades above a price, called the *implicit call price,* the bond is to be called. Also note that the more volatile the stock, the higher the implicit call price. So, from the previous description the spread between the implicit call price and the stated call price depends on the stock return volatility.

No investor would pay a price higher than the implicit call price, no matter how high the parity value rises. Refering to the value diagram, note that when the convertible bond rises in step with the higher parity value, it must rise at a slower rate as the value approaches the implicit call price. When the bond value reaches the implicit call price, the bond price must be the parity value because the investor should be indifferent about whether to hold the bond or to convert to equity. Referring to Exhibits 20–3 and 20–4, note how the call provision affects the bond values.

In Exhibit 20–4, the convertible bond value must be capped by the implicit call price. As the parity value rises, the convertible bond value rises in step. But as the convertible bond value approaches the implicit call price, the market anticipates the firm's calling the bond and the bondholders convert the bonds to the parity value.

For this reason, the market still trades the bond at the parity value. Exhibit 20–4 depicts this relationship between the parity value and the convertible bond value.

The Latent Call Option

The forced conversion of the bond introduces another option built into the convertible bond, the *latent call option*, denoted by C. This time, the issuer decides the optimal exercise of the option. In exercising the option, the issuer forces bondholders to convert the bond to equity. In so doing, the firm saves the present value of the coupons in subsequent years. If the convertible

EXHIBIT 20–4
Effect of the Implicit Call Price

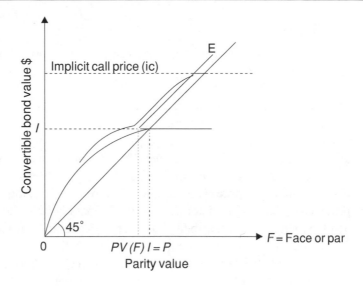

bond value does not rise above the implicit call price, the firm does not call the bond and the call option has little value. Therefore, the latent call option is valuable to the firm for saving the interest costs.

The most striking feature of the latent call option is that the option pricing behavior has to be significantly different than the stock option. The major difference is that no matter how high the underlying asset value (in this case, the convertible bond value), the value of the option is capped. It does not rise unbounded like the stock option because the latent call option allows the firm to save the interest cost, which has a maximum value.

In the presence of the call provision, the convertible bond has three components. The pricing formula is:

$$B = I + W - C \tag{2}$$

The impact of the call option on the convertible bond price is best illustrated by the example of the CBL bond again.

From Equation (2):

$$C = I + W - B \tag{3}$$

But it was argued earlier that the warrant value must exceed the parity value net of the present value of the dividends and the preset value of par. So $C > I + P - PV(d) - PV(\text{par}) - B$. But by definition,

$$C > P + PV(c) - PV(d) - B \tag{4}$$

Here, P is the parity value, $PV(c)$ the present value of the coupons out to the bond maturity, $PV(d)$ the present value of the dividends out to the bond maturity, and PV (par) the present value of par.

Now estimate the numbers for B, P, c, d, and $PV(\text{par})$. B is \$131. P is \$124.99. Assume a 7 percent discount rate (the prevailing 10-year rate) and a conservative estimate of a constant dividend of \$2.3214 per year. The present value of the annuity of the coupon net of the dividends over 19 years is \$58.696 (the present value annuity factor is 11.3343). Therefore using Equation (4), the latent call option has a value of more than \$52,686.

In the presence of the call provision, investors no longer believe they can hold the bond to maturity, as described above. They expect to be forced to convert. Therefore, the convertible bond price is not the sum of the parity and the present value of all the coupons. In the presence of the call provision, it is the sum of the parity and the present value of the coupons up to forced conversion. This line of argument can be used to calculate when the bond would be forced to convert. Let the time be b years. The present value of the coupons and dividends in b years is $PV(\text{coupons})$ and $PV(d)$. The bond value is B and the parity value is P. Therefore, the following equation must hold.

$$B = P + PV(\text{coupons}) - PV(d) \tag{5}$$

Using Equation (3) and the time b, it is relatively straightforward to calculate that the market expects the bond to be called. Notice that this is precisely the break-even analysis often used by convertible investors. Although this approach seems tractable and useful, there are several assumptions. Indeed, Equation (3) can be derived from Equation (2) if several assumptions are made. First, the latent warrant is traded sufficiently in the money that its value is approximated by the formula price of $P - PV(\text{strike price})$. Noting that the strike price is the par value:

$$W = P - PV(\text{par value}) \tag{6}$$

Also, if the premium of the latent call option is negligible (the market is quite certain about when the firm will call the bonds), the C (option value) is the present value of the coupons not paid to the investors.

$$C = PV(\text{coupon after } b) \tag{7}$$

Combining Equations (3), (6), and (7), Equation (5) is calculated.

The above analysis shows that in the break-even analysis issued to determine the expected time of forced conversion, it must be assumed that the warrant is very much in the money and the volatility of the latent call option is negligible.

THE PREMIUM DIAGRAM

Now consider two polar cases. When the stock prices are high so that the parity value is significantly higher than the investment value, the market should anticipate a forced conversion. For this reason, the convertible bond should be traded very near the parity value. On the other hand, when the stock value drops significantly so that the bondholder does not expect to convert the bond to equity, the convertible bond would trade near its investment value. These two polar cases of the convertible bond's performance are relatively straightforward.

Of course, the important part of pricing the convertible bonds occurs when the parity value is close to the investment value. In this region, the convertible bond value is influenced greatly by the latent warrant value and the latent call value; therefore, the convertible bond value is no longer a simple relationship to the parity and investment value. Pricing the convertible bond value in this case requires the modeling of the warrant value and the call option value.

There is much insight into the bond behavior if the fair value of the bond in the premium diagram, which is derived from the value diagram, is analyzed. While the value diagram is concerned with the absolute value of the bond, the premium diagram is concerned with the parity value and the convertible bond value as percentages to the investment's value (ratio). This way, the premium diagram focuses on the region where the parity value is close to the investment value. Also by normalizing the convertible bond values around the investment value it is possible to cross-compare different convertible bond pricing behaviors. Exhibit 20–5 provides a summary depiction.

Specifically, the x axis of the premium diagram is defined as the ratio of the parity value and the investment value. For example, when the x value is unity, the parity value is the same as the investment value. The y axis of the premium diagram is the ratio of the convertible bond value to the investment value. In essence, the premium diagram depicts the relationship between

EXHIBIT 20–5
Premium Diagram

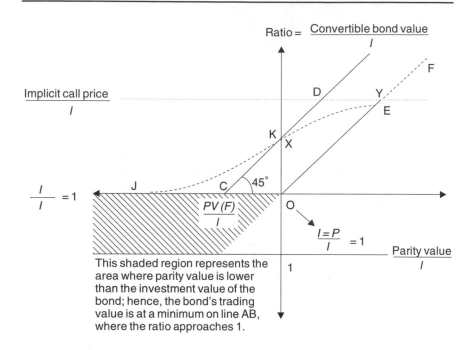

the convertible bond value and the parity value normalized by the investment value of the bond.

The Intrinsic Value

The premium diagram can be derived from Exhibit 20–4. The striking
result is that the premium seems to represent a call option as the normalized convertible bond value rises monotonically from 1 to a 45-degree
line. Perhaps this is the source of confusion in defining the latent warrant
because the value curve looks somewhat similar to a warrant value curve,
but as the analysis has shown, this curve represents two options. In addition, this curve is not specified by the standard parameters: expiration
date, exercise price, and volatility.

To illustrate this point, it is instructive to consider a special and somewhat
unrealistic case. Assume that there is no stock return uncertainty and, for
simplicity, assume that the stock does not pay any dividend. To be consistent

with the no arbitrage argument, the stock must appreciate at a risk-free rate, which also is assumed with certainty. Now the premium diagram of a convertible bond can be constructed.

The bond behavior is analyzed in four regions. First, when the parity value is low, the bond-to-the-investment-value ratio is unity; therefore, the value curve is depicted by *AB* in Exhibit 20–5. Point *C* is the present value of the exercise price of the latent warrant (divided by the investment value). When the parity ratio goes beyond point *C*, the bondholder is expected to convert the bond to equity at the bond maturity. That is, the convertible bond must now incorporate the intrinsic value of the latent warrant value. For this reason, the value curve must increase along the 45-degree line depicted by line *CD*.

As the parity ratio increases, the value curve also increases in step. But the value curve cannot go beyond the implicit call price. Indeed when the bond value reaches the call price, the bond price remains at the value even if the parity value continued to increase. This behavior is depicted by line *DE*, which indicates when the call option has value to the issuer. In this case, the issuer can call back the bonds and eliminate the ability of the bondholder to collect the coupons on the bond and to convert the bond to equity at maturity.

Finally, remember that the convertible bond cannot be traded below the parity value. Therefore when line *DE* meets the parity line, the convertible bond trades at parity. The explanation is quite simple. When the parity value is sufficiently high, the bond simply is traded at the parity anticipation of a forced conversion. When the firm calls the bond, the bondholder converts the bonds to equity without losing any value. In this region, the bond curve is represented by line *EF*.

The piecewise linear graph *ABCDEF* represents the intrinsic value of the convertible bond. To construct the intrinsic-value graph requires the (estimated) value of the parity, present value of the warrant exercise price, the investment value, and the call price (or implicit call price). The important point is that all these parameters can be measured, in principle, so the intrinsic-value graph can be constructed without developing complex mathematical models.

The Fair Value

The intrinsic value of the convertible bond is derived by assuming no uncertainty. In the presence of uncertainty, the convertible bond fair-value curve deviates from this intrinsic-value graph. It is a smooth curve because it is reasonable to assume that the uncertainty is resolved in a continuous and smooth manner. For this reason, the convertible bond value must relate to the parity value in a smooth fashion.

Such a fair-value curve is depicted in Exhibit 20–5 by XY. The curve must originate from point F because, under uncertainty, the bond is called when it reaches the implicit call price; at this point, the bond must be worth only the parity value. As the parity value drops, the bond value must drop because, in the world of uncertainty, the bond value can be, at most, the implicit call price. Meanwhile, if the parity value drops significantly to the region of CD, the bond value also drops. For this reason, the bond value has to come down instead of remaining at the call price as in the certainty case.

On the other hand, consider the region OA. In this instance, the minimum value of the bond is the investment value. But if the parity value increases substantially, the bond also incorporates the warrant intrinsic value. For this reason, the bond trades above the investment value. This resulting fair-value curve is depicted by JK. The complete fair-value curve must link curves XY and JK smoothly, as depicted by YJ.

The precise fair-value curve is determined by the level of stock-return uncertainty: the higher the uncertainty, the smaller the curvature of the fair-value graph. In any case, the intrinsic-value graph provides a valuable frame of reference for pricing or analyzing a convertible bond. Also, what is clear from this analysis is that the convertible bond fair-value curve is not a simple option-value curve because it is a combination of the latent warrant and the latent call option. Analysis that focuses on either the warrant value or the call option value (by using the break-even analysis) is misleading. The two aspects of the problem have to be studied together, and the convertible bond intrinsic-value graph provides such a framework.

CONCLUSION

This chapter provided a framework for ascertaining a convertible bond's fair value. It was shown that, for most convertible bonds traded in the market, the bond value incorporates both the warrant and call option values. It also was shown that, by constructing a graph depicting the intrinsic value of the convertible bond under different stock values, the capability of identifying and analyzing the effects of the warrant and call options is enhanced.

CURRENCY DERIVATIVES

Chapter Twenty-One

The Foreign Exchange Market
Spot, Forward, and Futures Contracts and Hedging Applications

David F. DeRosa
Swiss Bank Corporation

Foreign exchange is the largest of all the financial markets. Some estimates of the size of the trading volume are reported in parallel surveys undertaken during the month of April 1992 in cooperation with the Bank for International Settlements (BIS) and the New York Federal Reserve Bank. Earlier surveys were undertaken in April 1989. According to the 1992 survey, the global net turnover in the world's foreign exchange markets was estimated to be some $880 billion dollars per business day. This figure was adjusted for virtually all double-counting as well as for estimated gaps in reporting. The comparable number for April 1989 was $620 billion. The majority of transactions occur in the interbank market in the form of spot and forward deals. There is also a nontrivial dollar amount of trading done in listed futures contracts on a few of the major exchange rates, although the survey estimate is that it accounts for only 1 percent of total volume.

THE INTERBANK FOREIGN EXCHANGE MARKET

Foreign exchange is traded by a wide international network of dealers, most of whom are commercial banks and investment banking firms. London, New York, and Tokyo are the three largest centers for foreign exchange by volume of trading, but dealing institutions are located in many other cities throughout Asia, Europe, and America. The center of trading rotates around the globe throughout the day. New Zealand and Australia open the day in what is known as the Austral-Asian trading time zone. Six o'clock in the morning Sydney time is the official start of the foreign exchange day. Japan, Hong Kong, and Singapore join in a few hours later. Next, the center of trading moves to the European trading time zone. Trading takes place mainly in London but Zurich, Frankfurt, and Paris are also important. In the American trading time zone, New York dominates but Chicago, Los Angeles, Toronto, and Montreal are also sizable participants. Finally, trading for the day closes at five o'clock in the afternoon New York time.

Foreign exchange is a dealer's market. By definition, a dealer is a principal party who "makes a market"—that is, provides two-way quotes, both bid and offer, on foreign exchange in meaningful size (which is usually a minimum of $10 million worth of currency). As a principal, the dealer buys and sells for his or her own account (called the "book") by taking the other side of trades. When a counterparty buys, the dealer sells and when counterparty sells, the dealer buys. Profits arise from situations wherein the dealer can capture a small price advantage from the bid-offer spread or when the dealer's book is correctly positioned to benefit from directional moves in exchange rates. Dealing also means facing the risk of getting caught with a long position in a falling market or with a short position in a rising market. This is why being a dealer presumes a willingness to assume considerable financial risk and requires the commitment of large amounts of reserve capital to cover potential short-term losses. Consequently, not all banks are in a position to deal in foreign exchange. Still, many banks do have active roles in the market, not as market makers but as agents who arrange foreign exchange transactions for their customers. Putting up none of their own capital, they match each customer transaction back-to-back with a trade in the interbank market using exchange rates obtained from the market makers.

FOREIGN EXCHANGE RISK AND MARKET PARTICIPANTS

In the most common context, foreign exchange risk is the risk of exchange rate translation losses associated with any economic interest that is denominated in a foreign currency.

A U.S. dollar-based investor who acquires one million yen worth of shares in a Japanese company bears two risks. First, there is the risk that the shares might decline in value in their local currency. The shares might fall in value to 900,000 yen, for example. This risk is the local market risk that is born by every investor who owns shares; it has nothing to do with exchange rates. The second risk to the U.S. dollar-based investor is that the yen might decline in value against the dollar. This could erode any economic benefit from a positive rate of return from the Japanese stock market. It might even create a loss for the investor despite a rise in the yen value of the shares. Ordinarily, this is what is considered foreign exchange risk, but more subtle, less direct risks can be attributed to movements in exchange rates.

Foreign exchange risk is an unavoidable consequence of international investing. In the United States, tax exempt institutional investors—pension trusts, foundations, and endowment funds—had the equivalent of $262 billion international assets at the end of 1993. Pension funds of countries other than the United States had an exposure equal to $463 billion equivalent of international assets at the end of 1993 (see Exhibit 21–1). Mutual funds that specialize in international investing and that are distributed in the United States had $160 billion worth of overseas exposure at the end of 1994 (Exhibit 21–2). Given the size of the stakes, it is natural for there to be concern about currency risk. Foreign exchange risk can exert significant impact on investment performance. This can be affirmed by examination of the unhedged and currency hedged total returns on the FT-Actuaries World Stock Market Indexes (see Exhibit 21–3), which are popular performance benchmarks for international equity funds. Hedged returns are calculated using one-month currency forwards to hedge exchange rate risk. The perspective in Exhibit 21–3 is from that of German mark-based, Japanese yen-based and U.S. dollar-based investors. In each case, the stock market index excludes the investor's home market to focus the analysis on currency risk. Compound annual hedged returns are significantly different from unhedged returns. Roughly speaking, hedged returns are double or half of the corresponding unhedged returns, depending on which side of the currency the investor happens to be. Unhedged returns are more volatile than hedged returns, as can be seen by comparing the standard deviations of annual returns. Similar conclusions can be reached by examination of the data on unhedged and currency hedged versions of the Salomon Brothers World Government Bond Indexes (see Exhibit 21–4). Some investment managers cope with foreign exchange risk by hedging with forward cur-

EXHIBIT 21-1
Investments by Pension Funds in International Assets

A. *U.S. Tax-Exempt Assets Invested Overseas*
   (Billions of U.S. Dollars)

	1988	1989	1990	1991	1992	1993
Total U.S. tax-exempt	$2,067	$2,457	$2,410	$2,702	$3,319	$3,639
Assets invested overseas	$62	$86	$94	$127	$156	$262
Percent of total U.S. tax-exempt	3.00%	3.50%	3.90%	4.70%	4.70%	7.20%
Assets by category						
Equity	$53	$73	$74	$99	$117	$202
Fixed income	$9	$13	$17	$24	$34	$49
Other	—	—	$3	$4	$5	$11

B. *Non-U.S. Pension Fund Assets Invested Overseas, 1993*
   (Billions of U.S. Dollars)

	Japan	U.K.	Other	Total
Assets invested overseas	$92	$228	$143	$463
Percent of total assets	9.00%	28.00%	10.50%	14.48%

Source: InterSec Research Corporation. InterSec Research of Stamford Connecticut surveys investment managers. It cautions that these data exclude foreign investment holdings in accounts not designated as international or global strategies.

448

EXHIBIT 21–2
U.S. Foreign Mutual Fund Aggregate Net Assets
(Billions of U.S. Dollars)

	Stock Funds					Bond Funds		
	European	*Foreign*	*Pacific*	*World*	*Total*	*World*	*Short-Term World Income*	*Total*
1988	$0.65	$ 5.38	$ 1.15	$10.99	$ 18.17	$ 4.21	$ 0.14	$ 4.35
1989	1.32	7.37	1.42	13.36	23.47	4.49	0.38	4.87
1990	3.77	9.07	1.36	13.38	27.58	5.35	6.73	12.08
1991	3.52	12.82	1.83	17.73	35.90	7.14	21.20	28.34
1992	3.23	16.81	2.88	19.17	42.09	10.00	14.45	24.46
1993	5.29	52.89	12.50	34.70	105.37	19.94	12.21	32.15
1994	6.08	73.52	13.40	45.38	138.38	16.25	5.54	21.79

Notes: Data for mutual funds sold in the United States. European stock funds invest at least 65 percent in equity securities of European issuers.

Foreign stock funds invest primarily in equity securities of issuers located outside of the United States. Pacific stock fund's invest primarily in issuers located in countries in the Pacific Basin, including Japan, Hong Kong, Malaysia, Singapore, and Australia.

World stock funds invest primarily in equity securities of issuers located throughout the world, maintaining a percentage of assets (normally 25 percent to 50 percent) in the United States. World bond funds invest in bonds denominated in currencies other than the U.S. dollar.

Short-term world income funds invest primarily in various bonds not denominated in U.S. currency, usually with maturities of three years or less.

Source: Morningstar, Inc., 225 W. Wacker Dr., Chicago, IL 60606 (312) 696-6000.

EXHIBIT 21-3

Total Returns on FT-Actuaries World Stock Market Indexes
Unhedged and Currency Hedged, 1986–1994

	World Ex-Germany		World Ex-Japan		World Ex-U.S.	
	Hedged into DEM	*Unhedged DEM*	*Hedged into JPY*	*Unhedged JPY*	*Hedged into USD*	*Unhedged USD*
1986	42.34%	12.82%	28.17%	0.39%	39.81%	66.55%
1987	11.35	−2.29	5.05	−18.97	−0.52	26.25
1988	24.05	38.62	13.83	19.68	34.50	27.93
1989	23.49	11.44	23.30	49.03	26.09	12.17
1990	−22.25	−27.03	−11.73	−8.71	−30.38	−23.12
1991	19.54	21.96	24.63	14.84	4.85	13.32
1992	1.24	1.43	4.22	2.25	−11.03	−13.06
1993	22.24	30.91	20.17	8.84	26.25	32.25
1994	0.43	−5.47	−7.28	−10.26	−0.75	8.36
Compound annual return	12.14%	7.41%	10.29%	4.76%	7.51%	14.09%
Standard deviation of annual returns	18.57	20.12	14.39	20.23	23.28	26.26

Notes: Currency hedged returns calculated on the basis of rolling one-month forwards and includes the effect of bid-ask spread.
Hedged returns for Thailand, Brazil, South Africa, and Mexico are actually unhedged returns for lack of forwards data, but these countries are a minuscule part of the indexes.

Sources: Calculated by Goldman, Sachs & Co. and based on the FT-Actuaries World Indexes, which are jointly compiled by the Financial times, Ltd., Goldman, Sachs & Co., and NatWest Securities Ltd., in conjunction with the Institute of Actuaries and the Faculty of Actuaries.
Compound annual return and standard deviation of annual returns calculated by author.

EXHIBIT 21–4
Total Returns on Salomon Brothers World Government Bond Indexes
Unhedged and Currency Hedged, 1985–1994

	World Ex-Germany		World Ex-Japan		World Ex-U.S.	
	Hedged into DEM	*Unhedged DEM*	*Hedged into JPY*	*Unhedged JPY*	*Hedged into USD*	*Unhedged USD*
1985	12.49%	-1.98%	15.66%	-1.00%	11.14%	35.01%
1986	10.74	-3.57	11.18	-6.51	11.40	31.35
1987	2.17	-3.69	1.06	-14.15	9.27	35.15
1988	4.29	18.63	3.83	8.13	9.12	2.34
1989	6.55	-0.50	5.77	27.58	4.11	-3.41
1990	6.20	-1.74	5.58	6.40	3.32	15.29
1991	16.85	18.63	15.11	5.29	11.11	16.21
1992	14.39	12.47	8.50	4.37	8.03	4.77
1993	18.15	22.19	11.70	-1.29	13.42	15.12
1994	-2.47	-9.43	-6.25	-9.77	-4.02	5.99
Compound annual return	8.75%	4.54%	7.02%	1.33%	7.57%	15.03
Standard deviation of annual returns	5.69	11.01	5.06	11.55	3.38	14.35

Notes: Currency hedged returns calculated on the basis of rolling one-month forwards.

Sources: Salomon Brothers; compound annual return and standard deviation of annual returns calculated by author.

rency contracts. Others have developed expertise in using currency options in sophisticated strategies. Another solution is to engage the services of a specialist currency overlay manager who assumes responsibility for the portfolio's foreign exchange risk. Whatever the means, the sheer size of the assets at risk as well as the magnitude of exchange rate movements relative to local market returns mandates that the management of foreign exchange risk be made an integral part of the total investment process.

Many commodity trading advisors and hedge fund managers trade positions in foreign exchange and its related derivative instruments as a high-risk asset class. Capital is put at risk in an attempt to profit from having correctly anticipated directional moves in exchange rates. In a limited number of cases, performance has been brilliant. As a rule, return profiles have been volatile, which in part can be explained because of the use of substantial leverage. As such, a considerable amount of attention is now focused on monitoring and controlling the risk of trading positions in foreign exchange. Traditionally, risk control meant attempting to avoid steep capital drawdowns by concentrating on trades that have defined loss limits but are nonetheless attractive on a risk-reward basis. More recently, a new methodology based on probabilistic concepts, called "dollars-at-risk," has been moving quickly toward becoming the industry standard tool for risk management.

Foreign exchange risk is also a key concern in the everyday practice of doing business overseas. Corporate treasurers in the United States, Continental Europe, the United Kingdom, and Japan transacted over U.S.$6.6 trillion in foreign exchange in 1994.[1] Survey data show that the foremost concern of corporate treasurers who manage foreign exchange risk is associated with receivables and payables that derive from foreign operations. Treasurers are also concerned with the exchange rate exposure of their balance sheet when significant assets have been acquired in other countries or when financing has been obtained in overseas capital markets. Some

---

1 Source: Greenwich Associates, which conducts surveys of foreign exchange product endusers. The 1994 survey included 966 corporations, which was comprised of industrials, commercial enterprises, construction firms, services, and utilities. Total foreign exchange transactions in spot, forward, swaps, currency options, and currency futures were $1,526 billion (U.S.), $3,886 billion (top-tier Continental Europe), 477 billion pounds (U.K.), and $466 billion (Japan). Greenwich Associates also surveyed 351 financial institutions in the same four centers. Financial institutions included investment portfolio managers, investment banks, hedge funds, insurance companies and other financials. The survey estimates were $7,648 billion (U.S.), $1,642 billion (Continental Europe), 1,568 billion pounds (U.K.), and $546 billion (Japan).

corporations have taken foreign exchange risk management a step further with what has come to be known as "economic hedging." This term refers to the management of the foreign exchange risk implied by intangible economic property rights such as market position. For example, a German manufacturer of automobiles might hedge the economic value of his share of the U.S. market by buying dollar/yen, fearing that a stronger dollar (weaker yen) might enhance the competitive position of the Japanese manufacturers. But whatever the concern, corporate users tend to be hedgers, rather than speculators, and their process of managing foreign exchange risk usually requires careful planning as the entire process can be complicated by international tax, accounting, and legal considerations.[2]

Never to be overlooked are the central banks. Central banks are usually the economic agents of governmental policy with regard to exchange rates, notably in the context of their periodic direct intervention into currency markets. But central banks, like all financial institutions, have an interest in managing the foreign exchange risk attributable to their holdings of international assets, including foreign currency reserves.

SPOT AND FORWARD EXCHANGE RATES

Spot and forward exchange are traded in an over-the-counter market where money center banks act as the dealers. Usually, a bank is on the "other side" of every trade. The spot exchange rate is a quote for the exchange of two currencies in two business days (except in the case of the Canadian dollar versus the U.S. dollar, where delivery is in one business day). The spot rate is normally given as a bid-ask quotation. For example, a quote on the Japanese yen of 150.00/10 means that a dealer is willing to sell yen for dollars at 150.00 yen per dollar or buy yen for dollars at the rate of 150.10 yen per dollar. Unfortunately, two conventions for the quotation of spot and forward rates have evolved. In the American convention, currency is quoted in terms of U.S. dollars per unit of foreign exchange (i.e., one British pound equals $1.50). The British pound, Irish punt, Australian dollar, New Zealand dollar, and European Currency Unit (the ECU) are quoted American. All the other currencies are quoted European, which means they are quoted as

---

2 See Bruce H. Weinrib, Thomas J. Driscoll, and Peter J. Conners, "Final and Proposed Regulations Expand Available Foreign Hedging Opportunities," *Journal of Taxation,* August 1992, pp. 110–18.

the number of units of foreign currency equal to one dollar (e.g., 85 Japanese yen per one U.S. dollar or 1.70 German marks per one U.S. dollar). To make matters even more confusing, most exchange traded currency futures and options quote currencies American, even some that are quoted European in spot and forward markets.

The forward exchange rate is a quote for settlement (or "value") at a more distant date in the future than spot settlement. A forward rate can be negotiated for any settlement date, but indications are usually given for one month, three months, six months, or one year in the future.

The forward exchange rate, also called the outright, is sometimes quoted in two parts, one being the spot bid or ask, and the other part called the forward points. Forward points are either added or subtracted from the spot rate to arrive at the forward exchange rate. For example, if the forward points on yen for settlement in one year are quoted –2.97/–2.95, the outright would be 82.03/15, using 85.00/10 as the spot rate. Note that the negative sign indicates that the forward points should be subtracted from the spot bid or ask.

THE INTEREST PARITY THEOREM AND THE FORWARD EXCHANGE RATE

The interest parity theorem (IPT) is the linkage between forward exchange rates and interest rates. The basic concept is that the market sets the forward rate in relation to spot in order to absorb the interest rate differential between two currencies (known as the interest rate spread). This is a "no free lunch" idea: You cannot hop between currencies, pick up yield advantage, and lock up a guaranteed profit by using the forward market. The forward rate acts as the spoiler.

For example, suppose that a U.S. dollar-based investor were attracted by a substantial yield spread offered by the British pound over the U.S. dollar. If the investor were to convert dollars to pounds for the purpose of investing in high-yielding sterling paper, there would be no guarantee of any yield pickup because the future level of the spot exchange rate is unknown. That is the rate at which the investor would later have to exchange pounds back into dollars. The future spot might be higher than the initial spot, in which case the investor would make an even greater profit; or it might be lower than the initial spot, in which case some or all of the yield differential would be lost. If the spot exchange rate were to fall by a great enough amount, the investment might even suffer a negative return in dollars, meaning that the exchange rate loss had been greater than the interest earned on the pounds.

The exchange rate risk could be hedged by selling the future value of the pound versus the dollar in the forward market. But at what forward rate? If there were a 500 basis-point spread between pound and dollar one-year interest rates and if the spot exchange rate were $1.80 per pound, then the only one-year forward rate to make economic sense would be $1.7204. At any other rate, riskless arbitrage would be possible. To see this, take the example of $100.00. This converts to £55.56 British pounds at the spot rate. This sum invested at, say, 13 percent would become £62.78 pounds in one year. Comparing this to the alternative of keeping the funds in dollars at, say, 8 percent, and compounding to $108 after one year, we see that the forward rate must be:

$$\frac{108.00}{62.78} = 1.7204$$

What has just been described is called the interest parity theorem, which can be written mathematically as:

American quotation convention

$$F = Se^{(R_d - R_f)\tau}$$

European quotation convention

$$F' = S' e^{(R_f - R_d)\tau}$$

where

F is the forward rate quoted American convention with delivery in τ years

S is the spot rate quoted American

e is the base of the natural logarithm

R_d is the domestic interest rate

R_f is the foreign currency interest rate

F' and S' are the forward and spot rates for currencies quoted European convention. Note that these expressions use interest rates in their continuously compounded for algebraic simplicity.

The difference between the forward rate and the spot rate is called the forward points.

THE VALUATION OF FORWARD CONTRACTS

A currency forward contract is an agreement between two counterparties to exchange currencies at a fixed rate on a settlement day sometime in the future. In most instances, a forward contract is negotiated at the prevailing forward exchange rate; the initial value of such a forward contract is zero. Thereafter, the value of the contract assumes positive or negative values as a function of exchange rates, the domestic and foreign interest rates, and the remaining time to settlement. On settlement day, T, the value of a forward contract to buy one unit of foreign exchange, denoted as V_T, is equal to the spot rate at settlement, S_T, minus the forward rate that was established when the parties entered into the contract, F_0. This paradigm assumes American quotation.

To exit a forward contract, a second closing transaction must be executed. This second transaction can be executed any time before the settlement day and it forms the basis of how to value a forward contract. The closing transaction must also settle on the same settlement date. If the first contract bought foreign exchange, the closing contract must sell the same quantity of currency. If the first sold foreign exchange, the second must buy the same quantity of currency. Either way, on settlement day there will be some positive or negative residual of the other currency that must be settled. The net present value of this residual amount of currency is the value of the forward contract at any time before expiration.

Suppose that on day t, when time $\tau = (T - t)$ remains before settlement, we wish to value a forward contract to buy one unit of foreign exchange. There are two expressions that must be calculated. One is the present value of the deliverable quantity of currency specified in the closing contract, equal to F_t units of domestic currency, that can be expressed as F_t multiplied by the present value factor using continuously compounded domestic interest rate, $e^{-R_d \tau}$. This is equal to the spot rate, S_t, multiplied by the present value factor using the continuously compounded foreign interest rate, $e^{-R_f \tau}$.

The second expression is the present value of the deliverable quantity specified in the first contract, equal to F_0 multiplied by the present value factor using the continuously compounded domestic interest rate.

The net of these two terms is the present value of the forward contract:

$$V_t = S_t e^{-R_f \tau} - F_0 e^{-R_d \tau}$$

CURRENCY FUTURES CONTRACTS

Currency futures contracts are listed on the Chicago Mercantile Exchange's International Monetary Market [CME(IMM)], the Singapore Monetary Exchange (SIMEX), the Philadelphia Board of Trade, and the MidAmerica Commodities Exchange.[3] By trading volume, the most important currency futures exchange is the CME(IMM). It lists futures on the Australian dollar, British pound, Canadian dollar, French franc, German mark, Japanese yen, the Swiss franc, and the Mexican peso. The SIMEX currency futures are identical in all respects to CME(IMM) futures, except that SIMEX does not trade the Australian dollar, French franc, Swiss franc, Canadian dollar, or the Mexican peso.

Listed futures contracts have fixed specifications with respect to expiration date, size, and minimum price fluctuation (see Exhibit 21–5). For example, the CME(IMM)'s yen futures contract terminates trading on the second business day before the third Wednesday of the delivery month, has a notional value of 12,500,000 yen, and a minimum price fluctuation of $12.50 per contract.

The convention of the CME (IMM) is to quote all currencies in the American style. Currency futures are traded in pits in an "open outcry" environment similar to futures contracts on agricultural and other financial commodities.

Each futures exchange has a clearinghouse. The CME(IMM) and SIMEX own their clearinghouses. One role of a clearinghouse is to interpose itself between each buyer and seller of every currency futures contract in order to act as a guarantor of contract performance. In addition, traders can operate on a net basis whether or not their long and short positions were initiated against different counterparties. A long position involves the purchase of the futures contract, while a short position entails the sale of a contract.

The clearinghouse for each futures exchange sets initial and maintenance margin requirements. The term *margin* is misleading; *good faith deposit* is more accurate. Initial margin is the deposit that an investor must provide

---

3 Currency futures are also listed on São Paulo's Bolsa de Mercadonas and Futuros, the Sydney Futures Exchange, Barcelona's Mercado de Futuros Financieros, Amsterdam's Financial Futures Market, the New Zealand Futures Exchange, and the Tokyo International Financial Futures Exchange.

EXHIBIT 21-5
Listed Currency Futures Contracts

	Chicago Mercantile Exchange			Philadelphia Board of Trade		
Currency	Size	Minimum Fluctuation	Minimum Price Change	Size	Minimum Fluctuation	Minimum Price Change
Australian dollar	100,000	0.0001	$10.00	100,000	0.0001	$10.00
British pound*	62,500	0.0002	12.50	62,500	0.0001	6.25
Canadian dollar	100,000	0.0001	10.00	100,000	0.0001	10.00
ECU	NA	NA	NA	125,000	0.0001	12.50
French franc	500,000	0.00002	10.00	500,000	0.00002	10.00
German mark*	125,000	0.0001	12.50	125,000	0.0001	12.50
Japanese yen*	12,500,000	0.000001	12.50	12,500,000	0.000001	12.50
Swiss franc	125,000	0.0001	12.50	125,000	0.0001	12.50
Mexican peso	500,000	0.000025	12.50	NA	NA	NA

*Denotes SIMEX listing

Additional Specifications

Months	1, 3, 4, 6, 7, 9, 12 plus spot month	3, 6, 9, 12, and two additional near months
Last trading day	Second business day before third Wednesday	Friday before third Wednesday
First delivery day	Third Wednesday	Third Wednesday

upon opening a long or short position. Maintenance margin is the minimum allowable equity per contract in an investor's account.

More important than initial margin is daily variation margin by which gains and losses on futures are settled every day. Variation margin is based on the daily settlement price. In theory, the settlement price will be the last bona fide price at the close of a trading session. In practice, however, determination of a fair settlement price can be difficult because of the nature of the open outcry system in which many trades might occur simultaneously at the close. In this case, the settlement price can be the average of the highest and lowest trades done at the close. Also, when no trade is done at the close, special procedures may be in force that take into account the historical relationship between contract months.

Long positions in futures contracts receive positive variation margin and pay negative variation margin. Short futures positions do just the opposite; they pay positive variation margin and receive negative variation margin.

When a position is opened, the calculation of that day's variation margin is based on the spread between the traded price and the day's settlement price. Thereafter, the daily variation margin is based on the spread between the settlement price that day and the settlement price of the previous day. On a day when a position is closed, the amount required to settle is based on the spread between the traded price and the previous day's settlement price.

COMPARISON OF CURRENCY FUTURES CONTRACTS AND FORWARD CONTRACTS

Several differences between futures and forwards emerge from the previous discussion, but the distinguishing difference seems to turn on the practice of settling variation margin. Futures gains and losses are settled daily whereas there are no intermediate cash flows associated with forward contracts. How do futures contracts differ from forward contracts? More to the point, is there any reason to believe that the implicit forward rate embodied in the futures price should be systematically different from the actual forward exchange rate?

Suppose that on expiration day T, the futures price converges on the spot rate, which we can write:

$$f_T = S_T$$

Before expiration, the difference between the futures price and the spot exchange rate,

$$f_t - S_t$$

is defined as the futures basis.

The mark-to-market process resets the value of the futures contract to zero each day. Also, each day's cash flow from the mark to market must be invested in the case of a profit, or financed in the case of a loss.

The nature of the interest rate at which this can be done is the focus in the theoretical literature on the distinction between futures and forward contracts. In a simple case, one could assume that the interest rate is known with perfect certainty (i.e. it is nonstochastic).[4] Cox, Ingersoll, and Ross, building on earlier work by Black, demonstrate that the futures price must equal the forward exchange rate if this assumption holds.[5] Another way to express their conclusion is to say that if the interest rate were known with perfect certainty, the futures price, like the forward exchange rate, must obey the interest parity theorem. This means that the basis of the futures

---

4 Professor William Margrabe, at the Wharton School in 1976, is believed to be the first economist to understand the essential distinction between futures and forwards. Margrabe's insight was later incorporated into the classic mathematical economic treatment by John Cox, Jonathan Ingersoll, and Stephen Ross (1981). The distinction is that an investor in a futures contract (and not an investor in a forward contract) might be materially affected by random changes in short-term interest rates. Currency futures are exchange-traded instruments that require an initial margin and are "settled up" or marked to market every trading day. Maintaining a position in a futures contract involves paying and receiving funds every day, whereas a forward contract makes no demands for intermediate cash flows. Obviously, futures and forwards cannot be perfect substitutes because of the uncertainty about the day-to-day interest rates at which the initial margin and cash gains and losses from the futures position could be invested or need to be financed. The subtle point that Margrabe and Cox, Ingersoll, and Ross made was that this distinction between futures and forwards could only matter to the market if there were a systematic tendency for short-term interest rates to correlate, positively or negatively, with exchange rate movements. Otherwise, the extra uncertainty surrounding the reinvestment or financing of the daily settlement on the futures position would not amount to any additional "economic risk," meaning risk as it is priced in the market. In this case, futures contracts would sell at the same prices as corresponding forwards, commanding neither a risk premium nor discount. Unfortunately, Margrabe's insight may not be of great use to practitioners other than as a theoretical construct. Empirical evidence has not found a statistically significant difference between currency futures and forwards. Moreover, Cornell and Reinganum (1981) found no significant correlation between interest rates and exchange rates. This suggests that futures are no more or less risky than forwards in the Margrabe sense.

5 J. C. Cox, Jonathan E. Ingersoll, and Stephen A. Ross, "The Relationship between Forward and Futures Prices," *Journal of Financial Economics* 9 (Dec. 1981), pp. 321–46; Fischer Black, "The Pricing of Commodity Contracts," *Journal of Financial Economics* 3 (Jan.–March 1976), pp. 167–79.

would have to be equal to the forward points for settlement on the futures' expiration day.

Cox, Ingersoll, and Ross's proof of this theorem demonstrates that a rolling series of futures contracts can perfectly duplicate a forward contract, at least in the nonstochastic interest rate case. In their rollover futures hedge, the number of futures contracts is adjusted each day as a function of the known interest rate and the remaining time to expiration to be equal to $e^{-R_d \tau}$. In other words, at time, $t = 0$, the hedge would consist of $e^{-R_d T}$ contracts. The next day, an incremental amount of contracts would be added, making the total $e^{-R_d (T-1)}$. Finally, there would be one whole contract at expiration when $t = T$.

The following explanation of the Cox, Ingersoll, and Ross proof paraphrases Whaley and Stoll and Whaley.[6] Consider two portfolios, A and B. Portfolio A consists of a long forward contract negotiated at time $t = 0$ at the prevailing forward outright, F_0 (quoted American style), to receive one unit of foreign exchange on day T plus a long position in riskless zero coupon bonds that mature on day T. The bonds have maturity value equal to F_0 worth of domestic currency; their initial present value is equal to F_0 multiplied by present value factor using the continuously compounded domestic interest rate, $e^{-R_d \tau}$. On day T, when the bonds mature and the forward contract settles, portfolio A will be worth the spot exchange rate, S_T, because the forward contract will be worth the spot exchange rate minus the forward delivery price, F_0, and the bond will mature and pay an amount equal to F_0.

Portfolio B consists of a rollover futures position that expires on day T plus a long position in riskless zero coupon bonds that mature on day T. The initial futures price is denoted as f_0. Enough bonds are purchased to make their maturity value equal to f_0; their present value is equal to f_0 multiplied by $e^{-R_d \tau}$.

The daily mark to market in the rollover program is invested or financed at the domestic interest rate, R_d. The value of portfolio B on expiration day T will be equal to S_T because the profit or loss on the futures contracts will be marked to market each day in an amount equal to:

$$e^{-R_d (T-t)} (f_t - f_{t-1})$$

---

6   Robert E. Whaley, "Valuation of American Futures Options: Theory and Empirical Tests," *Journal of Finance* 61 (March 1986), pp. 127–49; Hans R. Stoll and Robert E. Whaley, "New Options Instruments: Arbitrageable Linkages and Valuation," *Advances in Futures and Options Research* (Greenwich, Conn.: JAI Press, 1986), pp. 25–62.

where

f_t is the futures price at the end of trading on day t
f_{t-1} is the futures price from the previous day

The future value of this amount on day T will be equal to:

$$e^{-R_d(T-t)} \, (f_t - f_{t-1})e^{+R_d(T-t)} = (f_t - f_{t-1})$$

The sum of all the future values of the daily mark-to-market will be equal to:

$$[f_1 - f_0]$$

plus $[f_2 - f_1]$

plus $\ldots$

plus $[S_T - f_{T-1}]$
       _____

which will equal $S_T - f_0$

Note that the futures price at expiration, f_T, is assumed to converge on the spot rate, S_T. When combined with the matured zero coupon bonds, with maturity value f_0, the value of portfolio B, like that of portfolio A, will be equal to S_T. Using the no arbitrage rule, Cox, Ingersoll, and Ross conclude that the futures price, f_0, must equal the forward exchange rate, F_0.

THE BASICS OF FOREIGN EXCHANGE HEDGING

This section concerns some of the basic hedging techniques that are applied by investment portfolio managers and corporate treasurers. Hedging programs attempt to immunize an exposure to currency movements, up or down. Hedging programs can be bilateral, where there is exposure to a single foreign currency, or multicurrency (also called multilateral), where there are exposures to several foreign currencies. Bilateral hedges can be implemented with forward contracts or with currency futures. Multicurrency hedges are more complicated. One version, called a matched hedge, calls for each foreign currency to be bilaterally hedged on a stand-alone basis.

Many times, especially in international portfolio management, there are exposures to 10, 20, or even more currencies. This is where an alternative to the matched hedge, called the basket hedge, becomes economical. The basket consists of three or four major currencies that are held in proportions designed to closely track the exposure to the greater number of currencies.

The final topic will be proxy hedging, a tool of active currency management which involves hedging an exposure to one exchange rate by taking a position in another exchange rate. This method has proved to be effective at times in fixed-income management, but in other instances it has been disappointing if not outright disastrous.

BILATERAL HEDGING WITH FOREIGN CURRENCY FORWARDS

Corporate treasurers use forward trades as anticipatory hedges for future foreign currency cash flows to avoid unwanted exposure to foreign exchange risk. The forward market affords them an opportunity to commit to a prearranged conversion rate. International equity and fixed-income portfolio managers use forwards as part of their currency hedging strategies. Take the example of a manager is long one billion yen worth of Japanese equities and who is concerned that the value of the yen might deteriorate over the next two months. A direct step would be to sell one billion yen forward for two months against dollars. This hedging transaction is called an "opening transaction." At a two month outright equal to 84.25, the trade would consist of a commitment to deliver one billion yen in two months and receive dollars in the amount equal to $11,869,436.20 since:

$$\frac{1 \ billion \ JPY}{84.25} = \$11,869,436.20$$

A sample trade ticket for this transaction is shown in Exhibit 21–6. The comment "no cash moves until day 60" is meant to serve as a reminder that a forward transaction generates no cash flow until value date.

The portfolio manager must make some decisions once the forward hedge is in place. Since portfolio hedgers rarely enter into forward contracts with the intention of making delivery of currencies, the hedge must be closed or rolled prior to settlement. A forward hedge can be closed anytime before the forward value date by means of a closing transaction, which is accomplished by reversing the original hedge with a second transaction that has the same original value date as the opening transaction. For example, the hedge might be closed one month later, day 30, by buying one billion

EXHIBIT 21–6
Forward Currency Transaction: Opening Trade from Customer's Perspective

Buy	Sell	Trade Date	Value Date
11,869,436.20 USD	1 yard JPY	Day 1	Day 60

Description of Trade			
Sell 1 yard JPY against USD for value in 60 Days			

Spot	Forward Points	Commission	Outright
84.95	−0.70	0	84.25

Settlement Instructions			
No Cash Moves Until Day 60 Pay 1 yard JPY to SBC Tokyo on Day 60 Receive 11,869,436.20 USD in Account at SBC NY on Day 60			

Counterparty	Dealer Code	Trader	
Swiss Bank New York	SBCN	D−Squared	

yen for settlement on day 60. The new forward rate would be a one-month rate because only one month would now remain until day 60. Suppose that the spot rate now is 84.00/10 and that the forward points are −26/−25. The outright for value in 30 days would be 83.74/85. The closing transaction would be a purchase of one billion yen against $11,941,724.39 at a rate of 83.74. If the opening and closing trades were done with two different banks, they would have to be settled in the usual way: To settle the opening trade, the portfolio manager must deliver one billion yen to the first bank and receive dollars on day 60; to settle the second trade, the portfolio manger must receive one billion yen from the second bank and receive dollars on day 60. However, the portfolio manager might be permitted to take net

EXHIBIT 21–7
Forward Currency Transaction: Closing Trade from Customer's Perspective

Buy	Sell	Trade Date	Value Date
1 yard JPY	11,941,724.39 USD	Day 30	Day 60
Description of Trade			
Buy 1 yard JPY against USD to close previous forward trade. Value Day 60			
Spot	Forward Points	Commission	Outright
84.00	−0.26	0	83.74
Settlement Instructions			
Net Settlement on Day 60 Pay 72,288.19 USD to SBC NY			
Counterparty	Dealer Code	Trader	
Swiss Bank New York	SBCN	J–Bone	

settlement in cases where both the opening and closing transactions have been made with the same bank. In the example, the net loss on the hedge is $72,288.19:

	Dollars	*Yen*
Opening trade 84.25	$11,869,436.20	(¥1,000,000,000)
Closing trade 84.74	($11,941,724.39)	¥1,000,000,000
	($72,288.19)	0

Under net settlement, this amount would have be wired directly to the portfolio manager's dealer counterparty on day 60 to complete settlement of both the opening and closing trades (see Exhibit 21–7).

On the other hand, the portfolio manager might wish to keep the yen hedge in place indefinitely. In a technique called rolling forwards, the manager does a spot transaction on day 58 to take care of the original forward transaction that settles on day 60 and simultaneously reestablishes the hedge with a new two-month forward trade. Gains or losses would be settled each time the hedge is rolled.

HEDGING MULTICURRENCY EXPOSURE

The previous section considered hedging a single foreign currency exposure using forward contracts. The discussion now turns to the management of multiple foreign currency exposures, a situation that is more relevant to international portfolio managers. One popular benchmark index is the FT-Actuaries World Index for international equities. Because benchmark indexes are capitalization-weighted, concentration forms in a handful of the major markets and currencies. This naturally leads to an application of portfolio theory and quadratic programming called basket hedging.

Matched Hedging

Matched hedging is a simple idea: Maintain a separate bilateral hedge for each currency exposure. This works well where the portfolio is exposed to only a small number of currencies. But if the number of currencies is large, a matched hedge may not be efficient. A large number of separate hedges can be cumbersome to manage, and opening and closing forward contracts on minor currencies can be expensive. Matched hedging is mentioned to show how a sledgehammer can be used to open the currency hedging nut. It is meant to increase appreciation for basket hedging, a technique that is more economical, which will now be introduced.

Basket Hedging

Basket hedging is an important tool in currency risk management. Two, three or four major currencies—usually the dollar, the mark, the pound sterling, and the yen—are combined to make a basket that tracks the currency exposure of the entire portfolio. The latter is usually referred to as the index. The objective is to minimize the forecast tracking error, which is defined as the difference between the currency return on the index and the basket.

The goal is to produce a set of weightings for two, three, or four currencies to make a basket that tracks the portfolio's currency exposure as closely as possible. It is assumed that the expected rates of return on all currencies are zero and that the problem is to minimize the variance of the tracking error between the basket and the portfolio's currency exposure. Exhibit 21–8 shows the basket hedge for a U.S. dollar-based investor's perspective for the FT-Actuaries World non-USA Index. The basket is composed of pounds, marks, and yen. The basket was constructed using the BARRA World Markets Model™. The FT-Actuaries World Index non-USA basket hedge is concentrated in yen, which would be expected given the weight that Japan has in the index. The projected tracking error is 1.044 percent, annualized. In constructing the actual basket hedge, the three currencies are sold forward one year against dollar. Two of these currencies, marks and yen, happened to be at premium to the dollar on April 12, 1995, when Exhibit 21–8 was constructed. The result is that the basket hedge has a net forward pickup equal to 2.68 percent, annualized. Of course, if the basket currencies were at a discount to the dollar, there would be a yield giveup instead of a pickup.

The Limitations of Basket Hedging

Basket hedging optimization depends on an assumed correlation matrix and a set of standard deviations; these are the Achilles' heel of basket hedging. If the correlation matrix is accurate as well as stable, optimization will produce a good basket hedge. This is more likely when the portfolio is dominated by exposures to the currencies of the larger, more stable economies. Otherwise, if the portfolio is heavily invested in unstable countries with rapidly changing economic environments, the correlation matrix is not likely to be at all indicative of the future currency interrelationships. Basket hedging might be quite off the mark.

Proxy Hedging

Proxy hedging refers to a technique wherein a short position in a stable, low interest rate currency is employed to hedge an exposure to a high interest rate currency. Interbank dealers and proprietary traders have used proxy hedging strategies for some time. To take an example, suppose that a dealer in dollar/Swiss is long dollars and short Swiss francs. One strategy would

EXHIBIT 21-8

Basket Hedge for FT-Actuaries World Index World Ex-USA, as of March 31, 1995
BARRA World Markets Model (5.0a). Data Base March 1995. Market Prices April 12, 1995

Basket

Currency	Raw Weight	Scaling	Adjusted Weight	Spot	Points	OutRight	Giveup Pickup
GBP	31.17%	0.9926	30.94%	0.6289	0.0047	0.6336	-0.74%
DEM	16.39	0.9926	16.27	1.4040	-0.0218	1.3822	1.58
JPY	52.44	0.9926	52.05	83.77	-4.03	79.74	5.05
Total	100.00%		99.26%		Weighted Average		2.68%

Estimated tracking error 1.044%

Index (as of December 30, 1994)

Country	Percentage
Australia	2.43%
Austria	0.22
Belgium	1.1
Canada	2.51
Denmark	0.58
Finland	0.48
France	5.59
Germany	5.74
Hong Kong	2.79
Ireland	0.25
Italy	2.25
Japan	46.48

Index (as of December 30, 1994)

Country	Percentage
Malaysia	1.7
Mexico	0.87
Netherlands	3.07
New Zealand	0.32
Norway	0.18
Singapore	0.96
Spain	1.55
Sweden	1.45
Switzerland	3.81
Thailand	0.35
U.K.	15.31
Total	99.99%

be to sell the position immediately in the interbank market. But conditions might not be opportune at that moment to make a sale. An alternative is to sell dollar/ mark in the full dollar amount of the position. This would leave the trader approximately hedged with a net long position in the relatively stable mark/Swiss cross-exchange rate.

Proxy hedging is fundamentally different from any of the hedging that has been discussed. In reality, it is a form of active currency management. Where the idea of proxy hedging proved disastrous was in the two exchange rate mechanism (ERM) crises of September 1992 and August 1993. A substantial market position had developed in what came to be known as the convergence play. This assumed that interest rates among the European Monetary System currencies would converge with exchange rates enjoying the protection of the ERM. When the ERM failed, the ensuing flight to marks obliterated any apparent but illusory yield advantage to holding the high interest rate currencies.

REFERENCES

Black, Fischer. "The Pricing of Commodity Contracts." *Journal of Financial Economics* 3 (Jan.–March 1976), pp. 167–79.

Cornell, Bradford, and Marc R. Reinganum. "Forward and Future Prices: Evidence from the Foreign Exchange Markets." *The Journal of Finance* 36 (December 1981), pp. 1035–45.

Cox, J. C., Jonathan E. Ingersoll, and Stephen A. Ross. "The Relationship between Forward and Futures Prices." *Journal of Financial Economics* 9 (Dec. 1981), pp. 321–46.

DeRosa, David F. *Managing Foreign Exchange Risk,* 2d ed. Burr Ridge, Ill.: Irwin Professional Publishing, 1996.

_____. *Options on Foreign Exchange.* Chicago: Probus Publishing, 1992.

Margrabe, William, "A Theory of Forward and Futures Pricing." Manuscript, The Wharton School, 1976.

Stoll, Hans R., and Robert E. Whaley. "New Options Instruments: Arbitrageable Linkages and Valuation." *Advances in Futures and Options Research* 1 (Greenwich, Conn.: JAI Press, 1986), pp. 25–62.

Whaley, Robert E. "Valuation of American Futures Options: Theory and Empirical Tests." *Journal of Finance* 61 (March 1986), pp. 127–49.

Weinrib, Bruce H., Thomas J. Driscoll, and Peter J. Connors, "Final and Proposed Regulations Expand Available Foreign Currency Hedging Opportunities," *Journal of Taxation* (August 1992), pp. 110–18.

Chapter Twenty-Two

The Foreign Exchange Market
Currency Options

David F. DeRosa
Swiss Bank Corporation

OPTION BASICS

The foreign exchange option market is the second largest option market. Only the option market for fixed-income securities and their derivatives is larger. The largest portion of the currency option market is the interbank market. But there are also listed, meaning exchange-traded, currency options. The Philadelphia Stock Exchange lists options on actual foreign currency. The Chicago Mercantile Exchange's International Monetary Market lists options on currency futures, which are referred to as futures options.

Currency options are either calls or puts. A currency call is the right, but not the obligation, to buy a sum of foreign currency at a fixed exchange rate, called the strike, on or before the option's expiration date. A currency put is an option to sell a sum of foreign exchange. Take the example of a dollar/mark call struck at 1.5400 on a face amount of $10 million. This option grants the right but not the obligation to buy 10 million dollars against 15.4 million marks. It is a call on dollars, but it is also a put on marks. To minimize the chance of a costly misunderstanding, the convention is to mention both currencies, tagging each with a call or a put identifier. The correct and unambiguous name for the option is "dollar call/mark put." European-style options can be exercised only on the exercise date, but American-style options can be exercised at any time before or on the expiration date.

THE INTERBANK CURRENCY OPTION MARKET

The interbank currency option market trades 24-hour per day alongside spot and forward foreign exchange. All of the top-tier foreign exchange dealers make markets in currency options for their customers and other dealing institutions. Most of the trading is done in options on the major currencies, but virtually any exchange rate can be traded as an option. The majority of trading is done in European exercise calls and puts. There is also a brisk and rapidly growing interest in exotic currency options, which are options with nonstandard features, such as barrier options, average rate options, and compound options.

Currency options are identified by five parameters, expiration, currency pair, option type, strike, and face amount.Unless otherwise specified, expiration is assumed to be European style at 10 A.M. New York time. A complete identification of the option in the example would be "European, three month, dollar call/mark put, 1.5400 strike on 10 dollars." Following the conventions of the spot market, "10 dollars" means 10 million dollars (see Chapter 21).

Traders also use an additional parameter, called delta, to identify options. Delta is the first derivative of the option price with respect to the exchange rate. The greater the delta, the more the option's value will change when the exchange rates moves. Delta is scaled between zero and 100. As a gross approximation, the delta of an option struck at the forward exchange rate (called "at-the-money-forward") is 50; the delta of an option stuck at advantage relative to the forward exchange rate (called "in-the-money-forward") is between 50 and 100; and the delta of an option struck at disadvantage relative to the forward exchange rate (called "out-of-the-money-forward") is between 50 and zero. For the option that has been serving as the example, the trader might have inquired for a "European, three month, 50 delta dollar call/mark put on 10 dollars."

Options in the interbank market are quoted in terms of implied volatility. The concept of implied volatility, like that of delta, goes back to option math. Implied volatility is a parameter in currency option models that is used to quantify the probable size of the future fluctuations in exchange rates as measured by standard deviation. As a rough measure, implied volatilities for options on major currencies range between 3 percent and 20 percent but in times of crisis they have been seen at much higher levels. The greater the implied volatility, the greater the worth of puts and calls. In a sample conversation, a client might ask

Client:

Three month, 50 delta dollar call/mark put on $10, please.

Dealer:

11.85 – 12.20 percent.

Client:

Mine at 12.20 percent.

Dealer:

I sell a European, three month, 50 delta dollar call/mark put at 12.20 on 10 dollars.

"11.85 – 12.20 percent" is the dealer's bid-offer quote. Because both put and call option values are positive functions of implied volatility, the smaller number, 11.85 percent, is known to be the volatility at which the dealer would buy the option. The larger number, 12.20 percent, is the volatility at which the dealer would sell the option. In this conversation, the client buys the dollar call/mark put by saying "mine" at the offer of 12.20 percent. Once the implied volatility is known, the exact price, called the option premium, can be calculated with the help of an option pricing model, given the level of the spot exchange rate and the forward points to option expiration date. This option can be quoted in at least five ways: total dollars or total marks, the percentage of face value, the number of dollar pips per mark, or the number of mark pips per dollar.

Interbank option exercise is marked at a date and a time (popular "cuts" are 10 A.M. New York and 3 P.M. Tokyo). Option exercise has the same format as a spot exchange deal. In the example, assume that the spot dollar-mark exchange rate has moved up to 1.5600. Through exercise, the holder of the dollar call/mark put would buy dollars and sell marks at an strike exchange rate of 1.5400 for settlement in two bank business days. The option holder might want to keep the long dollar/short mark spot position or immediately take the profit equal to:

$$10,000,000 \times \frac{(1.5600 - 1.5400)}{1.5600} = \$128,205.13$$

by selling dollars against marks for spot value.

The Listed Market for Currency Options

The Philadelphia Stock Exchange.   The Philadelphia Stock Exchange (the "Philly") lists options on foreign currencies that feature both the European and American exercise conventions. As in the case of over-the-counter (OTC) currency options, the Philly options deliver actual foreign currency upon exercise. Philly options clear through and are guaranteed by the Options Clearing Corporation. The exchange sets standardized contract sizes, fixes expiration dates, and establishes strikes (see Exhibit 22–1). Philly options are quoted in U.S. cents per unit of foreign exchange with two exceptions: the Japanese yen contract, which is quoted in hundredths of one cent per yen, and the French franc contract, which is quoted in tenths of one cent per franc. The value of a Philly option can be found by multiplying the contract face amount by the quoted option price. To take an example, the dollar value of a German mark call quoted at 0.66 is $412.50, since:

$$62,500 \text{ DEM} \times .66 \times .01 = \$412.50$$

The International Monetary Market (IMM). The International Monetary Market (IMM) of the Chicago Mercantile Exchange (CME) lists American-style options on its currency futures (see Exhibit 22–1). IMM currency futures options are guaranteed by the Chicago Mercantile Exchange Clearing House; it is the counterparty to every transaction. The IMM options match the specifications of the futures contracts with respect to quotation convention and size. The IMM futures options deliver currency futures only in the March–June–September–December cycle. For example, the October option would be exercised in the December futures contract. Upon exercise, the buyer of a long call or short put is credited with a long position in a currency futures contract. Likewise, the writer of a call or buyer of a put is debited with a futures contract at exercise. At exercise, there is a mark to market equal to the spread between the strike and the settlement price.

IMM currency futures options quotations work the same as those of the Philly currency options. The rule is to multiply the quoted price by the contract size. For example, a German mark call quoted at .55 would be worth $687.50, since:

$$125,000 \text{ DEM} \times .55 \times .01 = \$687.50$$

The Chicago Mercantile Clearing House operates a complex risk management program called the Standard Portfolio Analysis of Risk (SPAN) to determine option margin requirements. SPAN generates daily margin requirements based on portfolio risk analysis and scenario models of changing market conditions. The CME provides clearing firms with daily SPAN arrays for the calculation of minimum margin requirements.

EXHIBIT 22-1
Listed Currency Options and Futures Options

	Chicago Mercantile Exchange (IMM) Options on Futures			Philadelphia Stock Exchange Options on Foreign Exchange		
Currency	*Size*	*Minimum Fluctuation*	*Minimum Price Change*	*Size*	*Minimum Fluctuation*	*Minimum Price Change*
Australian dollar	1 futures contract	0.0001	$10.00	50,000	0.01	$5.00
British pound*	1 futures contract	0.0002	12.50	31,250	0.01	3.13
Canadian dollar	1 futures contract	0.0001	10.00	50,000	0.01	5.00
ECU	NA	NA	NA	62,500	0.01	6.25
French franc	1 futures contract	0.00002	10.00	250,000	0.02	5.00
German mark*	1 futures contract	0.0001	12.50	62,500	0.01	6.25
Japanese yen*	1 futures contract	0.000001	12.50	6,250,000	0.01	6.25
Swiss franc	1 futures contract	0.0001	12.50	62,500	0.01	6.25
Mexican peso	1 futures contract	0.000025	12.50	NA	NA	NA

Additional Specifications

Months	3, 6, 7, 9, 12 plus two serial months and four weekly expirations	3, 6, 9, 12 and two additional near months
Last trading day	Second Friday before third Wednesday*	Friday before third Wednesday
First delivery day	Exercise into currency futures contracts	Third Wednesday
Exercise	American	American and European

474

PUT-CALL PARITY FOR
CURRENCY OPTIONS

The value of European calls and puts having a common expiration and strike are related through the put-call parity theorem. To preclude profitable, riskless arbitrage, put-call parity must hold at all times in the lives of the options. The relationship states that the difference between the price of a European put and a call having the same strike and expiration is equal to the difference of (1) the present value of the strike and (2) the present value (using the foreign currency's interest rate) of the face amount of foreign currency.

There is a trick to understanding put-call parity. Assume that a trader were to buy a put and sell a call. At expiration, he would have a short position in the face amount of foreign currency and also a long position in cash equal to the strike, no matter which option finishes in the money. If the put finishes in the money, the trader would exercise, meaning he would deliver the face amount of foreign exchange and receive the strike. If the call finishes in the money, it would be exercised against him and he would be required to deliver the face amount of currency in exchange for the strike. If both options finish at the money, both would be worthless. On the other hand, the short position in foreign exchange would be exactly the long position in the domestic currency (the strike). The put-call parity relationship can be written algebraically.

Put-Call Parity for European Exercise

$$P - C = Ke^{-R_d\tau} - Se^{-R_f\tau}$$

where

C	is the price of the currency call
P	is the price of the currency put
K	is the strike
R_d	is the domestic interest rate
R_f	is the foreign interest rate
S	is the spot exchange rate, American quotation convention
τ	is the time remaining until expiration in years

Put-call parity for American currency options takes the form of an inequality.

Put-Call Parity American Exercise

$$C + K - S^{-R_f\tau} \geq P \geq C + Ke^{-R_d\tau} - S$$

VALUATION OF EUROPEAN CURRENCY OPTIONS

In 1983, Mark B. Garman and Steven W. Kohlhagen published a modification of the Merton (1973) version of the Black-Scholes model, which can value European options on foreign currencies. The result will be referred to as the BSGK (Black-Scholes-Garman-Kohlhagen) model. Like all theoretical models, BSGK requires some initial simplifying assumptions:

1. There are no taxes or transactions costs and all capital market and foreign exchange market participants are atomistic, price-taking competitors.

2. Foreign and domestic interest rates are riskless and constant over the option's life. Investors are assumed to be able to borrow and lend at these rates.

3. Instantaneous changes in spot foreign exchange rates are generated by a diffusion process of the form:

$$\frac{dS}{S} = \mu dt + \sigma dz$$

where

S is the spot exchange rate, quoted American convention
dS is an infinitesimally small change in S
μ is a drift term
dt is an instant time
σ is the standard deviation of the log returns in spot rates
dz is a white noise stochastic variable

dz is normally distributed with zero expectation and standard deviation equal to the square root of dt.

The first assumption is standard in many financial models and is sometimes called the frictionless markets condition. Note the inclusion of the foreign currency interest rate in the second assumption. This is Garman and Kohlhagen's principal modification to the earlier models for options on shares of common stock. The interest rate spread between the domestic and foreign rates plays a role analogous to the continuous dividend in the Merton's formulation of the Black-Scholes model. The third assumption directly implies that spot exchange rates are distributed lognormal and that the log return series,

$$\ln \frac{S_t}{S_{t-1}}$$

is normally distributed.

EXHIBIT 22–2
Put and Call Options on USD/DEM

Parameters	
Face in USD	$10,000,000
Face in DEM	15,400,000
Spot exchange rate	1.5400
Strike	1.5400
Days to expiration	32
USD interest rate	4.49%
DEM interest rate	4.84%
Implied volatility	12.20%

Valuation	USD Put/DEM Call	USD Call/DEM Put
USD pips	0.0092203	0.0094188
Total USD	$141,993	$145,049
DEM pips	0.0219	0.0223
Total DEM	218,670	223,376
Percentage of face	1.420%	1.450%

The heart of the model is the idea that a position in a currency option can be locally hedged under the frictionless market assumption by taking an opposite position in spot foreign exchange. By definition, a local hedge is supposed to operate on small, short-run price fluctuations. In Exhibit 22–2, the 10 million USD face USD put/DEM call struck at 1.5400 is worth $141,993 when spot is trading at 1.5400. This option would fall in value to $126,333 (a drop of $15,660) if the spot exchange rate were to rise to 1.5450. Suppose that one were to construct a local hedge with cash by going short dollars and long marks. If the spot exchange rate were to rise, the option would fall in value. On the other hand, the short dollar position would rise in value. The opposite would happen if the spot exchange rate were to fall; the option would become more valuable, but the spot hedge would lose value. The size of the short dollar position needed to hedge the USD put/DEM call varies with the level of the spot exchange rate. At a higher spot rate, a smaller cash position would be sufficient to hedge the put. But at a lower spot level, a greater cash position would be required.

If the size of the cash hedge could be adjusted continuously in response to exchange rate movements, the option position would be perfectly hedged —and the aggregate position consisting of the option plus the cash hedge would constitute a riskless investment.

The percentage of the option face that is required to correctly hedge movements in the spot exchange rate is the delta (δ) of the option as has been mentioned in the previous discussion. It can also be defined as the absolute amount by which the premium of the option rises or falls when the exchange rate changes by one unit. δ is bounded by zero and 1 for a call option and by -1 and zero for a put option. Traders have adopted the convention of multiplying call deltas by 100 and put deltas by -100.

Garman and Kohlhagen, following the Black-Scholes methodology and helped by an important lemma from stochastic calculus called Ito's lemma, derived the following partial differential equation that governs the pricing of a currency call:

$$\frac{1}{2} \sigma^2 S^2 \frac{\partial^2 C}{\partial S^2} - R_d C + (R_d S - R_f S) \frac{\partial C}{\partial S} - \frac{\partial C}{\partial \tau} = 0$$

This derivation requires that a perfect hedge be operated between the call and spot positions in currency. The resulting combination of options and cash constitutes a riskless investment, which, given first principles of economics, must earn no more nor less than the riskless interest rate.

By imposing the expiration day payoff function,

$$C_T = MAX \left[0, S_T - K \right]$$

as a boundary condition, Garman and Kohlhagen solved the partial differential equation to obtain the value of the call. The same approach was repeated to arrive at the value of a put option.

The exact BSGK equations for puts and call are:

$$C = e^{-R_f \tau} S N (x + \sigma \sqrt{\tau}) - e^{-R_d \tau} K N (x)$$

$$P = e^{-R_f \tau} S [N (x + \sigma \sqrt{\tau}) - 1] - e^{-R_d \tau} K [N (x) - 1]$$

$$x = \frac{\ln\left(\dfrac{S}{K}\right) + \left(R_d - R_f - \dfrac{\sigma^2}{2}\right) \tau}{\sigma \sqrt{\tau}}$$

where:

C is the premium on a European currency call
P is the premium on a European currency put
S is the spot exchange rate, American convention.
K is the strike
τ is the time in years to expiration

R_f is the foreign currency interest rate

Rd is the domestic interest rate

σ   is the standard deviation of currency returns

$N(\ )$ is the cumulative normal distribution function

Graphs of BSGK European USD/DEM put and call option premiums before expiration are displayed in Exhibit 22–3. The horizontal axis is the spot exchange rate. The vertical axis is the option premium. The premium is measured in units of dollars per marks of face. Each curvilinear line represents the value of the option given a fixed amount of time remaining to expiration. In general, the option curve shifts downward and becomes more convex as time elapses. The curve finally collapses onto the expiration locus at expiration.

THE SENSITIVITY OF OPTION PREMIUMS TO PARAMETERS

Exhibit 22–4 summarizes the effect that an increase in each of the BSGK variables has on the values of European calls and puts on foreign currency (spot quoted American convention).

The expressions in the table are partial derivatives, which, by definition, hold all other input variables constant. The precise change in the option's theoretical value in response to a change in some input variable y is given by

$$dC = \frac{\partial C}{\partial y} \, dy$$

where:

dc and dy are differentials of c and y.

In practice, traders work with discrete changes in parameters. The change in an option price can be approximated as:

$$\Delta \cong \frac{\partial C}{\partial y} \, \Delta y$$

where

ΔC and Δy represent discrete changes.

EXHIBIT 22–3
European Options on Dollar/Mark

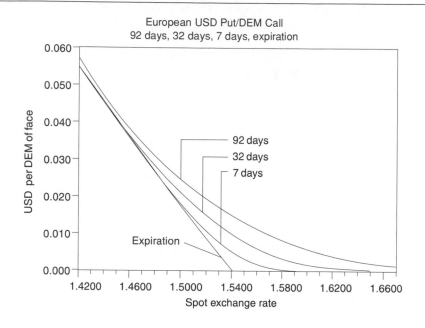

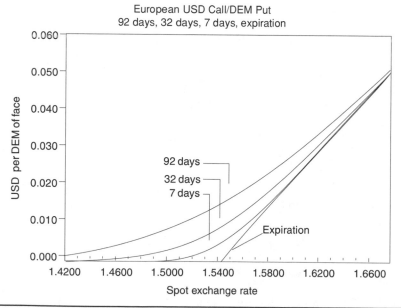

EXHIBIT 22-4
BSGK Partial Derivatives

Partial Derivatives	Calls	Puts
$\dfrac{\partial}{\partial S}$	↑	↓
$\dfrac{\partial}{\partial K}$	↓	↑
$\dfrac{\partial}{\partial \sigma}$	↑	↑
$\dfrac{\partial}{\partial R_d}$	↑	↓
$\dfrac{\partial}{\partial R_f}$	↓	↑

Some caution is in order because a sufficiently large Δy might imply a change in the partial derivative.

Delta and Gamma

Currency calls rise and currency puts fall with increases in the spot exchange rate (working with the American convention of spot quotation). Delta has been defined as the magnitude of the change in the option's value with respect to a change in the spot exchange rate. Deltas for calls and puts are given by the partial derivatives:

$$\delta_{call} \equiv \frac{\partial C}{\partial S} = e^{-R_f \tau} N(x + \sigma\sqrt{\tau})$$

$$\delta_{put} \equiv \frac{\partial P}{\partial S} = e^{-R_f \tau} [N(x + \sigma\sqrt{\tau}) - 1]$$

The deltas of calls and puts are bounded as follows:

$$0 \le \delta_{call} \le 1$$

$$-1 \le \delta_{put} \le 0$$

The delta of the USD put/DEM call in Exhibit 22–2 is equal to .5017. In practice, traders convert delta to units of one or the other face currencies, such as 5.017 million USD. In other words, given small moves in the spot rate, the value of the USD put/DEM call behaves like a short spot position of approximately 5 million USD/DEM. For example, if the spot exchange rate were to move up from 1.5400 to 1.5450, one would expect the value of the option to fall by $16,236, since:

$$\frac{(1.5400 - 1.5450)}{1.5450} \times \$5.017MM = -\$16,236$$

This of course is only an approximation. The actual movement in the option's value is equal to $15,660. Delta itself is a function of the spot exchange rate. Its partial derivative with respect to spot is called gamma (γ),

$$\gamma \equiv \frac{\partial \delta}{\partial S} = \frac{\partial^2 C}{\partial S^2}$$

Gamma is important to option traders; it is analogous to the concept of convexity in fixed-income analysis. Gamma is a negative function of time to expiration, meaning that short-dated options have the most convexity. The option with maximum gamma for any expiration is approximately struck at-the-money. Differentiating the equation for delta yields a formulation for gamma:

$$\gamma \equiv \frac{\partial^2 C}{\partial S^2} = \frac{e^{-R_f \tau} N' (x + \sigma\sqrt{\tau})}{S \, \sigma\sqrt{\tau}}$$

The term $N'(\;)$ in the formula is the probability density function for the normal distribution. In the general case for variable z with zero mean and unit standard deviation,

$$N'(z) = \frac{1}{\sqrt{2\pi}} \, e^{-\frac{z^2}{2}}$$

The gamma for the USD put/DEM call of Exhibit 22–2 is equal to 16.93. If the spot rate moved from 1.5400 to 1.5450, its change measured in American quotation terms would equal –0.0021 (i.e., .6474 – .6494). This amount multiplied by gamma equal to 16.93 yields –0.03612, which is an approximate change in delta from .5017 to .4656.

It is common practice to express gamma as the change in delta associated with one "big figure" of change in spot. For example, if spot were to rise to

1.5500 from 1.5400, the dollar delta of the option would fall from 5.070 MM USD to 4.308 MM USD, or by $709,258, since:

$$\gamma_{1\ Big\ Figure} = \left(\frac{1}{1.5500} - \frac{1}{1.5400} \right) \times 16.93 \times \$10\ MM\,USD \cong -\$709{,}258$$

Time Decay

Almost every European option loses value with the passage of time. This is called time decay. Options with little time to expiration decay proportionately the fastest. Also, out-of-the-money options decay faster than in-the-money options because time value instead of parity accounts for their value. Option traders estimate time decay with the partial derivative of the option's value with respect to the time remaining to expiration. This partial derivative is called theta (θ), and it is:

$$\theta_{call} \equiv \frac{\partial C}{\partial \tau} = -R_f\,e^{-R_f\tau}\,SN\,(x + \sigma\sqrt{\tau}) + R_d\,e^{-R_d\tau}\,KN\,(x) + \frac{e^{-Rd\tau}\,\sigma}{2\sqrt{\tau}}\,KN'\,(x)$$

To figure one day's worth of decay, divide theta by 365 and multiply the result by the face of the option. For the option in Exhibit 22–2, the time decay from day 32 to day 31 is equal to $2,177.

Some European options experience positive time decay. Normally, these are deep in-the-money, low-volatility options. Positive time decay can be induced by a sufficiently large spread between domestic and foreign interest rates.

The Relationship between Theta and Gamma

Theta and gamma are related, as can be seen by returning to the BSGK partial differential equation for currency call options,

$$\frac{1}{2}\,\sigma^2\,S^2\,\gamma - R_d\,C + (R_d\,S - R_f\,S)\,\delta - \theta = 0$$

where γ, δ, and θ replace the partial derivatives, with no change in meaning.

At a given level of delta, gamma and theta are related. This explains why options with high levels of gamma have fast time decay ("theta is the rent on gamma"). Short-date options are a good example.

Volatility

An increase in volatility leads to increases in the value of all European options because the greater the level of volatility, the greater the probability that any option will expire in the money. That there is also a greater probability that the option will expire out of the money is less important because the option holder's maximum loss is the premium. The partial derivative of the option price with respect to volatility is shown in the expression:

$$\kappa_{call} \equiv \frac{\partial C}{\partial \sigma} = e^{-Rd\tau} K \sqrt{\tau} N'(x)$$

In this chapter, this will be referred to as kappa (κ), but elsewhere it is called by many other names, including omega, tau, and vega. Kappa in the above expression shows the change in an option given a 1 percent change in volatility (i.e., 12.20 percent to 13.20 percent), which must be multiplied by the option face. For the USD put/DEM call in Exhibit 22–2, the kappa of the option is \$11,762. Kappa is greatest for long-dated options. It is also relatively larger in the case of at-the-money options.

Interest Rate Partials

Currency calls (e.g., USD put/DEM call) are a positive function of the domestic interest rate and a negative function of the foreign interest rate. The opposite is true for currency puts (e.g., USD call/DEM put) because, when the foreign currency interest rate rises, the present value of the face amount of foreign currency must fall. This will lower the value of a currency call, which receives the face amount of foreign currency upon exercise, and will increase the value of a currency put, which delivers foreign currency upon exercise. Similarly, when the domestic interest rate rises, the present value of the face amount of domestic currency falls. By the same logic, the value of a currency call will rise and the value of a currency put will fall.

The partial derivatives for currency calls are:

$$\frac{\partial C}{\partial R_d} = \tau e^{-Rd\tau} KN(x)$$

$$\frac{\partial C}{\partial R_f} = -\tau e^{-Rf\tau} SN(x + \sigma\sqrt{\tau})$$

THE NATURE OF CURRENCY
OPTION VOLATILITY

In the discussion of the BSGK model, the volatility parameter, σ, was defined as the standard deviation of the log return of the spot exchange rate. This parameter is not directly observable in the marketplace, unlike the spot exchange rate and the domestic currency and foreign currency interest rates, all of which are quoted in the market. But where there is a quoted price for an option, the model can be used in reverse to reveal the market level of "implied volatility." No mathematical inverse to the BSGK equation is known to exist. Iterative procedures, like Newton's method, can be used to estimate implied volatility.

As can be seen in Exhibit 22–5, option volatility can vary across term to expiration. Indeed, volatility for a specific expiration date can be greatly influenced by the future calendar of economic events. Dates for the release of important economic data or the scheduled dates for international trade talks, elections, central bank meetings, and economic and political summits are apt to command comparatively higher levels of implied volatility.

Implied volatility can possess subtle but usually ephemeral relationships with the level of the spot exchange rate. For example, consider the case of dollar/yen in 1994 when the spot rate broke below the 100 level for the first time. The Bank of Japan publicly expressed its concern that the yen had appreciated too much against the dollar. The market view was that if the dollar were to sink any lower, the Bank of Japan and possibly other central banks would have intervened to buy dollars against the yen. These concerns were reflected in the price of dollar/yen options. The level of volatility rose for short-dated expirations. More interesting was that a relationship between the level of the spot rate and volatility was built into the market. Volatility would rise whenever the dollar fell against the yen and it would fall whenever the dollar rose against the yen.

It is important to realize that when volatility changes, its term structure does not make parallel shifts. In fact, short-dated volatilities are more changeable than long-dated volatility. As a result, the term structure of implied volatility can have almost any shape; it can be positive sloping, negative sloping, or just plain flat. As a general rule, implied volatility rises during a crisis or whenever there is a good reason to believe that a sharp movement in spot rates is probable. Short-dated options are usually well bid in such an environment because they are rich in gamma. But when the excitement fades, short-dated volatility has been known to come down quickly.

EXHIBIT 22–5
Sample Currency Option Implied Volatility Quotations
(as of September 12, 1994, At-the-Money Forward Strikes)

Exchange Rate	1 Week	1 Month	3 Month	1 Year
USD/DEM	11.45 – 12.50	11.80 – 12.20	11.85 – 12.15	12.00 – 12.20
USD/JPY	9.65 – 10.75	10.70 – 11.00	11.15 – 11.45	12.00 – 12.20
USD/CHF OVER	0.30 – 0.60	0.30 – 0.60	0.30 – 0.60	0.30 – 0.60
GBP OVER	−3.80	−3.80	−3.50	−1.55
AUD	7.00 – 8.00	8.20 – 8.60	8.50 – 8.90	8.65 – 9.05
USD/CAD	6.50 – 7.50	5.70 – 6.20	5.85 – 6.35	6.00 – 6.50
DEM/JPY	8.70 – 9.70	9.80 – 10.10	10.50 – 10.80	11.20 – 11.45
DEM/CHF	4.50 – 5.50	4.40 – 4.80	4.35 – 4.75	4.30 – 4.70
GBP/DEM	7.50 – 8.50	7.30 – 7.70	7.30 – 7.70	7.30 – 7.70
DEM/ITL	7.50 – 9.50	8.50 – 9.50	8.70 – 9.70	9.00 – 9.80
DEM/FRF	1.00 – 2.00	1.80 – 2.30	2.50 – 3.00	3.20 – 3.60

A well-known empirical finding, commonly referred to as the "smile," is that out-of-the-money currency options can trade for higher volatilities than at-the-money options. This was the case with dollar/mark options on September 12, 1994 (see Exhibit 22–6). Note that options are identified in units of delta. To the left of the 50 delta option are the out-of-the-money USD puts/DEM calls and to the right are the out-of-the-money USD calls/DEM puts. What is the reason for the smile? The best answer is that it is an artifact of the leptokurtic nature of currency returns, which has been reported in numerous empirical studies.[1] Where there is an abundance of outliers, as with the leptokurtic distribution of currency returns, low delta options are particularly valuable to traders seeking to make low-cost, high-leverage speculative bets.

The smile in implied currency volatility is sometimes nonsymmetrical (i.e., a "crooked smile"). This phenomenon is called the "skew." Some skew is evident in the upper panel of Exhibit 22–6 with respect to the dollar/mark; much more skew is visible with the dollar/yen in the lower panel.

---

[1] See David Hsieh, "Testing for Nonlinear Dependence in Daily Foreign Exchange Rates," *Journal of Business* 62 (1989), pp. 339–68.

EXHIBIT 22–6
Implied Volatility and Delta, USD/DEM and USD/JPY
(as of September 12, 1994)

USD/DEM	15 Delta USD Put/FX Call	25 Delta USD Put/FX Call	50 Delta	25 Delta USD Call/FX Put	15 Delta USD Call/FX Put
1 week	11.40 – 13.15	11.45 – 12.80	11.45 – 12.50	11.35 – 12.70	11.25 – 13.00
1 month	12.00 – 12.45	11.90 – 12.30	11.80 – 12.20	11.85– 12.20	11.85 – 12.35
2 months	12.05 – 12.50	11.95 – 12.30	11.85 – 12.15	11.85 – 12.25	11.90 – 12.40
3 months	12.05 – 12.55	11.95 – 12.30	11.85 – 12.15	11.90 – 12.25	11.95 – 12.45
1 Year	12.00 – 12.30	12.00 – 12.20	12.00 – 12.20	12.05 – 12.30	12.10 – 12.40

USD/JPY					
1 week	10.55 – 12.25	10.25 – 11.60	9.65 – 10.75	9.05 – 10.45	8.60 – 10.65
1 month	11.45 – 11.95	11.20– 11.55	10.70 – 11.00	10.30 – 10.65	10.05 – 10.60
2 months	11.55 – 12.05	11.35 – 11.75	11.00 – 11.30	10.65 – 11.05	10.45 – 11.00
3 months	11.70 – 12.15	11.50 – 11.85	11.15 – 11.45	10.95 – 11.30	10.85 – 11.35
1 year	12.20 – 12.50	12.10 – 12.35	12.00 – 12.20	11.95 – 12.20	11.90 – 12.25

AMERICAN CURRENCY OPTIONS

American currency options can be exercised at any time before expiration, unlike European options, which can be exercised only at expiration. In all other respects, American and European options are identical. Because early exercise is permitted, the value of an American option should never be less than a similarly specified European option, making:

$$C' \geq C$$

$$P' \geq P$$

where the prime symbol denotes American exercise.

Also, an in-the-money American option should never trade for less than its intrinsic value,

$$C' \geq S - K$$

$$P' \geq K - S$$

because this value can be extracted by exercising the option at once. Early exercise notwithstanding, American options must obey the Black-Scholes partial differential equation provided assumptions 1, 2, and 3 (see page 476) are in force, with the implication that it is possible to locally hedge the options with spot trading. The Black-Scholes partial differential equation for American call options is:

$$\frac{1}{2}\,\sigma^2\,\frac{\partial^2 C'}{\partial S^2} - R_d\,C' + (R_d\,S - R_f\,S)\,\frac{\partial C'}{\partial S} - \frac{\partial C'}{\partial \tau} = 0$$

However, because early exercise is sometimes optimal, it is not possible to impose the expiration day payoff function as a boundary constraint (as was the case for European exercise options) to arrive at an analytical solution for American exercise options. Consequently, option theorists have turned to different classes of models.[2]

THE BINOMIAL MODEL FOR AMERICAN CURRENCY OPTIONS

The binomial option model proposed by J. C. Cox, Stephen A. Ross, and Mark Rubinstein (1979) values American options on dividend-paying common stocks with explicit recognition of early exercise. James N. Bodurtha, Jr. and Georges R. Courtadon (1987) modified the binomial model to work on currency options.

The Binomial Approach

In the binomial model, the spot exchange rate at a point in time is constrained to move or jump in one of two mutually exclusive paths: the one upward and the other downward. During the remaining time to expiration, designated as τ, the spot exchange rate must make a fixed number, N, of such jumps. N is a parameter; a greater value for N implies greater precision but slower speed of calculation. The size of each jump is a function of the domestic and foreign currency interest rates, the assumed volatility, and the number of jumps in the remaining time to expiration. The sizes of an up jump, u, and a down jump, d, are given by:

---

2 Notable are the binomial model of Cox, Ross, and Rubinstein (1979) and the quadratic approximation model of Barone-Adesi and Whaley (1987) and MacMillan (1986).

$$u = e^{(R_d - R_f)\frac{\tau}{N} + \sigma\sqrt{\frac{\tau}{N}}}$$

$$d = e^{(R_f - R_f)\frac{\tau}{N} - \sigma\sqrt{\frac{\tau}{N}}}$$

The spot exchange rate upon inception will be denoted as S_0. After the first jump, the spot rate will either be up, ^1S_u or down, ^1S_d,

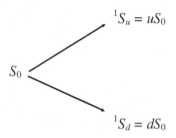

$$^1S_u = uS_0$$

$$S_0$$

$$^1S_d = dS_0$$

The presuperscript, 1 in this case, signifies the number of realized jumps.

Consider the case of the USD put/DEM call in Exhibit 22–2, now with American exercise. In the most simple case, assume that the spot rate could make only one jump in the remaining span of time before expiration on day 32. $N = 1$, in other words, and the magnitude of the up or down jumps would be:

$$u = e^{(4.49\% - 4.84\%)\frac{32}{365} + 12.2\%\sqrt{\frac{32}{365}}} = 1.03647$$

$$d = e^{4.49\% - 4.84\%)\frac{32}{365} - 12.2\%\sqrt{\frac{32}{365}}} = .96423$$

Expressed in the American quotation, the spot rate, S_0, is equal to .64935 (1 ÷ 1.5400). Accordingly, the spot rate on day 31, S_T will be either

$$S_T = {}^1S_u = uS_0 = 1.03647 \times .64935 = .67303$$

or

$$S_T = {}^1S_d = dS_0 = 0.96423 \times .64935 = .62612$$

This implies that the call option could have only one of two expiration values, depending on whether the spot moves up or down.

Up

$$^1C_u = Max\,(0, \,{}^1S_u - K) = .02368$$

Down

$${}^1C_d = Max\,(0,\,{}^1S_d - K) = 0$$

where the strike is at-the-money spot and the expiration values are denominated in dollars per one unit of mark face.

The value at time zero of this option can be calculated using an insight from Cox, Ross and Rubinstein. They show that the value at expiration of the option can be replicated by a portfolio that consists of borrowing a sum of dollars, B, and lending a sum of marks, DEM, to be repaid at option expiration, T. The future value at time T of the borrowed dollars is equal to

$$Be^{R_d\tau}$$

The value at time zero of the spot marks is

$$S_0 D$$

Interest would accrue at the rate R_f on the marks until expiration. Thereupon, the dollar value of the marks would depend on whether the spot rate moved up or down:

$${}^1S_u\,De^{R\frac{\tau}{N}} = uS_0\,De^{R\frac{\tau}{N}}$$

or

$${}^1S_d\,De^{R\frac{\tau}{N}} = dS_0\,De^{R\frac{\tau}{N}}$$

where the only unknown here is the spot exchange rate at expiration. If B and D are chosen as follows, the option payoff can be replicated:

$$B = \frac{u\,{}^1C_d - d\,{}^1C_u}{(u-d)\,e^{R_d\frac{\tau}{N}}} = -.31481$$

$$D = \frac{{}^1C_u - {}^1C_d}{(u-d)\,S_0 e^{R\frac{\tau}{N}}} = .502645$$

On expiration day, the value of this portfolio exactly matches the value of call:

	Call (^1C_u and ^1C_d)	Portfolio	
UP	.02368	Dollar loan	−.31605
		Marks	.33973
		Total	.02368
DOWN	0	Dollar Loan	−.31605
		Marks	+.31605
		Total	0

Since the payoff from the portfolio matches the payoff from the call, the two must be equivalent in value at time zero to eliminate the possibility of profitable riskless arbitrage. This makes the value of the call at time zero equal to:

$$C = B + S_0 D = .01158$$

The next step is to expand the number of jumps. The binomial model starts with the expiration values and progresses backward in time until time zero. In general, precision can be increased by choosing a greater value for N, but no matter how large N is, the procedure is always the same. First, evaluate the expiration values. Next, move back one jump to calculate the option values at the $(N - 1)$th node, checking for the possibility that early exercise might be optimal for American options. Then continue until the entire binomial tree has been evaluated to produce C_0.

THE QUADRATIC APPROXIMATION MODEL

Starting with the earlier work by Lionel W. MacMillan (1986), Giovanni Barone-Adesi and Robert E. Whaley (1987), discovered an efficient method of approximation for the value of an American option. The approach involves locating a critical value, S* at which early exercise is optimal. The value of an American call option would then be either

$$C' = (S - K), \ S \geq S^*$$

or

$$C' = C + A_2 \left(\frac{S}{S^*}\right)^{q_2}, \ S^* > S$$

where

$$A_2 = \frac{S^*}{q_2}\left[1 - e^{-R_d\tau} N\left(d_1(S^*)\right)\right]$$

$$q_2 = \frac{1}{2}\left[-(N - 1) + \sqrt{(N - 1)^2 + r\frac{M}{B}}\right]$$

$$N = 2\frac{(R_d - R_f)}{\sigma^2}$$

$$M = 2\frac{R_d}{\sigma^2}$$

$$B = 1 - e^{-R_d\tau}$$

$$d_1(S^*) = \frac{\ln\left(\frac{S^*}{K}\right) + \left(R_d - R_f + \frac{1}{s}\sigma^2\right)\tau}{\sigma\sqrt{\tau}}$$

$N(\ )$ is the cumulative normal density function. The only variable that is an unknown is S^*, the critical level of spot that triggers early exercise. Barone-Adesi and Whaley provide an algorithm that iteratively converges on S^* within an acceptable level of tolerance for error.

CURRENCY FUTURES OPTIONS

A currency futures option delivers a currency futures contract upon exercise, whereupon the in-the-money spread between the strike and futures price becomes an immediate credit or debit to long or short positions.

The futures options listed on the International Monetary Market division of the Chicago Mercantile Exchange have the American exercise convention. Early exercise is sometimes optimal for American futures options, especially for a deep in-the-money option trading at low implied volatility. John Hull (1991) showed that the binomial model can be adapted with little modification to work on American futures options, using up and down jumps equal to:

$$u = e^{\sigma \frac{\sqrt{\tau}}{N}}$$

$$d = e^{-\sigma \frac{\sqrt{\tau}}{N}}$$

Whaley (1986) adapted the Barone-Adesi and Whaley quadratic approximation method to handle American futures options (see DeRosa (1992)).

REFERENCES

Abramowitz, Milton, and Irene A. Stegun, eds. *Handbook of Mathematical Functions with Formulas, Graphs, and Mathematical Tables.* Applied Mathematics Ser. 55. Washington D.C.: National Bureau of Standards, 1972.

Barone-Adesi, Giovanni, and Robert E. Whaley. "Efficient Analytic Approximation of American Option Values." *Journal of Finance* 62 (June 1987), pp. 301–20.

Black, Fischer. "The Pricing of Commodity Contracts." *Journal of Financial Economics* 3 (Jan.–Mar. 1976), pp. 167–79.

Black, Fischer, and Myron Scholes. "The Pricing of Options and Corporate Liabilities." *Journal of Political Economy* 81 (May–June), pp. 637–59.

Bodurtha, James, N., Jr., and Georges R. Courtadon. *The Pricing of Foreign Currency Options.* Monograph Series in Finance and Economics, Monograph 1987–4/5. New York: New York University, 1987.

Cox, J. C., Stephen A. Ross, and Mark Rubinstein. "Option Pricing: A Simplified Approach." *Journal of Financial Economics* 7 (September 1979), 229–63.

DeRosa, David F. *Managing Foreign Exchange Risk*, 2d ed. Burr Ridge, Ill., Irwin Professional Publishing, 1996.

———. *Options on Foreign Exchange.* Chicago, Ill., Probus Publishing, 1992.

Garman, Mark B., and Steven W. Kohlhagen. "Foreign Currency Option Values." *Journal of International Money and Finance* 2 (December 1983), pp. 231–37.

Hsieh, David. "Testing for Nonlinear Dependence in Daily Foreign Exchange Rates." *Journal of Business* 62, (1989), pp. 339–368.

Hull, John. *Introduction to Futures and Options Markets*. Englewood Cliffs, N.J.: Prentice Hall, 1991.

———. *Options, Futures, and Other Derivative Securities*. Englewood Cliffs, N.J.: Prentice Hall, 1987.

MacMillan, Lionel W. "Analytic Approximation for the American Put Option." *Advances in Futures and Options Research*. 1 (1986) Greenwich, Conn.: JAI Press, 1986.

Merton, Robert C. "Theory of Rational Option Pricing," *Bell Journal of Economics and Management Science* 4 (Spring 1973), pp. 141–83.

Whaley, Robert E. "On Valuing American Futures Options." *Financial Analysts Journal* 42 (May–June 1986), pp. 194–04.

———. "Valuation of American Futures Options: Theory and Empirical Tests." *Journal of Finance* 61 (March 1986), pp. 127–49.

RISK
MANAGEMENT

## Chapter Twenty-Three

Managing the Market Risk of Derivatives

Steven L. Allen
Chemical Bank

Reflecting on the environment in which trading risks on derivatives must be managed, just after the end of the year 1994, one is conscious of strong cross-currents. On the positive side, the large losses that have shown up in the derivatives positions of some firms during 1994 have intensified the degree of effort and resources devoted to the measurement and mitigation of derivatives trading risks. On the negative side, some articles, particularly in the popular press, have taken to portraying the risks of derivatives as so large and unmanageable as to bring the effectiveness of the entire effort into question. The year 1994, after all, saw one major U.S. regional bank announce at a press conference that in derivatives it was "strictly a user not a dealer" (a phrase heretofore most prominent in plea bargains on narcotics violations). And a large money center bank took pains to point out that a sizable trading loss was due strictly to dealings in underlying instruments and not derivatives (thereby, we must suppose, making it an easier loss to bear).

IS DERIVATIVES TRADING TOO RISKY?

Does trading derivatives really give rise to risks that go beyond those of trading in underlying instruments? Many analysts have been quick to point out that for many of the more spectacular losses in derivatives, the loss-making positions could just as easily been put on in conventional underlying instruments. It has also been pointed out that some of the fears concerning derivatives are fed by the looseness of definition concerning what constitutes a derivative; for example, in counting up losses due to derivatives, some people will count all losses due to mortgage-backed securities, even those on straight pass-throughs. The word *derivative* in such instances comes to mean something close to "any instrument which has large risks."

There are, however, some aspects of derivatives which, at least in some instances, do give rise to greater difficulty in managing risk. The most prominent would be:

1. The long holding period of many derivatives. Unlike underlying instruments such as stocks and bonds, which generally allow for rapid liquidation of positions when desired, many derivatives give rise to positions that may need to be held for several years. This is not universally true of derivatives. Exchange-traded futures and options are among the most liquid of trading instruments. But custom-designed over-the-counter swaps and options may be nearly impossible to liquidate. Even if market risk can be offset, credit exposure and commitment to carry out payment and receipt operations can only be terminated by mutual consent of the contracting parties. This can result in the size of over-the-counter derivatives books building cumulatively over the years. The sheer number of outstanding positions makes understanding and monitoring the risks of the book a complex task.

2. The great virtue of derivatives, the flexibility with which they can be structured to meet a particular customer's needs, also results in a lack of standardization that adds to the complexity of understanding and monitoring risks.

3. The lack of readily available markets. This is not true for all derivatives; exchange-traded futures and options have virtually continuous price quotations. Nor is this unique to derivatives; many bonds do not have liquid price quotations available. However, this is a fairly common characteristic of many derivatives.

4. The difficulty in calculating how prices will respond to changes in market conditions is another difficulty in managing risk. While certainly not true of all derivatives (e.g., the futures contract on LIBOR has an extremely straightforward dependence of price on market rates), virtually all options and even many futures contracts (such as bond futures with multiple delivery options) require some form of modeling to track this relationship.

THE GROUP OF THIRTY RECOMMENDATIONS

These characteristics indicate a need for a systematic approach to the management of derivatives risk. A framework for such a systematic approach has been put forward in the July 1993 report of the Global Derivatives Study Group commissioned by the Group of Thirty, a multi-national organization of regulators, academics, and representatives from trading firms. The recommendations of this study are increasingly cited by regulatory bodies and industry groups, such as the International Swaps and Derivatives Association, as a model to follow in managing derivatives trading. As an example, the October 1993 Comptroller of the Currency banking circular on *Risk Management of Financial Derivatives* closely follows the Group of Thirty proposals. In this chapter I will follow the framework of the Group of Thirty recommendations that apply only to the management of trading risk.

I will refer to these recommendations according to the numbering system employed in the original Group of Thirty report. Each recommendation will be stated in full as given in that report and will be followed by a detailed discussion of implementation issues.

Recommendation 2: Marking to Market

Dealers should mark their derivatives positions to market, on at least a daily basis, for risk management purposes.

A policy of marking to market all derivatives positions, at least as often as the close of business each day, constitutes the essential foundation for managing trading risk. There are two primary reasons for this. First, without a nearly continuous mark to market, it would be possible that ineffective hedging strategies would not be recognized until long after their effectiveness had ceased. Second, without realistic marks to market, gains might be reported in one period which would later need to be reversed.

Methodologies for marking to market. The technique for marking to market must obviously differ by the type of derivative. For derivatives for which liquid market quotations are available, such as exchange-traded futures or options, there is no question that the proper mark to market is the price currently prevalent in the market. Traders may believe that the current price does not properly represent value; indeed, differences of opinion on proper value are what drive position taking. But any deviation between what traders believe a position to be worth and the amount that could be achieved by currently closing it out must be treated as a speculative profit that should be recognized only when it is actually realized.

For products on which liquid market quotations are not readily available, the situation is more complex. For some products, quotations are available but at somewhat irregular intervals or with doubt as to the real ability to get transactions done at these levels. For such products, it must be a matter of judgment based on historical experience whether quotations can be relied upon, or whether marks to market based on mathematical models should be employed. Other products are so individually tailored to particular client needs that recourse to a mathematical model is a necessity.

Mathematical models for derivatives have to account for two primary aspects of valuation. The first is the value to ascribe to cash flows scheduled for future dates. The second is how to account for the uncertain nature of future cash flows. The first problem has been solved in a way that can be regarded as virtually universally accepted, which is to assign a discounting factor to each future date and to discount any future cash flow on a particular date by the discounting factor assigned to that date (no matter what derivative product gives rise to the cash flow). While there remain some technical differences between competing methodologies about exactly how to build this set of discount factors, the differences in impact on mark-to-market values between them is small, owing to the common agreement that the scope of applicability of the discount factors should be universal. As a result, the discount factors, however selected, must closely agree with the liquid quotations readily available for such standard products as Treasury bonds and Eurodollar futures. Once such agreement has been arranged, not much room is left for disagreement between competing methodologies.

No such common ground exists for the valuation of uncertainty. Some products have models that are in such widespread and common use as to have become industry standards; for example, the Black-Scholes model for simple European-style options. Other products utilize models that are highly specific to a given firm and whose details are regarded as trade secrets. Such models give rise to a certain degree of skepticism about how reliable a mark to market based on such models can be. With different firms using different models for evaluation, and in the absence of liquid quotations, what confidence can there be that positions can really be unwound at values reasonably close to those being produced by the models? However, even if a model does not produce sound liquidation values it still may produce reasonable going-business values; that is, values which reflect the present value of future costs of hedging the position.

To achieve confidence in this going-business aspect of a model's values, it is necessary to be sure that the model's pricing is consistent with the methodology used to price any instruments (whether other derivatives or underlying instruments) which will be used for hedging purposes. One way of achieving this, which has been advocated by many theoreticians and some practitioners, is to build a single unified model that prices all transactions within a broad class of products (e.g., one model to price all interest rate derivatives and underlyings within a single currency, or one model to price all derivatives and underlyings related to a single commodity). There are several difficulties with such proposals, stemming from the variety of special solution techniques that need to be employed as models get built for increasingly complex derivatives. Some derivative products require lattice solution techniques to take account of complex conditional probabilities which are part of their valuation. Other products, which are highly dependent on the previous path of an underlying price, require Monte Carlo techniques. These Monte Carlo models may need to depend on two, three, or even more factors, and sometimes the set of factors needed to price one product is different from the set of factors needed to price another. While in theory it may be possible to build a single model covering all such variations, in practice it is usually too difficult from both the work involved in model construction and the computation time in arriving at model values. Firms that follow a single model approach often do so at the expense of creating simplifying probability assumptions, necessary to shoehorn a product into the unifying model without creating too high a level of difficulty, but unrealistic in terms of historical behavior of variables. Another danger is that the creativity of product development may be slowed down by denying model builders the full array of possible solution techniques.

An alternative approach is to allow a wide array of models, but to attempt to unify them by checking the mutual consistency of the probability assumptions underlying each model in use. This approach relies on the principle of "risk-neutral valuation," which states that as long as we are dealing with an instrument where risk is fully hedgable by a trading strategy involving some group of other instruments, then a single probability distribution exists (called the "risk-neutral probability distribution") which correctly prices all of these instruments. This pricing is calculated by taking expected values of future cash flow, using the probability weights of the risk-neutral distribution, and discounting all cash flows at risk-free discount factors.[1] It should be emphasized that this probability distribution does not represent any attempt to state the views of the firm on future market movements. It is simply a mathematical device for assuring that all products are being consistently priced based on their future hedging costs.

Assuring the consistency of probability assumptions used in marking to market. Two basic techniques can be used together in complementary fashion to assure that the probability assumptions of all models in use are consistent. The first is to measure directly the probability distribution underlying each model and check distributions between models. Thus, for example, the distributions of three-month LIBOR generated for various future dates by a Monte Carlo model could be directly compared with the distributions for the same dates generated by a lattice model. The second technique is to extend a model to price products which the model does not strictly need to handle, solely as a consistency check. For example, it is generally found to be computationally far too expensive to price ordinary caps and floors using either Monte Carlo or lattice techniques; the use of a Black commodity model is much faster and sufficiently accurate. But even a firm that prices all its caps and floors in inventory using a Black model, should also extend its Monte Carlo and lattice models to price a few standard caps and floors. If these standard structures do not price reasonably the same across all three types of models, then the probability distributions utilized in the three models must have significant differences.

The use of a common probability distribution across all models is an extension of and improvement on two other principles used in the pricing of option-type derivatives. One is the principle of using only "arbitrage-free" models in the more limited sense of assuring that the models correctly price the underlying instrument on which the derivative is based. The common probability distribution obviously includes this principle because the underlying instrument is one of the instruments which this distribution must correctly price. But it goes beyond this principle by insisting that not only the mean of the distribution (which is all that must be looked at to price the underlying instrument) be correct, but also the higher moments of the

---

1 A full statement and mathematical proof of this principle can be found in the first chapter of Darrell Duffie's *Dynamic Asset Pricing Theory*. Academic Press, 1988. A more intuitive and informal version of the argument can be found in John Hull's *Options, Futures, and other Derivative Securities,* 2d. edition, sections 10.8, 12.1, 12.3, 14.2, 19.3, Prentice Hall, 1993.

distribution, which are needed to assure consistency between the pricing of options with different terms.

The second principle is that of pricing less liquid instruments by interpolating from the available prices of more liquid instruments. For example, quotations might be readily available for four-year caps and five-year caps but not four-and-one-half year caps. In some way, the four-and-one-half year cap price should be interpolated from the price of the four-year caps and five-year caps. However, just knowing that interpolation should take place does not serve as guidance in choosing between different possible interpolation techniques. Should the price of a four-and-one-half year cap be interpolated from the price of a four-year cap and the price of a five-year cap? Or should a single volatility be established which correctly prices the four-year cap, another volatility which correctly prices the five-year cap, and then price the four-and-one-half year cap based on a volatility interpolated from these two volatilities?

The rules of using a common probability distribution across all models offers more specific guidance. The individual options that compose the four-year cap (the so-called "caplets") are exactly the same as the first four years of individual options that compose the four-and-one-half-year cap and five-year cap. Therefore, the rule of common probability distribution forces the first four years of individual options for the four-and-one-half-year cap and five-year cap to be priced at the market price of the four-year cap. Now only the last half year of options of the four-and-one-half-year cap needs to be priced, and they will be priced in a way consistent with the pricing of the last year of options on the five-year cap. This still leaves some room for choice of interpolation technique, but a very much narrowed one.

Another example of how the common probability distribution rule constrains the choice of interpolation technique can be seen by looking at options whose market quoted prices exhibit a "volatility smile," that is, the implied volatility (using a standard options model such as Black-Scholes) for options which are otherwise identical except for strike level is higher for in- and out-of-the-money options than for at-the-money options. One common approach to interpolating for such options—from strike prices at which market quotes are available to strike prices at which they are not—is to first calculate the implied volatilities for the strike prices at which quotes are known, interpolate from these volatilities to a volatility for an unknown strike, and then use this volatility to price the option at that strike. This methodology would not be acceptable under the criterion of using a common probability distribution, since the different volatilities used to price options at each strike imply different probability distributions. Examples of approaches that use a common probability distribution are models which assume volatility is itself a random variable with a probability distribution, and several recently proposed models in which the distribution of underlying is assumed to have fatter tails than the normal distribution, with the exact shape of the tails fitted to observed price quotes for options at different strikes.[2]

Input parameters for illiquid instruments.   What rules need to be followed in deriving input parameters for models used for marking to market illiquid instruments? The rule of pricing liquid and illiquid instruments using a common probability distribution will fix the values of some inputs within tight limits, but will offer little guidance on selecting other inputs. Consider, for example, a "quanto" option which pays off based on the U.S. dollar value of a Japanese stock index. The critical inputs needed to price this option are the volatility of the stock index, the volatility of the dollar/yen exchange rate, and the degree of correlation between the stock index and the exchange rate. There will be little freedom in choosing the volatilities because they will need to be consistent with the pricing of liquid options on dollar/yen exchange rates and liquid options on the stock index. But no liquid instruments are likely to exist which help to narrow down possible values of the correlation.

Two alternative approaches are available. One is to rely on historical values of the correlation. The other is to rely on forecasting models or predictions. This is not as sharp a contrast as might at first appear. Relying on historical values still requires judgment about the appropriate historical time period to choose and the proper weightings to be given to different time periods (e.g., recent history versus the more distant past, periods of economic turbulence versus calmer interludes). These choices amount, in effect, to selecting a forecasting model, while any forecasting model which is selected or even judgmental prediction made, is based to a large extent on historical experience. The more important distinction is who makes the choice of model or who is the source of the prediction. Relying on a source independent of the trading desk, such as a firmwide policy on selecting

---

2 For an example of the first type of model see Hull and White, "The Pricing of Options on Assets with Stochastic Volatilities," *Journal of Finance,* June 1987. For examples of the second type see the January 1994, February 1994, and January 1995 issues of *Risk* for articles by Dupire, Derman and Kani, and Rubinstein, respectively).

historical periods and weightings, or reliance on the forecasts of an economics department, has the advantage of removing a potential for trader manipulation of reported earnings.[3] Relying on the trading desk as the source of models or predictions allows greater sensitivity to factors driving particular markets. Whichever approach is chosen, it is important to maintain consistency across both transactions and time. In this example, consistency across transactions implies that the same correlation between the foreign exchange rate and the stock index must be used (for a given time period) for any transaction whose price depends on this correlation. This increases the incentive for hedging correlation risk by taking offsetting positions in different transactions, and it decreases the possibility of using the input to manipulate reported earnings. Consistency across time would mean that changes to forecasting models or rules for taking historical averages should be held to a minimum, and any changes made should be clearly labeled to management as to purpose and impact on reported earnings.

Recommendation 3: Market Valuation Methods

Derivatives portfolios of dealers should be valued based on midmarket levels less specific adjustments, or on appropriate bid or offer levels. Midmarket valuation adjustments should allow for expected future costs such as unearned credit spread, close-out costs, investing and funding costs, and administrative costs.

The Group of Thirty study recommends mark to market valuations based on either midmarket levels less specific adjustments, or on appropriate bid or offer levels. Either approach represents a means of adjusting the mark to market to reflect actual levels at which existing positions can be unwound. The approach based on bid or offer levels is geared more toward a liquidation approach, while the approach based on midmarket levels less specific adjustments reflects more of a going-business approach. One argument against an approach based on bid or offer levels is similar to that noted in the previous section in the discussion of a liquidation approach: the lack of confidence that reasonable liquidation values can be obtained for those derivatives for which liquid market quotations are not available. A second

---

3 It should be emphasized that this is only a proposal for marking to market; assumptions that determine position taking should always be derived from the traders responsible for the profit and loss (P&L) results.

argument is that an approach based on bid or offer levels requires a highly sophisticated computational technique for matching up transactions that substantially offset one another. Without such a computational ability, a trading book would get charged the full bid-offered spread on matched positions that would not need to be liquidated even in the event of wishing to unwind positions.

The specific adjustments approach, by contrast, can be applied at the portfolio level, largely based on summary portfolio statistics. The specific adjustments approach also offers a more flexible measure because it can distinguish between the cost of exposure to credit risk, exposure to future operating costs, and exposure to residual market risks not captured by the valuation models. The bid-offered spread reflects all of these costs, whereas actual positions may be exposed to some of these costs but not others.

The Group of Thirty study mentions four types of expected future costs for which specific adjustments should be allowed:

- Administrative costs
- Investing and funding costs
- Unearned credit spread
- Close-out costs

We will look at each of the four in turn, and discuss possible methodologies for estimating these costs. We will also discuss the desirability of making further adjustments against costs that are only potential rather than expected.

Administrative costs.   One of the identifying characteristics of many derivatives is the long time period over which payments must be made and received. Even when market and credit exposure has been eliminated, this commitment to future operations must be accounted for. As long as business continues to be booked at unchanged or increasing levels, future revenues would be available against which to charge these costs. But given the possibility of diminished levels of new business in the future, it is prudent to charge against current earnings the commitment to future operating costs that is needed to generate those earnings. This involves estimating the future administrative costs of the existing portfolio, including not only personnel expenses but also the computer systems and other infrastructure costs needed to support personnel. These costs are usually tied much more closely to the number of future payments to be made and received than to the notional size of transactions. The present value of future costs should be charged as an adjustment against the mark to market. In case of a diminished level of new business, the volume of future payments will decrease through time, lowering the size of this adjustment and thereby raising the mark-to-market value of the portfolio. This will give rise to a revenue stream against which the future costs can be changed.

Investing and funding costs.   Derivative books frequently give rise to large mismatches in the timing of receipt and distribution of cash. For example, a futures hedge against a forward position produces immediate cash flows that will eventually be offset when the forward position comes due. From a mark-to-market standpoint, this should not give rise to any variations, since proper futures hedges are leveraged to offset the discounted present value of the position to be hedged. But actual investing and funding may take place at rates different from those used in calculating the hedge. A forward position may be created by either borrowing or lending a security, and the supply and demand for the lending of particular securities may cause the lending rate to differ significantly from the rate being earned or charged on the cash from the futures hedge. Any costs which can be projected for the funding of mismatches in the timing of cash receipts, such as costs based on historical frequency and magnitude of higher or lower securities lending rates, should be included as a valuation adjustment.

Unearned credit spread adjustment.   The Group of Thirty study calls for projection of future credit losses based on (1) expected exposure to the counterparties, taking into account netting arrangements, (2) expected default experience for the credit rating of the counterparties, and (3) overall diversification of the portfolio.

A first cut at expected exposure to a counterparty is the current mark to market of that counterparty's positions (with amounts owed to the counterparty being allowed to offset amounts owed by the counterparty only if proper netting arrangements exist, and with reductions in exposure for any collateral held against the positions), since the mark to market represents the expected value of future cash flows under the risk-neutral probability distribution. However, there is no reason that the risk-neutral probability distribution needs to be used for this computation, since it does not involve pricing based on future hedging costs, and a probability distribution which represents the firm's expectations of future market conditions would be more appropriate. Also, credit defaults that occur will not all occur immediately, but will occur over time, after some of the expected cash flows which go into the current mark to market have already occurred. For both these reasons, it is desirable to have systems that allow the derivatives pricing models to be run for different forward points in time, using inputs that represent the firm's forecast for expected future market inputs.

Historical default experience is available from the major credit rating firms, referenced by credit rating and the total length of time of a credit exposure. From these figures, possibly modified for a firm's forecast of differing future credit climate or taking into account knowledge of any special characteristics of a firm's portfolio of counterparty exposures (e.g., industry or geographic concentration, or a firm's own historical experience of defaults of a particular class of borrowers), an expectation of defaults by year into the future for each counterparty credit rating can be derived. This can be combined with calculated exposures by a counterparty to produce an expected future credit loss, whose present value should be determined to obtain an adjustment against mark-to-market valuation.

Close-out costs. The Group of Thirty study states that this adjustment "represents the costs that would be incurred if all unmatched positions were closed out or hedged." An approach recommended in the study is to base these close-out costs on a one standard deviation adverse price move for a one-day time horizon for very liquid positions and a longer time horizon for less liquid positions. This approach appears quite sensible for those aspects of position that can be closed out, such as absolute interest rate exposures which could be closed out using exchange traded futures positions, or exposures to interest rate volatilities, which could be closed out using liquid cap and floor markets. But other exposures are not really candidates for closing out, since no liquid market exists. Examples would be exposure to correlation risk on quanto trades or exposure to mean reversion risk on path-dependent options. In such cases, the firm has committed itself to a long-term dynamic hedging strategy; what must be estimated is the expected cost of maintaining this long-term strategy.

There are two parts to the expected cost of a dynamic hedging strategy. The first is the personnel, systems, and infrastructure costs of maintaining a trading desk. What is being estimated is basically how much of this future cost will be necessary for hedging current positions as opposed to pricing and managing new positions. The second part is the bid-asked spreads that will need to be paid on expected purchase and sale of liquid instruments used in the dynamic hedge.[4] Projecting the cost of this bid-asked spread requires determination of:

1. The size of positions that need to be dynamically hedged.   Only net positions need be dynamically hedged; to the extent that the risk has been offset by putting on positions on the other side, dynamic hedging will not be necessary.

2. The frequency with which rehedges will be required.   This is in part a function of the volatility of the market indicator being hedged and in part a function of management's willingness to bear risk. If an attempt were made to truly hedge all market moves dynamically, no matter how small, as in the official assumptions for options models, bid-asked cost would increase without bound. It is therefore necessary in practice to assume some minimum threshold of price movement below which rehedging will not take place. The larger this threshold, the lower will be the expected bid-asked cost, but the larger will be the volatility of results achieved.[5]

3. The size of the bid-asked spread on the liquid instrument used for the dynamic hedge.   One product feature which should receive particular focus in estimating the expected cost of bid-asked spread is discontinuity in payouts. Examples of this feature are barrier options, gap options, digital options, and asset-or-nothing swaps. All have some trigger price or prices at which the option payout undergoes a large jump. All such products have certain scenarios (which may be of low probability), in which very large dynamic hedging positions may need to be bought and sold, leading to very high bid-asked spread cost.

Potential costs.   In addition to adjusting for expected costs, management must decide on the degree to which potential costs above the level of expected costs should be adjusted for. There does not appear to be any rationale for making such an adjustment for close-out costs for positions that can be hedged with liquid instruments or for administrative costs

---

4 Note that only the bid-asked spread must be accounted for; the expected cost of the "buy high, sell low" strategy of dynamic hedging should already be incorporated in the mark-to-market valuation through use of options models.

5 For more details, see Paul Wilmott's article in *Risk* (March 1994).

because both elements can be estimated to a reasonable degree of precision. But close-out costs for positions that require dynamic hedging, investing and funding costs, and credit costs are all subject to a significant degree of uncertainty. Management needs to make a decision concerning the degree of its willingness to recognize earnings in one time period and then later have these revenues reversed due to adverse market conditions. One factor in this decision will certainly be the opinion of the firm's accountants as to what constitutes acceptable reporting policy. But management must also decide whether it wishes to account for such potential costs differently for management accounting purposes than for financial accounting purposes. Relevant issues will be how the management accounting impacts decisions on which businesses to expand and contract, the risks of paying bonuses based on assumed profits which may later not be realized, and the incentive given to traders and marketers to pursue business which is probably but not certainly profitable. Once a firm has decided on a degree of risk it is willing to assume, expressed as a probability of having realized gains later reversed, this probability can be translated into a number of standard deviations of potential costs above expected costs.

When a number of standard deviations has been decided on, the process of calculating the potential exposures is a straightforward extension of the calculation of expected expenses for both investing/funding costs and credit costs. However, for dynamic hedging costs, in addition to costs of the bid-asked spread, one must look at the probability of being wrong about the underlying variable being hedged. On a quanto option, for example, one must look at the present value of losses that would occur if actual correlations proved to be different from expected correlations. This would need to rely on some historical analysis of the standard deviation of such values. A particular focus should be the potential dynamic hedging costs of products with discontinuities in payments, such as barrier and digital options, in the event that (possibly low probability) scenarios occur in which they are very sensitive to high volatilities over a short period of time.

One other potential cost factor to consider is model risk: the risk that models used for mark-to-market valuations are incorrectly specified. To the extent that this incorrect specification is simply a matter of different assumptions concerning input variables, such as the expected level of correlation on a quanto trade, this risk has already been considered in the above discussion. But to the extent that models exist which represent alternative probability distributions, any of which can price known liquid instruments correctly but which differ on pricing of nonliquid instruments, an additional potential cost factor exists. An example would be alternative models, one of which assumes normality of interest rate movements and another of which assumes lognormality of interest rates. The actual model that the firm uses may be selected based on which assumption the firm believes is economically more realistic, but it may also be selected primarily because of considerations of computational speed. To the extent feasible, there should be occasional pricings of the portfolio with alternative models, and a calculation of potential cost based on the standard deviation of differences between the model used for valuation and other possible models. A special case concerns any product priced using Monte Carlo simulation, where a potential cost may be calculated based on the standard deviation of the difference between results from a sufficiently large number of sample paths to assure stability (i.e., large enough that results from one randomly selected set of paths are reasonably close to the results from a different randomly selected set of equal size), and results from the number of paths that can be used in daily practice.

Recommendation 4: Identifying Revenue Sources

Dealers should measure the components of revenue regularly and in sufficient detail to understand the sources of risk.

The Group of Thirty study states that "measuring the components of profit helps participants to understand the profitability of various activities over time relative to the risk undertaken, as well as to gain insight into the performance of hedges." A basic justification of using mark-to-market valuation in the management of derivatives is that it will lead to early identification of ineffective hedging strategies, which can in turn trigger experimentation with alternative hedges or changes in the mix of products being offered. This can only happen if an effective and frequent analysis is made of what is causing changes in profit and loss (P&L). In particular:

1. P&L must be segregated by product line to identify which products may be encountering hedging difficulties.

2. P&L must be broken out into that part attributable to newly booked business versus that part due to hedging activity on existing business. This assures that hedging problems will not be masked by the offset of profits from new business. A persistent pattern of profitable new business offset by hedging losses is an indication either that traders have chosen to take positions which (at least temporarily) have had bad results, or that the adjustments made for expected future costs (discussed in the previous section) have been inadequate.

3. To distinguish between these two cases, it is important to identify what portion of hedging profits is due to movements against which risk factors, such as delta, gamma, vega, and theta. In this way, losses stemming from deliberately taken positions can be distinguished from those that arise from risks such as correlation exposure, which the trader cannot hedge. This analysis is also important in confirming that risk positions are reported correctly. If daily P&L swings cannot be accounted for by the reported size of risk positions and the daily changes in market variables, this is a warning that reported risk measurements may be incorrect. This should lead to investigations of whether some transactions have been misrepresented in the reporting systems, or whether additional or more detailed risk measures are required. Particular attention should be paid to unexplained P&L swings that take place around a date on which a payment is made or determined; if a model is not properly valuing a payment which has already been determined or is very close to it, the probability is very high that the trade has been misrepresented.

4. It is extremely important to highlight any P&L changes due to changes in those assumptions that cannot be directly tested against available market prices or changes in models. This eliminates the possibility that P&L due to such changes will mask the results of ineffective hedging strategies.

5. Significant differences between official P&L changes and informal trading desk estimation of these changes should be investigated. Such differences can be an indicator of hedges that are not performing as indicated.

The systems and personnel requirements to perform these analyses are very closely related to those needed to measure market risk (addressed in the discussion of Recommendation 5). Measures of exposure to different market risks need to be combined with a record of how much each model input changes from one day to another.

Recommendation 5: Measuring Market Risk

Dealers should use a consistent measure to calculate daily the market risk of their derivatives positions and compare it to market risk limits.

* *Market risk is best measured as "value at risk" using probability analysis based upon a common confidence interval (e.g., two standard deviations) and time horizon (e.g., a one-day exposure).*

> • *Components of market risk that should be considered across the term structure include: absolute price or rate change (delta); convexity (gamma); volatility (vega); time decay (theta); basis or correlation; and discount rate (rho).*

Controlling the risk of derivatives positions obviously requires the setting of limits on how much the valuation of the portfolio can change with a change in input variables to the mark-to-market models, and a frequent calculation of risk exposures to compare against these limits. The Group of Thirty study mentions a number of input variables for which sensitivity should be measured: the delta exposure to small changes in price levels, the gamma exposure to jumps in price levels, the vega exposure to changes in volatilities, the theta exposure to time decay, the rho exposure to changes in the discount rate, exposure to changes in the basis relationship between two prices, and exposure to changes in correlations. To these can be added exposures that are specific to given products, such as exposure to degree of mean reversion for path-dependent options.

The general technique for measuring all these exposures is simple to describe but may be computationally quite intensive. The most straightforward method is to vary each input variable in turn and to then reprice the portfolio, applying existing models to the new set of input variables. Since this requires a complete revaluation of the portfolio for each variable against which risk is to be computed, the amount of computer resources required for even an overnight run may be substantial. Where possible, faster analytic methods for computing exposures should be developed (though these should always be checked periodically against the slower but less error-prone method of rerunning the models with new inputs), but these analytic methods are often unavailable for Monte Carlo or lattice-type models.

The total number of variables for which the portfolio needs to be revalued is difficult to determine. Finer and finer time slices of variables such as interest rates and volatilities may be considered instead of simple parallel shifts. Since changes in variables often have nonlinear impacts on valuation, it may be necessary to measure the impact for several different magnitudes of shift for a given variable. Variables also frequently have interacting effects. For instance, a shift in price and shift in volatility may have a substantially different impact from the sum of the two effects taken individually. As a result, the movement of variables in pairs, or even triples, may need to be considered. It should be obvious that combining all of these refinements would quickly lead to computational infeasibility as well as a proliferation of risk reporting beyond what any manager could absorb. The only remedy is constant testing of the sensitivity of portfolio valuation to determine which time slices, nonlinear impacts, and variable interactions have large enough effects (relative to probability of occurrence) to require separate risk calculations. Risk reports should also be designed to differ by management level and by frequency. For example, senior managers might only see summary risk numbers on a daily basis and more detailed numbers on a weekly basis while trading desk heads receive the detailed numbers daily and a still more detailed report weekly.

The Group of Thirty report recommends that all risk exposures be reported based on a common denominator, the "value at risk." Value at risk is the loss that will occur from an adverse market move with a specified probability over a specified time horizon. To make all risk reporting comparable, the value at risk should be calculated for the same confidence interval and time horizon for all variables considered, with a time horizon of one day recommended as consistent with a daily mark-to-market policy. The use of value at risk as a common denominator also has the advantage of being compatible with the value at risk system employed by many financial institutions as a common risk measure across all business lines. It is important, however, that managers see both the size of market move being considered as well as the resulting loss, so that they can adjust for their own judgment about the likelihood of market moves.

The manner of calculating value at risk for a given confidence interval requires some care. Some institutions adopt the approach of taking the selected confidence interval, choosing up-and-down moves of prices and volatilities that correspond to this confidence interval, and then measuring the maximum change in valuation corresponding to these up-and-down moves. This approach does not work well either with variables that have nonlinear impacts on valuation or with variables that have interacting effects on one another, as the examples in Exhibits 23–1 and 23–2 illustrate.

Let us assume we are trying to determine value at risk for a two standard deviation confidence interval. In case (1a), a variable with linear impacts on valuation, simply looking at 2 standard deviation movements of the variable up and down is sufficient to determine that the value at risk is $12 million. In case (1b), a variable with nonlinear impacts on valuation, looking at 2 standard deviation moves of the variable up and down would show a 1 million value at risk, which is clearly an understatement.

Exhibit 23–2 shows two possible ways in which variables could have interacting effects. In case (2a), looking at 2 standard deviation movements

EXHIBIT 23–1
Calculating Value at Risk

Case 1a		Case 1b	
Value of variable (standard deviation)	Impact on mark to market (in $ millions)	Value of variable (standard deviation)	Impact on mark to market (in $ millions)
–3	$+18	–3	$+3
–2 1/2	+15	–2 1/2	+1
–2	+12	–2	(1)
–1 1/2	+9	–1 1/2	(3)
–1	+6	–1	(5)
– 1/2	+3	–1/2	(2)
+ 1/2	(3)	+ 1/2	(2)
+1	(6)	+1	(5)
+1 1/2	(9)	+1 1/2	(3)
+2	(12)	+2	(1)
+2 1/2	(15)	+2 1/2	+1
+3	(18)	+3	+3

of both variables up and down would result in a value at risk of $24 million. This would probably be an overstatement of the value at risk, since this large a loss could only occur with both variables moving down by two standard deviations. Unless these variables are highly correlated, this is an extremely unlikely event. On the other hand, in case (2*b*), looking at two standard deviation movements of both variables up and down would result in a value at risk of $8 million. This is probably an understatement of the value at risk, since larger losses can occur with a minus 2 standard deviation move of variable 1 and the current value of variable 2.

Accurate calculation of value at risk for such variables requires more detailed calculation of probabilities of valuations over a range of simulated values, possibly making use of Monte Carlo techniques. Some risk managers feel uncomfortable with this approach as opposed to a measurement of maximum change in valuation, because it appears to depend on using an exact value for the correlation between two variables and this value may be wrong. This objection may be overcome by treating the correlation as a random variable with a probability distribution of its own, and including this in the probability calculation of the valuation.

EXHIBIT 23–2
Interacting Effects of Variables

Case 2a

Value of Variable 2 (standard deviation)	Value of Variable 1						
	−3 Standard Deviation	-2 Standard Deviation	-1 Standard Deviation	Current Value	+1 Standard Deviation	+2 Standard Deviation	+3 Standard Deviation
-3	(51MM)	(31MM)	(11MM)	+9MM	+29MM	+49MM	+69MM
-2	(39MM)	(24MM)	(9MM)	+6MM	+21MM	+36MM	+51MM
-1	(27MM)	(17MM)	(7MM)	+3MM	+13MM	+23MM	+33MM
Current value	(15MM)	(10MM)	(5MM)	0	+5MM	+10MM	+15MM
+1	(12MM)	(9MM)	(6MM)	(3MM)	0	+3MM	+6MM
+2	(12MM)	(10MM)	(8MM)	(6MM)	(4MM)	(2MM)	0
+3	(12MM)	(11MM)	(10MM)	(9MM)	(8MM)	(7MM)	(6MM)

Case 2b

Value of Variable 2 (standard deviation)	Value of Variable 1						
	−3 Standard Deviation	-2 Standard Deviation	−1 Standard Deviation	Current Value	+1 Standard Deviation	+2 Standard Deviation	+3 Standard Deviation
−3	+6MM	+7MM	+8MM	+9MM	+10MM	+11MM	+12MM
−2	0	+2MM	+4MM	+6MM	+8MM	+10MM	+12MM
−1	(27MM)	(17MM)	(7MM)	+3MM	+13MM	+23MM	+33MM
Current value	(15MM)	(10MM)	(5MM)	0	+5MM	+10MM	+15MM
+1	(12MM)	(9MM)	(6MM)	(3MM)	0	+3MM	+6MM
+2	(10MM)	(8MM)	(7MM)	(6MM)	(5M)	(4MM)	(3MM)
+3	(6MM)	(7MM)	(8MM)	(9MM)	(10MM)	(11MM)	(12MM)

The source of probability distributions of variables that go into these simulations should be selected by the firm based on historical analysis or projections. Considerations affecting the selection of a method are similar to those discussed in the section on marking to market (Recommendation 2).

One exception which should be made to the recommendation of measuring all risks across a common time horizon of one day is the measurement of the gamma risk of price jumps. Since this is a risk only to the extent that jumps take place too quickly for dynamic rehedging to be done, it can properly be measured only over the minimum time horizon in which dynamic rehedging can be accomplished in a particular market, whether this turns out to be less than or greater than one day. There also can be a general argument for using a time horizon longer than one day as a common denominator, since even though marks to market may be reported on a daily basis, the realistic reaction time for management to analyze the changes in valuation and instruct a trader to alter a position may be considerably longer.

In addition to overnight measurements, market risk should be updated throughout the day. For any sizable book, this will require systems that calculate risk for new transactions only and then use these to update the previously measured overnight risk.

Recommendation 6: Stress Simulations

Dealers should regularly perform simulations to determine how their portfolios would perform under stress conditions.

While the analysis discussed in measuring market risk (Recommendation 5) gives a good idea of what the value at risk is over a large percent of market conditions, it cannot assess the maximum degree of losses that could be possible in extremely unlikely circumstances. While it might appear that these techniques could just be extended by raising the confidence level to a very high probability close to 100 percent, the value at risk approach almost certainly breaks down under such circumstances. First, almost all financial markets have historically shown a tendency to have rare violent moves on the order of 5 to 10 standard deviations or even more (see Exhibit 23–3, which compares the largest daily change over the period 1986 to 1994 with the standard deviation of daily changes over that period for a number of key economic variables; the analysis is also shown with the period of extraordinarily large changes during the fourth quarter of 1987 excluded). Such events are so rare and so large that statistical models do not throw much light on them. Second, during these violent fluctuations historical relationships between variables break down, and otherwise uncorrelated or negatively correlated markets may show close to perfect correlation. Third, under such circumstances normal market liquidity may disappear, invali-

EXHIBIT 23-3
Largest Daily Change and Standard Deviation of Key Economic Variables, 1986–1984

Index	1986–1994				Excluding 4th Quarter 1987			
	Standard Deviation	*Largest Change*	*Date*	*Number of Standard Deviations*	*Largest Change*	*Date*	*Number of Standard Deviations*	
U.S. equities (S&P 500)	1.03%	−22.90%	10/19/87	22.3	−7.01%	1/8/88	6.8	
U.K. equities (FTSE 100)	1.00	−13.03	10/20/87	13.0	5.44	4/10/92	5.4	
German equities (FAZ)	1.23	−14.32	10/16/89	11.6	−14.32	10/16/89	11.6	
Japanese equities (Nikkei)	1.37	−16.14	10/20/87	11.8	12.43	10/2/90	9.1	
U.S. 3M LIBOR	1.31	−10.69	10/20/87	8.2	−9.35	10/6/93	7.1	
U.S. long bond yield	0.76	−9.46	10/19/87	12.4	7.32	4/23/86	6.4	
U.K. 10-year bond yield	0.80	−6.17	4/10/92	7.7	−6.17	4/10/92	7.7	
German 10-year bond yield	0.74	−7.40	10/20/87	10.0	4.64	3/2/94	6.3	
Sterling/$ exchange rate	0.68	−3.29	9/16/92	4.9	−3.29	9/16/92	4.9	
DM/$ exchange rate	0.70	3.10	8/19/91	4.4	3.10	8/19/91	4.4	
Yen/$ exchange rate	0.65	−3.39	1/21/92	5.2	−3.39	1/21/92	5.2	
Gold price index	2.11	−20.03	10/20/87	9.5	−9.88	9/7/93	4.7	
Energy price index	1.78	−26.06	1/17/91	14.7	−26.06	1/17/91	14.7	

Source: DRI

dating the assumptions used when calculating close-out cost adjustments to valuation.

Despite these difficulties, it is important that a firm make some assessment of maximum loss to learn whether it has sufficient capital to cover the risks of an existing or planned level of participation in a market. With little guidance from statistical models, a firm must rely on its economists to produce scenarios of unlikely events to stress test its positions. Scenarios should be formulated with some consideration of the magnitude of past violent market moves, but also to draw on economic insights into what might be the degree of future movements under unlikely but still possible combinations of events. A scenario must also specify assumptions about the impact of unusual conditions on the frequency with which dynamic rehedging can be accomplished, which will have an impact on the measurement of gamma exposure. Once a set of scenarios has been specified, calculations of the impact on valuation are relatively straightforward using existing valuation models.

Recommendation 7: Investing and Funding Forecasts

Dealers should periodically forecast the cash investing and funding requirements arising from their derivatives portfolios.

Portfolios of derivatives can have reasonably large volumes of near-term cash flows that are known in advance, given the lags of three to six months often built in between the time payment sizes are calculated and when actual payments occur. Other near-term payments that are not yet set can still be projected to a fairly good degree of accuracy with the use of a probability range of future index values. Relatively straightforward computations can then be used to project funding surpluses or shortfalls by day and by currency. This information can be extremely useful to the firm's treasury function in developing strategies to minimize funding costs and to maximize investment returns.

Recommendation 8: Independent Market Risk Management

Dealers should have a market risk management function, with clear independence and authority, to ensure that the following responsibilities are carried out:

- *The development of risk limit policies and the monitoring of transactions and positions for adherence to these policies. (See Recommendation 4.)*
- *The design of stress scenarios to measure the impact of market conditions, however improbable, that might cause market gaps, volatility swings, or disruptions of major relationships, or might reduce liquidity in the face of unfavorable market linkages, concentrated market making, or credit exhaustion. (See Recommendation 5.)*
- *The design of revenue reports quantifying the contribution of various risk components, and of market risk measures such as value at risk. (See Recommendations 3 and 4.)*
- *The monitoring of variance between the actual volatility of portfolio value and that predicted by the measure of market risk.*
- *The review and approval of pricing models and valuation systems used by front- and back-office personnel, and the development of reconciliation procedures if different systems are used.*

This recommendation has a bearing on all of the other recommendations in the Group of Thirty report. In all of the areas of marking to market, market valuation methods, profit and loss component analysis, measurement of market risk, stress simulation, and investing and funding forecasts, it is important that management have access to experienced personnel whose reporting lines are independent of the trading desk and whose compensation is independent of trading desk performance. While the staff of the market risk management function cannot be expected to have the depth of understanding of individual markets, products, and models needed for the live trading functions, they should have sufficient understanding to be able to perform an independent check on the reasonableness and consistency of model assumptions. In addition to a formal role in approving models, designing stress scenarios, and monitoring risk limits and revenue explanations, this staff should also perform an informal role in encouraging a meaningful dialogue concerning risk and revenue between traders and senior managers.

Recommendation 16: Professional Expertise

Dealers and end-users must ensure that their derivatives activities are undertaken by professionals in sufficient number and with the appropriate experience, skill levels, and degrees of specialization. These professionals include specialists who transact and manage the risks involved, their supervisors, and those responsible for processing, reporting, controlling, and auditing the activities.

Recommendation 17: Systems

Dealers and end-users must ensure that adequate systems for data capture, processing, settlement, and management reporting are in place so that derivatives transactions are conducted in an orderly and efficient manner in compliance with management policies. Dealers should have risk management systems that measure the risks incurred in their derivatives activities, including market and credit risks. End-users should have risk management systems that measure the risks incurred in their derivatives activities based upon their nature, size, and complexity.

Historically, some of the largest losses in derivatives trading have resulted not from the uncertainties in models and assumptions used to measure the risk of positions, but from the inaccurate recording of the positions themselves. In some cases, this inaccuracy has been the result of oversights, in other cases the deliberate falsification of positions by traders. To guard against this it is necessary to ensure that:

1. Operational staff adequate in numbers and experience is assigned to the task of recording transactions and keeping these records up-to-date as events such as resets, unwinds, knockouts, options exercises, and amortizations take place. Staff levels should be sufficient to allow review of all input by an individual other than the one who prepared the input.

2. Systems that are capable of aggregating transactional positions into portfolio statistics must be developed and maintained. Constant monitoring of systems performance for possible errors is a necessity.

3. Operations and systems must be designed so that they are independent of the trading function. Operational staff need to be independent of the trading desk in reporting lines and compensation. Systems security needs to ensure that traders have no access to the records or programs used by the operations staff. The operations staff must produce the official mark to market, risk reports against limits, and earnings analyses. Safeguards in the form of cross-checks with customer confirmations, payments, and

collateral posting need to be designed to ensure that no trades are accidentally or deliberately hidden from the operations staff.

4. Operations staff needs to have independent access to all market information used in marking positions to market. In some cases this will be easy because prices come from exchange or publicly available screens. In other cases, the operations staff must be able to independently poll brokers or other market makers at selected intervals.

5. A review process prior to the introduction of new products is required to ensure that adequate operations and systems resources and procedures are in place.

Continuous vigilance is a necessity in this area. Any firm for which derivatives trading is a core business will always have the pace of product innovation run ahead of the slower tempo with which systems can be developed. As a result, some transactions will always have to be represented somewhat inaccurately for a time while systems personnel work to catch up to new developments. These transactions require constant attention from operations personnel to ensure that their representation remains reasonably accurate through time.

CONCLUSION

Managing the market risk of derivative products is a complex task due to the long-term hedging strategies that are required to support some derivatives. Firms engaging in this business must be prepared to make an ongoing commitment to employing the right level of expertise and to creating well-designed controls and procedures. The experience of firms which have made this commitment shows that with the proper policies, as reflected in the recommendations of the Group of Thirty, this risk can be managed successfully.

Chapter Twenty-Four

Interest Rate Risk Management: The Risk Point Method*

Ravi E. Dattatreya
Sumitomo Bank Capital Markets, Inc.

Raj S. Pundarika
Debt and Derivatives Marketer, Paribas Capital Markets

Institutions—that is, investors as lenders and corporations as borrowers—assume various types of financial risk. These include liquidity risk, credit risk, currency and interest rate risk, and option or convexity risk. In this chapter we will focus on interest rate risk. In addition, we will show how the concepts developed apply to many other types of risks.

It is important to view interest rate risk as an integral part of a comprehensive risk management program.[1] Risk management can be defined as a systematic approach that attempts to provide a degree of protection to the institution from risk and makes such risk acceptable. Any complete interest rate risk management program, therefore, should provide the necessary

---

* Adapted from *Advanced Interest Rate and Currency Swaps*, ed. Ravi E. Dattatreya and Kensuke Hotta (Burr Ridge, Ill.: Irwin Professional Publishing, 1994), pp. 219–45.

1 Risk management is known as asset liability management (ALM) in many contexts.

framework for the implementation of the Four Ms of risk management: measurement, monitoring, modification, and management.

Measurement defines exactly what types of risks will be managed under the program. For each risk, the appropriate risk measures and acceptable procedures for measurement are defined.

Monitoring sets forth the mechanics of locating which parts of the institution are sources of different forms and quantities of risk and the frequency with which these risks will be measured and reviewed. It puts in place the necessary systems and procedures to ensure that the information can be obtained when desired.

Modification provides the risk manager with the tools necessary to modify any particular risk to desired levels. For example, here is where we determine whether futures or swaps are appropriate instruments for the institution and the limits on quantities and purposes for which these will be used. In actual use, optimization by the risk manager (i.e., selection of tools and quantity) is also done here.

Management is the collection of policies and procedures for the exercise of the other three Ms. Here we define the upper and lower[2] bounds for each risk category as well as the conditions under which an action will be required to initiate the modification step. In addition to routine policy, this part of risk management includes some emergency powers for the risk manager and guidelines as to how and when these powers can be used. As an example, the emergency powers could include relaxation of the limits on the tools or amounts that can be employed.

In a way, we can compare risk management to a form of insurance. It can shield the institution from risk where its assumption is necessary. For example, in the absence of automobile insurance, we would probably find the risks of driving a car unacceptable. It is insurance that makes it possible for us to drive. The main function of risk management is similar: to enable the institution to be in business, that is, to assume the necessary risks. For example, it facilitates a bank to make long-term loans that are in demand

---

2 The goal of risk management is not risk elimination. Lower bounds for risk are required as risk and reward are interrelated. In most cases, risk cannot be eliminated, only transformed. This fact was realized best by corporations that issued (or converted via interest rate swaps to) fixed-rate debt just before the long rally in the bond market in the early 1990s. Even though these corporations had fixed-rate debt, which is considered a no-risk situation in most cases, they soon realized the risk in fixing as the market rates plummeted and they found themselves paying higher than market coupons on their debt or on interest rate swaps. One way to look at this situation is to consider both fixed rate and floating rate as risky: the former when rates fall, the latter when rates rise. For more discussion of this topic, see Ravi E. Dattatreya, Raj E. Venkatesh, and Vijaya E. Venkatesh, *Interest Rate and Currency Swaps*, (Burr Ridge, Ill.: Irwin Professional Publishing, 1994).

regardless of the availability of long-term funding for the loan, by providing acceptable techniques to hedge the resultant interest rate risk. It enables a multinational corporation to engage in business overseas, shielding the firm from changes in exchange rates. In general, the more leveraged an institution, the more critical risk management is to that institution because its net worth then is a small fraction of the size of its assets, and even modest market moves can result in wide swings in the net worth. Risk management is simply the process of preservation of net worth.

The function of risk management is not only protection from risk. The safety achieved through it also opens up opportunities for enhancing the net worth. An effective risk management program can make it possible for an institution to take on positions that would have been considered too large or too risky in the absence of the protection offered by risk management. Such a program can also enable an institution to enter into new business areas as the demands of the marketplace change and grow. In many cases these businesses would have been beyond the reach of the institution without the comfort of the insurance provided by risk management.

Every manager has two fundamental priorities. The first priority is to protect and preserve the existing business or investment and provide damage control.[3] The second priority is to enhance the returns, strengthen the business, and enrich the institution. Risk management, as discussed above, can be a vital ally to the manager in fulfilling these two needs.

There are several types of financial risk. These include interest rate risk, currency risk, credit risk, liquidity risk, and option or convexity risk. Among these risks, some (e.g., interest rate risk and option risk) fall neatly within the risk management framework, mainly because it is possible to quantify the risks easily and appropriate hedging vehicles are available. Any acceptable risk management policy will also help measure and monitor liquidity risk and provide suitable strategies for its management. Other risks are more complex to manage. Consider credit risk. It is difficult to manage it in the traditional sense. It is best controlled by limiting it before it is assumed.

The focus of our attention in this chapter will be the quantifiable risks, in particular, interest rate risk. As a consequence, we will be dealing mainly with risks associated with fixed-income assets and liabilities.

---

3 Damage control is the frequent use of emergency powers by the risk manager.

MEASURES OF INTEREST RATE RISK

As a first step in developing a framework for risk management, we have to define interest rate risk and determine an acceptable way to measure it.[4] Let us briefly review the basic definitions.

Interest Rate Risk

We measure interest rate risk by considering *price sensitivity,* that is, the change in the value of an asset or liability cash flow in response to a change in interest rates. More precisely, price sensitivity is expressed as the dollar change (or, some times, a percentage change) in value for a unit change in interest rates. This unit is most often one basis point or 100 basis points.

Different fixed-income instruments have different levels of interest rate risk. Various risk measures are available, each with its own advantages and problems.

Maturity

The term to maturity is an indicator of interest rate risk. Longer maturity bonds usually move more in price than shorter maturity bonds. However, this ordering does not always hold. Maturity takes into account only the timing of the final principal flow in a fixed-rate bond and ignores other important information such as the size and timing of other cash flows. The actual interest rate sensitivity depends on these factors; therefore, maturity, though sometimes useful, is only an approximate indicator of risk. Maturity is also not a cardinal measure, that is, it does not *quantify* risk.

Duration

It is possible to blend information contained in the size and timing of all cash flows into one number, called *duration,* that can be a more useful measure of risk. Duration is the weighted average time of all of the cash flows, the weights being the present values of the cash flows. For bonds with only one cash flow (e.g., zero-coupon bonds and money market

---

4 For a thorough discussion of interest rate risk measures and convexity, see Ravi E. Dattatreya and Frank J. Fabozzi, *Fixed Income Total Return Management,* 2d ed.(Burr Ridge, Ill.: Irwin Professional Publishing, 1994).

instruments), duration is equal to maturity. For others, duration will be shorter than maturity.

It turns out that by slightly adjusting duration by dividing by a factor $(1 + Y)$ where Y is the annual yield to maturity of the bond in decimal form, we get *modified duration* which is exactly equal to the price sensitivity of the bond as we have defined above. Since the adjustment factor is very close to one, duration and modified duration can be used interchangeably in most situations. This is also justified because duration is an approximate measure anyway. By this reasoning, we diligently avoid the common temptation to dwell on the (inconsequential) difference between the two durations.

We can also think of duration of a security as the maturity of a zero-coupon bond of equal price sensitivity.[5] This definition is a more general one in that it can be used with more complex securities such as options and with leveraged positions. For example, if the duration of an option is 150, it simply means that the price sensitivity of the option is equal to that of a zero-coupon bond of maturity equal to 150 years. Some instruments (e.g., options) can have negative duration, which can be represented by short positions in zero-coupon bonds.

Dollar Duration

Duration represents the *percentage* change in value in response to a change in rates. By weighting duration by the value of a holding, that is, by multiplying the market value of a holding by its duration (expressed as a decimal percentage), we get dollar-weighted duration. Known as *dollar duration,* this number represents the actual dollar change in the market value of a holding in a bond in response to a 100 basis point change in rates. When expressed as a dollar change per one basis point move in rates, dollar duration is sometimes called the *price value of a basis point,* or *PVBP*. Other than the factor of 100, there is little difference between dollar duration and *PVBP*.

The major advantage of using dollar duration is that it is additive. The concept therefore extends easily from individual securities to portfolios. The dollar duration of a portfolio is simply the (algebraic) sum of the dollar durations of the individual holdings.

---

5 We choose zero-coupon bonds for this comparison since these bonds, unlike coupon-bearing bonds, can have durations of arbitrary magnitude. In other words, there is a limit on how large the duration of a coupon bond can be; zero-coupon bonds have no such limit.

Convexity

Duration (or dollar duration) is not a constant. It changes as a result of changes in market rates and because of the passage of time. For simple fixed-coupon bonds, the dollar duration increases when the rates fall. That is, as the market rallies (i.e., as rates fall), for each successive basis point move down, the bond price increases at an increasing rate. Similarly, if rates increase and the market declines, the rate of decline slows down as the rates rise. This property is called *convexity*. It is a desirable property in an asset since the price sensitivity changes in a way beneficial to the holder of the asset.

There are certain securities with optionlike features such as callable corporate bonds and mortgage-backed securities[6] that show a contrary behavior: Their duration can fall in rallying markets and increase in falling markets. This property, called *negative convexity*, is not a desirable property in an asset unless suitably compensated, because the price sensitivity moves in a way not beneficial to the holder.

In most situations, convexity is a second order effect, that is, its influence on the price behavior of a bond is small compared with that of duration. However, for large moves in market rates, for highly leveraged positions, and where optionlike features are involved, convexity can be important.

YIELD CURVE RISK

Several years of use of the duration concept has enabled most financial institutions to all but eliminate market risk by means of prudent hedging activities. As a result, other residual risks have gained prominence, some of which can be dominant in many situations; among them, the most important is *yield curve risk,* which deserves a detailed treatment. In particular, yield curve risk can be significant in portfolios containing options, some mortgage derivatives, and most exotic securities.

As usually stated, duration of a fixed-income asset (or liability) is the price sensitivity relative to its own yield. Therefore, when we use duration for hedging purposes, we are implicitly assuming that the yield levels of the various assets and liabilities move in parallel (i.e., equal) amounts. How-

---

6 Most of the exotic securities in the current crop have negative convexity. To compensate the investor for this, they offer attractive, relatively higher current yields.

ever, different credit, coupon, or maturity sectors of the market move differently in terms of their yield. This difference is known as the *basis risk* among the sectors. Basis risk with respect to different maturity sectors is also known as *yield curve risk* and represents changes in the yield curve that are not parallel shifts. These include the so-called reshaping shifts (e.g., twists, pivoting moves, steepening, and flattening).

In general, basis risk is difficult to measure and hedge.[7] Most hedging vehicles address market risk,[8] (e.g., changes in the Treasury rates), not basis risk. It is possible to take the view that only market risk is hedgeable and treat basis risk as a prudent business risk that an institution has to take. This is the only approach in dealing with certain types of basis risk (e.g., credit risk).[9]

A risk measure can be considered more complete when compared with a simple measure such as duration if we can incorporate some of the important basis risks. Fortunately, it is possible to address yield curve risk in many acceptable ways. By necessity, such a broader risk measure will be more than just one number.

One method is to divide assets and liabilities into smaller maturity baskets and analyze each basket separately. If each basket covers a sufficiently small maturity range, then we can assume that the yield curve risk is acceptably small within that range. In a hedging application, we would use hedging instruments suitable for that maturity range to match dollar durations. In an asset/liability context, if each basket or sector is matched using appropriate hedges as required, then the assets and liabilities are matched as a whole because of the additive property of dollar duration. To the extent that the yields of all assets and liabilities and the hedging instruments used within a sector move in step, this approach is satisfactory.

There is a problem, however. It turns out that an asset of a given maturity might react to changes in rates in another maturity. Consider, for example, a 10-year bond with a coupon of 10 percent. The cash flow from this bond occurs every six months throughout its life. Since the value of a

---

7 In practice, basis risk refers to any risk that is not hedgeable or is not hedged. If a risk can be quantified and acceptably managed (e.g., yield curve risk in our case), then that risk is no longer a part of the generic basis risk.

8 This makes sense because a hedging instrument, to ensure its wide usage, should represent the broad market rather than a specific security or too narrow a sector. Otherwise, it would suffer a severe lack of liquidity, and the cost of hedging would be unacceptably high.

9 Derivative instruments for managing certain types of credit risk are being developed.

bond is simply the sum of the present values of the individual cash flows, the value of the 10-year bond could be influenced by rate changes not only in the 10-year maturity but also in all shorter maturities representing the cash flows.

In this context, it is appropriate to clarify what we mean by a "rate." In fixed-income analysis, we use two types of reference interest rates: full coupon rates and spot or zero-coupon rates. Full coupon rates are analogous to the yield to maturity on bonds trading at or close to par (e.g., the yield on an on-the-run (current coupon) Treasury). The spot rate for a given maturity, on the other hand, is the yield on a zero-coupon bond with that maturity. When dealing with individual cash flows (e.g., for discounting), it is appropriate to use spot rates; when dealing with bonds trading near par, a full-coupon rate can be used.

Since a bond is simply a collection of cash flows, its yield is a complex blend of the individual spot rates corresponding to the coupon and principal flows. Given the spot rate curve, we can easily determine the coupon yield curve. Conversely, a given spot rate is a complex blend of all shorter-maturity coupon rates. Given the coupon rate curve, we can determine the spot rate curve. In summary, a given spot rate depends on all intermediate coupon rates; a given coupon rate depends upon all intermediate spot rates.

The value of a 10-year par bond, then, responds to all intermediate spot rates, but depends only on the 10-year coupon rate. Thus, to hedge a 10-year par bond, all that we need is another 10-year bond (e.g., the current 10-year Treasury). If we wish to use zero-coupon bonds for hedging, then a 10-year zero-coupon bond and smaller amounts of all intermediate maturity zero-coupon bonds will be required for hedging. Similarly, a single cash flow occurring in the 10th year can be efficiently hedged by a 10-year zero-coupon bond. On the other hand, if we wish to use current coupon Treasuries for hedging. We will also need shorter-maturity Treasuries in addition to the 10-year Treasury.

If the bond we are hedging is not priced at par, then it behaves like the combination of a 10-year full-coupon bond and a 10-year zero-coupon bond. For example, a $100 million holding of a 9 percent bond selling at 90 can be viewed as the sum of $90 million of a 10 percent par bond and $10 million of a zero-coupon bond.[10] Thus the sensitivity of the 10-year discount bond is the sum of that of each of its components. The hedge for a bond not

---

10 In both cases, there is an annual cash flow of $9 million and a payment at maturity of $100 million.

near par, therefore, is a blend of the hedges for a zero and that for a full coupon bond.[11]

In summary, an asset (or a liability) of a given maturity might respond to spot or coupon rate changes in other shorter maturities. Therefore, we need to do more than simply group the assets and liabilities in maturity sectors.

One way to handle this problem is to first break down each asset and liability into its cash flow components. Then the individual cash flows can be grouped into maturity buckets. Now, the price sensitivity of each sector is more clearly defined, at least with respect to spot rates corresponding to each sector.

The cash flow approach provides very valuable insight into the relative natures of the assets and the liabilities. However, it represents risk in terms of the spot rate, that is, in terms of zero-coupon bonds, which are rarely used for hedging. A more sophisticated approach is the *risk point method*, discussed in the next section.[12]

TOWARD A MORE COMPLETE RISK MEASURE: THE RISK POINT CONCEPT

Since risk is a measure of change in value, it stands to reason that risk management and security valuation ought to be closely related. Therefore, it is advantageous to use a model that integrates these two aspects. The

---

11 Similarly, a 10-year premium bond can be decomposed into a slightly larger amount of a par bond and a short position on the zero-coupon bond.

12 Other approaches are available in literature. See, for example, D. Chambers and W. Carleton, "A Generalized Approach to Duration," in *Research in Finance,* vol. 7 (Greenwich, Conn.: JAI Press, 1988); Thomas S. Y. Ho, "Key Rate Durations: Measures of Interest Rate Risks," *Journal of Fixed Income,* September 1992; C. Khang, "Bond Immunization When Short-term Rates Fluctuate More Than Long-term Rates," *Journal of Financial and Quantitative Analysis* 14 (1979), pp. 1085–90; R. Litterman and J. Scheinkman, "Common Factors Affecting Bond Returns," *Journal of Fixed Income,* June 1991, pp. 54–61; Robert Reitano, "Non-Parallel Yield Curve Shifts and Durational Leverage," *Journal of Portfolio Management,* Summer 1990, pp. 62–67.

The discussion of the risk point concept here builds on the work reported in Ravi E. Dattatreya, "A Practical Approach to Asset Liability Management," Sumitomo Bank Capital Markets Report, 1989; Ravi E. Dattatreya, "A Practical Approach to Asset Liability Management," in F. Fabozzi and Atsuo Konishi, *Asset Liability Management,* (Chicago: Probus Publishing, 1991); and Ravi E. Dattatreya, Raj E. Venkatesh, and Vijaya E. Venkatesh, *Interest Rate and Currency Swaps,* (Burr Ridge, Ill.: Irwin Professional Publishing, 1994). See also: Ravi E. Dattatreya and Frank Fabozzi, *Fixed Income Active Total Return Management,* rev. ed., (Burr Ridge, Ill.: Irwin Professional Publishing, 1994); and Ravi E. Dattatreya and Scott Peng, *Structured Notes,* (Burr Ridge, Ill.: Irwin Professional Publishing, 1994).

risk point method attempts such integration. It also has the practical advantage that it measures risk relative to available hedging instruments.

We define the *risk point* of a security or portfolio with reference to a specific hedge instrument. For this reason, it can also be called *relative dollar duration*.[13] It represents the change in the value of the security or portfolio due to a one basis point change in the yield of the hedge. If we divide the risk point by the dollar duration or *PVBP* of the hedge, we get the dollar amount of the hedge instrument to be used as a hedge. This hedge amount will protect the portfolio against risk from small changes in the market sector represented by the hedge instrument.[14]

Unlike *PVBP* or dollar duration, which measures the *total* interest rate risk, the risk point measures only one component of the total risk. This component represents the risk due to a change in rates in a given maturity sector. Thus, to determine a complete risk or hedge, we need a full set of risk points relative to a set of hedge instruments. From this set of risk points we can determine the portfolio of hedge instruments that will hedge a given portfolio.

The risk point method consists of three main steps.

1. List the hedge vehicles that we are willing to use.

2. Apply a model that values the assets and liabilities relative to the prices of the hedge vehicles.

3. Change the yield or price of one of the hedge instruments by a small amount, keeping all other yields and prices the same. With the new yield, we revalue the portfolio. The change in its value (expressed as dollars per one basis point[15] change) is the risk point of the portfolio. We get the amount of the hedge instrument needed for hedging by simply equating the PVBP of the hedge to the risk point of the portfolio.[16]

---

13 We prefer, however, the former terminology. In the context of modern financial markets, the temporal meaning of duration is no longer relevant.

14 In defining the framework for risk measurement, we focus more on hedge instruments than on specific market segments or yield curve sectors because it is of little use to look at risk for which there is no tool for hedging or management. In addition, there is no loss of generality in our approach because almost all major sectors that are sources of risk are well represented by hedge instruments.

15 One basis point could refer to another appropriate small unit (e.g., 1 tick for Eurodollar futures, 1 percent for volatility in the case of options, etc.).

16 It is also possible to express the risk point as a hedge equivalent (i.e., the actual amount of the hedge required). The vector of risk points, would simply be the hedging portfolio. Representation of the risk point as a relative dollar duration has the advantage that alternative hedge instruments can be easily substituted.

This procedure is explained more fully in the next section.

AN IMPLEMENTATION
OF THE RISK POINT METHOD

The essential part of the risk point method is a model that values the assets and liabilities relative to the hedge instruments chosen. To be able to deal with a variety of assets and liabilities, the set of hedges chosen must also be broad. An example of a practical implementation of the method follows.

Hedge Instruments

For our example, we include all the current-coupon Treasury bonds and notes in the set of hedge instruments that we consider. T-bills are included to handle cash flows occurring in the short term.

Valuation Model

We will use a simple but effective valuation model. The procedure will be to value each financial instrument as the sum of the discounted present values of the cash flows generated by the instrument. We must first determine the *discount function,* that is, all the discount factors that will be used for this procedure. This is a two-step process.

In the first step, to obtain appropriate spreads to evaluate cash flows from corporate bonds, we include spreads from the interest rate swap market.[17] The composite rate (i.e., the sum of the Treasury yield and the spread), is called the *par bond yield* (see Exhibit 24–1).[18] It represents the yield on par bonds of the credit quality represented by the spreads used. We then use

---

17 By setting the spreads to zero, we can use the results to the Treasury market. Spreads from other markets (e.g., single-A corporate bonds) can be used if necessary.

18 The Treasury yields and swap spread used are obtained from market data as of 3.00 P.M. New York time on May 9, 1994. Each data point is represented on a semi-annual pay, 30/360 basis. Note that the familiar seven-year Treasury is absent because they are no longer planned to be issued.

Note that, it is possible to use LIBOR, in the short end, to determine the composite rate directly. In this case, care should be taken to ensure that the day count conventions are handled correctly.

EXHIBIT 24–1
The Hedging Instruments with Yields

Maturity (years)	Treasury Yield (percent)	Spread (basis points)	Total (percent)
0.5	4.932	28 bp	5.212
1.0	5.520	29	5.810
2.0	6.234	31	6.544
3.0	6.563	35	6.913
5.0	7.074	32	7.394
10.0	7.466	41	7.876

linear interpolation[19] to generate the *par curve*, that is, par bond yields at all maturities (see column 3, Exhibit 24–2).

The second step is to determine the zero curve, or, equivalently, the discount factors, from the par curve. Discount factors can be derived sequentially from the par curve one after another. This process is called *bootstrapping*. This procedure builds the zero curve in a step-by-step or inductive manner. For each maturity, it uses the fact that the price of a bond is the sum of the present values of all the cash flows (coupon and principal) from the bond. It is best illustrated using algebraic notation.

Suppose we have already determined the first n semiannual discount factors, $f_1, f_2, ..., f_n$. Then the discount factor for the next period, $f_{(n+1)}$, is determined using the following relationship:

$$1 = c \times f_1 + c \times f_2 + ... + c \times f_n + (1 + c) \times f_{(n+1)}$$

where the left-hand side, 1, represents the price of par, c is the semiannual coupon payment (one-half of the par rate), and $(1 + c)$ represents the final payment with principal and interest for a par bond maturing at the end of the $(n + 1)$th period. Each of the factors of the form $(c \times f_1)$ represents the present value of a cash flow. The relationship simply says that the sum of the present values of all cash flows is equal to the price of the bond. The required discount factor, $f_{(n+1)}$, is therefore given by:

---

19 We could use more sophisticated interpolation. However, linear interpolation gives acceptable results and is used widely in the interest rate swap market.

EXHIBIT 24–2
Bootstrapping: Getting the Zero Curve from the Par Curve

Maturity (years)	Par Yields (percent)	Interpolated Par Yields	Discount Factor	Cumulative Factor	Zero Rates
0.5	5.212%	5.212000	0.974602	0.974602	5.212000
1.0	5.810	5.810000	0.944257	1.918859	5.818712
1.5		6.177000	0.912552	2.831411	6.194689
2.0	6.544	6 .544000	0.878608	3.710019	6.576629
2.5		6.728500	0.846701	4.556720	6.768333
3.0	6.913	6.913000	0.814349	5.371069	6.964043
3.5		7.033250	0.783565	6.154633	7.091448
4.0		7.153500	0.752934	6.907567	7.221785
4.5		7.273750	0.722504	7.630071	7.354956
5.0	7.394	7.394000	0.692321	8.322392	7.490986
5.5		7.442200	0.665550	8.987942	7.541282
6.0		7.490400	0.639435	9.627377	7.593429
6.5		7.538600	0.613973	10.241350	7.647266
7.0		7.586800	0.589156	10.830505	7.702698
7.5		7.635000	0.564977	11.395483	7.759674
8.0		7.683200	0.541431	11.936914	7.818175
8.5		7.731400	0.518511	12.455425	7.878204
9.0		7.779600	0.496207	12.951632	7.939786
9.5		7.827800	0.474514	13.426147	8.002961
10.0	7.876	7.876000	0.453423	13.879569	8.067783

$$f_{(n+1)} = \frac{[1 - (c \times f_1 + c \times f_2 + \ldots + c \times f_n)]}{(1 + c)}$$

Or

$$f_{(n+1)} = \frac{[1 - c \times (f_1 + f_2 + \ldots + f_n)]}{(1 + c)}$$

Thus, given the par curve, if we know the first discount factor, we can compute all other discount factors sequentially. The first discount factor is easy to determine since the six-month par rate is also a six-month zero rate because a six-month (semiannual) bond has only one cash flow.

From the discount factors, it is easy to compute the zero rates. The nth zero rate, z_n, is related to the nth discount factor, f_n, via the relationship:

$$f_n \times \left(1 + \frac{z_n}{2}\right)^n = 1$$

assuming semiannual compounding. The interpolated par curve (column 3), the discount function (column 4), and the zero rates (column 6) are all shown in Exhibit 24–2.[20]

Once the discount function or the spot rate curve is known, the value of any security is simply the sum of the present values of its cash flows, discounted at the appropriate spot rate. This is shown in Exhibit 24–3 for a 10-year bond with a coupon of 10 percent. Each present value (column 5) is simply the product of the cash flow (column 4) and the corresponding discount factor (column 2). The total *PV*, 114.740102, is the value of the bond.

Determination of Risk Points

To determine the risk point corresponding to a given hedge, the following steps are taken: First, the yield on the hedge instrument is changed by one basis point. Then the spot rates are recomputed, using this new price for the particular hedge instrument, keeping the prices (and yields) for all other hedges the same as before. The value of the asset (or liability or portfolio) is now recomputed. The change in the value of the asset due to the change in the yield of the hedge gives us the risk point of the asset relative to that hedge instrument. This procedure is repeated for all hedge instruments in the set of hedges chosen. The risk point relative to a hedge can be used to determine the amount of the hedge to be bought (or sold) to hedge it against changes in the price of that hedge.

To illustrate this procedure, let us increase the yield on the 10-year Treasury from 7.466 percent (from Exhibit 24–1) by one basis point to 7.476 percent. The composite rate changes from 7.876 percent to 7.886 percent. The new discount functions and zero rates are recomputed as in Exhibit 24–4 (compare with Exhibit 24–2).[21] The computation of the new value of

---

20 The reader can obtain useful insight into the concepts and procedures by actually working out a number of examples. To facilitate this, we have also shown the intermediate values of the cumulative discount factors for ease of computation. In addition, we have provided all the values to several decimal places so that the reader can verify his or her work.

21 Note that the change in the 10-year rate impacts the discount function and the zero rates only beyond year 5.

EXHIBIT 24–3
Value of a 10%, 10-Year Bond

Maturity (years)	Discount Factor	Zero Rates	Cash Flow	Present Value
0.5	0.974602	5.212000	5.00	4.873009
1.0	0.944257	5.818712	5.00	4.721286
1.5	0.912552	6.194689	5.00	4.562759
2.0	0.878608	6.576629	5.00	4.393041
2.5	0.846701	6.768333	5.00	4.233503
3.0	0.814349	6.964043	5.00	4.071745
3.5	0.783565	7.091448	5.00	3.917823
4.0	0.752934	7.221785	5.00	3.764668
4.5	0.722504	7.354956	5.00	3.612519
5.0	0.692321	7.490986	5.00	3.461606
5.5	0.665550	7.541282	5.00	3.327749
6.0	0.639435	7.593429	5.00	3.197177
6.5	0.613973	7.647266	5.00	3.069864
7.0	0.589156	7.702698	5.00	2.945778
7.5	0.564977	7.759674	5.00	2.824887
8.0	0.541431	7.818175	5.00	2.707157
8.5	0.518511	7.878204	5.00	2.592553
9.0	0.496207	7.939786	5.00	2.481037
9.5	0.474514	8.002961	5.00	2.372570
10.0	0.453423	8.067783	105.00	47.609370
			Total PV:	114.740102

the 10 percent bond under study is shown in Exhibit 24–5 (compare with Exhibit 24–3). The value of the bond has fallen from 114.740102 to 114.667571, that is, by 0.072531. This number is the change in dollars for every $100 par holding of the bond. This is the risk point for the 10 percent bond relative to the 10-year Treasury.

The risk point is usually computed for a given par holding of a security. In analytical situations where the par holding is hypothetical, it is convenient to express it as dollars per $10,000 par holding.[22] This makes the risk point

_____

22 Change in value for a 1 bp move on a $10,000 par holding is equal to 100 times the change in value for a 1 bp move on a $100 holding. The latter represents the *PVBP* or dollar duration.

EXHIBIT 24–4
New Zero Curve after Incrementing 10-Year Yield

Maturity (years)	Par Yields (percent)	Interpolated Par Yields	Discount Factor	Cumulative Factor	Zero Rates
0.5	5.212%	5.212000	0.974602	0.974602	5.212000
1.0	5.810	5.810000	0.944257	1.918859	5.818712
1.5		6.177000	0.912552	2.831411	6.194689
2.0	6.544	6.544000	0.878608	3.710019	6.576629
2.5		6.728500	0.846701	4.556720	6.768333
3.0	6.913	6.913000	0.814349	5.371069	6.964043
3.5		7.033250	0.783565	6.154633	7.091448
4.0		7.153500	0.752934	6.907567	7.221785
4.5		7.273750	0.722504	7.630071	7.354956
5.0	7.394	7.394000	0.692321	8.322392	7.490986
5.5		7.443200	0.665506	8.987898	7.542511
6.0		7.492400	0.639344	9.627243	7.595897
6.5		7.541600	0.613830	10.241072	7.650990
7.0		7.590800	0.588957	10.830029	7.707698
7.5		7.640000	0.564721	11.394750	7.765973
8.0		7.689200	0.541114	11.935864	7.825799
8.5		7.738400	0.518130	12.453994	7.887182
9.0		7.787600	0.495762	12.949756	7.950151
9.5		7.836800	0.474003	13.423759	8.014749
10.0	7.886	7.886000	0.452845	13.876605	8.081033

number roughly comparable to duration or dollar duration. The risk points for this bond relative to all the other hedges are shown in Exhibit 24–6 (column 5) on this basis, that is, for a $10,000 par holding. Also shown here are a few other results that should be of interest to risk managers. Column 6 shows the fraction (as a percentage) of the total risk represented by any given sector. For example, approximately 95.4 percent of the risk in this bond is in the 10-year sector. Column 7 expresses the risk point as a percentage of the total value of the bond. The numbers in this column are similar to duration. These two columns, along with the risk points themselves, form a more complete picture of the risk in the 10 percent bond under consideration. Exhibit 24–11 shows a graphical depiction of risk points. We call the collection of risk points the *risk profile* or the *risk point profile*.

EXHIBIT 24–5
Change in the Value of the 10%, 10-Year Bond

Maturity (years)	Discount Factor	Zero Rates	Cash Flow	Present Value
0.5	0.974602	5.212000	5.00	4.873009
1.0	0.944257	5.818712	5.00	4.721286
1.5	0.912552	6.194689	5.00	4.562759
2.0	0.878608	6.576629	5.00	4.393041
2.5	0.846701	6.768333	5.00	4.233503
3.0	0.814349	6.964043	5.00	4.071745
3.5	0.783565	7.091448	5.00	3.917823
4.0	0.752934	7.221785	5.00	3.764668
4.5	0.722504	7.354956	5.00	3.612519
5.0	0.692321	7.490986	5.00	3.461606
5.5	0.665506	7.542511	5.00	3.327532
6.0	0.639344	7.595897	5.00	3.196721
6.5	0.613830	7.650990	5.00	3.069148
7.0	0.588957	7.707698	5.00	2.944785
7.5	0.564721	7.765973	5.00	2.823603
8.0	0.541114	7.825799	5.00	2.705569
8.5	0.518130	7.887182	5.00	2.590650
9.0	0.495762	7.950151	5.00	2.478812
9.5	0.474003	8.014749	5.00	2.370017
10.0	0.452845	8.081033	105.00	47.548774
			New PV	114.667571
			Old PV	114.740102
			Change:	–0.072531

PROPERTIES OF RISK POINTS

Exhibit 24–6 also shows the sum of all the risk points, called the *total risk*.[23] This number, 7.600610, is similar[24] to the PVBP for the bond, as it represents the change in the value of the bond due to a parallel move up of

---

23 Note, however, that because some risk points can be negative and some positive, the magnitude of total risk does not always indicate the risk level of an instrument.

24 Similar, but not exactly equal, since the *PVBP* computation starts with a flat yield curve.

EXHIBIT 24–6
Risk Points for the 10% Bond

Maturity (years)	Treasury Yield (percent)	Spread (basis points)	Total	Risk Point	Percent of Total Risk	Percent of Total PV
0.5	4.932%	28 bp	5.212	–0.002566	0.033757	–0.002236
1.0	5.520	29	5.810	–0.009118	0.119968	–0.007947
2.0	6.234	31	6.544	–0.021308	0.280349	–0.018571
3.0	6.563	35	6.913	–0.055563	0.731037	–0.048425
5.0	7.074	32	7.394	–0.258960	3.407101	–0.225693
10.0	7.466	41	7.876	–7.253094	95.427787	–6.321324
			Totals:	–7.600610	100.000000	–6.624196

the yield curve by one basis point. If this is expressed as a percentage of total value of the bond (Exhibit 24–6, column 7, last row), then we get a number similar to the duration of the bond.

At first blush, it seems as though total risk will increase or decrease based on the selection of hedge instruments. However, the risk point method is quite robust and, under most conditions, handles arbitrary selection of hedge instruments well. For example, let us delete the five-year Treasury from the hedge instrument list and recompute the par curve, zero curve, and the risk points. Exhibit 24–7 shows the new risk points and total risk. Note how the risk in the 7-year sector has been redistributed between the 3-year and the 10-year sectors.

The risk points have another interesting property. Consider again the 10 percent coupon, 10-year bond. The collection of risk points actually represents a portfolio of hedging Treasuries, called the *hedge portfolio*. This portfolio has the property that its risk is the same as that of the bond. When a portfolio is designed so as to match the risk of another, then the former is called an *immunizing* or *duration-matching* portfolio. In addition, the cash flow from this portfolio is close to that of the bond. When a portfolio is designed so that its cash flows match that of another, the former is called a *dedicated* portfolio. The hedge portfolio is always immunizing or duration matching. The larger the number of hedge instruments, the closer the hedge portfolio comes to a fully dedicated portfolio.

There is one difference between the dedicated portfolio in this context and the one used in structured investments. In the latter, only positive

EXHIBIT 24–7
Risk Points with a Smaller Set of Hedges

Maturity (years)	Treasury Yield (percent)	Spread (basis points)	Total	Risk Point	Percent of Total Risk	Percent of Total PV
0.5	4.932%	28 bp	5.212	–0.002584	0.033865	–0.002251
1.0	5.520	29	5.810	–0.009182	0.120353	–0.007999
2.0	6.234	31	6.544	–0.021457	0.281247	–0.018692
3.0	6.563	35	6.913	–0.242119	3.173593	–0.210917
5.0						
10.0	7.466	41	7.876	–7.353835	96.390943	–6.406137
			Totals:	–7.629176	100.000000	–6.645995

holdings are considered, whereas in our hedging portfolio, negative holdings (i.e., short positions) are quite common.

Finally, risk points are additive, in two ways. The risk point in any sector for a portfolio can be computed easily by simply adding the risk points in that sector of all bonds in the portfolio. In addition, we can quickly compute the risk point for a broader sector by adding the risk points for all the smaller sectors within.

Exhibits 24–8 and 24–9 show the risk points for various common fixed income investments.[25]

It is interesting to look at the risk profile for an exotic structure.[26] In Exhibit 24–10, we show the profile for a three-year note that pays coupons equal to the five-year swap rate less a fixed spread. Such a note is called a CMS note or constant maturity swap rate note. The coupon on the note is reset semiannually. Simple duration analysis will treat the note essentially as a floating rate instrument, implying a small duration or risk. The risk point profile (Exhibit 24–10, column 5, and Exhibit 24–11), however, reveals that the CMS note has negative and positive risks. The note is bullish on rates up to three years and bearish on rates beyond that. In particular, the note has risk in the five- and 10-year maturities even though it has only a three-year maturity.

---

25 The data in Exhibit 24–9 for mortgage-backed securities were computed by Thomas Ho of Global Advanced Technology Corporation, New York.

26 The risk point analysis of exotic securities is covered in detail in Ravi E. Dattatreya and Scott Peng, *Structured Notes,* (Burr Ridge, Ill.: Irwin Professional Publishing, 1994).

EXHIBIT 24–8
Risk Points Profile of Some Common Investments

Maturity (years)	10-Year Par Bond	10-Year 3% Bond	10-Year 15% Bond	10-Year 0% Bond	14.50% Annuity	5-Year Par Bond	3-Year Par Bond	3, 10 Dumbbell
0.5	0.000000	0.005890	-0.008606	0.009514	-0.017515	0.000000	0.000000	0.000000
1.0	0.000000	0.020933	-0.030583	0.033812	-0.062249	0.000000	0.000000	0.000000
2.0	0.000000	0.048917	-0.071469	0.079013	-0.145466	0.000000	0.000000	0.000000
3.0	0.000000	0.127555	-0.186362	0.206034	-0.379316	0.000000	-2.685351	-1.753771
5.0	0.000000	0.594487	-0.868566	0.960251	-1.767856	-4.160751	0.000000	0.000000
10.0	-6.938302	-6.215646	-7.994128	-5.771025	-2.148999	0.000000	0.000000	-2.406980
Totals:	-6.938302	-5.417864	-9.159714	-4.482402	-4.521401	-4.160751	-2.685351	-4.160751

EXHIBIT 24–9
Risk Points for Mortgage-Backed Securities

Maturity (years)	Sequential PO	Sequential IO	Companion PAC Bond	Z-PAC Bond	Z Bond
1.0	2.712990	−1.067860	−0.087954	−0.227987	0.084370
2.0	0.105150	−0.751634	−0.312604	−0.462619	0.176150
3.0	−0.881439	0.727920	−1.991636	−0.900864	0.408440
5.0	−0.791930	−0.190383	−8.828908	−0.149317	1.440020
10.0	−8.551698	6.211113	−10.083130	0.164040	−17.569742
Totals	−8.137903	5.143436	−26.806461	−1.725013	−14.650842

APPLICATIONS OF THE RISK POINT METHOD

The risk point method, being a more complete and comprehensive measure of interest rate risk, can be used wherever other simple measures such as duration are currently used. We provide here a brief review.

Hedging

This is the most common use of duration and therefore of risk points. Common duration analysis not only gives us only a crude approximation for the hedge, but it also fails to provide critical information about which hedge instruments are optimal to use. On the other hand, the risk point method correctly identifies the major risks in a portfolio and directly generates the portfolio of hedge instruments best suited for the hedging task. Since the starting point for the risk point method is the selection of hedge instruments, we have full control over which hedge instruments will be considered for hedging from the outset.

The par amount of any hedge instrument required to hedge a portfolio can be determined by dividing the risk point of the portfolio by the $PVBP$[27] of the hedge instrument. For example, consider the 10-percent coupon bond

---

27 Note that the *PVBP* of a hedge is equal to its risk point relative to itself. For example, from Exhibit 24–8, the *PVBP* of the 10-year Treasury is $6.938302. Note that this *PVBP* is slightly different from the traditional definition. One reason is that the latter starts out with a flat yield curve instead of the actual yield curve.

EXHIBIT 24–10
Risk Point for a CMS Note

Maturity (years)	Treasury Yield (percent)	Spread (basis points)	Total	Risk Point
0.5	4.932%	28 bp	5.212	–0.058520
1.0	5.520	29	5.810	–0.208950
2.0	6.234	31	6.544	–0.484468
3.0	6.563	35	6.913	–2.831432
5.0	7.074	32	7.394	2.280450
10.0	7.466	41	7.876	1.512276
			Total:	0.209356

again. For every $100 of the bond, we need $104.5370 (7.253094/6.938302) of the 10-year Treasury as a component of the hedge.

Indexing

As a structured portfolio methodology, indexing is quite common. Indexing requires one to manage a portfolio in such a way that the returns from the portfolio track that from a given bond index (e.g., various Lehman Brothers indexes or the Merrill Lynch Government Bond Index). A common technique is to purchase, as far as possible, the same bonds as in the index in the same proportions. The effectiveness of this technique is limited because indexes almost always have too many bonds in them and most of these are not available at fair prices in the quantities required. An alternative is to manage the portfolio duration to match the published duration of the index as closely as possible. This technique allows the manager to pick bonds that are relatively cheap for the portfolio.

Situation. A portfolio manager is running an indexed fund tied to an index with a duration of five years. Given the bearish mood of the market, the manager decides to keep the duration of the fund short, at 4.5 years. Rates do climb. However, the manager finds that the fund has barely kept up with the index instead of outperforming the index as expected. Further analysis reveals that the yield curve has steepened as the rates rose. The fund holds a relatively large amount of 10-year bonds, which have suffered a loss. Thus, duration matching in normal situations and using a

EXHIBIT 24–11
Risk Point Profile of a CMS Note

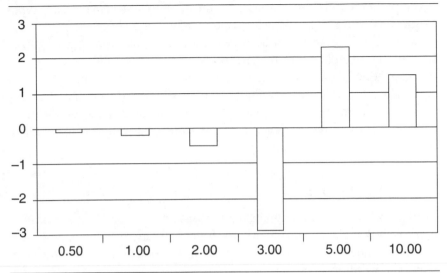

shorter duration in a bearish market provide no guarantee that expected results will be obtained. The reason is that duration is an oversimplification.[28]

A superior way to index is to first determine the full risk point profile of the index and then manage the fund against this profile as a guide.[29] Then the manager will know what types of yield curve bets are implied in the fund's portfolio.

Immunization and Dedication

Another popular application of duration is in immunization. If we are managing a portfolio to meet a specific liability in the future, immunization

---

28 In this context, we can compare duration to the mean of a distribution. A normal distribution with small variance can be represented satisfactorily by its mean. This is an ideal situation. If the variance is large, or if the distribution is skewed, then we need more parameters to describe or represent the situation. The farther the distribution from the ideal, the less meaningful the mean. Similar is the case with duration.

29 In the absence of published information on the risk points for an index, the profile can be estimated by looking at a simplified portfolio representative of the index.

calls for balancing the portfolio, so that the duration of the portfolio equals the duration of the liability. This procedure is based on a parallel shift assumption for yield curve moves. Therefore, it is subject to the same types of surprises suffered by the index fund manager above.

A more robust approach is to determine the risk point profile of the liability and match this to the risk profile of the portfolio. In this sense, immunization is not much different from index fund management.

In dedicated portfolios, a common strategy is to cash match in the early years and use immunization in later years. Again, this strategy can be made more robust by using risk point matching rather than duration matching in the back years.

Benchmarking

In many industrial corporations, the performance of the liability portfolio is measured against a benchmark portfolio. In many ways, this procedure resembles indexing. We recommend use of the risk point profile for managing the liabilities. Perhaps the creation of the benchmark portfolio itself can benefit from this method.

Scenario Analysis

One use of duration is in scenario analysis. Under parallel shift assumptions, we can quickly determine the change in the value of a portfolio from its duration. This use of duration is limited to parallel shifts and fails to reveal risks due to reshaping shifts of the yield curve. Using the risk point profile of the portfolio, it is easy to carry out scenario analysis, including yield curve twists and other reshaping shifts.

In the case of the 10-percent coupon bond (Exhibit 24–6), if the 10-year rate moves up by 10 bp and the five-year rates move up by 5 bp and the other rates are unchanged, then the change in the value of a $10,000 holding can be estimated to be $73.825740 ($10 \times \$7.253094 + 5 \times \$0.258960$).

Bond Swap Transactions

A common bond swap transaction is to swap a bond (a bullet) for a pair of bonds (the dumbbell) in such a way that the duration of the dumbbell is equal to that of the bullet. Even though it is difficult to match the risk point profiles of the bullet and the dumbbell, the profiles provide accurate clues as to where the risks and bets in the transaction might be.

EXTENSIONS

The application of the risk point method is not limited to securities with simple, known, and fixed cash flows. It is a general approach and can be used to hedge virtually all instruments. As long as a security can be valued relative to a set of hedge instruments, the method is applicable. For example, suppose that we are considering an option on a 10-year zero-coupon bond. We can easily determine the risk point for the option by first determining the change in the price of the zero relative to the current 10-year Treasury. Second, we determine the corresponding change in the price of the option due the change in the zero price. This directly gives us the risk point of the option relative to the current 10-year Treasury.[30]

The concept can also be extended to include risks other than interest rate risk. For example, suppose that we would like to hedge the option on the 10-year zero-coupon bond against changes in volatility. We would choose a hedge instrument that responds to volatility, such as an option on the current 10-year Treasury. To determine the risk point, called the *volatility risk point,* we compute the change in the value of the hedge as well as the option on the zero per unit change in the volatility. The ratio of the two represents the risk point of the option relative to the hedge with respect to volatility. This number is the number of units of the hedge instrument required to hedge the option on the zero to protect against changes in volatility.

In addition to volatility risk, we can similarly define risk points for stock market risk, exchange rate risk, commodity price risk, credit risk, and so on. The two key factors in such extensions are the availability of appropriate hedge instruments and a valuation model.

Convexity

We can also extend the idea of duration like risk point to convexity. Convexity basically measures the nonlinear relationship between the cause (change in the reference rate) and the effect (value or price of a security). One way to measure the nonlinearity is to look at the difference between a linear estimate and the actual value. In Exhibit 24–12, we show the difference between the change in the value of the 10 percent bond for a 10 basis

---

30 The risk point for the option relative to the 10-year Treasury is the product of (1) the risk point of the option relative to the zero and (2) the risk point of the zero relative to the 10-year. Mathematically, we can restate this relationship as follows: $d(\text{option})/d(10\text{-year UST}) = [d(\text{option})/d(\text{zero})] \times [d(\text{zero})/d(10\text{-year UST})]$.

EXHIBIT 24–12
Convexity Points—I

Maturity (years)	Treasury Yield (percent)	Spread (basis points)	Total	Risk Point	Convexity Points
0.5	4.932%	28 bp	5.212	−0.002566	0.000011
1.0	5.520	29	5.810	−0.009118	0.000043
2.0	6.234	31	6.544	−0.021308	0.000118
3.0	6.563	35	6.913	−0.055563	0.000405
5.0	7.074	32	7.394	−0.258960	0.003621
10.0	7.466	41	7.876	−7.253094	0.137062
			Totals:	−7.600610	0.141261

point change in the yield of a hedge (column 6) and 10 times the change in value for a 1 basis point change in yield (i.e., the risk point, column 5). The result, Column 7, can be called the *convexity points*.

There is another way to determine convexity (see Exhibit 24–13). We can move the entire yield curve[31] by a small amount (10 basis points) and recompute the risk points. The difference between the risk points computed before (column 5) and after (column 6) is the parallel shift. The result will represent a type of convexity points.[32]

It is difficult to pinpoint exactly how the convexity points ought to be used, because convexity itself is a second-order effect. Nonetheless, we recommend their use, if only for monitoring purposes, by the risk manager. This is especially so when exotic securities are involved.

MARKET VOLATILITY AND VALUE-AT-RISK ANALYSIS

The risk points are static numbers in the sense that they are properties of securities, not of the market. However, it is straightforward to incorporate data that describe market dynamics such as variance (or volatility) and covariance of prices and yields.

---

31 There are a number of degrees of freedom in selecting the type and magnitude of the yield curve shift. The actual shift chosen is influenced by specifics of any particular situation.

32 This set of convexity points is considered more useful in certain circumstances.

EXHIBIT 24–13
Convexity Points—II

Maturity (years)	Treasury Yield (percent)	Spread (basis points)	Total	Risk Point Before	Risk Point After	Change or Convexity
0.5	5.032%	28 bp	5.312	−0.002566	−0.002420	0.000145
1.0	5.620	29	5.910	−0.009118	−0.008604	0.000514
2.0	6.334	31	6.644	−0.021308	−0.020116	0.001192
3.0	6.663	35	7.013	−0.055563	−0.052492	0.003072
5.0	7.174	32	7.494	−0.258960	−0.245042	0.013919
10.0	7.566	41	7.976	−7.253094	−7.205489	0.047605
			Totals:	−7.600610	−7.534163	0.066447

One way to include volatility is to simply multiply the risk point relative to a hedge by the standard deviation for that hedge. For example, suppose that the risk point for a portfolio is $10,000 per basis point change in the five-year Treasury. Suppose, also, that the yield of the five-year Treasury changes about three basis points per day on average. Then we can say that the value of the portfolio changes about $30,000 (three basis points times $10,000 per basis point) per day on the average due to changes in the yield of the five-year Treasury.

We can extend this idea further. Value-at-Risk (VAR) of a portfolio represents the amount of loss that could result with a given probability. Suppose that the probability that a portfolio can lose more than $2 million over a one-week horizon is less than 3 percent. Then the VAR for the portfolio is $2 million, that is, with 97 percent confidence, we can say that the loss in the portfolio is going to be less than $2 million over the one-week horizon. Different confidence bands and horizon periods are used in different contexts. In order to estimate the VAR of a portfolio, we not only have to estimate the price volatility of each security in the portfolio, but also the correlation for each pair of securities. In order to limit the task of data estimation to a manageable level, that is, to reduce the number of pair-correlations that need to be estimated, some type of mapping is usually applied. The RiskMetrics methodology includes one such mapping. In this context, a mapping is a representation of the portfolio in a simpler, more tractable format.

The risk point concept also leads to an efficient mapping. Recall that the vector of risk points represents a portfolio, called the equivalent portfolio, of hedge instruments with equal risk. If the hedge instruments, relative to which the risk points are computed, are carefully chosen, then the equivalent portfolio is an excellent representative portfolio or mapping for VAR computation. Since the risk point concept is driven by a valuation model, this approach ensures that the mapping is not ad hoc as in other methodologies, but is based on robust and valid analytical reasoning. In addition, VAR analysis based on the risk point concept can handle more complex securities in the portfolio including options.

CONCLUSION

In this chapter, we have presented the risk point concept as a more complete measure of interest rate risk than other commonly used measures such as duration. The concept adds value in almost all situations where duration is used, including: hedging, immunization, dedication, indexation, bond swapping, and scenario analysis. The risk point concept is especially valuable in the management of portfolios including options and most of the complex modern financial instruments. We recommend that the risk point method be used as an integral part of a comprehensive risk management program.

In risk management, as in most important situations, our policy is to reject the black box approach. By providing more insight into the nature of risk, the risk point method takes us one step away from the black box, one step closer to our ideal.

Chapter Twenty-Five

Ten Important Risk Management Steps for End-Users

Leslie Rahl and Tanya Styblo Beder

Capital Market Risk Advisors, Inc.

Nineteen ninety-four was a watershed year for the derivatives industry. The well-publicized losses at Metallgesellschaft ($1.340 billion), the Askin funds ($600 million), Procter & Gamble ($157 million), Gibson Greetings ($19.7 million), Harris Trust ($51.3 million), Glaxo Holdings ($150 million), and Piper Jaffray ($700 million), to name just a few of the losses in excess of $10 million that were reported for that year, have made derivatives a household word (see Exhibits 25–1, 25–2, and 25–3).

Derivatives have been discussed on the *Today* show, *Time* and *Newsweek* magazines, and even in the onboard magazine of United Airlines. This is in sharp contrast to the 1980s, when it was a struggle to get the press to pay attention to derivatives. Now *derivatives* has become a familiar word. For some, a witch-hunt has commenced for the "D" word.

Although there is general agreement that poorly managed derivatives can cause problems, there is some disagreement about what a derivative is. The International Swap and Derivatives Association (ISDA) has traditionally surveyed the volumes of interest rate swaps; currency swaps; caps, collars and floors; and swaptions. This universe is sometimes the definition of "derivatives." But away from ISDA, many other instruments are classified as derivatives (see Exhibit 25–4).

EXHIBIT 25–1
Publicly Disclosed Derivatives Losses as of December 31, 1994

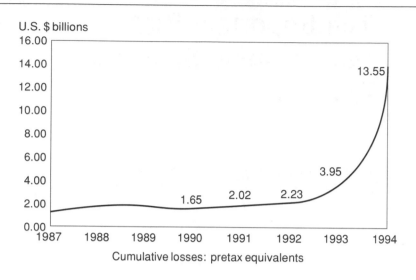

EXHIBIT 25–2
Losses by Market Segment, 1994

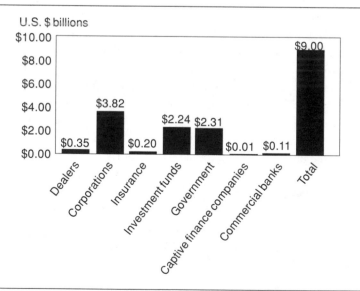

EXHIBIT 25–3
Losses by Type of Derivative, 1994

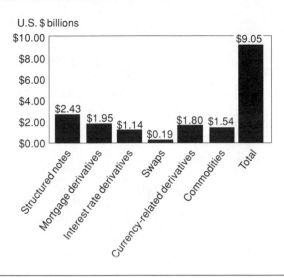

EXHIBIT 25–4
Derivatives Universe

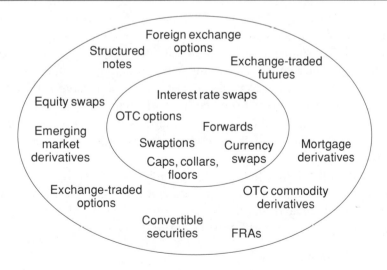

EXHIBIT 25–5
Interest Rate Swaps

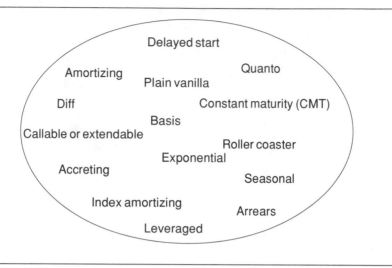

In turn, each of these "products" is a family of instruments with vastly different risk profiles within the family. See the interest rate swaps family in Exhibit 25–5.

Clearly, the risk profile of a plain vanilla swap is very different from the risk profile of a highly leveraged swap tied to LIBOR squared. To lump all derivatives into a single category of risk is as inappropriate as grouping the stock of a blue chip company with the stock of a bankrupt company. There are derivative instruments such as plain vanilla interest rate swaps that have liquidity and price characteristics similar to transparent cash markets. There are also derivative and cash market instruments that have difficult and complex valuation issues. From both a risk management and a policy perspective, it is preferable in many situations to group transactions by complexity, liquidity, and price transparency instead of by derivatives versus cash markets.

There is a silver lining, however, in the cloud over derivatives. Many end users and dealers alike heard a wake-up call for better risk management, and they have learned from the market's losses. The key culprits behind the $9 billion of publicly disclosed losses during 1994 were:

- Insufficient oversight.
- Model and/or assumption problems.

- Improper hedging techniques.
- Too much risk relative to capital.
- Fraud.

This is consistent with the results of a survey of 80 dealers and 80 end users conducted by the Group of Thirty, a prestigious Washington-based group headed by Paul Volcker, in January 1993 and published in March 1994. The study identified eight key causes of negative profit-and-loss (P&L) variances in derivatives transactions:

- Market discontinuity (88 percent).
- Illiquidity (84 percent).
- Inexperienced trader (84 percent).
- Input error in model (68 percent).
- Trader exceeded limits (61 percent).
- Model error—algorithms (61 percent).
- Model error—programming (61 percent).
- Systems failure (58 percent).

Note that five of the eight reasons relate to the derivatives model or the assumptions in the model. Also note that credit losses do not appear on the list of causes of negative P&L variation. This substantiates the ISDA findings that credit losses in OTC derivatives have been de minimus to date.

Many end users have stepped up oversight of their derivatives activities. We worked with them during 1994 to limit their chances for loss, and developed 10 steps to assist end users in properly controlling derivatives risks.

1. PROVIDE IN-DEPTH TRAINING FOR SENIOR MANAGEMENT AND THE BOARD OF DIRECTORS

Regulators have made it clear that they are looking to senior management and to the board of directors to understand, manage, and control the use of powerful but risky derivatives. The Group of Thirty survey found that 29 percent of end users believed that their board had "little understanding" of derivatives and had significant work to do to improve their knowledge. The Bank of England in its April 1993 paper, "Derivatives: Report of an Internal Working Group," recommended that: supervisors should consider the extent to which senior management do (or are likely to) understand the derivatives area of a firm's business. A guiding principle might be that, where this activity is important to a bank, at least two members of the Board (including the Finance Director) should be sufficiently knowledgeable to be able to ensure that the business is controlled effectively. In addition, managers at any level who receive "risk reports" should be able to interpret and evaluate them.

When Dennis Weatherstone, the chairman of Morgan Guaranty Trust and the chairman of the Group of Thirty Study Committee on Derivatives presented the study in July 1993, he commented that Recommendation 1 was the single most important of 24 recommendations.

Box 25–1

Group of Thirty Recommendation #1

Dealers and end users should use derivatives in a manner consistent with the overall risk management and capital policies approved by the Board of Directors and reviewed as business and market circumstances change. Policies governing derivatives use should be clearly defined, including purposes for which these transactions are to be undertaken. Senior management should approve procedures and controls to implement these policies, and management at all levels should enforce them.

On March 7, 1994, *The Wall Street Journal* published "Directors: Control Your Derivatives," an op-ed piece by former Securities and Exchange Commission Chairman Richard Breeden. The piece was an indictment of corporate complacency about derivatives practices. Breeden warned senior management and directors that they needed to shape up or face a "one-way ticket to financial disaster."

The *BASLE Risk Management Guidelines* (July 1994) and the *IOSCO Risk Recommendations* (July 1994), echoed the recommendations of the Group of Thirty. Specialized trade organizations, such as the Investment Company Institute (ICI) for mutual funds and the GFOA for municipal finance officers, published similar guidelines for their membership.

EXHIBIT 25–6
What Depth of Understanding of Derivative Products and Associated Risks Is Possessed by Your Board of Directors?

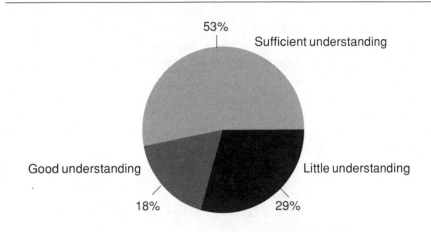

One encouraging sign is that corporate and fund managers alike as well as the dealer community appear to be taking the role and responsibility of the board and senior management increasingly to heart. Although training at senior management levels has always been a component of our consulting practice, we have seen a dramatic increase in the request for in-depth training at senior management and board levels as well as increased involvement at the highest levels.

When respondents in the original Group of Thirty study were asked about the directors' understanding of derivatives, 29 percent indicated that their board of directors had "little understanding" (see Exhibit 25–6).

2. CONDUCT A SELF-ASSESSMENT/RISK MANAGEMENT AUDIT

One of the first steps toward improved management is a comprehensive and brutally honest assessment of how your firm's risk management practices measure up against current "best practice." Note that "best practice" is constantly evolving, so that a risk management audit needs to be ongoing. Just over a decade ago, swaps were priced as bonds and all mortgages were assumed to have a 12-year average life. Today these practices are grossly out of date.

The recommendations released by the Group of Thirty Study Committee in July 1993 form an excellent basis for assessing your practices compared with "best practice" in the market at large and ensuring that detailed programs are in place to manage risk. In fact, the Group of Thirty recommendations have formed the basis for most regulatory reports on derivatives over the past 18 months.

Many regulators have stated that companies should conduct their own risk assessment. Rating agencies increasingly are focusing on this area when evaluating the creditworthiness of corporations, insurance companies, and mutual funds as well as banks and investment banks.

3. DEVELOP POLICIES FOR THE USE OF DERIVATIVES

Articulate a strategy for the use of derivatives. It is essential that every user of derivatives have written policies providing guidance for the use of derivatives. The type of issues that should be addressed include:

A. What derivatives are "approved" and in what size?

B. Which applications are allowable and which are not? For example, are both hedging and speculation allowed?

C. Who is authorized to commit the firm to a derivative transaction?

D. What counterparties are acceptable for which type of transactions, in what size, and for what maturity?

E. How will new derivatives be approved?

F. How will new applications be approved?

G. How will counterparty limits be measured, monitored, and updated?

H. What type of leverage is permitted?

I. What type of credit enhancement is required/permitted?

J. What are the acceptable concentration limits?

K. What are the risk limits?

L. Who is authorized to modify the procedures and limits?

M. What risk reports will be provided to whom and how often?

N. Which accounting approach will be used?

O. What type of stress testing will be performed? How often?

P. What systems will be used to:

1. Assess the appropriateness of the initial price?
2. Mark to market (or mark to model)?
3. Track credit and risk exposures?
4. Stress test?
5. Track and manage collateral (if any)?
6. Track and process payments and settlements?

Q. What forms of documentation will be acceptable and how will documentation be negotiated and tracked?
R. What early warning systems will be implemented to identify problems?
S. How often will written policies be reviewed and updated?
T. What exogenous events will trigger a review of policies and procedures?

4. IMPLEMENT A STRONG INDEPENDENT RISK OVERSIGHT (IRO) FUNCTION

Many end-users have discovered that two vital functions, if performed, provide a safety net for risk gone awry: risk management and risk measurement. (See Box 25–2).

5. INSTITUTE STRESS TESTING AND SIMULATION

Another key function of independent risk oversight is stress testing. Proper stress testing can help answer the following five questions:

1. What variables, given a small move, cause a large move in price or risk valuation?
2. Which variables important to your portfolio have a high likelihood of change?
3. What variables or exposures are considered to offset each other? By how much?
4. How wide is the variance of results produced by other commonly used models compared with yours?

Box 25–2

Safety Net for Risk

Risk Management

The activities of the professionals who price and transact the firm's products plus retain or hedge away resultant risks. Products include not only derivatives, but *all* activities of the firm.

Risk Measurement

The oversight activities of management who evaluate, monitor, and contain, when necessary, the risk management activities of the firm.

The creation of a strong, independent risk measurement or independent risk oversight function can provide an important safety net for the use of derivatives and other complex products. One of the vital functions of independent risk oversight is to ensure the integrity of the mark to market (or mark to model as we prefer to call it) process. The independent risk oversight (IRO) function should be independent of line management with authority, analytical tools, and policies for managing risk gone awry. The risk management functions should regularly assess the methodologies, models, and assumptions used to measure risk and to limit exposures. An institution should not become involved in a product at significant levels until senior management and all relevant personnel (including those in risk management, internal control, legal, accounting and auditing) understand the product and are able to integrate the product into the institution's risk measurement and control systems. In large dealer shops and among end-users with large, complex portfolios, independent risk oversight is an incremental check and balance above and beyond the traditional role of internal and external audit. In such institutions, internal auditors are expected to evaluate the independence and overall effectiveness of the institution's risk management functions in the same way they audit line functions. Among end-users with smaller and or less sophisticated portfolios, independent risk oversight is sometimes the responsibility of the audit or comptroller's division instead of a separate function.

5. What is your model's acceptance in the marketplace? Do the majority of models use the same data inputs and modeling assumptions?

Every portfolio has its Achilles' heel. Stress testing can help find the vulnerability and provide the knowledge to hedge away risk as necessary *before* a confluence of undesirable events occurs. One of the key recommendations by the Group of Thirty, and echoed subsequently by the OCC, IOSCO and the BASLE Committee, is that the portfolio of both dealers and end-users should be regularly stress tested. The Group of Thirty explained that an independent risk oversight function should be responsible for the design of stress scenarios to measure the impact of market conditions, *however improbable*, that might cause market gaps, volatility swings, or disruptions of major relationships, or might reduce liquidity in the face of unfavorable market linkages, concentrated market making, or credit exhaustion. In our experience, the + 100 bp, −100 bp type of "stress testing" falls far short of meeting this key recommendation. Given the role of models in causing losses, we also recommend that stress testing include sensitivity to the type of model and assumptions in addition to sensitivity to market moves. Items we frequently implement include:

- Sensitivity to yield curve level and shape.
- Sensitivity to volatility curve level and shape.
- Sensitivity to assumptions about the relationship between ATM and OTM volatility.
- Sensitivity to swap spread levels and shape of curve.
- Sensitivity to basis risk.
- Sensitivity to foreign exchange risk.
- Sensitivity to yield curve creation methodology.
  - Cross-over point between futures and cash.
  - Number of points on yield curve.
  - Interpolation methods (i.e., straight versus spline)
  - Smoothing versus "raw" curve.
- Sensitivity to correlation assumptions.
- Sensitivity to model; for example, Black-Scholes compared with other options models.

There are three common approaches to stress testing.
- Static, single scenario.
- Static, multiple scenario.
- Dynamic, simulation.

In most cases, some form of stress testing is better than none at all. However, subjecting a portfolio to a single stress test (typically a 50 or 100 bp parallel yield curve shift), often fails to identify the key risks to which the portfolio is vulnerable. While selecting multiple scenarios is an improvement, there are two major flaws:

1. What if an important scenario with significant implications to the portfolio has been deliberately or accidentally overlooked?
2. What if the scenario happens sometime in the future rather than today? In even the simplest portfolio, a + 100 bp parallel shift can have a very different impact on the portfolio at different points in time.

Multiple scenario analysis can be improved by using some sort of mathematical process (e.g., random number generation) to select scenarios to test above and beyond the scenarios selected by independent risk oversight. (e.g., yield curve inversion, volatility curve steepening). The process can also be enhanced by supplementing the scenarios selected by IRO at random with historical scenarios that have been particularly stressful (e.g., the stock market crash, the Iranian Oil crises, the ERM crises).

Monte Carlo simulation provides one of the most sophisticated approaches for stress testing in today's market. When simulations are dynamic over time, this type of analysis is probably the most powerful. However, the compute-intensive nature of Monte Carlo simulation, coupled with its mathematical complexity, probably place it out of reach for all but the largest and most sophisticated end-users.

The ability to analyze how capital at risk changes under both predictable and adverse conditions is critical. Many regulators emphasize that instruments such as structured notes should be subject to stress testing and that risk management be performed on a companywide basis, including an analysis of both derivative and nonderivative risks. In addition, stress testing should include quantitative exercises that compute potential losses or gains and more qualitative analyses of the actions that management plans to take under particular scenarios.

6. MARK TO MARKET REGULARLY

Mark all financial transactions, including derivatives, to market regularly (even when "hedge accounting"). To the degree that your positions rely on subjective assumptions and nonstandard models, be aware that you are "marking to model" instead of "marking to market." Assumptions are unavoidable in pricing, sizing, and monitoring risk. Alternate assumptions

EXHIBIT 25–7
How Does Your Mark-to-Model Exposure Break Down by Price Type?

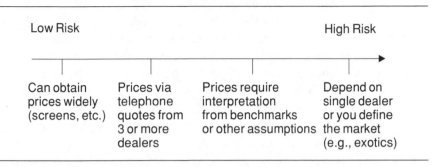

Low Risk			High Risk
Can obtain prices widely (screens, etc.)	Prices via telephone quotes from 3 or more dealers	Prices require interpretation from benchmarks or other assumptions	Depend on single dealer or you define the market (e.g., exotics)

can change the risk picture dramatically. We often recommend that end users profile all of their financial risks and P&L according to price transparency characteristics. Categorizing the liquidity and price transparency characteristics of a portfolio provides important insight into how far actual, attainable market prices might vary from the mark-to-model value (see Exhibit 25–7).

- Transparent. Can obtain prices from publicly available sources (e.g., data feeds, newspapers, screens).
- Multiple execution quotes. Can obtain prices from three or more dealers "on the wire."
- Requires assumptions. Can obtain prices by breaking the transaction into pieces or assuming "it trades like a reality-priced instrument."
- Theoretical model dependence. Can obtain prices based only on a theoretical model. End users who depend on a single dealer for mark-to-model valuation often fall into this category.

Important questions to be answered by independent risk oversight include a price reality check:

What percentage of your portfolio falls in each price category?

How has the distribution changed over time?

How does the distribution change with the addition of other risk dimensions?

- Credit?
- Market?
- Maturity?

7. ESTABLISH ADEQUATE RESERVES

One recommendation of the Group of Thirty was that portfolios should be "valued based on midmarket levels less specific adjustments, or on appropriate bid or offer levels. Midmarket valuation adjustments should allow for expected future costs such as unearned credit spread, close-out costs, investing and funding costs, and administrative costs." The concept of reserves is foreign to many end users. When assessing the risk management practices of even large, sophisticated end users, we frequently hear comments such as "Reserves are for banks not for our corporation/fund." This misconception is often clarified by explaining that the goal is to ensure that mark-to-market values are truly a best-effort reflection of where positions could be liquidated (on an orderly basis). Some end users learned this lesson the hard way: The Louisiana State Pension Fund suffered a $25 million loss in 1994 when a portfolio of IOs and POs was liquidated that it had diligently marked to market by getting dealer quotes that reflected only a midmarket price instead of the bid.

Another common end-user adjustment is exposure to risk. To the degree that you rely on your own pricing models to value transactions or rely on a single dealer to provide valuations (often the one who sold you the deal), you are exposed to the risk that if you terminate the transaction before maturity, the actual price at which you could execute an unwind or an offsetting transaction in the marketplace could vary considerably from the theoretical value at which you carry it. Different pricing models (e.g., Hull and White versus Black-Scholes), different assumptions (e.g., yield curve construction), and different supply and demand characteristics can materially influence actual market quotes.

8. ESTABLISH CREDIT, PRODUCT, AND PORTFOLIO SENSITIVITY LIMITS

Create an appropriate limit structure and ensure that limits are reviewed regularly. Limits should include credit limits, market risk limits, and basis or mismatch limits. Although credit losses in derivatives have been de minimus, proper attention to credit risk is vital. Limits on the amount of risk you are willing to take with each counterparty should reflect the creditworthiness of the counterparty as well as concentration of counterparty credit exposure mix (commercial bank versus investment bank, U.S. versus foreign, etc.). Credit exposure should be calculated as current mark-to-market value plus an estimate of potential risk for the remaining maturity and it should be monitored on a regular basis. Market risk limits should consider outright exposure as well as concentrations, sensitivity to volatility and yield curve, and leverage. Basis and mismatch limits should clearly articulate such policy issues concerning the degree to which you are comfortable hedging a five-year issuance or investment with a three-year hedge and the degree to which you are comfortable hedging commercial paper with six-month LIBOR or the Swedish krona with Belgian franc.

Limits need to be reviewed on a regular basis. Circumstances change. Limit setting, measurement, and monitoring need to be a dynamic process. It is also critical to establish policies on actions to be taken if exposure exceeds the limits previously established. The best time to think through the handling of a problem is before a crisis occurs.

9. DEFINE ROLES AND RESPONSIBILITIES

Ensure that there is clear accountability. When conducting a forensic review of loss situations, we often discover finger pointing rather than clear authority and responsibility. From the boardroom to the back office, issues of authority, responsibility, limits, policies, and procedures should be fully understood. Of course, this advice is not unique to derivatives transactions.

10. ESTABLISH EARLY WARNING SYSTEMS

With twenty-twenty hindsight, we know this area deserves significant self-criticism and updating. The reversals that occurred in the financial markets during the spring of 1994 not only caught many participants by surprise, but also caught many end users ignoring the massive "sea change" that was occurring. This is particularly evident in the structured note and mortgage-backed securities markets where end users were slow to observe the inadequacies of bull market products and models in the emerging bear market. Early warning systems designed with knowledge gained from stress testing should encompass all changes that should trigger a reassessment of limits, models, assumptions, policies, and procedures.

Depending on the degree and complexity of derivatives and other financial transactions in your firm, implementing these 10 steps and updating them on an ongoing basis can be a daunting challenge. But the rewards are clear: They should place you 10 very long steps away from the unexpected losses of the future.

Chapter Twenty-Six

Corporate Exposure Management: An Alternative Approach

Azam Mistry
Marine Midland Bank

The management of market exposure by corporations—defined as hedging and related activities in the foreign exchange, interest rate, and commodity markets—is now a widely accepted function of treasury departments in most multinationals. However, controversy and debate continue to surround most of the activities undertaken by these groups in the interest of reducing risk to the corporation and its shareholders. Criticisms range from accusations of unhealthy and needless speculation to views that espouse financial market efficiency and denounce attempts to manage exposure as misdirected or even futile. Senior management disquiet and suspicion are abundant: dissatisfaction with the prospect of cash flow losses on hedge transactions matched solely by accounting profits; reproach for hedging activities that in retrospect invariably look unnecessary or badly timed; the impression that certain risks are being managed to the deliberate exclusion of others; and a feeling that financial and other market-related risks will average out over time, leaving the true profitability of the corporation to be determined by the performance of its mainstream activities.

The views expressed by the author in this chapter are entirely his own and do not represent the views of his current or previous employers. Reprinted from *Advanced Interest Rate and Currency Swaps,* ed. Ravi E. Dattatyreya and Kensuke Hotta (Burr Ridge, Ill.: Irwin Professional Publishing, 1994), pp. 191–218.

These are muddy waters. Is there some form of clear thinking or appeal to first principles that may be useful? Specifically, what are the legitimate aims and parameters of a policy of exposure management? Is there a conceptual theme that one may usefully develop?

DEFINING THE MULTINATIONAL FIRM

Let's go back to basics. It seems reasonable to define today's global corporation as an entity generating both positive and negative cash flows in a variety of currencies in addition to its own base currency, and possessing assets and liabilities dispersed geographically and by currency of original denomination. The interaction of these assets and liabilities creates cash flows whose expected magnitude and uncertainty represent the value of the firm as embodied in the price of its stock.

The corporation employs some element of choice between differing asset and liability "mixes" in terms of the cash flows that may be expected to arise directly from their usage. This is no easy choice because the cash flows resulting from differing mixes are difficult to predict.

Further, the magnitude and uncertainty of the cash flows themselves may be impacted directly by various decisions. Such decisions involve issues like input costs and output pricing, including agreements to fix either of these magnitudes for varying periods of time.

Thus defined, the multinational firm's value is a dynamic function of its expected cash flows and asset-liability mix. Management seeks to influence this value through decisions made at various levels and by different functional groups. Strategic choices relating to mainstream corporate activities, such as manufacturing, input sourcing, equipment configuration, marketing and distribution, capital expenditure, research and development, human resource optimization, and so forth, serve to alter the mix and efficiency of assets and liabilities, to impact costs and revenues, and to vary the speed and magnitude of cash flows.

However, focusing purely on financial decisions made in treasury and related departments, it is easy to see that exposure management through foreign exchange, interest rate, and commodity market activities can have a major impact on the cash flows and asset-liability configuration of the corporation. Foreign exchange hedging may be used to fix the value in base currency of future cash inflows and outflows at either positive or "negative" cost; it may also serve to protect the base-currency translated value of net investments abroad. Interest rate market activity through debt issues, cash management, swaps, and other transactional hedges is capable of locking in (or varying) the level of interest rate costs or earnings for different periods of time. Commodity market activities can fix the cost of input materials and hedge against fluctuations in output prices for varying periods of time.

Viewed in this manner, exposure management activities represent an additional set of levers for use by management in varying the expected return and variability of the firm's stock price. While these activities are subject to the same shortcomings as other control mechanisms, they may be operated somewhat independently, although within the constraints imposed by mainstream corporate operations. Significantly, through altering the configuration of risk and reward that ultimately represents the appeal of the stock to investors, exposure management may serve as an instrument that aligns the corporation's risk-reward configuration with the preferences of its stockholders.

THE CONVENTIONAL APPROACH
AND ITS EVOLUTION

The conventional style of exposure management finds its origins in the micro approach to managing risk. Exposure is recognized and eliminated on a transaction-by-transaction basis or in a manner that treats every major corporate project or program as an individual and separable event in the organization's life. This is most clearly demonstrated by activities that aim at covering foreign exchange exposure arising from purchases of raw materials and components from overseas, or equivalently, by hedging through forward foreign exchange contracts the exposure arising from firm sales commitments denominated in a nonbase currency. In addition, corporations often tend to view specific projects or ventures as individual profit activities, which require for evaluation purposes that exposure directly relating to the venture be hedged in its entirety.

This form of itemized thinking has led to an attempt to view the balance sheet and income statement—indeed, the entire activity of the corporation—as something amenable to a checklisting of exposure and nonexposure items. More damaging, such thinking has in the past engendered the feeling that it is both possible and desirable for all exposure-entailing items to be hedged in their entirety. The tendency here has been to focus primarily on the objective of risk elimination with somewhat less emphasis on the costs involved. Note that these costs are variable over time and can be high. For example, the hedging forward of high interest rate foreign currency receivables, the locking in of input materials through commodity hedging in a positive price curve environment, and the decision to pay fixed interest rates on long-term debt in a steep yield curve situation can entail high costs relative to current levels. In some cases, it is conceivable that the high cost of covering exposure would make it preferable to accept a certain degree of risk. Cost considerations must enter into the determination of both the amount and the manner of hedging activity undertaken.

These issues have long since led to changes in the rationale and practice of exposure management, encompassing the three areas of foreign exchange, interest rate, and commodity market activities.

Foreign Exchange Management

In the field of foreign exchange management, the now common practice of aggregating and netting out exposure across activities and functional divisions aims at reducing the number of hedging transactions and the costs involved. Secondly, a methodology of hedging foreign exchange risk using proxy currencies has evolved. This involves the use of a smaller basket of currencies in which hedges are placed, such currencies representing a proxy for the actual currencies in which exposure arises. Again, the objective is to reduce costs through finding hedge currencies that are both closely correlated with the exposure currencies and that involve lower hedging costs. A further refinement involves netting revenues against costs where these items are denominated in closely correlated foreign currencies. An example might involve a U.S. corporation that earns revenues in EMS (European Monetary System) member currencies from sales in Europe and also pays import or other costs denominated in similar EMS currencies; in this situation, the costs may be netted against the revenues, leaving only the balance to be hedged.

Further, both the time horizon and scope of foreign exchange exposure management have increased. Risk reduction activities in this area now encompass not merely transactional exposure but also translation and foreign earnings exposure in future years. It is argued that the translation of net overseas investment represents a risk to the corporation in more than a pure year-end accounting sense. This is clearly seen if one regards a foreign investment as an asset potentially disposable at any point in time; from this perspective, foreign exchange hedges that protect the value in base currency of this asset are justified.

With regard to foreign earnings, the need to provide protection against future overseas profits deteriorating in base currency terms seems reasonable. Typically, these exposures are managed through the use of currency swaps, utilizing both the principal re-exchange and the coupon flows as the operational components of the hedge. Clear choices exist as to the currency, maturity, and custom configuration of the hedge; all of these have a direct bearing on hedging costs and efficiency.

The key issues here that require treasury management consideration relate to (1) the specific amounts of net overseas investment and future earnings from offshore operations that should be hedged back into the base currency and (2) the future period of time over which both translation and foreign earnings exposure should be eliminated through hedging activities. Any judgment on these matters must make implicit assumptions about the accuracy of forecasts about future foreign cash flows and continuing ownership of foreign assets. The inevitable uncertainty involved implies that decisions taken regarding these parameters will ultimately reflect to some degree the risk tolerance and cost-conservatism of the treasury department and that of the corporation's senior management.

Interest Rate Management

In the field of interest rate management, attention is focused primarily on the cost and configuration of debt, and—to a lesser extent—on the liquidity and return profile of surplus funds. The key issues involve the appropriate fixed-floating interest rate proportion of debt carried by the corporation and the tenor of this debt. These magnitudes may be varied through the use of interest rate and currency swaps that enable flexible switching between fixed- and floating-rate obligations in a variety of currencies. Additionally, interest rate swaps and related instruments like futures and FRAs (forward rate agreements) are increasingly being used on both the debt and asset side to optimally manage the short-term profile and liquidity of the corporation.

Treasury management teams face difficult decisions relating to the appropriate mix of fixed and floating interest rate debt obligations carried and the maturities of such debt. Differing mixes and maturities entail different interest rate costs and risks; these change as the slope and position of the yield curve alter over time. In a given situation, a conservative corporation may choose to maintain nearly 100 percent of its debt in long maturities at fixed interest rates, and it may accordingly execute swap strategies designed to enable it to reach this position. In the same circumstances, a less conservative company may decide instead on a 50-50 mix.

However, in a steeply positive yield curve environment the high cost of taking the 100 percent option may perhaps cause the first institution to realign its strategy towards a partial floating-rate debt portfolio. Arguably, the second corporation may similarly change its tactics in the interest of achieving lower interest costs through an increased floating-rate debt strategy operated at the short end of the yield curve. Of course, in both cases the immediate reduction in cost is likely to be accompanied by an increment of risk through possible higher interest costs in the future, as indeed the shape of the yield curve implies.

The point really is that the specific response of any institution in these or other circumstances is virtually impossible to predict because few objective guidelines exist for the appropriate fixed-floating rate proportion, even for a given environment with rigorously defined parameters. In actual practice, most corporations tend to reach their equilibrium positions largely through judgmental criteria and the weight of precedence.

Commodity Market Management

The newest area of exposure management involves the use of commodity market derivatives, especially commodity swaps, futures, and options. These instruments are typically used to fix the cost of input materials purchased by corporations and to hedge against declines in the price of output products, especially where the commodity component of these products is high. For example, a corporation that purchases large quantities of aluminum on a monthly basis, invoiced regularly against a market index, may elect to enter an aluminum swap whereby it pays a fixed price over the period of the swap in return for receiving a monthly average price relating to the same index. This effectively locks in the cost of purchasing aluminum during this period. Similar transactions may be executed using options, futures, or hybrid derivative structures to hedge commitments on purchased inputs or on sales of output. Again, the key issues involve the period of time for which costs or output prices are fixed, and the proportion of total commitments that are fixed through hedge mechanisms such as these.

It is clear that the evolution and wider scope of exposure management has forced treasury departments to face certain thorny issues and difficult choices. Much of the confusion stems from a failure to recognize the wider role and perspective of exposure management and a reluctance to award these activities their true role. The conceptual inconsistency that results leads directly to contradictions and the incessant debate familiar to participants in the field.

CONVENTIONAL CONFUSION

The state of conflict and debate is best seen through a review of the comments often heard in treasury and related circles:

"We Hedge Everything. We Never Speculate."

This seemingly innocuous policy statement makes strong claims. In its most rigorous interpretation, it enjoins certain ground rules:

- It is inappropriate to undertake market transactions not directly related to exposure faced by the corporation.
- All firm commitments must be fully hedged in an efficient manner.
- Hedges should not be subject to removal and replacement during a period of continuing exposure.
- Attempts to optimally time the execution of hedges are improper and futile.

The first imperative seems reasonable enough: In general, it is not appropriate for an institution to speculate in financial or other markets unless this activity is part of its stated mission. However, the second instruction makes unrealistic demands. It is often impractical or even impossible to hedge certain exposures completely. In some cases, the necessary instruments or markets may not exist or may not be fully developed, making it necessary to execute an imperfect hedge that substitutes a residual but lower risk for the original exposure. Examples include proxy-currency and proxy-instrument hedging as well as the use of mismatched dates or amounts between the exposure and the hedging vehicle (as in futures hedging). In addition, cost considerations may influence the hedging decision. If the cost of a perfect hedge is inordinately high, the wisdom of executing such a strategy may be legitimately questioned; instead, a less perfect hedge structure that provides what is judged to be adequate protection may be selected.[1]

Clearly, corporations do not "hedge everything." For instance, most institutions borrow funds in the money markets on a floating-rate basis, implicitly "speculating" on the future trend in interest rates. They choose to

---

1 There is clear evidence that conservative corporations have followed this line of thinking. In the mid-1980s, several structures were developed to enable corporations to cover forward foreign exchange risk in developing country currencies, including the Mexican peso. These hedges involved exorbitant forward exchange rate costs due to high foreign interest rates, and it is significant that few institutions chose to enter such transactions.

leave unhedged portions of their anticipated earnings flows denominated in foreign currencies, thereby tacitly taking views on future foreign exchange movements. They also choose not to fix in advance the prices of their input raw materials and supplies over the foreseeable future, thereby assuming that future price movements will not unduly damage profitability. This inaction is usually a response to the uncertainty regarding future corporate cash flows and needs as well as the cost of executing longer hedges. Is there not a degree of speculation in the decision to do nothing or in the decision to hedge only on a partial basis?

Imperfect and partial hedges such as those described above neither fulfill the requirements of a stated policy of "full and efficient" hedging nor comply with the strictures of a policy intended to be entirely free of speculative elements. For instance, the reduction of pure market risk through imperfect hedges leaves behind residual risk of a somewhat different nature. The strategy relies for its success on the assumption that certain market relationships will continue to hold or else change only in a favorable manner and direction. Tactics like these essentially involve an element of speculation about market magnitudes.

Again, a decision to hedge partially or not at all will usually reflect unavoidable constraints and necessarily involve speculative issues and judgments. Such actions are both necessary and prudent. If they appear improper in any sense, it is only because the field of exposure management is more complex than it seems. A fuller appreciation of the underlying issues reveals the hollowness of statements that blindly espouse the need to hedge completely and avoid speculative considerations in their entirety.

With regard to the last two statements, it should be acknowledged that a great deal of controversy exists regarding the "active" management of hedging activities, that is, the attempts to initiate, raise, and replace hedges at appropriate times to maximize gains or minimize losses. Those who oppose these practices usually refer to considerations of market efficiency and the often misstated conviction that it is impossible to "beat the market" consistently. This is the incorrect formulation of a sophisticated argument (for one thing it seems to suggest the strange conclusion that it is impossible to underperform the market as well!). The truth (or at least the theory) is that in the long run it is impossible to beat the market while accepting the same degree of risk that market movements entail. If one wishes to beat the market, it is necessary to undertake higher levels of risk. In the context of hedging activity, this implies that a policy of active management of hedges will experience a greater proportion of failures (and successes); that is, there will be more hits and misses than a passive hedging policy would entail.

In the long run, active hedge management will reflect a higher degree of risk than passive hedging activities and will provide higher returns (or reduced hedging costs) commensurate with this risk. This means that the choice of hedging strategy adopted (which in general aims first and last at the reduction of risk to the corporation) itself has a bearing on the degree of risk reduction achieved. In commonsense terms, this has intuitive appeal: An exposure management policy that allows for hedge removal and replacement in accordance with judgments about future market movements may result in lower hedging costs, but will do so only through the acceptance of a risk greater than that entailed by a policy of passive hedging. This is a provocative area that goes to the heart of arguments that follow, but it is not appropriate to enter into it at present. For the moment, it is sufficient to note that, once again, these considerations show that exposure management is not really amenable to the kind of black-and-white thinking that one may easily be seduced into adopting.

"Why Did You Hedge?"

This is invariably a retrospective statement. It usually represents a response to circumstances where a specific hedge appears to have been unnecessary due to market movements resulting in a favorable outcome for the underlying exposure and a loss-making consequence for the hedge strategy. In a nutshell, and with the benefit of hindsight, the hedge was not needed. Or was it?

This common statement reflects either a futile lamentation or a serious misconception about the role and function of hedging activities. It is important to accept the nature of any individual or collective set of hedges as a form of insurance policy against risks that may or may not arise. To the extent that such risks do not materialize, it is appropriate to view the cost of hedging, (i.e., the loss made on the hedge and other related outgoings) as an insurance premium paid to reduce risk. From this perspective, the claim that a given hedge appears in retrospect to have been unnecessary is like asserting that an individual carrying a life insurance policy has wasted money because he or she is still alive and should not have undertaken the insurance.

Hedging activities, like insurance, are to be regarded as necessary costs paid to mitigate risk to the entity concerned. The value of these is clearly seen if one considers that these actions enable a risk-reducing entity such as a corporation to achieve a greater degree of certainty in future successful economic performance, albeit at a cost. Ultimately, such activities are of value to parties with an interest linked to the success and continued healthy existence of the entity whose protection is achieved.

However, two significant issues need to be recognized. First, the cost should not be such that these parties would consider it inappropriate or excessive in any sense. Obviously, different parties may have differing perceptions about what constitutes an appropriate cost. Second, and closely linked to the first issue, the degree of risk reduction should be in some sense congruent with that desired by the interested parties. These are difficult issues that raise complex questions; however, a correct stance taken on both issues—however arrived at—can provide a cost-risk trade-off that correctly aligns the entity insured or hedged with the disposition and objectives of interested parties.

"In the Long Run, It Will Even Out. These Levels Will Come Back."

This statement seems to embody a naive faith in the cyclical nature of market movements, based on observations that certain market magnitudes tend to revert to equilibrium levels over time. There is perhaps some truth to the premise that financial markets experience mean reversion in the long run, particularly with regard to real rather than nominal magnitudes. However, the suggestion is that hedging activity is to some degree unnecessary since these allegedly symmetrical market fluctuations will ensure that, for a relatively unhedged firm, the good years will cancel out the bad ones, leaving a satisfactory picture in the long run. Quite apart from the fact that this statement places blind faith in the regularity and timing of market fluctuations, it ignores the very real problem of risk arising to the corporation in the short term.

If the position of an unhedged or underhedged corporation is "correct" in some long-term sense, it is only correct in the same sense that a stopped clock is correct twice a day, or indeed, 730 times a year. In the real world, a corporation is judged at least partly by its short-term viability and performance, as evidenced by fluctuations in its stock price. The need to provide continuous or ongoing protection of some sort cannot be ignored.

The statement does, however, have a deeper implication: It seems to suggest that a degree of risk acceptable to the corporation exists. This point is worth further discussion.

"Our Investors Want This Risk."

This is a sophisticated argument that goes to the heart of the issues involved. The point made is that investors who acquire the shares of a corporation do so to earn returns commensurate with the acceptance of a certain degree of risk and, more specifically, make their investment decision in anticipation of precise types of risks.

For example, consider a shareholder who purchases the stock of a U.S. corporation that relies for most of its revenues on profitable exports to other countries or through successful operation of its overseas subsidiaries. Such an investor may have made the investment decision based on clear expectations about various magnitudes, including perhaps a perception that the U.S. dollar will weaken against the currencies of the corporation's trading partners. If the corporation then chooses to hedge forward all its foreign currency revenues into dollars or to hedge a substantial part of its future foreign earnings, these actions would directly contradict the objectives of the investor. To put it more broadly, when an investor chooses to purchase the stock of a U.S. corporation that prospers when the dollar depreciates against other currencies, he or she may be making the decision on the basis that the stock is equivalent in part to a short-dollar foreign exchange position, and that such a position is an appropriate addition to a diversified investment portfolio. Hedging actions by the corporation aimed at neutralizing or reducing the impact of a depreciating dollar on its operations may work directly against the investor's overall objectives.[2]

Another example might include a shareholder purchasing stock in a highly leveraged corporation in the belief that interest rates will fall, raising the price of the stock through decreased interest costs and improved cash flow. If this corporation decided to fix the interest rates on all or a large portion of its debt through the use of, say, interest rate swaps, this would again frustrate the investor's objectives, especially if the implicit investment assumption made was that the corporation would maintain the existing

---

2 Arguments of this genre have long been common in academic circles. The area of most debate has involved diversification of corporate activities through acquisitions and mergers. The theoretical view has been that corporations acting purely in the interest of their shareholders should not diversify or switch activities on a large scale, since investors have clearly made a decision to invest specifically in the existing operations of the corporation. In other words, a chemical company should not move into the natural gas exploration business through acquisition or otherwise, since its shareholders have demonstrated that their investment is directed toward the chemical business only. If these shareholders wished to diversify their investment portfolios, they would do so through direct acquisition of shares in natural gas exploration companies.

portion of its debt portfolio on a floating-rate basis in order to take advantage of declining interest rates.

If one accepts the spirit of this argument (and it is a compelling argument), several important issues present themselves. Since any given policy of exposure management entails differing risks and costs, the choice of the appropriate strategy raises several difficult questions. The corporation is faced with the near-impossible problem of determining the specific objectives and risk-reward preferences of the majority of its shareholders. The question that needs answering relates to the image of the corporation in the eyes of its investors, and raises issues concerning information flow to the investment community and the resulting correctness of perceptions about the corporation's activities. Does the investor view the corporation as an entity that benefits from a strengthening or weakening dollar? Is the stock perceived as one that responds favorably to bullish or bearish interest rate scenarios? Does the corporation's shareholder community see its investment as a play on commodity price levels? Assuming that such information is available, should the corporation direct its activities toward satisfaction of the objectives of its existing shareholder base or should it focus its exposure management activities (and perhaps other efforts) so as to attract other types of investors? If information flows are near-perfect, implying that investors are fully aware of the risks being accepted commensurate with the current hedging policy (or lack of it), should any changes be made at all, even if adherence to this policy may entail severe performance problems for the corporation?

The comments reviewed above will sound all too familiar to those involved in corporate treasury activities. The issues raised serve to emphasize that the real challenge in exposure management relates not to the choice of hedging structure adopted from the wide menu of simple and hybrid mechanisms now available from commercial and investment banking institutions, or to the issues of timing and active management of hedges, but to inevitable decisions regarding the amount of exposure hedged and the period of time for which hedge protection is appropriate. If the corporation is viewed as a vehicle that exists primarily to serve the interests of its shareholders, these decisions must be made against the backdrop of assumptions about the objectives of these shareholders, the efficacy of information flows to these individuals and institutions, and, finally, the legitimacy of actions taken by the corporation to shift its investor base toward alternative entities.

To arrive at criteria upon which to base these decisions, it is useful to acquaint ourselves with the basics of formal portfolio management theory, especially as it describes the actions of investors seeking to develop optimal investment strategies in their portfolios.

A PRIMER ON PORTFOLIO THEORY

Classic portfolio theory states that an investor equipped with the requisite information will make rational choices among alternative investment opportunities based solely on the expected return and the risk attached to each. If two (or more) investment alternatives exist, each with the same degree of risk but differing expected returns, the investor will choose the investment with the higher return. Similarly, if two investment opportunities offer the same expected returns but differing risks, the investor will select the investment that entails less risk. Obviously, the investment that offers a higher return with lower risk than another will invariably be chosen. However, if one investment has a higher expected return and a higher risk, the choice is not clear; ultimately, the decision will depend on the investor's preferences, that is, his or her attitude to risk and return. Since this is a matter involving the personal characteristics of the investor, the outcome cannot be objectively forecast: It is a function of the individual's evaluation of risk versus return.

Exhibit 26–1 summarizes these conclusions. The vertical axis denotes the expected returns of stocks A, B, C, and D. The horizontal axis plots the risk associated with each stock, embodied by the standard deviation, a statistical measure of the volatility of stock price returns (the standard deviation represents the square root of variance, which is the average of the squared deviations from the mean stock price return).

In Exhibit 26–1, stocks B and C are clearly preferred to stock A: stock B has the same return as stock A with lower risk, while stock C has the same risk as stock A but a higher expected return. Stock D has a higher return and lower risk than stock A and is therefore the preferred investment. However, a clear choice cannot be made between stocks B, C, and D: stock B has a lower degree of risk but also a lower return than stocks C and D. Stock C has a higher return than both B and D, but also entails a higher risk. Note that a simple graphical rule may be adopted here: If a stock on the graph lies in the quadrant to the northwest of another stock, it will be

EXHIBIT 26–1

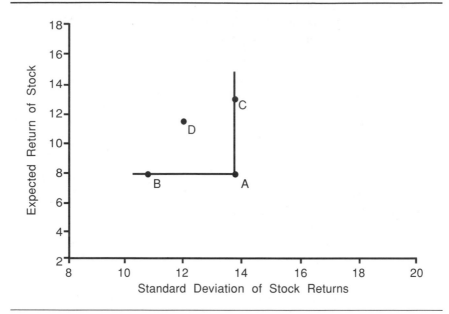

unambiguously chosen over that stock. This is clearly displayed by the choice of stocks B, C, and D over stock A. As stated earlier, the choice made by an investor between stocks B, C, and D cannot be objectively forecast. The outcome will depend on the investor's personal risk-return preferences.

The theory is extended to apply to combinations of "portfolios" of stocks and other investment instruments, with the same rules regarding return and risk being observed. Exhibit 26–2 shows portfolios of investments graphed according to their expected (portfolio) returns and volatility.

Using the northwest rule described earlier, it is possible to identify those portfolios that would be chosen by a rational investor over other portfolios; these would be the portfolios with the most northwesterly positions on the graph. Portfolio theory denotes these as "efficient" or "undominated" portfolios, since they are superior to other investment portfolios. The line connecting these portfolio positions on the graph is called the "efficient frontier," denoted in Exhibit 26–2 as the line *EF*. The portfolios lying along this line are sometimes described as being "mean-variance efficient." A rational investor would choose only between portfolios of stocks falling along this frontier; any other portfolio chosen would represent a suboptimal investment decision. The exact portfolio selected along the frontier would

EXHIBIT 26–2

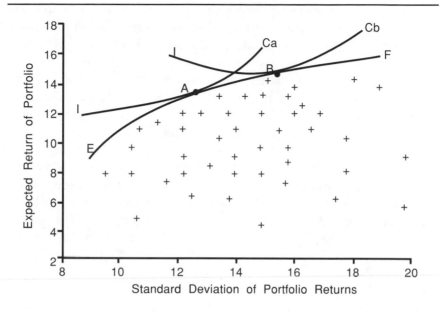

depend on the investor's risk-return preference, that is, the rate at which the investor would accept increased risk for increased return. This is illustrated graphically by the investor's indifference curve, a tool of traditional microeconomic theory, shown in Exhibit 26–2 as IC_a. The point of tangency between the indifference curve and the efficient frontier represents the portfolio chosen by a given investor. Thus investor A, with preferences denoted by indifference curve IC_a, would select portfolio A, while investor B, who has a greater tolerance for risk as denoted by indifference curve IC_b, would choose portfolio B.

APPLICATION TO EXPOSURE MANAGEMENT

Investors with access to information about the expected returns and risks of investment opportunities are assumed to behave in accordance with the tenets of this theory. In particular, it is assumed that an investor would select an investment portfolio chosen only from those located along the efficient frontier and, further, that the specific choice would reflect the investor's risk-return preferences and objectives. In making this decision, the investor would rely on the expected return and risk associated with each stock in the portfolio and the historical relationship between these stocks, revealed through (1) historical stock volatilities and correlations in the past, and/or (2) explicit information, statements, and analyses relating to each corporation whose stock is considered for inclusion in the portfolio.

In actual practice, institutional investors make formal application of the theory to establish efficient investment portfolios and to define for their own investors/beneficiaries the degree of risk associated with these investments. Mathematical techniques such as portfolio optimization are usually employed, utilizing historical data regarding stock returns and volatilities over varying periods of the past in order to identify appropriate efficient portfolios. An investment fund will often explicitly state its policy regarding risk in either qualitative or quantitative terms and sometimes estimate in advance the return expected in exchange for accepting this degree of risk. Even if investors do not explicitly or quantitatively identify expected returns and risks, it is obvious that investment decisions tacitly recognize them. To these investors, it is important that corporations whose stocks are included in the portfolio follow policies designed to maintain the risks and expected returns associated with their stocks. Specifically, actions taken by the corporation to reduce risk at the cost of decreased returns (or to increase risk in the interest of achieving higher returns) may be inappropriate as far as investor objectives and preferences are concerned. One absurd extreme, for example, would involve a corporation that reduces risk and return to a degree that approaches the return on risk-free investments such as U.S. government Treasury bills.

What are the implications for exposure management policy? Since exposure management activities aim specifically at reducing risk to the corporation with a concomitant incurrence of cost, it is clear that these activities are capable of making inappropriate adjustments in risk and return as far as investor interests are concerned. A corporation with major overseas activities may, for example, "overhedge" its currency exposures, resulting in an investment profile incongruent with the perception of its investors that it is a stock well geared to overseas growth and foreign currency appreciation. A debt-laden corporation that employs hedging strategies to fix the interest rates on its borrowings prior to the onset of a period of falling yields will frustrate the intention of investors who see it as an entity whose stock price is likely to appreciate due to lower interest charges. A corporation utilizing large amounts of raw materials that establishes substantial commodity hedges to lock in the price levels of its future requirements will fail to adequately exploit a period of falling commodity prices, frustrating investors who believe that such declines would substantially increase its profitability. Conversely but equivalently, a corporation that fails to hedge itself adequately in an environment of potentially adverse market conditions would mislead investors who believed in its ability to appropriately safe-guard its profits.

Exposure management policies (indeed, all corporate policies) should optimally aim at achieving no more and no less than that expected by investors. In an ideal world with perfect information flows and absolute efficiency of control by management, it may be argued that a corporation would be managed exactly in line with shareholder objectives. Manufacturing, marketing, pricing, acquisition and disposal of business—all corporate activities would be coordinated to result in the expected return-risk configuration that all or a majority of shareholders have clearly expressed themselves as desiring. Exposure management policy would be directed so as to facilitate achievement of this overall risk-reward profile; the interaction of alternative hedging policies with other corporate actions would be known, and the optimal exposure management policy would be clearly identified.

Unfortunately, such an ideal world does not exist. Mainstream corporate activities like manufacturing, marketing, capital investment, and so forth, are incapable of fine tuning; furthermore, the potential effects upon stock price volatility and returns from varying decisions relating to these is unknown, perhaps even unknowable, due to the limited experience of the past and the near impossibility of carrying out controlled experiments. Consequently, these policies must be treated to some extent as given parameters. Exposure management, however, may be utilized as an "overlay" to such mainstream corporate policies and may be directed toward a role of neutrality as far as the overall risk-return profile of the corporation is concerned. If this rationale is adopted, it means that the selection of an appropriate mix of hedging strategies must ignore mainstream corporate policies and focus on providing the hedge policy that results *in itself* in a degree of risk equivalent to that desired by the corporation's shareholders.

What is the practical application of this statement? Consider the question of interest rate policy relating to the appropriate mix of floating-rate and fixed-rate debt obligations. If the history of stock price action or (for the moment) some other appropriate analysis of investor preference has shown that the shareholders of a corporation desire, or are willing to accept, a risk or volatility reflected by a standard deviation of stock price returns of, say, 14 percent, then the correct proportion of fixed- to floating-rate debt would be that which has historically shown a volatility of 14 percent. Effectively, it is assumed that the cost implied by the adoption of such an interest rate policy would be acceptable to shareholders.

Consider the area of translation exposure or future foreign earnings exposure. The leading question relates to the proportion of total foreign exposure that should be hedged. If a hedge ratio of, say, 70 percent of total exposure would have in the past resulted in a volatility or risk measured by a standard deviation of 14 percent, equivalent to that deemed acceptable to shareholders, then that 70 percent ratio is the appropriate policy parameter. The hedging costs implied by the adoption of such a 70-30 ratio would implicitly be those acceptable to shareholders. In a similar fashion, the appropriate hedging policy for commodity exposure management could be identified; the same analysis could be applied to find the appropriate ratio of hedged and unhedged commodity exposures that should be adopted by the corporation.

A more sophisticated application, using certain assumptions, could assist in finding the proper mix of proxy currencies used to hedge foreign earnings and translation exposure, and to identify the appropriate duration of hedge instruments and the time horizon over which protection should be maintained. In selecting these parameters, the tenets of portfolio theory would be closely followed and an efficient frontier of hedge strategies would be identified, as shown in Exhibit 26–3. (Note that this diagram is the same as that in Exhibit 26–2, except that the y axis shows negative expected return, i.e., expected hedging costs, plotted against standard deviation along the x axis.) If a given hedge strategy involved the same risk as other strategies but at lower expected cost, then it would be selected over these. This is shown in Exhibit 26–3, where hedging structure A located on the efficient frontier EF is clearly preferable to strategies B and C. In general, only efficient hedge strategies (i.e., mean-variance efficient structures) would be employed.

Restricting the selection of hedge strategies to those located on the efficient frontier provides an initial decision rule to assist in setting exposure management policy. For example, if a corporation that has historically employed a 70-30 fixed-floating rate debt strategy were to find that a 60-40 ratio resulted in either lower risk at the same cost, the same risk at lower cost, or lower risk at lower cost, then the corporation could legitimately change its policy in the interest of its shareholders. If this rationale were applied to different areas of exposure management, the corporation would

EXHIBIT 26–3

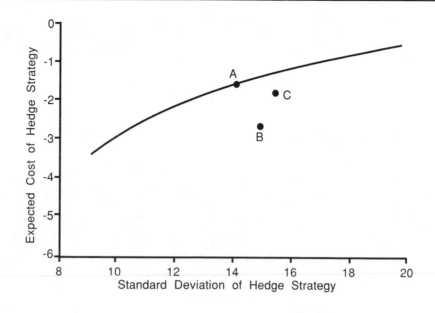

employ only those hedging policies that were found to be mean-variance efficient, that is, found to lie along the efficient frontier.

SERVING DIFFERENT MASTERS

Difficult and provocative questions arise, however, when one attempts to choose between strategies located *along* the frontier. In theory, the appropriate policy would be found at the point of tangency between the collective indifference curves of the corporation's shareholders and the efficient frontier, as described earlier. However, it is not easy to define a collective indifference curve for all shareholders because different investors possess varying risk-reward preferences. Exhibit 26–4 shows theoretical equilibrium points for different groups of investors. Which of these alternative policies should the corporation choose? Or, to put it another way, which group of investors may legitimately have its interests served by the management of the corporation?

EXHIBIT 26–4

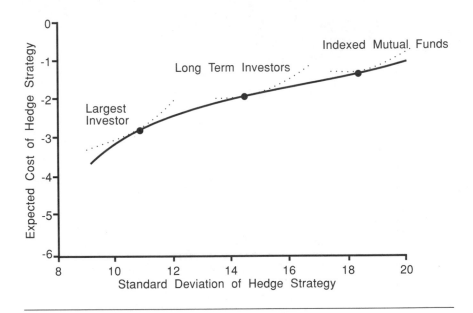

Identifying correctly those shareholders who represent the most important beneficiaries of the corporation is difficult. The management of a company may judge that the interests of its largest shareholders legitimately represent the higher priorities for the setting of policy. Communication with these shareholders to ascertain their objectives and preferences may provide a useful guide to corporate policy, including exposure management policy; this is particularly true if these shareholders are institutions that can clearly articulate their aims. Alternatively, corporations may find it appropriate to respond to the objectives of their longer-term investors, choosing policies that sacrifice short-term gains and accept a higher degree of more immediate risk in exchange for successful long-term performance. Or again, a corporation may choose to prioritize the interests of a broad band of investors, whose preferences and objectives are reflected directly by the behavior of a wide equity market index; in this case, the company may adopt policies that embody the same degree of risk or volatility as that displayed by the index over time.

There are other means by which a corporation may seek to identify appropriate exposure management policies. These center around the issue of information—the accuracy of information disseminated by the corporation about its activities and policies and the information relating to preferences implicitly or explicitly disclosed by shareholders. For example, a corporation with heavy involvement in energy and related activities would constitute a stock judged by investors to be an energy sector investment. To the extent that these shareholders expect risk (and returns) consistent with energy stock price movements, the corporation may adopt hedging policies with the same degree of volatility as that displayed by an energy sector index. If the corporation is a conglomerate with diversified operations, it might be possible for its management to adopt a risk profile comparable to that displayed by a competitor with a similar portfolio of businesses.

Alternatively, the company may choose to maintain the degree of volatility that its own stock return has experienced in the recent past during periods of outstanding performance or wide share ownership. In such instances, the corporation is effectively seeking to align itself with the preferences revealed by existing and potential investors through price action in the markets.

A more direct approach may involve publicizing the corporation's exposure management policies: Management may reveal in investor briefings and press releases that the corporation intends to conduct hedging policies to maintain, for example, an earnings profile that responds favorably to dollar declines in foreign exchange markets, interest rate declines in the domestic economy, or upward trends in certain commodity price levels. If this idea seems peculiar, it is worth noting that these are essentially the same informational parameters that professional investment managers are obliged to provide to their (large) investors; whether communicated in quantitative or qualitative terms and whatever the degree of freedom allowed to the manager in deviating from such stated policies, these investment guidelines are invariably sketched for investors in some detail. In practice, however, few corporations provide such specific information, relying instead on investor efforts and experience allied with stock analysts' findings to adequately inform their shareholders.

The crux of these arguments is that the choice of hedging strategy need not be overly concerned with issues like "beating the market," seeking to identify and eliminate as much exposure as possible, adopting complex hybrid strategies that provide an implicit play on future market direction, attempting to optimally time the execution and raising of hedges, or analyzing in retrospect the wisdom of loss-making hedge strategies. Emphasis should be placed instead on the objectives of defining shareholders' risk tolerance and return expectations, communicating the true profile of the corporation's operations (including hedging strategies), and formulating exposure management policies that align the institution's performance profile with shareholder expectations.

IMPLEMENTING AN "INVESTOR-FRIENDLY" POLICY

The specifics of the process described above may now be made clearer.

1. The corporation should identify the prevalent perceptions of its investor community about the risk level of its stock price. This may be done through recognizing the relevant groups of shareholders that the corporation feels legitimately represent its priority ownership and by acknowledging the expectations, objectives, and preferences of these groups. Alternatively, the corporation may choose to examine the impressions relating to its image among investors in general, namely, the perceptions concerning the primary industrial sector(s) in which it operates, the extent to which it is viewed as an institution with interests geared to world markets, the prevailing opinions held by existing and potential investors about the sensitivity of its costs and revenues to changing conditions in interest rate, foreign exchange, and commodity markets. Various sources for such information exist, including stock analyst opinions, shareholder discussions, published stock betas, inclusion in certain market indices, and so on.

2. Following step 1, the corporation will be in a position to identify the degree of risk or volatility that the external investor world associates with its stock price. A specific risk level or a risk band may then be assigned as a target exposure volatility which senior management should seek to maintain.

3. This target volatility or risk may then be used to derive investor-appropriate exposure management policies. The corporation would examine its interest rate, foreign exchange, and commodity hedging strategies to determine what mix of the exposure management policies employed in each area would achieve the required target risk level. To achieve this, mathematical optimization techniques utilizing historical data relating to interest rate, foreign exchange, and commodity price volatilities and correlations over an appropriate period in the past would be employed. Ideally, each functional exposure area would not be

analyzed in isolation. Instead, due attention would be given to the interaction, or correlation, between rates and prices in the three markets.

For example, the optimization would take note of the manner in which a particular foreign currency interest rate has fluctuated with the exchange rate of that currency against the base currency, or the tendency of a certain commodity price to move in line with a particular currency exchange rate. The result would be an efficient frontier of hedge policies, each embodying a different combination of interest rate, foreign exchange, and commodity management policies. This would illustrate the different levels of risk and return that would have been achieved in the past through different combinations of hedging strategies.

An example of this output is provided in Exhibit 26–5 and graphed in Exhibit 26–6. Note that strategies D and F do not lie on the efficient frontier in Exhibit 26–6, implying that they are not viable candidates. The strategies A, B, C, E, G, H, and I are mean-variance efficient and represent legitimate choices, depending on which level of risk is considered suitable. Note further that the example assumes a hedge horizon of five years for all strategies; this is adopted for simplicity. In practice, the period of the hedge strategy could itself be optimized in a similar manner, although this may involve some data constraints.

In this example, if the corporation wished to maintain a risk level equivalent to a standard deviation of 14 percent, it would adopt strategy E as shown in Exhibit 26–5, implying a hedging cost of 2.75 percent per annum. This would involve an optimal exposure management policy that hedged 43 percent of translation exposure and 63 percent of foreign earnings exposure over the five-year hedging horizon; the corresponding interest rate policy adopted would require that 60 percent of the corporation's debt be carried on a fixed interest rate basis, and 43 percent of commodity exposures would be covered.

THEORETICAL AND PRACTICAL PROBLEMS

The rationale proposed does present certain problems, both from a theoretical and an implementational point of view.

1. The methodology described ignores the volatility arising directly from the mainstream activities of the corporation (i.e., the volatility of costs and revenues), both domestic and overseas, relating to the everyday business of the institution. Consequently, all correlations

EXHIBIT 26–5
Hedging Strategies for Exhibit 26–6

Hedging Strategies	Foreign Exchange		Interest Rate	Commodity Exposure	Expected Hedging Costs per Annum (percent)	Standard Deviation of Hedging Policy
	Translation Exposure (percent hedged)	Foreign Earnings Exposure (percent hedged)	Percent of Total Debt Fixed	Percent of Total Hedged		
A	35%	93%	92%	56%	−4.50%	9.15
B	39	85	84	67%	−3.70%	11.20
C	38	70	71	55%	−3.30%	12.50
D	50	54	76	58%	−4.28%	13.20
E	43	63	60	43%	−2.75%	14.01
F	49	61	51	41%	−3.60%	14.86
G	59	48	42	32%	−2.33%	15.75
H	63	39	49	25%	−2.18%	17.03
I	72	28	59	29%	−2.10%	18.05

between these excluded cash flows and the market rates and prices included in the analysis are omitted. While this exclusion is less than satisfactory, it is justifiable owing to the near impossibility of accurately estimating these volatilities and correlations.[3]

2. No consideration is given to the possible "feedback" effect of an optimal exposure management policy on the behavior of the stock price itself. It is conceivable that such an effect may cause an undesirable shift in the risk-return profile of the stock. While the magnitude of any possible shift is impossible to estimate in advance, the corporation may be able to avert sharp variations in stock price behavior by avoiding sudden changes in its current exposure management policy. A good indicator for monitoring alterations in stock price action is the beta value, a measure of the correlation between the stock price movements and changes in an equity market index, such as the S&P 500 Index.

3. No mention has been made of the period over which market volatilities should be measured for inclusion in the optimization. This period should be lengthy enough to cover different trends in market magnitudes, but not so long as to reflect institutional structures and circumstances no longer prevailing. In general, a period in the recent past covering three to five years would be considered appropriate for this analysis.[4]

4. Another important question relates to the frequency of adjustments made to hedging policy in response to subsequent optimizations carried out. The initial optimization will be based on the original profile of exposure carried by the corporation; as these exposures change, new optimizations will have to be run in order to adjust hedging policy. A monthly reexamination of the exposure policy through regular optimization would appear to be sufficient. It is important for the corporation to avoid frequent changes in policy since these may prove to be expensive: Transactional costs in the

---

3 The same problem arises in the area of portfolio management. Fund managers who hold investment portfolios of foreign equities, bonds, and other overseas assets often tend to base their initial investment decisions solely on foreign currency-denominated returns and risks; subsequently, they implement foreign exchange hedges as an overlay strategy, usually employing optimization criteria. In doing this, they implicitly ignore the correlations between foreign currency-denominated asset returns and exchange rate movements. This is identical to the approach described above.

4 A related problem involves the degree of confidence that should be placed on the stability of volatilities and correlations over time. The implicit assumption made is that future volatilities in market rates and prices will continue to resemble those observed in the period from which optimization data are drawn. To put it another way, it is assumed that the period over which market volatilities are measured is sufficiently representative of the future period in which optimization results are to be applied.

EXHIBIT 26–6

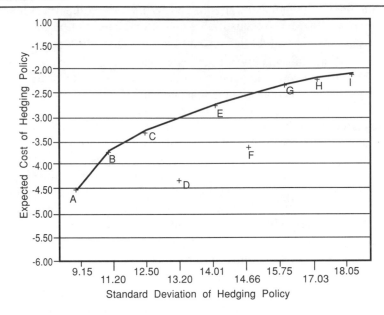

form of bid-offer spreads may be excessive, and undesirable cash outflows may result from the frequent raising of loss-making hedge strategies.

5. A potential problem may arise if the optimal exposure management policy selected results in a risk level for the stock incongruent with its current return. If the risk level is "correctly" chosen by management, but appears too high in relation to the expected return (implying that the corporation is in some sense underhedged), the return will rise through a fall in the stock price, other things being equal. Conversely, if the risk level is too low, resulting in an excessive stock return in relation to the risk involved, the return will fall through an appreciation in the stock price. In both cases, the market will ensure that the appropriate level of return is achieved, although some changes in the composition of the corporation's shareholder group may result. The price assumption here is that the corporation's management has made a correct identification of the level of risk that may be legitimately associated with the stock. Given the correctness of this assumption, modest changes in shareholder composition should be regarded as acceptable.

6. The most basic issue involved in this approach, however, relates to the separate existence of the corporation and the separation of management and ownership that the corporate structure provides. Senior management thinking and action may sometimes be unrelated to the direct interests of shareholders. This may be evidenced not only in the relatively straightforward situation where management and shareholder interests are directly opposed, but also in the case where management views itself as a better judge of what is beneficial to the corporation (and therefore its shareholders) than the shareholders themselves.

For example, consider the situation where the pursuance of an investor-appropriate exposure management policy is likely to lead to performance problems for the corporation over a period of time. Management may judge that the shareholders are somehow incorrect in requiring (through their implicit or explicit preferences) that such a policy be followed, and may consequently ignore the preferences of these shareholders by adopting an alternative policy. This may ultimately lead some of the corporation's shareholders to either mandate a change in senior management or to sell their stock in the company and invest the proceeds elsewhere; the latter seems to imply that management may be able to direct its shareholder composition toward the kind of investors it deems appropriate.

It is difficult to judge if the corporation's management is acting legitimately in taking such actions. Clearly, however, this issue arises in other areas of corporate policy, including the decision to diversify operations, divest business segments, reduce or augment dividends, and undertake large capital expenditures. Perhaps the best thing to say is that if one accepts some role for senior management in guiding and interpreting shareholder intentions in the light of the former's better-informed position, it is permissible to allow some degree of latitude to management in applying and fine-tuning exposure management and other policies, subject to the broad consensus of shareholders.

CORPORATE APPLICATION OF THESE TECHNIQUES TODAY

This chapter has argued for an application of portfolio theory and practice to the area of exposure management. Such an application provides a solution to current controversies regarding exposure management policy, or at least a clearer perspective of the role and scope of hedging activities. The question arises as to what extent this theory is actually being utilized by corporations today.

In many institutions, the functions of treasury exposure management and pension fund management are getting closer. This collaboration has been encouraged by the increased use of derivatives and other hedging instruments by pension fund managers and the realization that both functions utilize the same markets and counterparties. The similarity between treasury departments engaged in the hedging of translation and foreign earnings exposure arising from overseas operations and pension fund managers covering similar exposure from foreign bond and equity portfolios has not gone unnoticed. Exchange of ideas and personnel resources has also facilitated greater cooperation. This interaction has resulted in attempts to apply the tenets of portfolio theory to exposure management and efforts to transplant techniques used in exposure management to pension fund activities.

Several commercial and investment banks now offer optimization techniques and advisory services supporting the application of portfolio theory to their corporate treasury customers. Some of these are comprised purely of optimization methods applied to different exposures faced by the corporation and aimed at identifying the efficient frontier of hedging strategies as a menu for treasury decisions to focus upon. Others include quantitative and qualitative (even judgmental) techniques that embody directional forecasts for market magnitudes. Treasury departments are free to incorporate these techniques into their exposure management methodology, or even to mandate the advising financial institution to execute and manage the chosen hedge strategy.

Corporate treasuries are notoriously secretive about their hedging strategies. However, several large corporations now appear to be experimenting with optimization methods drawn directly from classic portfolio theory. At a minimum, these institutions may be utilizing the methodology to determine the position of their current strategies in mean-standard deviation space, and perhaps to adjust these policies to achieve efficient frontier positions. Beyond this, it may be surmised that some corporations are employing these techniques to justify altering their positions along the frontier, with the objective of changing the cost-risk trade-off between alternative strategies. One can only speculate on the rationale utilized by corporations to determine which optimal exposure management policy to adopt, but it is more than likely that considerations such as those described here are receiving serious attention.

Chapter Twenty-Seven

Credit Derivatives: A Primer

J. Gregg Whittaker and Sumita Kumar
Chemical Securities Inc.

In the vast and ever-changing landscape of financial derivatives, credit derivatives are among the most recent and most rapidly growing innovations. Just as other derivatives allow for management of market factors such as interest rate or currency risks, credit derivatives permit investors to manage credit exposures by separating their view on credit from other market variables. In this chapter, we will define credit derivatives, address why they are used and who is currently using them, and describe a number of specific products and their applications. Finally, we will consider the possibilities for the future development of this powerful new market.

WHAT ARE CREDIT DERIVATIVES?

Broadly defined, a credit derivative is a financial contract outlining a potential exchange of payments in which at least one leg of the cash flows is linked to the "performance" of a specified underlying credit-sensitive asset or liability. The underlying markets include bank loans, corporate debt, trade receivables, emerging market and municipal debt, and the credit exposure generated from other derivatives-linked activities. The performance of such market credits reflects perceived risk and the cost of a potential default.

As in other more traditional derivative markets, swap, note, and option-based products form the foundation for all credit derivative products. For example, a credit option or credit-linked note can be structured to pay the purchaser upon a default or credit downgrade. Moreover, credit derivatives can also take the form of financial swaps where a counterparty exchanges the total return of a certain credit in return for some spread over a specified benchmark, such as LIBOR.

WHY USE CREDIT DERIVATIVES?

Credit derivatives provide users with an efficient, tailor-made, on- or off-balance-sheet means of attaining or hedging credit risk. Credit derivatives offer tremendous flexibility in terms of tailoring a structure to meet individual specifications, thereby enabling users to overcome a variety of market and nonmarket impediments in order to achieve their desired investment and hedging objectives. By reducing capital requirements and greatly easing the back-office administrative burdens, these derivatives are often a cleaner, lower-cost alternative to the underlying cash markets. Moreover, they can provide access to investors who may be otherwise precluded from the underlying cash markets. Users can also choose the degree of leverage that best suits their particular investment and risk management style.

From a hedging standpoint, credit derivatives are powerful and innovative credit risk management tools. Credit derivatives represent the first broad-based market designed specifically for the management of credit risk. In 1994 alone, over $1 trillion in new bank loans and corporate bonds were issued and over $4 trillion of swap-related activity. Popular methods to hedge the associated credit risk have typically been the incorporation of covenants into the agreements, collateralization, and portfolio diversification. While effective to varying degrees, all are limited and fail to fully immunize the creditor. The limitations of traditional credit risk management strategies can be seen when considering the "credit paradox." Most institutions have limited credit-related resources and must specialize to maximize their efficiency. This specialization inherently results in a concentrated credit exposure. For example, a regional bank may lend predominantly to corporations within a limited geographical area, a certain industry, or both, while an automobile parts manufacturer has trade receivables outstanding to a highly concentrated, highly cyclical group of auto-related companies. However, modern portfolio theory, not to mention common sense, dictates that a diversified portfolio is required to achieve an optimal risk/return profile, that is, to reach the efficient frontier. Covenants and collateral, even if implemented, provide partial protection at best, and cash market diversification may not be practical. The regional bank must maintain and enhance its existing relationships, which may be endangered by selling its loans. Similarly, the auto parts manufacturer may have no other outlets for its products.

Credit derivatives can be used to diversify credit exposure from an economic perspective, while allowing the user to continue its on-balance-sheet activities unabated, thereby solving the credit paradox. The risk management capabilities of credit derivatives will be discussed more fully in later sections of this chapter.

From an investment standpoint, credit derivatives offer users efficient access to the underlying credit-sensitive markets. Efficiency here is defined as increased flexibility and leverage along with decreased cash, regulatory capital, and back-office requirements. Moreover, the prudent use of credit derivatives can enable users to minimize their tax liabilities, especially in cross-border situations. The overall result can be significantly enhanced performance relative to the available cash market alternatives.

Users of Credit Derivatives

The universe of potential users of credit derivatives is as vast as the number of institutions that are exposed to or that seek exposure to credit risk. This includes commercial banks, insurance companies, corporations, money managers, mutual funds, hedge funds, and pension funds. These institutions may use these innovative products for either investment or risk management applications.

CREDIT DERIVATIVE STRUCTURES

As mentioned earlier, credit derivatives include credit swaps, credit-linked notes, and credit options. The following section provides an overview of these general structures and a brief description of some of the specific products. The next two sections, on investment and risk management applications, will further expand on these concepts through a series of case studies.

Credit Swaps

A credit swap is an agreement between two counterparties to exchange disparate cash flows, at least one of which must be tied to the performance of a specified credit-sensitive asset, or a portfolio or index of such assets.

The other cash flow is usually tied to some floating rate index such as LIBOR, a fixed rate, or linked to some other credit-sensitive asset(s).

While there are a number of variations of a credit swap, we will describe only two.

- Total return swap
- Default swap

Total return swap. A total return swap is a swap agreement in which the total return of a bank loan or credit-sensitive security is exchanged for some other cash flow, usually tied to LIBOR or some other loan or credit-sensitive security. While no principal amounts are exchanged and no physical change of ownership occurs, the total return swap allows participants to "effectively" go long or short the underlying security. As such, a total return swap can be considered a synthetic loan or security.

The maturity of the total return swap need not match that of the underlying security, and the swap can typically be terminated at any time. Moreover, at termination many such structures allow the user to purchase the underlying loan or security at the initial price in lieu of a cash settlement of the swap. However, if the swap is cash settled, the termination payment is typically determined by means of a dealer poll of the prevailing underlying market value.

Default swap. A default swap is a swap agreement in which a periodic fixed-rate payment or up-front fee is exchanged for the promise of some specified payment(s) to be made only if a particular, predetermined credit event occurs. The default swap can be structured on a single credit name or a basket of names. A credit event is typically defined as a default or a credit downgrade, where a default could include bankruptcy, insolvency, or failure to make payments within a predetermined amount of time. A lowering of the credit by public rating agencies below a certain prespecified level would constitute a downgrade.

A default swap, then, is comparable to a credit-wrapper. The default payment can be structured in a number of ways. It can be linked to the price movement of a particular security, it can be set at a predetermined recovery rate (binary payoff), or it can be in the form of an actual delivery of the underlying security at a predetermined price. Regardless of the form, a default swap allows for the transference of credit risk from one swap counterparty to the other.

Credit-Linked Notes

Credit-linked notes provide investors with a cost-effective means of monetizing credit views and provide hedgers with an innovative credit risk management tool. These notes come in a variety of forms, but the common thread between them is the link between return and the credit-related performance of the underlying. Credit-linked notes are loans or securities, typically issued by an investment grade entity, with coupon, redemption, and maturity provisions like traditional note structures. Unlike standard notes, however, the performance of a credit-linked note is a function of the performance of the underlying asset, in addition to the performance of the issuer. Therefore, the redemption value of the credit-linked note is directly dependent on the redemption value of the underlying asset. While there are many types of credit-linked notes, we will briefly describe only a few of these innovative structures.

- BLAST Note[sm]
- DEMO Note[sm]
- DISCO Note[sm]
- CLEAR Note[sm]

BLAST note[sm]—Bank loan asset-backed secured trust note[sm]. A BLAST Note[sm] is an investment-grade debt or loan obligation of a trust or creditworthy entity that provides high yields, leveraged upside and limited downside returns relative to a diversified loan portfolio. The trust uses the note proceeds to purchase Treasury securities, which are then used to collateralize the "effective" purchase of bank loans. From an economic perspective, the note holders are long both the Treasuries and the underlying bank loans. The collateralization may be as low as 10 percent, allowing investors to achieve an upside leverage of up to 10 to 1, with yields topping 20 percent per annum. However, unlike other leveraged transactions, there are no margin calls with a BLAST Note[sm], so the investor can lose no more than the initial investment amount.

From an investment perspective, BLAST Notes[sm] are the economic equivalent of purchasing a diversified portfolio of loans on margin, but without the risk of margin calls. Moreover, due to its innovative structuring, the note itself will carry an investment-grade rating even though the underlying portfolio is leveraged and has an average rating that is clearly noninvestment grade.

From a risk management perspective, BLAST Notes[sm] can be issued as a means of hedging the credit risk of an existing portfolio. These notes provide the issuer with "first loss" protection on the underlying loans.

DEMO note[sm]—Default expectation monetizing obligation note[sm]. DEMO Notes[sm] are debt or loan obligations that pay investors an enhanced return in consideration for compounded credit risk. DEMO Notes[sm] are overcollateralized by a portfolio of underlying loans or credit-sensitive securities. In the event of a default of any one of the loans or securities, the DEMO Note[sm] is terminated and the defaulted loan or security is "put" to the note holder. The note can be cash settled as well, based either on the post-default market value of the underlying or on some pre–agreed-upon recovery rate. These notes enable investors to monetize their outlook more fully concerning the default risk of the underlying assets while providing first-loss credit risk protection on the underlying portfolio to the issuer.

DISCO note[sm]—Default immunized secured credit obligation note[sm]. DISCO Notes[sm] are debt or loan obligations that allow investors to participate in any upside price performance of some underlying bank loan or credit-sensitive security while providing full principal protection. These notes are designed for the risk-averse investor looking to capitalize on the potential upside of "risky" loans or securities. Note holders participate in the upside price performance of the underlying asset with total immunization against downside losses in consideration for reduced coupon payments. Consequently, the DISCO Note[sm] will outperform a direct investment in the underlying asset during a downturn in the market and will show a much more stable overall payoff profile. From a risk management perspective, the DISCO Note[sm] is an innovative variation on the more traditional covered call writing strategy for the issuer.

CLEAR note[sm]—Credit-Linked Enhanced Asset Return Note[sm]. CLEAR Notes[sm] are debt or loan obligations that provide investors with enhanced returns relative to some underlying bank loan or credit-sensitive security in consideration of forgoing all or part of the recovery value in the event of default. Therefore, this note enables users to monetize their outlook more fully concerning the default risk of these assets. The issuer of the CLEAR Note[sm] is not the underlying borrower, but some other investment-grade entity. Further, in the event of default of the underlying, the CLEAR Note[sm] is terminated at some pre–agreed-upon redemption value, which may be as low as zero, with no further recourse to either the note issuer or the underlying borrower. In consideration of forgoing any further claim to the recovery value, the CLEAR Note[sm] yield is significantly higher than that of the underlying asset.

Credit Options

A credit option is a privately negotiated, over-the-counter option contract between two counterparties, which can be customized to meet the specific credit-related hedging or investment objectives of the client. A credit call option gives the purchaser the right, but not the obligation, to buy an underlying credit-sensitive asset or credit spread at a predetermined price for a predetermined period of time. A credit put option gives the purchaser the right, but not the obligation, to sell the underlying asset or credit spread at a predetermined price for a prespecified period of time. These basic option structures provide the groundwork for building more exotic credit option structures.

Credit options can be used as both a hedging and an investment vehicle. Purchasing credit options enables investors and hedgers to participate in price or credit spread movement while risking no more than the option premium. Selling credit options can be a valuable source of fee income for those who are looking to enhance portfolio returns. As in other markets, there are a myriad of credit option products, but all fall into one of the following two broad categories.

- Standard credit options
- Exotic credit options

Standard credit options.   The standard credit option gives the purchaser the right, but not the obligation, to buy (call) or sell (put) an asset or credit spread at a stated price (strike) for a specified period of time (expiration). These structures allow investors to take a view solely on credit-related performance, without any exposure to the absolute level of yields or to any other noncredit market factor. For example, if an investor has the view that a particular credit spread is going to widen in the next year, he or she can purchase a one-year call option on that credit spread. The option will be in the money at expiration if the credit spread does indeed widen beyond the strike. If it does not, the investor's loss is limited to the premium paid for the call.

Exotic credit options.   Exotic credit options are defined as credit options that break at least one of the rules of a standard option with respect to time, price, position, or underlying asset. The most common forms of exotic credit options are the barrier and digital options.

Barrier credit options involve a contingent credit-related mechanism that serves to activate or inactivate the option. In other words, the trigger that turns the option "on" or "off" is a function of the credit quality of the underlying asset. Refer again to the example above of an option on a credit spread, but now consider a "down-and-out" call. The down-and-out call is structured similarly to the standard call, except that this option ceases to exist if the credit spread narrows below a prespecified knockout level. Consequently, the premiums for barrier credit options are typically lower than for like standard options. Other forms of barrier credit options include down and ins, up and outs, and up and ins.

Digital (or binary) credit options have payouts at expiration of either zero, if the option expires out of the money, or some pre–agreed-upon fixed amount, if the option expires in the money. The fixed payment, unlike a standard option, is independent of how deep in-the-money the option actually is. For example, a digital put option on a bank loan could pay the par amount if the borrower defaulted or nothing if the borrower continued to perform as scheduled, regardless of the underlying market price.

INVESTMENT APPLICATIONS

The following section takes a closer look at the various credit derivative structures defined in the previous section by developing and working through a number of investment applications.

Synthetic High-Yield Debt Trading

Assume an investor seeks to attain $10 million of exposure to an outstanding high-yield bond or a bond in syndication. However, this investor has limited access to the cash bond market, limited back-office capabilities, or needs to invest off-balance-sheet. The investor can use a total return swap to gain exposure to the bond while keeping it off the balance sheet (see Exhibit 27–1).

Assume that an investor chooses to leverage her cash investment 10 times by holding in reserve, or pledging to Chemical, only $1 million

EXHIBIT 27–1
Total Return Swap to Attain Desired Exposure

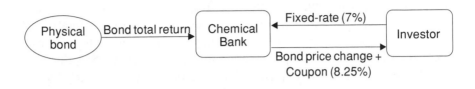

against the $10 million underlying exposure. Further, assume that the underlying bond yield paid to the investor is 8.25 percent, while the fixed swap payment to Chemical Bank is 7.0 percent. This 125 basis point spread is leveraged 10 times to 12.5 percent in respect of the client's investment. Add to this the cash yield on the $1 million of, say, 6 percent, and the swap generates a current annual income of 18.5 percent. Moreover, the swap enables the investor to avoid the compliance and back-office burdens of bond ownership.

Building a Loan Portfolio

Bank loans are an underutilized asset class that have historically generated relatively stable, attractive returns. The leveraged (noninvestment grade) bank loan market remains a largely untapped source of high-yield paper, with over $250 billion in syndicated leveraged loans outstanding but only $10 billion held by institutional investors. Between January 1993 and May 1995, the leveraged bank loan annual return was 10.43 percent, compared with 11.18 percent and 12.16 percent for high-yield securities and the S&P 500 Index respectively. Moreover, because these loans are senior-secured, floating rate assets, they are far less volatile than high-yield bonds. Over this same time period, the annual volatility of loans was only 2.17 percent compared to 4.52 percent for high yield and 8.39 percent for the S&P. Consequently, bank loans have provided attractive, highly competitive returns that have only a fraction of the volatility that has prevailed in the high yield and equity markets. Credit derivatives in the form of swaps, notes, or options provide efficient access to this historically strong, underutilized asset class.

Consider a life insurance company that is seeking to better utilize its credit analysis capabilities by investing in leveraged par loans. However, to the relatively high capital requirements for noninvestment grade assets coupled with the administrative burdens inherent in the cash loan market, diminish the appeal of this investment strategy.

The solution to this problem for many is the BLAST Note[sm]. A total return swap, while appealing at first blush, is inappropriate since life insurance companies can only use swaps and other like derivatives for "risk management" purposes. The BLAST Note[sm], on the other hand, is allowable for investment purposes because it is a rated, investment-grade debt obligation. Moreover, the note can be structured to meet the investor's leverage requirements, or lack thereof, and it can be accomplished with relatively simple back-office administrative demands. Consequently, the BLAST Note[sm] offers clients an allowable, efficient mechanism for investing in a diversified portfolio of bank loans.

For example, assume the insurance company purchases a $10 million BLAST Note[sm], issued by a trust, which uses the note proceeds to purchase T-notes. The T-notes are then pledged to Chemical Bank as collateral for a swap paying the total return on a $100 million loan portfolio yielding LIBOR plus 250 basis points. In consideration, the trust makes a swap payment of LIBOR plus 125 basis points to Chemical (see Exhibit 27–2).

The swap spread here of 125 basis points on $100 million notional is leveraged 10 times to 12.5 percent in respect to the note holder's $10 million investment. Add to this the 6 percent T-note yield, and the BLAST Note[sm] generates current annual income of 18.5 percent.

Trading Credit Spreads

Suppose an investor is bullish on, say, Mexican par bonds and seeks to profit from any narrowing of their credit spread relative to U.S. Treasury yields. This can be accomplished by purchasing a knockout (up-and-out) put on the credit spread. The premium for this put is moderated by two factors: the knockout feature and the character of forward credit spreads. First, as discussed previously, the knock-out feature reduces option premiums relative to standard options. Second, the fact that forward credit spreads are wider than spot spreads (a function of the positive net carry resulting from buying the underlying emerging market debt and shorting the US Treasuries, that is, the dealers hedge), likewise tends to reduce put premiums (see Exhibit 27–3).

EXHIBIT 27–2
BLAST Note^{sm} to Attain Desired Exposure

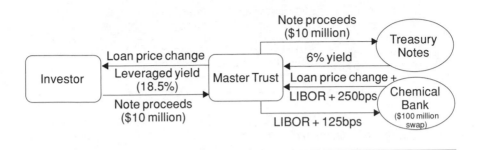

EXHIBIT 27–3
Up-and-Out Put Option

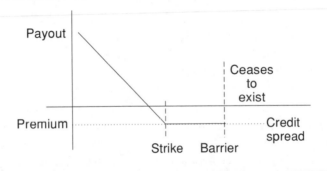

The investor profits as credit spreads narrow between Mexican par bonds and U.S. Treasury notes below the strike. If spreads are above the strike but below the barrier, the option has no intrinsic value, but the potential remains that the option could expire in the money. However, if spreads ever rise above the barrier (i.e. if the investor is sufficiently incorrect about spreads narrowing) the knockout put ceases to exist and the investor realizes a loss equal to the premium paid.

Bearish spread strategies can be implemented as well, but they are often less efficiently priced than their bullish counterparts because of, again, the character of forward credit spreads and the potential difficulty and cost of shorting the underlying emerging market debt.

EXHIBIT 27–4
Total Return Swap to Arbitrage Capital Structure Mispricings

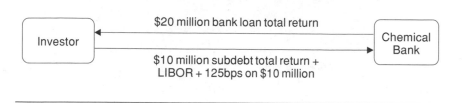

Capital Structure Arbitrage

Investors can use total return swaps to arbitrage a perceived mispricing between bank loans and subordinated debt of the same issuer. For example, suppose that both assets are priced at par, but the loan yields LIBOR plus 375 basis points while the debt yields LIBOR plus 275 basis points. Clearly, in the absence of some overriding technical or other nonmarket factor, a mispricing exists since the senior, secured asset yields more than the subordinated asset. To efficiently exploit this opportunity, a total return swap can be executed to effectively go long the bank loan and go short the subordinated debt at a ratio of, say, two to one.[1]

This swap (see Exhibit 27–4) generates a net spread of 175 basis points [(100bps × $10 / $20) + (250bps × $10 / $20)] on $20 million. Assuming a $2 million cash investment, this spread is leveraged 10 times into a 17.5 percent return. Add this to the return on the cash itself of, say, 6 percent, and this structure generates a yield of 23.5 percent per annum.

Creating a Guaranteed Fund

Suppose a pension fund wishes to attain bank loan exposure but has strict guidelines regarding asset credit quality and principal preservation. DISCO Notes[sm] can be issued by a creditworthy entity and customized to provide participation in any underlying bank loan price appreciation, but with limited or no associated downside risk.[2]

---

1 The ratio of two to one, though somewhat arbitrary in this example, reflects the tendency of subordinated bonds to be more credit sensitive than their bank loan counterparts.

2 For those familiar with the equity derivative market, the DISCO Note[sm] is the structural equivalent of a protected equity note (PEN), but it is linked to bank loans instead of equity.

For example, a pension fund purchases a two-year, $50 million DISCO Note^{sm} from Chemical Bank that pays the investor 100 percent of any underlying distressed loan portfolio price appreciation over the life of the note, payable at maturity, plus a coupon of 1 percentz per annum.

Thus, if the underlying loan prices appreciate by 20 percent over the next two years, the total return paid to the investor is 20 percent of the notional ($10 million) plus the coupons or about 11 percent per annum. On the other hand, if the loan prices fall by 20 percent, the investor is fully protected and receives a total return of 1 percent per annum, the minimum return guaranteed by Chemical Bank under the terms of the DISCO Note^{sm}.

Creating Synthetic Assets with Desired Risk Profiles

A fund manager can use a DEMO Note^{sm} to create assets synthetically with the desired risk/return profile. For example, assume that the manager wishes to attain exposure to a certain noninvestment-grade sector of the market, but is unable to find the desired paper due to a lack of supply. Higher-grade paper, which we will assume is more readily available, can be put into a DEMO Note^{sm} structure to create the desired noninvestment-grade exposure with the associated higher yields.

Specifically, assume that the fund manager seeks two-year, B-rated credit exposure, but cannot source the paper. However, BB/Ba paper is readily available. A two-year, $10 million, B-rated DEMO Note^{sm} yielding LIBOR plus 400 basis points can be structured with four underlying BB/Ba loans, each valued at $10 million and with an average yield of LIBOR plus 275 basis points. The note is illustrated in Exhibit 27–5.

The investor is taking on compounded credit risk in that the DEMO Note^{sm} effectively defaults if "any" of the underlying loans default. According to Moody's, the likelihood of a BB/Ba credit defaulting within two years is about 4 percent. Therefore, the likelihood of any one of four BB/Ba credits defaulting within two years, assuming zero correlation, is about 15 percent ($1.0 - 96\%^4$), which is about equal to the likelihood of a B credit defaulting within two years. In other words, the investor has created a B-rated type security yielding LIBOR plus 400 basis points.

From the issuers standpoint, the note provides first-loss protection on the underlying loan portfolio. The cost of the protection, the 400 basis-point spread on the DEMO Note^{sm} over the bank's funding cost of LIBOR, results in a 100 basis-point decline in the margin earned on each of the four underlying loans. In the event that any of the loans default, the DEMO

EXHIBIT 27–5
DEMO Note^{sm} *to Create Desired Exposure*

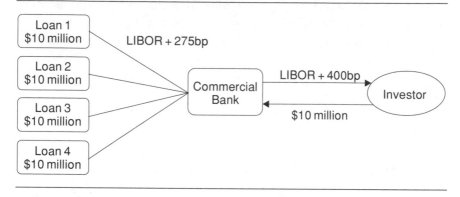

Note^{sm} is terminated, the bank keeps the $10 million of note proceeds, and the defaulted loan is put to the investor. Consequently, the bank is made whole and the investor bears the risk of the first default. However, any subsequent defaults are the sole responsibility of the bank. The investor can then sell the defaulted underlying loan or hold on to it and go through the workout process.

RISK MANAGEMENT APPLICATIONS

In addition to the investment applications described in the previous section, credit derivatives can be used as an effective risk management tool. The following case studies illustrate a few of the myriad of hedging strategies available to participants in this powerful new derivatives market.

Hedging Default Risk

Credit derivatives can be used to provide default protection in respect to a single, specified credit-sensitive asset or a portfolio of such assets. Assume a commercial bank has exposure to a loan for which it is seeking default protection. The bank enters into a default swap in which it receives some agreed-upon amount in the event that the underlying borrower defaults in consideration for making a fixed quarterly swap payment (see Exhibit 27–6).

EXHIBIT 27–6
Default Swap to Hedge Risk of Loan Default

The bank has thereby exchanged the credit risk of the borrower for that of the swap counterparty in consideration for reducing the margin on the loan by an amount equal to the periodic swap fee.

This fee will depend primarily on the amount to be paid in the event of default as well the definition of "default" itself. The swap may be structured so that, in the event of default, the underlying loan is put to Chemical Bank at a price equal to the agreed-upon market value of the loan at the inception of the trade. Or the price paid by Chemical might alternatively be struck at par. On the other hand, the default swap might be cash settled based on some pre–agreed-upon fixed amount or based on the prevailing post-default market value.

Moreover, the definition of default is another key to the default swap and its pricing. A default may include bankruptcy, insolvency, or merely the failure to make payments within a predetermined amount of time. A downgrade of the credit by a public rating agency below a certain prespecified level might also constitute a default. In short, the more broadly default is defined, the higher the default swap fees, and vice versa.

The bank could also issue a DEMO Note[sm] or a CLEAR Note[sm] to provide first-loss default protection for a portfolio of bank loans. Referring to the discussion of DEMO Notes[sm] in the previous section, these notes provide the issuer with full protection against loss in the event that any of the underlying loans default. However, any losses due to subsequent defaults are borne solely by the issuer. Similarly, CLEAR Notes[sm] on the individual underlying loans would provide protection for any and all defaulted loans, but each payout is fixed, implying the issuer receives first loss protection only to the extent of the pre–agreed-upon payouts.

Diversifying Concentrated Portfolios

Consider another total return swap, this time one used as a hedging tool instead of an investment vehicle. As discussed previously, many institutions face the problem we define as the credit paradox. Restated briefly, most institutions have limited credit-related resources and must specialize to maximize their efficiency. This specialization results inherently in a concentrated credit exposure. However, a diversified portfolio is required to achieve an optimal risk/return profile. For a variety of reasons, including relationship maintenance and underlying market illiquidity, traditional cash market mechanisms fail to fully address the problem. Credit derivatives, on the other hand, can be used to diversify credit exposure from an economic perspective, while allowing the user to continue its on-balance-sheet activities unabated.

Consider a commercial bank that, like most banks, can best leverage its limited origination and credit-related resources by specializing in a few specific industries, geographical locations, or both, resulting in a concentrated loan portfolio that it seeks to diversify. However, because its clients expect it to hold the loans on balance sheet, the bank cannot diversify by traditional secondary loan market trading. In this case, the bank can enter into a total return swap to diversify its risk without actually selling the underlying loans (see Exhibit 27–7).

As a result of the swap, the commercial bank has effectively diversified its concentrated loan portfolio as desired, while retaining the original loans on its balance sheet to maintain good client relations, thereby pushing out toward the efficient frontier and solving the credit paradox.

Freeing Up Credit Lines

Credit derivatives can also be used to free up internal credit lines to borrowers, trading partners, or traditional derivatives counterparties. Assume a commercial bank has reached its internal lending limit with a certain client, but it must continue to provide for the upcoming funding needs of the client to maintain a strong relationship. To address this problem, the bank enters into a total return swap tied to the underlying loans. Under the swap, the bank pays the total return on the existing loan position in consideration for a LIBOR-based payment. In so doing, while the underlying loans stay on the books, the bank has effectively swapped the borrower's credit risk for that of the swap counterparty.

EXHIBIT 27-7
Total Return Swap to Diversify Concentrated Loan Portfolio

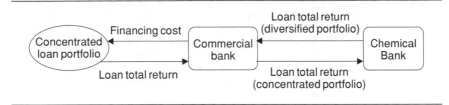

From the perspective of internal risk management, the commercial bank's credit exposure to the borrower has been reduced or eliminated and the corresponding credit lines freed up, but it has been replaced by exposure to the swap counterparty. Therefore, it is critical that the bank executes such swaps only with highly creditworthy dealers to which it has, or can establish, significant credit guidelines.

Hedging Credit Spreads

Consider an investor who is long floating-rate LDC paper and wishes downside credit protection while retaining upside potential. In other words, the investor seeks protection in the event that a deterioration in the underlying credit leads to an increase in the credit spread relative to U.S. Treasury notes. Consequently, the investor purchases a credit spread call (see Exhibit 27–8).

As the credit spread rises and the relative value of the paper falls, the increased call payout serves as a hedge for the investor.

Hedging Credit Downgrades

A variation of the default swap can be used to hedge the risks associated with the downgrade of assets in a portfolio. Suppose a fund manager is limited by charter to maintaining the credit quality of each of the fund's investments to BB/Ba2 or better. Typically, to avoid the pitfalls associated with a forced liquidation in the event of a credit downgrade, the manager may buy higher-rated paper than is minimally required. For example, the fund manager may purchase only BBB-/Baa3 assets. The cost to the fund manager is the yield given up by purchasing the higher-rated, higher-priced assets as opposed to BB/Ba2 assets.

EXHIBIT 27–8
Call Option to Hedge Credit Spreads

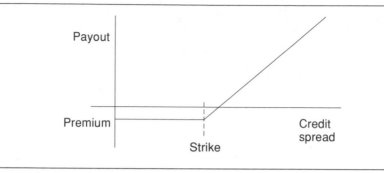

The fund manager could use a default swap that pays off in the event of a rating downgrade. If the swap fee paid by the fund is less than the forgone yield spread defined above, then the default swap may be a more cost-effective means of managing the risk of a credit downgrade.

FUTURE MARKET DEVELOPMENT

Credit derivatives are currently growing at an exponential rate and have the potential to become a trillion dollar plus market, given the expanse of the underlying credit markets combined with the compelling investment and risk management applications these products provide. Virtually all aspects of the underlying credit markets and market players point to continued and sustained growth. Corporate bond outstandings grew at a compound annual rate of 11 percent from 1982 to 1993,[3] domestic C&I bank loan syndications totaled $665 billion in 1994,[4] and junk bond issuances increased dramatically after hitting a low in 1990. Moreover, corporate bonds are a large percentage of the holdings of insurance companies, pension funds, and mutual funds. Corporations and regional, commercial, and Ex-Im banks should also become major users of credit derivatives as the market continues to evolve.

Further, we expect that as the market becomes more efficient and further develops, a variety of customized products will emerge as users begin to

---

3 Source: Flow of Funds Account, Federal Reserve Board.

4 Source: Loan Pricing Corporation.

better understand the possibilities and the varied uses of credit derivatives. Various market indexes will develop to aid market participants in tracking performance. And the growth of the credit derivatives market will see the increased use of loan indexes, corporate bond indexes and bond sector indices as investment and hedging benchmarks. Consequently, a liquid over-the-counter market should develop for options and other derivative products tied to these indexes and to the more widely traded underlying bonds and loans themselves.

One of the most dramatic outcomes from the continued development of credit derivatives will be the creation of a market for credit. Currently, the pricing of credit risk is often a subjective undertaking dependent upon an analyst's interpretation of the available financial information. In the not too distant future, however, pricing credit risk will be as simple as pulling up a screen on your PC, with trading opportunities created when your own views differ from those of the market. Efficient credit risk hedging capabilities will be available and affordable to virtually all end users.

However, one of the impediments to the complete development of credit derivatives is the lack of a credible information infrastructure. Currently only limited historical credit information is available for users. Typically, it is the banks and other such credit issuers who have tracked credit performance, but even here the information is generally fragmented and incomplete. So, for the market to sustain its growth, banks must continue their efforts to enhance and consolidate their analysis, and nonbank users will have to gain access to this information.

In addition, the accounting and regulatory environment for credit derivatives will have to become more certain before many of the potential players are willing to participate and take full advantage of these products. For example, hedge accounting and regulatory capital relief for institutions using these products for risk management purposes is vital to the development of the market in this area.

CONCLUSION

The credit derivatives market provides clean, efficient access to underlying credit-sensitive markets, thereby providing an effective means by which users can attain their investment and risk management objectives. These derivatives, whether in the form of swaps, notes, or options, provide users with a more cost-effective means of reaching their investment goals through reduced cash, capital, and back-office requirements along with increased leverage potential. In addition, they offer the risk manager powerful new hedging tools, capable of isolating credit risk from other market risks.

Because credit derivative structures encompass a variety of markets, a broad array of potential users exits for whom this market fills a myriad of important investment and risk management needs. The underlying markets include everything from bank loans, corporate and sovereign debt, and municipal bonds to the credit risks inherent in other more traditional derivative markets. Consequently, the list of current and potential users includes commercial banks, insurance companies, corporations, money managers, mutual funds, hedge funds, and pension funds.

The credit derivatives market will almost certainly continue to develop rapidly for the foreseeable future. However, its long-term prospects hinge on the development of a sound regulatory environment, more readily available historical information, and a better understanding among participants about the advantages and versatility of these products.

Chapter Twenty-Eight

Portfolio Simulation Model Analysis of Derivative Product Credit Risk

Augustus Moore
Sumitomo Bank Capital Markets, Inc.

THE NEW WAVE OF RISK ANALYSIS

The initial wave of expansion of the derivative products markets over the past decade is now being followed by a second wave of risk analysis. Just as the first wave relied on relatively complex analytical tools to properly price and hedge its products, the second wave requires complex tools to effectively manage the individual counterparty and portfolio risks associated with these products. For financial institutions familiar with relatively static credit exposures, management's initial response was to rely on simulation models to capture only the worst-case exposures of individual derivative product contracts. For day-to-day credit exposure management, these worst-case numbers are generally applied as fixed percentages of notional amount for each transaction type. As the products and markets mature, however, only firms with the ability to capitalize on the dynamic nature of the business will continue to find profitability between the increasingly thin market spreads.

The Purpose of Credit Control

If we consider credit risk to be primarily defined by the risk of loss due to counterparty default, the function of the credit department in the derivative products context is twofold. While the traditional role as assessor of counterparty credit quality and transaction suitability remains, we are also faced with the additional need to properly estimate the magnitude of potential loss when default might occur. This second problem is essentially defined by the structure and tenor of the derivative contracts in question and the volatility of the underlying rates or indexes that determine their value. This dilemma has been widely discussed, and models for calculation of this risk on an individual transaction basis have been developed and generally accepted. Practically speaking, however, very few dealers assess these risks effectively on a portfolio basis.

Most likely and worst-case estimates of credit losses.   As in any other business, when management is faced with an uncertain future, it requests two basic scenarios upon which to base investment decisions: the expected scenario and the worst-case scenario. Derivative products credit managers have historically ignored the expected and focused on the worst-case scenario. At the same time, in an effort to fit the derivative product into a loan analysis context, they have represented the exposure of that product as a fixed amount from inception to maturity, which the product would only exceed in particularly exceptional market conditions.

The method of calculation of this credit exposure has been examined and well defined by the academic, business, and regulatory communities. Using a plain vanilla interest rate swap for illustration and defining the worst case as a two standard deviation move in the underlying interest rates, we can map out the potential credit exposure to that swap by valuing the transaction under two standard deviation shifts of the rates (in the exposure producing direction) until maturity. Exhibit 28–1 shows the results of such an excercise with annual analysis points for a 10-year plain vanilla interest rate swap. This picture is now quite familiar and has been used in various regulatory and industry group papers on the subject. Fundamentally, Exhibit 28–1 shows that despite the potential for ever-increasing shifts in interest rates over time, the potential exposure in an interest rate swap actually begins to decrease after the first third of its tenor, since the number of remaining payment exchanges reduces the impact of the shifting rates on overall deal value. Potential exposure abruptly drops to zero after the final payments are made.

Although this limited application of simulation analysis has been widely understood and accepted, the next step, which is to capture the benefits of portolio diversification, has not. Instead of undertaking this excercise for

EXHIBIT 28–1
Worst-Case Potential Exposure: Interest Rate Swap

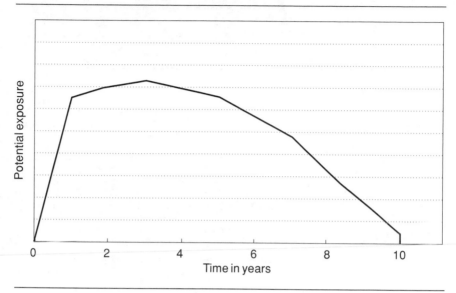

each new deal to make the credit exposure understandable to conventional lending-oriented credit managers, the traditional next step (see Exhibit 28–2) has been to convert the worst-case exposure into a fixed amount that covers the worst case over the life of the deal. To further simplify the calculation for the purposes of day-to-day operations, the fixed amount can be expressed as a percentage of the notional amount that would vary according to tenor and underlying rate volatility (more commonly tenor alone). According to this methodology, additional transactions are converted to fixed amounts in the same manner and exposures are summed for both single counterparty and portfoliowide credit management purposes.

Losses due to counterparty default. The cost of oversimplification is evident even in this simple case, when we factor in the reality that the probability for counterparty default increases with the passage of time. For contrast, we can look at a cross-currency swap, with principal exchanges on the start and maturity dates, using the same worst-case exposure methodology. For this transaction, we have to consider the potential movement of each currency's interest rate and the foreign exchange rate between the

EXHIBIT 28–2
Worst-Case Potential Exposure: Interest Rate Swap

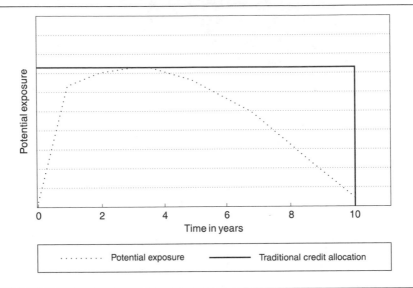

two currencies. Exhibit 28–3 shows the worst-case exposure of a generic cross-currency swap. The overriding source of potential exposure for this transaction is the volatility of the foreign exchange rate in relation to the final principal exchange. This causes worst-case exposure to continue to rise, despite the declining number of remaining interest payment exchanges, because the final principal exchange is one of relatively large amounts. According to the original methodology, however, this meant only that for a specific tenor a larger percentage of the notional amount was assigned to cross-currency swaps when determining their fixed credit exposure allocation.

The shortcomings of the fixed credit exposure methodolgy become apparent through comparison of Exhibits 28–2 and 28–4. Assume a choice between an interest rate swap and a cross-currency swap of equal tenor with counterparties of equal credit quality. Assume also that the notional amount of the interest rate swap is sufficiently large relative to that of the currency swap to make the fixed percentage exposure numbers of the two transactions equal. This would make the traditional decision maker indifferent between the two transactions. Since the counterparty may be two to five times as

EXHIBIT 28–3
Worst-Case Potential Exposure: Cross-Currency Swap

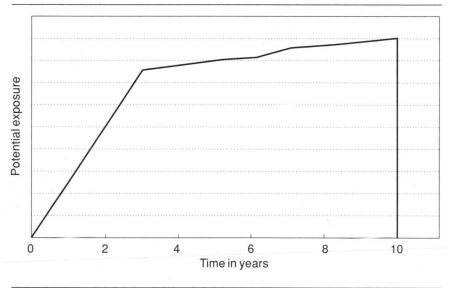

likely to default in ten years as they are in three, in the long run the firm that fails to charge an additional credit spread for the cross-currency transaction will suffer significantly higher losses relative to its profits.

Credit exposure limits.   Rather than having a tenor-tiered system of potential exposure limits, however, it makes more sense to remove this element of the decision-making process from the credit function and simply build potential loss logic for each type of transaction into the returns required of the trading desk. This allows the credit department to have its traditional function of determining a counterparty's credit quality and allows traders to pursue maximum profitability within prudent confines based on that determination.

The Basic Components of a Simulation Model

Portfolio simulation analysis takes the process one step further and creates a standard of evaluation for a range of transactions. This is beneficial not only when examining a portfolio of transactions with a single counterparty,

EXHIBIT 28–4
Worst-Case Potential Exposure: Cross-Currency Swap

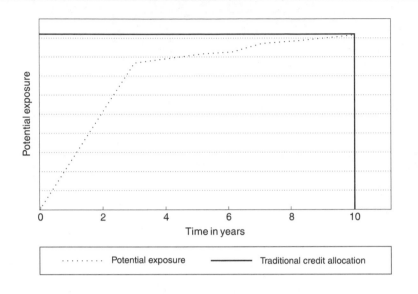

but also in evaluating a portfolio of counterparties of varying credit quality. In its raw form, simulation analysis gives the user a sample of the wide spectrum of possible outcomes as well as a level of confidence regarding the probability of those outcomes. The basic components of a simulation model can be divided into three groups: (1) the subjects to be evaluated, in this case a portfolio of derivative contracts; (2) the spectrum of conditions under which the subjects will be evaluated, in this case the probable economic futures; and (3) statistical analysis of the results.

Exhibit 28–5 shows the results of a simulation analysis of a plain vanilla interest rate swap using only 20 randomly generated probable future economic paths at annual intervals. Each line represents the valuation of the transaction under one such economic path. The dark line represents the 95 percent confidence level of exposure, which, since we have only 20 paths, could be considered as the worst-case credit exposure. Using this basic framework, one can vary the composition of the portfolio to be analyzed and the corresponding economic elements to be simulated, and maintain a consistent standard of measurement across transactions and ultimately

EXHIBIT 28–5
Standard Simulation Analysis

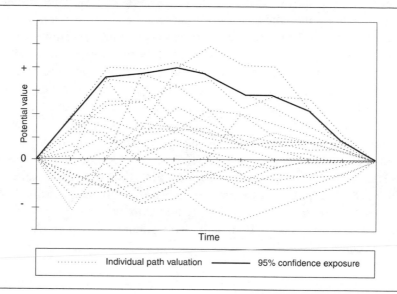

across counterparties to more effectively manage credit exposure on an individual counterparty and portfoliowide basis. The benefits of expanding the application of simulation analysis from the individual deal to the counterparty portfolio level and the dealer's entire portfolio level are potentially very large given the various diversification effects that will be described in some detail next.

APPLICATION OF SIMULATION MODEL ANALYSIS

If a derivative products dealer had only one transaction, or iterations of the same transaction, with each of its counterparties, it might be sufficient to use a fixed-percentage method to control credit exposure. However, this is rarely the case. The more diverse a counterparty's portfolio of transactions is, the less accurate a fixed percentage method will be in capturing the actual risks being taken. This discepancy grows even greater when considering an entire portfolio of transactions across all counterparties.

Individual Counterparty Analysis

One of the basic appeals of fixed-percentage credit exposure measurements is the simplicity that allows traders and marketers to determine whether a new deal is acceptable in a matter of seconds or minutes. However, over-simplification can result in the loss of important distinctions between currencies or rates involved in valuing different deals. The more significant drawback is that the various portfolio effects that reduce exposure in the real world are lost and profitable buiness may be forgone due to overesti-mation of incremental exposure. Simply put, diversification of the portfolio creates potential for offsetting valuation movement of individual deals. Finally, each distinct deal structure decreases the likelihood that the worst-case scenario will occur for all of the deals in the portfolio at the same time, which is the hidden basic assumption of any fixed-percentage methodology.

These portfolio effects can be divided into four categories—timing, netting/offsetting, correlation, and diversification—which will be de-scribed below.

Timing of exposure. Returning to our examples of the plain vanilla interest rate and cross currency swaps of Exhibits 28–1 through 28–4, it is clear that different structures produce their peak potential expo-sure values at different points in their tenor. We are now faced with the question of how to evaluate a portfolio of one interest rate swap and one currency swap transacted with the same counterparty. Exhibit 28–6 illus-trates how a fixed-percentage approach will ignore the timing of the exposures, treating the peak exposure of the first transaction as the base of analysis for the second. When the timing effect is taken into account (see Exhibit 28–7), we see the countervailing effects of the declining exposure in the interest rate swap and the increasing exposure in the currency swap resulting in a lower combined peak potential exposure level.

Offsetting value movement and netting of multiple deal values. Perhaps the most significant source of overestimation of credit exposure by fixed-percentage methods of credit control is the ignorance of offsetting effects of market movement on the individual deals within an individual counterparty's portfolio. The ability to offset deal values under bankruptcy conditions, subject to proper legal documentation, for a growing number of counterparties in a growing number of countries, only heightens the impor-tance of this factor. To make the best illustration of this point, assume a

EXHIBIT 28–6
Exposure Timing Effect: Traditional Combination

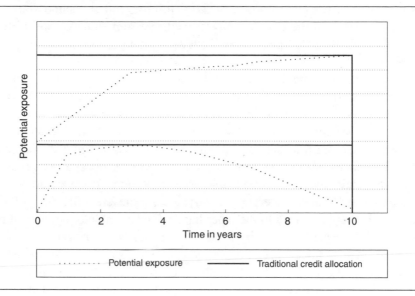

EXHIBIT 28–7
Exposure Timing Effect: Actual Combination

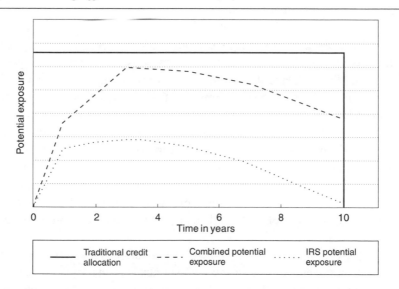

counterparty whose portfolio consists of two transactions that perfectly offset one another. To be specific, we'll assume two 10-year interest rate swaps with a notional amount of $100 million and the same start and maturity dates. In the first, we pay a fixed rate semiannually and receive six-month LIBOR; in the second, we receive that same fixed rate and pay LIBOR.

The traditional method (see Exhibit 28–8) would again simply add the two peak exposures. This would make sense if we were paying or receiving the fixed rate in both deals, but since the payment and receipt of the fixed rate offset one another, deal value will follow suit as the LIBOR rate moves over the life of the transaction. Exhibit 28–9 demonstrates how the potential positive values of the first transaction will be offset by negative values of the other under even the worst case market conditions. If we are not able to net exposures to the counterparty, the true peak exposure will be that of only one of the transactions. On the other hand, if we are able to net exposures, these two transactions actually create no exposure whatsoever. This effect is reduced as the deals offset one another less perfectly (i.e., if one deal's tenor is greater or less than the other, the payment dates do not match perfectly, or the fixed rate or spread on the floating side differ), but the effect is still significant where applicable. Where netting is legally enforceable, the remarkable implication of this example is that certain transactions can actually reduce potential exposure to a counterparty, perhaps making a negative credit spread advisable.

Interest and currency exchange rate correlation.   Correlation of rate movements is another source of credit risk reduction in diversified portfolios. If we replace the interest rate swap in which we receive fixed U.S. dollars in the previous example with one in which we receive fixed Canadian Dollars on an equivalent notional amount (roughly Canad. $137 million at current rates), there would be no change in the fixed percentage analysis as shown in Exhibit 28–10 and compared to Exhibit 28–8. In reality, however, there will be a strong offsetting tendency in the value of the U.S. dollar and Canadian dollar interest rate swaps due to the roughly 50 percent correlation between interest rate movements. Exhibit 28–11 shows the how the potential exposure of the two deals is reduced on a combined basis.

Diversification.   As a portfolio's diversity grows, the benefits of using simulation analysis to measure and control credit exposure also grow. Beyond the basic forces described above, the simple benefit of diversifica-

EXHIBIT 28–8
Offsetting Deal Effect: Traditional IRS Combination

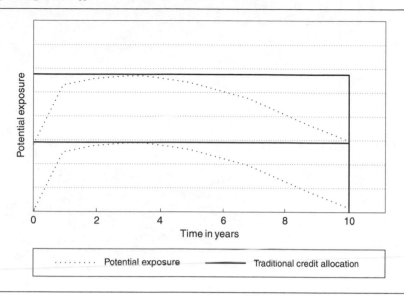

EXHIBIT 28–9
Offsetting Deal Effect: Actual IRS Combination

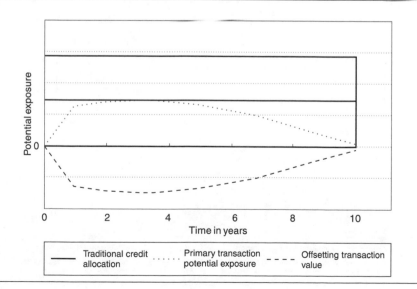

EXHIBIT 28–10
Correlation Effect: Traditional Canadian Dollars/U.S. Dollars

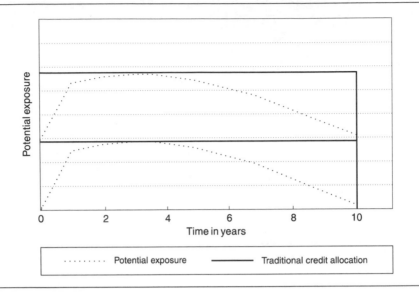

EXHIBIT 28–11
Correlation Effect: Actual Canadian Dollars/U.S. Dollars

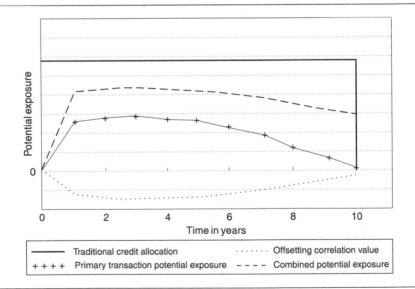

EXHIBIT 28–12
Combined Portfolio Effects: Large Counterparty Portfolio

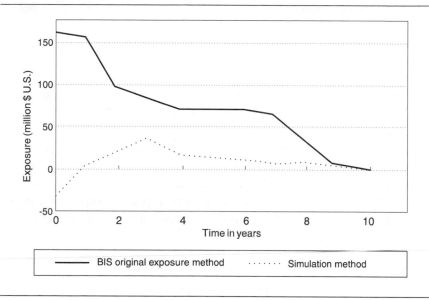

| BIS original exposure method | ⋯⋯⋯ Simulation method |

tion derives from the addition of relatively independent variables to the statistical mix. While the worst case for one transaction is improbable, the coincidence of the worst case for two independent transactions is even more so. As transactions that depend on additional indexes for their valuation are added to the portfolio, the probability of a worst-case coincidence continues to drop.

For a more practical example of the combined effect of all these influences on potential exposure of a diversified portfolio, consider the outstanding transactions between a bank derivative products subsidiary, Any Bank Capital Markets, Inc. (ABCM), and an investment bank, Someone's Brothers, Inc. (SBI). The portfolio has a current market value of $28 million in favor of SBI and consists of more than 100 interest rate swaps, currency swaps, and FRAs with a combined notional amount of $2.5 billion, final maturity of 9.8 years, and involves seven currencies and 12 interest rate indexes. Exhibit 28–12 shows this portfolio's credit exposure from both the fixed-percentage perspective of the BIS original exposure risk asset conversion method and the simulation-based potential exposure analysis method. Relying on the fixed-percentage method to measure credit exposure, ABCM might be very near the limit of its credit risk appetite to SBI, while the simulation analysis shows that the potential exposure of the portfolio has barely begun to approach the numbers produced by the other method.

Portfoliowide Analysis

The above described potential exposure appears to be the best measurement of the individual counterparty credit risk because the amount lost due to default will be the market value of the transactions with that counterparty at the time of default. When considering the credit risk of a dealer's entire portfolio across all counterparties, however, measurement of each counterparty's probability of default should be factored in as an additional independent variable. This probability can be estimated by simply comparing a credit grading system to historical defaults and applying it to the future in a similar manner.

Futher benefits of diversification. In this case, as in the one described above, the addition of an independent variable creates a corresponding reduction in potential losses. In addition to the fact that in a diversified portfolio the market conditions that create maximum potential exposure to one counterparty are unlikely to also create maximum potential exposure to a second or third counterparty, the probable dispersion of default timing further reduces risk.

Portfolio credit risk limits. Ideally, management should set credit risk limits on a portfolio basis, based on the amount of capital dedicated to support the portfolio. The portfolio limits will then dictate individual counterparty limits. In the simulation analysis context, a counterparty's credit grade will translate statistically into a scale of default probability. This means that credit management need only create one set of exposure limits according to the credit grade, and let the individual grading process dictate each counterparty's limit.

Within this framework, relatively small or unsophisticated counterparties may be given lower limits to bar them from inappropriately large transactions. Coupled with appropriate credit spread guidelines built into the minimum pricing requirements, this methodology will ensure sufficient credit quality of the portfolio while leaving the traders free to pursue profit opportunities as they appear in the marketplace.

Practical Matters

All of this additional information does not come without an added cost. The complex technology required to price derivatives is merely the necessary foundation for a simulation model to analyze them. The revaluation process that keeps trade support staff working late on a nightly basis in offices around the world must be repeated thousands of times under a multitude of market scenarios, and the results must be analyzed in short order for the results to still have meaning. While by no means insurmountable, the task requires additional effort and understanding on all fronts, making implementation difficult.

A product of your assumptions. Ultimately, the simulation analysis is nothing more than a product of built-in assumptions that are input to the model. For example, since simulated values are really nothing more than the product of normally distributed variations around the base case, expected values can be nothing more than an indicator of the model's ability to revert back to its base case. Whether you use historical or current market implied volatilities and correlations to generate your simulated economic futures, you remain vulnerable to the eventuality that the markets will move differently in the future than they have in the past or are currently expected to move. A straightforward first test of any model is to go back in time and check its predictions against actual historical results. However, even this type of testing can create false confidence. While the relatively complex assumptions of a simulation model bring great improvements when compared with the simple assumptions of a fixed-percentage method, further improvements always remain to be made. It is important to gain some level of comfort regarding the sensitivities and tolerances of a specific model.

Trading money and time for information. Compromises must be made between the amount of resources devoted to development of a model and the value of the information derived from the model. The basic vulnerability of simulation model is sampling error—in other words, the potential for the economic conditions produced by the model to unfairly represent the possible range of conditions. Beyond the organizational requirements discussed below, seemingly simple trade-offs must be made that can have significant results on the quality of information. The most basic examples of this are choosing the spacing of time points for your analysis and the number of future economic paths to be generated. Obvi-

EXHIBIT 28–13
IRS Potential Exposure: Same Deal One Week Later

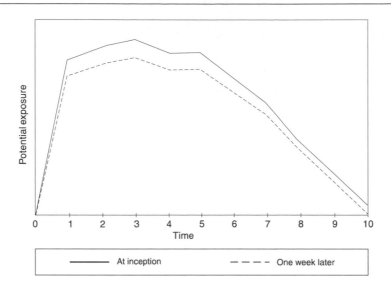

ously, in both cases more is better, but the supply will invariably be limited by the time frame in which the information produced remains relevant. Additionally, while it is usually possible to improve the speed at which a model will produce by purchasing additional computer hardware, the cost of that hardware must be balanced against the value of the reduction in sampling error.

Exhibit 28–13 graphs the results of two potential exposure simulations done on the same interest rate swap transaction. Both worst-case scenarios are based on simulations that generated the same number of future economic paths. The only difference between them is that the higher line is the result of an annual analysis beginning two days before the start date of the transaction while the lower line is the result of one beginning a week after. This shatters the commonly held picture of the potential exposure of the interest rate swap because the actual potential exposure is jagged rather than smooth. The intuition behind this lies in the fact that each payment exchange abruptly reduces the impact of potential rate fluctuations on deal value. This can be seen more clearly in Exhibit 28–14, which compares the results of a monthly analysis of the first three years of this same interest rate swap to the annual analysis shown in all of the exhibits up to this point.

EXHIBIT 28–14
Monthly Time Point Analysis: Three-Year Interest Rate Swap

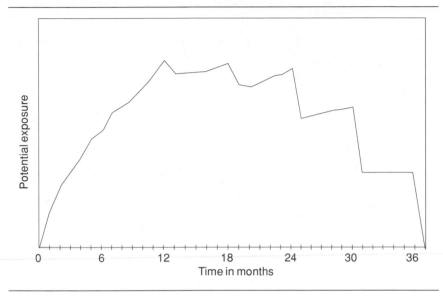

The number of future economic paths created can also significantly alter results. Exhibit 28–15 shows the worst-case potential exposure for three simulations of the same interest rate swap. One line represents the result of a 100-path simulation. A second line represents the results of a 200-path simulation. The third line represents the results of a 1,000-path simulation. It is clear from this picture that the sampling error can cause either overestimation or underestimation of potential exposure; however, the magnitude of the error correction may not be as valuable as the additional time or hardware required to generate it.

Organizational requirements.   During the initial period of financial innovation, the traditional derivative products dealer focused its most competent (and generally most expensive) personnel in the marketing and trading of its products. Implementation of simulation analysis on a portfolio basis will require dealers to push some of that competence back into the credit or risk management area. While the traditional systems of fixed percentage estimation were relatively easy to understand, portfolio simulation analysis requires a broader understanding of the financial forces at play for the credit officer to maintain confidence in the values being reported and controlled. The other alternative is blind acceptance, which is

EXHIBIT 28–15
IRS Potential Exposure: Same Deal Different Number of Paths

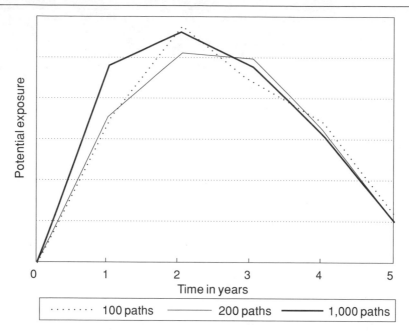

essentially a relinquishment of credit control altogether and therefore undesirable.

CONCLUSION

As the derivatives products markets continue to mature, successful competition will hinge not only on product innovation, but also on more effective pricing and risk management. From the credit perspective, derivatives are unique compared with traditional lending and investing activities not only in their inherent market value volatility, but in their potential for portfolio dynamics even on the level of the individual counterparty. In the long run, sophisticated players in these markets who fail to recognize these effects in their credit control systems and pricing will penalize themselves and unnecessarily drain profitability. Portfolio simulation model analysis allows credit management the opportunity to maintain conservative, worst-case limits that more closely reflect the risks at hand while at the same time requiring traders to secure greater returns when it is advisable for them to do so.

In this light, the present-day derivative products dealer can be equated to an insurance company, which may be able to gradually drive its competitors out of business by redefining policies. Companies that are able to discount lower-risk transactions and drive higher-risk business to a competition that may unwittingly accept inadequate profits, will eventually find themselves with higher-quality portfolios and more than sufficient retained earnings upon which to build future growth. While the costs of developing and implementing a portfolio simulation model may be formidable, the costs of not properly understanding the risks taken will inevitably be larger.

Chapter Twenty-Nine

Triple-A Derivative Product Vehicles

Jennifer White
Sumitomo Bank Capital Markets, Inc.

The swap market has grown rapidly over the last 10 years and has become an integral part of the international capital markets. The derivative products business, which has been extremely innovative in cross-border risk management in recent years, relies on the creditworthiness of the providers of the product. Making decisions about risk management and arbitrage possibilities is complex; making a credit decision about the provider or projecting the credit quality of the counterparty over the life of a transaction adds risk to any decision to use derivative products.

Banks are the main providers of derivative products, both as principal dealers and as intermediaries for investment banks, and credit ratings of the major banks have fluctuated in recent years. A counterparty entering into a long-term agreement may experience a change in the risk rating of the derivative product provider during the life of a deal. Many entities that use swaps for their hedging requirements, particularly sovereigns and large corporations, are mandated to deal only with top-rated providers. As bank ratings began to change, these entities began to express a need for creditworthiness and stability to ensure that their hedging programs remained stable.

To address the end users' concerns, 10 financial institutions have established separate enhanced derivative product companies over the past three years to give counterparties the credit ratings and stability that they need. Each vehicle is designed to provide a constant triple-A rating for all of its transactions and to remove the credit uncertainty attached to entering into a derivative transaction. This certainty helps to stabilize the derivatives business from the point of view of both customers and providers, and allows the customers renewed access to much of the expertise, innovation, and technology investment that these financial institutions have made in developing their derivatives businesses.

Standard & Poor's and Moody's have each established a rating process for reviewing, approving, and monitoring the triple-A vehicles, and the establishing entity must go through a process of negotiation with the rating agencies. Although each vehicle differs depending on the objectives and constraints of its parent organization, each complies with some general rules: (1) the parent must have substantial experience in and management understanding of the derivative products industry; (2) the parent must have established technology and operations support of derivative products; and (3) the parent must develop a detailed and complete plan for the establishment and operation of the vehicle. Beyond these general requirements, further criteria must be met. However, since each vehicle has been developed with different objectives in mind, these criteria can be met using a variety of methods.

STRUCTURES

There are two general types of triple-A vehicle at this point: the continuation structure and the termination structure. A continuation structure maintains its portfolio of swap transactions to maturity. In the case of the downgrade of the parent below certain levels, a continuation type triple-A is required to retain a "contingent manager" to handle the day-to-day operations of the vehicle's swap portfolio. The contingent manager must be a knowledgeable participant in the derivatives markets and, in almost all cases, must be engaged and familiar with the vehicle's operations prior to assuming management. The contingent manager's objective is to hedge and manage all swap transactions to maturity while minimizing the risks in the portfolio.

A termination structure is required to cash settle all of its swap transactions in the event that one of a number of trigger events occurs. These trigger events include certain downgrades of the parent, bankruptcy of the parent, and failure to increase capital or collateral when required. The existing triple-A vehicles fall into these two categories as shown in Exhibit 29–1.

EXHIBIT 29–1
Two Categories of Triple-A Vehicles

Continuation Structures	*Termination Structures*
SBCM Derivative Products Limited (The Sumitomo Bank, Limited)	Credit Lyonnais Derivatives Program (Credit Lyonnais)
Merrill Lynch Derivative Products Inc. (Merrill Lynch & Co., Inc.)	Morgan Stanley Derivative Products Inc. (Morgan Stanley Group)
Lehman Brother Financial Products Inc. (Lehman Brothers Inc.)	Paribas Dérive's Garantis (Compagnie Financière de Paribas)
GS Financial Products L.P. (Goldman Sachs Group)	Salomon Swapco Inc. (Salomon Brothers Holding Co.)
Tokai Derivative Products Ltd. (The Tokai Bank. Limited)	Westpac Derivative Products Ltd. (Westpac Banking Corporation)

A subset of the termination group is the guarantee structure (Paribas and Credit Lyonnais.) These vehicles do not maintain their own portfolios of swap transactions but rather guarantee a portion of the swap portfolios of their parents.

LEGAL AND REGULATORY REQUIREMENTS

In all cases, the triple-A vehicle is designed as a bankruptcy-remote subsidiary. The rating agencies' primary concern is that, in the event of the bankruptcy of the vehicle's parent, the assets of the vehicle would not be consolidated into the parent organization. The operations of the vehicle must be organized in a way as to maintain this separateness. The vehicle's parent and related entities often provide marketing services to the vehicle as agent for which the vehicle pays an arm's-length fee.

In addition to legal requirements, each vehicle must comply with the regulatory requirements of its country and often the country of its parent. Where the parent is a bank, the vehicle may be regulated by both a banking commission or ministry of finance and the body regulating other financial institutions. In most cases, considerable negotiations have been made to ensure that the regulators are comfortable with the vehicle.

CAPITAL AND INVESTMENT OF CAPITAL

The structure of each vehicle and the intended composition of the vehicle's derivatives portfolio determine the amount of capital put into the company. The capital must be sufficient to address, at a triple-A level, the financial risks faced by the vehicle, particularly the risk of counterparty default and the ensuing effect on the remaining portfolio of the vehicle.

The capitalization of the 10 existing triple-A vehicles ranges from $150–350 million for continuation structures and from $140–200 million for the termination structures. Permissible investments generally include all triple-A-rated securities. Other investment grade securities may also be allowed. All investments are subject to discount factors determined by the rating agencies. These discount factors effectively reduce the capital available in order to take into account the potential for any change in the securities' market value should they need to be liquidated.

PORTFOLIO COMPOSITION

The triple-A vehicles currently established have permission to enter into some or all of interest rate, currency, and equity swaps and options thereon. These products are limited to currencies and indexes that have liquid markets, so that rehedging or liquidation costs, if such action were required, would not compromise the vehicle's status. The scope of these vehicles' product capabilities is expected to grow as markets develop and as client requirements expand.

The triple-A vehicles' counterparties are generally rated single A or higher; however, each vehicle has different restrictions on its client base depending on the way in which its capital requirements are calculated. In certain circumstances lower-rated counterparties, if permitted, may be required to post collateral. Other vehicles have restrictions not only on the rating of a counterparty at the time a transaction is executed, but also require assignment or termination of transactions should a counterparty be downgraded. Certain characteristics of a client, such as the enforceability of netting in the relevant jurisdiction(s), documentation requirements, and the form of guarantee should one be provided, also have an impact on the acceptability of the counterparty.

Each of the vehicles has established counterparty, country, and product limits. These limits are imposed in order to maintain a diversified portfolio

EXHIBIT 29–2
Mirror Transactions Structure

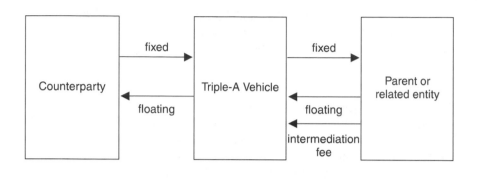

and to reduce the effect of single counterparty's default, the imposition of currency controls in a particular country, or the sudden illiquidity of the market in a particular index or product type. It is the intent of each triple-A vehicle to maintain a portfolio with no market risk and to dedicate the majority of its resources to the management of the credit risk of its portfolio and the maintenance of a triple-A likelihood of default. Each triple-A vehicle has separated credit risk from market risk and, in general, has hedged its market risk by entering into exactly offsetting transactions with its parent or a related entity. Exhibit 29–2 shows the "mirror" structure when the vehicle receives a fixed rate from a counterparty and pays a floating rate.

A capital allocation is made to reserve for costs of rehedging the portfolio in case of default by the parent (continuation structure) or the acceleration of the portfolio (in a termination structure.) The exposure to the parent or related entity resulting from these "mirror" transactions generally requires a conservative capital allocation due to the nature of this exposure and the potential impact of the liquidation of this portfolio.

USE OF CAPITAL AND PROTECTION AGAINST CREDIT RISK

One of the most significant components of the structure of a triple-A vehicle is the quantification and management of credit risks. In most cases, the vehicles have each built mathematical models to simulate the changing requirements of a portfolio of derivative transactions over a period of time. These models use current market conditions, historical default rates based on counterparties' credit quality (determined by the rating agencies), the appropriate net or gross treatment of each counterparty, and volatilities and correlations to determine the amount of capital required to protect against potential credit loss.

The models are also used to determine the potential exposure to the parent or related entity with which the vehicle hedges its market risk. While the potential exposure to a counterparty in a continuation structure is measured over the life of the counterparty's portfolio, the exposure to the parent uses a shorter time horizon to maintain capital sufficient to cover the change in the value of the hedge should the parent default. In a termination structure, a shorter time horizon is used for the entire portfolio as the trigger events would require all transactions to be liquidated at mid-market or similar levels.

RELATIONSHIP WITH THE RATING AGENCIES

Each of the triple-A vehicles maintains ongoing relations with the rating agencies. The rating agencies each receive frequent reports on the vehicle's operations and portfolio from both the vehicle's management and from outside auditors. The outside auditors verify the calculations of the credit risk model, the capital requirements, and the valuation of the vehicle's portfolio. They also ensure that the vehicle is operating within the limits and other requirements set forth in its operating policies. The rating agencies and the outside auditors are involved in any decision to change limits or add to the list of permitted products or counterparties, or to revise the operating policies in any other way.

MANAGEMENT

Although each of the triple-A vehicles has a close relationship with its parent, the structure includes separate management, generally in the form of a board of directors and employees. Included in the board are outside directors who have no other ownership or employment contract with the parent or its affiliates. A majority or unanimous vote of these outside directors is required to make any significant change to the operations of the vehicle, and to take any decision with regard to the declaration of bankruptcy or insolvency. The vehicle's activities are generally severely restricted if the number of directors and outside directors falls below the required levels. The board meets periodically to ensure that all operating guidelines are being met, and all periodic internal and auditor reports are directed to the board.

CONCLUSION

The triple-A vehicles are highly controlled entities with specific require-ments. The objectives of each vehicle differ; however, the basic parameters applied to each are meant to maintain an entity which provides triple-A credit stability for clients in their derivative products markets.

INVESTMENT, HEDGING, AND TRADING STRATEGIES

Chapter Thirty

How to Use the Holes in Black-Scholes*

Fischer Black
Goldman, Sachs & Co.

The Black-Scholes formula is still around, even though it depends on at least 10 unrealistic assumptions. Making the assumptions more realistic hasn't produced a formula that works better across a wide range of circumstances. In special cases, though, we can improve the formula. If you think investors are making an unrealistic assumption like one of those we used in deriving the formula, there is a strategy you may want to follow that focuses on that assumption.

The same unrealistic assumptions that led to the Black-Scholes formula are behind some versions of "portfolio insurance." As people have shifted to more realistic assumptions, they have changed the way they use portfolio insurance. Some people have dropped it entirely or have switched to the opposite strategy.

People using incorrect assumptions about market conditions may even have caused the rise and sudden fall in stocks during 1987. One theory of the crash relies on incorrect beliefs, held before the crash, about the extent to which investors were using portfolio insurance and about how changes in stock prices cause changes in expected returns.

* This article appeared in *Journal of Applied Corporate Finance* 4 (Winter, 1989).

THE FORMULA

The Black-Scholes formula looks like this:

$$w\,(x,t) = xN(d_1) - cd^{-r(t^* - t)}\,N(d_2)$$

where $d_1 = \dfrac{ln(x/c) + (r + 1/2v^2)\,(t^*\!-\!t)}{v\sqrt{t^*\!-\!t}}$

and $\quad d_2 = \dfrac{ln(x/c) + (r - 1/2v^2)\,(t^*\!-\!t)}{v\,\sqrt{t^*\!-\!t}}$

In this expression,

w is the value of a call option or warrant on the stock,
t is today's date,
x is the stock price,
c is the strike price,
r is the interest rate,
t^* is the maturity date,
v is the standard deviation of the stock's return
N is the "cumulative normal density function" (You can approximate N using a simple algebraic expression.)

The value of the option increases with increases in the stock's price, the interest rate, the time remaining until the option expires, and the stock's volatility. Except for volatility, which can be estimated several ways, we can observe all of the factors the Black-Scholes formula requires for valuing options.

Note that the stock's expected return doesn't appear in the formula. If you are bullish on the stock, you may buy shares or call options, but you won't change your estimate of the option's value. A higher expected return on the stock means a higher expected return on the option, but it doesn't affect the option's value for a given stock price.

This feature of the formula is very general. I don't know of any variation of the formula where the stock's expected return affects the option's value for a given stock price.

HOW TO IMPROVE THE ASSUMPTIONS

In our original derivation of the formula, Myron Scholes and I made the following unrealistic assumptions:

- The stock's volatility is known and doesn't change over the life of the option.
- The stock price changes smoothly; it never jumps up or down a large amount in a short time.
- The short-term interest rate never changes.
- Anyone can borrow or lend as much as he or she wants at a single rate.
- An investor who sells the stock or the option short will have the use of all the proceeds of the sale and receive any returns from investing these proceeds.
- There are no trading costs for the stock or the option.
- An investor's trades do not affect the taxes he or she pays.
- The stock pays no dividends.
- An investor can exercise the option only at expiration.
- There are no takeovers or other events that can end the option's life early.

Since these assumptions are mostly false, we know the formula must be wrong. But we may not be able to find any other formula that gives better results in a wide range of circumstances. Here we look at each of these 10 assumptions and describe how we might change them to improve the formula. We also look at strategies that make sense if investors continue to make unrealistic assumptions.

Volatility Changes

The volatility of a stock is not constant. Changes in the volatility of a stock may have a major impact on the values of certain options, especially far-out-of-the-money options. For example, if we use a volatility estimate of 0.20 for the annual standard deviation of the stock, and if we take the interest rate to be zero, we get a value of $0.00884 for a six-month call option with a $40 strike price written on a $28 stock. Keeping everything else the same, but doubling the volatility to 0.40, we get a value of $0.465.

For this out-of-the-money option, doubling the volatility estimate multiplies the value by a factor of 53.

Since the volatility can change, we should really include the ways it can change in the formula. The option value will depend on the entire future path that we expect the volatility to take and on the uncertainty about what the volatility will be at each point in the future. One measure of that uncertainty is the "volatility of the volatility."

A formula that takes account of changes in volatility will include both current and expected future levels of volatility. Though the expected return on the stock will not affect option values, expected changes in volatility will affect them. And the volatility of volatility will affect them too.

Another measure of the uncertainty about the future volatility is the relation between the future stock price and its volatility. A decline in the stock price implies a substantial increase in volatility while an increase in the stock price implies a substantial decrease. The effect is so strong that it is even possible that a stock with a price of $20 and a typical daily move of $0.50 will start having a typical daily move of only $0.375 if the stock price doubles to $40.

John Cox and Stephen Ross have developed two formulas that take account of the relation between the future stock price and its volatility.[1] To see the effects of using one of their formulas on the pattern of option values for at-the-money and out-of-the money options, let's look at the values using both Black-Scholes and Cox-Ross formulas for a six-month call option on a $40 stock, taking the interest rate as zero and the volatility as 0.20 per year. For three exercise prices, the values are as follows:

Exercise Price	Black Scholes	Cox-Ross
40.00	2.2600	2.2600
50.00	0.1550	0.0880
57.10	0.0126	0.0020

The Cox-Ross formula implies lower values for out-of-the-money call options than the Black-Scholes formula. But putting in uncertainty about the future volatility will often imply higher values for these same options. We can't tell how the option values will change when we put in both effects.

---

[1] See John Cox and Stephen Ross, *Journal of Financial Economics* (Jan./Mar. 1976).

What should you do if you think a stock's volatility will change in ways that other people do not yet understand? In addition, suppose that you feel the market values options correctly in all other respects. You should "buy volatility" if you think volatility will rise, and "sell volatility" if you think it will fall. To buy volatility, buy options; to sell volatility, sell options. Instead of buying stock, you can buy calls or buy stock and sell calls. Or you can take the strongest position on volatility by adding a long or short position in straddles to your existing position. To buy pure volatility, buy both puts and calls in a ratio that gives you no added exposure to the stock; to sell pure volatility, sell both puts and calls in the same ratio.

Jumps

In addition to showing changes in volatility in general and changes in volatility related to changes in stock price, a stock may have jumps. A major news development may cause a sudden large change in the stock price, often accompanied by a temporary suspension of trading in the stock.

When the big news is just as likely to be good as bad, a jump will look a lot like a temporary large increase in volatility. When the big news, if it comes, is sure to be good or is sure to be bad, the resulting jump is not like a change in volatility. Up jumps and down jumps have different effects on option values than symmetric jumps, where there is an equal chance of an up jump or a down jump.

Robert Merton has a formula that reflects possible symmetric jumps.[2] Compared with the Black-Scholes formula, his formula gives higher values for both in-the-money and out-of-the-money options and lower values for at-the-money options. The differences are especially large for short-term options.

Short-term options also show strikingly different effects for up jumps and down jumps. An increase in the probability of an up jump will cause out-of-the-money calls to go way up in value relative to out-of-the-money puts. An increase in the probability of a down jump will do the reverse. After the crash, people were afraid of another down jump, and out-of-the-money puts were priced very high relative to their Black-Scholes values while out-of-the-money calls were priced very low. This fear continues to affect option values.

---

2 See John Cox, Robert Merton, and Stephen Ross, *Journal of Financial Economics* (Jan./Mar. 1976).

What should you do if you think jumps are more likely to occur than the market thinks? If you expect a symmetric jump, buy short-term out-of-the-money options. Instead of stock, you can hold call options or more stock plus put options. Or you can sell at-the-money options. Instead of stock, you can hold more stock and sell call options. For a pure play on symmetric jumps, buy out-of-the-money calls and puts, and sell at-the-money calls and puts.

For up jumps, use similar strategies that involve buying short-term out-of-the-money calls, selling short-term out-of-the-money puts, or both. For down jumps, do the opposite.

Interest Rate Changes

The Black-Scholes formula assumes a constant interest rate, but the yields on bonds with different maturities tell us that the market expects the rate to change. If future changes in the interest rate are known, we can simply replace the short-term rate with the yield on a zero-coupon bond that matures when the option expires.

But future changes in the interest rate are uncertain. When the stock's volatility is known, Robert Merton has shown that the zero-coupon bond yield will still work, even when both short-term and long-term interest rates are shifting.[3] At a given point in time, we can find the option value by using the zero-coupon bond yield at that moment for the short-term rate. When both the volatility and the interest rate are shifting, we will need a more complex adjustment.

In general, the effects of interest rate changes on option values do not seem nearly as great as the effects of volatility changes. If you have an opinion on which way interest rates are going, you may be better off with direct positions in fixed-income securities rather than in options.

Your opinion may affect your decisions to buy or sell options. Higher interest rates mean higher call values and lower put values. If you think interest rates will rise more than the market thinks, you should be more inclined to buy calls, and even more inclined to buy more stocks and sell puts, as a substitute for a straight stock position. If you think interest rates will fall more than the market thinks, these preferences should be reversed.

---

3 Robert Merton, *Bell Journal of Economics and Management Science* (1977).

Borrowing Penalties

The rate at which individuals can borrow, even with securities as collateral, is higher than the rate at which they can lend. Sometimes their borrowing rate is substantially higher than their lending rate. Also, margin requirements or restrictions put on by lenders may limit the amount they can borrow.

High rates and limits on borrowing may cause a general increase in call option values, because calls provide leverage that can substitute for borrowing. The interest rates implied by option values may be higher than lending rates. If this happens and you have borrowing limits but no limits on option investments, you may still want to buy calls. But if you can borrow freely at a rate close to the lending rate, you may want to get leverage by borrowing instead of buying calls.

When implied interest rates are high, conservative investors might buy puts or sell calls to protect a portfolio instead of selling stock. Fixed-income investors might even choose to buy stocks and puts, and sell calls, to create a synthetic fixed-income position with a yield higher than market yields.

Short-Selling Penalties

Short-selling penalties are generally even worse than borrowing penalties. On U.S. exchanges, investors can sell a stock short only on or after an uptick. They must go to the expense of borrowing stock if they wants to sell it short. Part of their expense involves putting up cash collateral with the person who lends the stock; they generally get no interest or interest well below market rates on their collateral. Also, investors may have to put up margin in cash with their broker, and they may not receive interest on cash balances with the broker.

For options, the penalties tend to be much less severe. Investors need not borrow an option to sell it short. There is no uptick rule for options. And investors lose much less interest income in selling an option short than in selling a stock short.

Penalties on short selling that apply to all investors will affect option values. When even professional investors have trouble selling a stock short, we will want to include an element in the option formula to reflect the strength of these penalties. Sometimes we approximate this by assuming an extra dividend yield on the stock, in an amount up to the cost of maintaining a short position as part of a hedge.

Suppose you want to short a stock but face penalties if you sell the stock short directly. Perhaps you're not even allowed to short the stock directly. You can short it indirectly by holding put options or by taking a naked short position in call options. (Most investors who can't short stock directly also can't take naked short positions.)

When you face penalties in selling short, you often face rewards for lending stock to those who want to short it. In this situation, strategies that involve holding the stock and lending it out may dominate other strategies. For example, you might create a position with a limited downside by holding a stock and a put on the stock, and by lending the stock to those who want to short it.

Trading Costs

Trading costs can make it hard for an investor to create an optionlike payoff by trading in the underlying stock. They can also make it hard to create a stocklike payoff by trading in the option. Sometimes they can increase an option's value and sometimes they can decrease it.

We can't tell how trading costs will affect an option's value, so we can think of them as creating a "band" of possible values. Within this band, it will be impractical for most investors to take advantage of mispricing by selling the option and buying the stock or by selling the stock and buying the option.

The bigger the stock's trading costs are, the more important it is to choose a strategy that creates the payoffs you want with little trading. Trading costs can make options especially useful if you want to shift exposure to the stock after it goes up or down.

If you want to shift your exposure to the market as a whole rather than to a stock, you will find options even more useful. It is often more costly to trade in a basket of stocks than in a single stock. But you can use index options to reduce your trading in the underlying stocks or futures.

Taxes

Some investors pay no taxes; some are taxed as individuals, paying taxes on dividends, interest, and capital gains; and some are taxed as corporations, also paying taxes on dividends, interest, and capital gains, but at different rates.

The very existence of taxes will affect option values. A hedged position that should give the same return as lending may have a tax that differs from the tax on interest. So, if all investors faced the same tax rate, we would use a modified interest rate in the option formula.

The fact that investor tax rates differ will affect values too. Without rules to restrict tax arbitrage, investors could use large hedged positions involving options to cut their taxes sharply or to alter them indefinitely. Thus, tax authorities adopt a variety of rules to restrict tax arbitrage. There may be rules to limit interest deductions or capital loss deductions, or rules to tax gains and losses before a position is closed out. For example, most U.S. index option positions are now taxed each year—partly as short-term capital gains and partly as long-term capital gains—whether or not the taxpayer has closed out his or her positions.

If you can use capital losses to offset gains, you may act roughly the same way whether your tax rate is high or low. If your tax rate stays the same from year to year, you may act about the same whether you are forced to realize gains and losses or are able to choose the year you realize them.

If you pay taxes on gains and cannot deduct losses, you may want to limit the volatility of your positions and have the freedom to control the timing of gains and losses. This will affect how you use options, and may affect option values as well. I find it hard to predict whether it will increase or decrease option values.

Investors who buy a put option will have a capital gain or loss at the end of the year or when the option expires. Investors who simulate the put option by trading in the underlying stock will sell after a decline and buy after a rise. By choosing which lots of stock to buy and which lots to sell, they will be able to generate a series of realized capital losses and unrealized gains. The tax advantages of this strategy may reduce put values for many taxable investors. By a similar argument, the tax advantages of a simulated call option may reduce call values for most taxable investors.

Dividends and Early Exercise

The original Black-Scholes formula does not take account of dividends. Yet dividends reduce call option values and increase put option values, at least when there are no offsetting adjustments in the terms of the options. Dividends make early exercise of a call option more likely and early exercise of a put option less likely.

We now have several ways to change the formula to account for dividends. One way assumes that the dividend yield is constant for all possible stock price levels and at all future times. Another assumes that the issuer has money set aside to pay the dollar dividends due before the option expires. Yet another assumes that the dividend depends in a known way on the stock price at each ex-dividend date.

John Cox, Stephen Ross, and Mark Rubinstein have shown how to figure option values using a "tree" of possible future stock prices.[4] The tree gives the same values as the formula when we use the same assumptions, but the tree is more flexible and lets us relax some of the assumptions. For example, we can put on the tree the dividend that the firm will pay for each possible future stock price at each future time. We can also test, at each node of the tree, whether an investor will exercise the option early for that stock price at that time.

Option values reflect the market's belief about the stock's future dividends and the likelihood of early exercise. When you think that dividends will be higher than the market thinks, you will want to buy puts or sell calls, other things being equal. When you think that option holders will exercise too early or too late, you will want to sell options to take advantage of the opportunities the holders create.

Takeovers

The original formula assumes the underlying stock will continue trading for the life of the option. Takeovers can make this assumption false.

If firm A takes over firm B through an exchange of stock, options on firm B's stock will normally become options on firm A's stock. We will use A's volatility instead of B's in valuing the option.

If firm A takes over firm B through a cash tender offer, there are two effects. First, outstanding options on B will expire early. This will tend to reduce values for both puts and calls. Second, B's stock price will rise through the tender offer premium. This will increase call values and decrease put values.

However, when the market knows of a possible tender offer from firm A, B's stock price will be higher than it might otherwise be. It will be between its normal level and its normal level increased by the tender offer.

---

4 John Cox, Mark Rubinstein, and Stephen Ross, "Option Pricing: A Simplified Approach," *Journal of Financial Economics* 7 (1979), pp. 229–63.

If A then fails to make an offer, the price will fall or will show a smaller than normal rise.

All these factors work together to influence option values. The chance of a takeover will make an option's value sometimes higher and sometimes lower. For a short-term out-of-the-money call option, the chance of a takeover will generally increase the option value. For a short-term out-of-the-money put option, the chance of a takeover will generally reduce the option value.

The effects of takeover probability on values can be dramatic for short-term out-of-the-money options. If you think your opinion of the chance of a takeover is more accurate than the market's, you can express your views clearly with options like these.

The October 19, 1987, crash is the opposite of a takeover as far as option values go. Option values then, and since, have reflected the fear of another crash. Out-of-the-money puts have been selling for high values, while out-of-the-money calls have been selling for low values. If you think another crash is unlikely, you may want to buy out-of-the-money calls, sell out-of-the-money puts, or do both.

Now that we've looked at the 10 assumptions in the Black-Scholes formula, let's see what role, if any, they play in portfolio insurance strategies.

PORTFOLIO INSURANCE

In the months before the crash, people in the United States and elsewhere became more interested in portfolio insurance. As I define it, portfolio insurance is any strategy in which you reduce your stock positions when prices fall and increase them when prices rise.

Some investors use option formulas to figure how much to increase or reduce their positions as prices change. They trade in stocks or futures or short-term options to create the effect of having a long-term put against stock or a long-term call plus T-bills.

You don't need synthetic options or option formulas for portfolio insurance. You can do the same thing with a variety of systems for changing your positions as prices change. However, the assumptions behind the Black-Scholes formula also affect portfolio insurance strategies that don't use the formula.

The higher your trading costs, the less likely you are to create synthetic options or any other adjustment strategy that involves a lot of trading. On

October 19, 1987, the costs of trading in futures and stocks became much
higher than they had been earlier, partly because the futures were priced
against the portfolio insurers. The futures were at a discount when portfolio
insurers wanted to sell. This made all portfolio insurance strategies less
attractive.

Portfolio insurance using synthetic strategies wins when the market
makes big jumps without much volatility. It loses when market volatility is
high, because an investor will sell after a fall and buy after a rise. The
investor loses money on each cycle.

The true cost of portfolio insurance is a factor that doesn't even affect
option values. It is the mean reversion in the market: the rate at which the
expected return on the market falls as the market rises.[5]

Mean reversion is what balances supply and demand for portfolio insurance. High mean reversion will discourage portfolio insurers because it will
mean they are selling when expected return is higher and buying when
expected return is lower. For the same reason, high mean reversion will
attract "value investors" or "tactical asset allocators," who buy after a
decline and sell after a rise. Value investors use indicators like price-earn-
ings ratios and dividend yields to decide when to buy and sell. They act as
sellers of portfolio insurance.

If mean reversion were zero, more investors would want to buy portfolio
insurance than to sell it. People have a natural desire to try to limit their
losses. On balance, there must be as many sellers as buyers of insurance.
What makes this happen is a positive normal level of mean reversion.

THE CRASH OF 1987

During 1987, investors shifted toward wanting more portfolio insurance.
This increased the market's mean reversion, but mean reversion is hard to
see; it takes years to detect a change in it. So investors did not understand
that mean reversion was rising. Since rising mean reversion should restrain
an increase in portfolio insurance demand, this misunderstanding caused a
further increase in demand.

---

5 For evidence of mean reversion, see Eugene Fama and Kenneth French, "Permanent and
Temporary C omponents of Stock Prices," *Journal of Political Economy* 96, no. 2 (Apr. 1988), pp.
246–73; and James Poterba and Lawrence Summers, "Mean Reversion in Stock Prices: Evidence
and Implications," *Journal of Financial Economics* 22, no. 1 (Oct. 1988), pp. 27–60.

Because of mean reversion, the market rise during 1987 caused a sharper than usual fall in expected return. Investors at first didn't see this. They continued to buy, as their portfolio insurance strategies suggested. Eventually, though, they came to understand the effects of portfolio insurance on mean reversion, partly by observing the large orders that price changes brought into the market.

Around October 19, 1987, the full truth of what was happening hit investors. They saw that at existing levels of the market, the expected return was much lower than they had assumed. They sold at those levels. The market fell, and expected return rose, until equilibrium was restored.

MEAN REVERSION AND STOCK VOLATILITY

Now that we've explained mean reversion, how can you use your view of it in your investments?

If you have a good estimate of a stock's volatility, the stock's expected return won't affect option values. Since the expected return won't affect values, neither will mean reversion, but mean reversion may influence your estimate of the stock's volatility. With mean reversion, day-to-day volatility will be higher than month-to-month volatility, which will be higher than year-to-year volatility. Your volatility estimates for options with several years of life should be generally lower than your volatility estimates for options with several days or several months of life.

If your view of mean reversion is higher than the market's, you can buy short-term options and sell long-term options. If you think mean reversion is lower, you can do the reverse. If you are a buyer of options, you will favor short-term options when you think mean reversion is high and long-term options when you think it is low. If you are a seller of options, you will favor long-term options when you think mean reversion is high and short-term options when you think it's low.

These effects will be most striking in stock index options, but they will also show up in individual stock options through the effects of market moves on individual stocks and through the influence of "trend followers." Trend followers act like portfolio insurers, but they trade individual stocks instead of portfolios. When the stock rises, they buy; when it falls, they sell. They act as if the past trend in a stock's price is likely to continue.

In individual stocks, as in portfolios, mean reversion should normally make implied volatilities higher for short-term options than for long-term options. (An option's implied volatility is the volatility that makes its Black-Scholes value equal to its price.) If your views differ from the market's, you may have a chance for a profitable trade.

Chapter Thirty-One

Using Derivative Products to Manage the Risk and Return of Life Insurance Companies

Thomas A. McAvity, Jr.
Lincoln Investment Management, Inc.

This chapter describes how derivative products can help life insurance companies manage risk and return within an asset-liability management (ALM) framework. We begin by examining this ALM framework and then provide a brief overview of derivative products and markets. The heart of the chapter consists of case studies that illustrate how derivative product strategies have met the needs of insurers.

ASSET-LIABILITY MANAGEMENT FRAMEWORK

Besides offering traditional risk-transfer products like life and health insurance, insurers provide investment products that allow customers to accumulate capital for retirement and other needs. Hybrid products such as universal life offer a combination of life insurance and capital accumulation.

Since these investment and hybrid products have been growing more rapidly than other products, insurers have experienced dramatic growth in their invested assets, in the ratio of invested assets to surplus, and in the portion of net operating income generated by investment spreads. Many insurers find that managing the level and downside risk of investment spreads has become their most important challenge.

Managing an Investment Spread Business

Insurers operate as investment intermediaries when they sell fixed-invest-ment products backed by the general account. Most of the money invested is funded by customer deposits and premiums. The insurer uses the invest-ments to manufacture the cash flows required by the liabilities. The insurer's net investment revenue or margin is the spread between investment income and the income credited to the customers. Over the lives of the liabilities and the related assets, the insurer's financial goal is to earn sufficient margin to recoup acquisition costs and periodic expenses and to earn sufficient profit to achieve the desired return on capital and other resources employed.

With a fixed product, the insurer guarantees an interest rate (or specified index for computing return) at time of sale. The rate may be explicitly stated or implicitly used in calculating the size of the deposit required to fund the stream of future benefits that the insurer is obligated to pay (e.g., a pension buyout annuity, structured settlement, or typical immediate annuity). The rate may be committed for the entire term of the product (e.g., a guaranteed investment contract or GIC) or for a portion of the term, subject to adjust-ment by the insurer from time to time thereafter (e.g., a single-premium deferred annuity or SPDA). Such adjustments may be based on the insurer's experience with the underlying investment portfolio or simply on market requirements.

Operating as an investment intermediary can be viewed as a special case of operating as a risk intermediary. Consider an insurer that sells GICs and buys a diversified portfolio of fixed-income investments with cash flows that match the liability cash flows, including the extra spread required to cover expenses and profit. The incremental yield obtained on the fixed-in-come investments in relation to U.S. Treasuries can be viewed as premiums covering the risks of default, rating downgrade, and spread widening. These premiums are analogous to premiums collected on term life insurance. In each case, the premium should cover not only the expected claims or losses but also compensate the insurer for bearing downside risk.

By diversifying the specific risks of issuers and industries, the insurer narrows the probability distribution of future default experience, just as a term insurance writer diversifies mortality risk. In each case, no matter how well diversified the population, the insurer is left with the systematic risks of rising general levels of default or mortality as the result of system-wide changes or events (e.g., the arrival of an epidemic or of a deep recession). These systematic risks can be measured by simulating future cash flows for a set of scenarios that spans the range of uncertainty for each systematic risk.

Managing Return and Risk to Net Worth

Asset-liability management should focus on managing economic net worth under uncertainty while satisfying constraints. For a life insurance company engaged in more than one investment spread business, management of net worth requires a two-tier financial engineering approach: (1) for each product line, create integrated investment and product strategies with a desirable performance profile across all possible scenarios and (2) for each scenario, roll up all product lines into the corporate "portfolio" and reconsider the respective levels of activity and component strategies in light of the aggregate performance profile. Derivative products can be valuable tools for enhancing risk-reward profiles at both levels.

The performance profile of the strategy for a single product line must be evaluated in the context of the whole portfolio of product lines because total risk is reduced to the extent that risk exposures are weakly or negatively correlated across the portfolio. At the levels of the legal entity and holding company, the portfolio of product-line activities should be balanced to achieve the most attractive profile of economic results while meeting constraints over the natural time horizon of the business.

A company's capacity for risk is proportional to its capital. For a given level of capital, its appetite for risk is a function of management philosophy and constraints imposed by constituents. The optimal weighting of product-line activities and the optimal mixture of strategies will vary with capital, risk aversion, management's views of likely future events, and its level of confidence in those views.

The traditional concept of an efficient frontier of optimal asset allocations based on the prospective mean and variance of asset returns is inappropriate for two reasons. First, return on assets must be combined with return on liabilities to determine whether the company has increased net worth. Instead of maximizing asset returns in relation to asset risk, insurers should maximize return on net worth in relation to risk to net worth. The risks assumed at the asset or liability level are levered at the surplus level by the ratio of assets or liabilities to net worth. For example, a one-year duration mismatch between assets and liabilities translates into a 15-year surplus duration if invested assets are 15 times net worth.

Second, the use of variance as a proxy for downside risk is appropriate only for symmetric return distributions. Variance is the average of the squared deviations from the mean, whether up or down. For many insurance product lines, the profile of results combining assets and liabilities has more downside risk than upside potential because of options embedded in both assets and liabilities. To isolate downside risk, the insurer must consider the entire distribution or use more discriminating measures like downside semivariance, which averages the squared downside deviations from the mean, deviations from a specified target or threshold, rather than the mean.

Variable Products

Like an open-ended mutual fund, a variable product passes through to the end user the experience of a managed pool of money. The risk of underperformance is passed through to the customer along with the potential for outperformance. A variable annuity or variable universal life insurance policy offers the functionality of a mutual fund or family of mutual funds within the "wrapper" of an annuity or a life insurance policy.

Although fixed and variable products pose very different risks to the insurer and the customer, they address a common challenge to the insurer: to create an investment strategy that meets customer needs and expectations while avoiding unnecessary and uncompensated risks. To create the cash flows necessary to meet a given set of customer needs, the insurer must identify the most suitable investment strategy or style, select or create a benchmark index representing that style, and manage the investment strategy in relation to that benchmark.

Regulatory, Accounting, and Tax Frameworks

Insurers operate within regulatory, accounting, and tax frameworks that differ from those governing commercial and investment banks and nonregulated corporations. These differences represent material advantages and disadvantages in the competition for the sale of investment products and investment management services.

State insurance laws and regulations are intended to protect the customer by requiring fair products, realistic benefit illustrations, and reasonable sales compensation and by mitigating the risk of insolvency. The latter objective is addressed through reserve requirements, cash flow testing, risk-based capital (RBC), and constraints on the use of asset classes perceived as risky. Guarantee fund associations provide a safety net for customers by redistributing insolvency losses to competitors.

Regulators and rating agencies evaluate the financial stability, profitability, and claims-paying ability of life insurers through the lens of statutory accounting, which differs markedly from the accounting models applied to commercial banks, investment banks, and nonregulated financial corporations. Liabilities are valued using a combination of legally required methods and discount rates and the Actuarial Standards of Practice.

Actuaries are required to perform cash flow testing to ensure that statutory reserves are adequate to cover potential future obligations in a variety of interest rate and economic scenarios.

The amount of risk-based capital required is a function of the liability profile and the mixture and diversification of invested assets. Regulators will monitor the ratio of available capital to required capital and take measured action to the degree that this RBC ratio falls too low.

The National Association of Insurance Commissioners (NAIC) has created a new Model Investment Law that updates and broadens the existing restrictions on investments, including derivative products. Part of the impetus behind the law is to close some barn doors that allowed a few companies to self-destruct. Close examination of these defaults shows a common cause—an abusive disregard of the need to diversify risks. This restrictive tone, however, is being attenuated by the valuable process of discussion and mutual education taking place between the industry and the regulators as work progresses on possible amendments.

In the area of derivative products and other innovations, the education process is critical not only to regulators but also to senior management and members of the board of directors. Before the education process progressed, some regulators tended to view derivatives and other innovations as risky and requiring much tighter restrictions than other more familiar practices that are actually much riskier. For example, earlier drafts of the Model Investment Law were liberal in the permitted concentration of exposure to the credit risk of a single domestic issuer (3 percent of invested assets for a BBB-rated issuer) but more restrictive in the exposure to the credit risk of a swap counterparty or foreign issuer (1 percent for an AAA-rated counterparty). This anomaly has been corrected.

Insurers and their products are subject to unique tax rules. Life insurance products provide customers with a tax advantage called "inside buildup"; for example, earnings credited to an annuity contract are typically not taxed until they are distributed to the customer. The death benefit paid on life insurance is not taxable income to the estate of the person dying. Life insurers are also taxed differently than competitors under the Internal Revenue Code.

The Challenge: Building Economic Net Worth While Meeting Expectations of Constituents

Insurers must manage risk and return in the context of not only economic reality but also the perceptions of constituents, including regulators, rating agencies, distributors, agents, customers, and shareholders. While real risk may be measured in terms of downside exposure to the economic value of the firm's net worth, perceived risk is measured primarily in terms of the adequacy of surplus and the pattern of reported net income determined under generally accepted accounting principles (GAAP) and statutory accounting rules.

Regulators and rating agencies use measures of risk and formulas for estimating required capital that are based on simplified ratios and rules of thumb using information required on the statutory accounting "blank." These measures necessarily fall short of the economic realism attainable with a well-conceived in-house risk management and capital allocation system grounded in more detailed data and more discriminating segmentation of products.

We can view "cosmetic capital" as the amount of capital necessary to comply with the expectations of these external constituents, and "internal" or "economic" capital as the amount necessary to absorb downside risk in the company's own decision models. They will typically not be equal. Cosmetic capital requirements represent constraints that must be met along any scenario.

Reinsurance

For a growing company, available surplus can be an important constraint. Insurers may use reinsurance to avoid undue concentration of risk and to allow a limited amount of surplus to support a larger and more diversified book of business. For example, an insurer may have life insurance in force in amounts ranging from $10,000 to $50,000,000. For policies on any one life with exposure exceeding the company's retention limit, say $1,000,000, the company may obtain reinsurance for the excess, avoiding undue concentrations of risk and stabilizing the volatility of potential claims in any single year. The reduction in risk achieved through this "excess-loss" reinsurance, combined with reduced requirements for reserves and surplus, allow the company to insure more lives, achieving greater diversification of risk and economies of scale. Unless the cost of the reinsurance is too high relative to the price at which the underlying policies have been sold, the potential profile of the company's future operating results has been improved.

Reinsurance is not always structured as "excess-loss" over a deductible amount. With "quota-share" reinsurance, the reinsurer participates pro rata or symmetrically in the profits and losses of a block of business, albeit with possible variations in profitability resulting from how the allowances and profit sharing are negotiated. Ceding companies constrained by limited capital use quota-share reinsurance to expand their in-force business to realize economies of scale and build market share and franchise value.

The next section shows how derivative products can be used to reduce risk in ways very similar to reinsurance. Derivatives include instruments with symmetric payoffs, like quota-share reinsurance, and asymmetric payoffs, like excess-loss reinsurance.

OVERVIEW OF DERIVATIVE PRODUCTS

The use of derivative products to transfer risk started many years ago with forward contracts on commodities. Forward contracts are bilateral agreements that allow a buyer and a seller to reduce their risk by fixing the price of a transaction prior to the delivery date. Terms of a forward contract may be customized to suit both parties. They are over-the-counter as opposed to exchange-traded derivative products.

Over-the-Counter Derivatives

In the past decade, the over-the-counter (OTC) derivatives market has grown from less than $1 trillion to over $10 trillion. Some of the most common products are forwards, swaps, options, caps, and floors. Most OTC derivative transactions or "deals" are made between a customer and a dealer. Brokers provide a means for dealers to trade with one another without giving up as much information about market prices, flows, and buy and sell interest.

In the OTC market, each party to the transaction relies on the creditworthiness of the counterparty to honor future obligations. The amount of counterparty risk at a given time in the future is simply the replacement cost (i.e., market value) of the deal if the counterparty should default at that time. Most swaps provide only for exchange of periodic payments based on differentials between two interest rates or returns, not of principal. As a result, the market value of a swap is generally a modest percentage of notional amount. Dollar for dollar, counterparty risk is greater for longer-dated transactions, for options purchased from the counterparty, and for currency swaps, which include final payments representing currency-driven changes in the value of the notional amount.

Generally, OTC trades are documented on a standard confirmation form that is linked to a master agreement between the parties. In the United States and an increasing number of foreign jurisdictions, laws honor the provision typically set forth in the master agreement providing for netting of obligations across all deals between the two parties, thereby reducing the probable size of the counterparty risk over time. This risk is further diminished by agreements between the parties to put up collateral for some or all of the amount at risk.

Forward Contracts

Consider agricultural commodities. In the spring, it is uncertain what the price of a crop will be in the fall. The prevailing or "spot" price in the spring is irrelevant, because the crop can't be delivered until fall. This uncertainty creates risk for both farmers and users of the crop. Each growing season, a farmer's ability to cover costs and earn an adequate income is at risk if prices are too low at the time of delivery. A processor's costs are at risk if prices are too high.

For each party, entry into a forward contract locks in a mutually agreeable price. The forward contract is an example of a symmetric derivative product. From the farmer's perspective, it eliminates the risk that the spot price may be lower at harvest time, but sacrifices the opportunity for incremental profit if the spot price turns out to be higher. The processor also eliminates risk but forsakes potential savings. Since each party is averse to risk, there is room for both parties to feel that they are getting a good deal.

To illustrate this point, let's assume that the farmer and the processor have the same subjective probability distribution for the price per bushel at harvest time:

Probability	*Price*
10%	$4.00
25	5.00
30	6.00
25	7.00
10	8.00
Expected price	$6.00

Using this distribution, they would agree on its $6.00 expected value (the probability weighted average).

Let's define the "certainty equivalent" as the price at which each party is indifferent between the alternatives of locking in a sure thing or retaining the risk. Risk aversion is subjective; it depends on individual circumstances and attitudes. The more risk-averse the farmers are, the lower the price they will accept as a certainty equivalent; in this case, farmers may be willing to accept a price as low as $5.25 to remove their risk. Likewise, the more risk-averse the producers are, the higher the forward price they are willing to agree to pay, perhaps $6.35 in this case. For each party, the difference between the expected value and the certainty equivalent is the premium they are willing to pay to hedge the risk. For two risk-averse parties with the same view of the probability distribution of prices at delivery, there is a range of prices satisfactory to both.

Exchange-Traded Futures

Like forward contracts, exchange-traded futures contracts have a symmetric payoff. When futures began trading on exchanges, the buy and sell interest provided by hedgers was supplemented by market makers ("locals") and speculators, improving liquidity. Liquidity is critical to allow continuous trading and stable prices even when hedgers don't enter the market simultaneously.

Exchange-traded contracts require a certain trading volume to be viable, as illustrated by the failure of three contracts on NASDAQ-traded OTC stocks in the mid-1980s. When a new contract fails to attract trading volume, potential users avoid taking positions out of fear of poor liquidity, including wide bid-ask spreads and the risk of adverse market impact should they elect to offset their positions.

Conversely, high volume tends to be self-sustaining. The most successful exchange-traded contracts are designed to track closely the price performance of heavily traded underlying markets. Variety is sacrificed because of the need to focus trading volume in one or at most a few standardized contracts for each broad market.

The available times to expiration are limited to the extent of active buy and sell interest and are generally shorter than those available in the over-the-counter market. Eurodollar contracts are traded at quarterly intervals out to 10 years, with volume and liquidity declining as the term to expiration increases beyond five years. The U.S. Treasury bond contract is traded in quarterly expiration dates out to two years but has significant volume and open interest only in the first year. The U.S. 10-year note contract is traded out only one year, and interest in the last two quarterly contracts is minimal.

The futures exchanges protect participants from counterparty risk through the use of initial and variation margin. Initial margin is like a good-faith deposit. Variation margin is the daily settlement in cash of any profit or loss based on marking to market buyers' and sellers' positions. Suppose that an insurer buys a future at a price of $100. If the price rises to $104, the company will receive variation margin of $4. If the price then drops to $101, the insurer will have to pay variation margin of $3.

There is a symbiotic relationship between the OTC and exchange-traded markets. OTC dealers use exchange-traded futures and options to hedge or replicate many of the OTC products they provide to customers. The growth in the OTC derivatives market has contributed to, rather than subtracted from, the growth of the listed futures and options markets. In each of these markets, volume is large compared to trading volume in many of the underlying cash markets.

Futures contracts exist or are in the process of being created on most of the active debt and equity markets around the world. Volume on foreign exchanges is growing even faster than in the United States and is already almost as great. Futures and options trading abroad totaled 517.6 million contracts in 1993, up 33.5 percent from 1992. In the United States, 1993 volume totaled 521.3 million, up 13.3 percent. Of the total of 1.039 billion contracts traded worldwide in 1993, 774 million or 74.5 percent were financial futures. Of the financial futures, interest rate futures accounted for the largest share (510 million or 65.9 percent) and the fastest growth rate (up 29.1 percent from 1992).

Options

Options may be traded on an exchange or over the counter. Options provide asymmetric payoffs. Suppose that instead of selling his crop forward at $5 per bushel, a farmer buys the option to sell the crop at $5 per bushel. If the final price is less than $5 per bushel, the farmer exercises the option and sells his crop to the writer of the option for $5 per bushel. However, if the price exceeds $5 per bushel, the farmer lets the option expire worthless and sells the crop in the spot market for the higher price. The asymmetric payoffs of options are like excess-loss reinsurance, in which the reinsurer assumes responsibility for paying the excess of any claim over the amount of risk retained by the ceding company.

The asymmetric payoff patterns provided by options are not typically available in the underlying cash markets. There exist exchange-traded options on many individual stocks as well as on many stock and bond indexes. The over-the-counter derivatives market can provide virtually any conceivable customized option, and it provides times-to-expiration that extend much longer than listed markets.

Insurers buy assets with embedded options like mortgage-backed securities and callable bonds. They also embed options in many of their products. For example, in a typical single-premium deferred annuity (SPDA), the customer has the option to withdraw 10 percent of the account value annually with no penalty and the balance at a declining penalty that disappears after five to eight years. Like the prepayment options embedded in residential mortgages, these withdrawal options are not efficiently exercised by customers. One of the biggest challenges for the insurer is to estimate how customers will exercise these options under various interest rate scenarios. Big moves in interest rates can actually change market practices, as we have seen in the residential mortgage industry.

Fixed annuity and universal life products provide that the credited rate will not fall below a guaranteed minimum, typically 3 percent to 6 percent. With falling interest rates, these floors become valuable to customers and costly to insurers.

Listed and OTC options allow an insurer to hedge many of the risks assumed in existing investment strategies and product designs. Even if they don't use these tools, insurers can examine the cost of hedging embedded options as a rational basis for evaluating the richness or cheapness of investment opportunities and for pricing their products.

The market price of options on bonds and interest rates is a function of forward rates and the volatility or uncertainty surrounding the rate on which the option's value will be determined. Volatility is usually expressed in percentage terms. For example, if the one-year Treasury yield is 4 percent and the implied volatility of an option on that note is 25 percent, then that volatility is equivalent to 25 percent of 4 percent, or 100 basis points. Usually, the volatility of the yield of a Treasury note is higher for shorter maturities and lower for longer maturities.

HEDGING A FIXED DEFERRED ANNUITIES BUSINESS AGAINST THE RISK OF RISING INTEREST RATES

Single, flexible, and periodic premium deferred annuities (SPDAs, FPDAs, PPDAs) have provided much of the growth of general account investment portfolios in the U.S. life insurance industry in the last decade. They now account for a major portion of investable assets for many life insurers, and the surplus allocated to them typically accounts for a major part of total company surplus. The substantial downside risk of these products represents an important strategic problem for many insurers. This case study illustrates how derivatives can be used to improve the risk-reward profile of an important line of business.

A typical SPDA guarantees an interest rate to the customer for the first year. Because this "new money rate" is the primary basis of competition for new deposits, it is often more generous than would be supported by prevailing investment yields, given the spread that the insurer must earn over time to recoup acquisition costs and make the desired profit. The extra amount might take the form of an explicit bonus or "teaser."

After the first year, the insurer has the valuable option of deciding what "renewal rate" to credit, providing considerable leeway in recouping any teaser and in managing the interest rate margin under normal conditions. This option is constrained, however, by two boundaries. If rates fall, renewal rates may not be reduced below the guaranteed minimums. If rates rise, an insurer must set renewal rates keeping in mind the customer's option to withdraw his or her money and the adverse effect that grossly uncompetitive renewal rate practices would have on new sales.

Withdrawal and Surrender Options

Most SPDAs grant customers the option to withdraw their money. Although cash withdrawals are subject to tax, a competitor can arrange a convenient tax-free exchange to another deferred annuity. SPDAs typically permit free partial withdrawal annually and surrender at any time of the full account value less a surrender charge. Surrender charges are typically structured to recapture the unamortized portion of acquisition costs over the first five to eight years after issuance. A typical surrender charge schedule begins at 7 percent for the first year and declines 1 percent per year to 1 percent in the seventh year.

Some surrenders will occur because customers become disabled or unemployed or simply need the cash. This base level of withdrawals will be increased by interest-sensitive withdrawals when the insurer's renewal rate is not competitive with the new money rate offered by competitors.

For SPDA providers who invest in relatively long maturities, uncompetitive renewal rates are most likely to occur in the event of a sustained uptrend in interest rates. Suppose that over the past five years, an insurer has invested the proceeds of each annuity sold into 7- and 10-year notes. The insurer now has a laddered portfolio with maturities ranging from 2 to 10 years. If interest rates rise over a sustained period, the effective rate at which income is generated by such a portfolio of fixed-rate investments (the "portfolio earned rate") will increase only to the extent that cash generated by new deposits and by maturities, prepayments, and interest from in-force assets can be reinvested at higher prevailing market rates. Hence, the yield on the portfolio will lag behind prevailing market yields, and the market value of the portfolio will fall below its book value, creating a dilemma for the insurer.

If the insurer maintains a constant margin between the portfolio earned rate and the renewal rate, that rate will become increasingly uncompetitive and withdrawals will increase. Although surrender charges will offset most of the write-off of the unamortized balance of deferred acquisition costs for GAAP purposes, the insurer still has to cope with funding cash outflows with the sale of bonds whose market value is less than book value. This policy is also likely to reduce the sales of new annuities.

If the insurer sets the renewal rate higher than would be permitted by a policy of maintaining a constant net interest margin, current statutory and GAAP net income will suffer. If rates rise fast and long enough, the required subsidy may exceed the amount of gross margin for which the product was originally priced, causing a negative gross margin.

The resolution of the dilemma is to strike a balance that achieves the least unattractive trade-off between high current operating losses and excessive surrenders. The shortfall in operating income will be proportional to the gap that opens up between (1) the rate actually credited and (2) the renewal rate that the insurer can afford to pay, which depends on the portfolio earned rate. Within this framework, we can isolate the need for cash flows from a hedging strategy as those necessary to keep the shortfall within desired tolerances and to cover losses on bonds sold to fund withdrawals and surrenders.

Hedging with CMT and CMS Caps

The role of a hedge is to generate the cash flows needed to offset potentially adverse experience. It is helpful to visualize the operation of the hedge along those scenarios in which projected shortfalls exceed tolerances. In this case, out-of-the-money caps on the 5-, 7-, and 10-year constant maturity Treasury (CMT) and swap (CMS) rates allow an insurer to limit the size of its downside risk to an acceptable level at a cost of about 15 basis points per year. The hedge serves a function similar to excess-loss reinsurance, in which the ceding company retains the first loss but uses reinsurance to limit that loss to a tolerable level.

Although the most common interest rate caps are driven by LIBOR, caps based on CMT and CMS rates are more suitable for this hedge and are usually cheaper. CMT and CMS rates are suitable because they track the new money rates offered on competing annuities. To back newly sold SPDAs, insurers usually buy bonds and mortgages with maturities of 5 to 10 years, typically gravitating toward the highest yield attainable. To address the possibility that the yield curve may invert in the future, some caps may be bought on the two-year CMT or CMS and/or LIBOR.

Setting the size and strike prices of the cap hedge is a financial engineering problem best solved with a comprehensive simulation model of the assets and liabilities managed according to specified decision rules over time. Such a model provides the framework for considering not only cap hedges but also all of the other "knobs" that may be adjusted in the investment strategy, product design, and strategy for setting new money and renewal rates to be credited to customers. Another "knob" is the possible use of traditional and financial reinsurance.

Hedging with Yield Curve Swaps

Some insurers address the risk of rising rates by shortening duration, and then seek to make up for the lost yield through other strategies or a less competitive credited rate policy. One straightforward method of shortening the duration of a fixed-income portfolio is to enter into an interest rate swap in which the insurer pays a fixed rate and receives a floating rate. Such a swap transforms part of the fixed-rate portfolio to a floating-rate portfolio.

The floating rate is equal to a fixed spread over or under the prevailing constant-maturity Treasury (CMT) or swap rate (CMS) for maturities of 5, 7, or 10 years. The insurer can select a swap with the desired term (or "tenor"). By selecting a swap with a delayed start, an insurer can achieve a more attractive spread than with an immediate start under most market conditions.

Let's illustrate the idea with an example in which the rate received by the insurer floats with the prevailing yield on the five-year Treasury note over a five-year term. As time passes, new five-year notes are issued and replace the old notes for purposes of the calculation. The yield received by the insurer tracks fairly well the yield offered by competitors on new SPDAs.

The spread over or under the Treasury varies with the slope of the yield curve and the term of the swap. In April 1994, when the yield curve was steeply sloped, the market for this trade was to pay three-month LIBOR and to receive the five-year CMT minus 130 basis points. In December 1995, when the yield curve was much flatter, the market was to receive five-year CMT minus 20 basis points.

The insurer can pay either a fixed rate or LIBOR floating rate. Paying fixed allows the insurer to acquire and retain fixed-rate investments with attractive spreads to underlie the swap. The insurer could pay LIBOR in the swap, and find a floating or short-duration investment that offers a positive spread over LIBOR. If that spread were 50 basis points, then the all-in result of the short-term investment program and the yield curve swap would be 5 CMT plus 30 basis points, given market prices as of December 1995.

Like "ground" in an electrical circuit, LIBOR represents "home base" for the U.S. dollar swap market; most swaps represent an exchange of LIBOR for some other rate or return. If the insurer pays a fixed rate instead of LIBOR, that fixed rate will be the market swap rate for a fixed-for-floating swap of that tenor. In contrast to caps, CMT and CMS swaps have symmetric payoffs. By allowing the portfolio earned rate to fall as well as rise, they may undermine performance in the event of a sustained drop in interest rates. The optimal mixture of fixed-rate bonds, caps, and CMT or CMS swaps will depend on the age of the in-force block and the current level and slope of the yield curve, as well as other factors.

HEDGING ASSET AND LIABILITY COMMITMENTS

In the market for guaranteed interest contracts (GICs) and other guaranteed pension products, rate competition requires providers to work for a narrow gross margin. By managing interest rate risk carefully, an insurer can minimize the allocation of surplus, thereby increasing the ratio of invested assets to surplus and allowing a modest interest margin to create an attractive return on equity.

Unlike retail products, which are sold in an almost continuous flow of smaller transactions, GICs and other guaranteed institutional products require larger discrete commitments. GICs are sold when the opportunity is available to achieve a favorable rate. Likewise, assets with the desired maturity, yield, and structure become available sporadically, typically not at the same time as the opportunity to sell a GIC.

The sale of a GIC can be hedged by the purchase of U.S. Treasury notes or STRIPs, selecting maturities that have interest rate exposures most similar to those of the GICs being hedged. As commitments are made to acquire long-term investments, an appropriate amount of these Treasuries can be sold.

Hedging with Interest Rate Futures

As a substitute for buying Treasuries, an insurer can hedge a GIC by buying exchange-traded interest rate futures on 2-, 5-, and 10-year U.S. Treasury notes. Futures provide liquidity, low transaction costs, and the ability to avoid putting up cash that may not yet have been received from the GIC deposit. Using futures instead of Treasuries also provides the benefit of hedge accounting under SFAS No. 87; under this statement, any gain (loss) on unwinding the hedge is credited (debited) to the carrying value of the asset(s) purchased.

Alternatively, the insurer can warehouse an "inventory" of assets in anticipation of selling GICs. The short sale of Treasuries to hedge such an inventory is not permitted under insurance law. The most attractive hedge is to sell futures whenever an asset is purchased and to offset the appropriate amount of this short position when a GIC is sold. At any given time, the outstanding futures position is a mirror image of the asset inventory. SFAS No. 87 calls for incorporating the gain or loss on the hedge into the assets being hedged.

Each of these strategies hedges against changes in interest rates but not against changes in the spreads available in the bond and GIC markets, which are closely correlated. An insurer carrying a large inventory of hedged assets would be helped (hurt) if spreads on assets and GICs narrowed (widened) in the interval of time before GICs were sold against them. As a result, an insurer may vary the size of the inventory and tilt to positive or negative inventory positions, depending on their view of the future trend in spreads on fixed-income assets and GICs.

HEDGING THE RISK OF WIDENING SPREADS

Spreads on noncallable corporate bonds have fluctuated widely over the past 10 years. Such fluctuations introduce risk and opportunity into the management of a fixed-income portfolio within an asset-liability framework.

Consider a block of single-premium deferred annuities sold over the past six years, on which surrender charges are declining 1 percent per year as the block ages. These SPDAs might be supported by a fixed-income portfolio consisting of 60 percent corporate bonds and private placements, 25 percent mortgage-backed securities (MBSs), and 15 percent commercial mortgages. Recall that as renewal rates on these SPDAs fall short of SPDA new-money rates, customers have an increasing incentive to surrender. If the yield spreads in the market should widen, a competitor attempting to lure away these deposits will have the advantage of using higher-yielding assets over and above the effects of any increase in interest rates.

Spreads on corporate bonds are correlated with swap spreads, which are defined as the spread between the fixed side of a fixed-for-LIBOR swap and the equivalent maturity Treasury yield. Swap spreads tend to widen when the yield curve flattens and tighten when it steepens. When the curve steepens, investors prefer to receive fixed to earn a higher rate. Corporations prefer to receive fixed and pay floating to reduce the cost of fixed-rate debt. The midmarket swap spread can be viewed as the equilibrium level at which two AA-rated counterparties are indifferent between receiving or paying fixed. The difference between the swap spread and the single-A or BBB corporate bond spread can be isolated as the incremental premium for term default risk.

Hedging with Spread Locks

In 1993, the yield curve was steep, but the outlook for low corporate default rates was strong. Swap spreads were very tight by historical standards. If the primary concern was that a flattening of the yield curve would cause corporate and swap spreads to widen, an insurer could use spread locks as a hedge and as a means of actively expressing the view that swap spreads are likely to widen. A spread lock is an over-the-counter derivative transaction that specifies the tenor of the swap whose spread is being measured and the term over which the customer expects that spread to widen (or narrow). The dealer will offer to set the lock at the end of the term at a certain spread, which may be wider than the spot spread.

At the end of the term, if the spread is wider than the lock, the dealer owes money to the insurer. If the spread is narrower than the lock, the insurer owes money to the dealer. The amount owed is typically equal to the product of three terms: (1) the notional amount of the transaction, (2) the spread difference (actual level versus the lock), and (3) the duration of a swap of that tenor.

For example, suppose that an insurer is concerned that 10-year single-A spreads, which are 70 basis points, may widen. With spot 10-year swap spreads at 35 basis points, the insurer puts a spread lock of $100 million notional amount on the 10-year swap spread for one year at a spread of 38 basis points. After a year, corporate spreads and swap spreads widen by 15 basis points to 90 and 55 respectively. The cash settlement on the spread lock would be based on a favorable spread of 17 basis points and be calculated as follows:

$$\$100,000,000 \times .0017 \times 6.85 = \$1,164,500.$$

That payoff would offset most of the effect on market value of the 20 basis point widening of $100 million of the insurer's corporate bonds.

Spread locks may be European style, that is, exercisable only at the termination date, or they may allow the customer a window during which the lock can be exercised. Even before the window or termination date, a customer can typically unwind the lock at a mutually agreeable level, which will be a function of the forward swap spread then prevailing in the market.

Hedging with CMT/CMS Swaps

Another way to hedge against spread widening is to enter into a floating-to-floating swap in which the insurer pays the CMT rate plus a specified spread and receives the CMS rate for the same maturity. The specified spread will be based on the forward swap spreads implied by the current prices in the swap and Treasury markets. The trade is attractive if the insurer believes that swap spreads will be wider than those implied spreads. The CMT/CMS swap accomplishes the same result as a series, or "strip," of European-style spread locks.

HEDGING THE RISK OF FALLING RATES

For portfolios backing fixed cash flows like GICs and long-tailed fixed annuities, the use of callable corporate and mortgage-backed securities creates reinvestment risk. As conditioned as we might be to focus on inflation and high interest rates as our main fear, we must consider the possibility of an era of disinflation and even lower interest rates. Even for liabilities like SPDAs, on which the insurer enjoys the option of resetting the renewal rate, there is the danger of penetrating the level of the minimum guaranteed rate.

Sometimes, securities with call or prepayment risk are priced attractively in relation to noncallable securities of similar duration and quality. In the case of SPDAs, it may be attractive to use some current coupon or discount MBS pass-throughs and CMO tranches with some shortening risk but little or no lengthening risk, trading off some call risk to obtain more yield.

Such strategies leave some need to hedge against an extreme rally in interest rates. Insurers have used various tools to meet this need, including interest rate floors, prepayment caps, and bond warrants.

Interest Rate Floors

Interest rate floors are the mirror image of caps. They usually consist of a quarterly or semiannual series of options ("floorlets") on a yield index like LIBOR, CMT, or CMS. On each reset date, the yield is observed; if the yield is less than the strike yield, the floorlet entitles the owner to receive an amount of revenue equal to the notional amount times the excess of the strike yield over the observed yield, adjusted to a quarter- or half-year.

Floorlets are priced in relation to the forward rate for the respective index. When the yield curve is upwards-sloping, forward rates rise more steeply than the yield curve itself, making floors an economical way to protect portfolios from reinvestment risk.

Simulations show that the prepayment risk requires more than a simple floor structure. Payoffs must be souped up, either by having the notional amount increase as the index drops or by purchasing a ladder of strikes to accomplish the same objective in a piecewise linear fashion.

Floors may also be used as part of a defensive strategy. An insurer with long-dated liabilities could replace some long assets with shorter assets plus floors driven by a long-maturity CMT or CMS. If rates drop significantly, the floors rise in value at an accelerating rate, protecting the portfolio from reinvestment risk and helping the combined strategy to outperform the original assets if the move is substantial. Conversely, if rates rise significantly, the floor loses value at a decelerating rate, allowing the combination to lose less value than the original assets. Only if rates are fairly stable will this strategy underperform the original long assets.

Prepayment Caps

Using floors to hedge MBS prepayments requires the investor to make assumptions about the prepayment behavior of the underlying residential mortgages. Prepayments have proven to be difficult to estimate in recent years. An alternative hedge is to use prepayment caps, which pay the owner an amount designed to meet the hedging need at each realized level of prepayments. In effect, the insurer is synthetically selling the mortgage-backed securities by using this hedging method, and the dealer is stepping into the insurer's shoes in bearing the prepayment risk.

The investor has a choice between floors and other more complex products driven solely by interest rates and products that are driven by experience in the MBS market. One criterion for making this choice is the investor's view of whether the market is overvaluing or undervaluing the prepayment option in relation to pure interest rate options.

Bond Warrants

Bond warrants are long-dated call options on specific bonds to be issued upon exercise, typically by a corporate issuer with an investment-grade rating. Bond warrants are often cheaper than OTC swaptions of similar structure. Unfortunately, limited availability tends to restrict an end user's ability to diversify the credit risk of such options. At least the credit risk is mitigated by the insurer owning the option: if the credit spread widens, the insurer can consider this in deciding whether to exercise the option. This situation is the opposite of that encountered with callable bonds, where the call option works against the investor with respect to changes in interest rates and the creditworthiness of the issuer.

CREATING SYNTHETIC ASSETS

Many insurance company investment departments have developed confidence in their expertise and access to opportunities in certain traditional sectors of the domestic fixed-income markets, particularly fixed-rate public and private corporate obligations, commercial mortgages, and mortgage-backed securities. Unfortunately, continued adherence to this menu limits opportunities for diversification, leaving insurers with undue concentrations of exposure to the systematic risks of interest rate movements and defaults in the United States. The swap market allows insurers and other investors to diversify the risk exposures of their portfolios while continuing to earn excess returns in the cash markets where they have expertise.

The swap market also allows insurers to seek relative value in new market sectors that may be less efficiently priced than traditional sectors. Foreign markets have become very attractive to some insurers and leading independent money managers. Asset swaps allow the investor to achieve these benefits without retaining currency risk.

Asset Swaps

An asset swap combines an existing bond or note with a swap to create a new synthetic asset suitable for an investor. If the asset is denominated in a foreign currency, the swap wraps around the asset and converts it into a dollar-based investment with either a fixed or floating interest rate. We illustrate the idea with an investment made in February 1993 and sold in February 1994.

The underlying security was a LYON (a zero-coupon convertible bond) issued by SKF, a Swedish manufacturer. The bond is denominated in European currency units (ECUs). When combined with the swap, it had the characteristics of a coupon-bearing, dollar-denominated corporate bond offered at a spread of 300 basis points over a par Treasury maturing on the put date. In February 1994, the insurer sold the bond and unwound the swap, taking advantage of appreciation of the hedged position to 150 basis points over Treasuries. Part of the appreciation was attributable to a substantial increase in the price of the stock during the one-year holding period.

Total Return Swaps

Some dealers offer swaps in which the insurer pays LIBOR or a fixed rate and receives the total return on a defined index or group of securities. For example, insurers have done total return swaps in which they receive the return on a bond index, a class of mortgage-backed securities (e.g., all FNMA 7 pass-through securities issued during the first quarter of 1994), or a specified portfolio of bank loans.

By using a swap structure, the insurer can invest its cash in floating- or fixed-rate assets to create the cash flows required by the pay side of the swap. Depending on the riskiness of the swap, the insurer might use high-quality assets or attempt to achieve an excess return by taking advantage of the strengths of its style and capabilities (e.g., with origination of private placements or consumer finance loans).

Equity-Linked Structures

In domestic and foreign equity markets, OTC derivatives can curtail downside risk by providing asymmetric exposures not available in the cash markets. An insurer can combine a zero-coupon bond with a long-dated call on an index of domestic or foreign equities to create a downside-protected exposure to the market. This same exposure can also be bought in the form of a "protected equity note," in which the option and the zero-coupon obligation are embedded in a note issued by the dealer or an unrelated third-party issuer.

An equity swap paying the return on a foreign equity index provides a result that is difficult and costly for an insurer to reproduce in the cash markets. The swap may be on a highly diversified index of equities in a country or in a "basket" of country indexes. Transaction costs, in the form of the spread charged by the dealer, may be less than would be paid by the insurer in the cash markets if the dealer or its customers enjoy preferred access, regulatory status, or tax treatment in the countries involved.

An insurer can use such exposures to enhance the returns and diversification of its invested assets and achieve a more efficient allocation of surplus. It can also use these tools to create similar benefits for customers.

Structured Notes

Structured notes are a very broad and fast-growing class of investment products that combine the flexibility of over-the-counter derivative transactions with the regulatory and accounting treatment afforded to traditional notes. Under current regulations and reporting requirements, a structured note with no risk to principal is treated like any other note issued by that issuer. No extra risk-based capital is assigned to the underlying coupon risk.

Structured notes are a delivery vehicle for OTC derivatives. They offer the advantages of convenient packaging and user-friendly regulatory treatment. Unfortunately, they usually cost more than the equivalent structure unbundled because the issuer must be induced to provide the note structure and sometimes to guarantee the performance of the counterparty on the embedded swap.

The NAIC is currently considering whether insurers should be allowed to use such unbundled derivative strategies to replicate the risk-reward exposures now allowed only in the form of cash market investments and structured notes.

CONCLUSION

The case studies illustrate how insurers can use derivative products to reduce the risks inherent in their existing asset-liability spread businesses or to enhance the profile of return versus risk across scenarios that realistically capture the major sources of risk. The suitability of risk-reducing or hedging applications is generally accepted by major insurers and regulators at this stage. However, there is still a gap in awareness that may retard the use of derivatives for equally suitable enhancement of an insurer's risk-reward profile.

Insurers are already in the business of taking risks in the products they sell and in the relationship of their investment strategies to the liability cash flows that will be required in various scenarios. Why is the risk assumed in a derivative product different? The core issue is not where the risk is taken but what overall portfolio of risks is assumed.

One issue the regulators are considering is whether insurers should be allowed to use derivatives to replicate exposures that might otherwise be assumed in the cash markets. Replication transactions would have to be reported based on substance rather than form; that is, based on the exposures assumed rather than to swaps or options per se. It is ironic that regulators are more concerned with permitting suitable, portfolio-enhancing replication transactions like total-return swaps while they ignore much larger risks to net worth assumed in large duration mismatches between assets and liabilities and excessive dependence on single classes of risky assets.

Of all the current regulatory requirements, the most all-encompassing, holistic measure of aggregate risk is cash flow testing. In a perfect world, these cash flow tests would be a by-product of an insurer's own proprietary simulation capabilities, which would be used for financially engineering investment and product strategies at the product line and corporate levels, considering not only the statutory results but also the economic and GAAP results, taking taxes into account. In this world, insurers would be aware of the lessons of modern finance and portfolio theory as they seek to achieve the optimal mix of activities.

If regulators encouraged insurers to develop such advanced risk management capabilities, they could rely on the application of these capabilities as the primary safety net protecting customers from insolvency. With more stringent and economically rational standards for cash flow testing in place, the calculations of required risk-based capital could be based on actual risks assumed rather than coarse rules of thumb. The integrity of the cash flow testing procedures and supporting data could be strengthened by requiring representations by the valuation actuaries and members of senior management and independent audits.

Chapter Thirty-Two

Derivative Embedded Securities—Structural Aspects

Satyajit Das
Financial Derivatives and Risk Management

A derivative embedded security is usually defined as a conventional fixed-income debt combined with a derivative transaction. The derivative element is generally incorporated into the normal fixed-income security structure by linking either the redemption and/or the coupon value to movements in the underlying asset price by means of financial market variables such as interest rates, currencies, equity market indexes, and commodities. Traditionally, this element tended to take the form of either a symmetric position, such as a forward contract, or an asymmetric position, such as an option. Increasingly, however, nonstandard hybrid and exotic option structures are incorporated into derivative embedded security structures.

While derivative embedded securities have proliferated in recent times, there has been a long history of fixed-income securities embedded with derivative elements. The most common of such *traditional* derivatives include fixed-income bonds with call options, which give the issuer the ability to retire the securities before their scheduled maturity, or equity convertible securities with embodied call options on the equity of the issuer. The key distinguishing feature of a modern derivative embedded security

Earlier versions of this paper have appeared in *IFR Swaps Weekly* and *Capital Market Strategies*.
© Copyright Satyajit Das, 1994.

compared with its traditional counterpart is the role played by the derivative element.

In a traditional configuration such as a callable or a convertible bond, the call option is utilized as a "sweetener" to make the security more attractive to investors as part of an overall investment package. In contrast, the incorporated derivative element in modern derivative embedded securities is highly engineered to allow specifically for the creation and the transfer of the risk that is embodied in the derivative component. This may entail, for example, an investor creating the derivative element, which is then securitized through the security structure with the issuer transferring the derivative element to a derivative market maker. The market maker in turn reallocates the risk element to end users of that particular instrument. In this way, modern derivative embedded securities are utilized as a complex basis for the transfer of risk through an often long chain of transactions.

Using the collared floating rate note (FRN) issue as an example, this chapter looks at certain structural aspects of derivative embedded securities including the rationale for such structures, the credit implications of these arrangements, and their pricing implications.

STRUCTURAL ELEMENTS

Appendix 32-1 illustrates an example of a collared FRN transaction that emerged in 1992 and 1993 to take advantage of the relatively steep slope of the U.S. dollar interest rate yield curve during that period. The basic economics of the collared FRN was driven by combining a standard FRN structure with both a cap and a floor on the US$ LIBOR interest rate. Thus, in addition to purchasing a FRN, an investor would have effectively sold a cap and purchased a floor (or equivalently sold an interest rate collar on the US$ LIBOR) to the issuer.

The following key structural elements of this transaction should be noted:

- The issuer of the securities was typically a highly rated entity (usually AA rated or better).
- The issuer in these transactions did not, as a general rule, position or absorb the risk of the derivative elements created through the FRN structure. The issuer typically onsold the derivative elements or, in turn, hedged its exposure to the derivative elements through the derivative markets. The issuer's primary motivation was the margin that could be made from the derivative elements captured through

the sale of the security and the price for which the derivative elements could be hedged, repackaged, or sold in the capital markets. The overall result to the issuer was an attractive total cost of funds that was based on the margin earned from the purchase and the onsale of the derivative element that acted as a subsidy on its overall borrowing cost.

- The maturity of the derivative embedded security in the case of collared FRNs was quite long—up to 10 or 12 years, a contrast to the more common derivative embedded security structures which usually entailed shorter maturities (typically one to three years) although longer transactions are not unknown.

- Key elements in the cash flow structuring of the security were central to the efficacy of the arrangement. In the case of the collared FRN, the transaction entailed the investor's execution of the following package: purchase of both a normal FRN and a US$ LIBOR interest rate floor at a minimum interest rate level of 5 percent per annum, and sale of a cap on US$ LIBOR at a maximum rate of 10 percent per annum. Thus, in addition to purchasing a FRN, the structure required the investor to purchase and sell both the option elements from and to the issuer.

The mechanics involved were a crucial element of the structure. They facilitated a shift in the performance obligations to the issuer (who as noted was highly rated and considered relatively free of credit or default risk). This is crucial in the case of the cap that was sold by the investor to the issuer, where there is normally a performance obligation on the writer of the option to make cash payments whenever US$ LIBOR exceeded the cap level. The structure, however, obviated this requirement by requiring the *issuer* to effectively assume the credit risk of the option writer.

In the case of the collared FRN, this is achieved by the issuer paying only the maximum interest rate of 10 percent to the investor. Any payment related to the inherent value of the cap (i.e., reflecting a difference between the US$ LIBOR and the maximum rate whenever LIBOR was above the maximum rate) was made to the ultimate purchaser of the cap. In this manner, the performance obligations under the derivative element was shifted to the issuer, so that the issuer's credit risk could be substituted for that of the investor's. In the reverse case, when the investor purchased a floor, the performance obligation rested with the issuer from the outset.

The above identified elements are all present in the transactions described in Appendix 32–1. The importance of the cash flow structuring in the shifting of the performance obligation to the issuer is illustrated by the second transaction (see Exhibits 32–2A and 32–2B in the appendix, the World Bank transaction that entailed a securitization of the collared FRN). In this transaction, the issue of the FRNs was combined with a maximum interest rate, but it was sold in conjunction with the detachable issues of the floor certificates, which were effectively the minimum interest rate elements of the transaction. The economic benefit of such an arrangement was the ability of the investor to freely and quite separately trade the floor certificates from the capped FRN.

From the viewpoint of cash flow structuring, the two option elements—the cap *written by the investor* and the floor *purchased by the investor*—could be treated differently. The floor element, in which the performance obligation was on the issuer as the grantor of the option, could be freely securitized. In contrast, the cap element, in which the performance obligation was on the investor as the grantor of the cap, cannot be similarly structured because this would prevent the transfer of the performance obligation from the investor to the issuer.

While the above discussion about the structural elements of the derivative embedded securities relate to the collared FRN example, in practice almost all derivative embedded securities transactions must necessarily embody similar structural features.

RATIONALE FOR DERIVATIVE EMBEDDED SECURITIES

There are four possible explanations for the use of such structures:

1. Regulatory arbitrage where investors and, less frequently, issuers utilize derivative embedded structure to circumvent barriers to trading in the relevant derivatives directly.
2. Utilizing such structures to monetize position/expectations in a particular manner.
3. Utilizing such structures to provide credit enhancement to facilitate participation in the derivatives market.
4. Allowing derivative transactions to be undertaken in denominations that might otherwise not be feasible.

There is some evidence that derivative embedded securities are utilized to circumvent regulations that would otherwise prevent an investor or, alternatively, an issuer from undertaking the underlying derivative transaction itself. There is nothing sinister about the use of derivative embedded securities to circumvent barriers when dealing in derivatives. In fact, the capacity to utilize derivatives in this format is a necessary means for issuers and investors who would otherwise be prevented from managing their financial risk to the fullest extent possible. This is particularly true of investors who may be constrained by legal papers created in an era before the availability of derivatives, which may be difficult and cumbersome to change. In a sense, investors' use of derivative embedded securities to purchase or sell securities as part of their normal functions are a means of overcoming the transaction costs of effecting the necessary change in the constituent documents of the relevant entity. Although it is difficult to get direct evidence of the regulatory arbitrage element that motivates derivative embedded securities, anecdotal evidence suggests that this element is indeed significant. In addition, the identity of major buyer groups, namely European and Asian investors, alone suggests that this as a strong motivation for such transactions.

Derivative embedded securities are also utilized frequently to monetize positions and/or expectations about capital market variables. The advantage of derivative embedded securities in this regard is that they allow investors or issuers to monetize their market view in a customized fashion. The major elements of these monetizing aspects include:

- Transactions that allow value to be captured by essentially allowing, say, an investor's expectation regarding particular values of financial assets to be embedded in the derivative. For example, a collared FRN or a reverse or inverse FRN structure can be characterized as monetizing an investor's view that forward rates currently implied by an yield curve are significantly above the actual rate that will prevail in the future.

- Monetizing positions or expectations through derivative embedded securities may allow a degree of liquidity/tradeability that cannot be achieved otherwise. For example, in the case of a collared FRN, the investor can effectively trade a series of options to embody views on the forward interest rates. This can be done by purchasing and selling the FRNs without entering into a complex series of transactions requiring the availability of credit facilities and counterparty risk lines. The liquidity or tradeability potential (at least, in theory) is an important incentive to utilize derivative embedded securities to monetize such positions and expectations.

- Utilizing derivative embedded securities to create interesting combinations of positions. An example of this concept is evident in a reverse FRN where in essence the security combines a fixed bond with an interest rate swap in which the investor receives a fixed rate and pays a floating rate. Under this combined structure, the investor has several sources of value including (1) the realized short-term money market rates relative to those embodied in the current yield curve, and (2) the movement in the term swap rate and interest rate swap values that will fluctuate according to the increase or decrease of term swap rates.

This particular combination of expectations/views may in practice allow value to be created from combinations of positions in a unique way. Importantly, creating such instruments in a package which is, potentially, both tradeable and liquid may enhance the value of the transaction.

As discussed earlier, the cash flow structuring entailed in a derivative embedded security allows the investor to transfer the credit exposure of the transaction to the issuer, which effectively utilizes the credit quality in such derivative transactions. This is particularly important for investors dealing in small amounts of derivatives or investors whose structure, such as a mutual or pooled fund, may make it difficult for such entities to have access to the required credit arrangements to participate in derivative transactions more generally.

A related issue may be termed a denomination feature. The use of derivative embedded securities allows investors, in particular, to participate in the derivatives market in denominations that are significantly lower than those that might be achieved through direct participation. In capped FRN transactions, which are not atypical, the low denominations of the FRNs themselves would allow investors to purchase and sell derivative elements for relatively modest amounts (e.g., $500,000 and above), thereby allowing retail participation in the derivatives market within a wholesale and institutional market structure.

PRICING IMPLICATIONS

The structural elements and rationale for derivative embedded securities have direct implications on the price of such transactions. These implications exist at two levels:

1. Value capture issues.
2. The apportionment of value between various parties that are involved in the transactions.

Given the nature of the transactions, an investor who is seeking to purchase or to sell the derivative element incorporated in a security structure, particularly if there are no alternative means of participating in the derivative market, will likely be price insensitive. In addition, it is probable that the investor will be prepared to pay a premium for a structure that allows the monetization of a particular position or expectation in a desirable manner. The investor will also be required to pay an additional premium for the credit enhancement elements of the transaction as well as for the denomination-reduction process, which implicitly allows for a more widespread participation. Against this background, investors typically will pay, as in the case of the collared FRN, a higher price for the derivatives than that based on a theoretical value under normal market trading conditions.

Value in this context for the overall transaction will be driven by several elements:

- The investor's desired position and the value that the investor accords to the structure.
- The issuer's target cost of funds and the value the issuer places on its credit enhancement role in the transaction.
- The return objectives of the intermediary arranging the overall package.

Predictably, there is significant competition between investors, issuers, and intermediaries to create a volatile market for such structures. Moreover, the value-exchange equation is dynamic and would alter depending on changes in any one or more of the variables identified.

FUTURE FOR DERIVATIVE EMBEDDED SECURITIES

Derivative embedded securities are now an established part of the activity in capital markets. They fulfill a fundamental and necessary part, facilitating a particular form of risk transfer in the derivatives market. The market has evolved with the increasing movement of derivative embedded securities, from the public to the private placement market, particularly in the context of continuously offered debt issuance programs such as medium-term note issuance facilities. The flexibility of such arrangements, particularly the capacity to accommodate reverse enquiry processes whereby dealers can respond to investor requirements for particular security packages and procure issuers for such transactions, has made derivative embedded securities essential vehicles for such activities.

A possible growth component is the use of derivative embedded security structures by issuers, particularly corporations, with underlying risk positions that might utilize the security package to simultaneously generate cost-effective funding while managing its financial risk profile. A primary motivation for such transactions may be the increased efficiency in managing financial risks in combination with funding transactions.

Appendix 32–1
COLLARED FLOATING RATE NOTES (FRNs)

Background/Origins

The collared FRN structure has its origins in the capped FRN and Mini-Max FRN transactions completed in the mid-1980s. The collared FRN market emerged around August 1992 when Kidder Peabody, the US investment bank, reintroduced the concept with issues for, among others, J.P. Morgan and Credit Local de France. The market re-emerged in an environment of declining U.S. interest rates. A particular feature of the market, at this time, was the relatively steep slope of the U.S. dollar interest rate yield curve.

Structure and Economics

1. Structure.   The basic structure of the collared FRN entails a normal FRN structure with an interest coupon related to US$ LIBOR (either three or six months). The interest rate coupon is subject to a minimum and maximum interest rate level of 5 percent per annum and 10 percent per annum respectively. The initial issues were undertaken for maturities of 10 years.

The initial transactions were subordinated FRNs (designed to be treated as Tier 2 capital for Bank of International Settlement (BIS) capital adequacy purposes). However, a number of subsequent issues were senior rather than subordinated issue structures. Exhibit 32–1A sets out the term of the J.P. Morgan issue, one of their first transactions to be undertaken.

2. Economics.   The basic economics of the collared FRN is driven by the fact that it combines a standard FRN transaction with a US$ LIBOR interest rate cap and floor. Based on the structure described, the investor's package consists of:

- The purchase of a normal 10-year, US$ LIBOR related coupon FRN.
- The sale of a cap on US$ LIBOR at the maximum interest rate (say, 10 percent per annum).
- The purchase of a US$ interest rate floor at the minimum interest rate level (say, 5 percent per annum).

The sale of the cap and purchase of the floor is equivalent to the sale of an interest rate collar on US$ LIBOR.

The position of the issuer is the exact opposite to that of the investor. The issuer has borrowed, utilizing a US$ LIBOR-based FRN while simultaneously purchasing

EXHIBIT 32–1A
J.P. Morgan and Co., Inc.

Amount	U.S. $200 million of subordinated FRNs
Maturity	10 years (due August 19, 2002)
Spread	Three-month LIBID flat
Fixed re-offer price	99.85
Minimum interest	5%
Maximum interest	10%
Amortisation	Bullet
Call option	None
Denominations	U.S. $5,000, U.S. $100,000
Commissions	0.50% (management and underwriting 0.25%; selling 0.25%)

Source: *International Financing Review* 56, no. 940 (August 1, 1992).

a US$ LIBOR interest rate cap and selling a US$ LIBOR-based floor (a purchased interest rate collar on US$ LIBOR). As described below in detail, the issuer hedges the exposure due to the collar by selling the cap and purchasing the floor to generate normal US$ LIBOR-based funding.

The economics of the transaction are driven substantively by the shape of the U.S. dollar yield curve. The strongly positive nature of the yield curve means that forward rates in U.S. dollars are significantly above the prevailing rates for particular maturities. For example, the rate for U.S. dollars three- or six-month LIBOR in 3, 6, 9, 12, and so forth, months is significantly above the prevailing LIBOR or bank borrowing rates for the corresponding maturities. This merely reflects the steepness of the yield curve itself.

The steepness of the yield curve and the fact that the US$ LIBOR forward rates implied from the curve are significantly above the observed yield curve dictate the respective values of the cap and floor which, in turn, dictate the economics of the transaction. That forward US$ LIBOR rates are significantly above the current yield curve means that the US$ LIBOR floors purchased by the investors while significantly in the money during the initial periods are out of the money for much of the life of the transaction. In contrast, the higher US$ LIBOR forward rates implied by the yield curve dictate that the US$ interest rate cap is closer to the strike price of the maximum interest rate level (effectively, the cap strike level) of the collared FRN structure. This relativity of the minimum and maximum rates (effectively, the strike rates for the floor and cap respectively) determines their relative value.

At the time these transactions were undertaken, based on the yield curves prevailing, the market price of the 5 percent floor was significantly below that of the 10 percent cap. The inputed value of the cap and floor suggest that investors were forgoing approximately 50 basis points per annum in value from the transaction; in other words, collared FRN had an implied yield of approximately LIBOR minus 50 basis points per annum. This forgone value effectively allowed the issuer to create an attractively priced funding as described below.

Investor perspective.   The major demand for these collared FRNs came from money market investors, primarily money market funds seeking the benefit of a minimum coupon. With the U.S. dollar short-term interest rate at historically low levels and, at that time, apparently headed lower, investors were prepared to tradeoff the forgone profit of the cap for the high short-term current coupon income generated by the floor implicit in the minimum interest level. Investors were willing to sell the cap at a level lower than theoretical value, due to the fact that a greater emphasis was first placed on current income and then their views on the market.

Initial demand for collared FRNs were concentrated among the Swiss and Far Eastern money market investors. However, as the market developed rapidly, German, UK, and US investors joined in the purchase of these collared FRN transactions.

Issuer perspective.   From the perspective of the issuer, these transactions were fully hedged into normal US$ LIBOR-based funding, typically at relatively attractive borrowing rates. The issuer who had effectively purchased a U.S. dollar interest rate cap at the maximum rate and sold the investor an interest rate floor at the minimum interest rate hedged its exposure by simultaneously onselling the interest rate cap and purchasing a corresponding interest rate floor to immunize against the risk of the transaction. These interest rate cap and floor transactions were typically undertaken by the issuer directly with the arranger of the transaction or alternatively a third-party cap/floor trader.

As noted above, the attractive funding cost for the issuer was generated by the fact that the investor valued the collar element of the transaction at a level that was lower than the economic value of the separate interest rate cap and floor. This allowed issuers to typically onsell the interest rate cap and purchase the interest rate floor for premiums that generated a net cash inflow to the issuer, which reduced their borrowing costs in some cases by as much as 50 basis points per annum.

From the issuer's perspective, the transactions were particularly attractive as they generated attractively priced long-term funding, typically 10 years, at a time when arbitrage opportunities in traditional bond markets were relatively scarce. An additional advantage, particularly for banks, was the capacity to structure a number of these transactions as subordinated issues, thereby allowing these institutions to raise cost-effective Tier 2 capital to enhance their capital adequacy positions.

Market Evolution and Product Variations

As the market evolved, an interesting product variation focused on securitizing the option elements of the structure. Under this arrangement, the issue of FRNs was combined with a maximum interest rate, but it was sold in conjunction with the issue by the borrower of floor certificates. These detachable floor certificates, which were effectively the minimum interest rate elements of the transaction allowed the investor free trading access independent of the capped FRNs. Exhibits 32–2A and 32–2B illustrate an example of this variation by detailing the terms of an issue for the World Bank completed in March 1993.

The structure was, in addition, interesting for a number of other features including:

- The deferral of the maximum interest level, which operated only from the beginning of the fifth interest rate period (effectively, 2.5 years into the term of the 10-year transaction), reflecting that DM LIBOR was higher than the maximum rate at the time of issue.

- The maximum interest rate which was lower than the then prevailing DM LIBOR rate, reflecting the inverse slope of the DM yield curve and the different implied pattern of forward DM LIBOR rates.

- The structure of the floor certificates had a strike rate of 7 percent (which is unusually close to the maximum interest rate level) and operated for the full life of the transaction, again reflecting the particular shape of the DM yield curve.

Exhibit 32–2A
World Bank: Capped FRN

Amount	DM 200 million of FRNs
Maturity	10 years (due April 28, 2003)
Coupon	Six-month LIBOR plus 0.25% payable semiannually on April 28 and October 28
Maximum interest	$7\frac{1}{4}$% as from the beginning of the fifth interest period
First interest determination date	April 26
Issue price	100%
Amortisation	Bullet
Call option	None
Denominations	DM 10,000 and DM 250,000 (global note)
Commissions	0.20% (management and underwriting combined 0.10%)

Source: *International Financing Review* 72, no 970 (March 13, 1993).

EXHIBIT 32–2B
World Bank: Floor Certificates

Issuer	World Bank
Number	20,000 certificates
Exercise	Each certificate entitles the holder to payment on April 28 and October 28 corresponding to the positive difference between 7% and six-month LIBOR. Each certificate relates to DM 10,000
Issue price	DM 695 per certificate
Expiration	April 28, 2003
Selling concession	0.25%

Source: *International Financing Review* 72, no 970 (March 13, 1993).

## Chapter Thirty-Three

Use of Options and Futures for Tactical Asset Allocation

Roger G. Clarke
TSA Capital Management

Several basic elements are required for an effective tactical asset allocation process. First, the investor must have a view of market direction and the time frame over which the movement might occur. Second, the investor must be willing to take action based on that view. The investor must have an idea of what positions to take and have the discipline to act. Being timid about taking positions will not produce the desired results. Finally, implementation of the new allocation must be done in a cost-effective way or the potential value added will be dissipated through transactions costs.

Options and futures provide a very cost-effective way to implement tactical changes in asset allocation. In the major stock and bond markets around the world, options and futures generally provide a less expensive alternative for changing broad market exposure than trading individual physical securities. Though many different variations of derivatives are available today, including index-return swaps, equity-linked notes, and other structured products, this chapter will focus on implementation using simple futures and options.

BASIC USES OF DERIVATIVES IN ASSET ALLOCATION

The three principal uses of options and futures in tactical asset allocation are creating additional market exposure, hedging existing market exposure, and structuring automatic, market-driven changes in market exposure.

Additional market exposure can be created by purchasing futures contracts or call options. For example, if the investor wants to increase market exposure in the U.S. equity market by $10 million, an equivalent amount of U.S. futures contracts can be purchased on the S&P 500 Index instead of purchasing $10 million worth of individual stocks. Alternatively, $10 million worth of market exposure could be obtained by purchasing an appropriate number of call options on the S&P 500 Index.

Alternatively, if the investor wants to reduce market exposure by $10 million, the desired change can be made by hedging. The reduction in exposure can be accomplished by selling $10 million in futures contracts or by purchasing an appropriate number of put options.

Finally, automatic changes in asset mix at predetermined market levels can be triggered by selling options. A reduction in market exposure can be achieved by selling call options. An increase in market exposure can be achieved by selling put options.

An important characteristic of options relative to futures is captured in their asymmetric response to market moves. Call options are more sensitive to market rallies while put options are more sensitive to market declines. On the other hand, futures are equally sensitive no matter which way the market moves. Consequently, options provide somewhat greater flexibility in designing specialized strategies to alter the risk/return characteristics of a portfolio. Exhibit 33–1 briefly summarizes these characteristics.

Structuring Linear Return Patterns

The most common use of futures is either to create additional market exposure or to reduce market exposure. (Hedging risky asset exposure can also be thought of as increasing the cash position in a portfolio). The purchase of a futures contract increases market exposure to the underlying index or security driving the futures contract while the sale of a futures contract reduces exposure. To illustrate how futures can be used to affect an asset allocation shift, consider a portfolio of U.S. stocks and bonds depicted in Exhibit 33–2. If exchange-traded futures are used to alter the mix, a small cash reserve must be set aside to post as collateral with the exchange and to use in the daily settlement of gains and losses on the contracts. The initial margin and daily mark to market are designed to reduce the risk that an investor might build up sizable losses over time and then not be able to pay. Daily settlement of gains and losses forces investors to have adequate cash on hand to fund losses or else be forced to close out their positions so no further losses can accumulate. In Exhibit 33–2, the cash

EXHIBIT 33–1
Basic Uses of Derivatives in Asset Allocation

	Linear Patterns	*Nonlinear Patterns*
Create exposure	• Buy futures • Buy calls and sell puts	• Buy call options • Buy call options spreads • Replicate a call option with a dynamic futures position
Reduce (or hedge) exposure	• Sell futures • Buy puts and sell calls	• Buy put options • Buy put option spreads • Replicate a put option with a dynamic futures position
Automatic change in exposure	• NA	• Sell call options • Sell put options • Replicate options with a dynamic futures position

reserve amounts to $10 million or 10 percent of the total portfolio, leaving $45 million each to be invested in individual stocks and bonds.

If the investor wants to keep the portfolio fully invested with a 50/50 mix of stocks and bonds, additional market exposure can be created using the cash reserve as collateral by purchasing $5 million each of stock and bond futures. This overlay of futures on top of the cash portfolio will create a combined portfolio that will behave as if it had a 50/50 mix of stocks and bonds even though the underlying assets are invested in $45 million each of stocks and bonds and $10 million in cash. The $5 million in equity index futures plus the interest earned on $5 million in cash will generate a return approximately equal to the index return on stocks associated with the equity index futures contract. Interest on the remaining $5 million in cash plus the $5 million in bond futures contracts will behave similarly to $5 million in physical bonds. Futures contracts are priced so that this correspondence generally holds without much tracking error. The section on pricing futures and options contracts contains a brief review of the fair pricing of futures contracts and the arbitrage that keeps the futures fairly priced.

If the investor now wants to change the effective mix in the portfolio to $60 million in stocks and $40 million in bonds, the investor would purchase another $10 million in equity index futures and sell $10 million in bond

EXHIBIT 33–2
Portfolio Allocation Using Futures

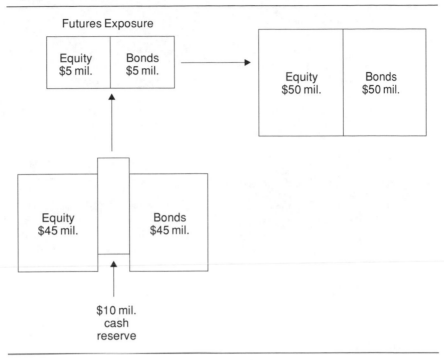

futures. The net futures positions that create an effective 60/40 mix of stocks and bonds would require a long position of $15 million in equity futures and a short position of $5 million in bond futures. The $45 million in individual stocks plus $15 million in futures will generate returns equivalent to $60 million in equity exposure. Conversely, the $45 million in bonds less the $5 million net short position in bond futures will generate returns equivalent to $40 million in bonds. This is illustrated in Exhibit 33–3.

Asset allocation using futures contracts often combines two applications of the use of derivatives. Long positions create additional market exposure while short positions reduce or hedge existing market exposure. Futures are linear in their impact on the return distribution of the portfolio. They respond in equal magnitude to market rallies as they do to market declines.

This symmetry is illustrated in Exhibit 33–4. If the 45-degree straight line represents the return on the market exposure when the underlying market moves, the addition of short futures positions to hedge the market

EXHIBIT 33–3
Asset Allocation Shifts Using Futures

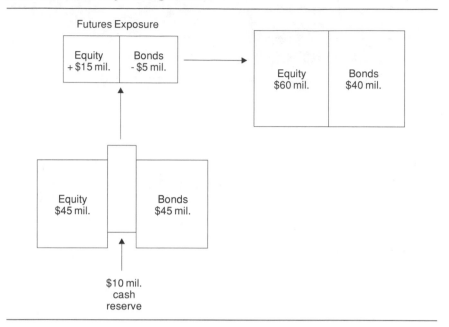

EXHIBIT 33–4
Return Profiles for Hedged Portfolios

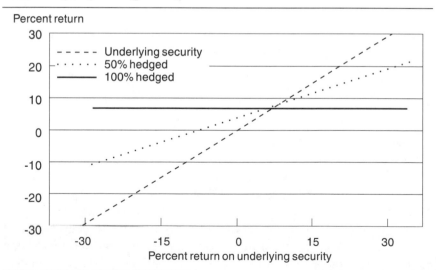

risk will flatten the slope of the return line until it becomes horizontal using a full hedge. A fully hedged position generates a constant return equivalent to investing in a riskless asset whose return is independent of what the market does. A partially hedged position will have a positive return slope but will be less than that of full market exposure.

Though individual options are nonlinear in their exposure characteristics, a combination of a long call and a short put with the same strike price and maturity also produces a linear return pattern. This option combination is conceptionally equivalent to purchasing a futures contract to create market exposure. The long call position creates market exposure as the market rises while the short put position creates market exposure as the market falls. The combination creates a linear payoff pattern consistent with the returns from using a futures contract.

A simple way to calculate the number of futures contracts needed to reallocate asset exposure is to divide the desired change in asset exposure by the index value per futures contract; that is,

$$n = \frac{\Delta A}{I} = \frac{A\,(P_T - P_C)}{I} \tag{1}$$

where

n = Number of futures contracts
ΔA = Desired change in asset exposure
A = Total value of assets,
P_T = Target proportion in stocks or bonds,
P_C = Current proportion in stocks or bonds, and
I = Index value per futures contract

For example, suppose an investor has a $100 million portfolio and wants to change it from 40 percent equity exposure to 60 percent exposure. Assume each S&P contract is worth about $200,000. As shown below, this investor would need about 100 contracts to move the equity mix in the portfolio from 40 percent to 60 percent. Buying 100 S&P contracts creates additional equity exposure without actually buying individual physical securities.

$$n = \frac{100,000,000\,(.60 - .40)}{200,000} = 100 \text{ contracts}$$

The calculation of the number of futures contracts is slightly more complex if the risk of the underlying assets is different than the risk characteristics of the futures index. The number of futures contracts will be greater or less depending on whether the risk of the underlying asset is greater than or less than that of the futures index. To make the risk adjustment the change in asset exposure needs to be multiplied by the ratio of relative risks between the underlying assets and the futures index

$$n = \frac{\Delta A}{I} \left(\frac{R_A}{R_I} \right) \tag{1a}$$

where R_A represents the risk of the underlying assets and R_I represents the risk of the futures index. For equity portfolios, the risk is usually represented by the portfolio beta. For fixed-income portfolios, the risk is usually represented by the duration of the portfolio.

Continuing with the previous example, consider that the equity portfolio has a beta of 1.05 while the beta of the S&P 500 is equal to 1.0. The number of futures contracts needed to create 20 percent more equity exposure equivalent to that of the underlying portfolio would be:

$$n = \frac{100,000,000 \,(.60 - .40)}{200,000} \left(\frac{1.05}{1.0} \right) = 105 \text{ contracts}$$

More futures contracts are required than before because of the greater volatility of the underlying assets. The same percentage move in the futures index will likely be associated with a larger move in the underlying assets. To match the larger move, more contracts are needed. Similarly, if the underlying assets are less risky than the futures index, fewer contracts would be needed to produce the same return effect.

If a combination of put and call options is used instead of futures contracts (a put/call combo), the number of options needs to match the exposure in the requisite number of futures contracts in order to replicate the linear payoff.

The use of foreign futures contracts for global asset allocation are structured in a similar way. Exhibit 33–5 illustrates how this process works. However, when investors buy futures contracts on, say, the Nikkei 225, they are buying Japanese equity market exposure without the currency exposure associated with the notional or principal amount of that equity contract. The investor is buying hedged equity exposure in the foreign country. If the investor wants the currency exposure, which is naturally associated with the

EXHIBIT 33–5
Separation of Asset and Foreign Exchange Decisions Using Futures

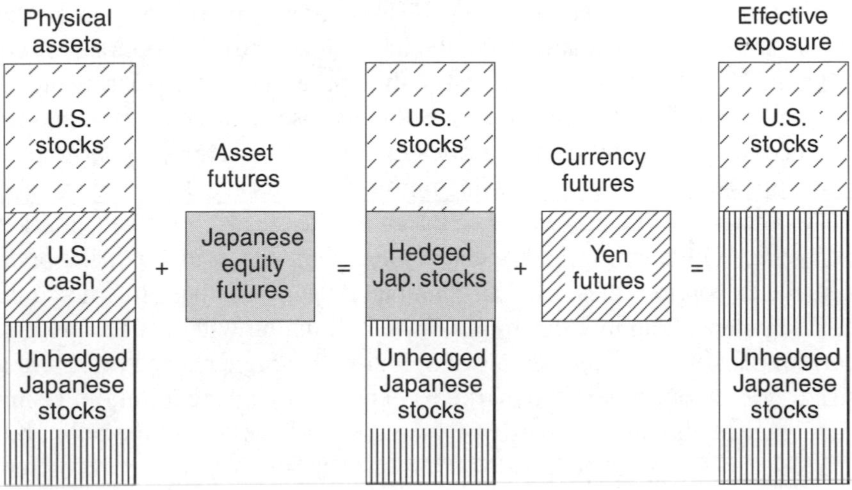

purchase of physical securities, yen futures contracts or forwards must be purchased to create the currency exposure. This is an interesting characteristic of using futures contracts for global asset allocation, because only the daily changes in value in the contract are denominated in the foreign currency, not the principal amount itself. Even these gains and losses can be converted to the investor's home currency on a daily basis so that little currency exposure results over the life of the contract.

Structuring Nonlinear Return Patterns

Options offer another alternative for implementing asset allocation strategies. Individual put and call options offer nonlinear return patterns, whereas the return pattern from a futures contract is linear. (However, we noted earlier that a put/call combination can be substituted for a futures contract and creates a linear payoff).

Besides being used to mimic a futures contract, options can be used in several nonlinear applications in asset allocation, including creating additional market exposure, hedging existing market exposure, and triggering changes in exposure.

Creation of additional market exposure. Two common option positions used to create new market exposure are buying calls and buying call spreads. To add equity market exposure to a portfolio, the investor can buy call options on an equity index. If, for example, extra exposure to the Japanese equity market is desired, the investor can buy call options on the Nikkei 225. If the market appreciates, the option will increase in value. If the market declines, the most the investor can lose is the cost of the option. The cost of the call option is the price the investor must pay to participate in the upside market potential while limiting the loss in a declining market.

An alternative strategy would be to buy a call spread to create the market exposure. With a call spread, investors buy calls with a lower strike price than the call options they sell. For example, if the market has only moderate upside potential, an investor might buy a call option with a strike price at current market levels and sell a call option with a higher strike price—at a strike price above where the market is expected to be at expiration. Using a call spread, the investor participates in the market only up to a point, but at a reduced cost because the sale of the out-of-the-money call option offsets the cost of the long call option.

The payoff profiles at expiration for these two strategies, compared to buying a futures contract, are illustrated in Exhibit 33–6. If investors buy futures contracts, they will participate to the full extent of the market increase or decrease. If they buy a call option to create exposure, they participate if the market goes up; if the market goes down, they will not suffer the full decline. The gap between the option and futures payoff on the upside represents the cost of the call option. If an investor's view about the market is positive, but not excessively bullish, the lower-cost call spread creates additional exposure but caps the market participation beyond a certain point.

The effects of using options are somewhat different if the market moves right after the options are purchased, before the full effect of the time decay in the option premium is realized. Exhibit 33–7 illustrates what occurs before option expiration. The valuation curves smooth out if the market moves right after the investor puts the position on. In this example, the options expire in 60 days. With the call option, the investor participates smoothly as the market moves away from its current security price, in this case at 100. On the way up, it will always lag behind the futures contract, but it will not decline as sharply if the market goes down right after the option is put on. It is not a straight line because the natural exposure of the option changes as the security price moves. The call option spread creates

EXHIBIT 33–6
Creating New Market Exposure with Options (Value at Expiration)

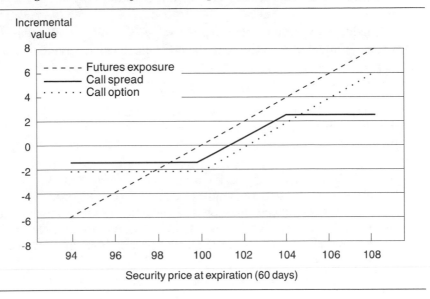

EXHIBIT 33–7
Creating New Market Exposure with Options (Current Value)

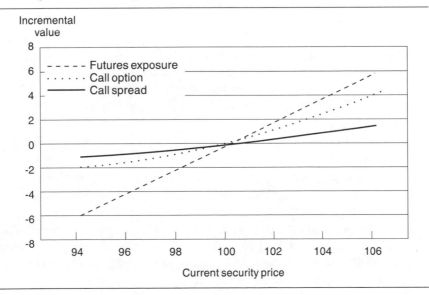

a flatter profile. It does not participate as much in the full market move as the single call option and declines less when the market falls.

Hedging existing market exposure.   A second use of options is to protect existing market exposure in the portfolio. Typical strategies used for this purpose include buying puts, buying a put spread, using a zero-premium collar, and using a zero-premium put spread collar.

- *Buying puts.* Buying puts may be attractive if the investor believes the market has high downside risk and is willing to pay for protection. The price of protection is the price of the put option.
- *Buying a put spread.* Buying a put spread is similar to buying a call spread. A put option with a strike price close to current market levels is purchased, and a put option with a lower strike price is sold. The put spread can be used when the investor views the market as having moderate downside risk. In this case, the investor pays less for protection from moderate market declines than the cost of a put option.
- *The zero-premium collar.* This strategy is constructed by selling a call option with a large enough premium to fund the purchase of a put option. As long as an investor believes the market will likely stay within a trading range on the upside, this strategy is attractive. Investors get full market participation within the trading range; if the market runs outside of that range, the strategy will underperform on the upside but do better on the downside.
- *The zero-premium put spread collar.* This strategy is constructed by buying a put spread and selling a call option, as in the zero-premium collar. This strategy works well if an investor believes the market will stay in a trading range and not appreciate or depreciate greatly. It provides higher upside participation but restores market exposure after a substantial decline.

The portfolio protection these strategies provide is diagramed in Exhibit 33–8 which shows the payoff profile of selected strategies. The futures exposure is a straight 45-degree line. The other strategies have exposure on one or the other side of the futures line. Using these strategies changes the beta of an equity portfolio or the duration of a fixed-income portfolio. The beta or duration of a portfolio is related to the slope of payoff profiles. The profiles flatten as the market falls and offer the portfolio protection against negative market returns if the market moves soon after the positions are put in place (see Exhibit 33–9).

EXHIBIT 33–8
Protecting Existing Market Exposure (Value at Expiration)

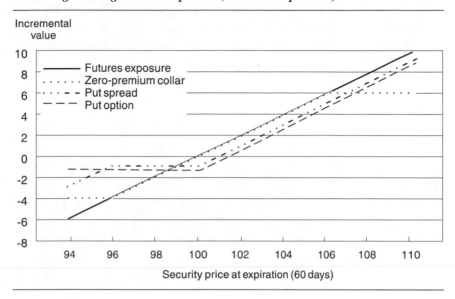

Security price at expiration (60 days)

EXHIBIT 33–9
Protecting Exiting Market Exposure (Current Value)

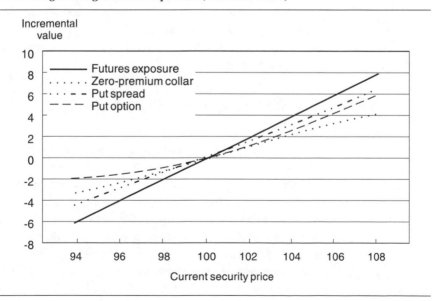

Current security price

Automatic changes in market exposure. Changes in market exposure can be triggered automatically as the market moves by selling options. The sale of a call option will truncate market participation above the option's strike price if the market reaches that level by the expiration date of the option. The receipt of the option premium effectively pays the investor for making the decision to sell in advance.

Conversely, the sale of a put option will allow the investor to prepurchase a position in the market at the put option's strike price. The sale of options are frequently used in asset allocation strategies to automatically reposition the portfolio if certain market levels are reached. Selling call options on 10 percent of the portfolio's exposure will automatically reduce the exposure by 10 percent if the market rallies up to the level of the call option's strike price at expiration. Selling put options on 10 percent of the portfolio exposure will automatically increase the exposure by 10 percent if the market falls to the level of the put option's strike price. At that point, the investor can replace the option position with an equivalent futures position to make the shift permanent.

The purchase of additional market exposure or the hedging of existing market exposure, using options referred to in the previous sections, can also be thought of as creating automatic changes in market exposure. The purchase of call options allows the investor to increase market exposure as the market rises while the purchase of put options allows the investor to decrease market exposure as the market falls. The options automatically adjust their levels of participation as the market reaches the options' strike prices and goes in the money. The nonlinear payoff pattern of an option creates this automatic adjustment feature.

Synthetic Option Positions Using Dynamic Hedging

We noted earlier that a put/call combination can be used to replicate the linear payoff of a futures contract. The return characteristics of an option can also be mimicked using futures or forward contracts to adjust exposure in a systematic way as the price of the underlying security moves. Selling more futures contracts as the price falls creates the protection a put option provides. Buying futures as the price rises reduces the impact of the hedge and allows some upside participation in market returns. On the other hand, selling futures contracts as the price rises will create the effect of having sold a call option to truncate upside returns. Investors may prefer to construct an option position using dynamic hedging instead of purchasing options directly because the available options may not have the exact parameters in maturity or strike price needed by the investor. The investor may also expect the market to have a different volatility going forward than the market consensus found in the current option prices. If realized volatility turns out to be less than the volatility implied by the initial option prices, dynamic hedging will be less expensive than the outright purchase of an option.

The effectiveness of the dynamic hedge to mimic the price movement of an option depends on knowing how the price of the option will respond to a change in the underlying security price and on being able to effectively change the futures hedge smoothly. Both the actual option position and the synthetic option position protect the portfolio against adverse market returns and allow the benefit of favorable returns to be captured. The synthetic option created through dynamic trading achieves its goal with some uncertainty, however, because it is only an approximation. If the ex post volatility of security prices is less than the volatility implied in pricing the actual option, the synthetic option will generally be less expensive. Actual volatility greater than the implied volatility will increase the cost of the synthetic option. Sharp market moves or gaps do not allow the investor to change the hedge ratio smoothly and the tracking error of the synthetic option will increase relative to that of the actual option, thus increasing the cost of the dynamic replication.

The problems associated with gapping markets and the subsequent difficulty in adjusting the hedge ratio was particularly noticeable in the stock market break in October 1987. Dynamic hedging strategies were being used quite extensively by many investors who had difficulty in revising their hedge ratios smoothly. As a result, the option positions their hedges were designed to mimic were not replicated very accurately.

Dynamic option creation requires a few calculations to provide protection with a specific floor return for the portfolio as a whole. This occurs because the return floor usually includes the original cost of the option position as part of the portfolio protection. For example, consider the total value of a portfolio to be equal to n units of the underlying security (valued at S_0) plus the value of the put option used to create the hedge (valued at P_0).

$$V_0 = n(S_0 + P_0) \tag{2}$$

The number of units of the security which can be held given a fixed initial investment V_0 is:

$$n = \frac{V_0}{S_0 + P_0} \tag{3}$$

For the total value of the portfolio at the expiration of the options (time t) to be equal to a specified floor value V^* if the market declines sufficiently, it must be the case that:

$$V^* = n[S_t + (K_P - S_t)] \qquad \text{for } S_t < K_P$$

$$= nK_P$$

$$= \frac{K_P V_0}{S_0 + P_0}$$

Choosing V^* does not automatically determine the strike price of the put option to be used since the number of units invested in the security is also a function of the put's strike price K_P through its dependence on P_0. The choice of the correct strike price for the put option usually requires an iterative calculation until the appropriate strike price K_P can be found given the values for V^*, V_0, and S_0. A similar procedure would have to be used if a call option was being used to cap the appreciation.[1]

$$V** = n\ [S_t - (S_t - K_C)] = nK_C = \frac{K_C V_o}{S_o - C_o} \tag{4}$$

Exhibit 33–10 illustrates the procedure for a simple portfolio with a security valued at $100. The security is assumed to have an annualized volatility of 15 percent, the maturity of the option is 90 days, and the current annualized interest rate is 6.0 percent with a yield on the security of 2.0 percent. The total value of the portfolio to be protected is currently $10,000,000 while the floor value is set at $9,500,000. Notice that the strike price on the put option needs to be set at 96.02 for the total portfolio value to be protected below $9,500,000.

Once the composition of the portfolio is established with the appropriate strike price on the put option, the dynamic hedge can be created. To see how

---

1 The choice of the correct strike price of the call option again requires an iterative calculation since C_0 depends on the choice of K_C. For example, for $S_t > K_C$, we would have:

$$V^{**} = n[S_t - (S_t - K_C)] = nK_C = \frac{K_C V_o}{S_o - C_o}$$

EXHIBIT 33–10
Calculation of Put Option Strike Price for Portfolio Protection

Put Option Strike Price	Option Price	Put Option Delta	Protected Floor (000s)	Portfolio Shares (000s)	Initial Portfolio Value (000s)
$90	$0.19	-0.06	$8,983	99.82	$10,000
91	0.26	-0.08	9,076	99.74	10,000
92	0.36	-0.10	9,167	99.63	10,000
93	0.48	-0.13	9,255	99.52	10,000
94	0.64	-0.16	9,340	99.36	10,000
95	0.84	-0.20	9,421	99.17	10,000
96	1.07	-0.24	9,498	98.94	10,000
96.02*	1.08	-0.24	9,500	98.94	10,000
97	1.35	-0.28	9,571	98.67	10,000
98	1.68	-0.33	9,638	98.35	10,000
99	2.06	-0.38	9,700	97.98	10,000
100	2.49	-0.43	9,757	97.57	10,000

*The put option strike price must be set at this level to protect a $10 million portfolio at $9.5 million with a 90-day investment horizon. The put option is priced using a modified Black-Scholes model for a European option assuming that the current security price is $100, volatility is 15 percent, the annualized 90-day interest rate is 6 percent and the annualized dividend yield is 2 percent.

this can be done, suppose an investor wants to mimic the change in the portfolio value over time as the price of the underlying security changes. Taking the change in value using equation (2) gives:

$$\Delta V_t = n(\Delta S_t + \Delta P_t) \tag{5}$$

Dynamic hedging can be done by configuring a portfolio composed of the underlying security (or a synthetic security) and cash reserves. As the security price changes, the change in the value of the replicating portfolio which holds cash, shares of the underlying security and H futures contracts would be:

$$\Delta R_t = m_t \Delta S_t + H_t \Delta F_t \tag{6}$$

where ΔR_t is the change in the aggregate value of the replicating portfolio, m_t is the number of shares held at time t, H_t is the number of futures contracts held at time t and ΔF_t is the change in the price of a futures contract.

The change in value at time t for the hedged portfolio and the replicating portfolio will be equal if the number of shares in the replicating portfolio and the number of futures contracts are set so that the change in value is the same for both positions. That is,

$$n(1 + \Delta^t_{put})\Delta S_t = m_t \Delta S_t + H_t \Delta F_t \qquad (7)$$

where Δ^t_{put} represents the delta of the associated put option at time t which is to be replicated in creating the hedge.

If no futures contracts are used in adjusting market exposure ($H_t=0$), the proportion of shares needing to held in the replicating portfolio is:

$$\frac{m_t}{n} = 1 + \Delta^t_{put} \qquad (8)$$

Consequently, the proportion of the replicating portfolio held in the risky asset is:

$$\frac{m_t S_t}{V_t} = \frac{n(1 + \Delta^t_{put})S_t}{V_t}$$

$$= \frac{V_o}{V_t} \frac{S_t(1 + \Delta^t_{put})}{(S_o + P_o)} \qquad (9)$$

The remainder of the replicating portfolio would be held in cash.

On the other hand, if no actual shares are held in the replicating portfolio, but futures are used to mimic the return on the shares (thereby creating a synthetic security), the proportion of futures contracts held in the replicating portfolio relative to the shares being replicated is:

$$\frac{H_t}{n} = (1 + \Delta^t_{put})\left(\frac{\Delta S_t}{\Delta F_t}\right) \qquad (10)$$

where $\Delta S_t / \Delta F_t$ can be thought of as the security's market sensitivity (or beta) relative to the futures contract.

As the market price of the underlying security fluctuates over time, the delta of the appropriate put option will also change, causing a need to rebalance either the number of shares in the replicating portfolio or the number of futures contracts. It is this rebalancing over time which creates the dynamic replication of the hedged portfolio. As the market falls, the delta of the put option will approach −1.0 causing the dynamic hedge to reduce the number of shares or futures contracts held in the replicating portfolio and increase the allocation to cash. The reverse happens as the market rises. More shares are held and less is allocated to cash as the delta on the put option approaches zero, resulting in an increased allocation to the risky asset. If a collar is being replicated, the delta of the call option will approach 1.0 as the market rises and gradually reduce the portfolio allocation to the risky asset.

Exhibit 33–11 shows the results of implementing a dynamic hedge using the parameters in Exhibit 33–10. Using these values in equation (8) indicates that 75,486 shares of stock are initially held in the replicating portfolio, leaving $2,451,400 in cash (no futures contracts are used). The protective put strategy increases the proportion of the portfolio allocated to the risky asset as it increases in value and decreases the proportion as it falls in value. The portfolio value can actually fall below the floor before the expiration of the option, but since the portfolio is nearly all cash at that point, the interest earned on the cash up to the expiration date will bring the portfolio back up to the floor value.

SETTING UP A TACTICAL ASSET ALLOCATION PROGRAM

An effective tactical asset allocation requires a view of the relative attractiveness of markets, a portfolio construction mechanism, and cost-effective way to implement portfolio changes.

Assessing Relative Market Attractiveness

One of the most important ingredients for a tactical asset allocation program is an assessment of the relative attractiveness of markets. A simple three-way asset allocation program evaluates the attractiveness of stocks, bonds, and cash. A variety of techniques have been used to determine the attractiveness of one market over another. Some investors use quantitative tools to forecast a specific numeric return for each market. Other techniques may score markets in a less precise way, but still produce a ranking of expected relative market performance. Whatever system is used, the goal is to distinguish the attractiveness of one market from another.

EXHIBIT 33–11
Dynamic Portfolio Allocation to Replicate a Protected Portfolio

			Beginning of Period			
Day	Security Price	Put Option Delta	Shares in Replicating Portfolio (000s)	Portfolio Value (000s)	Portfolio Cash (000s)	Percent of Portfolio in the Risky Security
0	$100	−0.24	75.49	$10,000	$2,451	75.5%
1	101	−0.20	79.44	10,076	2,053	79.6
2	102	−0.16	82.96	10,156	1,693	83.3
3	103	−0.13	86.05	10,239	1,376	86.6
4	102	−0.16	83.14	10,153	1,672	83.5
5	101	−0.19	79.76	10,070	2,014	80.0
6	100	−0.23	75.89	9,991	2,402	76.0
7	99	−0.28	71.51	9,915	2,835	71.4
8	98	−0.33	66.66	9,844	3,311	66.4
9	97	−0.38	61.38	9,778	3,825	60.9
10	96	−0.44	55.72	9,717	4,368	55.1
11	95	−0.50	49.81	9,662	4,931	49.0
12	94	−0.56	43.75	9,613	5,501	42.8
13	93	−0.62	37.70	9,571	6,065	36.6
14	92	−0.68	31.80	9,534	6,608	30.7
15	91	−0.74	26.21	9,503	7,118	25.1
16	90	−0.79	21.06	9,478	7,583	20.0
17	89	−0.83	16.46	9,458	7,993	15.5
18	88	−0.87	12.50	9,443	8,343	11.7
19	87	−0.91	9.21	9,432	8,631	8.5
20	86	−0.93	6.57	9,424	8,859	6.0
21	85	−0.95	4.54	9,419	9,033	4.1
22	84	−0.97	3.05	9,416	9,160	2.7
23	83	−0.98	2.01	9,414	9,248	1.8
24	82	−0.99	1.31	9,414	9,306	1.1
25	81	−0.99	0.87	9,414	9,343	0.8
26	80	−0.99	0.61	9,415	9,366	0.5
27	79	−1.00	0.46	9,416	9,379	0.4
28	78	−1.00	0.38	9,417	9,387	0.3
29	77	−1.00	0.34	9,418	9,392	0.3
30	76	−1.00	0.32	9,419	9,395	0.3

Portfolio Construction

Once the investor has developed an assessment of which markets are more attractive than others, the relative market rankings need to be converted into a portfolio allocation. Some investment managers have used a formal optimization procedure to structure the portfolio while others develop their own rules of thumb for translating market rankings into portfolio positions. Formal optimization routines typically take the correlation between various markets into account in the portfolio formation process, while more heuristic approaches may or may not use a specific risk structure. In any event, the investor must develop a procedure to allocate the portfolio toward the most attractive markets and away from the least attractive markets.

The portfolio construction process also needs to accommodate any specific constraints with regard to maximum and minimum exposures in specific markets or combinations of markets that the investor wants to impose. In addition, many investors have a specific benchmark in mind for the portfolio. The benchmark serves as the neutral position when the ranking process yields no strong view about the relative attractiveness of markets. The benchmark also serves as the performance standard to measure whether the allocation process has added value relative to a static portfolio allocation.

A sample portfolio benchmark and constraint set is shown in Exhibit 33–12. In this example, the portfolio benchmark includes a balance of not only U.S. stocks and bonds, but also some international stock and bond exposure. The range of allowable exposure is wider for the larger benchmark allocations than it is for the smaller allocations, reflecting differences in market liquidity and transactions costs. The size of the ranges helps control the size of the incremental exposures that can be introduced and helps control the magnitude of the tracking error relative to the benchmark. Care must be used in setting the ranges so that there are no inconsistencies between the maximum and minimum ranges for the various markets. Otherwise, some desired allocations may not be feasible.

Notice also that benchmark positions and ranges can be established for currency exposures as well as for asset market exposures. If the benchmark currency exposure is unhedged, the currency benchmark positions will be equal to the asset benchmark positions. A fully hedged benchmark would place all of the currency benchmark allocation in the investor's home currency with no allocation to foreign currency positions. Finally, it is not uncommon for the currency positions to be constrained by the asset expo-

EXHIBIT 33–12
Sample Portfolio Benchmark and Ranges

	Minimum (%)	Benchmark (%)	Maximum (%)
Stocks			
U.S.	25.0	50.0	75.0
U.K.	0.0	3.0	6.0
Japanese	0.0	4.0	8.0
French	0.0	3.0	6.0
German	0.0	3.0	6.0
Canadian	0.0	1.0	3.0
Australian	0.0	1.0	3.0
Total stocks	25.0	65.0	85.0
Bonds			
U.S.	15.0	30.0	75.0
U.K.	0.0	1.0	5.0
Japanese	0.0	1.0	5.0
French	0.0	1.0	5.0
German	0.0	1.0	5.0
Canadian	0.0	0.5	3.0
Australian	0.0	0.5	3.0
Total bonds	15.0	35.0	75.0
Total assets		100.0	
Currencies			
U.S. dollar	40.0	80.0	100.0
U.K. pound	0.0	4.0	11.0
Japanese yen	0.0	5.0	13.0
French franc	0.0	4.0	11.0
German mark	0.0	4.0	11.0
Canadian dollar	0.0	1.5	6.0
Australian dollar	0.0	1.5	6.0
Total currencies		100.0	

sures in the portfolio, so that no foreign currency exposure is larger than the underlying asset exposure.

Exhibit 33–13 shows the recommended portfolio mix using the associated expected returns and risk. The portfolio recommendations are gener-

EXHIBIT 33-13
Recommended Deviations from Benchmark Exposures

	Portfolio Exposure (%)			Expected Return	Standard Deviation
	Recommended	Benchmark	Incremental		
Stocks					
U.S.	53.0	50.0	3.0	17.8	21.1
U.K.	5.5	3.0	2.5	17.3	21.9
Japanese	0.0	4.0	−4.0	10.2	23.7
French	1.0	3.0	−2.0	12.1	25.2
German	3.0	3.0	0.0	17.0	23.4
Canadian	2.0	1.0	1.0	17.2	22.1
Australian	0.0	1.0	−1.0	15.0	24.9
Total stocks	64.5	65.0	−0.5		
Bonds					
U.S.	25.0	30.0	−5.0	10.0	19.0
U.K.	0.0	1.0	−1.0	12.0	17.1
Japanese	3.0	1.0	2.0	16.1	13.8
French	0.5	1.0	−0.5	13.0	13.7
German	3.5	1.0	2.5	16.5	13.2
Canadian	2.0	0.5	1.5	15.8	17.3
Australian	1.5	0.5	1.0	16.0	16.8
Total bonds	35.5	35.0	0.5		
Total assets	100.0	100.0	0.0		
Currencies					
U.S. dollar	84.5	80.0	4.5	6.5	NA
U.K. pound	4.5	4.0	0.5	6.7	11.8
Japanese yen	3.0	5.0	−2.0	3.2	11.7
French franc	0.0	4.0	−4.0	1.0	11.6
German mark	6.5	4.0	2.5	7.0	11.8
Canadian dollar	0.0	1.5	−1.5	5.1	4.6
Australian dollar	1.5	1.5	0.0	6.5	10.1
Total currencies	100.0	100.0	0.0		

ated by a mean-variance optimization relative to the benchmark. The altered positions could easily be achieved by buying and selling futures contracts in the appropriate amounts.

Available Exchange-Traded International Derivatives

Exhibit 33–14 shows the major exchange-traded international equity index futures and options contracts along with their respective trading volume in 1994. In every contract except the Osaka Nikkei 225, futures volume in U.S. dollars increased, and in most markets growth exceeded 30 percent. Options volume declined in most markets with the exception of the United States, Spain, Austria, and Hong Kong. With the increase in futures volume relative to the underlying stocks, the ratio of futures and options volume to stock volume continues to grow. In nearly every market the ratio exceeds one and in more than half the ratio exceeds two. The most active markets are France, Japan, and the United States by this measure (see Exhibit 33–15).

The indexes underlying the major equity index futures contracts generally track quite closely to the commonly used benchmark indexes. Exhibit 33–16 shows the annualized tracking error for the local index futures contracts compared to the respective MSCI (Morgan Stanley Capital International) and FT (Financial Times) indexes. Low tracking error allows the futures and options contracts to be used effectively either to hedge or to create market exposure without introducing substantial tracking error into the performance of the aggregate portfolio.

Exhibit 33–17 shows the most liquid futures markets available for long-term bonds along with the contract size in the foreign currency. Futures contracts for the major currencies are also available as shown in Exhibit 33–17. Volume in the currency futures markets is dwarfed by the volume of trading done in the interbank market using forwards. This also applies to currency options. The volume of over-the-counter currency options exceeds the exchange-traded volume by a wide margin.

Comparative Advantages and Disadvantages in Using Derivatives

Exhibit 33–18 summarizes the major advantages and disadvantages of using options and futures in implementing asset allocation strategies. The most obvious advantages relate to speed of execution, liquidity, reduced transactions costs, the need for little net investment, and the flexibility to create nonlinear return patterns. Speed and liquidity are typically good because the volume of trading in the major markets exceeds that of the underlying securities. Furthermore, there is no settlement delay in using derivatives because no cash changes hands for the principal amount of the transaction.

EXHIBIT 33–14

Comparison of Average Daily Volume in Dollars for Stock, Futures, and Options Markets* (Expressed in Millions of Dollars)

Country	Index	*Stock* 1994 Avg. Daily	*Stock* Percent Change 1993–94	*Futures* 1994 Avg. Daily	*Futures* Percent Change 1993–94	*Options* 1994 Avg. Daily	*Options* Percent Change 1993–94
U.S.	S&P 500	$10,585	9%	$16,803	43%	$ 9,450	229%
	S&P 500					13,870	31
Canada	TSE 35	723	41	33	65	16	–74
U.K.	FT-SE 100	1,340	–3	2,001	46	347	–23
France	CAC-40	535	–20	2,039	32	404	–38
Germany	DAX	1,503	–3	2,651	55	604	–28
Switzerland	SMI	358	0	662	127	129	–27
Netherlands	AEX	245	–5	178	60	124	–32
Spain	IBEX	207	9	271	174	70	141
Belgium	BEL-20	53	–5	21	73	10	–12
Sweden	OMX	148	–10	97	234	334	79
Denmark	KFX	57	24	27	33	5	–2
Austria	ATX	32	25	13	164	48	140
Japan	TOPIX	3,274	–10	1,656	35		
	OSE NIK225			4,902	–17	3,357	–21
	SIM NIK225			2,227	25		
	CME NIK225			233	78		
	Nikkei 300			546			
Hong Kong	Hang Seng	560	–6	1,043	126	151	118
Australia	All Ords	368	23	381	42	124	–13

*Options volume is expressed in terms of the exercise value of contracts traded.

Source: Goldman Sachs

Additional delays are also avoided because no time is needed to configure a particular portfolio of individual securities before implementing a change in broad market exposure.

Changing broad market exposure using derivatives usually involves considerably lower transaction costs than trading individual securities. Market impact and commissions are generally lower while transfer and

EXHIBIT 33–15
Ratio of Futures and Options to Stock Volume

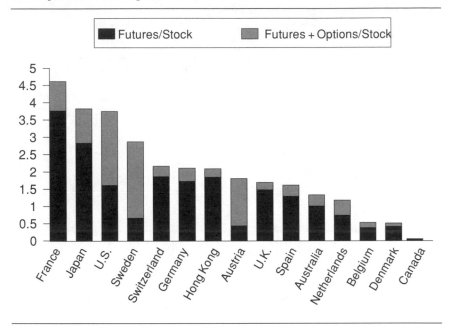

EXHIBIT 33–16
Tracking Error of Local Equity Index Futures versus FT and MSCI Indexes

Country	Local Index Futures	Annualized Tracking Error (%)	
		versus FT-AWI	*versus MSCI*
U.S.	S&P 500	NA	0.9
U.K.	FTSE 100	1.0	1.7
Japan	TOPIX	2.3	3.9
France	CAC 40	1.9	2.2
Australia	ALLORDS	2.2	2.8
Germany	DAX 30	1.8	2.1
Netherlands	EOE 20	5.5	5.8
Switzerland	SMI	1.8	4.2

Source: Morgan Stanley and Goldman Sachs

EXHIBIT 33–17
Selected Exchange-Traded International Fixed Income and Currency Futures

Fixed Income Contract	Contract Size
U.K. Gilt	50,000 BP
French notionnel	500,000 FF
U.S. bond	100,000 USD
German bund (LIFFE)	250,000 DM
Japanese bond	100,000,000 JY
Australian bond	100,000 AUD
Canadian bond	100,000 CD
Italian bond	200,000,000 IL

Foreign Exchange Contract	Contract Size
U.K. pound	62,500 BP
Swiss franc	125,000 JF
French franc	250,000 FF
German mark	125,000 DM
Japanese yen	12,500,000 JY
Canadian dollar	100,000 CD
Australian dollar	100,000 AUD
Dutch guilder	125,000 DG

withholding taxes assessed against individual securities are usually avoided. Exhibit 33–19 summarizes the estimated costs of trading futures in the major markets relative to trading underlying equity securities. Approximate cost advantages of derivatives range from one-fifth to one-tenth relative to the underlying stocks.

Because no cash changes hands between parties for the principal amount of the transaction when using futures or options, only a small amount of capital needs to be set aside to implement an asset allocation program. Futures require initial margin as a "good faith" deposit while the purchase of options requires cash to pay the option premium. In addition, daily mark to market for futures positions requires some liquidity in the portfolio to settle up any short-term losses generated. Depending on the size of the futures positions taken, from five to 10 percent of the aggregate portfolio is usually set aside as a short-term cash reserve to fund initial margin requirements, purchase options, and accommodate daily margin cash flows.

EXHIBIT 33–18
Advantages and Disadvantages of Using Options and Futures

Advantages

- Speed of execution
- Liquid markets
- Reduced transactions costs
- Little capital required
- No disruption of underlying asset management
- Flexibility to create nonlinear return patterns

Disadvantages

- Potential tracking error relative to the underlying portfolio or benchmark
- Cash reserve required for liquidity and margin
- Replaces active security returns on cash reserve with indexlike performance
- Need to replenish cash reserve if depleted
- Cash flow mismatch between realized and unrealized returns
- Daily back-office monitoring of mark to market
- Lack of familiarity and understanding by staff

As a result of the need for only a limited amount of capital, the asset allocation program can be performed as an overlay on top of the underlying assets. This allows the underlying assets to be fully managed using an active value-added strategy, if desired, without costly disruption by changes in broad asset allocation. Ordinarily a change in asset mix from stocks to bonds would require that selected equity securities be sold before bonds could be purchased. The use of futures and options avoids this disruption. Equity exposure can be reduced simultaneously with an increase in bond exposure by using derivatives without selling the underlying securities. The separation of specific asset selection from broad market exposure also allows for a separation of investment decision making. One investment manager can select individual securities while another can make the asset allocation decision.

Another application of this ability to separate security selection from asset allocation is the potential to create synthetic index funds. The under-

EXHIBIT 33–19
Estimated Transactions Costs of Cash versus Futures

	Cost (bps)			
	Commissions	*Market Impact*	*Taxes*	*Total*
Stocks				
U.S.	14	55	0	69
Japan	20	70	30	120
U.K.	20	90	50	160
France	10	55	0	65
Germany	10	50	0	60
Equity futures				
U.S.	1	5	0	6
Japan	6	5	0	11
U.K.	2	10	0	12
France	4	10	0	14
Germany	3	5	0	8

Source: Goldman Sachs

lying assets could conceivably all be kept in short-term cash reserves to maximize liquidity while the purchase of equity index, fixed-income, and currency futures or forwards could create an international portfolio without purchasing individual securities and incurring the resulting custody and transactions costs.

Finally, the direct use of options or the dynamic creation of optionlike returns using futures allows the investor to create nonlinear return patterns not normally available by purchasing underlying securities. This gives the investor the flexibility to make more precise trade-offs between risk and return in the portfolio.

However, using options and futures has a number of disadvantages. We noted earlier that there is likely to be some tracking error between the index used for the futures contract and the underlying portfolio benchmark. This slippage may either benefit or hurt the performance of the fund, depending on the particular time period, but the lack of perfect correlation will create some tracking error in the performance of the portfolio.

The need for a cash reserve requires that some assets be set aside to fund the margin and cash flow requirements of the derivatives. As a result, the cash reserve fund will not participate in any value added from active management of the underlying stocks and bonds. The daily mark to market of futures contracts also imposes some back office and accounting responsibilities to settle daily futures gains and losses. Though funding for the derivatives requires only a fraction of the initial portfolio, the cash reserve might become depleted and have to be replenished. When this occurs, some disruption of the underlying asset management will occur as assets are liquidated to generate cash to replenish the cash reserve.

Gains and losses on futures contracts are realized daily while gains and losses on underlying securities are realized only periodically. This causes a mismatch in the timing of cash flows in the portfolio. The depletion of the cash reserve can occur as losses from derivatives are realized while offsetting gains are unrealized. Even though one may offset the other in total return, there is a tendency for investors to fail to view the portfolio in its total context and to misunderstand the need to replenish the cash reserve. This mismatch between realized and unrealized gains can cause confusion for those who are unfamiliar with the cash flow consequences. The lack of understanding of derivatives and how they work is often an impediment to the use of derivatives in asset allocation strategies.

PERFORMANCE ATTRIBUTION WHEN DERIVATIVES ARE USED FOR ASSET ALLOCATION

The use of derivative contracts (options, futures, and forwards) allows the investor to change the asset and currency exposure without altering the physical asset mix in the underlying portfolio. Since the underlying asset mix may not represent the effective exposure once derivatives are added in, this sometimes makes performance attribution difficult to do. This section describes a technique that can be used to do performance attribution from data available to the investor when derivatives are used.

To capture the effect on performance from the use of derivative instruments, we can write the total return to the portfolio as:

$$R = (1 - m)(R_B + \alpha_u) + mR_c + \sum_i D_i^A + \sum_j D_j^c + e \tag{11}$$

where

m	=	Proportion of the total fund segregated in a cash reserve at the beginning of the period to service margin requirements
R_B	=	Benchmark return
α_u	=	Value added through management of the underlying assets
R_c	=	Average interest earnings rate on the cash reserve
D_i^A	=	Net gains or losses on derivative contracts during the period (converted to the investor's base currency) for asset market i as a percent of the initial total fund value
D_j^C	=	Net gains or losses on derivative contracts during the period (converted to the investor's base currency) for currency market j as a percent of the initial value of the total portfolio
e	=	Residual error term reflecting tracking error on derivatives contracts relative to benchmark returns, the interest earned on realized gains or losses during the measurement period and currency translation gains or losses from daily margin flows

The value added of the fund relative to the benchmark can be written as:

$$R - R_B = (1 - m)\alpha_u - m(R_B - R_c) + \sum_i D_i^A + \sum_j D_j^c + e \tag{12}$$

$$= (1 - m)\alpha_u + \sum_i \left[D_i^A - mw_i^B \ (r_i^B + f_i - R_c) \right] + \sum_j \left[D_j^c - mH_j^B \ (r_j^c - f_j) \right] + e \tag{13}$$

where

w_i^B	=	The benchmark portfolio weight in asset i
r_i^B	=	The local asset return of asset i in the benchmark
f_j	=	The forward premium for currency j
H_j^B	=	The currency exposure to currency j in the benchmark
r_j^c	=	The currency return (change in spot rate) for currency j

The transformation of equation (12) to equation (13) results from decomposing the benchmark returns into their component parts and regrouping terms.

The value added for the total portfolio in equation (13) is composed of several different parts. The first term represents the fact that m proportion

---

Box 33–1

Performance Analysis with the Use of Derivatives

To illustrate the performance attribution of a portfolio using derivatives consider the basic portfolio data in the example below using U.S. and Japanese stocks. Assume that the underlying asset portfolio has outperformed the benchmark by 1.0 percent due to the management of the underlying assets.

r_{Yen}	=	3.0%	D_{JP}^A	=	–0.2%
f_{Yen}	=	0.3	D_{Yen}^c	=	–0.3
r_{US}^B	=	4.0	R_B	=	2.0
r_{JP}^B	=	–3.0	m	=	15.0
R_c	=	3.2	w_{US}^B	=	50.0
α_u	=	1.0	w_{JP}^B	=	50.0
D_{US}^A	=	1.2	H_{Yen}^B	=	50.0

The total return on the portfolio, including the derivatives positions is:

$$R = (1 - m)(R_B + \alpha_u) + mR_c + D_{US}^A + D_{JP}^A + D_{Yen}^c$$

$$= (1 - 0.15)(0.02 + 0.01) + 0.15(.032) + 0.012 - 0.002 - 0.003$$

$$= 3.73\%$$

giving a total value added relative to the benchmark of:

Value added = 3.73 – 2.0 = 1.73%

(continued)

---

of the portfolio set aside in the cash reserve does not participate in any incremental return received from the management of the underlying asset portfolio. The cash reserve is assumed to be overlaid with derivative exposure invested at benchmark weights in the respective asset and currency markets, which earn the benchmark return before any active positions are taken.

The second term in equation (13) represents the contribution to total value added from an incremental allocation to each asset market. This contribution is captured by the total net gain or loss in the respective derivative positions for the period. A slight adjustment is needed to account for the fact that some of the total gains or losses may be generated by the derivatives contracts used to keep the cash reserve fully invested at benchmark weights before any active allocation is done.

Box 33–1 *(concluded)*

The components of this value added are:

Underlying Assets

$$(1-m)\,\alpha_u = (1.0 - 0.15)(1.0) = 0.85\%$$

Asset Allocation

U.S. stocks: $D_{US}^A - mw_{US}^B \ (r_{US}^B - R_c) = 1.2 - (.15)(0.5)(4.0 - 3.2) = 1.14$

Japanese stocks:

$$D_{JP}^A - mw_{JP}^B \ (r_{JP}^B + f_{Yen} - R_c) = -0.2 - (.15)(.5)(-3.0 + 0.3 - 3.2) = 0.24$$

Currency Management

Japanese yen: $D_{Yen}^c - mH_{Yen}^B \ (r_{Yen} - f_{Yen}) = -0.3 - (.15)(.5)(3.0 - 0.3) = -0.50$

Error Term $= 0.0$

                                                                      Total $= 1.73\%$

Notice that the underlying assets have contributed 0.85 percent to the value added of the portfolio even though the management of the underlying assets has resulted in outperformance of 1.0 percent. The difference lies in the fact that a portion of the total assets were set aside in a cash reserve to service any margin requirements for the derivative positions and earned benchmark returns. Asset allocation decisions on U.S. and Japanese stocks have added a total of 1.38 percent while currency decisions have subtracted 0.50 percent, resulting in a net value added for the portfolio of 1.73 percent.

The third term in equation (13) represents a similar contribution from active currency management. The total net gains or losses in derivative positions for each currency are again adjusted for the fact that part of the gains or losses may represent flows from currency contracts used to keep the cash reserve fully invested at benchmark weights before any active allocation is done.

The last term in the equation captures any residual error in the performance calculation. This error can result from tracking error in the pricing of the derivatives contracts relative to the benchmark returns, accounting for the interest earned on any realized gains or losses during the measurement period, and accounting for currency translation gains or losses on daily margin flows. This residual term is typically small relative to the other terms.

Equation (13) reduces to a particularly simple form if only assets in the investor's home country are included in the portfolio. This gives a value added equal to:

$$R - R_B = (1 - m)\alpha_u + \sum_i \left[D_i^A - mw_i^B (r_i^B - R_c) \right] + e \qquad \textbf{(13a)}$$

This simplification occurs because all of the terms involving the translation of foreign currency returns to the investor's base currency are eliminated when no foreign assets or currencies are used. The value added can be calculated from the total gains or losses on derivatives. These are again adjusted because some contracts may be held to keep the cash reserve invested at the benchmark mix before active positions are taken.

PRICING FUTURES AND OPTIONS CONTRACTS

Futures and Forwards

A *forward contract* provides an opportunity to contract now for the purchase or sale of an asset or security at a specified price but to delay payment for the transaction until a future settlement date. A forward contract can be either purchased or sold. An investor who purchases a forward contract commits to the purchase of the underlying asset or security at a specified price at a specified date in the future. An investor who sells a forward contract commits to the sale of the underlying asset or security at a specified price at a specified date in the future.

The date for future settlement of the contract is usually referred to as the *settlement* or *expiration date*. That the price is negotiated now but payment is delayed until expiration creates an *opportunity cost* for the seller in receiving payment. The opportunity cost is the interest the investor might have received by receiving the payment now and investing it until the maturity of the forward contract. As a result, the negotiated price for future delivery of the asset is usually different from the current cash price in order to reflect the cost of waiting to get paid.

For example, if an investor sells stock currently worth $1,000,000 but has to wait 30 days to actually be paid, the opportunity cost or interest lost over that 30-day period at a current interest rate of 6 percent would be:

Opportunity cost = $1,000,000 (.06)(30/360) = $5,000

The fair price for the stock if payment is deferred by 30 days would be:

$1,000,000 + $5,000 = $1,005,000

Strictly speaking, such a contract is referred to as a forward contract. a *futures contract* contains many of the same elements as a forward contract, but any gains or losses that accrue as the current price of the asset fluctuates relative to the negotiated price in a futures contract are realized on a day-to-day basis. This daily realization is referred to as the *mark to market*. The total gain or loss is generally the same for a futures contract as for a forward contract with the same maturity date, except that the accumulated gain or loss is realized on a daily basis with the futures contract instead of at the forward contract's settlement date. Futures contracts also require the posting of a performance bond or deposit with the broker to initiate the trade. The purpose of this deposit is to reduce the chance that one of the parties to the trade might build up substantial losses and then default. This performance bond is referred to as *initial margin*. The amount of initial margin varies for different futures contacts, but it usually amounts to between 2 and 10 percent of the contract value, depending on the volatility of the specific market or underlying security. More volatile contracts usually require higher margins than less volatile contracts.

Another difference between forward and futures contracts is that futures contracts have standardized provisions specifying maturity date and contract size so they can be traded interchangeably on organized exchanges such as the Chicago Board of Trade or the Chicago Mercantile Exchange. Most contracts that are traded actively are futures contracts, although an active forward market for foreign exchange exists through the banking system. Futures markets are regulated by the Commodity Futures Trading Commission, but forward markets are not. Exhibit 33–20 provides a brief summary of the differences between futures and forward contracts.

Although forward and futures contracts are not exactly the same, the two terms are often used interchangeably. Research shows that, if interest rates are constant and the term structure[2] is flat, the two will be priced the same.

---

2 The *term structure* of interest rates refers to the pattern of interest rates according to the maturity of the obligation. A flat term structure would indicate that borrowing funds for one year would be at the same annualized interest rate as borrowing for 10 years, for example.

EXHIBIT 33–20
Comparison of Futures and Forward Contracts

	Futures	*Forward*
Contract/Size	Standardized	Flexible
Maturity	Fixed maturities usually in three month increments	Flexible
Pricing	Open outcry process at the futures exchange	Bid and offer quotes by each bank or broker
Collateral	Initial margin and daily mark to market	Standing lines of credit
Counterparty	Exchange serves as the guarantor of the trade	Individual bank or broker with whom the contract was negotiated
Commissions	Fixed rate per contract paid to the broker	Usually embedded in the bid/offer quotation
Settlement	Position is usually reversed by an offsetting transaction in the futures market	Often settled in cash at the expiration of the contract. Some contracts require physical delivery.

These conditions are not met precisely in practice, but the difference in price between a futures and forward contract is usually small.[3]

The fair pricing of a futures or forward contract is usually maintained because market mechanisms provide the opportunity to create a riskless position for a gain if the contract is mispriced in excess of any transactions costs incurred to structure the arbitrage. This pricing relationship is driven by the cash and carry arbitrage. The arbitrage relationship creates an equivalence between the return from either investing directly in the security itself or purchasing a futures contract while holding an equivalent amount of cash in an interest-bearing cash reserve. The creation of the equivalent return pattern using the futures contract is sometimes referred to as having

---

3 See J. C. Cox, J. E. Ingersoll, and S. A. Ross, "The Relation between Forward Prices and Futures Prices," *Journal of Financial Economics*, Dec. 1981, pp. 321–46; B. Cornell and M. Reinganum, "Forward and Future Prices: Evidence from Foreign Exchange Markets," *Journal of Finance*, Dec. 1981, pp. 1035–45; and H. Y. Park and A. H. Chen, "Differences between Futures and Forward Prices: A Further Investigation of Marking to Market Effects," *Journal of Futures Markets*, Feb. 1985, pp. 77–88.

created a *synthetic security*. One behaves like the other in its risk and return characteristics; that is, the two sides of the relationship in equation (14) have the same risk and return profile.

Forward contract + Cash reserve ⟷ Underlying security   **(14)**

At times the investor may find it more advantageous to create the risk/return profile of the security by using the futures or forward contracts instead. Futures and forwards provide a convenient and cost-effective way to create quick exposure to selected foreign exchange, fixed income, equity, and commodities markets.

The cash and carry arbitrage relationship shows that the fair price of a forward contract can be represented as:

F_0 = Current security price + Interest opportunity cost − Cash
      distribution paid by the security

$$= S_0 (1 + rt) - C_t \qquad\qquad (15)$$

where

F_0 = current price of the forward contract
S_0 = current price of the underlying security
r = annualized riskless interest rate corresponding to maturity date
     t (reflecting the interest the seller loses by waiting to be paid)
t = maturity of the forward contract (fraction of a year)
C_t = cash distribution from the underlying security paid through date
     t (i.e., dividends or interest)

The fair price of a forward contract in equation (15) represents the current price of the security adjusted for the opportunity cost of delayed settlement. The seller of the security is compensated for waiting to receive the money by earning interest on the current value of the security. In addition, the forward price is reduced by any cash distributions the seller receives before settlement while still owning the security. This adjustment to the current security price to arrive at the fair forward price is sometimes referred to as the *net cost of carry* or *net carry*. If the forward contract is not priced in this way, one of the alternatives for achieving the security returns in equation (14) will dominate the other.

For any given forward price, the investor can infer what interest rate the buyer has to pay to compensate the seller. This rate is usually referred to as the *implied repo rate*. The market tends to price the forward contract so that the implied rate equals a fair market interest rate. The rate usually varies between the short-term Treasury bill rate and the Eurodollar rate. If the implied rate is greater than the market rate, investors could create a riskless arbitrage to capture the increased return. A rate higher than the market rate could be earned by selling an overvalued forward contract and buying the security. Funds could be borrowed below market rates by buying an undervalued forward contract and selling the security.[4]

By using this pricing relationship, we can see how a synthetic security can be created by purchasing the forward contract and investing an equivalent amount of cash in an interest bearing account earning at rate r until time t. The value of the cash reserve at the maturity of the forward contract will be $S_0(1+rt)$. The gain or loss on the forward contract at maturity will be equal to (F_t-F_0). At expiration the price of the forward contract will converge to the price of the security. Using this relationship allows us to write the value of the synthetic security at expiration as:

$$\text{Value of the synthetic security at } t = S_0 (1 + rt) + (F_t - F_0)$$

$$= S_0 (1 + rt) + \{S_t - [S_0 (1 + rt) - C_t]\}$$

$$= S_t + C_t \tag{16}$$

The term $(S_t + C_t)$ represents the value the investor would have at time t if the underlying security had been purchased initially and the investor subsequently received the interest or dividends. The investor has created the same risk and return characteristics with a forward contract as with the underlying security.

Futures and forwards also provide a convenient and cost-effective way to hedge risk in each of their respective markets. Rearranging the synthetic security relationship in equation (14) shows how derivatives can be used for hedging.

---

4 For some securities or commodities, selling the futures or forward contract is easier than shorting the underlying security. This can create asymmetry in the arbitrage conditions. The forward price rarely goes to excess on the upside, but it sometimes goes to excess on the downside because creating the downside arbitrage by buying the forward contract and selling the security may be more difficult. Thus, futures or forward prices can be more easily underpriced relative to their fair value than overpriced, as indicated by implied repo rates that are sometimes less than riskless market interest rates.

$$\underset{\text{security}}{\text{Underlying}} - \underset{\text{contract}}{\text{Forward}} \longleftrightarrow \underset{\text{cash reserve}}{\text{Synthetic}} \qquad (17)$$

The insight from Equation (17) comes by noting that holding the underlying security and selling a forward contract results in creating a *synthetic cash reserve*; that is, the risk in the underlying security is offset by a short position in the forward contract. The arbitrage relationship in the pricing of the forward contact is such that the return earned on the hedge is consistent with a riskless rate.

Using the fair price of the forward contract also allows us to see how hedging can eliminate the risk in the underlying security. The gain or loss on the short forward position cancels out the risk in the underlying security, giving the value of the hedged position at expiration as:

$$\begin{aligned}
\text{Value of the hedged} & \\
\text{position at expiration} &= S_t + C_t - (F_t - F_0) \\
&= S_t + C_1 - \{S_t - [S_0(1 + rt) - C_t]\} \\
&= S_0(1 + rt) \qquad (18)
\end{aligned}$$

Notice that the value of the hedged position is not dependent on the value of the underlying security at expiration. All of the risk has been eliminated by creating a synthetic cash reserve earning a rate r so that the value of the position at expiration including interest is $S_0(1+rt)$.

In essence, creating a hedged position is an attempt to eliminate the primary risk in the underlying security and shift it to others in the futures market willing to bear the risk. The risk can always be shifted by doing away with the underlying security position, but this may interfere with the nature of the investor's business or disrupt a continuing investment program. The futures or forward market provides an alterative way to temporarily control or eliminate much of the risk in the underlying security position while continuing to hold the security.

Equity index futures pricing.   The fair price of an equity index futures contract is established according to the cash and carry arbitrage relationship:

$$\begin{aligned}
F_0 &= \text{Index} + \text{Interest} - \text{Dividend income} \\
&= S_0(1 + rt) - D_t \qquad (19)
\end{aligned}$$

where

F_0 = fair value futures price
S_0 = equity index
r = annualized financing rate (money-market yield)
D_t = value of dividends paid before expiration
t = time to expiration (fraction of a year)

Because dividend yields are often less than short-term interest rates, the equity index futures price is often greater than the index price.

Consider, as an example, a contract on the S&P 500 Index that is traded on the Chicago Mercantile Exchange with quarterly expiration dates ending in March, June, September, and December. The size of the contract is equal to $500 times the value of the S&P 500 Index. The contract does not require the purchase or sale of actual shares of stock but is cash settled in an amount equal to the value of the shares. Assume that the index is at 600, and the expiration time for the contract is 34 days hence. The financing rate is 6.6 percent a year, and expected dividends through expiration in index points are 1.24. Thus, according to the general form for the price of an equity index futures contract,

$$F_0 = 600\left[1 + \frac{0.066(34)}{360}\right] - 1.24 = 602.50$$

If the actual futures price is quoted at 602.22, the future would appear to be underpriced by 0.28 index points relative to fair value. Whether this difference is material enough to be arbitraged away by market participants depends on the transactions costs of constructing the arbitrage.

Treasury bond and note futures pricing.   The pricing of a note or bond futures contract is somewhat more complicated than it is for an equity index contract:

F_0 = (Price + Interest cost – Coupon income)/Delivery factor

$$= \frac{P_0(1 + rt) - Bc(t + a)}{f} \tag{20}$$

where

B = par value of the cheapest-to-deliver note or bond

P_0 = market price of note or bond B + accrued interest
r = annualized financing rate (money market yield)
c = annualized coupon rate
t = time to expiration (fraction of a year)
a = period of accrued interest for bond B (fraction of a year)
f = delivery factor of note or bond B

Equation (20) indicates that the fair price of a Treasury note or bond contract is equal to the current security price plus the interest opportunity cost less the coupon interest paid all of which is adjusted by the *delivery factor*. Treasury Bond futures contracts are traded on the Chicago Board of Trade with quarterly expiration dates ending in March, June, September, and December. The size of the contract is equal to $100,000 face value of eligible Treasury bonds having at least 15 years to maturity and not callable for at least 15 years.[5] The contract requires the actual purchase or sale (called *delivery*) of Treasury bonds if it is held to expiration.

Because different notes and bonds have different coupon payments and maturities, the actual Treasury note or bond which can be selected for delivery by the short seller is adjusted in price by a delivery factor to reflect a standardized 8 percent coupon rate. This adjustment normalizes the Treasury notes and bonds eligible for delivery, so that the short seller has some flexibility in choosing which note or bond might actually be delivered to make good on the contract. The factor associated with any note or bond is calculated by dividing by 100 the dollar price that the note or bond would command if it were priced to yield 8 percent to maturity (or to first call date if the note or bond is callable). The pricing of the futures contract generally follows the price of the note or bond that is the cheapest to deliver at the time. The futures price itself is quoted in 32nds, with 100 as the price of an 8 percent coupon note or bond when its yield to maturity is also equal to 8 percent.

The fair price of the Treasury note and bond futures contract is also a function of the interest opportunity cost $(P_0 rt)$ and the size of the coupon payments up to the expiration date of the futures contract $[Bc(t + a)]$. Thus, the theoretical price of the Treasury bond future with 98 days to expiration is:

---

5 Treasury note futures contracts are priced in the same way as Treasury bond futures contracts except that the eligible notes for delivery must have at least six and one-half years to maturity at the time of delivery.

Current market price	(7.25% due in 2016)	78.16
+ Interest cost	78.16(.066)(98/360)	= 1.40
− Coupon income	−100(.0725)(98+9)/360	= −2.16
		77.40
÷ Delivery factor		0.9167
= Theoretical futures price		84.43 or 84 14/32

The actual price of this contract is 84 12/32, a mispricing that is equal to −2/32.

If the short-term interest rate is less than the coupon rate on the cheapest-to-deliver (CTD) note or bond, the futures price will be less than the note or bond's price. If the short-term interest rate is greater than the coupon rate on the note or bond, the futures price will be greater than the bond's price. Because short-term rates are generally lower than long-term rates, the futures price is often less than the note or bond's market price.

Foreign currency futures pricing. Futures contracts in foreign currencies are traded on the International Monetary Market with the same expiration cycle of March, June, September, and December. Each contract has an associated size relative to the foreign currency as noted previously in Exhibit 33–17. Settlement at expiration involves a wire transfer of the appropriate currency two days after the last trading day.

The fair pricing of a foreign exchange futures contract follows the same arbitrage process as that of the other futures contracts resulting in the relationship:

$$F_0 = \frac{S_0(1 + r_d t)}{(1 + r_f t)}, \tag{21}$$

where r_f is the annualized foreign interest rate of maturity t, r_d is the annualized domestic interest rate, and S_0 is the spot exchange rate. This arbitrage relationship is often called *covered interest arbitrage*. Equation (21) indicates that the fair price of a foreign exchange futures contract is equal to the current spot exchange rate times the ratio of one plus the interest rate in the respective countries.

To understand this relationship, consider the following investment alternatives. In the first case, one unit of the domestic currency is invested for t fraction of a year at an annualized rate of r_d. As an alternative, the investor could convert the domestic currency to the foreign currency at a spot exchange rate of S_0 ($/foreign currency), receive interest at the foreign interest rate, and then contract to convert back to the domestic currency at the forward foreign exchange rate F_0. Each investment is invested in riskless securities and the currency risk has been neutralized, so both strategies should generate a riskless return. To avoid one riskless return from dominating the other, both should result in the same value at time t. Equating the two values gives

$$(1 + r_d t) = \frac{F_0(1 + r_f t)}{S_0}.$$ (22)

The forward foreign exchange rate would have to be set at its fair value for both strategies to give the same rate of return. If the forward exchange rate deviated from this fair value, the difference could be arbitraged to give profits with no risk. Solving for the appropriate forward exchange rate from the equation above gives the price which eliminates arbitrage profits:

$$F_0 = \frac{S_0(1 + r_d t)}{(1 + r_f t)}.$$ (23)

The calculation of a fair forward exchange rate, given interest rates in Japan and the United States and using the covered interest rate arbitrage relationship, is shown below. Assume the Japanese interest rate is 3.5 percent, the U.S. interest rate is 6.2 percent, and the time to expiration is 35 days. The exchange rate is .00960 dollars per yen or 104.16 yen per dollar. The fair forward foreign exchange rate is:

$$F_0 = \frac{0.00960\left(1 + \frac{.062(35)}{360}\right)}{\left(1 + \frac{.035(35)}{360}\right)} = 0.00963 \text{ \$/yen, or } \frac{1}{0.00963} = 103.89 \text{ yen/\$}$$

The futures price reflects the relative difference in interest rates between countries over the time period. The higher interest rate in the United States results in a higher forward exchange rate of 0.00963 for future delivery as against the spot rate of 0.00960 in terms of dollars/yen.

Options

The two basic types of options are a *call option* and a *put option*. The call option gives the investor the right to buy a security at a specified price within a specified period of time. For example, a call option on the S&P 500 gives an investor the right to buy units of the S&P 500 Index at a set price within a specified amount of time. In contrast, the put option gives the investor the right to sell a security at a specified price within a particular period of time.

Options have several important characteristics. One is the *strike* or *exercise price*. This price gives the value at which the investor can purchase the underlying security. The *maturity* of the option defines the time period within which the investor can buy or sell the security at the exercise price.

Three terms—*at the money*, *in the money*, and *out of the money*—identify where the current security price is relative to the strike or exercise price. An option in the money refers to an option that would result in a positive value to the investor if exercised. For example, a call option that has a strike price of $100 when the security price is $120 is in the money because the investor can buy the security for less than its market price. Similarly, a put option with a strike price of $100 while the security is priced at $90 would be in the money because the investor can sell the security for more than its current market price.

Some options can be exercised early, but some can only be exercised on the specific maturity date. An option that can be exercised early is called an *American* option; an option that can be exercised only at the maturity date is a *European* option. Most of the options traded on organized U.S. exchanges are American options, although a few European option contracts also are traded.

Analysts have come to think of the option price or premium as being composed of two parts—the *intrinsic value* and the *time value* (see Exhibit 33–21). The intrinsic value depends on the relationship between the security price and the exercise price of the option. The intrinsic value of a call option is the maximum of either zero or the difference between the security price and the exercise price $(S - K)$. If $(S - K)$ is positive, the call option is in the money and has a positive intrinsic value. If $(S - K)$ is negative, the call option is out of the money and has zero intrinsic value. The intrinsic value of a put option is just the reverse: The maximum of zero or $(K - S)$. If $(K - S)$ is positive, the put option is in the money. If $(K - S)$ is negative, the put option is out of the money and has zero intrinsic value.

For example, suppose the current foreign exchange rate between the U.S. dollar and the deutsche mark is 0.62 US$/DM. A put option with a strike price of 0.64 US$/DM would have an intrinsic value of:

$$\text{Put intrinsic value} = \max(0, K - S)$$

$$= \max(0, 0.64 - 0.62)$$

$$= 0.02 \text{ US\$/DM}$$

EXHIBIT 33–21
Option Price

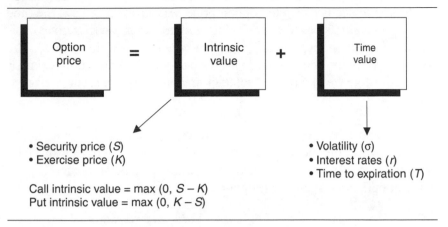

- Security price (*S*)
- Exercise price (*K*)

Call intrinsic value = max (0, *S* – *K*)
Put intrinsic value = max (0, *K* – *S*)

- Volatility (σ)
- Interest rates (*r*)
- Time to expiration (*T*)

If the size of the option contract covers 62,500 DM, the dollar amount of the intrinsic value would be:

$$0.02 \text{ US\$/DM} \times 62,500 \text{ DM} = \$1,250$$

On the other hand, the intrinsic value of a call option with the same strike price would be zero.

$$\text{Call intrinsic value} = \max (0, S - K)$$
$$= \max (0, 0.62 - 0.64)$$
$$= 0$$

In this instance, the put option would be in the money while the call option would be out of the money.

The time value of an option is a function of the security's volatility, or risk (σ); the current level of interest rates (*r*); and the option's maturity, or time to expiration (*T*).

The volatility of the underlying security and the time to expiration are particularly important to the price of an option. Volatility is important because the higher the volatility of the underlying security, the greater the potential payoff of the option if it expires in the money. Therefore, an option on a more risky security should be worth more than an option on a less risky security. Time to expiration is also important. An option with a short time to expiration has less time to reach a value where the option will pay off.

Consequently, an option with more time to expiration will be worth more than an option with only a short time to expiration.

The difference between the option price and intrinsic value is the time value. The option's positive time value gradually approaches zero at expiration, with the option price at expiration equal to its intrinsic value. The convergence of the option price to its intrinsic value at expiration is similar to the convergence of a futures contract to the underlying security price at expiration.

Payoff profiles.   Insight into the characteristics of options can be obtained by looking specifically at how options behave and what value they have at expiration. The matrix below is a simple technique for showing the value of option positions at expiration.

	Value at Expiration	
	$S < K$	$S > K$
Call	0	$S - K$
Put	$K - S$	0
Security	S	S

At the expiration of the put or call option, its intrinsic value depends on whether the security price is more or less than the exercise price. The value of the underlying security is the same, S, whether it is below or above the option's exercise price. These values form the basic building blocks for option strategy analysis.

Exhibit 33–22 illustrates the payoff pattern at expiration for a call option. The security price is plotted on the horizontal axis. The vertical axis measures the payoff at expiration. The trivial case representing the security's value is shown by the dashed line. For example, if the security ends with a value of K dollars, then the security will have a payoff of K dollars. The call option has a value of zero until the security price reaches the exercise price K, after which the call option increases one for one in price as the security price increases. The investor, however, must first purchase the option. So the net payoff from buying a call option is negative until the security price reaches the exercise price, and then it starts to rise (the dotted line). This line represents the payoff the investor receives net of the cost of the option. The investor breaks even with zero net profit at the point where the security price equals the strike price plus the call option premium.

Note that the call option has a kinked or asymmetric payoff pattern. This feature distinguishes it from a futures contract. The future has a payoff

EXHIBIT 33–22
Payoff Profile of a Call Option

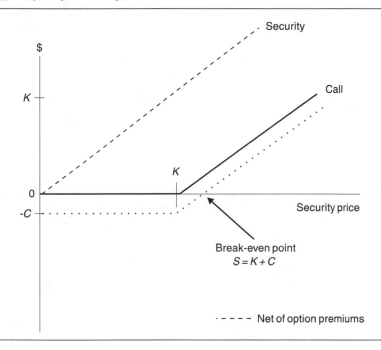

pattern that is a straight line, as does the underlying security. This payoff asymmetry allows the option to create specialized return patterns that are unavailable when using a futures contract.

Exhibit 33–23 illustrates the behavior of a put option. The put option has an intrinsic value of zero above the exercise price. Below there, it increases one for one as the security price declines. If an investor buys a put option, the net payoff of the option is the dotted line. The investor breaks even, with zero net profit, at the point where the security price equals the strike price less the put option premium.

Pricing an option: The Black-Scholes model. The   Black-Scholes model for pricing a call option was first published by F. Black and M. Scholes in 1973.[6] Our understanding of options and how to price them

---

6 F. Black and M. Scholes, "The Pricing of Options and Corporate Liabilities," *Journal of Political Economy*, May–June 1973, pp. 637–59.

EXHIBIT 33–23
Payoff Profile of a Put Option

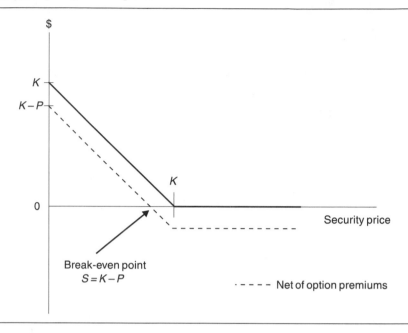

has been one of the most important developments in finance in the last 25 years. The Black-Scholes model also became the most common method for valuing options. The pricing formula is relatively difficult to calculate by hand, but many computer programs are available and are easy to use.

The Black-Scholes model for a call option can be written as

$$C = S_0 N(d) - Ke^{-rT}N(d - \sigma\sqrt{T}), \tag{24}$$

where

$$d = \frac{ln(S_0 / K) + (r + 1 / 2\sigma^2)T}{\sigma\sqrt{T}}$$

$N(d)$ = cumulative normal distribution

The Black-Scholes model indicates that the call option is equal to the security price (S_0) times a probability $N(d)$ minus the present value of the exercise price (Ke^{-rt}) times another probability $[N(d - \sigma\sqrt{T})]$. The probabilities are given by the cumulative normal distribution represented in Exhibit 33–24.

EXHIBIT 33–24
Standard Normal Curve
Total Area under Curve = 1.0

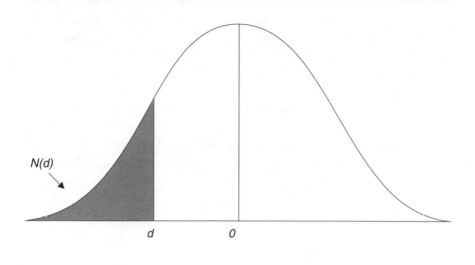

$N(d)$

d 0

Notice that the call price depends on the current security price (S_0) and the exercise price K; it also depends on the rate of interest (r), the time to expiration (T), and the risk of the underlying security (σ). As noted previously when discussing the payoff of an option, the intrinsic value is dependent on both the security price and the strike price of the option. Furthermore, the potential size of the payoff, and the probability of being in the money are affected by the volatility of the underlying asset. Finally, it is not surprising that the time to achieve the threshold of the strike price is another factor which has a bearing on the price of the option.

The price of the put option can be found from the Black-Scholes model by using the *put/call parity relationship.*[7]

$$P = C - S_0 + Ke^{-rT}$$

$$= S_0\,[N(d) - 1] - Ke^{-rT}\,N(d - \sigma\sqrt{T})\qquad(25)$$

---

7 The put/call parity relationship is the arbitrage relationship that keeps the prices of the put and call options tied to the price of the underlying security. It is constructed in a way similar to the cash-and-carry arbitrage relationship for a forward contract.

where d and $N(d)$ are defined as in the Black-Scholes equation for a call option. By substituting the price of the call option developed by Black-Scholes, we can derive the price of the put option. The formula is similar to the call option formula: The security price times a probability minus the present value of the strike price times another probability. The associated probabilities are again drawn from the cumulative normal distribution. A table of values for the cumulation normal distribution is given in the appendix (page 748).

To illustrate the calculation of option prices using the Black-Scholes model, assume the security price (S_0) is $100, the strike price ($K$) is also $100, the riskless rate ($r$) is 5 percent, and the volatility of the security price (σ) is 22 percent. For an option with a maturity (T) of one year, d would equal 0.34; $N(d)$, 0.6331; and $N(d - \sigma\sqrt{T})$, 0.5478. The price for the call option is:

$C = 100(0.6331) - 100(0.9512)(0.5478) = \$11.20,$

and the price for the put option is:

$P = 100(-0.3669) - 100(0.9512)(-0.4522) = \$6.32$

For a call option with one quarter of a year to expiration, d equals 0.17; $N(d)$, 0.5675; $N(d - \sigma\sqrt{T})$, 0.5239. The prices for the call and put options are

$C = 100(0.5675) - 100(0.9876)(0.5239) = \$5.01,$

$P = 100(-0.4325) - 100(0.9876)(-0.4761) = \$3.77.$

The use of the Black-Scholes model requires a knowledge of the current security price, the exercise price, the expiration date, the current interest rate, and the volatility of the underlying security (represented by the standard deviation of returns). The first three parameters are well defined and readily observable. The interest rate generally used in the formula corresponds to a riskless rate with a horizon equal to the expiration date of the option. Strictly speaking, the interest rate should be a continuously compounded rate. Thus, to convert a simple annualized rate R to a continuously compounded rate r, the following relationship can be used:

$ln(1 + R) = r$

Although the continuously compounded rate will always be lower than the simple interest rate, any mispricing in an option with a short maturity caused by the use of the simple rate instead of the continuous rate will generally be small because the option price is not overly sensitive to the interest rate assumption for short horizons.

The annualized volatility of returns for the underlying security is the last parameter in the model. It is represented by the standard deviation of the continuously compounded return on the security. In pricing options, analysts typically use some measure of historical volatility, such as daily, weekly, or monthly returns. If daily returns are used to estimate annual volatility, the daily variance is typically multiplied by 250 (the number of trading days in a year) to obtain an annualized number. If weekly returns are used, the variance is multiplied by 52. If monthly returns are used, the variance is multiplied by 12.

The Black-Scholes model allows us to examine one other important relationship used in designing hedge relationships. It is important to know how the price of an option changes with respect to the price of the underlying security. This change in option price as the underlying security price changes is called the option's *delta* and was used in equation (7) to replicate an option. For example, if a call option has a delta of 0.4, this would imply that if the security price increases by $1, the option price will increase by $0.40 ($1 \times 0.40 = 0.40$). It can be shown that the delta of a call option using the Black-Scholes model is equal to the cumulative normal probability:

$$\Delta_{call} = N(d) \tag{26}$$

It follows from the put/call parity relationship that the delta of a put option is equal to the delta of a call option minus one in which the put and the call options have the same strike price and maturity.

$$\Delta_{put} = \Delta_{call} - 1$$
$$= N(d) - 1 \tag{27}$$

Since the cumulative normal probability can take on values from zero to one, the delta of the call option will range from zero to one and the delta of a put option will range from zero to -1. A deep out-of-the-money option will have a delta close to zero, indicating that the option price will not change in value much as the security price changes. This implies that a deep in-the-money call option will have a delta close to 1.0 and a deep in-the-money put option will have a delta close to -1.0 such that they move nearly dollar for dollar with a change in the security price. At-the-money call options have a delta of approximately 0.5 while at-the-money put options have a delta of approximately -0.5. The delta on such options would indicate that for every $1 increase in the underlying security price, the call option would increase in value by $0.50 and the put option would decrease in value by $0.50.

Assumptions and modifications of the Black-Scholes model.
The Black-Scholes model depends on several assumptions. It was originally developed with the assumption that returns for the security are lognormally distributed and independent over time. In addition, it is assumed that the underlying security has constant risk, or variance, and that the interest rate is constant over time. The model also assumes no instantaneous price jumps in the security; that is, over a very short period of time, the security can move a little but not a large amount. The original model also assumed no dividends or cash payments from the security and no early exercise. The model was developed for pricing a European-style option. Researchers have tried to develop models to relax most of these assumptions. Many of today's models are variations of the original 1973 Black-Scholes model.

The easiest assumption to relax is probably that of no cash distributions. If known dividends are to be paid on a stock before expiration of the option, the price of the option will adjust for the dividend payments. For known discrete dividends, the current stock price needs to be adjusted by the present value of the dividends before being used in the Black-Scholes model. For example, suppose the current stock price is S_0 with an expected dividend of D_T at time T. The adjusted stock price to use at each place in the Black-Scholes formula to price the option is:

$$S_0^* = S_0 - D_T\, e^{-rT} \tag{28}$$

The incorporation of the dividend payment in a pricing model reduces the price of the call option and increases the price of a put option.

Another approach to adjusting the stock price is to assume that the dividend is paid continuously at a known yield.[8] This assumption might approximate the dividends on a stock index; because of the many different stocks in an index, looking at each dividend separately is difficult. In this case, if y represents the aggregate annual dividend yield, the adjusted stock price used to price an option with expiration date T is:

$$S_0^* = S_0 e^{-yT} \tag{29}$$

Options on foreign exchange can also be put into this framework, in which the assumption is that the foreign currency pays continuous interest at rate r_f. The pricing of a foreign currency option can be found by using the Black-Scholes model with the following modification: If S_0 represents the current exchange rate, the modification involves substituting:

---

8 See R. Merton, "The Theory of Rational Option Pricing."*Bell Journal of Economics and Management Science*, Spring 1973, pp. 141–83.

EXHIBIT 33–25
Modifications to the Black-Scholes Model

Discrete cash payout

$$S_0^* = S_0 - D_T e^{-rT}$$

D_T = payout at time T from the security

Continuous cash payout

$$S_0^* = S_0 e^{-yT}$$

y = rate of continuous payout or yield from the security

Currency option

$$S_0^* = S_0 e^{-r_f T}$$

r_f = foreign interest rate

Futures option

$$S_0^* = F_0 e^{-(r-y)T}$$

$F_{0üòçòF}$ [:0é $= futures\ price$

y = rate of continuous payout or yield from the security

Note: The standard Black-Scholes model can be used to price European options on securities with cash payouts, options on currencies, or options on futures contracts by substituting S_0^* for S_0 in the standard Black-Scholes formula.

$$S_0^* = S_0 e^{rT} \tag{30}$$

for each occurrence of S_0 in the standard Black-Scholes formula.

The dividend and foreign exchange adjustments presented here assume that the options cannot be exercised early, but variations of the Black-Scholes model for American options allow for early exercise.[9] The techniques used to price American options are typically more complex than those for European options and often require substantial numerical analysis for a solution.

Relaxing some of the other assumptions of the Black-Scholes model is more difficult than it is for those discussed here. Some attempts have been made to develop models in which the underlying security price is not

---

9 Interested readers might consult R. Roll, "An Analytic Valuation Formula for Unprotected American Call Options on Stocks with Known Dividends," *Journal of Financial Economics*, Nov. 1977, pp. 251–58; R. Geske, "A Note on an Analytic Formula for Unprotected American Call Options on Stocks with Known Dividends," *Journal of Financial Economics*, Dec. 1979, pp. 375–80; and R. Whaley, "On the Valuation of American Call Options on Stocks with Known Dividends," *Journal of Financial Economics*, June 1981, pp. 207–12.

log-normally distributed.[10] Relaxing the assumptions of constant variance and interest rates is yet more difficult. Specialized models for fixed-income options have been developed, however, by relaxing the assumption of constant interest rates.[11] Exhibit 33–25 summarizes the modifications that can be made to the Black-Scholes model to price various types of European options.

CONCLUSION

Options and futures provide a cost-effective way to implement tactical changes in asset allocation. In the world's major stock and bond markets, options and futures generally provide a less expensive alternative for changing broad market exposure than trading individual securities.

There are three principal uses of options and futures in tactical asset allocation: creating additional market exposure, hedging existing market exposure, and structuring automatic, market-driven changes in market exposure. The use of futures and forwards generally produce a symmetric impact on the return profile of a portfolio while options produce asymmetric effects. However, in some cases they can be structured to be interchangeable, so that futures positions can be dynamically adjusted to mimic the asymmetry of an option while combinations of options can be structured to mimic the symmetry of a futures or forward contract.

REFERENCES

Black, F., E. Derman, and W. Toy. "A One-Factor Model of Interest Rates and Its Application to Treasury Bond Options." *Financial Analysts Journal*, Jan.–Feb. 1990, pp. 33–39.

Black, F., and M. Scholes. "The Pricing of Options and Corporate Liabilities." *Journal of Political Economy*, May–June 1973, pp. 637–59.

---

10 For example, R. Bookstaber and J. McDonald, in "A Generalized Option Valuation Model for the Pricing of Bond Options," *Review of Futures Markets* 4 (1985), pp. 60–73, have developed models with more general probability distributions, of which the lognormal is a special case.

11 See R. Dattatreya and F. Fabozzi, "A Simplified Model for Valuing Debt Options," *Journal of Portfolio Management*, Spring 1989, pp. 64–73; F. Black, E. Derman, and W. Toy, "A One-Factor Model of Interest Rates and Its Application to Treasury Bond Options," *Financial Analysts Journal*, Jan.–Feb. 1990, pp. 33–39.

Bookstaber, R., and J. McDonald. "A Generalized Option Valuation Model for the Pricing of Bond Options." *Review of Futures Markets 4* (1985), pp. 60–73.

Chance, D. *An Introduction to Options and Futures*. Chicago: Dryden Press. 1989.

Clarke, R. *Options and Futures: A Tutorial*. Charlottesville, Va.: Association for Investment Management Research, 1993.

Clarke, R., and M. Kritzman, *Managing Currency Risk: Concepts and Practices*. Charlottesville, Va.: Association for Investment Research, 1996.

Cornell, B., and M. Reinganum. "Forward and Futures Prices: Evidence from Foreign Exchange Markets." *Journal of Finance*, Dec. 1981, pp. 1035–45.

Cox, J. C., J. E. Ingersoll, and S. A. Ross, "The Relation Between Forward Prices and Futures Prices." *Journal of Financial Economics*, Dec. 1981, pp. 321–46

_____. "A Note on an Analytic Formula for Unprotected American Call Options on Stocks with Known Dividends." *Journal of Financial Economics*, Dec. 1979, pp. 375–80.

Dattatreya, R., and F. Fabozzi. "A Simplified Model for Valuing Debt Options." *Journal of Portfolio Management*, Spring 1989, pp. 64–73.

Dengler, W. H., and H. P. Becker. "10 Option Strategies and When To Use Them." *Futures*, June 1984.

Geske, R. "A Note on an Analytic Formula for Unprotected American Call Options on Stocks with Known Dividends." *Journal of Financial Economics*, Dec. 1979, pp. 375–80.

Hull, J. *Options, Futures, and Other Derivative Securities*. 2nd ed. Englewood Cliffs, N.J.: Prentice Hall, 1993.

Merton, R. "The Relationship Between Put and Call Option Prices: Comment." *Journal of Finance*, March 1973, pp. 183–84.

_____. "The Theory of Rational Option Pricing." *Bell Journal of Economics and Management Science*, Spring 1973, pp. 141–83.

Park, H. Y., and A. H. Chen. "Differences between Futures and Forward Prices: A Further Investigation of Marking to Market Effects." *Journal of Futures Markets*, Feb. 1985, pp. 77–88.

Roll, R. "An Analytic Valuation Formula for Unprotected American Call Options on Stocks with Known Dividends." *Journal of Financial Economics*, Nov. 1977, pp. 251–58.

Whaley, R., "On the Valuation of American Call Options on Stocks with Known Dividends," *Journal of Financial Economics*, June 1981, pp. 207–12.

Appendix

Standard Normal Distribution

d	0.00	0.01	0.02	0.03	0.04	0.05	0.06	0.07	0.08	0.09
0.0	.5000	.5040	.5080	.5120	.5160	.5199	.5239	.5279	.5319	.5359
0.1	.5398	.5438	.5478	.5517	.5557	.5596	.5636	.5675	.5714	.5753
0.2	.5793	.5832	.5871	.5910	.5948	.5987	.6026	.6064	.6103	.6141
0.3	.6179	.6217	.6255	.6293	.6331	.6368	.6406	.6443	.6480	.6517
0.4	.6554	.6591	.6628	.6664	.6700	.6736	.6772	.6808	.6844	.6879
0.5	.6915	.6950	.6985	.7019	.7054	.7988	.7123	.7157	.7190	.7224
0.5	.6915	.6950	.6985	.7019	.7054	.7988	.7123	.7157	.7190	.7224
0.6	.7257	.7291	.7324	.7357	.7389	.7422	.7454	.7486	.7517	.7549
0.7	.7580	.7611	.7642	.7673	.7704	.7734	.7764	.7794	.7823	.7852
0.8	.7881	.7910	.7939	.7967	.7995	.8023	.8051	.8078	.8106	.8133
0.9	.8159	.8186	.8212	.8238	.8264	.8289	.8315	.8340	.8365	.8389
1.0	.8413	.8438	.8461	.8485	.8508	.8531	.8554	.8577	.8599	.8621
1.1	.8643	.8665	.8686	.8708	.8729	.8749	.8770	.8790	.8810	.8830
1.2	.8849	.8860	.8888	.8907	.8925	.8943	.8962	.8980	.8997	.9015
1.3	.9032	.9049	.9066	.9082	.9099	.9115	.9131	.9147	.9162	.9177
1.4	.9192	.9207	.9222	.9236	.9251	.9265	.9279	.9292	.9306	.9219
1.5	.9332	.9345	.9357	.9370	.9382	.9394	.9406	.9418	.9429	.9441
1.6	.9452	.9463	.9474	.9484	.9495	.9505	.9515	.9525	.9535	.9545
1.7	.9554	.9564	.9573	.9582	.9591	.9599	.9688	.9616	.9625	.9633
1.8	.9641	.9649	.9656	.9664	.9671	.9678	.9686	.9693	.9699	.9706
1.9	.9713	.9719	.9726	.9732	.9738	.9744	.9750	.9756	.9761	.9767
2.0	.9772	.9778	.9783	.9788	.9793	.9798	.9803	.9808	.9812	.9817
2.1	.9812	.9826	.9830	.9834	.9838	.9842	.9846	.9850	.9854	.9857
2.2	.9861	.9864	.9868	.9871	.9875	.9878	.9881	.9884	.9887	.9890
2.3	.9893	.9896	.9898	.9901	.9904	.9906	.9909	.9911	.9913	.9916
2.4	.9918	.9920	.9922	.9925	.9927	.9929	.9931	.9932	.9934	.9936
2.5	.9938	.9940	.9941	.9943	.9945	.9946	.9948	.9949	.9951	.9952
2.6	.9953	.9955	.9956	.9957	.9959	.9960	.9961	.9962	.9963	.9964
2.7	.9965	.9966	.9967	.9968	.9969	.9970	.9971	.9972	.9973	.9974
2.8	.9974	.9975	.9976	.9977	.9977	.9978	.9979	.9979	.9980	.9981
2.9	.9981	.9982	.9982	.9983	.9984	.9984	.9985	.9985	.9986	.9986
3.0	.9987	.9987	.9987	.9988	.9988	.9989	.9989	.9989	.9990	.9990

Chapter Thirty-Four

Global Portfolio Optimization

Fischer Black and Robert Litterman
Goldman, Sachs & Co.

Investors with global portfolios of equities and bonds are generally aware that their asset allocation decisions—the proportions of funds they invest in the asset classes of different countries and the degrees of currency hedging—are the most important investment decisions they make. In deciding on the appropriate allocation, they are usually comfortable making the simplifying assumption that their objective is to maximize expected return for a given level of risk (subject in most cases to various types of constraints).

Given the straightforward mathematics of this optimization problem, the many correlations among global asset classes required in measuring risk, and the large amounts of money involved, one might expect that in today's computerized world quantitative models would play a dominant role in the global allocation process. Unfortunately, when investors have tried to use quantitative models to help optimize the critical allocation decision, the unreasonable nature of the results has often thwarted their efforts.[1] When investors impose no constraints, the models almost always ordain large short positions in many assets. When constraints rule out short positions,

---

1 For some academic discussions of this issue, see R. C. Green and B. Hollifield, "When Will Mean-Variance Efficient Portfolios Be Well Diversified?" *Journal of Finance,* forthcoming, and M. J. Best and R. R. Grauer, "On the Sensitivity of Mean-Variance Efficient Portfolios to Changes in Asset Means: Some Analytical and Computational Results," *Review of Financial Studies* 4 (1991), pp. 16–22.

the models often prescribe "corner" solutions with zero weights in many assets, as well as unreasonably large weights in the assets of markets with small capitalizations.

These unreasonable results stem from two well-recognized problems. First, expected returns are very difficult to estimate. Investors typically have knowledgeable views about absolute or relative returns in only a few markets. A standard optimization model, however, requires them to provide expected returns for all assets and currencies. Thus investors must augment their views with a set of auxiliary assumptions, and the historical returns they often use for this purpose provide poor guides to future returns.

Second, the optimal portfolio asset weights and currency positions of standard asset allocation models are extremely sensitive to the return assumptions used. The two problems compound each other; the standard model has no way to distinguish strongly held views from auxiliary assumptions, and the optimal portfolio it generates, given its sensitivity to the expected returns, often appears to bear little or no relation to the views the investor wishes to express. In practice, therefore, despite the obvious conceptual attractions of a quantitative approach, few global investment managers regularly allow quantitative models to play a major role in their asset allocation decisions.

This chapter describes an approach that provides an intuitive solution to the two problems that have plagued quantitative asset allocation models. The key is combining two established tenets of modern portfolio theory— the mean-variance optimization framework of Markowitz and the capital asset pricing model (CAPM) of Sharpe and Lintner.[2]

Our approach allows the investor to combine his views about the outlook for global equities, bonds and currencies with the **risk premiums** generated by Black's global version of CAPM equilibrium.[3] These equilibrium risk premiums are the **excess returns** that equate the supply and demand for global assets and currencies.

As we have noted and will illustrate, the mean-variance optimization used in standard asset allocation models is extremely sensitive to the

---

2 H. Markowitz, "Portfolio Selection," *Journal of Finance*, March 1952; J. Lintner, "The Valuation of Risk Assets and the Selection of Risky Investments in Stock Portfolios and Capital Budgets," *Review of Economics and Statistics*, Feb. 1965; and W. F. Sharpe, "Capital Asset Prices: A Theory of Market Equilibrium Under Conditions of Risk," *Journal of Finance* Sept. 1964.

3 F. Black, "Universal Hedging: How to Optimize Currency Risk and Reward in International Equity Portfolios," *Financial Analysts Journal,* July/Aug. 1989.

expected return assumptions the investor must provide. In our model, **equilibrium** risk premiums provide a neutral reference point for expected returns. This, in turn, allows the model to generate optimal portfolios that are much better behaved than the unreasonable portfolios that standard models typically produce, which often include large long and short positions unless otherwise constrained. Instead, our model gravitates toward a balanced—that is, market-capitalization-weighted—portfolio that tilts in the direction of assets favored by the investor.

Our model does not assume that the world is always at CAPM equilibrium, but rather that when expected returns move away from their equilibrium values, imbalances in markets will tend to push them back. We think it is reasonable to assume that expected returns are not likely to deviate too far from equilibrium values. This suggests that the investor may profit by combining his or her views about returns in different markets with the information contained in equilibrium prices and returns.

Our approach distinguishes between the views of the investor and the expected returns that drive optimization analysis. Equilibrium risk premiums provide a center of gravity for expected returns. The expected returns used in our optimization will deviate from equilibrium risk premiums in accordance with the investor's explicitly stated views. The extent of the deviations from equilibrium will depend on the degree of confidence the investor has in each view. Our model makes adjustments in a manner as consistent as possible with historical covariances of returns of different assets and currencies.

Our use of equilibrium allows investors to specify views in a much more flexible and powerful way than is otherwise possible. For example, rather than requiring the investor to have a view about the absolute return on every asset and currency, our approach allows the investor to specify as many or as few views as he or she wishes. In addition, the investor can specify views about relative returns and can specify a degree of confidence about each view.

A set of examples illustrates how the incorporation of equilibrium into the standard asset allocation model makes it better behaved and enables it to generate insights for the global investment manager. To that end, we start with a discussion of how equilibrium can help an investor translate his or her views into a set of expected returns for all assets and currencies. We then follow with a set of applications of the model that illustrate how the equilibrium solves the problems that have traditionally led to unreasonable results in standard mean-variance models.

EXHIBIT 34–1
Historical Excess Returns, January 1975–August 1991*

	Germany	France	Japan	U.K.	U.S.	Canada	Australia
Total Mean Excess Return							
Currencies	−20.8	3.2	23.3	13.4		12.6	3.0
Bonds	15.3	−2.3	42.3	21.4	−4.9	−22.8	−13.1
Equities	112.9	117.0	223.0	291.3	130.1	16.7	107.8
Annualized Mean Excess Return							
Currencies	−1.4	0.2	1.3	0.8		0.7	0.2
Bonds	0.9	−0.1	2.1	1.2	−0.3	−1.5	−0.8
Equities	4.7	4.8	7.3	8.6	5.2	0.9	4.5
Annualized Standard Deviation							
Currencies	12.1	11.7	12.3	11.9		4.7	10.3
Bonds	4.5	4.5	6.5	9.9	6.8	7.8	5.5
Equities	18.3	22.2	17.8	24.7	16.1	18.3	21.9

*Bond and equity returns in U.S. dollars, currency hedged and in excess of the London interbank offered rate
(LIBOR); returns on currencies are in excess of the one-month forward rates.

NEUTRAL VIEWS

Why should investors use a global equilibrium model to help make their
global asset allocation decisions? A neutral reference is a critically important input in making use of a mean-variance optimization model, and an
equilibrium provides the appropriate neutral reference. Most of the time
investors have views—feelings that some assets or currencies are overvalued or undervalued at current market prices. An asset allocation model can
help them to apply those views to their advantage. But it is unrealistic to
expect investors to be able to state exact expected excess returns for every
asset and currency. The equilibrium, however, can provide investors an
appropriate point of reference.

Suppose, for example, that investors have no views. How then, can they
define their optimal portfolio? Answering this question demonstrates the
usefulness of the equilibrium risk premium.

In considering this question, and others throughout this chapter, we use
historical data on global equities, bonds and currencies. We use a seven-
country model with monthly returns for the United States, Japan, Germany,

France, the United Kingdom, Canada, and Australia from January 1975 through August 1991.[4]

Exhibit 34–1 presents the means and standard deviations of excess returns and Exhibit 34–2 the correlations. All the results in this article are given from a U.S. dollar perspective; use of other currencies would give similar results.[5]

Besides equilibrium risk premiums, there are several other naive approaches investors might use to construct an optimal portfolio when they have no views about assets or currencies. We examine some of these: the historical average approach, the equal mean approach, and the risk-adjusted equal mean approach.

Historical Averages

The historical average approach assumes, as a neutral reference, that excess returns will equal their historical averages. The problem with this approach is that historical means provide very poor forecasts of future returns. For example, Exhibit 34–1 shows may negative values. Exhibit 34–3 shows what happens when we use such returns as expected excess return assumptions. We may optimize expected returns for each level of risk to get a

---

4 In actual applications of the model, we typically include more asset classes and use daily data to measure more accurately the current state of the time-varying risk structure. We intend to address issues concerning uncertainty of the covariances in another paper. For the purposes of this chapter, we treat the true covariances of excess returns as known.

5 We define excess return on currency-hedged assets to be total return less the short rate and excess return on currency positions to be total return less the forward premium. In Exhibit 34–2, all excess returns and volatilities are percentages. The currency-hedged excess return on a bond or equity at time t is given by:

$$E_t = \frac{P_{t+1}/X_{t+1}}{P_t/X_t} \cdot 100 - (1 + R_t)FX_t - R_t$$

where P_t is the price of the asset in foreign currency. X_t the exchange rate in units of foreign currency per U.S. dollar, R_t the domestic short rate and FX_t the return on a forward contract, all at time t. The return on a forward contract or, equivalently, the excess return on a foreign currency, is given by:

$$FX_t = \frac{F_t^{t=1} - S_{t+1}}{X_t} \cdot 100,$$

where F_t^{t+1} is the one-period forward exchange rate at time t.

EXHIBIT 34-2
Historical Correlations of Excess Returns, January 1975–August 1991

	Germany			France			Japan		
	Equities	*Bonds*	*Currency*	*Equities*	*Bonds*	*Currency*	*Equities*	*Bonds*	*Currency*
Germany									
Equities	1.00								
Bonds	0.28	1.00							
Currency	0.02	0.36	1.00						
France									
Equities	0.52	0.17	0.03	1.00					
Bonds	0.23	0.46	0.15	0.36	1.00				
Currency	0.03	0.33	0.92	0.08	0.15	1.00			
Japan									
Equities	0.37	0.15	0.05	0.42	0.23	0.04	1.00		
Bonds	0.10	0.48	0.27	0.11	0.31	0.21	0.35	1.00	
Currency	0.01	0.21	0.62	0.10	0.19	0.62	0.18	0.45	1.00
U.K.									
Equities	0.42	0.20	−0.01	0.50	0.21	0.04	0.37	0.09	0.04
Bonds	0.14	0.36	0.09	0.20	0.31	0.09	0.20	0.33	0.19
Currency	0.02	0.22	0.66	0.05	0.05	0.66	0.06	0.24	0.54
U.S.									
Equities	0.43	0.23	0.03	0.52	0.21	0.06	0.41	0.12	−0.02
Bonds	0.17	0.50	0.26	0.10	0.33	0.22	0.11	0.28	0.18
Canada									
Equities	0.33	0.16	0.05	0.48	0.04	0.09	0.33	0.02	0.04
Bonds	0.13	0.49	0.24	0.10	0.35	0.21	0.14	0.33	0.22
Currency	0.05	0.14	0.11	0.10	0.04	0.10	0.12	0.05	0.06

EXHIBIT 34–2 (concluded)

	Germany			France			Japan		
	Equities	Bonds	Currency	Equities	Bonds	Currency	Equities	Bonds	Currency
Australia									
Equities	0.34	0.07	-0.00	0.39	0.07	0.05	0.25	-0.02	0.12
Bonds	0.24	0.19	0.09	0.04	0.16	0.08	0.12	0.16	0.09
Currency	-0.01	0.05	0.25	0.07	-0.03	0.29	0.05	0.10	0.27

	United Kingdom			United States		Canada			Australia	
	Equities	Bonds	Currency	Equities	Bonds	Equities	Bonds	Currency	Equities	Bonds
U.K.										
Equities	1.00									
Bonds	0.47	1.00								
Currency	0.06	0.27	1.00							
U.S.										
Equities	0.58	0.23	-0.02	1.00						
Bonds	0.12	0.28	0.18	0.32	1.00					
Canada										
Equities	0.56	0.27	0.11	0.74	0.18	1.00				
Bonds	0.18	0.40	0.25	0.31	0.82	0.23	1.00			
Currency	0.14	0.13	0.09	0.24	0.15	0.32	0.24	1.00		
Australia										
Equities	0.50	0.20	0.15	0.48	-0.05	0.61	0.02	0.18	1.00	
Bonds	0.17	0.17	0.09	0.24	0.20	0.21	0.18	0.13	0.37	1.00
Currency	0.06	0.05	0.27	0.07	-0.00	0.19	0.04	0.28	0.27	0.20

EXHIBIT 34–3
Optimal Portfolios Based on Historical Average Approach

	Germany	France	Japan	U.K	U.S.	Canada	Australia
Unconstrained							
Currency							
Exposure (%)	–78.7	46.5	15.5	28.6		65.0	–5.2
Bonds (%)	30.4	–40.7	40.4	–1.4	54.5	–95.7	–52.5
Equities (%)	4.4	–4.4	15.5	13.3	44.0	–44.2	9.0
With Constraints against Shorting Assets							
Currency							
Exposure (%)	–160.0	115.2	18.0	23.7	77.8	–13.8	
Bonds (%)	7.6	0.0	88.8	0.0	0.0	0.0	0.0
Equities (%)	0.0	0.0	0.0	0.0	0.0	0.0	0.0

frontier of optimal portfolios. The exhibit illustrates the frontiers with the portfolios that have 10.7 percent risk, with and without shorting constraints.[6]

We can make a number of points about these "optimal" portfolios. First, they illustrate what we mean when we claim that standard mean-variance optimization models often generate unreasonable portfolios. The portfolio that does not constrain against shorting has many large long and short positions that bear no obvious relation to the expected excess return assumptions. When we constrain shorting, we have positive weights in only 2 of the 14 potential assets. These portfolios are typical of those generated by standard optimization models.

The use of past excess returns to represent a "neutral" set of views is equivalent to assuming that the constant portfolio weights that would have performed best historically are in some sense neutral. In reality, they are not neutral at all, but a very special set of weights that go short assets that have done poorly and go long assets that have done well in the particular historical period.

---

6 We choose to normalize on 10.7 percent risk here and throughout the chapter because it happens to be the risk of the market-capitalization-weighted 80 percent currency-hedged portfolio that will be held in equilibrium in our model.

EXHIBIT 34-4
Optimal Portfolios Based on Equal Means

	Germany	France	Japan	U.K.	U.S.	Canada	Australia
Unconstrained							
Currency							
Exposure (%)	14.5	−12.6	−0.9	4.4		−18.7	−2.1
Bonds (%)	−11.6	4.2	−1.8	−10.8	13.9	−18.9	−32.7
Equities (%)	21.4	−4.8	23.0	−4.6	32.2	9.6	10.5
With Constraints against Shorting Assets							
Currency							
Exposure (%)	14.3	−11.2	−4.5	0.2		−25.9	−2.0
Bonds (%)	0.0	0.0	0.0	0.0	0.0	0.0	0.0
Equities (%)	17.5	0.0	22.1	0.0	27.0	8.2	7.3

Equal Means

The investor might hope that assuming equal means for returns across all countries for each asset class would result in an appropriate neutral reference. Exhibit 34-4 gives an example of the optimal portfolio for this type of analysis. Again, we get an unreasonable portfolio.[7]

One problem with this approach is that equal expected excess returns do not compensate investors appropriately for the different levels of risk in assets of different countries. Investors diversify globally to reduce risk. Everything else being equal, they prefer assets whose returns are less volatile and less correlated with those of other assets.

Although such preferences are obvious, it is perhaps surprising how unbalanced the optimal portfolio weights can be, as Exhibit 34-4 illustrates, when we take "everything else being equal" to such a literal extreme. With no constraints, the largest position is short Australian bonds.

Risk-Adjusted Equal Means

Our third naive approach to defining a neural reference point is to assume that bonds and equities have the same expected excess return per unit of

---

7 For the purposes of this exercise, we arbitrarily assigned to each country the average historical excess return across countries, as follows—0.2 for currencies, 0.4 for bonds, and 5.1 for equities.

EXHIBIT 34–5
Optimal Portfolios Based on Risk-Adjusted Means

	Germany	France	Japan	U.K.	U.S.	Canada	Australia
Unconstrained							
Currency							
Exposure (%)	5.6	11.3	−28.6	−20.3		−50.9	−4.9
Bonds (%)	−23.9	12.6	54.0	20.8	23.1	37.8	15.6
Equities (%)	9.9	8.5	12.4	−0.3	−14.1	13.2	20.1
With Constraints against Shorting Assets							
Currency							
Exposure (%)	21.7	−8.9	−14.0	−12.2		−47.9	−6.7
Bonds (%)	0.0	0.0	0.0	7.8	0.0	19.3	0.0
Equities (%)	11.1	9.4	19.2	6.0	0.0	7.6	19.5

risk, where the risk measure is simply the volatility of asset returns. Currencies in this case are assumed to have no excess return. Exhibit 34–5 shows the optimal portfolio for this case.

Now we have incorporated volatilities, but the portfolio behavior is no better. One problem with this approach is that it hasn't taken the correlations of the asset returns into account. But there is another problem as well, perhaps more subtle but also more serious.

This approach, and the others we have so far used, are based on what might be called the "demand for assets" side of the equation—that is, historical returns and risk measures. The problem with such approaches is obvious when we bring in the supply side of the market.

Suppose the market portfolio comprises two assets, with weights 80 percent and 20 percent. In a simple world, with identical investors all holding the same views and both assets having equal volatilities, everyone cannot hold equal weights of each asset. Prices and expected excess returns in such a world would have to adjust as the excess demand for one asset and excess supply of the other affect the market.

The Equilibrium Approach

To us, the only sensible definition of neutral means is the set of expected returns that would "clear the market" if all investors had identical views. The concept of equilibrium in the context of a global portfolio of equities, bonds and currencies is similar, although currencies do raise a complicating question: How much currency hedging takes place in equilibrium? The answer is that, in a global equilibrium, investors worldwide will all want to take a small amount of currency risk.[8]

This result arises because of a curiosity known in the currency world as "Siegel's paradox." The basic idea is that, because investors in different countries measure returns in different units, each will gain some expected return by taking some currency risk. Investors will accept currency risk up to the point where the additional risk balances the expected return. Under certain simplifying assumptions, the percentage of foreign currency risk hedged will be the same for investors of different countries—giving rise to the name "universal hedging" for this equilibrium.

The equilibrium degree of hedging, the "universal hedging constant, depends on three averages: the average across countries of the mean return on the market portfolio of assets, the average across countries of the volatility of the world market portfolio, and the average across all pairs of countries of exchange rate volatility.

It is difficult to pin down exactly the right value for the universal hedging constant, primarily because the risk premium on the market portfolio is a difficult number to estimate. Nevertheless, we feel that universal hedging values between 75 percent and 85 percent are reasonable. In our monthly data set, the former value corresponds to a risk premium of 5.9 percent on U.S. equities, while the latter corresponds to a risk premium of 9.8 percent. For this chapter, we will use an equilibrium value for currency hedging of 80 percent. Exhibit 34–6 gives the equilibrium risk premiums for all assets, given this value of the universal hedging constant.[9]

---

8 See Black, "Universal Hedging."

9 The "universal hedging" equilibrium is, of course, based on a set of simplifying assumptions, such as a world with no taxes, no capital constraints and no inflation. Exchange rates in this world are the rates of exchange between the different consumption bundles of individuals of different countries. While some may find the assumptions that justify universal hedging overly restrictive, this equilibrium does have the virtue of being simpler than other global CAPM equilibriums that have been described elsewhere. (See B. H. Solnik, "An Equilibrium Model of the International Capital Market," *Journal of Economic Theory*, Aug. 1974, or F. L. A. Grauer, R. H. Litzenberger and R. E. Steble, "Sharing Rules and Equilibrium in an International Capital Market Under Uncertainty," *Journal of Financial Economics* 3 (1976), pp. 233–56.) While these simplifying assumptions are necessary to justify the universal hedging equilibrium, we could easily apply the basic idea of this chapter—combining a global equilibrium with investors' views—to another global equilibrium derived from a different, less restrictive, set of assumptions.

EXHIBIT 34–6
Equilibrium Risk Premiums
(Percent Annualized Excess Returns)

	Germany	France	Japan	U.K.	U.S.	Canada	Australia
Currencies	1.01	1.10	1.40	0.91		0.60	0.63
Bonds	2.29	2.23	2.88	3.28	1.87	2.54	1.74
Equities	6.27	8.48	8.72	10.27	7.32	7.28	6.45

Consider what happens when we adopt these equilibrium risk premiums as our neutral means when we have no views. Exhibit 34–7 shows the optimal portfolio. It is simply the market-capitalization portfolio with 80 percent of the currency risk hedged. Other portfolios on the frontier with different levels of risk would correspond to combinations of risk-free borrowing or lending plus more or less of this portfolio.

By itself, the equilibrium concept is interesting but not particularly useful. Its real value is to provide a neutral framework to which the investor can adjust according to his or her own views, optimization objectives, and constraints.

EXPRESSING VIEWS

Investors trying to use quantitative asset allocation models must translate their views into a complete set of expected excess returns on assets that can be used as a basis for portfolio optimization. As we will show here, the problem is that optimal portfolio weights from a mean-variance model are incredibly sensitive to minor changes in expected excess returns. The advantage of incorporating a global equilibrium will become apparent when we show how to combine it with an investor's views to generate well-behaved portfolios, without requiring the investor to express a complete set of expected excess returns.

We should emphasize that the distinction we are making–between investor views on the one hand and a complete set of expected excess returns for all assets on the other—is not usually recognized. In our approach, views represent the subjective feelings of the investor about

EXHIBIT 34–7
Equilibrium Optimal Portfolio

	Germany	France	Japan	U.K.	U.S.	Canada	Australia
Currency							
Exposure (%)	1.1	0.9	5.9	2.0		0.6	0.3
Bonds (%)	2.9	1.9	6.0	1.8	16.3	1.4	0.3
Equities (%)	2.6	2.4	23.7	8.3	29.7	1.6	1.1

relative values offered in different markets.[10] If an investor does not have a view about a given market, he or she should not have to state one. And if some views are more strongly held than others, the investor should be able to express the differences.

Most views are relative. For example, investors may feel one market will outperform another. Or they may feel bullish (above neutral) or bearish (below neutral) about a market. As we will show, the equilibrium allows investors to express their views this way, instead of as a set of **expected excess returns.**

To see why this is so important, we start by illustrating the extreme sensitivity of portfolio weights to the expected excess returns and the inability of investors to express views directly as a complete set of expected returns. We have already seen how difficult it can be simply to translate no views into a set of expected excess returns that will not lead an asset allocation model to produce an unreasonable portfolio. But suppose that the investors have already solved that problem, using equilibrium risk premiums as the neutral means. They are comfortable with a portfolio that has market capitalization weights, 80 percent hedged. Consider what can happen when these investors now try to express one simple, extremely modest view.

Suppose an investor's view is that, over the next three months, the economic recovery in the United States will be weak and bonds will perform relatively well and equities poorly. The investor's view is not

---

10 Views can represent feelings about the relationships between observable conditions and such relative values.

EXHIBIT 34–8
Optimal Portfolios Based on a Moderate View

	Germany	France	Japan	U.K.	U.S.	Canada	Australia
Unconstrained							
Currency Exposure (%)	−1.3	8.3	−3.3	−6.4		8.5	−1.9
Bonds (%)	−13.6	6.4	15.0	−3.3	112.9	−42.4	0.7
Equities (%)	3.7	6.3	27.2	14.5	−30.6	24.8	6.0
With Constraints against Shorting Assets							
Currency Exposure (%)	2.3	4.3	5.0	−3.0		9.2	−0.6
Bonds (%)	0.0	0.0	0.0	0.0	35.7	0.0	0.0
Equities (%)	2.6	5.3	28.3	13.6	0.0	13.1	1.5

very strong, and he or she quantifies it by assuming that, over the next three months, the U.S. benchmark bond yield will drop 1 basis point rather than rise 1 basis point, as is consistent with the equilibrium risk premium.[11] Similarly, the investor expects U.S. share prices to rise only 2.7 percent over the next three months, rather than to rise the 3.3 percent consistent with the equilibrium view.

To implement the asset allocation optimization, the investor starts with expected excess returns equal to the equilibrium risk premiums and adjusts them as follows. He or she moves the annualized expected excess returns on U.S. bonds up by 0.8 percentage points and the expected excess returns on U.S. equities down by 2.5 percentage points. All other expected excess returns remain unchanged. Exhibit 34–8 shows the optimal portfolio, given this view.

Note the remarkable effect of this very modest change in expected excess returns. The portfolio weights change in dramatic and largely inexplicable ways. The optimal portfolio weights do shift out of U.S. equity into U.S. bonds, as might be expected, but the model also suggests shorting Canadian and German bonds. The lack of apparent connection between the view the investor is attempting to express and the optimal portfolio the model

---

11 In this chapter, we use the term "strength" of a view to refer to its magnitude. We reserve the term "confidence" to refer to the degree of certainty with which a view is held.

generates is a pervasive problem with standard mean-variance optimization. It arises because there is a complex interaction between expected excess returns and the volatilities and correlations used in measuring risk.

COMBINING INVESTOR VIEWS WITH MARKET EQUILIBRIUM

How our approach translates a few views into expected excess returns for all assets is one of its more complex features, but also one of its most innovative. Here is the intuition behind our approach.

1. We believe that there are two distinct sources of information about future excess returns: investor views and market equilibrium.
2. We assume that both sources of information are uncertain and are best expressed as probability distributions.
3. We choose expected excess returns that are as consistent as possible with both sources of information.

The above description captures the basic idea, but the implementation of the approach can lead to some novel insights. We will now show how a relative view about two assets can influence the expected excess return on a third asset.[12]

Three-Asset Example

Let us first work through a very simple example of our approach. After this illustration, we will apply it in the context of our seven-country model. Suppose we know the true structure of a world that has just three assets, A, B and C. The excess return for each of these assets is known to be generated by an equilibrium risk premium plus four sources of risk—a common factor and independent shocks to each of the three assets. We can express this model as follows:

$$R_A = \pi_A + \gamma_A Z + \upsilon_A,$$

$$R_B = \pi_B + \gamma_B Z + \upsilon_B,$$

$$R_C = \pi_C + \gamma_C Z + \upsilon_C,$$

---

12 We try here to develop the intuition behind our approach using some basic concepts of statistics and matrix algebra. A more formal mathematical description is given in Appendix A.

where:

R_i = the excess return on the ith asset

π_i = the equilibrium risk premium on the ith asset

γ_i = the impact on the ith asset of Z

Z = the common factor

υ_i = the independent shock to the ith asset

In this world, the covariance matrix, Σ, of asset excess returns is determined by the relative impacts of the common factor and the independent shocks. The expected excess returns of the assets are a function of the equilibrium risk premiums, the expected value of the common factor, and the expected values of the independent shocks to each asset. For example, the expected excess return of asset A, which we write as $E[R_A]$, is given by:

$$E[R_A] = \pi_A + \gamma_A E[Z] + E[\upsilon_A].$$

We are not assuming that the world is in equilibrium (i.e., that $E[Z]$ and the $E[\upsilon_i]s$ are equal to zero). We do assume that the **mean** $E[R_A]$, is itself an unobservable random variable whose distribution is centered at the equilibrium risk premium. Our uncertainty about $E[R_A]$ is due to our uncertainty about $E[Z]$ and the $E[\upsilon_i]s$. Furthermore, we assume the degree of uncertainty about $E[Z]$ and the $E[\upsilon_i]s$ is proportional to the volatilities of Z and the $\upsilon_i s$ themselves.

This implies that $E[R_A]$ is distributed with a covariance structure proportional to Σ. We will refer to this covariance matrix of the expected excess returns as $\tau\Sigma$. Because the uncertainty in the mean is much smaller than the uncertainty in the return itself, τ will be close to zero. The equilibrium risk premiums together with $\tau\Sigma$ determine the equilibrium distribution for expected excess returns. We assume this information is known to all; it is not a function of the circumstances of any individual investor.

In addition, we assume that each investor provides additional information about expected excess returns in the form of views. For example, one type of view is a statement of the form: "I expect asset A to outperform asset B by Q," where Q is a given value.

We interpret such a view to mean that the investor has subjective information about the future returns of A relative to B. One way we think about representing that information is to act as if we had a summary statistic from a sample of data drawn from the distribution of future returns, data in which all we were able to observe is the difference between the returns of A and B. Alternatively, we can express the view directly as a probability distribution for the difference between the means of the excess returns of A and B. It doesn't matter which of these approaches we use to think about our views; in the end we get the same result.

In both approaches, though, we need a measure of the investor's confidence in his or her views. We use this measure to determine how much weight to give to the view when combining it with the equilibrium. We can think of this degree of confidence as determining, in the first case, the number of observations that we have from the distribution of future returns or as determining, in the second, the standard deviation of the probability distribution.

In our example, consider the limiting case: The investor is 100 percent sure of his or her view. We might think of this as the case where we have an unbounded number of observations from the distribution of future reruns, and where the average value of $R_A - R_B$ from these data is Q. In this special case, we can represent the view as a linear restriction on the expected excess returns:

$$E[R_A] - E[R_B] = Q$$

In this special case, we can compute the distribution of $E[R] = \{E[R_A], E[R_B], E[R_C]\}$ conditional on the equilibrium and this information. This is a relatively straightforward problem from multivariate statistics. To simplify, assume a normal distribution for the means of the random components.

We have the equilibrium distribution for $E[R]$, which is given by Normal $(\pi, \tau\Sigma)$, where $\pi = \{\pi_A\, \pi_B\, \pi_C\}$. We wish to calculate a conditional distribution for the expected returns, subject to the restriction that the expected returns satisfy the linear restriction $E[R_A] - E[R_B] = Q$. We can write this restriction as a linear equation in the expected returns:[13]

$$P \bullet E[R]' = Q,$$

where

P is the vector $[\mathbf{1}, \mathbf{-1}, \mathbf{0}]$.

The conditional normal distribution has the following mean:

$$\pi' + \tau\Sigma \bullet P' \bullet [P \bullet \tau\Sigma \bullet P']^{-1} \bullet [Q - P \bullet \pi']$$

---

13 A "prime" symbol (e.g., P') indicates a transposed vector or matrix.

which is the solution to the problem of minimizing:

$$(E[R] - \pi)\tau\Sigma^{-1}(E[R] - \pi)'$$

subject to $P \bullet E[R]' = Q$

For the special case of 100 percent confidence in a view, we use this conditional mean as our vector of expected excess returns.

In the more general case where we are not 100 percent confident, we can think of a view as representing a fixed number of observations drawn from the distribution of future returns. In this case, we follow the "mixed estimation" strategy described in Theil.[14] Alternatively, we can think of the view as directly reflecting a subjective distribution for the expected excess returns. In this case, we use the Black-Litterman approach, given in the appendix.[15] The formula for the expected excess returns vector is the same from either perspective.

In either approach, we assume that the view can be summarized by a statement of the form $P \bullet E[R]' = Q + \varepsilon$, where P and Q are given and ε is an unobservable, normally distributed random variable with mean 0 and variance Ω. Ω represents the uncertainty in the view. In the limit, as Ω goes to zero, the resulting mean converges to the conditional mean described above.

When there is more than one view, the vector of views can be represented by $P \bullet E[R]' = Q + \varepsilon$, where we now interpret P as a matrix, and ε is a normally distributed random vector with mean 0 and diagonal covariance matrix Ω. A diagonal Ω corresponds to the assumption that the views represent independent draws from the future distribution of returns, or that the deviations of expected returns from the means of the distribution representing each view are independent, depending on which approach is used to think about subjective views. The appendix gives the formula for the expected excess returns that combine views with equilibrium in the general case.

Now consider our example, in which asset correlations result from the impact of one common factor. In general, we will not know the impacts of the factor on the assets—that is, the values of γ_A, γ_B and γ_C. But suppose the

14 H. Theil, *Principles of Econometrics* (New York: John Wiley and Sons, 1971).

15 F. Black and R. Litterman, "Asset Allocation: Combining Investor Views with Market Equilibrium" (Goldman, Sachs & Co., Sept. 1990).

unknown values are [3, 1, 2]. Suppose further that the independent shocks are small, so that the assets are highly correlated with volatilities approximately in the ratios 3:1:2.

Suppose, for example, the covariance matrix is as follows:

$$\begin{bmatrix} 9.1 & 3.0 & 6.0 \\ 3.0 & 1.1 & 2.0 \\ 6.0 & 2.0 & 4.1 \end{bmatrix}$$

Assume also, for simplicity, that the percentage equilibrium risk premiums are equal—for example, [1, 1, 1]. There is a set of market, capitalizations for which that is the case.

Now consider what happens when the investor expects A to outperform B by 2 percent. In this example, virtually all of the volatility of the assets is associated with movements in the common factor, and the expected return of A exceeds that of B by more than it does in equilibrium. From this, we clearly ought to impute that a shock to the common factor is the most likely reason A will outperform B. If so, C ought to perform better than equilibrium as well. The conditional mean in this case is [3.9, 1.9, 2.9]. Indeed, the investor's view of A relative to B has raised the expected return on C by 1.9 percentage points.

But now suppose the independent shocks have a much larger impact than the common factor. Let the Σ matrix be as follows:

$$\begin{bmatrix} 19.0 & 3.0 & 6.0 \\ 3.0 & 11.0 & 2.0 \\ 6.0 & 2.0 & 14.0 \end{bmatrix}$$

Suppose the equilibrium risk premiums are again given by [1, 1, 1]. Now assume the investor expects that A will outperform B by 2 percent.

This time, more than half of the volatility of A is associated with its own independent shock. Although we should impute some change in the factor from the higher return of A relative to B, the impact on C should be less than in the previous case.

In this case, the conditional mean is [2.3, 0.3, 1.3]. Here the implied effect of the common-factor shock on asset C is lower than in the previous case. We may attribute most of the outperformance of a relative to B to the independent shocks; indeed, the implication for $E[R_B]$ is negative relative to equilibrium. The impact of the independent shock to B is expected to dominate, even though the contribution of the common factor to asset B is positive.

Note that we can identify the impact of the common factor only if we assume that we know the true structure that generated the covariance matrix of returns. That is true here, but it will not be true in general. The computation of the conditional mean, however, does not depend on this special knowledge, but only on the covariance matrix of returns.

Finally, let's look at the case where the investor has less confidence in his view. We might say $(E[R_A] - E[R_B])$ has a mean of 2 and a variance of 1, and the covariance matrix of returns is, as it was originally:

$$\begin{bmatrix} 9.1 & 3.0 & 6.0 \\ 3.0 & 1.1 & 2.0 \\ 6.0 & 2.0 & 4.1 \end{bmatrix}$$

In this example, however, the conditional mean is based on an uncertain view. Using the formula given in the appendix, we find that the conditional mean is given by:

[3.3, 1.7, 2.5].

Because the investor has less confidence in his or her view, the expected relative return of 2 percent for $A - B$ is reduced to a value of 1.6, which is closer to the equilibrium value of 0. There will also be a smaller effect of the common factor on the third asset because of the uncertainty of the view.

Seven-Country Example

Now we will attempt to apply our view that bad news about the U.S. economy will cause U.S. bonds to outperform U.S. stocks to the actual data. The critical difference between our approach here and our earlier experiment that generated Exhibit 34–8 is that here we say something about expected returns on U.S. bonds versus U.S. equities and we allow all other expected excess returns to adjust accordingly. Before we adjusted only the returns to U.S. bonds and U.S. equities, holding fixed all other expected excess returns. Another difference is that here we specify a differential of means, letting the equilibrium determine the actual levels of means; above we had to specify the levels directly.

Exhibit 34–9 shows the complete set of expected excess returns when we put 100 percent confidence in a view that the differential of expected excess returns of U.S. equities over bonds will be 2.0 percentage points below the equilibrium differential of 5.5 percentage points. Exhibit 34–10 shows the optimal portfolio associated with this view.

EXHIBIT 34–9
Expected Excess Annualized Percentage Returns
Combining Investor Views with Equilibrium

	Germany	France	Japan	U.K.	U.S.	Canada	Australia
Currencies	1.32	1.28	1.73	1.22		0.44	0.47
Bonds	2.69	2.39	3.29	3.40	2.39	2.70	1.35
Equities	5.28	6.42	7.71	7.83	4.39	4.58	3.86

EXHIBIT 34–10
Optimal Portfolio Combining Investor Views with Equilibrium

	Germany	France	Japan	U.K.	U.S.	Canada	Australia
Currency Exposure (%)	1.4	1.1	7.4	2.5		0.8	0.3
Bonds (%)	3.6	2.4	7.5	2.3	67.0	1.7	0.3
Equities (%)	3.3	2.9	29.5	10.3	3.3	2.0	1.4

These results contrast with the inexplicable results we saw earlier. We see here a balanced portfolio in which the weights have tilted away from market capitalizations toward U.S. bonds and away from U.S. equities. We now obtain a portfolio that we consider reasonable, given our view.

CONTROLLING THE BALANCE OF A PORTFOLIO

In the previous section, we illustrated how our approach allows us to express a view that U.S. bonds will outperform U.S. equities, in a way that leads to a well-behaved optimal portfolio that expresses that view. In this section we focus more specifically on the concept of a "balanced" portfolio and show an additional feature of our approach: Changes in the "confidence" in views can be used to control the balance of the optimal portfolio.

We start by illustrating what happens when we put a set of stronger views, shown in Exhibit 34–11 into our model. These happen to have been the short-term interest rate and exchange rate views expressed by Goldman

EXHIBIT 34–11
Economists' Views

	Germany	France	Japan	U.K.	U.S.	Canada	Australia
Currencies							
July 31, 1991							
Current Spot Rates	1.743	5.928	137.3	1.688		1.151	1.285
Three-Month Horizon Expected Future Spot	1.790	6.050	141.0	1.640	1.000	1.156	1.324
Annualized Expected Excess Returns	−7.48	−4.61	−8.85	−6.16		0.77	−8.14
Interest Rates							
July 31, 1991 Benchmark Bond Yields	8.7	9.3	6.6	10.2	8.2	9.9	11.0
Three-Month Horizon Expected Future Yields	8.8	9.5	6.5	10.1	8.4	10.1	10.8
Annualized Expected Excess Returns	−3.31	−5.31	1.78	1.66	−3.03	−3.48	5.68

Sachs economists on July 31, 1991.[16] We put 100 percent confidence in these views, solve for the expected excess returns on all assets, and find the optimal portfolio, shown in Exhibit 34–12. Given such strong views on so many assets, and optimizing without constraints, we generate a rather extreme portfolio.

Analysts have tried a number of approaches to ameliorate this problem. Some put constraints on many of the asset weights. We resist using such artificial constraints. When asset weights run up against constraints, the portfolio optimization no longer balances return and risk across all assets.

Others specify a **benchmark portfolio** and limit the risk relative to the benchmark until a reasonably balanced portfolio is obtained. This makes sense if the objective of the optimization is to manage the portfolio relative

---

16 For details of these views, see the following Goldman Sachs publications: *The International Fixed Income Analyst* Aug. 2, 1991, for interest rates and *The International Economics Analyst* July/Aug. 1991, for exchange rates.

EXHIBIT 34–12
Optimal (Unconstrained) Portfolio Based on Economists' Views

	Germany	France	Japan	U.K.	U.S.	Canada	Australia
Currency Exposure (%)	16.3	68.8	–35.2	–12.7		29.7	–51.4
Bonds (%)	34.5	–65.4	79.2	16.9	3.3	–22.7	108.3
Equities (%)	–2.2	0.6	6.6	0.7	3.6	5.2	0.5

to a benchmark.[17] We are uncomfortable when it is used simply to make the model better behaved.

An alternative response when the optimal portfolio seems too extreme is to consider reducing the confidence expressed in some or all of the views. Exhibit 34–13 shows the optimal portfolio that results when we lower the confidence in all of our views. By putting less confidence in our views, we generate a set of expected excess returns that more strongly reflect equilibrium. This pulls the optimal portfolio weights toward a more balanced position.

We define balance as a measure of how similar a portfolio is to the **global equilibrium portfolio**—that is, the market-capitalization portfolio with 80 percent of the currency risk hedged. The distance measure we use is the volatility of the difference between the returns on the two portfolios.

We find this property of balance to be a useful supplement to the standard measures of portfolio optimization, expected return and risk. In our approach, for any given level of risk there will be a continuum of portfolios that maximize expected return depending on the relative levels of confidence that are expressed in the views. The less confidence the investor has, the more balanced his or her portfolio will be.

Suppose an investor does not have equal confidence in all his or her views. If the investor is willing to rank the relative confidence levels of his or her different views, then the investor can generate an even more powerful result. In this case, the model will move away from strongly held views more quickly than from the more strongly held ones.

We have specified higher confidence in our view of yield declines in the United Kingdom and yield increases in France and Germany. These are not

---

17 We discuss this situation later.

EXHIBIT 34–13
Optimal Portfolio with Less Confidence in the Economists' Views

	Germany	France	Japan	U.K.	U.S.	Canada	Australia
Currency Exposure (%)	−12.9	−3.5	−10.0	−6.9		−0.4	−17.9
Bonds (%)	−3.9	−21.0	19.6	2.6	7.3	−13.6	42.4
Equities (%)	0.8	2.2	24.7	7.1	26.6	4.2	1.2

EXHIBIT 34–14
Optimal Portfolio with Less Confidence in Certain Views

	Germany	France	Japan	U.K.	U.S.	Canada	Australia
Currency Exposure (%)	−10.0	−0.4	−4.8	−2.8		−6.2	−7.8
Bonds (%)	−10.3	−34.3	25.5	1.6	22.9	−2.4	28.1
Equities (%)	0.1	2.3	25.9	7.0	26.3	6.0	1.3

the biggest yield changes that we expect, but they are the forecasts that we most strongly want to represent in our portfolio. We put less confidence in our views of interest rate moves in the United States and Australia.

When we put equal confidence in our views, we obtained the optimal portfolio shown in Exhibit 34–13. The view that dominated that portfolio was the interest rate decline in Australia. Now, when we put less than 100 percent confidence in our views, we have relatively more confidence in some views than in others. Exhibit 34–14 shows the optimal portfolio for this case.

BENCHMARKS

One of the most important, but often overlooked, influences on the asset allocation decision is the choice of the benchmark by which to measure risk. In mean-variance optimization, the objective is to maximize return per unit of portfolio risk. The investor's benchmark defines the point of origin for measuring this risk. In other words, it represents the minimum-risk portfolio.

In many investment problems, risk is measured as the volatility of the portfolio's excess returns. This is equivalent to having no benchmark, or to defining the benchmark as a portfolio 100 percent invested in the domestic short-term interest rate. In many cases, however, an alternative benchmark is called for.

Many portfolio managers are given an explicit performance benchmark, such as a market-capitalization-weighted index. If an explicit performance benchmark exists, then the appropriate measure of risk for the purpose of portfolio optimization is the volatility of the tracking error of the portfolio vis-à-vis the benchmark. And for a manager funding a known set of liabilities, the appropriate benchmark portfolio represents the liabilities.

For many portfolio managers, the performance objective is less explicit, and the asset allocation decision is therefore more difficult. For example, a global equity portfolio manager may feel his or her objective is to perform in the top rankings of all global equity managers. Although the manager does not have an explicit performance benchmark, his or her risk is clearly related to the stance of the portfolio relative to the portfolios of competitors.

Other examples are an over-funded pension plan or a university endowment where matching the measurable liability is only a small part of the total investment objective. In these types of situations, attempts to use quantitative approaches are often frustrated by the ambiguity of the investment objective.

When an explicit benchmark does not exist, two alternative approaches can be used. The first is to use the volatility of excess returns as the measure of risk. The second is to specify a **"normal" portfolio** one that represents the desired allocation of assets in the absence of views. Such a portfolio might, for example, be designed with a higher-than-market weight for domestic assets in order to represent the domestic nature of liabilities without attempting to specify an explicit liability benchmark.

An equilibrium model can help in the design of a normal portfolio by quantifying some of the risk and return trade-offs in the absence of views. The optimal portfolio in equilibrium is market-capitalization-weighted and is 80 percent currency hedged. It has an expected excess return (using equilibrium risk premiums) of 5.7 percent and an annualized volatility of 10.7 percent.

A pension fund wishing to increase the domestic weight of its portfolio to 85 percent from the current market capitalization of 45 percent, and not wishing to hedge the currency risk of the remaining 15 percent in international markets, might consider an alternative portfolio such as the one

EXHIBIT 34–15
Alternative Domestic-Weighted Benchmark Portfolio

	Germany	France	Japan	U.K.	U.S.	Canada	Australia
Currency							
Exposure (%)	1.5	1.5	7.0	3.0		2.0	0.0
Bonds (%)	0.5	0.5	2.0	1.0	30.0	1.0	0.0
Equities (%)	1.0	1.0	5.0	2.0	55.0	1.0	0.0

shown in Exhibit 34–15. The higher domestic weights lead to an annualized volatility 0.4 percentage points higher than and an expected excess return 30 basis points below those of the optimal portfolio. The pension fund may or may not feel that its preference for domestic concentration is worth those costs.

IMPLIED VIEWS

Once an investor has established his or her objectives, an asset allocation model establishes a correspondence between views and optimal portfolios. Rather than treating a quantitative model as a black box, successful portfolio managers use a model to investigate the nature of this relationship. In particular, it is often useful to start an analysis by using a model to find the implied investor views for which an existing portfolio is optimal relative to a benchmark.

For example, we assume a portfolio manager has a portfolio with weights as shown in Exhibit 34–16. The weights, relative to those of his or her benchmark, define the directions of the investor's views. By assuming the investor's degree of risk aversion, we can find the expected excess returns for which the portfolio is optimal.

In this type of analysis, different benchmarks may imply very different views for a given portfolio. Exhibit 34–17 shows the implied views of the portfolio shown in Exhibit 34–16, given that the benchmark is, alternatively, (1) a market-capitalization-weighted portfolio, 80 percent hedged, or (2) the domestic-weighted alternative shown in Exhibit 34–15. Unless a portfolio manager has thought carefully about what his or her benchmark is and where the allocations are relative to it, and has conducted the type of analysis shown here, he or she may not have a clear idea of what views the portfolio represents.

EXHIBIT 34–16
Current Portfolio Weights for Implied-View Analysis

	Germany	France	Japan	U.K.	U.S.	Canada	Australia
Currency							
Exposure (%)	4.4	3.4	2.0	2.2		2.0	5.5
Bonds (%)	1.0	0.5	4.7	2.5	13.0	0.3	3.5
Equities (%)	3.4	2.9	22.3	10.2	32.0	1.7	2.0

EXHIBIT 34–17
Annualized Expected Excess Returns Implied by a Given Portfolio

	Germany	France	Japan	U.K	U.S.	Canada	Australia
Views Relative to the Market-Capitalization Benchmark							
Currencies	1.55	1.82	−0.27	1.22		0.63	2.45
Bonds	0.30	−0.30	−0.58	1.03	−0.13	−0.01	1.22
Equities	2.82	3.97	−0.30	6.73	4.15	5.01	5.88
Views Relative to the Domestic-Weighted Benchmark							
Currencies	0.05	0.20	0.50	0.54		0.01	0.90
Bonds	−0.01	0.21	0.72	0.85	−1.45	−1.01	0.18
Equities	2.24	2.83	5.24	4.83	−1.49	0.28	2.38

QUANTIFYING THE BENEFITS OF GLOBAL DIVERSIFICATION

While most investors demonstrate a substantial bias toward domestic assets, many recent studies have documented a rapid growth in the international components of portfolios worldwide. It is perhaps not surprising, then, that investment advisers have started to question the traditional arguments that support global diversification. This has been particularly true in the United States, where global portfolios have tended to underperform domestic portfolios in recent years.

Of course, what matters for investors is the prospective returns from international assets, and as noted in our discussion of neutral views, the historical returns are of virtually no value in projecting future expected excess returns. Historical analyses continue to be used in this context simply

EXHIBITS 34–18
The Value of Global Diversification
(expected excess returns in equilibrium at a constant 10.7% risk)

	Domestic	Global	Basis-Point Difference	Percentage Gain
Without Currency Hedging				
Bonds Only	2.14	2.63	49	22.9
Equities Only	4.72	5.48	76	16.1
Bonds and Equities	4.76	5.50	74	15.5
With Currency Hedging				
Bonds Only	2.14	3.20	106	49.5
Equities Only	4.72	5.56	84	17.8
Bonds and Equities	4.76	5.61	85	17.9

because investment advisers argue there is nothing better to measure the value of global diversification.

We would suggest that there is something better. A reasonable measure of the value of global diversification is the degree to which allowing foreign assets into a portfolio raises the optimal portfolio frontier. A natural starting point for quantifying this value is to compute it based on the neutral views implied by a global CAPM equilibrium.

There are some limitations to using this measure. It assumes that there are no extra costs to international investment; thus relaxing the constraint against international investment cannot make the investor *worse* off. On the other hand, in measuring the value of global diversification this way, we are also assuming that markets are efficient and therefore we are neglecting to capture any value that an international portfolio manager might add through having informed views about these markets. We suspect that an important benefit of international investment that we are missing here is the freedom it gives the portfolio manager to take advantage of a larger number of opportunities to add value than are afforded by domestic markets alone.

We use the equilibrium concept here to calculate the value of global diversification for a bond portfolio, an equity portfolio and a portfolio containing both bond and equities (in each case both with and without allowing currency hedging). We normalize the portfolio volatilities at 10.7 percent–the volatility of the market-capitalization-weighted portfolio, 80 percent hedged. Exhibit 34–18 shows the additional return available from including international assets relative to the optimal domestic portfolio with the same degree of risk.

What is clear from Exhibit 34–18 is that global diversification provides a substantial increase in expected return for the domestic bond portfolio manager, both in absolute and percentage terms. The gains for an equity manager, or a portfolio manager with both bonds and equities, are also substantial, although much smaller as a percentage of the excess returns of the domestic portfolio. These results also appear to provide a justification for the common practice of bond portfolio managers to hedge currency risk and of equity portfolio managers not to hedge. In the absence of currency views, the gains to currency hedging are clearly more important in both absolute and relative terms for fixed-income investors.

HISTORICAL SIMULATIONS

It is natural to ask how a model such as ours would have performed in simulations. However, our approach does not in itself produce investment strategies. It requires a set of views; any simulation is a test not only of the model but also of the strategy producing the views.

One strategy that is fairly well known in the investment world and has performed quite well in recent years, is to invest funds in high-yielding currencies. Below, we show how a quantitative model such as ours can be used to optimize such a strategy. In particular, we will compare the historical performance of a strategy of investing in high-yielding currencies with two other strategies: (1) investing in the bonds of countries with high bond yields and (2) investing in the equities of countries with high ratios of dividend yield to bond yield.

Our purpose is to illustrate how a quantitative approach can be used to make a useful comparison of alternative investment strategies. We are not trying to promote or justify a particular strategy. We have chosen to focus on these three primarily because they are simple, relatively comparable, and representative of standard investment approaches.

Our simulations of all three strategies use the same basic methodology, the same data, and the same underlying securities. The strategies differ in the sources of views about excess returns and in the assets to which those views are applied. All the simulations use our approach of adjusting expected excess returns away from the global equilibrium as a function of investor views.

In each of the simulations, we test a strategy by performing the following steps. Starting in July 1981 and continuing each month for the next 10 years, we use data up to that point in time to estimate a covariance matrix of returns on equities, bonds, and currencies. We compute the equilibrium risk premiums, add views according to the particular strategy, and calculate the set of expected excess returns for all securities based on combining views with equilibrium.

We then optimize the equity, bond and currency weights for a given level of risk with no constraints on the portfolio weights. We calculate the excess returns that would have accrued in that month. At the end of each month, we update the data and repeat the calculation. At the end of 10 years, we compute the cumulative excess returns for each of the three strategies and compare them with one another and with several passive investments.

The views for the three strategies represent very different information but are generated using similar approaches. In simulations of the high-yielding currency strategy, our views are based on the assumption that the expected excess returns from holding a foreign currency are above their equilibrium value by an amount equal to the forward discount on that currency.

For example, if the equilibrium risk premium on yen, from a U.S. dollars perspective, is 1 percent and the forward discount (which, because of covered interest rate parity, approximately equals the difference between the short rate on yen-denominated deposits and the short rate on dollar-denominated deposits) is 2 percent, then we assume the expected excess return on yen currency exposures to be 3 percent. We compute expected excess returns on bonds and equities by adjusting their returns away from equilibrium in a manner consistent with 100 percent confidence in the currency views.

In simulations of a strategy of investing in fixed-income markets with high yields, we generate views by assuming that expected excess returns on bonds are above their equilibrium values by an amount equal to the difference between the bond-equivalent yield in that country and the global market-capitalization-weighted average bond-equivalent yield.

For example, if the equilibrium risk premium on bonds in a given country is 1 percent and the yield on the 10-year benchmark bond is 2 percentage points above the world average yield, then we assume the expected excess return for bonds in that country to be 3 percent. We compute expected excess returns on currencies and equities by assuming 100 percent confidence in these views and adjusting returns away from equilibrium in the appropriate manner.

EXHIBIT 34–19
Historical Cumulative Monthly Returns
U.S.-Dollar-Based Perspective

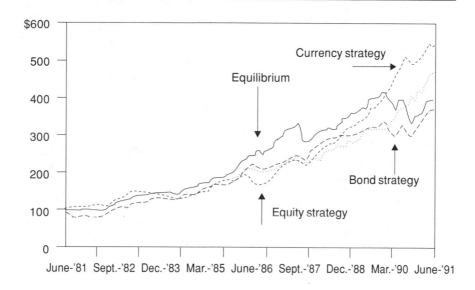

In simulations of a strategy of investing in equity markets with high ratios of dividend yield to bond yield, we generate views by assuming that expected excess returns on equities are above their equilibrium values by an amount equal to 50 times the difference between the ratio of dividend to bond yield in that country and the global market-capitalization-weighted average ratio of dividend to bond yield.

For example, if the equilibrium risk premium on equities in a given country is 6.0 percent and the dividend to bond yield ratio is 0.5 with a world average ratio of 0.4, then we assume the expected excess return for equities in that country to be 11 percent. We compute expected excess returns on currencies and bonds by assuming 100 percent confidence in these views for equities and adjusting the returns away from equilibrium in the appropriate manner.

Exhibits 34–19 and 34–20 show the results graphically. The former compares the cumulative value of $100 invested in each of the three strategies as well as in the equilibrium portfolio, which is a global market portfolio of equities and bonds, with 80 percent currency hedging. The

EXHIBIT 34–20
Historical Risk/Return Trade-Offs, July 1981–August 1991

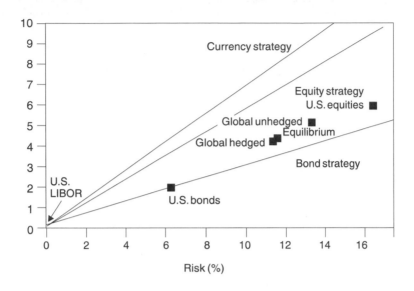

strategies were structured to have risk equal to that of the equilibrium portfolio. While Exhibit 34–19 gives a clear picture of the relative performances of the different strategies, it cannot easily convey the trade-off between risk and return that can be obtained by taking a more or less aggressive position for any given strategy.

Exhibit 34–20 makes such a comparison. Because the simulations have no constraints on asset weights, the risk/return trade-offs obtained by combining the simulation portfolios with cash are linear and define the appropriate frontier for each strategy. We show each frontier, together with the risk/return positions of several benchmark portfolios—domestic bond and equity portfolios, the equilibrium portfolio, and global market-capitalization-weighted bond and equity portfolios with and without currency hedging.

What we find is that strategies of investing in high-yielding currencies and in the equity markets of countries with high ratios of dividend yields to bond yields have performed remarkably well over the past 10 years. By contrast, a strategy of investing in high-yielding bond markets has not added value. Although past performance is certainly no guarantee of future performance, we believe that these results, and those of similar experiments with other strategies, suggest some interesting lines of inquiry.

CONCLUSION

Quantitative asset allocation models have not played the important role that they should in global portfolio management. We suspect that a good part of the problem has been that users of these models have found them difficult to use and badly behaved.

We have learned that the inclusion of a global CAPM equilibrium with equities, bonds, and currencies can significantly improve the behavior of these models. In particular, it allows us to distinguish between the views of the investor and the set of expected excess returns used to drive the portfolio optimization. This distinction in our approach allows us to generate optimal portfolios that start at a set of neutral weights and then tilt in the direction of the investor's views. By adjusting the confidence in his or her views, the investor can control how strongly the views influence the portfolio weights. Similarly, by specifying a ranking of confidence in different views, the investor can control which views are expressed most strongly in the portfolio. The investor can express views about the relative performance of assets as well as their absolute performance.

We hope that our series of examples—designed to illustrate the insights that quantitative modeling can provide—will stimulate investment managers to consider, or perhaps to reconsider, the application of such modeling to their own portfolios.

Appendix A

1. n assets—bonds, equities, and currencies—are indexed by:

$i = 1, ..., n$

2. For bonds and equities, the market capitalization is given by M_i.
3. Market weights of the n assets are given by the vector:

$W = \{W_1, ..., W_n\}$

We define the $W_i s$ as follows:

If asset i is a bond or equity:

$$W_i = \frac{M_i}{\sum_i M_i}$$

If asset i is a currency of the ith country:

$$W_i = \lambda W_i C$$

where $W_i C$ is the country weight (the sum of market weights for bonds and equities in the ith country) and λ is the universal hedging constant.

4. Assets' excess returns are given by a vector:

$$R = \{R_1, ..., R_n\}$$

5. Assets' excess returns are normally distributed with a covariance matrix Σ.

6. The equilibrium-risk-premiums vector Π is given by

$$\Pi = \delta \Sigma W$$

where δ is a proportionality constant based on the formulas in Black.

7. The expected excess return, $E[R]$, is unobservable. It is assumed to have a probability distribution that is proportional to a product of two normal distributions. The first distribution represents equilibrium; it is centered at Π with a covariance matrix $\tau \Sigma$, where τ is a constant. The second distribution represents the investor's views about k linear combinations of the elements of $E[R]$. These views are expressed in the following form:

$$PE[R] = Q + \varepsilon$$

Here P is a known $k \bullet n$ matrix, Q is a k-dimensional vector, and ε is an unobservable normally distributed random vector with zero mean and a diagonal covariance matrix Ω.

8. The resulting distribution for $E[R]$ is normal with a mean $E[R]$:

$$E[R] = [(\tau\Sigma)^{-1} + P'\Omega^{-1}P]^{-1}$$

$$[(\tau\Sigma^{-1}\Pi + P'\Omega^{-1}Q].$$

In portfolio optimization, we use $E[R]$ as the vector of expected excess returns.

Glossary

asset excess returns In this chapter, returns on assets less the domestic short rate (see formulas in footnote 5).

balance A measure of how close a portfolio is to the equilibrium portfolio.

benchmark portfolio The standard used to define the risk of other portfolios. If a benchmark is defined, the risk of a portfolio is measured as the volatility of the tracking error—the difference between the portfolio's returns and those of the benchmark.

currency excess returns Returns on forward contracts (see formulas in footnote 5).

equilibrium The condition in which means (see below) equilibrate the demand for assets with the outstanding supply.

equilibrium portfolio The portfolio held in equilibrium; in this article, market capitalization weights, 80 percent currency hedged.

expected excess returns Expected values of the distribution of future excess returns.

means Expected excess returns.

neutral portfolio An optimal portfolio given neutral views.

neutral views Means when the investor has no views.

normal portfolio The portfolio that an investor feels comfortable with when he or she has no views. The investor can use the normal portfolio to infer a benchmark when no explicit benchmark exists.

risk premiums Means implied by the equilibrium model.

Chapter Thirty-Five

Opportunities for Hedging and Trading with Catastrophe Insurance Futures and Options

Joseph B. Cole and Richard L. Sandor
Centre Financial Products Limited

Not since the introduction of GNMA and T-bill futures has the futures market traded such an innovative and exciting hedging and trading instrument as the Chicago Board of Trade's (CBOT) catastrophe insurance contract. This contract offers traders the opportunity to participate in the convergence of the financial and insurance markets through novel hedging and trading strategies. Moreover, this instrument represents a true "zero-beta" asset for investors and commodity funds managers for the purposes of portfolio diversification.

This chapter will begin with a brief description of the property reinsurance market. The subsequent section provides an overview of CBOT contract specifications and illustrates the hedging and trading uses of this new instrument through several examples. The last section discusses of the zero-beta characteristics of catastrophe futures and options and offers suggestions for study and further research.

Reinsurance is utilized by insurers to reduce volatility in operating results, increase capacity, and provide financing. The relationship between insurance and reinsurance may be illustrated by the schematic in Exhibit 35–1. The primary insurance market is characterized by the sale of insurance

EXHIBIT 35–1
The Insurance, Reinsurance, and Retrocession Markets

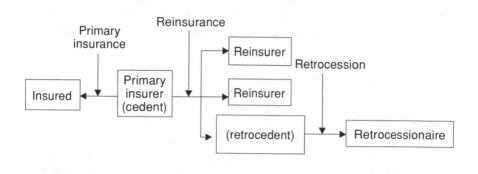

policies, such as automobile or homeowners policies, from a primary insurer to the insured. Primary insurers may "cede" or pass on some or all of the insurance risk to another insurer, called the reinsurer. Reinsurers, in turn, may retrocede or pass on portions of their reinsurance risk to other insurers called retrocessionaires. Similar to "forward contracting," the market for reinsurance generally consists of bilateral contracts which are negotiated individually between the reinsured and reinsurer and are sometimes facilitated by a reinsurance broker. The market for catastrophe reinsurance enables insurers to hedge against catastrophic losses and to more effectively manage their finances, thereby reducing earnings volatility and optimizing the use of capital.

Placement of reinsurance is usually done on a treaty or facultative basis. Treaty reinsurance for property risks can be written on either a proportional (prorata) or nonproportional (excess) basis. In either case, the ceding insurer and the reinsurer agree on what types of risks are covered by the reinsurance. In contrast, facultative reinsurance often involves one certain type of risk or one specific policy. Accordingly, catastrophe reinsurance is often provided on a treaty basis since it is designed to provide the reinsured broad coverage against an accumulation of losses.

Nonproportional treaties have many characteristics that are similar to option hedging strategies. A "stop-loss" cover, for instance, provides a ceding company with protection above an agreed-upon dollar amount or ratio of losses and, thus, is similar to the purchase of a call option. An excess-of-loss treaty insures the reinsured for a stated amount of protection above an agreed upon retention amount. For example, a $10 million excess of $30 million loss treaty would require the reinsurer to pay up to, but no more than, $10 million of additional losses beyond the initial $30 million in losses retained by the reinsured. Thus, an excess-of-loss policy is similar to a call option spread where the reinsured is long a "$30 million/$40 million bull call option spread" relative to claims payments.

Although reinsurance treaties are written and purchased to control losses, they cannot prevent them. The severe catastrophic losses of the last four years has had a substantial impact on the earnings and surplus positions of many property insurers. Industries that experience a high degree of stress in the form of earning volatility and increased risks often respond in three ways. First, since higher risks often mean rewards, new entrants are attracted to the industry through capital infusions or new start-up companies. Second, standardization and commoditization occur in the industry's products, increasing homogeneity and the trading and transfer of risks. Third, efficient hedging mechanisms and risk management tools are developed.

The property reinsurance industry is exhibiting all three of these responses. During the 12 months following Hurricane Andrew, over $3 billion of new capital was raised for property insurance companies, mostly in the form of offshore reinsurance entities. Some evidence of reinsurance standardization may also be found in the increasing use of industry loss warranties that employ indexes or measures of industry catastrophic losses for the purposes of "double trigger" reinsurance treaties and other nontraditional covers. The third response, the development and use of efficient hedging mechanisms, is the topic of this chapter.

THE FUTURES CONTRACT

Catastrophe insurance futures and options contracts started trading on December 11, 1992, at the Chicago Board of Trade. Generally, a futures contract is a standardized agreement to buy or sell a financial instrument or commodity on an organized exchange at some time in the future for a price agreed upon today. The basis for the catastrophe insurance futures is an index tracking the losses of approximately 25 (minimum of 10) property/casualty insurers who report their data to ISO Data, Inc. (Isodata), an independent data collection agency. Exhibit 35–2 presents the current composition of contributing insurers who collectively represent about 23 percent of the U.S. property insurance industry.

EXHIBIT 35-2
The Board of Trade of the City of Chicago:
Catastrophe Futures Included Insurers for Quarterly Contracts
(Covering Accident Quarters (Q1 '94–Q4 '94))

American Financial Group	Kemper Corporation/Group
AMICA Mutual Insurance Group	Kemper National Insurance
CIGNA Group	Companies
CNA Insurance Companies	Liberty Mutual Group
Commercial Union Insurance	Lincoln National Group
Companies	Royal Insurance Group
Continental Insurance Companies	Safeco Insurance Group
Employers Mutual Companies	St. Paul Group
Fireman's Fund Companies	Transamerica Corporation Group
General Accident Group	United States F&G Group
Hanover Insurance Group	USAA Group
ITT Hartford Group	Westfield Companies
	Zurich Insurance Group—U.S.

Source: CBOT

As with other futures contracts, the catastrophe insurance futures contracts may only be traded by qualified futures commission merchants (FCMs) on the floors of exchanges regulated by, Commodity Futures Trading Commission (CFTC). An initial margin must be posted; thereafter, each counterparty is responsible for a daily variation margin representing the change in value of the futures position, otherwise known as the mark to market. The contract has a cash settlement because the underlying instrument, the index value, cannot be physically delivered. The Board of Trade Clearing Corporation (BOTCC) acts as the ultimate guarantor of all trades, ensuring the creditworthiness of the counterparties. Overall, these strict rules permit insurers and reinsurers to hedge the systematic risk component of their insurance liabilities as related to the index compiled by Isodata.

The primary purpose of using catastrophe insurance futures and options is to provide more effective risk management to insurers facing potentially large payouts in the property line of insurance. The Eastern, Midwestern, Western, and National catastrophe futures and options contracts are now available and trading. Each contract's underlying index, as reported by Isodata, takes into account losses caused by the following: earthquake, flood, hail, riot, and wind across applicable lines as shown in Exhibit 35–3.

EXHIBIT 35–3
Catastrophe Futures Contracts

Applicable Lines	Wind	Hail	Earthquake	Riot	Flood
Homeowners	◆	◆			
Earthquake			◆		
Fire	◆	◆		◆[1]	
Allied	◆	◆		◆[1]	
PP auto physical damage	◆	◆	◆	◆	◆
Commercial auto physical damage		◆	◆	◆	◆
Farm owners	◆	◆		◆	
Inland marine	◆[1]	◆[1]	◆[1]		◆
Commercial multiple peril	◆	◆		◆	

[1] Commercial portion only.
Source: CBOT

As shown in Exhibit 35–4, the futures index value is calculated by multiplying the $25,000 unit of trading by the incurred catastrophic losses "standardized" by the earned property premium. Thus, the futures value represents, in essence, an industry loss ratio multiplied by $25,000 of "coverage." It is important to note that the changes in futures prices will be mostly due to unexpected catastrophic losses, since the premium is established, or fixed, in advance and therefore only the numerator is uncertain. Exhibit 35–5 presents the estimated quarterly premiums assumed for each of the four contract regions.

Exhibit 35–6 presents calculation and settlement methods for the catastrophe futures contracts. Three important time periods occur during the trading cycle of a CBOT catastrophe contract. The "loss period" encompasses the quarter one full quarter before the contract date. The "reporting period" spans the six-month period that includes the loss quarter and the quarter following the contract date. The "calculation period" comprises the three months and five calendar days following the reporting period. Cash settlement of the futures and options contract occurs at the end of the calculation period.

In the case of the March 1994 contract, trading began on October 6, 1993, and will continue until cash settlement on October 5, 1994. The loss period for this contract is the first quarter of 1994, or from January 1, 1994 through March 31, 1994. Isodata calculations employ losses that occur in this loss

EXHIBIT 35–4
Catastrophe Insurance Futures Index Value
(Unit of Trading)

= $25,000 × (Incurred Catastrophic Losses/Earned Property Premium)

Incurred Catastrophic Losses
Total losses reported as incurred at the end of the quarter following the catastrophe quarter.

Earned Property Premium
Estimated quarterly premium based on the most recent statutory annual statements filed by the reporting companies.

Source: CBOT

EXHIBIT 35–5
Estimated Premiums of Catastrophe Futures Contract Regions

	1993 Contracts[1]	1994 Contracts[2]
National	$12,242,060,112	$12,984,325,717
Eastern	$5,718,769,160	$6,052,961,404
Midwestern	$3,968,805,577	$4,237,619,841
Western	$2,848,444,165	$3,006,003,081

For Settlement Value of CBOT Contracts

[1] 1993: March, June, September, December (March '94 Renamed)
[2] 1994: March, June, September, December
Source: Chicago Board of Trade

period and are reported for the six months including the loss period and three months following the contract date, in this case, January 1, 1994, through June 30, 1994. The reporting period spans six months because of the time consumed filing claims and assessing damages. After losses are incurred during the loss period and filed during the reporting period, Isodata calculates, compiles, and issues the final settlement price three months and five calendar days after the month.

EXHIBIT 35–6
Catastrophe Futures Time Line Calculations and Trading Schedule

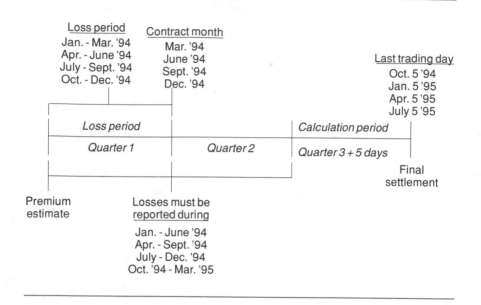

A Futures Hedging Example

Suppose an insurance company is interested in hedging third quarter '93 catastrophic losses in the Eastern region. An effective way of doing so would be to purchase September Eastern catastrophe futures sometime in July. Details of this sample hedge are shown in Exhibit 35–7. The hedge would be undertaken to lessen the financial impact on the company during summer months when hurricanes frequently come ashore. Assume that the company has $28.5 million in Eastern region premiums for 0.5 percent market share. Actuarial estimates for the company's third quarter losses are $10.0 million while industry premium and loss estimates are $5.7 billion and $2.0 billion, respectively.

The September contract price in July may be calculated by dividing industry estimated and reported losses by the CBOT Eastern catastrophe contract premium. Assuming 75 percent of the industry's $2 billion in losses are employed by Isodata to calculate the estimated settlement price, a hypothetical September Eastern futures price of $6,575 would result. To hedge $28.5 million of insurance premiums, the insurer would need to buy 1,520 contracts.

EXHIBIT 35–7
Company XX Hedging Strategy

- ♦   Limit the impact of catastrophic losses due to the frequency and severity of hurricanes, which commonly occur in August and September on the eastern seaboard.
- ♦   Early July: By September Eastern Catastrophe Futures

Actuarial Forecasts: Catastrophe Quarter July-September

	Company XX	*Industry*
Incurred losses	$10.0 million	$2.0 billion
Premiums	$28.5 million	$5.7 billion
Percent of incurred losses reported by September 30	75%	75%

Price of September Futures
(In July)

$25,000 × (Industry Estimated Loss/Industry Estimated Premium)
$25,000 × ([$2.0 billion × 75%]/$5.7 billion) = $6,575

Number of Contracts Company XX Needs to Buy

([Company Premium/Contract Size] × [Hedged Losses/% Reported])
([$28.5 million/$25,000] × [1.00/0.75]) = 1,520 contracts

September Eastern Catastrophe Final Settlement Price
(In March)

$25,000 × (Industry Reported Losses/Industry Estimated Premium)
$25,000 × [($3 Billion × 75%)/$5.7 Billion] = $9,875

Evaluating Company XX's Hedge

3rd Quarter Results	
Expected incurred results	$10,000,000
Actual losses incurred	15,000,000
Increase in losses:	$ 5,000,000
Futures Results	
Purchased September futures @	$ 6,575
September futures settlement @	9,875
Futures gain per contract:	$ 3,300
Contracts purchased:	× 1,520
Total futures gain:	$ 5,016,000

Now, assume that on the last day of trading, April 5, 1994, the industry reported losses equaling $3.0 billion and that 75 percent were reported and entered in the Isodata calculations. The final settlement price of the contract would thus be $9,875 ($25,000 × ([$3.0 billion × 75%]/$5.7 billion). Given the company's 0.5 percent market share, third quarter property claims would be approximately $15.0 million. Upon evaluation of the hedge, it is evident that without the futures position, the company's actual incurred losses would have exceeded expected incurred losses by $5,000,000. The futures gain of $3,300 per contract would result in a total futures gain of $5,016,000, thereby offsetting unanticipated losses of $5,000,000 by almost $16,000 for a small basis gain.

CALCULATING A HEDGING LAYER FOR SYNTHETIC REINSURANCE

The catastrophe insurance options contracts at the Chicago Board of Trade (CBOT) may also be employed by insurers and reinsurers to create synthetic excess-of-loss reinsurance policies. The following example, summarized in Exhibits 35–8 and 35–9, illustrates the calculations and assumptions necessary for an insurer creating a synthetic excess-of-loss reinsurance policy.

The objective of the insurer is to hedge $40 million of loss exposure above $40 million in losses. In other words, the insurer wishes to hedge the $40 million to $80 million layer of potential underwriting losses. The insurer's book of insurance is assumed to be fairly similar (correlation of 100 percent) in terms of line and region to the CBOT National catastrophe futures contract. The insurer also has a 2 percent market share of industry.

Due to contract design and specifications, not all of the industry's ultimate loss for a catastrophe in a given quarter are "passed through" to the futures contract. As shown in Exhibit 35–9, quarterly industry losses are assumed to be incurred and reported at 75 percent of the ultimate industry loss. By dividing these reported losses by the National contract premium of $12.2 billion, a range of loss ratios given various quarterly catastrophe totals may be computed. This range is further adjusted upward by 5 percent since the calculation procedure performed by Isodata for the CBOT settlement prices introduces normal quarterly losses of a like amount. This 5 percent "normal loss load" occurs since Isodata employs a calculation method that incorporates losses by state and line, which may include incidental losses

EXHIBIT 35–8
Calculating the Hedging Layer for a Synthetic Reinsurance Contract

Objective:	An insurance (reinsurance) company wishes to hedge $40 million in exposure above $40 million in returned losses.
Assumptions:	Company has 2 percent market share on National basis.
	Correlation between company and industry losses is 100 percent.
	75 percent of National incurred and reported losses impact. settlement prices of CBOT catastrophe futures contracts.
	Normal or average quarterly losses at 5 percent influence CBOT catastrophe futures settlement prices.
Solution:	$40MM excess $40MM coverage is approximated by 17 percent/30 percent bull call option spread.

EXHIBIT 35–9
Calculating the Hedging Layer for a Synthetic Reinsurance Contract

Industry Ultimate Loss ($billions)	CBOT Catastrophe Futures			Company Market Share Losses ($millions)
	Reported Loss (×0.75)	Reported Loss Ratio (/$12.2 billion)	CBOT Strike (+5%)	
1.00	0.75	6.1%	11.1%	20
2.00	1.50	12.3	17.3	40
3.00	2.25	18.4	23.4	60
4.00	3.00	24.6	29.6	80
5.00	3.75	30.7	35.7	100
6.00	4.50	36.9	41.9	120
7.00	5.25	43.0	48.0	140
8.00	6.00	49.2	54.2	160
9.00	6.75	55.3	60.3	180
10.00	7.50	61.5	66.5	200

not associated with large industry catastrophes as defined by Property Claim Services.

An examination of Exhibit 35–9 shows that an insurer with a 2 percent market share would experience $40 million in losses when the industry incurs $2 billion in losses. The appropriate "attachment points" for the company's $40 million to $80 million loss layer are approximately 17 percent and 30 percent. To hedge this layer, the insurer would simultaneously buy 17 percent strike call options and sell 30 percent strike call options. The 17 percent/30 percent bull call option spread would "mirror" industry losses of $2 to $4 billion and, by assumption, the company's $40 million of exposure above $40 million in returned losses.

CALCULATING EXPECTED WIN/LOSS RATIOS FOR 60/80 "HURRICANE" OPTION SPREADS

In addition to creating novel hedging strategies, the new Chicago Board of Trade's insurance futures and options are providing unique trading opportunities. Trading activity in "hurricane" option spreads is spurring additional study by speculators and traders. Specifically, the five-to-one risk/reward ratio of the Eastern September 60/80 bear call spread appears to offer substantial opportunities for profit with limited risk.

As discussed earlier, the CBOT's catastrophe insurance futures contracts are designed to track quarterly catastrophic loss ratios for the property insurance industry. The September 1994 Eastern catastrophe contract is based, for example, on insured losses incurred during July 1, 1994, through September 30, 1994, and reported from July 1, 1994, through December 31, 1994. These losses are divided by a predetermined quarterly industry premium and the result is the quarterly loss ratio. An Eastern futures value of 27.0 represents the expectation of a 27 percent loss ratio by the insurance industry for the Eastern region. Traders often refer to the Eastern September catastrophe contract as the hurricane future since the loss period encompasses the majority of seasonal hurricane activity.

Reflecting contract specifications, a 60/80 call spread represents a loss ratio range of 20 percent. This range approximates $4.8 to 6.5 billion in industry losses, assuming $6.1 billion in Eastern premium and a 75 percent reporting rate.[1] With the underlying September Eastern futures contract at 27.0, the lower leg of the spread is 122 percent out of the money.[2]

---

1 By assumption, the six month reporting period for the CBOT settlement procedure captures 75 percent of total industry. Thus, a 60 percent futures index priced represents $3.63 billion in incurred and reported losses and $4.8 billion (3.63/0.75) in total industry losses.

2 One hundred twenty-two percent is arrived at by calculating the quantity (60.0-27.0)/27.0.

EXHIBIT 35–10
60/80 "Hurricane" Bear Call Spread

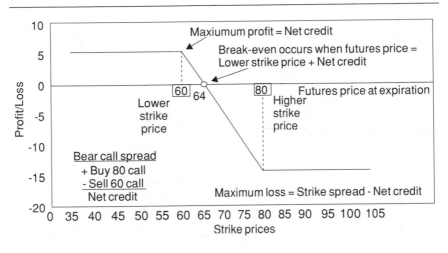

The profit and loss potential of a 60/80 bear call spread priced at a 4.0 net credit is illustrated in Exhibit 35–10. This spread has a five-to-one risk/reward ratio with a $1,000 premium credit and $4,000 maximum loss since the contract multiplier equals $25,000. Note that as long as the September futures remains below 64.0 representing $5.2 billion in reported and incurred losses, the spread writer earns a profit. The maximum loss is also represented in Exhibit 35–10 and equals 16 points or $4,000 per spread.

Twenty-six intense hurricanes (category 3 or higher) have hit the Eastern region since 1949 (see Exhibit 35–11), including two of the largest, Hugo and Andrew, in the last six years. After adjusting the insured loss estimates for inflation, only Andrew, with a simulated loss ratio of 178.9, would have created a loss for the spread writer. Hugo, with a simulated loss ratio of 48.3, would still have returned 4.0 points in profit or $1,000, since the 60/80 spread would not have been hit.

Exhibit 35–12 presents a range of possible expected win/loss ratios by adjusting maximum loss and maximum return by probabilities of occurrence. Recent prices for the 60/80 Eastern September call spread are around 4 points, with 20 points of risk. Therefore, the market is pricing the spread at a five-to-one risk/reward ratio. As shown in the Exhibit 35–12, the expected (**probability-weighted**) cost of the spread is 3.20, and equals 16

EXHIBIT 35–11

Intense Hurricanes, 1949–1992 (Category ≥ 3)

Date	Hurricane	Class	Inches Pressure	Insured/PCS CPI-Adjusted	CBOT Simulated Setlmt.Ratios
August 31, 1949	SE FL	3	28.17	$ 53,386,611	
October 13, 1950	KING (SE FL)	3	28.20	68,357,239	
August 25, 1954	CAROL	3	28.35	780,534,645	
October 5, 1954	HAZEL	4	27.70	700,185,490	
September 2, 1954	EDNA (NEW ENGLAND)	3	28.17	66,001,091	
September 10, 1955	IONE	3	28.35	25,922,427	
August 3, 1955	CONNIE	3	28.41	145,165,591	
June 25, 1957	AUDREY	4	27.91	179,003,630	
September 20, 1959	GRACIE	3	28.05	69,213,159	
August 29, 1960	DONNA	4	27.46	477,897,136	
September 3, 1961	CARLA	4	27.49	518,155,319	
September 28, 1964	HILDA (CENTRAL LA)	3	28.05	114,934,789	
August 26, 1965	BETSY	3	27.99	2,345,979,793	
September 5, 1967	BUELAH	3	28.05	150,345,496	
August 14, 1969	CAMILLE	5	26.84	659,974,896	
July 30, 1970	CELIA	3	27.91	1,168,557,920	
August 29, 1974	CARMEN (CENTRAL LA)	3	28.11	45,188,545	
September 15, 1975	ELOISE	3	28.20	326,379,398	
August 29, 1979	FREDERIC	3	27.94	1,574,944,232	
July 31, 1980	ALLEN	3	27.91	107,022,664	
August 15, 1983	ALICIA	3	28.41	982,628,185	
September 8, 1984	DIANA	3	28.02	50,454,278	
August 27, 1985	GLORIA	3	27.82	564,092,038	
September 16, 1985	ELENA	3	28.32	731,467,407	
September 10, 1989	HUGO	4	27.58	4,939,159,757	48.3%
August 16, 1992	ANDREW	4	27.23	$15,949,500,000	178.9%

EXHIBIT 35–12
Calculating Expected Win/Loss Ratios for Short 60/80 Call Spread

Eastern Sep 60 Call @ 16.0
Eastern Sep 80 Call @ 12.0
$\overline{\qquad}$ 4.0 pts credit
20.0 pts risk

"Odds of Occurrence"	*(1)* *Expected Loss* *(16) ∗ Prob (Loss)*	*(2)* *Expected Return* *(4) ∗ Prob* *(No Loss)*	*(2)/(1)* *Expected* *Win/Loss Ratios*
Market (1:5) = 0.20	(3.20) = 16 ∗ 0.20	3.20 = 4 ∗ 0.80	0%
Recent (1:7) = 0.1429	(2.28) = 16 ∗ 0.1429	3.43 = 4 ∗ 0.8571	150% = 3.43/2.28
(1:14) = 0.0714	(1.14) = 16 ∗ 0.0714	3.71 = 4 ∗ 0.9286	325% = 3.71/1.14
Hurricane Data (1:26) = 0.0385	(0.61) = 16 ∗ 0.0385	3.85 = 4 ∗ 0.9615	631% = 3.85/0.61

times the probability of loss (0.20). The expected (**probability-weighted**) profit is also 3.20 and equals 4.0 times the probability of no loss (0.80). Thus, the expected win/loss ratio is 0 percent as it should be since the market prices all option spreads to an expected return of zero. In other words, equilibrium option pricing is a fair game and provides no probability of gain to either the seller or buyer.

Employing recent hurricane data from 1989 to date, historical odds of seven to one may be used to similarly value the potential expected win/loss ratio for the 60/80 call spread at 150 percent. If recent historical data suggesting 14-to-1 odds are used to evaluate possibilities, the expected win/loss ratio for shorting the 60/80 Eastern September call spread exceeds 300 percent. Using inflation-adjusted hurricane data from 1949, the potential expected win/loss ratio of this short position approaches 600 percent since out of 26 hurricanes only Hurricane Andrew would have created a loss.

The previous "odds" also should be adjusted for demographics as well as the inflation component. This expected win/loss ratio method of assessing the risk/return potential of a short 60/80 Eastern September call spread does, however, offer valuable insight into these exciting new futures and options contracts.

EXHIBIT 35–13
Efficient Frontier (Risk-Return Trade-Off Opportunities)

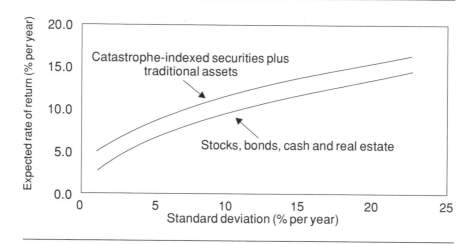

CATASTROPHE FUTURES AS ZERO BETA ASSETS

Catastrophe-indexed securities, such as the CBOT catastrophe insurance futures and option contracts, may offer investors an effective way to diversify existing investment allocations while providing relatively high expected returns. Since returns on catastrophe-indexed securities are generally uncorrelated with the economy, these instruments will enhance portfolio performance so long as their expected return exceeds the risk-free rate.

Most investors maintain a diversified portfolio of traditional assets including stocks, bonds, real estate, and cash. According to modern portfolio theory, investors manage their portfolios with respect to their risk and return preferences by shifting between assets to achieve higher returns with less risk. As a result, investors are constantly in search of combinations of assets defined by the "efficient frontier."

The efficient frontier consists of all optimal combinations of minimum risk and highest return available to investors, as shown in Exhibit 35–13. Risk may be measured by standard deviation of return with higher standard deviations representing higher risk. Return is measured by the total holding period return for the portfolio over a particular time period. Movements

EXHIBIT 35–14
Catastrophe Losses versus S&P500 Index
(Comparison of Annual Percentage Changes)

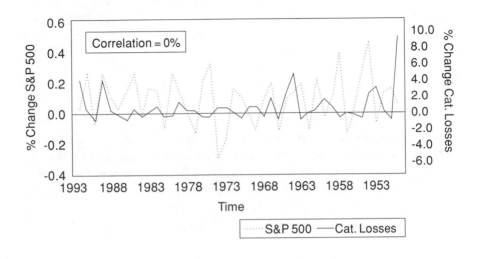

along the efficient frontier are accomplished by adding new assets that enhance the portfolio's risk/return trade-offs. Thus, assets with low correlation and high returns are valuable for both portfolio diversification and yield enhancement.

Catastrophe-indexed securities may be considered zero-beta assets since their payoffs are generally uncorrelated with the economy or almost any existing investment class. Indeed, little correlation exists between stocks and bonds and such catastrophic events as earthquakes, tornadoes, or hurricanes. The correlation of annual percentage changes of the S&P500 Index and catastrophe losses, illustrated in Exhibit 35–14, is zero over the 1949 through 1992 period. Therefore, securities that have returns linked to catastrophic events may be considered zero-beta assets.

The value of a high-yield, zero-beta asset is especially apparent when diversification benefits are examined in terms of the Sharpe Ratio. The Sharpe ratio is defined as the ratio of excess return (above the risk-free rate) to standard deviation. Generally speaking, alternative investments should be added to a portfolio if:

$$\begin{bmatrix} \text{Sharpe ratio of} \\ \text{alternative asset} \end{bmatrix} \geq \begin{bmatrix} \text{Correlation coefficient} \\ \text{of alternative asset} \end{bmatrix} \times \begin{bmatrix} \text{Sharpe ratio} \\ \text{of portfolio} \end{bmatrix}$$

Since a zero-beta asset, such as a synthetic reinsurance contract utilizing CBOT catastrophe options, is generally uncorrelated with the market, the right-hand side of the above equation reduces to zero. Thus, catastrophe-indexed instruments will enhance portfolio performance if its expected return exceeds the risk-free rate of interest.

CONCLUSION

This chapter has reviewed several hedging and trading uses of the new CBOT catastrophe futures and options contract. Although current trading activity is relatively low, many insurance and financial market participants are studying the new contracts and are initiating pilot programs. Regulatory impediments imposed by state insurance commissions in the United States are also being reduced or eliminated in states such as New York and California.

From a hedging perspective, the opportunity to employ a new risk management tool for property losses is timely. The last several years have been the costliest in terms of losses for the property insurance industry. As a result, reinsurance coverage is much more costly, tripling since 1990, and much more difficult to achieve due to capacity restrictions.

The difficulties of the reinsurance industry may be fortuitous, however, for investors and speculators. Given the well-defined features of the CBOT catastrophe insurance contracts, their overnight variation margining, and their characteristics as a zero-beta asset, catastrophe insurance futures and options represent a tremendous opportunity for investors and commodity fund managers.

Chapter Thirty-Six

Turning Positive
Convexity into Dollars

Laurie S. Goodman
PaineWebber

During the three years of the 1990–1993 rally, it was virtually impossible to find positive convexity in the mortgage market. Securities came only in two flavors: negatively convex and more negatively convex. The reason for this ultimately painful situation was that there were no outstanding pass-through classes priced substantially under par. At any given point in time, the lowest coupon traded was the current coupon which generally had a price above 98. The rally was so sharp that in some periods there were no coupons under par. Consequently, the only positively convex securities were the higher coupon interest only securities (IOs).

By contrast, when the market sold off in 1994, sizable amounts of 30-year 6.5s, 7s, 7.5s and 8s were left outstanding—all priced below par. By the summer of 1994, 30-year pass-throughs with coupons of 6.5 percent and under have positive convexity on our optional-adjusted spread (OAS) model. Furthermore, selected CMO tranches backed by this lower coupon collateral possess considerable positive convexity. For example, principal only securities (POs) and structured PO bonds backed by this collateral have little extension risk from their current levels, and high contraction risk is a very good thing: The price moves toward par very quickly as the bond shortens. This asymmetry is picked up in the convexity measures. Similarly, inverse floaters often have a great deal of positive convexity, particularly the long-average-life tranches priced at a discount. Investors win if the market rallies because the security contracts *and* the coupon increases. If the market trades off, the security should not extend much because prepayment rates do not have much room to slow further from the very slow levels used to price the mortgage securities. Moreover, because the coupon could never go below zero, the inverse floaters had relatively little downside from the forward rates implicit in the July 1994 yield curve. That is, the coupon on many inverse floaters reaches zero when LIBOR is between 7 percent and 8 percent. In fact, forward LIBOR in July 1994 was well above that level.

The problem stopping many investors in such an environment from adding convexity to their portfolios is that there is a cost to the convexity, and that cost is usually a lower base-case yield. Many investors are reluctant to buy instruments with a great deal of positive convexity because they yield less than comparable instruments with less positive convexity. In the following discussion, I make the point that instruments with a great deal of positive convexity allow the portfolio manager to hold higher-yielding instruments with negative convexity, producing, in effect, an attractive combination. Alternatively, the holding of positively convex instruments allows the portfolio manager to write call options against the position. In either view, the result is the same: Positive convexity essentially means the investor has purchased an option and the value of this embedded option can be monetized by writing options against the position.

CONVEXITY: WHAT DOES IT MEASURE?

Convexity is one of the least understood concepts among fixed-income professionals. Most investors believe that positive convexity is a good thing and negative convexity is a bad thing. Understanding the value of this characteristic of debt instruments often ends there.

Positively Convex Securities

The technical definition of convexity is that it is the second derivative of price with respect to yield. Most investors are very familiar with the first derivative of price with respect to yield, or duration—the relative change in price for a small change in yield. However, for large changes in yield, bond prices are not as well behaved as they are for small changes, because duration is also changing. The most intuitive way to think about convexity is the actual price move in a security for a large interest rate change minus the price move explained by duration. This is illustrated in Exhibit 36–1. If duration completely captured the price movements of the security, and

EXHIBIT 36–1
Impact of Convexity

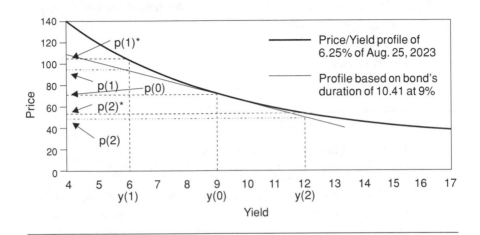

interest rates move down from Y(0) to Y(1), we could have expected prices to move up from P(0) to P(1). As can be seen from the figure, the actual price is P(1)*, higher than P(1). Similarly, as yields move higher, from Y(0) to Y(2), we would expect, based on duration alone, that the price of the security would move down from P(0) to P(2). In fact, prices in this figure move down by less, to P(2)*. Thus, we speak about the security illustrated in Exhibit 36–1 as being positively convex because the security actually performs better than we could have estimated from duration alone; as rates rise, the price of the security declines less than we would have expected, and as rates fall, the price of the security rises more than we would have expected.[1]

Negatively Convex Securities

By contrast, a negatively convex security is one whose price *depreciates more* than would have been expected from duration alone and *appreciates less* than would have been expected from duration alone. Prices of mort-

---

1 This is actually an approximation, because *duration* is the first term of the Taylor series expansion of price and *convexity* is the second term. Higher order moments also will have a slight effect.

gage pass-throughs with near-par or premium prices are negatively convex: As rates rise, the securities' cash flows extend and durations
lengthen, increasing potential for price depreciation; as rates fall, the
securities' cash flows contract and durations shorten, decreasing the potential for price appreciation.

Interpreting Convexity

Even for the most seasoned fixed-income professionals, convexity is a
difficult number to interpret. The approximate price change attributable to
convexity is given by equation (1):

Approximate % price change due to convexity =
$$(0.5) \times \text{convexity} \times (\text{Yield Change})^2 \tag{1}$$

Note that for an instrument with positive convexity, the approximate
change in price attributable to convexity is *positive* for either an increase or
decrease in yield, reflecting that the yield change term is squared, which
gives that term a positive sign. The opposite is true for an instrument with
negative convexity: The approximate change in price attributable to convexity is negative for either an increase or decrease in yield.

To see how to apply this, take the Treasury long bond, with a convexity
of 2.30. Using equation (1), a 100 basis point drop in yields would raise the
price of the security by more than would be expected from duration alone:

$$0.5 \times 2.30 \times 1 = 1.15\%$$

Using the calculator, the actual price change on the security for a 100-ba-
sis-point drop in rates is 12.953 percent; an 11.706 percent rise in price
would have been expected based on duration alone. Thus, the security
performs better by 1.247 percent. Of that, 1.15 percent can be explained by
convexity. For a 300-basis-point rise in yield, the convexity effect would
raise the price (above the level predicted by the duration of the security) by
an estimated:

$$0.5 \times 2.30 \times 9 = 10.35\%$$

For a 300-basis-point rise in rates, the security should fall in price by
35.117 percent based on duration alone, whereas in the calculation it
actually falls by only 26.816 percent. The effect of convexity, at 10.35
percent, accounts for the bulk of the difference between actual price
performance and performance based on duration alone.

In PaineWebber's SuperBond System and many other analytical systems, the reported convexity numbers are already scaled by 0.5. This simplified interpretation of what we refer to as the SuperBond convexities is indicated in equation (2):

Approximate % price change due to convexity =

SuperBond convexity × (Yield change)^2 (2)

To give some feeling for the magnitude of convexities, indicative convexities of Treasury securities and of selected mortgage securities are shown in Exhibit 36–2 (the calculations were performed using the PaineWebber SuperBond system). Thus, a mortgage security, such as FNR 93-152 C, a PAC PO backed by 8 percent collateral, offered (as of close on July 28, 1994) at around 71, has convexity of 2.1; this is approximately twice the convexity of a Treasury long bond. Similarly, a security such as FHR 1455 WB, an inverse floater with a price of 41.50 backed by Gold 7 percent collateral, has a convexity of 5.36, far more positively convex than a 30-year Treasury zero. Many mortgage securities are, of course, negatively convex. For instance, FNR 92-270 M, a PAC IO backed by 15-year 8s, has a convexity of –2.95, and FHR 1552 JC, a PAC IO backed by 30-year 7s, has a modestly positive convexity of 0.97. Also included in Exhibit 36–2 are Gold 7s and 8s , with convexities 0 and –0.57, respectively.

For investors who still find convexity unintuitive, we can look at instantaneous price changes under different scenarios to capture the same notion. For example, note the instantaneous price changes shown on each of the securities in Exhibit 36–2. On the Treasury long bond, as interest rates go up 200 basis points, the security will decline in price by $17.05; as rates go down 200 basis points, the security will rise in price by $25.29. Note that on the positively convex securities, the price increases more as rates fall than it decreases as rates rise. This is particularly true on FHR 1455 WB; the price increases by $40.76 and decreases by only $18.94. We can think of the amount the security increases versus the amount the security decreases as an alternative measure of convexity. With the negatively convex securities on the other hand, the price decreases are much greater than the price increases for a 200-basis-point move.

Note that on FHR 1552 JC, the relative price changes in the plus- and minus-200-basis-point scenarios indicate negative convexity, but the convexity measure is positive. This anomaly arises because convexity is actually measured for a small change in rates. For a small change in rates, this PAC IO behaves like a fixed-rate bond and exhibits positive convexity.

EXHIBIT 36–2
Convexity Characteristics of Treasury Securities and Selected Mortgage Securities (as of July 28, 1994)

Description	Coupon	Maturity	Yield	Duration	Convexity	Price +200	Price unchg.	Price −200	Price Change +200 -unch.	Price Change −200 -unch.	Impact of Convexity*
Treasury Securities											
2-yr. Treasury	6.125	7/31/1996	6.20	1.85	0.02	96.25	99.86	103.65	−3.61	3.79	0.18%
3-yr. Treasury	6.500	5/15/1997	6.47	2.49	0.04	95.17	100.06	105.27	−4.89	5.21	0.31
5-yr. Treasury	6.875	7/31/1999	6.95	4.17	0.11	91.80	99.70	108.45	−7.91	8.74	0.84
7-yr. Treasury	5.500	4/15/2000	6.96	4.70	0.14	84.77	93.20	102.65	−8.43	9.45	1.09
10-yr. Treasury	7.250	5/15/2004	7.28	6.83	0.30	87.10	99.78	114.91	−12.68	15.13	2.46
30-yr. Treasury	6.250	8/15/1923	7.55	11.71	1.15	67.77	84.83	110.11	−17.05	25.29	9.70
30-yr. Treasury Zero	0.000	8/15/1923	7.46	28.00	3.94	6.82	11.91	20.91	−5.09	9.00	32.82
Selected Mortgage Securities											
7.0% Gold collateral	7.000	30yr	8.13	5.84	.00	83.77	93.97	103.81	−10.20	9.84	−0.38
8.0% Gold collateral	8.000	30yr	8.28	4.95	−.57	88.54	99.03	106.08	−10.49	7.05	−3.48
FHR 1455 WB (Inverse Floater)	4.675 − 0.5 × 1mo LIB		11.72	33.66	5.36	22.56	41.50	82.26	−18.94	40.76	52.56
FNR 93-152 C PAC PO	0.000		9.79	11.27	2.10	60.03	71.00	83.30	−10.97	12.30	1.87
FNR 92-270 M PAC IO	1,139.68		14.25	−4.42	−2.95	3,557	3,503	2,544	54	−959	−25.84
FHR 1522 JC PAC IO	7.00		8.88	2.26	.97	29.81	31.25	29.25	−1.44	−2.00	−11.00

* [(Px chng in −200) + (Px chng in +200)] / Initial Price

806

For a large drop in rates the security turns highly negatively convex. The results in plus- and minus-200-basis-point shifts reflect this effect.

ENHANCING INTERIM PERFORMANCE

Many portfolio managers may realize when positive convexity is very cheap, but they may be reluctant to buy it because the security will under-perform as long as the low-volatility environment continues. Typical of this thinking is a conversation we had with a money manager, who said: "OK, now I see that I have a great deal of positive convexity in my portfolio. How do I convert this into dollars *now*? I don't want to wait for interest rates to move 200 basis points before the value of my trade is realized. I get marked to market every month. I need to show performance on an interim basis."

Writing Options against the Position

Positive convexity behaves effectively like an option: The security does better than its duration would suggest in some scenarios, and performs in line with its duration in others. The way to convert this positive convexity into dollars is to write options against the position. This can be done *explicitly* by writing options or *implicitly* by purchasing negatively convex securities.

Exhibit 36–3 shows the results of this analysis pairing the inverse floater (FHR 1455 WB) with PAC IOs (Combination 1). The combination of FHR 1455 WB and FHR 1552 JC, the PAC IO backed by 30-year Gold 7s is compared with 30-year Gold 7 percent collateral. As can be seen, this combination outperforms Gold 7 percent collateral in all scenarios from –200 basis points to +200 basis points. The combination outperforms in the base case by 165 basis points. On an expected-return basis, the combination outperforms by 267 basis points, reflecting the greater positive convexity on the combination. The expected-return results assume a 15 percent yield volatility on the 10-year note yield—roughly the average level over the five-year period from July 1989 through July 1994.

In Exhibit 36–3, you can also look at a combination of FNR 93-152 C, the PAC PO backed by 8 percent collateral, and FNR 92-70 M, a PAC IO backed by 15-year 8s. This combination (Combination 2) is compared with Gold 8 percent collateral. As can be seen, in the base case, the portfolio

EXHIBIT 36–3
Combining Positively Convex Security with PAC IOs to Enhance Yield

		Interest Rate Scenario							Expected TROR
		−200	−100	−50	unchg.	+50	+100	+200	
Combination 1									
FHR 1455 WB	Price	64.53	63.49	51.66	43.62	37.28	32.05	24.05	
Inverse Floater	TROR	92.98	51.35	28.89	10.77	−4.82	−18.79	−42.90	15.58
FHR 1552 JC	Price	25.01	27.49	27.27	27.03	26.81	26.57	26.06	
PAC IO	TROR	8.83	10.38	9.75	9.10	8.47	7.82	6.36	8.94
Combo 1	TROR	23.55	18.10	13.22	9.39	6.21	3.42	−1.37	10.34
Comparison for Combination 1									
Gold 7%	Price	103.81	99.47	96.80	94.05	91.35	88.72	83.76	
Collateral	TROR	15.89	12.94	10.41	7.74	5.08	2.46	−2.59	7.68
Combo 1 less Gold 7%		7.67	5.16	2.81	1.65	1.13	.96	1.22	2.67
Combination 2									
FNR 93-152 C	Price	89.70	87.25	83.70	79.22	75.51	72.43	67.60	
PAC PO	TROR	24.80	21.71	17.15	11.26	6.25	2.01	−4.85	11.69
FNR 92-70 M	Price	2,825	3,256	3,462	3,581	3,636	3,659	3,645	
PAC IO	TROR	−23.43	−1.60	6.08	10.77	13.23	14.54	15.22	6.82
Combo 2	TROR	13.77	16.12	14.44	11.14	8.02	5.21	.36	10.61
Comparison for Combination 2									
Gold 8%	Price	106.08	103.69	101.56	99.14	96.52	93.85	88.53	
Collateral	TROR	11.67	11.63	10.27	8.16	5.72	3.18	−1.99	7.48
Combo 2 less Gold 8%		2.10	4.49	4.17	2.98	2.30	2.03	2.35	3.13
Probabilities*		6.1	18.4	18.6	19.0	15.5	14.1	8.3	

* Based on 15% Vol on 10yr Yield for 1yr Horizon

EXHIBIT 36–4
Writing Options against a Positively Convex Mortgage Security
(A Long Position in an Inverse Floater Plus a Short Position in an
OTC Call Option on the 10-yr. Note)

PORTFOLIO

	Face	Price	Accrued Interest	Proceeds
Inverse*	1,000,000	41:16	0.0853	415,853
Call**	−1,000,000	1:30	0.0000	−19,375
				396,478

	Interest Rate Scenario						
	−200	−100	−50	Unchg.	+50	+100	+200
ROR							
Inverse	92.98	51.35	28.89	10.77	−4.82	−18.79	−42.90
Portfolio	75.67	43.99	27.27	15.86	−.11	−14.42	−39.11
TERMINAL VALUE							
Inverse	892,392	656,807	544,670	461,846	396,050	341,385	256,586
Call	−139,163	−66,744	−32,694	0	0	0	0
Portfolio	753,229	590,063	511,976	461,846	396,050	341,385	256,586
7.25% 5/15/04 at Horizon Date							
Yield	5.28	6.28	6.78	7.28	7.78	8.28	9.28
Price	113.71	106.47	103.06	99.79	96.65	93.64	87.95

*The inverse floater used here is FHR 1455 WB.
**This is a 1-yr. option on a 10-yr. Treasury (7.25% 5/15/04) struck at-the-money: that is the strike yield is "7.28%, the same as the yield as of the close of Thursday, 7/28/94."

outperforms by 298 basis points. On an expected total rate of return basis, Combination 2 outperforms by 313 basis points. The message remains: Adding negatively convex instruments to the portfolio can monetize positive convexity by increasing the base-case yield or by increasing the return in situations where the positively convex security does poorly.

Writing Options to Offset Embedded Options

Another alternative is to write options to offset the embedded options the investor has purchased with the mortgage security. Assume an investor has purchased FHR 1455 WB, the very positively convex inverse floater discussed above. We can monetize these options by writing an at-the-money one-year call option on a 10-year note. That is, we write an option such that if the yield on the 7.25 percent Treasury note of May 15, 2004, is lower than the 7.28 percent yield as of July 28, 1994, the call will be exercised. The compensation for writing this option is the premium of 1 $\frac{30}{32}$ points up front. This can significantly raise the total return on the portfolio in the base case and in cases in which interest rates rise (see Exhibit 36–4). As can be seen, the base case return on the inverse FHR 1455 WB, is 10.77 percent. Adding $1 million face of options for each $1 million face of the inverse floater improves the base-case rate of return by over 500 basis points. If rates rally substantially, the options entail a cost, but the cost is less than the upside on the inverse. Thus, the investor is lowering the upside in a major market rally to cushion the downside. The total rate of return in Exhibit 36–4 vividly illustrates this point. If rates fall 200 basis points, the total rate of return after writing the options is only 75.67 percent rather than 92.98 percent without writing the options.

CONCLUSION

Investors who hold positively convex securities need not simply pray for a major rally so that positive convexity can be turned into dollars. Rather, they can add negatively convex, higher-yielding securities, or they can add options. In both cases, investors are trading away superior performance that would be realized if rates move significantly in order to attain a higher base-case return or a more stable return profile.

## Chapter Thirty-Seven

Evaluating Inverse Floaters

Laurie S. Goodman,
Jeffrey Ho, and
Linda L. Lowell
PaineWebber

Investors evaluate mortgage inverse floating rate products from a variety of approaches, each of which has advantages and disadvantages. No single approach tells the whole story. Five major approaches can be used to gauge relative value:

- Traditional—yield and average-life profile
- Re-creation value
- Option adjusted spread analysis
- Yield to forward LIBOR
- Unbundling of options

The surge of interest in mortgage derivatives by sophisticated investors in 1994—particularly in inverse floaters and inverse IOs—generated some lively discussion about the application and limitations of these different approaches to valuation, especially on the part of the large number of investors considering opportunities in this market for the first time. In this chapter, we review the various approaches and compare the advantages and disadvantages of each. Each approach can add to a basic understanding of the behavior of complex securities as well as indicate where good relative values exits. We recommend they all be employed by investors in this market sector.

TRADITIONAL MORTGAGE CASH FLOW MEASURES: THE YIELD AND AVERAGE-LIFE PROFILE

Investors first approached mortgage derivatives by evaluating them the same way they would other mortgage products, using a price/yield table or an inverse table (index/yield table). The first is widely used with fixed rate mortgage-backed securities (MBSs), displaying yields and average lives given different prices on one axis and prepayment speeds on the other (or, alternatively, displaying prices with yield as a variable on one axis). In the case of variable rate securities, the coupon at the current level of the index rate is assumed. Alternatively, inverse tables display yields, given a price, with different levels of the index on one axis and different prepayment speeds on the other. These tables indicate the sensitivity of the security's average life and yield to different prepayment speeds; given an average life, it is also an easy matter to evaluate the sensitivity of yield spread to Treasuries for different prepayment speeds.

An example of an inverse table, for FNR 93-183 S, an inverse floater backed by 30-year 6.5s, is given in Exhibit 37–1 (priced as of the close of August 3, 1994). The coupon on this inverse floater resets according to the formula:

$$22.89 - (3.27 \times 1\text{-month LIBOR})$$

In August 1994, with the 1-month LIBOR rate at 4.5 percent, the security had a coupon of 8.2 percent. In the base case, at 130 percent PSA—the Bloomberg Street consensus speed for this collateral at the time—the security had an average life of 7.35 years and, priced at 53 points, a yield of 25.93 percent. This base-case yield is shaded in the center column (LIBOR = 4.5 percent, 130 percent PSA). If LIBOR remained unchanged, and speeds came in at 145 percent PSA (corresponding to the consensus projection for this collateral if interest rates fell 100 basis points), the security's yield would increase to 42.01 percent and the average life would contract to 2.90 years. A more likely scenario at the time, however, would have been faster prepayments accompanied by a lower LIBOR rate: For instance, at LIBOR of 3.5 percent, the expected yield on this security is 48.35 percent. Accordingly, most investors look at the diagonal from the lower left-hand corner (high LIBOR, slow prepayments) to the upper right-hand corner (low LIBOR, fast prepayments) to gain an idea of how the security behaves. The scenarios implied by the diagonal to the other

EXHIBIT 37–1
Inverse Floater Yield Table—FNR 93-183 S
Px = 53 on 8/3/94; 8/10/94 settle; Coupon = 22.89 – (3.27 × 1-month LIBOR);
Collateral = 30yr 6.5s

	Interest Rate Scenario						
	+300	+200	+100	unch	–100	–200	–300
Speed (% PSA)	10	105	120	130	145	225	630
LIBOR							
1.500	36.26	36.30	38.93	46.35	61.55	62.45	120.99
2.500	29.52	29.60	32.16	39.37	54.87	55.82	114.28
3.500	23.06	23.17	25.65	32.56	48.35	49.37	107.70
4.500	16.95	17.11	19.47	25.93	42.01	43.10	101.25
5.500	11.29	11.49	13.67	19.55	35.85	37.01	94.92
6.500	6.14	6.36	8.30	13.46	29.88	31.11	88.72
7.500	3.75	3.97	5.77	10.54	26.96	28.23	85.66
Average Life	17.29	16.36	11.81	7.35	2.90	2.73	0.92
Window	6/09–3/14	4/08–6/13	8/94–10/10	8/94–8/08	8/94–7/01	8/94–11/99	8/94–9/95

corners are fairly unlikely—fast speeds such as 630 percent PSA accompanied by a dramatic rise in LIBOR (reflecting a steeply inverted yield curve) or a sharp fall in LIBOR and very slow speeds.

Yield leverage is often used as a thumbnail measure of the risk of the security. Yield leverage is the difference between the base case yield and the yield at LIBOR 100 basis points higher. In this instance, the base-case yield is 25.93 percent; if LIBOR rises 100 basis points, the yield falls to 19.55 percent. The difference (25.93 percent – 19.55 percent) amounts to a yield leverage of 6.38 percent.

The problem with inverse or yield tables is that they cannot indicate how much an investor should be compensated for the complex risks in the inverse floater. Is a yield of 25.93 percent adequate compensation for the higher leverage and the average-life variability? We know, from theory, that investors in leveraged positions should be compensated for the additional risk. If an investor had purchased 4.27 Treasury notes (T 7.5 11/15/01) at a yield of 6.92 percent and financed 3.27 of them at then-typical financing

rates (one-month LIBOR – 25, or 4.25 percent), the position would yield
15.64 percent [(4.27 × Treasury note rate) – (3.27 × financing rate] = 29.55
– 13.90 = 15.69).[1] Is the difference between the inverse's base-case yield
of 25.93 percent and the yield of 15.64 percent on a comparably leveraged
Treasury position adequate compensation for the average life uncertainty?

RE-CREATION ANALYSIS

Given the limitations of inverse tables in determining relative value, it was
natural that investors should want a measure of relative value that could also
be used as a pricing guide. Many investors use "re-creation" or recombination values for month-end marking; others use the recombination technique
to evaluate month-end marks they get from dealers. Furthermore, dealers
often use re-creation value as a guide when bidding a security. To perform
this analysis, the floater and the inverse are recombined to form the
underlying fixed-rate tranche. If this underlying security—a PAC, TAC or
companion structure of some type—is traded, then it can be priced. The
prices of both the underlying and the floater uniquely determine the recombination value of the inverse.

To see how this would be implemented, we use as an example FNR
93-179 SG. This bond was created by taking a 5.85 percent TAC backed by
30-year 7s and tranching it into a floater and an inverse. This is shown in
Figure 37–1. We know the floater, FNR 93-179 FA pays LIBOR plus 50
up to an 8.5 percent cap. This floater would trade at a dollar price of 98.5
points, which corresponds to a discount margin of 92 basis points at 150
percent PSA. The underlying bond would trade at +105/three-to-five-year
blend at 150 percent PSA. As of the close on August 3, 1994, the interpolated
rate on the three- and five-year Treasury was 6.47 percent. Thus the
underlying bond would yield 7.52 percent, at 150 percent PSA, corresponding to a price of 94.75 points. Using a little algebra we can easily find the
price of the inverse floater:

$$\frac{2.2077 \, (Price_{FA}) + Price_{SG}}{1 + 2.20755} = Price_{\text{Underlying Fixed-Rate Tranche}}$$

---

1 This is comparable to the leveraged position embodied by the inverse floater. Recall that the
inverse floater is equivalent to a leveraged position in an underlying fixed-rate bond funded at the
floater rate, plus some caps on the implied floating rate expense.

FIGURE 37–1
Re-Creation Value

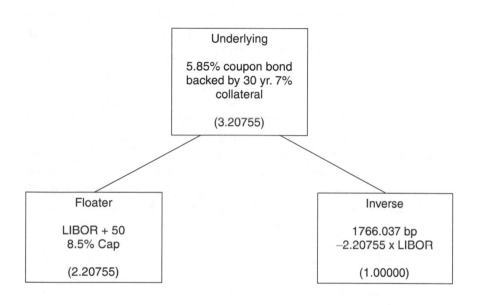

We know that

$$\frac{2.20755 \; (98.5) + Price_{SG}}{3.20755} = 94.75$$

Therefore,

$Price_{SG} = 86.47.$

Thus, the recombination price of 86.47 (86:15) points is considerably higher than the offered price of 82 points, indicating this inverse is very cheap to its re-creation value.

Finding the re-creation value assumes that we know where the floater and the underlying fixed-rate tranche trade with a fair degree of certainty. In the case of FNR 93-179 FA and SG, this was true because the underlying was well structured; that is, it is a fairly stable bond. Where the security is less well-structured, there can be considerable pricing uncertainty on both the underlying fixed rate and the floater. This pricing uncertainty is magnified by the degree of leverage when solving for the price of the inverse floater.

All the problems of re-creation valuation are illustrated by performing the analysis on FNR 93-183 S. First, the bond has a fair amount of average-life variability: The underlying structure is a scheduled bond with third priority to principal paydowns. This imparts pricing uncertainty to both the floater and the underlying fixed-rate tranche. Moreover, the underlying fixed-rate tranche in this case was actually divided into three bonds: a floater, an inverse floater, and a two-tiered index bond (TTIB). This was a very common structuring strategy in 1993 deals. The collateral used to create such structures was primarily 6.5s and 7s. With coupons this low, it was difficult to simultaneously create both a floater with a cap high enough to be salable *and* an inverse floater with enough leverage—and hence enough yield—to be salable. Typically, if the structurer created a salable floater, the inverse floater had leverage that was too low and, consequently, too low a yield to be appealing. The solution, as it turned out, was the introduction of two-tiered index bonds.

When a TTIB is also part of the structure, we can still perform the recombination, but the analysis is less useful because of the considerable uncertainty about where the TTIB would actually trade; this type of bond is typically much less liquid and harder to value than the inverse floater. In these cases, a recombination analysis should be viewed as "garbage in, garbage out."

The most important objection to re-creation value is that it simply prices the bonds (the underlying, the floater and the inverse) relative to each other. It is not a guide to relative value within the mortgage market. For example, consider a situation in which, given the price of the underlying fixed-rate bond and the floater, the inverse floater is found to be several points cheap to creation value. If the underlying bond is inherently rich and the floater too cheap, the fact that the inverse is calculated to be cheap to creation value may not indicate relative value. That is, the investor may still be purchasing a rich security relative to the universe of alternatives.

The final problem with recombination analysis is that there is no reason why an inverse floater (or any bond, for that matter) cannot trade cheap to re-creation value for a long period of time. When, as happened in August 1994, there is an adequate supply of secondary bonds trading cheap to re-creation value, the selling of new inverses is precluded. If inverses were trading expensive to recombination values, the pace of new issuance would be such that the price of the securities would quickly realign.

OPTION-ADJUSTED SPREAD ANALYSIS

While recombination allows investors to judge relative value of the inverse versus its re-creation value, it does not allow investors to gauge relative value in inverses against other securities, especially long-duration alternatives. By contrast, the option-adjusted spread (OAS) was introduced into the mortgage market specifically for comparisons between securities. Before discussing the advantages and disadvantages of this approach, we provide a brief review.

All market participants use a Monte Carlo approach to calculate option-adjusted spreads for mortgage securities. The results, however, can be very different from firm to firm. The two major sources of variation are the determination of the probability distribution of interest rates and prepayment function estimation .

The first step in an OAS analysis is to generate a probability distribution of interest rates over time. This is done first by deriving spot and implied forward Treasury rates for Treasury securities of different maturities. Some firms use on-the-run Treasury securities for this derivation, other firms use all Treasury coupon securities, and still others use all-coupon issues plus Treasury strips.[2] After the spot-rate yield curve is calculated, a probability distribution is selected for short-term Treasury rates. This probability distribution is selected so that it is consistent with spot rates on the calculation date. Loosely speaking, this means it will be centered near forward rates. The selection of the probability distribution can be very different across models; implicit in the distribution is the volatility and the degree of mean reversion. Some models use the normal distribution, others use a log-normal distribution. The log-normal distribution ensures that interest rates will never be negative; a normal distribution coupled with mean reversion ensures that interest rates will never get very negative. The variance of the distribution can be either assumed or estimated.

The probability distribution is then used to generate interest rate paths. In Monte Carlo simulations, a large number of interest rate paths are chosen randomly from the interest rate distribution. For each path, the cash flows of the mortgage security are generated. This is based on an embedded prepayment model, which gives the prepayment rate at each point in time.

---

2 Generally, the more market information incorporated, the better. However, the result can occur that individual on-the run Treasuries are rich to the generalized Treasury yield structure when run through the model—which some users of OAS models may find disconcerting the first time they encounter it.

EXHIBIT 37–2
FNR 93-183 SG: Sensitivity of OAS to Prepayment Model

OAS	OAD	Convexity
90% of PW Prepayment Model		
51.60	38.70	8.19
100% of PW Prepayment Model		
173.80	37.20	7.24
110% of PW Prepayment Model		
341.70	35.46	6.98

The OAS is found using an iterative search. A spread is assumed (guessed) and the present value along each path is calculated. The present values are then averaged and compared with the market price of the bond. If they are equal, the assumed spread is the option-adjusted spread. If the values are not equal, other spreads are tried until one is found that equals the market price of the bond.

ADVANTAGES AND DISADVANTAGES OF OAS ANALYSIS

Option-adjusted spread is a powerful tool for relative value analysis. It is the only methodology that is internally consistent and captures both the shape of the yield curve and the value of the embedded options in a single summary number. Moreover, by running a large number of interest rate paths, both favorable and unfavorable to the security, the structure of the tranche is fully taken into account. Any priority switches, rapid call or extension, or strange behavior under certain interest rate prepayment scenarios will be captured. The problem with OAS lies not in the number but in the interpretation.

It is very easy to misinterpret OAS numbers. First, OAS users must realize that OAS is heavily dependent on models. Small differences in the prepayment model can make large differences in the OAS. Exhibit 37–2 shows the OAS, as well as the option-adjusted duration and convexity of FNR 93-183 S at different multiples of the PaineWebber prepayment model.

EXHIBIT 37–3
Divergence in Prepayment Models

	Interest Rate Scenario								
	–300	*–200*	*–100*	*–50*	*unch.*	*+50*	*+100*	*+200*	*+300*
PSA projection									
Street median	629	221	150	138	131	124	118	109	102
PaineWebber	776	340	153	127	116	110	106	102	100
Absolute deviation									
Nine-firm average	170	44	7	6	7	8	8	11	13
PaineWebber	147	119	3	11	15	14	12	7	2
Absolute deviation as percentage of street median									
Nine-firm average	27%	20%	4%	5%	5%	6%	7%	10%	13%
PaineWeber	23%	54%	2%	8%	11%	11%	10%	6%	2%

At 100 percent of the prepayment model, the security has an OAS of 174; an OAS of 342 at 110 percent of the model and an OAS of 52 at 90 percent. Note that at 90 percent of the prepayment model, the inverse floater has a lower OAS than some pass-throughs (at a normal multiple of 100 percent). This alone should make investors wary about relying exclusively on OAS analysis. There are wide differences in prepayment models at different firms, and this can make a large difference in the results.

Furthermore, by means of some simple comparisons, we can show that 10 percent is a normal variation between models. Exhibit 37–3, above, shows the median speed that is estimated by nine dealers in mortgage securities on FNMA 6.5s for seven interest rate scenarios. This information is compiled by Bloomberg, and is referred to as street consensus speeds. It also indicates the amount that the individual projections of the nine firms contributing to the consensus differed from the consensus. These differences are summarized as the mean absolute deviation and mean percentage deviation across firms. Thus, in the base case, the Bloomberg median is 131 percent PSA. The average absolute deviation was 7 percent PSA; that is, firms were, on average different from the consensus by 7 percent PSA. The difference amounts to 5 percent of the consensus speed. Obviously, some firms were higher and some were lower. Note that the mean percentage deviation on the security is smaller in the base case and for modest interest rate shifts and higher in cases in which interest rates go up or down substantially. Compared with the average prepayment model, the Street median (as compiled by Bloomberg) understates the variation of any individual firm. The table also compares the PaineWebber results with the Street median numbers. In the base case, PaineWebber is lower than the Street average by 11 percent.When yields shift down 300 basis points, it is 23 percent higher than the Street average. To summarize, a 10 percent difference between prepayment models is somewhere between realistic and conservative as an estimate of model uncertainty. Applied to the OAS analysis of volatile derivatives, however, this normal variation in prepayment models can make the difference between the security looking very attractive, marginally attractive, or unattractive.

A second disadvantage: OAS is a less meaningful number for leveraged securities. Clearly, any model error is magnified as a result of the leverage. Moreover, the OAS on a leveraged security should be higher, as the OAS on the financing should be low. For example, if the OAS on FNMA 6.5s is 48 and we are able to finance at 0 OAS, then the OAS on a position in which we owned 4.27 FNMA 6.5s and financed 3.27 of them would be 205 (48 × 4.27).

Third, a security will never actually earn its OAS. Depending on the path that materializes, the security can significantly outperform or significantly underperform Treasury securities. Thus, the OAS will not correspond to the ex-post profit on the trade. More importantly, the distribution of path-dependent prices is never provided with OAS numbers, so that one does not have a good idea of how wide the variation is across paths. If the path-dependent prices were highly concentrated, the security would have less risk than if the path dependent prices were all over the map. This uncertainty is not priced.[3]

Our conclusion regarding OAS numbers is that they should be used cautiously as measures of relative value. Run the prepayment model at different multiples and test the sensitivity. The less sensitive the OAS output is to multiplying the prepayment model, the more credence that can be placed on the results.

On the other hand, we believe that OAS can serve to be a very valuable guide (1) to the price risk of the security and (2) to the possible upside on the security if interest rates remain at current levels. By holding OAS

---

3 An excellent and very readable discussion of the disadvantages of OAS analysis can be found in Robert Kopprasch, Option Adjusted Spread Analysis: Going Down the Wrong Path?" in the *Financial Analysts Journal*, May/June 1994.

EXHIBIT 37–4
Instantaneous Price Sensitivity Analysis on FNR 93-183 S

				Interest Rate Scenario			
	–200	*–100*	*–50*	*unch*	*+50*	*+100*	*+200*
Price	101.91	76.44	63.09	53.00	45.05	38.61	29.09

constant and calculating instantaneous price changes under different scenarios, we can get an idea of the price risk. For instance, using our FNR 93-183 S example in early August 1994, if interest rates had gone up 100 basis points, holding the OAS constant, the price of the security would have declined by 14.39 points or 27.15 percent. The instantaneous price changes under different interest rate scenarios are shown in Exhibit 37–4. Investors should make sure they can handle this degree of risk. This also illustrates the positive convexity on the security. Note that if rates had fallen 100 basis points, the security would have risen in price by 23.44 points. This is far larger than the price drop of 14.39 points if rates had risen 100 basis points. Finally, this analysis allows investors to gauge the impact of mispricing. If, for example, with the market at those levels, we believed the OAS on FNR 93-183 S could tighten 100 basis points from 174 to 74, we could determine that the security would instantaneously increase in price from 53:00 to 57:15 points. Was a 4:15 point gain enough compensation for the bid-asked spreads in the market? The investor must decide.

YIELD TO FORWARD LIBOR

Many investors have been frustrated in a steep-yield-curve environment by the ambiguity that surrounds the evaluation of inverses using yield or inverse tables. When the curve is upward sloping, a more highly leveraged portfolio should have a higher yield. This can be seen by using the swap market to convert an inverse floater into a fixed-rate bond (in effect, swapping out the implied LIBOR financing). An investor who did so would find that the yield on the swapped inverse floater is far lower than the base-case yield indicated, say, for the example in Exhibit 37–1. That is, swapping the security would mean purchasing an amortizing swap in which the investor receives LIBOR and pays a fixed rate. The fixed rate paid on this amortizing swap reflects the steep forward LIBOR rates of August 1994. An equivalent alternative to an amortizing swap would be to use Eurodollar futures to convert the LIBOR component of each cash flow into a fixed-rate component; the fixed rate that would be received at each point in time would be forward LIBOR. The economic effect of these transactions can be replicated by using forward LIBOR to find the cash flows on the inverse floater for different prepayment speeds; the yields on these cash flows can then be compared with those on comparable fixed-rate structures.

The mechanics of the yield to forward LIBOR calculation are quite simple: Each coupon is converted to a fixed-rate equivalent by assuming that LIBOR is equal to forward LIBOR as of each coupon reset date. The coupon formula for FNR 93-183 S is:

$$22.89 - 3.27 \times LIBOR$$

Thus, if forward LIBOR for a particular month was 6.5 percent, the bond would be assumed to pay a coupon of 1.64 percent, or a monthly coupon of 1.64 percent divided by 12 and then multiplied by the outstanding amount on the tranche. Note that the assumed fixed coupon will be different each month as forward LIBOR changes. The yield to forward LIBOR is simply the internal rate of return on this cash flow stream.

This analysis is provided in Exhibit 37–5 for FNR 93-183 S at the same prepayment speeds as in Exhibit 37–1, as well as those projected by the PaineWebber Prepayment Model. As can be seen from this analysis, the yield to forward LIBOR is lower than the yield to current LIBOR at all prepayment speeds, but the differential increases in the slower prepayment scenarios, where the inverse is heavily dependent on coupon income for its cash flow performance. In the case of FNR 93-183 S, the security has a 0 percent coupon as long as LIBOR is 7 percent or above. We call 7 percent the "LIBOR strike." Forward LIBOR is higher than 7 percent after December 1996.

SHORTCOMINGS OF YIELD-TO-FORWARD LIBOR

The problem with a yield to forward LIBOR analysis is that many investors believe that they have created a fixed-rate bond in which the yield profile is comparable to a Treasury security or a fixed-rate bond with a similar structure. This is not true for two reasons. First, even an amortizing swap

EXHIBIT 37–5
Yield to Forward LIBOR versus Current LIBOR on FNR 93-183 S
(Price = 53)

	% PSA							PW Prepayment Model
	100	105	120	130	145	225	630	
Yield to forward LIBOR	4.29	4.54	6.64	12.30	30.79	32.14	94.09	7.27
Yield to current LIBOR	16.95	17.11	19.47	25.93	42.01	43.10	101.25	19.22
Average life (yrs.)	17.29	16.36	11.81	7.35	2.90	2.72	0.91	10.33

(what we have created here, in effect) does not reflect the uncertainty of the mortgage cash flows. If yields rise, slowing prepayments, the inverse is underswapped, and additional swaps have to be added but at a greater cost, reflecting the higher fixed rate. On the other hand, if yields decline, accelerating prepayments, the combination is now overswapped, and some swaps have to be paired off but at a lower fixed rate. Either outcome will always hurt the inverse. It follows that in the absence of other considerations, inverse floaters should trade cheaper than fixed-rate cash flows.

The other reason that the swapped inverse position is not fully comparable to a fixed-rate bond is that the inverse contains a valuable embedded LIBOR option that is not priced by this procedure. This option can be viewed as a cap on the implied LIBOR funding if we construe an inverse floater as equivalent to a long position in the underlying fixed-rate bond funded at the coupon rate of the sibling floater. We can also demonstrate the presence of this option by considering that, if forward rates are realized, the investor will be receiving a 0 percent coupon after December 1996. However, at that point, the coupon rate can only go up from there; it cannot decline. If rates go below 7 percent, the coupon will be restored; if LIBOR stay above 7 percent, the coupon stays at 0 percent. That is, the coupon can never go negative. In effect, the investor is essentially long a cap. More precisely, the investor is long a leveraged amount of caps—3.27 caps struck at 7 percent. Owing to these extremely valuable options, the yield to forward LIBOR should be lower than on a comparable fixed-rate bond.

In other words, when we compare an inverse floater's yield to forward LIBOR profile to that of a similarly structured fixed-rate bond under the same prepayment profiles, the result is obscured by two contradictory effects: The value of the inverse floater is overstated because we miss the added cost to the swap imposed by average life variability, and the value of the inverse floater is understated because we ignore the value of the LIBOR option. As a result, this technique is best for those situations where both these problems are minimized. The effect of implicitly over- and underswapping is minimized for bonds with stable cash flows over a wide range of interest rate scenarios; for example, inverses backed by low-coupon balloon collateral and 30- or 15-year backed inverses with stable structures such as PACs. The value of the LIBOR cap is minimized in bonds with high LIBOR strikes; this corresponds to inverses in which the cap on the sibling floater is high. That is, the 0 percent floor on the inverse coupon is exercised when the floater hits its cap and is receiving all interest cash flow from the underlying fixed-rate bond. Similarly, the higher the cap and the shorter the life on the floater, the less important valuing the floor on the inverse will be.

EXPLICITLY PRICING THE LIBOR OPTION

Market participants do attempt to explicitly capture the value of the LIBOR option when evaluating inverse floaters. In the first approach, the inverse is combined with a position in a swap and the cap is sold. On occasion—and FNR 93-183 S proves to be one of those occasions—the net payment on the inverse-swap combination can be negative, and standard calculators cannot find a yield. In this example, the fixed rate on the swap would be 7.12 percent. Thus, using the fixed rate on the swap is greater than the LIBOR strike. The second approach is conceptually equivalent and has the same drawbacks, so we confine our demonstration to it, using FNR 93-183 S for continuity.

In the second approach, market participants effectively price and strip off the cap, and then compare the resultant yield to the yield on a synthetic inverse floater with the same average life as in the base case. The synthetic is created using a Treasury security and swaps. For example, we could replicate FNR 93-183 S at the base-case prepayment assumption with a Treasury maturing in 7.35 years entering into 3.27 swaps in which the investor receives fixed and pays floating. As of August 3, that would mean purchasing UST 7.5 11/15/01, at a yield of 6.92 percent, and entering into 3.27 swaps in which we receive a fixed rate of 7.12 percent and pay LIBOR:

Receive: 6.92% on the Treasury

                  23.28% on the fixed side of the swap

                  (3.27×7.12)

Pay: $3.27 \times LIBOR = 14.72\%$

                  $(3.27 \times 4.50\%)$

Net yield: 15.48%

Net-net, the yield on the synthetic combination is 15.48 percent (6.92 + 23.28 − 14.72). Notice that the yield on this synthetic is much lower than the base case yield of 25.93 percent on FNR 93-183 S. Actually, it is very close to the yield on FNR 93-183 S at 100 percent PSA without considering the option value.

Next, we account for the fact that the coupon on the inverse can never go below zero; whereas, it can do so on the synthetic combination. To adjust for this difference, we gross up the base-case yield on the inverse to account for the value of the caps, selling 3.27 caps with a 7 percent strike and a 7.35-year average life, assuming 18 percent yield volatility, at 5.92 points. Altogether, 3.27 caps would be worth 19.36 points. We lower the price of the inverse floater by 19.36 points to get a new price of 33.64 points (from 53.00) and then calculate a new yield of 47.97 percent.

Assuming the average life of the inverse is very stable, we can compare it to the synthetic inverse floater. Thus, we would be comparing a yield of 47.97 percent on the inverse to 15.49 percent on the synthetic. In the case of FNR 93-183 S, the inverse is sufficiently unstable, so that we are significantly overstating the value of the inverse. Even so the 47.97 percent is so much better than 15.82 percent that it appears the inverse floater is a good buy relative to the synthetic.

The problem with these techniques is that, as interest rates move, a swapped position is either under- or overswapped; adjusting the swap to compensate entails an additional cost in either case. Selling off the cap partially corrects for the problem. As rates rise, the average life extends on the implied cap which is embedded in the inverse, increasing its value even more than typically would occur in a rising rate environment.[4] Obviously,

---

4 This is reinforced by considering the floater sibling who has written the caps. It is well known that the caps the investor is short go up dramatically in value as the security extends, dragging down the price of the floater.

the average life of the cap the investor has written remains constant. Similarly, as rates fall, the average life falls on the caps the investor is long, where as the average life is constant on the caps that have been written against the inverse.

UNBUNDLING THE OPTIONS

We have pointed out the difficulties that arise when we try to use swaps to evaluate inverse floaters with volatile average life. Swap-based analyses also have the drawback of failing to capture the PO-like optionality in many inverse floaters. To account for this option value as well as the LIBOR option, we take a different approach to decomposing the inverse floater into its economic constituents. To do this, we divide an inverse floater into its coupon payment stream and its principal payment stream. It should be immediately apparent that the principal cash flows are a PO. We then show that the coupon payment stream is an IO inverse, which in turn is equivalent to a floor. Once again, we base our example on FNR 93-183 S. Assume an amount of $10 million, which we strip into two parts as follows:

1. The $10 million in principal; this is a scheduled PO backed by 30-year 6.5s.
2. The interest, which is computed according to the formula:

22.89 percent – (3.27 × 1-month LIBOR)

   on a notional balance of $10 million.

Now we can easily create the same cash flows by thinking of a security with a larger notional amount and less leverage as follows:

Receive 22.89		Receive 7.0
Pay 3.27 × LIBOR	=	Pay LIBOR
on $10 million		on $32.7 million

Note that the second set of cash flows comprises exactly those on an IO inverse (7.0 percent – LIBOR, 0 percent floor). Note also that the interest payments on the bond are equal to those on $32.7 million interest rate swaps with one important difference: *The cash flows from the inverse can never be negative.* The reason: the investor is long a 7.0 percent cap, acquired from the floating rate tranche.

EXHIBIT 37–6
Cap/Floor/Swap Parity

	Condition	Payment
Floor	IF index > $X\%$	0
	IF index < $X\%$	$X\%$ – index
Cap	IF index > $X\%$	Index – $X\%$
	IF index < $X\%$	0
Swap		
(Receive X	IF index > $X\%$	$X\%$ – Index
Pay Index)	IF index < $X\%$	$X\%$ – Index
Conclusion:	$F - C = S => F = S + C$	

Now it can easily be shown that an inverse interest only security (IIO) is a floor. The payment on a floor is shown in Exhibit 37–6. If the index (LIBOR) is less than the strike (7 percent), the position will pay the strike less the index (7 percent – index). If the index is higher than the strike, the position will pay zero. This is exactly the payout on an inverse IO.

It can also be shown, as we do in Exhibit 37–6, that a floor is equal to a swap plus a cap. That is, a long swap position nets the investor the fixed rate minus the index, regardless of the index level. The cap pays the index minus the fixed rate as long as the index is above the fixed rate. Thus, a swap (S) plus a cap (C) pays zero if the index is greater than the fixed rate, and it pays the fixed rate minus the index if the index is less than the fixed rate. This is equivalent to a floor (F). We can summarize these notions in equation form below.

$$F = S+C$$

or F = IO inverse

This analysis tells us that an inverse floater is a structured PO plus a floor, or a structured PO plus an IO inverse. The difficulty with this methodology is that now that we have done the decoupling, we need to know where each of the component parts trades. We know where the PO trades, but it is very difficult to value the IO Inverse with these characteristics. However, we can easily value a floor that has a maturity equal to the average life of the security or, alternatively, we can value an amortizing floor.

EXHIBIT 37–7

Valuation of an Inverse Floater as a Structured PO and Floor

Floor cost per $100		Price of PO	
Single 7.0% floor	5.32	Orig. Px of inverse floater	53.00
× 3.27	17.39	Gain from writing floors	17.39
		Price of structured PO	35.60

			Interest Rate Scenario				
	+300	*+200*	*+100*	*Unch.*	*100*	*–200*	*–300*
PSA	100	105	120	130	145	225	630
Yield*	6.15	6.51	9.90	20.41	51.23	52.97	160.01
Avg Life	17.29	16.36	11.81	7.35	2.90	2.73	.92

*This yield table was calculated assuming the bond is a PO with a price of 35.60.

Many investors assume that if we are really long a floor, we should be able to sell it off and reduce the purchase price of the PO by that amount. Exhibit 37–7 shows this analysis on FNR 93-183 S. We assume that we have sold off 3.27 floors with a 7 percent strike and received 5.32 points for each of them. The purchase price of the PO is then reduced by 17.39 points (3.27 × 5.32), from its original price of 53 to 35.60 points. The price/yield table on this PO is also shown in Exhibit 37–7. (To do this in the price/yield table calculator, we set LIBOR high enough that the coupon is zero, so that we are valuing the PO).

This approach is intuitively appealing in that it allows the investor to break down the options and evaluate exactly the bets that are implicit in the security. The problem with this approach is that the floor, which is embedded in the inverse floater and in which we are implicitly long, is not identical to the floor that we can write in the derivatives market. More precisely, the floor we are long is prepayment-rate dependent. As rates fall, the floor in which we are implicitly long disappears, limiting its potential for price appreciation, while the floor in which we are short increases in value dramatically. To see this, consider the floor we have written on FNR 93-183 S. If rates were to instantaneously fall 100 basis points, each floor that we are short would be worth 9.06 points rather than its initial value of 5.32 points. Each floor in which we are implicitly long would be worth only 4.66

points rather than its initial value of 5.32 points because it becomes a floor for only 2.90 years rather than 7.35 years. The contraction in average life has more than offset the price appreciation the floor would otherwise experience. In this case, the PO option kicks in.[5]

Similarly, as rates rise, the floor you are implicitly long gets longer, and depreciates less in price than it otherwise would. In the case of FNR 93-183 S, the floor extends in average life from 7.35 years to 11.82 years, and declines from 5.38 points to 4.09 points. Meanwhile, the value of the floor you are short decreases in value to 2.49. To summarize, the investor is implicitly long a floor in the inverse floater, but the value of the floor cannot be accurately captured in the derivatives market. Pricing it in the derivatives market attributes to it too much premium income, which is then used to reduce the cost of the PO. Thus, the PO is purchased too cheaply in this analysis.

CONCLUSION

At least five different approaches are used to evaluate inverse floaters: the traditional yield and average life tables, recombination (or re-creation) analysis, OAS analysis, yield to forward LIBOR (or swap-based) analysis, and unbundling the options. Each of these methods adds to our understanding of the instruments, and each has a set of well-defined problems. The major advantages and disadvantages of each are summarized in Exhibit 37–8. The important point is that all methods should be used for what each contributes to a clearer evaluation of the security. If a security appears to represent good relative value on all measures, investors should feel comfortable that they have purchased a cheap bond. If, on the other hand, an inverse floater looks cheap on some measures and less appealing on others, further work must be done to see if the techniques by which the security looks good are techniques that we use to bias the answer upward, or if the techniques by which the security looks poor are techniques that we use to bias the answer downward.

---

5 There is the added difficulty in a steep rally for an investor who actually writes a floor against an inverse floater. At high enough speeds, the inverse is called away, leaving the investor with a naked floor. The payoff on the PO option should provide adequate compensation.

EXHIBIT 37–8
Advantages and Disadvantages of Different Evaluation Methods

Method of Evaluation	Advantages	Disadvantages
Traditional: yield and average life profile	Readily available on Bloomberg	Difficult to use for relative value analysis
		Doesn't tell what security should yield in base case as compensation for its risk
Re-creation value	Valued in light of underlying structure	Often hard to realistically price on the floater or underlying, further complicated when a TTIB is present
	Options in inverse do not have to be valued explicitly	Doesn't reveal anything about relative value—price on underlying or floater may be rich or cheap
Option-adjusted spread analysis	Captures option values and shape of Treasury yield curve in a consistent manner	Heavily dependent on prepayment model
	Structure of bond is explicitly considered	
Yield to forward LIBOR	Captures impact of the forward curve on coupon	Security really can't be swapped as a result of average life variability as prepayment rates change
		Doesn't take account of implicit long cap
		Doesn't tell what base-case yield should be
Unbundling the options	Captures options and turns inverse into a less complicated PO	Tends to overstate value of floor, making inverse look too attractive

## Chapter Thirty-Eight

Restructuring Adjustable-Rate Mortgages

Venkat T. Ramdev
BZW Securities Inc.

Lev Borodovsky
Credit Suisse

Matthew C. Baber
BZW Securities Inc.

The volatile interest rate environment that prevailed in the mid-1990s had a pronounced effect on the mortgage market. The rising interest rate environment that resulted from the Federal Reserve's tight money policy had severe adverse effect on the mortgage market and especially on structured mortgage securities (derivatives). This led to upheavals in this sector and the demise of several institutions that were key players in this area. When interest rates rise, the prepayments of the underlying mortgages slow down, causing the average life of securities to increase. This reduces the value of the fixed flows and changes the value of the securities considerably. Furthermore, liquidity issues that arise with the sale of these securities in a depressed market contribute to the deterioration in their value.

Adjustable-rate mortgages (ARMs) were considered to be somewhat immune to rising interest rates. That did not turn out to be the case, especially as short-term rates rose rapidly and a liquidity crunch in the fixed-rate mortgage sector rippled across the markets for all mortgage-backed securities. A number of devastating and highly publicized losses by public funds and other institutions prompted many holders to abandon the ARM market. Street dealers resolved the problem of floating-rate mortgages by configuring them into option-free floating-rate instruments that pay a spread to the LIBOR index. ARM holders were willing to pay up in order to convert their holdings into a liquid index without any embedded optionality.

Similar to a floating-rate note, the owner of an ARM pays a rate, which is set periodically based on a benchmark index, plus a spread. These securities are expected to remain close to par even as rates fluctuate. The resets generally happen annually or semiannually, though the period can sometimes be longer. The indexes are usually short-term Treasury yields (constant-maturity treasuries, or CMTs), cost of funds for thrifts, or sometimes the prime rate. To protect homeowners as well as pools of mortgages from rates rising to extremely high levels or rising too quickly, caps are always built into these mortgages. Floors are put on to cover some of the cost of the caps. In the early 1990s, the buyers of adjustable-rate mortgages dismissed the value of the caps because the caps were deep out of the money in a low and stable interest rate environment. Investors searched for high floating coupon securities. The built-in optionality (the caps) surprised investors as the risk profile of ARMs changed in a rising rate environment, making them behave like fixed-income securities.

INTEREST RATE SENSITIVITY OF ADJUSTABLE-RATE MORTGAGES

Adjustable mortgages always have some or all of the following embedded options: (1) periodic caps, (2) periodic floors, (3) lifetime cap, and (4) sometimes a lifetime floor. These embedded options have a significant effect on the risk profile and price sensitivity to fluctuations in interest rates.

The *periodic cap and floor* restrict fluctuations of the adjustable mortgage rate, preventing an increase (decrease) from one period to the next from exceeding the level determined by the periodic cap (floor). The periodic cap can be thought of as a series of European calls whose strike rates are set at the beginning of the reset period and whose options expire at the end of the reset period or are exercised based on the rate at that time. The cap is sold to the mortgage payer as protection against an unexpected rise in rates while the mortgage payer sells back the floor to reduce the cost of the cap. Effectively, the investor who owns an ARM is *short* the periodic and lifetime cap and *long* the periodic floors. In an extremely volatile interest rate environment, periodic caps and floors have a significant value

EXHIBIT 38–1
Effects of Interest Rate Fluctuations on the Price of a 6.5 Percent ARM

Mortgage: 6.0% GNMA II ARM
Coupon: 6.0%
Periodic cap: 1%
Periodic floor: 1%
Cap and floor reset: annually
Lifetime cap: 11.0%

Time Period (years)	Change in Mortgage Index (%)	ARM Rate (%)	Effective Options
0	0	6.0%	None
1	+1.50%	7.0	Periodic cap
2	+1.00	8.0	Periodic cap
3	−2.00	7.0	Periodic floor
4	+0.50	7.5	None
5	+2.50	8.5	Periodic cap
6	+1.25	9.5	Periodic cap
7	+1.50	10.5	Periodic cap
8	+0.75	11.0	Lifetime cap

because they limit sudden large increases or declines in rates. The *lifetime cap* (a series of European calls) offers protection to the homeowner by capping the maximum adjustable mortgage rate during the life of the mortgage. The lifetime cap has a significant value when interest rates increase considerably above the level at which the mortgage was initially issued. The *lifetime floor* is sometimes sold by the mortgage payer to reduce the cost of the cap, thus effectively purchasing a collar on the rates.

Investors in a standard ARM have the following positions:

- Long the floating cash flows.
- Short the prepayment option.
- Short periodic cap.
- Short lifetime cap.
- Long periodic floor.
- Long lifetime floor (if one exists).

Exhibit 38–1 illustrates the effect of the interest rate fluctuations on the price of an ARM.

EXHIBIT 38–2
Capped ARM versus a Fixed-Rate Security

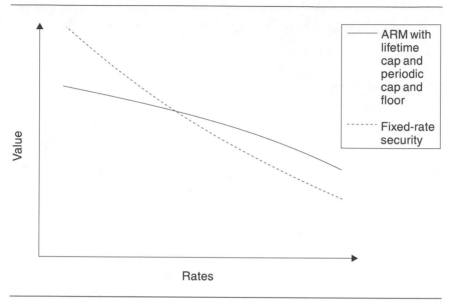

MECHANICS OF ARMs AND THE
RATIONALE FOR RESTRUCTURING

Investors anticipating rising rates purchase floating-rate structures as protection. A sudden increase in rates by the Fed raised the current and anticipated coupon on their investment, preventing the ARM from declining in value in a way that a fixed-income security declines. However, this assumption proved to be erroneous. When short-term interest rates increased significantly (more than what the periodic cap would permit), the caps became in the money, restricting the coupon from rising further. Once periodic caps were reached, the security offered no added protection against further interest rate hikes within that reset period. In addition, as the longer-term rates rose, the lifetime cap become more valuable. The price sensitivity to rates of these adjustable-rate mortgages began to resemble that of a fixed-rate mortgage (see Exhibit 38–2), and their value dropped. It is important to note that the rise in both the long- and the short-term rates reduces the value of an ARM by capping *current* as well

EXHIBIT 38–3
Duration of Capped ARM

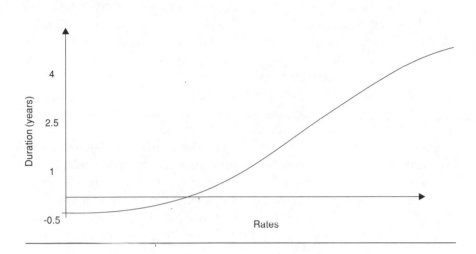

as the *expected* coupon, while the present value of the cash flows decreases. Investors simply overlooked the effects of the built-in optionality that they had sold to the mortgage payers.

Most managers of fixed-income funds track the effective duration of their portfolio. ARM securities have durations of under a year while the yield is relatively high. Due to built-in caps, which represent a short call option position on interest rates, the securities have a strong negative convexity, causing duration to rise rapidly with increasing rates because the embedded caps represent a short convexity position on interest rates (i.e., when interest rates fall, the coupon size of the adjustable-rate mortgage drops and prepayments pick up, lowering the value of the security). Managers who thought they had a low duration portfolio found their portfolios durations increasing to four or five years in a rising rate environment. Exhibit 38–3 shows the effect of rising rates on a typical capped ARM security's duration.

Investors in these securities faced two alternatives: (1) Sell their portfolio of adjustable rate mortgages at a loss in an illiquid depressed market or (2) restructure them by means of a swap into an option-free floating-rate instrument indexed to LIBOR.

RESTRUCTURING A GNMA II ADJUSTABLE-RATE MORTGAGE

Investors who hold distressed adjustable-rate mortgages such as 6.0 percent GNMA II ARMS (e.g., Coupon 1 CMT + 150 bp, annually resetting periodic cap and floor of +100 bp and −100 bp respectively, lifetime cap of 11 percent) are willing to pay for swapping the cash flows from the adjustable-rate mortgage for option-free floating-rate payments. The float-ing-rate payments are indexed to LIBOR (paying a spread over it) and are not subjected to the embedded options that exist in the underlying mortgage (i.e., periodic cap and floor and the lifetime cap and floor).

An investor who owns this type of GNMA II ARM pass-through cer-tificate enters into an interest rate swap with a counterparty which results in an uncapped, amortizing LIBOR floating-rate note that pays a spread over LIBOR. In effect, the investor buys back the collar or the lifetime cap or both, which he or she had sold to the homeowner from the coun-terparty, and converts the yearly reset of monthly payments based on the CMT into a monthly floating rate linked to the more liquid LIBOR index. The new monthly adjusting index allows the investor to fully participate in the increases in the rates on a monthly basis. Exhibit 38–4 details the transaction.

An investor who owns a distressed GNMA II ARM security can restruc-ture it into a floating-rate security that pays a spread over LIBOR by entering into the following transaction.

The investor enters into an amortizing swap (often called an index principal swap or an IPS) with a counterparty such as a bank or financial institution. In this transaction, the investor pays the cash flows that result from the GNMA adjustable-rate mortgage and receives a floating rate, which is a spread to LIBOR. The cash flow from the GNMA II ARM is 150 bp over the one-year constant maturity treasury rate, subject to the annually resetting periodic caps and periodic floors (+100 bp and −100 bp respec-tively) and the life time cap (11 percent). The notional outstanding of the swap amortizes according to a predetermined set schedule that is derived from the prepayment estimate forecasts for the adjustable-rate mortgage pool under consideration. The counterparty pays the investor a spread over the one-month LIBOR rate, which is devoid of any caps or floors. In addition, the investor pays the counterparty the difference between the par value and the bid price of the GNMA ARM. This transforms the swap into a par-par swap.

EXHIBIT 38–4
Restructuring a GNMA II ARM

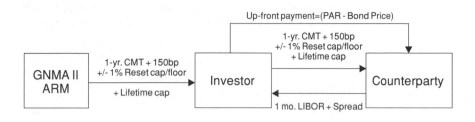

The spread over the LIBOR rate that the investor receives depends on the intrinsic value of the embedded options in the GNMA ARM at the commencement of the transaction, the forward curve of the one-month LIBOR, and the forward curve of the one-year constant maturity treasury. Higher value of the embedded options in the ARM at the time of restructuring would imply a lower spread over LIBOR than the investor receives.

RISKS IN RESTRUCTURING

The amortization schedule of the notional balance on the swap is based on the outstanding notional and is determined using the long-term forecasted PSA estimates for the prepayments on the GNMA pool. When interest rates fall, the prepayment speed increases, causing the outstanding mortgage to prepay faster than originally anticipated, thereby shortening the average life. The converse is true should interest rates rise. This presents an issue to the investor because of a mismatch between the actual principal outstanding on the GNMA mortgage, which determines the cash stream to the investor, and the outstanding principal on the swap, which dictates the amount the investor pays out. Hence, the investor bears the prepayment risk.

The swap transaction is often designed for a 10-year maturity, as in this example. However, the underlying mortgage is a 30-year instrument. Therefore, in the event the mortgage does not completely prepay by the end of the 10-year horizon, the above transaction matures and the investor bears the *tail risk*.

Variations to the Restructuring Trade

There may be a few variations to the above structure. Instead of uncapping all the embedded options in the GNMA ARM completely, investors may choose to uncap one or a combination of the embedded options in the ARM and swap the cash flows into a LIBOR floater with the remaining options.

Uncapping the lifetime cap.   The floating leg of the swap rate is subject only to the periodic caps and floors. The maximum interest rate on the floater is not bounded. The investor who believes that rates may rise dramatically over the long term due to inflationary pressures would buy back the lifetime cap. In the example, the investor may feel that rates may gradually move above 11 percent over a longer period of time.

Uncapping the periodic cap.   An investor who believes that rates are mean reverting (i.e., the tendency of rates to revert to their historical average over time) and will stay within a range, even though rates may be volatile from one year to the next, may buy back only the periodic collar (i.e., the periodic caps and floors). As long as rates don't approach 11 percent, the investor fully participates in the rising rates.

Exhibit 38–5 shows the sensitivity of the security to rates as the caps are taken off. Note that the drop in value at lower rates is due to prepayments in the underlying mortgage, giving capped ARM a high negative convexity. (In Exhibit 38–5, the three securities are assumed to have the same initial value.)

- Uncapping only the periodic cap allows one to swap into LIBOR plus 35 bp (the holder is still subjected to the lifetime cap).
- Uncapping only the lifetime cap allows one to swap into LIBOR plus 80 bp (the holder is still subjected to the periodic caps and floors).
- Uncapping both the lifetime and the periodic cap allows one to swap into LIBOR plus 25 bp.
- Without uncapping, the swap results in LIBOR plus 150 bp for the investor, with the risk of receiving small fixed payments if the index hits the caps.

In this example, the value of both caps together is 125 bp, while apart they are 115 bp and 70 bp (or 185 bp). If the lifetime cap becomes in the money, the periodic cap would no longer be valuable because the lifetime cap now restricts the payments from rising further, independent of the year-to-year changes in rate. The caps are therefore not independent and are less valuable together than they would be if priced separately.

EXHIBIT 38–5
Uncapping an ARM Security

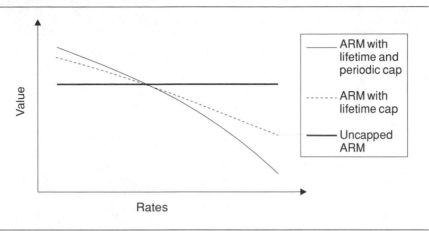

Moving the strike.   In some instances, it may be too expensive to buy back the optionality fully. Investors may just buy back a *call spread*, which would shift the periodic cap from 1 percent a year to, say, 2 percent a year or a lifetime cap to possibly 13 percent.

This variation is usually adopted by regional banks and thrifts, which do not want to cap the maximum rate they receive at, say, 11 percent. These institutions would like a higher cap, such as 13 percent in order to benefit from a higher interest rate environment prevailing at the time of execution of the swap transaction because that would reflect directly in their cost of funds. Effectively, the investor is buying back the 11 percent lifetime cap and selling a 13 percent lifetime cap (*call spread*).

All of the above structures give the investor a cheaper alternative, thus a higher spread received over LIBOR.

Swapping from a one-year LIBOR basis instead of one-year CMT basis into a one-month basis.   Another variation is a structure in which the investor pays a rate indexed to one-year LIBOR instead of the one-year constant-maturity treasury (CMT) rate. The investor then pays a spread over the one-year LIBOR to the counterparty on the swap, even though the one-year CMT rate is the index used to determine the cash flows for GNMA adjustable-rate mortgages. In this variation, the investor takes the basis spread risk between the one-year CMT and the one-year LIBOR.

EXHIBIT 38–6
Comparison of the Results of Uncapping the Periodic Cap and Floors and the Lifetime Cap

GNMA II ARM:
Periodic cap and floor = 1.0% (annually resetting)
Lifetime cap = 11%
Initial coupon = 6%

Time Period (years)	Change in Mortgage Index (%)	ARM Rate (%)	ARM Rate (%) Uncapped Periodic Caps and Floors	ARM Rate (%) Uncapped Lifetime Cap
0	0	6.00%	6.00%	6.00%
1	+1.00%	7.00	7.00	7.00
2	+1.50	8.00	8.50	8.00
3	−0.50	7.50	8.00	7.50
4	+0.50	8.00	8.50	8.00
5	+2.00	9.00	10.50	9.00
6	+1.25	10.00	11.00	10.00
7	+1.50	11.00	11.00	11.00
8	+0.75	11.00	11.00	11.75
9	+0.50	11.00	11.00	12.25
10	+0.50	11.00	11.00	12.75

Transferring the prepayment risk. In the proposed structure, the investor takes the risk that the GNMA ARM pool will prepay faster or slower than the forecasted speeds. This transaction may result in a mismatch between the actual notional outstanding on the mortgage and that on the swap. This risk could be transferred to the counterparty by reconfiguring the notional on the swap to amortize at the actual prepayment rate of the mortgage pool and not a predetermined amortization rate. This would result in an additional charge to the investor.

Difficulties with restructuring. In a volatile environment, embedded options can be costly to buy back. Some of the caps may be in or close to the money as rates rise or the yield curve steepens. The dealers often charge a considerable spread to swap investors into LIBOR from a less liquid index. In addition, it can be costly to get out of the prepayment risk.

EXHIBIT 38–7
Market Effects on Value of Built-in Options to an ARM

	Values of the				
Scenario	Lifetime Cap	Lifetime Floor	Periodic Cap	Periodic Floor	Prepayment Option
Increase in volatility	Increases	Increases	Increases	Increases	Increases
Parallel, upward shift in the yield curve	Increases	Decreases	Increases	Decreases	Decreases
Yield curve steepens	Increases	Decreases	Increases	Decreases	Decreases
Yield curve inverts	Decreases	Increases	Decreases	Increases	Increases

As most mortgage dealers are long the prepayment risk and would not like to put additional risk to their portfolio, they often charge high spreads.

EFFECT OF MARKET MOVEMENTS

Exhibit 38–7 illustrates general changes in value of all the built-in options to an ARM as the market environment changes.

The value of the built-in options fluctuates with movements in the short-term rates as well as the long-term rates and the expected volatility of rates. In addition, change in prepayment speed due to interest rate fluctuations and sectoral and demographical shifts affect the value of the ARM.

EFFECT OF YIELD CURVE SHIFTS

Parallel Shifts in the Yield Curve

Parallel shifts affect the value of periodic caps by changing the value of the first cap and by increasing the absolute volatility of forward rates. For example, when the short-term rates are at 4 percent, a 1 percent cap has little value because rates would have to move relatively by 25 percent from their current level to hit the strike. If short-term rates are near 10 percent, the effective relative move would correspond to 10 percent, which is much more likely. In addition, the probability of prepayment drops as rates rise, increas-

EXHIBIT 38–8
Parallel Shift

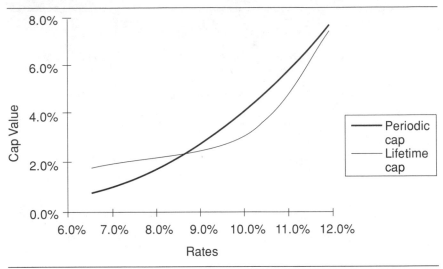

ing the value of caps. Lifetime caps rise in value as rates move them closer to at the money. Exhibit 38–8 shows the sensitivity of a periodic cap to parallel shifts in rates (while the implied volatility is kept constant):

Sensitivity to Yield Spread between the Short and Long Rates

ARM investors received a relatively high yield because they were implicitly selling periodic and lifetime caps in the steep yield curve environment that prevailed in the early 1990s. A steep curve implies larger forward rates affecting the lifetime caps and rising forward rates that affect the periodic caps. Exhibit 38–9 shows the sensitivity of the caps to the spread between the long- and short-term rates (1 percent periodic cap, 11 percent lifetime cap).

It is important to note that in an upward-sloping yield curve environment, the value of a lifetime cap comes from the options (caplets) that are farther out (greater than two years), whereas the periodic caplets are generally flat throughout the 10-year period, dropping off due to discounting (see Exhibit 38–10).

As noted earlier, the two caps in combination are worth less than the sum of the individuals.

EXHIBIT 38–9
Yield Curve "Steepness"

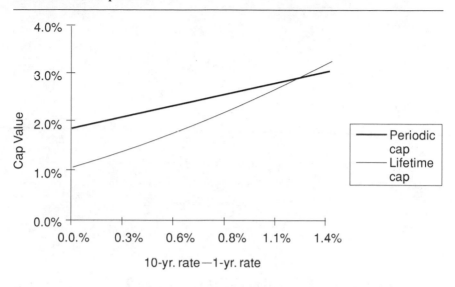

EXHIBIT 38–10
Caplet Value

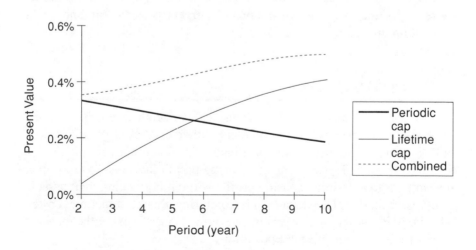

EXHIBIT 38–11
Volatility Sensitivity

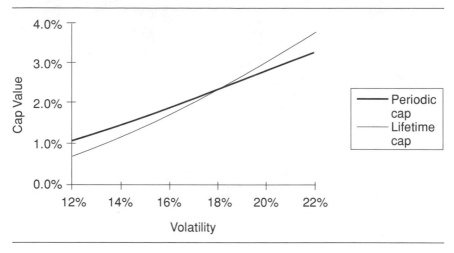

EFFECT OF INCREASED INTEREST RATE VOLATILITY

The lifetime cap increases with volatility considerably faster than the periodic cap because the periodic cap is only sensitive to the rate variance during a single period. Vega (sensitivity of the option price to volatility) of the longer dated caplets of the lifetime cap is larger compared to the vega of the periodic caplets. Exhibit 38–11 compares responses to volatility increases of the two types of options (1 percent periodic cap and an 11 percent lifetime cap).

CONCLUSION

The built-in optionality of ARM securities can produce unexpected and often dramatic response to the markets. Other distressed securities with built-in optionality, such as inverse floaters, are sometimes restructured in a similar fashion. Transactions of this type permit investors to tailor their investments to a desired exposure profile without liquidating their asset in a depressed market. This manner of restructuring, though sometimes costly, adds liquidity into these markets by providing alternatives for the management of fixed-income investor portfolios.

Chapter Thirty-Nine

Exploring Prepayment Functions in OAS Models

Jeffrey Ho
PaineWebber

The single most important component of any mortgage OAS model is the prepayment function. It is also the single most important source of differences between the option-adjusted spreads, durations, convexities and other measures of risk and reward generated by different OAS models. Market participants model prepayments using actual historical data, and most use a similar set of explanatory variables, but they employ a wide variety of statistical estimation procedures doing so. The result is a very wide range in prepayment estimates for the same securities in the same interest-rate scenarios. Most users of OAS models understand that the output is highly dependent on the prepayment function, and some OAS users even attempt to relate a particular prepayment model's biases to the resultant OA-output, but that is usually as far as it goes. OAS has been around so long now, that many users seem to take it for granted and do not dig beneath the surface to get a feeling for how inputs and parameters drive the numbers.

We believe option-adjusted analysis of MBS can be a very powerful tool, but an effective use of this tool requires a more systematic and general understanding of how differences in prepayment models affect the OAS results. This article attempts to do that by specifying a simplified, generalized form of the prepayment function, which we then calibrate to produce two prepayment functions: one implied by the Street Median prepayment projections, and a second implied by IO/PO prices. Armed with these simple, implied prepayment functions, we can examine the sensitivity of

OAS results by changing the shape of the function. This experiment captures most of the typical variation seen between prepayment models. We also are able to introduce prepayment uncertainty not correlated with interest rates and study its impact on OAS results. Finally, we test these systematic adjustments to the prepayment function on a full range of pass-through, IO, PO, and fixed-rate CMO securities.

THE PREPAYMENT FUNCITON

The first step in our analysis is to specify a prepayment function that captures the key determinants of prepayments included in the great host of prepayment models currently in use on the Street, by third-party analytic services and by large mortgage investors. This function is the mathematical equivalent of a sentence that says: "Prepayments are faster or slower depending on the age of the underlying loans and the interest rate savings possible if borrowers refinance or move." Expressing it mathematically allows us to change the coefficients and other parameters of the equation to reflect the most typical differences between prepayments. Our simplified prepayment function is spelled out below.

$$CPR = \frac{TOP}{1 + e^x}$$

$$X = INTC + AGE \times (1 - e^{RHO \times age}) + REFI \times$$
$$MAX[MIN[MAX[refi,LOWER],UPPER]-LOWER,0]$$

Subject to a minimum PSA speed:

$$CPR = MAX[CPR,[MIN[age,30] \times 0.2] \times \frac{PSA}{100}]$$

where

TOP	=	highest CPR speed possible
PSA	=	lowest PSA speed possible
INTC	=	an interecept term
RHO	=	coefficient to transform age
AGE	=	coefficient for sensitivity to age
REFI	=	coefficient for sensitivity to refinancing incentive
LOWER	=	lower breakpoint in refinancing curve

EXHIBIT 39–1
Street Median Prepayment Model

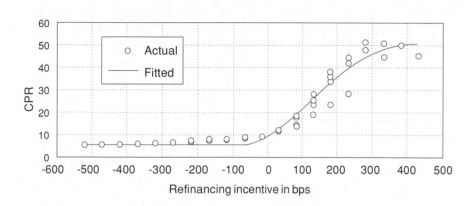

UPPER = upper breakpoint in refinancing curve
age   = age in months
refi   = refinancing incentive in bps

This formulation allows us to capture the response of prepayments to the rate incentive and aging. Most prepayment analysts consider prepayments to be primarily a function of rate, or refinancing along with mobility, incentive, seasoning, or age, seasonality and burnout. We ignore the effects of seasonality and burnout for simplicity's sake, because the lion's share of variability in prepayments can be explained by the first two, and because it allows us to bypass any debate about the magnitude or timing of these lesser factors.

Our function has the typical S-curve shape (see Exhibit 39–1, described below, to see what we mean) which we get when we plot actual or projected prepayments against the rate incentive. Mortgages which face a negative incentive to prepay are predicted to pay at a low rate, reflecting the fact that even when borrowing costs are very high, some households still move. In other words, some amount of mobility is interest-rate insensitive. This is the bottom turn of the reclining "S." Prepayments quickly increase from this "base rate" as the incentive becomes neutral and then positive. At some point, further increases in incentive generate only modest increases in prepayment response. This plateau is the top of the "S." When mortgage market participants speak of "the steepness" of the prepayment curve, or function, they are referring to the mostly linear portion of the plotted curve that connects the base rate to plateau rate. The more responsive (jumbo as opposed to conforming conventional loans, for instance) to rate savings, the steeper is this portion of the curve, or in other words, the smaller the savings required to get the mortgages to prepay at the plateau rate. A "slower" model takes greater incentives to get from base to plateau speeds and plateaus at lower speeds. The coefficients TOP, INTC, REFI, LOWER and UPPER allow us considerable freedom in setting the shape the curve. Seasoning enters into the prepayment equation in such a way that its influence plateaus out after a while (typically around 20-40 months).

THE OAS MODEL

The ins and outs of OAS modeling are not our subject, but a brief description of our OAS model is in order. We use a plain vanilla, Black-Derman-Toy approach. The term structure used to generate the OAS results for this paper is represented by a single-factor, arbitrage-free model that describes a log-normal diffusion of a short-term rate.[1] The diffusion process is calibrated to return on-the-run Treasury prices observed on April 3, 1995. Additionally, the volatility of the diffusion process is calibrated to return observed cap prices as of the same valuation date. Next, a stratified sampling of paths is taken from this calibrated diffusion process. The mortgage securities are then valued by generating cash flows along these paths using the prepayment function and summing the probability weighted present values of the security along the sample paths. This stratified sampling approach avoids any sampling bias and reduces computational time.[2]

A STREET MEDIAN PREPAYMENT FUNCTION

One stratagem the market has developed for sorting through the large number of apparently valid prepayment models is to reflect the median of

---

1 F. Black; E. Derman; and W. Toy. "A One-Factor Model of Interest Rates and Its Application to Treasury Bond Options." *Financial Analysts Journal*, 46 (Jan.–Feb. 1990), pp. 33–39.

2 Thomas S. Y. Ho. "Managing Illiquid Bonds and the Linear Path Space." *Journal of Fixed Income*, June 1992, pp. 80–93.

Street prepayment projections in static cash flow evaluations of MBSs. As a result, the Street median has become a critical component of aggregate prepayment expectations and, in turn, market value.

We can turn this process on its head, by finding the prepayment function implied by Street median projections for various coupons and degrees of seasoning and then incorporating that prepayment function in an OAS analysis. Interesting in its own right, this undertaking also gives us a point of comparison for option-adjusted evaluation using the prepayment function implied by IO/PO prices. In this case we derived a general form of an agency conventional 30-year prepayment model based on the Street Median prepayment projections current rates and instantaneous yield shifts of plus or minus 50, 100, 200, and 300 basis points for FNMA 6s through 9.5s as of April 3, 1995. These PSAs are shown in Exhibit 39–1, along with refinancing incentives estimating by subtracting the current coupon rate (8.16 percent as of April 3, 1995) from the security coupon. The PSAs were then converted to CPRs. The prepayment function implied by these data points was found by iteratively adjusting the coefficients in our generalized prepayment function to minimize the squared difference between forecast and actual CPRs. A plot of the implied Street Median prepayment function, assuming age equal to 30 months, is shown in Exhibit 39–2, along with actual Street Median projected CPRs. The coefficients of this representative model are shown in Exhibit 39–3 under the heading "Street."

IMPLIED PREPAYMENT FUNCTION

Much as the market can derive implied volatilities from option prices, we can inspect the prepayment function implied by current mortgage security prices. For example, some market participants look for multipliers which can be applied to an existing prepayment model to equalize OASs on IOs and POs off the same collateral. The trouble with this simple approach is that a different multiplier is required for different coupon IOs and POs. It can, however, lend some insight into whether a particular prepayment model over- or underestimates speeds for a particular coupon.

A more robust approach is to find a single prepayment function that minimizes the differences in OASs between IOs and POs for all coupons. We do that by finding the coefficients in our prepayment function which minimize the OASs modeled as described above, using pricing for benchmark trusts as of April 3, 1995. The resulting coefficients are listed in

EXHIBIT 39–2
Street Median Prepayment Estimates as of 4/3/95

					Shifts				
Cpn	−300	−200	−100	−50	0	50	100	200	300
					Median PSA				
6.00	302	164	134	124	117	109	104	95	92
6.50	481	191	141	132	124	115	108	98	94
7.00	611	317	156	143	133	124	116	104	96
7.50	753	474	209	154	144	136	128	112	102
8.00	812	633	314	206	160	146	136	121	112
8.50	860	720	424	244	191	163	149	128	117
9.00	852	857	584	400	252	198	160	140	128
9.50	773	737	477	404	326	241	205	157	139
				Refi Incentive with 8.16 Cur Cpn					
6.00	84	−16	−116	−166	−216	−266	−316	−416	−516
6.50	134	34	−66	−116	−166	−216	−266	−366	−466
7.00	184	84	−16	−66	−116	−166	−216	−316	−416
7.50	234	134	34	−16	−66	−116	−166	−266	−366
8.00	284	184	84	34	−16	−66	−116	−216	−316
8.50	334	234	134	84	34	−16	−66	−166	−266
9.00	384	284	184	134	84	34	−16	−116	−216
9.50	434	334	234	184	134	84	34	−66	−166

Exhibit 39–2 under the heading "Implied." In addition, we derive two additional sets of coefficients, one for a model which is uniformly slower than the "Implied" and another for a model which is steeper than the "Street." They are shown in Exhibit 39–3 under the headings "Slower" and "Steeper." Projected CPRs are plotted against prepayment incentive for all four derived models in Exhibit 39–4. Exhibit 39–5 shows projected CPRs plotted against age for the four models.

Coefficients of the slower model were selected to correspond uniformly to a slowing as envisioned by the Street. Coefficients of the "Steeper" curve were selected so that 30-year FNMA 8s would have the same expected average life as under the "Street" model, while lower coupons extend and higher coupon contract. This steeper curve is indicative of the interest rate sensitivity we would expect a whole loan prepayment model to exhibit.

EXHIBIT 39–3
Coefficients for Various Prepayment Models

	Street	*Implied*	*Slower*	*Steeper*
TOP	53.6	26.5	26.5	62.0
INTC	6.2	5.0	4.6	7.0
AGE	−1.56	−1.56	−1.56	−1.56
RHO	−0.1	−0.1	−0.1	−0.1
DIS	−0.0115	−0.0090	−0.0091	−0.0135
LOWER	−269	−390	−300	−269
UPPER	439	300	300	439
PSA	92	118	75	95

EXHIBIT 39–4
CPR as a Function of Refinancing Incentive Given Age of 10 Months

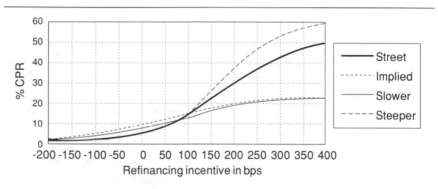

OAS RESULTS

Exhibit 39–6 shows the OAS results from using these different models. Results calculated using the derived models include option-adjusted spread (OAS), option-adjusted duration, option adjusted convexity, and expected WAL (probability weighted across paths). We also calculate zero OAS prices under each model. The zero prices are those implied by holding OAS at zero and are included to provide another way of measuring the effect of differences in the prepayment function on OAS modeling and option-adjusted measures of risk and reward.

EXHIBIT 39–5
CPR as a Function of Age Given Refinancing Incentive of 100 bps

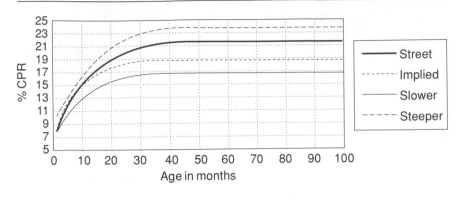

One thing readers may notice is that, under the "Implied" model, the OASs on the IOs and POs are far from being equal. Recall the implied model was the one which *minimized* the differences between OAS on IOs and POs with the same collateral. The OASs on IOs and POs are much closer than we would observe in an econometric model estimated directly from historical data or than those calculated using the "Street" model, since the firm models underlying the "Street model" were in turn estimated from historical data. Note also that the durations and convexities for collateral, IOs and POs using the implied model are what we would expect. In fact, it is somewhat surprising that so simple a model produces such adequate results. The other characteristic of this implied prepayment function we find quite interesting is that it is more gently sloping than one might expect. This is depicted in Exhibit 39–4. Models calibrated from historical data tend to change curvature more dramatically.

Just as we would expect, the "Slower" model produces higher OASs as well as higher zero OAS prices for IOs and premium coupon collateral and lower OASs and zero OAS prices for POs and discounts. This effect of prepayment function shape is the basic, critically important result we wanted to derive from this experiment. It is summarized in Exhibit 39–7.

We also see differences in the option-adjusted measures when we compare results produced under the "Street" and "Steeper" functions. For example, under the steeper model, as the average life on the discount collateral shortens up, the discount-backed POs benefit (look more attrac-

EXHIBIT 39–6
OAS Results Given Various Prepayment Models (Prices as of 4/3/95)

Type	Actual Cpn	Actual Price	Street Median zPx*	OAS	Dur	Cx	WAL	Implied zPx*	OAS	Dur	Cx	WAL	Slower zPx*	OAS	Dur	Cx	WAL	Steeper zPx*	OAS	Dur	Cx	WAL	Prepayment Uncertainty zPx*	OAS	Dur	Cx	WAL
FNMA 30yr	6.50	91:20	93:24	38	5.9	0.2	10.3	94:16	53	5.9	0.5	9.1	94:20	54	5.8	0.5	9.4	93:26	38	5.8	0.2	10.1	94:16	54	5.8	0.5	9.1
FNMA 30yr	7.00	94:14	96:10	34	5.7	0.4	9.9	97:05	51	5.7	0.1	8.9	97:09	51	5.7	0.3	9.1	96:07	32	5.5	0.3	9.7	97:05	51	5.7	0.1	8.8
FNMA 30yr	7.50	96:30	98:25	34	5.6	0.0	9.6	99:24	55	5.2	-1.2	8.2	99:28	53	5.4	-0.5	8.9	98:18	30	5.5	0.4	9.4	99:23	55	5.2	-1.2	8.2
FNMA 30yr	8.00	99:04	101:04	39	4.9	-2.0	9.0	101:31	60	4.4	-1.5	7.3	102:09	60	4.7	-1.5	8.2	100:30	34	4.9	-1.9	9.0	101:30	60	4.4	-1.5	7.3
FNMA 30yr	8.50	101:04	103:03	42	3.7	-2.9	7.6	103:27	61	3.7	-1.1	6.6	104:10	65	4.0	-1.4	7.4	102:28	37	3.6	-3.7	7.7	103:26	61	3.7	-1.1	6.5
FNMA 30yr	9.00	102:25	104:10	39	2.3	-2.7	6.1	105:13	64	3.2	-0.8	5.9	105:31	71	3.3	-1.1	6.5	104:00	31	1.9	-3.3	5.8	105:12	63	3.1	-0.8	5.8
FNMA 30yr	9.50	104:05	104:03	0	1.0	-1.3	4.1	106:05	55	2.8	-0.3	4.9	106:21	64	2.7	-0.3	4.9	103:16	-26	0.4	-1.3	3.6	106:03	54	2.8	-0.2	4.9
FNS 249 IO	6.50	35:20	38:28	169	0.1	0.3	9.9	36:11	40	1.5	-4.0	8.9	36:31	71	2.4	0.3	9.0	38:20	145	-1.0	0.7	9.8	36:05	30	1.5	-4.1	8.8
FNS 240 IO	7.00	36:03	40:03	206	0.7	1.4	9.5	38:02	105	-4.4	-24.1	8.6	38:26	141	1.8	-3.3	8.8	39:18	171	-0.1	1.6	9.2	37:27	95	-4.5	-24.1	8.5
FNS 254 IO	7.50	36:06	41:22	276	-4.3	-22.7	9.2	37:23	86	-13.5	-12.2	7.8	40:21	224	-5.5	-27.6	8.6	40:31	235	-1.1	-7.6	8.9	37:16	75	-13.6	-12.2	7.8
FNS 251 IO	8.00	35:00	40:21	305	-18.3	-35.9	8.2	35:26	52	-17.1	1.5	6.8	39:11	238	-14.9	-8.6	7.6	41:12	301	-15.5	-54.4	8.3	35:18	36	-17.3	1.8	6.7
FNS 7 IO	8.50	30:12	34:05	308	-31.4	-10.1	5.9	32:11	166	-15.4	6.2	5.4	35:07	352	-16.4	3.0	5.9	34:14	301	-36.5	-20.8	5.9	32:04	149	-15.5	6.2	5.3
FNS 42 IO	9.00	30:11	29:11	-59	-38.6	5.9	4.6	31:09	87	-12.8	7.6	4.8	33:22	275	-15.0	6.2	5.2	28:10	-217	-49.4	8.1	4.4	31:02	67	-12.8	7.3	4.8
FNS 2 IO	9.50	30:16	25:03	-686	-40.6	21.4	3.7	31:00	47	-9.7	8.0	4.5	32:31	213	-12.6	8.2	4.8	22:18	-1,272	-53.7	36.1	3.2	30:23	21	-9.8	8.4	4.5
FNS 249 PO	6.50	56:03	55:11	-21	9.7	0.2	9.9	58:27	79	8.1	3.4	8.9	58:12	65	7.6	0.4	9.0	55:30	-5	10.1	-0.3	9.8	59:02	85	8.1	3.5	8.8
FNS 240 PO	7.00	58:15	56:21	-53	8.9	1.4	9.5	59:25	39	11.7	15.8	8.6	59:05	19	7.9	2.9	8.8	57:13	-31	9.0	-0.5	9.2	60:00	45	11.7	15.8	8.5
FNS 254 PO	7.50	61:00	57:15	-105	12.3	16.7	9.2	62:21	52	16.1	5.4	7.8	59:27	-34	12.4	17.9	8.6	58:10	-82	9.7	6.1	8.9	62:28	58	16.0	5.3	7.8
FNS 251 PO	8.00	64:18	60:26	-119	19.8	20.6	8.2	66:23	72	15.5	-3.0	6.8	63:15	-35	16.4	2.9	7.6	60:07	-137	18.3	34.0	8.3	66:30	80	15.4	-3.0	6.7
FNS 7 PO	8.50	70:31	69:01	-69	20.1	1.0	5.9	71:25	30	11.6	-4.1	5.4	69:11	-56	13.5	-3.2	5.9	68:30	-73	22.4	5.1	5.9	72:00	37	11.6	-4.1	5.3
FNS 42 PO	9.00	72:21	74:22	85	17.8	-5.5	4.6	74:07	61	9.4	-3.9	4.8	72:09	-14	11.2	-4.0	5.2	75:25	134	20.3	-6.9	4.4	74:14	69	9.4	-3.9	4.7
FNS 2 PO	9.50	73:29	79:10	263	14.3	-8.5	3.7	75:19	69	7.8	-3.5	4.5	74:02	7	9.4	-4.1	4.8	81:14	403		-11.6	3.2	75:25	77	7.7	-3.5	4.5
2yr SEQ	7.71	100:00	100:04	6	1.8	-2.4	2.2	100:06	13	1.4	-0.9	1.7	100:00	18	1.7	-1.3	2.0	100:04	6	1.8	-3.0	2.2	100:06	12	1.4	-0.9	1.6
5yr SEQ	7.93	100:00	100:15	10	4.6	-3.6	6.0	101:09	33	3.8	-1.6	4.8	101:12	33	4.4	-1.9	5.9	100:12	8	4.7	-4.3	6.1	101:09	33	3.8	-1.6	4.8
10yr SEQ	8.09	100:00	101:29	28	6.3	-3.8	11.5	103:17	54	5.8	-2.0	9.5	103:24	54	6.6	-2.3	11.6	103:16	22	6.3	-4.2	11.7	103:16	54	5.7	-2.1	9.4
20yr SEQ	8.41	100:00	106:06	67	7.9	-0.2	19.1	108:31	91	8.6	-0.7	18.5	109:08	91	9.0	0.0	20.8	108:30	60	7.7	0.0	18.7	108:30	91	8.6	-0.7	18.4
2yr PAC	7.32	100:00	100:04	5	2.2	0.0	2.4	100:02	15	2.2	0.0	2.4	100:02	15	2.3	0.0	2.4	100:02	3	2.2	-0.1	2.3	100:10	14	2.2	0.0	2.4
5yr PAC	7.53	100:00	100:10	7	4.0	-0.3	5.5	101:11	28	4.3	-0.2	5.8	101:15	31	4.6	-0.1	5.8	100:03	2	4.0	-0.8	5.5	101:10	27	4.3	-0.2	5.8
5.8 10yr PAC	7.73	100:00	101:19	23	5.7	-1.0	10.1	103:10	44	6.6	0.1	10.9	103:22	48	6.9	0.5	10.9	101:02	16	5.6	-1.4	9.7	103:08	43	6.5	0.1	11.0
20yr PAC	7.88	100:00	104:21	48	7.9	-1.5	17.1	106:22	62	9.2	-0.8	19.0	107:01	64	9.6	-0.8	19.1	103:25	41	7.4	-2.4	16.3	106:20	62	9.2	-0.9	19.0
2yr SUP	8.50	99:24	99:31	11	1.6	-3.9	2.9	99:31	20	0.9	0.0	1.4	99:32	24	1.8	-3.9	2.3	99:32	11	1.6	-4.4	3.1	100:00	24	0.9	-0.2	1.3
5yr SUP	8.50	98:20	101:11	47	3.3	-8.4	10.2	101:05	91	2.7	-8.3	3.8	101:00	83	3.4	1.8	3.8	101:22	48	3.1	-12.9	11.4	101:04	91	2.6	-7.9	3.8
10yr SUP	8.50	96:18	102:05	77	3.8	-12.1	14.1	100:15	93	3.5	5.1	6.9	100:11	85	3.8	-10.9	6.9	101:31	75	4.3	-10.6	14.4	100:18	99	3.5	3.8	6.6
20yr SUP	8.50	93:13	102:16	117	4.8	-8.7	17.5	102:28	137	3.5	-6.9	14.3	102:09	131	5.0	-5.8	18.3	102:07	114	4.4	-10.8	17.5	102:24	138	3.5	-6.6	14.0

* Zero OAS Price

EXHIBIT 39–7
When to Expect the Obvious

	BENEFITS*	*HURTS***
SLOWER (Longer WAL)	IOs, PREMIUMs	POs, DISCOUNT
FASTER (Shorter WAL)	POs, DISCOUNTs	IOs, PREMIUMs

* Higher OAS holding price constant, and higher price holding OAS constant.
** Lower OAS holding price constant, and lower price holding OAS constant.

tive) from higher OAS and higher zero OAS prices than under the Street function, while the discount-backed IOs are hurt (look richer), displaying lower OASs and lower zero OAS prices.

The effect of a steeper prepayment function on the option-adjusted convexity is more interesting. The more negative a securities' convexity, the better its carry and horizon TROR in an unchanged yield curve scenario, and the worse its performance is rising or declining yield environments. Convexity is most negative in the slight premium pass-throughs, and either less negative or positive for lower or higher coupons. This effect is amplified by the steeper prepayment curve. Under a steeper prepayment curve, an investor in current coupon mortgages sees a better base case yield by being short at-the-money prepayment options with a higher gamma (option terminology for being more short on volatility). A similar effect is seen in the IOs, where the 8 percent- and 8.5 percent-backed IOs are much more negatively convex under the steeper model than under the Street model, and IOs backed by both lower and higher coupons are more positively convex than under the Street model. As we would expect, just the opposite can be seen with in the POs: the 8 percent- and 8.5 percent-backed POs are much more positively convex under the steeper prepayment function than under the Street model, while POs backed by both lower and higher coupons are less positively convex under the steeper prepayment function than under the Street model.

INTRODUCING PREPAYMENT UNCERTAINTY

Prepayments are not a certain function of refinancing incentive and aging for several reasons. First, some uncertainty is inherent in any attempt at an econometric statistical estimation. That is to say, any estimation of a combination of explanatory variables results in a regression error. The error of the regression indicates the residual uncertainty remaining after the explanatory variables are taken into account.

Another source of uncertainty arises from the fact that prepayment functions typically project prepayments as percentage mortality rates whereas mortgage pools experience prepayments in integral numbers of loans of different sizes. That means that even a right-on-target long-term projected prepayment rate will differ significantly, month by month, from observed prepayments. Actual prepayments will appear as short-term spikes and troughs from the most accurate projection. This problem tends to be exaggerated in pools made up of smaller numbers of loans.

A third important source of uncertainty arises in option-pricing models and reflects the fact that the prepayment process is largely driven by long-term rates, but long-term rates are not perfectly correlated with short rates. However, most term-structure valuation systems model the diffusion of the short rate only (i.e., one factor models), which imposes some additional risk in forecasting prepayments in an OAS model.

In other words, prepayment functions estimated statistically can predict the mean, but actual prepayments can vary dramatically from predicted prepayments. We can model the sort of effect this error or uncertainty has on option-adjusted measures of spread and price sensitivity by introducing proportional volatility into the results from one of our models. For this experiment we select the "Implied" prepayment function. The proportional volatility function is described as follows:

$$X = (1 - \frac{CPR}{100})^{\frac{1}{12}}$$

$$SMM = X \times e^{\sigma \times dz}$$

where dz is a normally distributed random variable with a mean of zero and variance σ^2 of one, while σ (sigma) is the volatility.

As formulated, prepayment uncertainty is assumed to be log-normally distributed. Among other things, this assumption means prepayments can't go below zero. We treat the output from our prepayment function as the median for this random distribution. Applying a 20 percent volatility to the output of the implied prepayment function results in the option-adjusted spreads, durations, and so forth given in the last set of columns in Exhibit 39–6. Note that increasing the variability of prepayment projections results in a systematic decrease in OASs and zero OAS prices on IOs and increases in OASs and zero OAS prices on POs. The largest change in the zero OAS price is a difference of 9 ticks between the market price and the zero OAS price on the 9.5 percent IOs.

Is this result reasonable? We need to consider what goes on with each sample path taken in an OAS calculation. An individual path produces a set of cash flows that is discounted to a present value. The expected value of the security is simply the probability weighted average of values across many paths. This process can be difficult for non-modelers (regular investors, traders and analysts) to visualize or conceive intuitively. To assist our readers, we simplify the process in Exhibit 39–8, by illustrating the present value calculation of IO and PO cash flows generated for a highly simplified amortizing security over three paths, or vectors, of CPRs, a base case, a faster speed path and a slower speed path. The same discount rates are used over all three paths. In the top section of the table which we consider as our base case, the IO and PO have a present value of $447,838 and $362,873 respectively. In the middle section, we multiply our base case CPRs by exp(20 percent), and the IO and PO have a present value of $434,321 and $392,367, respectively. Finally, in the bottom section, we multiply our base case CPRs by exp(-20 percent), and the IO and PO have a present value of $460,487 and $334,934, respectively. When we average the present values of the IO and PO from the higher CPR and lower CPR cases (assigning equal weight to each path), the present value of the IO is lower than in the base case ($447,404 compared to $447,838); the present value of the PO is also higher than in the base case ($363,650 compared to $362,873). If we assume for the sake of illustration that the base case represents valuations that would result if prepayments were a particular function of interest rates, we can interpret the average valuations across the higher and lower CPR paths as incorporating prepayment volatility or uncertainty. We conclude that introducing multiplicative prepayment volatility gives us lower zero OAS prices for IOs (and premiums) and higher zero OAS prices for POs (and discounts). We would derive a similar general result using any other discount rates, base-case CPRs and volatilities.

We would have thought that the introduction of prepayment uncertainty would be favorable for POs, unfavorable for IOs, exactly the result that is shown in the zero OAS prices. However, the order of magnitude is much smaller that we would have thought. A comparison of the durations, convexities and expected average lives produced under the implied prepayment function and the prepayment volatility scenario (Exhibit 39–6) indicates that including prepayment uncertainty does not significantly change these measures. This result is noteworthy, given the high degree of prepayment volatility (20 percent) introduced. That is to say, each monthly CPR

EXHIBIT 39-8
Impact of Prepayment Volatility

		Base Case CPR Vector Scenario			
cpr	io cf	io pv	po cf	po pv	bal
		447,838		362,873	1,000,000
10.0	80,000	470,800	100,000	381,478	900,000
9.0	72,000	411,350	81,000	296,280	819,000
8.0	65,520	357,642	65,520	226,884	753,480
7.0	60,278	308,253	52,744	170,275	700,736
6.0	56,059	261,996	42,044	124,176	658,692
5.0	52,695	217,853	32,935	86,884	625,758
4.0	50,061	174,932	25,030	57,143	600,727
3.0	48,058	132,427	18,022	34,056	582,705
2.0	46,616	89,586	11,654	17,025	571,051
1.0	45,684	45,684	5,711	5,711	565,341
		Higher CPR Scenario			
cpr+ *	io cf	io pv	po cf	po pv	bal
		434,321		392,367	1,000,000
11.05	80,000	456,589	110,517	412,485	889,483
9.95	71,159	396,392	88,473	317,847	801,010
8.84	64,081	342,765	70,820	241,738	730,190
7.74	58,415	294,073	56,489	180,356	673,701
6.63	53,896	248,982	44,673	130,870	629,028
5.53	50,322	206,374	34,759	91,185	594,269
4.42	47,541	165,288	26,271	59,765	567,998
3.32	45,440	124,871	18,832	35,521	549,166
2.21	43,933	84,343	12,138	17,721	537,027
1.11	42,962	42,962	5,935	5,935	531,092
		Lower CPR Scenario			
cpr- *	io cf	io pv	po cf	po pv	bal
		460,487		334,934	1,000,000
9.05	80,000	484,097	90,484	352,106	909,516
8.14	72,761	425,347	74,067	275,380	835,449
7.24	66,836	371,590	60,476	212,164	774,974
6.33	61,998	321,583	49,086	160,065	725,888
5.43	58,071	274,262	39,409	117,254	686,479
4.52	54,918	228,701	31,058	82,350	655,422
3.62	52,434	184,068	23,722	54,328	631,700
2.71	50,536	139,599	17,148	32,458	614,552
1.81	49,164	94,571	11,121	16,257	603,431
0.90	48,274	48,274	5,460	5,460	597,971
		Average PVs from Higher and Lower CPRs			
	io	447,404	po	363,650	

Note: io assumes coupon of 8%, and period discounting starts, at 5% and increment 0.125% per period
* cpr+ =base case cpr*exp(20%), cpr- =base case cpr*exp(-20%)

was shocked by 20 percent, and yet the largest change in constant OAS price was only 9 ticks. We would have thought that introducing prepayment volatility would have had more of an effect. Stated differently, within the context of an OAS model and by not specifically incorporating risk-adversity, prepayment volatility—an effect that is not normally captured—turns out to be relatively unimportant.

IMPACT ON FIXED RATE CMOs

This analysis can also be applied to CMOs. To test the sensitivity in CMOs of option-adjusted measures of risk and reward to reasonable differences between prepayment functions and to prepayment uncertainty, we use a generic PAC and sequential deal structured from 8.5 percent FNMA 30yr collateral as described in Exhibit 39–9. We stripped the coupons on the bonds where necessary to avoid prices above par at current market spreads and speeds. Coupons were limited to 8.5 percent, the coupon on the collateral. As a result, the support bonds have discount prices at current market spreads and speeds. Yield and average life profiles of the various bonds are shown in the table as well. The OASs and other option-adjusted measures under each prepayment function are shown in the last twelve rows of Exhibit 39–6.

When we compare the slower prepayment function to the implied function, we find that all the sequentials, the PACs and the 2-year support benefit from the slower prepayments with higher OASs and zero OAS prices. This is to be expected since the full price (that is, including accrued interest) of these securities is above par. The longer discount support bonds suffer with lower OASs and zero OAS prices.

With a steeper prepayment function, most bonds have lower OASs, zero OAS prices and durations than under the Street median function. Note that the steeper prepayment curve is very negative for intermediate and long sequentials and longer PACs. The OASs on the 10-year sequential and PAC are 28 basis points and 23 basis points, respectively, under the Street median scenario. They are 22 basis points and 16 basis points, respectively, with the steeper curve. The effect is very modest for the longer support bonds: The 10-year support is lower by only 2 basis points, from 77 basis points to 75 basis points. Intuitively, in a steeper curve, the PAC schedule does not provide as much prepayment protection to PACs; thus, the supports actually suffer less than the PACs.

EXHIBIT 39-9
Generic CMO Deals

PAC DEAL

Bond	Type	%	Coup	WAL	Sprd	Price
1	PAC	19.60	7.32	2.40	49	100:00
2	PAC	19.25	7.53	5.90	55	100:00
3	PAC	20.58	7.73	10.90	65	100:00
4	PAC	2.46	7.88	18.10	58	100:00
5	SUP	14.88	8.50	2.40	179	99:24
6	SUP	7.55	8.50	5.90	185	98:20
7	SUP	3.83	8.50	10.90	195	96:18
8	SUP	11.85	8.50	19.75	198	93:13

8.5% FNCL collateral, priced at 200 PSA, collars of 100-300 PSA.

			PSA					
Bond		75	100	150	200	300	500	900
1	Yield	7.26	7.23	7.23	7.23	7.23	7.22	7.17
	WAL	2.83	2.40	2.40	2.40	2.40	2.32	1.82
2	Yield	7.56	7.55	7.55	7.55	7.55	7.52	7.46
	WAL	7.18	5.90	5.90	5.90	5.90	4.24	2.68
3	Yield	7.80	7.79	7.79	7.79	7.79	7.77	7.72
	WAL	12.41	10.90	10.90	10.90	10.90	7.13	4.03
4	Yield	7.96	7.96	7.96	7.96	7.96	7.95	7.92
	WAL	18.10	18.10	18.10	18.10	18.10	13.76	7.21
5	Yield	8.62	8.62	8.58	8.53	8.47	8.39	8.25
	WAL	18.21	14.37	4.83	2.40	1.54	1.03	0.68
6	Yield	8.74	8.75	8.76	8.85	9.01	9.18	9.43
	WAL	22.54	20.00	13.80	5.90	2.90	1.87	1.24
7	Yield	8.95	8.96	8.99	9.09	9.63	10.19	10.92
	WAL	24.62	22.58	17.60	10.90	3.69	2.21	1.45

SEQUENTIAL DEAL

Bond	Type	%	Coup	WAL	Sprd	Price
1	SEQ	34.50	7.71	2.40	88	100:00
2	SEQ	26.90	7.93	5.90	96	100:00
3	SEQ	24.92	8.09	10.90	102	100:00
4	SEQ	13.68	8.41	19.90	112	100:00

8.5% FNCL collateral, priced at 200 PSA.

			PSA					
Bond		75	100	150	200	300	500	900
1	Yield	7.71	7.69	7.65	7.62	7.57	7.49	7.36
	WAL	4.48	3.73	2.87	2.40	1.89	1.43	1.02
2	Yield	8.00	7.99	7.98	7.96	7.93	7.88	7.81
	WAL	12.08	9.99	7.39	5.90	4.30	2.96	2.04
3	Yield	8.18	8.18	8.17	8.16	8.14	8.11	8.04
	WAL	20.22	17.70	13.64	10.90	7.71	4.92	2.99
4	Yield	8.51	8.51	8.50	8.50	8.49	8.47	8.43
	WAL	27.25	26.07	23.07	19.90	14.80	9.24	5.04

Prepayment uncertainty has little effect on sequentials and PACs. Shorter bonds gain nothing to a tick in zero OAS prices at the expense of longer bonds. PACs gain a tick or two in zero OAS prices at the expense of supports.

APPLICATIONS

This analysis should serve as a guide to investors seeking to judge the biases imposed by prepayment function on option adjusted measures of risk and reward in mortgage-backed securities. This paper shows, first, that by ignoring prepayment uncertainty, we are ignoring a minor effect. Second, it is important to "calibrate" in the user's mind any OAS model that is employed. For instance, to determine whether a high OAS on a security really indicates good relative value, investors can ask for output from the option pricing model for IOs and POs backed by a range of coupons. Where IOs have large positive OASs, and the related POs have large negative OASs, it could indicate that the prepayment function in the option pricing model is too slow over that range of prepayment incentives (rather than indicate that the POs are rich to the IOs). By testing the output of specific OAS models in this way, we have a benchmark for comparison across models.

Chapter Forty

Efficient Procedures for Valuing European and American Path-Dependent Options*

John Hull and Alan White
University of Toronto

Researchers during the last 20 years have devoted considerable attention to the development of efficient numerical procedures for pricing options when analytic results are not available. A popular procedure suggested in 1979 by J. Cox, S. Ross, and M. Rubinstein (CRR) represents movements in the asset price in the form of a binomial tree. Another proposed in 1977 by P. P. Boyle uses Monte Carlo simulation.

The CRR procedure involves working backward in time, evaluating the price of the option at each node of the tree. It can handle American-style options, but so far it has not been used in many situations where payoffs depend on the history of the asset price as well as its current value because the history of the asset is not known when calculations are carried out at a node.

In contrast, Monte Carlo simulation involves working forward, simulating paths for the asset price. It can handle options where the payoff is path-dependent, but it cannot handle American options because there is no way of knowing whether early exercise is optimal when a particular stock price is reached at a particular time.

---

* This article was first published in *Journal of Derivatives* 1, no. 1 (Fall 1993), pp. 21–31.

We show how tree approaches such as CRR can be extended to value some types of path-dependent options. One interesting application is to European and American options on the arithmetic average price of an asset, the so-called Asian options. No numerical procedures have up to now been available for American options on the average price of an asset. For European average price options, the approach we describe is faster than Monte Carlo simulation and more accurate than the lognormal approximation suggested by E. Levy and S. Turnbull and L. Wakeman. A second application is to the valuation of mortgage-backed securities and indexed-principal swaps.

THE FIRST EXTENSION OF CRR

We begin by assuming that the value of a derivative security at time t is a function of t; not the price of the underlying asset, S; and some function of the path followed by the asset price between time zero and time t, $F(t, S)$. The notation is as follows:

$S(t)$	Price of the asset at time t
$F(t,S)$	Function of the path followed by S between time zero and time t that underlies the price of the derivative security
$v(S,F,t)$	Value of the derivative at time t when the asset price is S and the path function has value F
r	Risk-free interest rate (assumed constant)
T	Life of the derivative security

The principle of risk-neutral valuation shows that the value of the derivative security is independent of the risk preferences of investors. This means that we may with impunity assume that the world is risk-neutral. We suppose that the process followed by S in a risk-neutral world is geometric Brownian motion:

$$dS = \mu S\, dt + \sigma S\, dz$$

where μ, the drift rate, and σ, the volatility, are constant. (When the asset is a nondividend-paying stock, $\mu = r$; if the stock pays a continuous proportional dividend at an annual rate δ, $\mu = r - \delta$; when the asset is a foreign currency, μ is the excess of the domestic risk-free rate over the foreign risk-free rate; and so on.)

This process can be represented in the form of a Cox, Ross, and Rubinstein binomial tree, where the life of the option is divided into n time steps of length Δt ($\Delta t = T/n$). In time Δt, the asset price moves up by a proportional amount u with probability p, or down by a proportional amount d with probability $1 - p$, where:

$$u = e^{\sigma\sqrt{\Delta t}}; \qquad d = \frac{1}{u};$$

$$a = e^{\mu\Delta t}; \qquad p = \frac{a - d}{u - d}$$

For example, suppose that T is three months, $S(0)$ is 50, σ is 40 percent per year, and r is 10 percent per year. Exhibit 40–1 shows the tree obtained with only three time steps ($\Delta t = 0.0833$). In this case, $u = 1.1224$, $d = 0.8909$, $a = 1.0084$, and $p = 0.5073$.

In general, there are $i + 1$ nodes at time $i\Delta t$ in a tree such as that shown in Exhibit 40–1. We denote the lowest node at time $i\Delta t$ by $(i, 0)$, the second lowest by $(i, 1)$, and so on. The value of S at node (i, j) is $S(0)u^j d^{i-j}$ ($j = 0, 1, ..., i$); at node B in Exhibit 40–1 [that is, node $(3, 2)$], the value of S is $50 \times 1.1224^2 \times 0.8909 = 56.12$.

If we were valuing a regular option, we would work back from the end of the tree in Exhibit 40–1 to the beginning, calculating a single option value at each node. To value a path-dependent option, one approach is to value the option at each node for all alternative values of the path function $F(t, S)$ that can occur.

There are two requirements for this method to be feasible:

1. It must be possible to compute $F(t + \Delta t, S)$ from $F(t, S)$ and $S(t + \Delta t)$. This means that the path function is Markov.

2. The number of alternative values of $F(t, S)$ must not grow too fast with the size of the tree.

We denote the kth value of F at node (i,j) by $F_{i,j,k}$ and define $v_{i,j,k}$ as the value of the security at node (i,j) when F has this value. The value of the derivative security at its maturity, $v_{n,j,k}$, is known for all j and all k. To calculate its value at node (i, j) where $i < n$, we note that the stock price has a probability p of moving up to node $(i + 1, j + 1)$ and a probability $1 - p$ of moving down to node $(i + 1, j)$.

We suppose that the kth value of F at node (i,j) leads to the k_uth value of F at node $(i + 1, j + 1)$ when there is an up movement in the stock price, and

EXHIBIT 40–1
The CRR Tree for Stock Price Movements

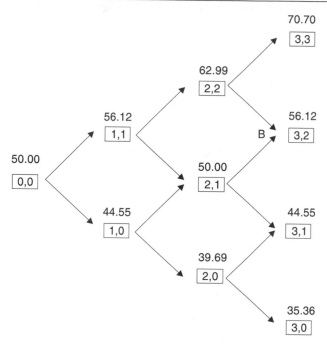

The initial stock price is $50; the time step is one month; the continuously compounded risk-free interest rate is 10 percent per year; and the volatility is 40 percent per year. The probability of an up-movement at each node is 0.5073 and the probability of a down-movement is 0.4927. At each node, the values of (i,j) are shown within the box. The stock price is shown above the box.

to the k_dth value of F at node $(i + 1, j)$ when there is a down movement in stock price.[1] For a European-style derivative security, this means that:

$$v_{i,j,k} = e^{-r\Delta t}\left[pv_{i+1,j+1,k_u} + (1 - p)v_{i+1,j,k_d}\right] \tag{1}$$

If the derivative can be exercised at node (i, j), the value in equation (1) must be compared with the early exercise value, and $v_{i,j,k}$ must be set equal to the greater of the two.

---

1 We are assuming here that the first of the two conditions just given holds; that is, we are assuming that the value of F at time $(i + 1)\Delta t$ can be calculated from the value of F at time $i\Delta t$ and the value of S at time $(i + 1)\Delta t$.

We illustrate the approach by considering a three-month American lookback put option on the nondividend-paying stock portrayed in Exhibit 40–1. This pays off the amount by which the maximum stock price observed during the option's life exceeds the asset price at the time of exercise. We set $F(t,S)$ equal to the maximum stock price realized between time zero and time t. (The purpose of this example is to illustrate a general approach; there are more efficient ways of valuing lookback options in practice.)

Exhibit 40–2 shows the results of the rollback calculations. The top number at each node is the stock price. The next row of numbers shows the alternative values of F at the node. The final row of numbers shows the corresponding values of v:

Look at nodes A, B, and C to see the way the tree is used. At node A [that is, node (2,1)], the value of F, the maximum stock price to date, is either 56.12 or 50.00. That is:

$$F_{2,1,1} = 56.12; F_{2,1,2} = 50.00$$

Similarly, for node B [that is, node (3,2)] and node C [that is, node (3,1)], we obtain

$$F_{3,2,1} = 62.99: F_{3,2,2} = 56.12$$
$$F_{3,1,1} = 56.12; F_{3,1,2} = 50.00$$

The payoff at node B when $F = 62.99$ is the excess of 62.99 over the current stock price:

$$v_{3,2,1} = 62.99 - 56.12 = 6.87$$

Similarly $v_{3,2,2} = 0$. At node C we obtain:

$$v_{3,1,1} = 11.57; v_{3,1,2} = 5.45$$

Consider now the situation at node A and $F = 50.00$ (that is, $k = 2$). If there is an up-movement so that we move from node A to node B, F changes from 50.00 to 56.12. In the notation of equation (1), this means that $k_u = 2$. If there is a down-movement, so that we move from node A to node C, F stays at 50.00. In the notation of equation (1), this means that $k_d = 2$.

According to equation (1), the value of being at node A when $F = 50$ is:

$$[v_{3,2,2} \times 0.5073 + v_{3,1,2} \times 0.4927]e^{-0.1 \times 0.08333}$$
$$= (0 \times 0.5073 + 5.45 \times 0.4927)e^{-0.1 \times 0.08333}$$
$$= 2.66$$

EXHIBIT 40–2

Tree for Valuing an American Lookback Put Option on a Stock Price

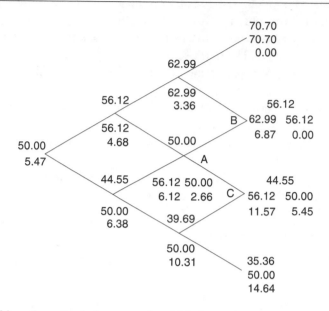

The payoff from the option is the amount by which the maximum stock price achieved to date exceeds the current stock price. The tree has three time steps. The tree parameters are the same as in Exhibit 40–1. The upper number at each node is the stock price; the middle numbers are the alternative values for the maximum stock price to date; the lower numbers are the corresponding option prices.

Example of calculations: Consider node A when the maximum stock price is 50. There is a probability 0.5073 that the stock price will move up to 56.12. In this case, the maximum stock price is 56.12, and the payoff is zero. There is a probability 0.4927 that the stock price will move down to 44.55. In this case, the maximum stock price remains at 50 and the payoff is 5.45. With an interest rate of 10 percent and a time step of one month, the value of being at node A when the maximum is 50 is therefore $(5.073 \times 0 + 0.4927 \times 5.45)e^{-0.08333 \times 0.1} = 2.66$.

Clearly, it is not worth exercising at node A when $F = 50$, as the payoff from doing so would be zero.

A similar calculation for the situation where the value of F at node A is 56.12 gives $k_u = 2$ and $k_d = 1$. The value of the derivative security at node A, without early exercise, is:

$$v_{3,2,2} \times 0.5073 + v_{3,1,1} \times 0.4927]e^{-0.1 \times 0.08333}$$

$$= (0 \times 0.5073 + 11.57 \times 0.4927)e^{-0.1 \times 0.08333}$$

$$= 5.65$$

In this case, early exercise is optimal, as it gives a value of 6.12.

Working back through the tree, repeating these types of calculations at each node gives the value of the derivative security at time zero as $5.47.

THE SECOND EXTENSION OF CRR

The approach described is computationally feasible when the number of alternative F-values at each node does not grow too quickly as n, the number of time steps, is increased. The example of the lookback option presents no problems, because the number of alternative values for the maximum or the minimum asset price at a node in a binomial tree with n time steps is never greater than n. An option on the arithmetic average would be very difficult to value using this approach, because the number of alternative arithmetic averages that can be realized at a node grows very quickly with n.

An extension to the approach that places no constraints on the number of F-values involves computing $v(S,F,t)$ at a node only for certain predetermined values of F, not all of those that can occur. The value of $v(S,F,t)$ for other values of F is computed from the known values by interpolation as required.

We illustrate this approach by using it to calculate the prices of European and American options on the arithmetic average of the stock price. In this case, F at a node is defined as the arithmetic average of the asset prices from time zero to the node.

The first step is to choose the values of F for which the option prices will be calculated. Somewhat arbitrarily, we choose to use values that have the following form:

$$S(0)e^{mh}$$

where h is a constant, and m is a positive or negative integer.[2]

The values of F that are considered at time $i\Delta t$ must span the full range of possible Fs at that time. This is determined by inspection, using forward induction. To illustrate the approach, we return to the tree in Exhibit 40–1; now suppose that we choose $h = 0.1$

The maximum and minimum averages achievable at time Δt are $(50.00 + 56.12)/2 = 53.06$ and $(50.00 + 44.55)/2 = 47.275$. To cover these, we

---

2 We make this choice because S follows geometric Brownian motion. In other situations, other choices to span the range of possible values of F may be more appropriate, and some trial and error may be necessary to determine a good way of specifying the F's.

should let m range from -1 to $+1$ at time Δt so that the "averages" considered are 45.24, 50.00, and 55.26. Given that averages of 45.24 and 55.26 are being considered at time Δt, the maximum and minimum average that are possible at time $2\Delta t$ are:

$$(2 \times 55.26 + 62.99)/3 = 57.84$$

and

$$(2 \times 45.24 + 39.69)/3 = 43.39$$

To cover these, we must let m range from -2 to $+2$ at time $2\Delta t$, so that the averages considered are 40.94, 45.24, 50.00, 55.26, and 60.07. Similar calculations are carried out for later nodes.[3]

Equation (1) still holds. The difference is that the values of $v_{i+1,j+1,ku}$ and $v_{i+1,j,kd}$ are not necessarily calculated when the nodes at time $(i + 1)\Delta t$ are considered. We determine $v_{i+1,j+1,ku}$ by interpolating between $v_{i+1,j+1,k1}$ and $v_{i+1,j+1,k2}$ where k_1 and k_2 are chosen so that $F_{i+1,j+1,k1}$ and $F_{i+1,j+1,k2}$ are the closest values of F to $F_{i+1,j+1,ku}$ that have the form $S(0)e^{mh}$ and are such that $F_{i+1,j+1,kt} \leq F_{i+1,j+1,ku} \leq F_{i+1,j+1,k2}$. We determine $v_{i+1,j,kd}$ similarly.

Exhibit 40–3 illustrates the way calculations are carried out. We suppose that a stock price has a 0.5 probability of moving from a node X where the stock price is 40 to node Y where it is 44, and a 0.5 chance of moving from node X to node Z where the stock price is 36.36. In this example, $h = 0.08$: the values of F considered at node X are 36.92, 40.00, and 43.33; and the values of F considered at nodes Y and Z are 34.09, 36.92, 40.00, 43.33, and 46.94.

We suppose that the values of v corresponding to these values of F are 0.10, 0.90, 1.80, 3.00, and 4.60 at node Y, and 0.01, 0.50, 1.10, 1.80, and 2.80

---

3 Formally, the calculations are as follows. If $S(0)e^{m_1h}$ is the highest value of F considered at time $i\Delta t$, the highest value considered at time $(i + 1)\Delta t$ is the smallest value of m for which:

$$e^{mh} > \frac{(i + 1)\, e^{m_1h} + u^{i+1}}{i + 2}$$

Similarly if $S(0)e^{m_2h}$ is the lowest value of F considered at time $i\Delta t$, the lowest value considered at time $(i + 1)\Delta t$ is the largest value of m for which:

$$\frac{(i + 1)\, e^{m_2h} + d^{i+1}}{i + 2} > e^m$$

EXHIBIT 40–3
Part of a Tree for Valuing a Call Option on an Average Stock Price

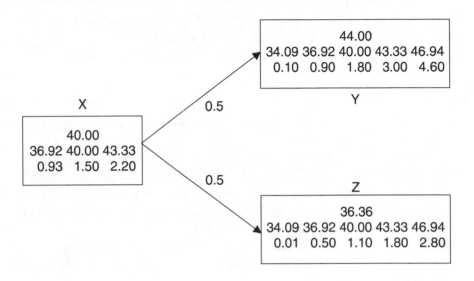

At each node, we consider certain predetermined values of the average. The upper number at each node shows the stock price; the middle numbers are the values of the average considered; the lower numbers are the values of the option. Node X is assumed to be at time $2\Delta t$; each time step is three months; and the probability of an up- or down-movement is 0.5.

Example of calculations: Consider node X when the average (calculated from three observations) is 43.33. There is a 0.5 probability of moving up to node Y where the average becomes 43.50. Using linear interpolation, the value of the option is then 3.08. There is a 0.5 probability of moving down to node Z where the average becomes 41.59; using linear interpolation, the value of the option is 1.43. The value of the option at node X when the average is 43.33 is therefore $(0.5 \times 3.08 + 0.5 \times 1.43)e^{-0.25 \times 0.1} = 2.20$.

at node Z. We also assume that the averages at node X are calculated over two time steps (using three values of the stock price), that each time step is three months, and that the risk-free interest rate is 10 percent per year.

Consider the calculation of v at node X when $F = 43.33$. There is a 0.5 probability that the stock price will move up to node Y, in which case the average stock price becomes $(3 \times 43.33 + 44.00)/4 = 43.50$. We interpolate to obtain the value of v for this value of F. The number 43.50 is 4.7 percent of the way between 43.33 and 46.94. Our estimate of the value of v at node when $F = 43.50$ is therefore $3.0 + 0.047 \times 1.6 = 3.08$.

There is a 0.5 probability that the stock price will move down to node Z, in which case the average stock price becomes 41.59. We interpolate between 1.1 and 1.8 to estimate the value of v at node Z, when $F = 41.59$, to be 1.43. The value at node X when $F = 43.33$ is therefore $(3.08 \times 0.5 + 1.43 \times 0.5)e^{-0.25 \times 0.1} = 2.20$. (This assumes no early exercise.)

Exhibit 40–4 shows the results of using this approach to value a variety of American and European options that pay off:

$$\max[A(t) - X, 0]$$

where X is the strike price, and $A(t)$ is the arithmetic average of the asset price between times 0 and t.

It also provides Monte Carlo estimates of the European option prices. The Monte Carlo simulations are based on 40 time steps and 100,000 simulation runs, and make use of the antithetic variable technique. This is a procedure for controlling sampling so as to reduce the standard error of the answer for a given number of runs. (The standard error is shown in parentheses.) The tree results are based on 40 time steps and a value for h of 0.005. In all cases, the beginning and ending asset prices are included in calculation of the average.

The European results for the tree approach and for Monte Carlo simulation are very close. The mean of the differences between the two is 0.003. 65 percent, 90 percent, and 100 percent of the Monte Carlo values are within one, two, and three standard deviations of the tree estimates, respectively. These results do not allow rejection of the hypothesis that the tree value is the true value.

Exhibit 40–4 also shows European option prices calculated using the analytic approximation recommended by E. Levy and by Turnbull and Wakeman (LTW), assuming that for the purposes of calculating the average the stock price is observed with the same frequency as for the Monte Carlo simulation and tree results.[4] This procedure, which calculates the mean and standard deviation of the arithmetic average and then assumes that the distribution is lognormal, although faster, is much less accurate than the procedure we propose. Sixty percent of the Monte Carlo values are greater

---

4 We do not incorporate the Edgeworth series adjustment suggested by Turnbull and Wakeman. An alternative analytic approximation for calculating the prices of European options on the arithmetic average has been suggested by Curran. This involves considering the probability distribution of the arithmetic average conditional on the geometric average. In the limit, our procedure will give more accurate European option prices than any analytic approximation.

EXHIBIT 40–4
Value of Options on the Average Price of a Nondividend-Paying Stock

Life of Option (Years)	Options*	40	45	Strike Price 50	55	60
0.5	Amer/Bin	12.115	7.261	3.275	1.152	0.322
	Euro/Bin	10.755	6.363	3.012	1.108	0.317
	Euro/LTW	10.764	6.379	3.012	1.094	0.307
	Euro/MC	10.759	6.359	2.998	1.112	0.324
		(0.003)	(0.005)	(0.007)	(0.005)	(0.003)
1.0	Amer/Bin	13.153	8.551	4.892	2.536	1.208
	Euro/Bin	11.545	7.616	4.522	2.420	1.176
	Euro/LTW	11.573	7.652	4.542	2.415	1.159
	Euro/MC	11.544	7.606	4.515	2.401	1.185
		(0.006)	(0.008)	(0.010)	(0.009)	(0.007)
1.5	Amer/Bin	13.988	9.652	6.199	3.771	2.194
	Euro/Bin	12.285	8.670	5.743	3.585	2.124
	Euro/LTW	12.332	8.728	5.786	3.601	2.116
	Euro/MC	12.289	8.671	5.734	3.577	2.135
		(0.008)	(0.010)	(0.012)	(0.012)	(0.010)
2.0	Amer/Bin	14.713	10.623	7.326	4.886	3.171
	Euro/Bin	12.953	9.582	6.792	4.633	3.057
	Euro/LTW	13.021	9.662	6.861	4.675	3.070
	Euro/MC	12.943	9.569	6.786	4.639	3.055
		(0.010)	(0.013)	(0.014)	(0.015)	(0.013)

Notes: Initial stock price is 50, the risk-free interest rate is 10 percent per year, and the stock price volatility is 30 percent per year. Averaging is between the beginning of the life of the option and the exercise date. Tree calculations are based on 40 time steps and a value for h equal to 0.005. The Monte Carlo simulations are based on 40 time steps and 100,000 trials using the antithetic variable technique.

*Amer/Bin = American option valued using a binomial tree.

EXHIBIT 40–5

Value of Options on the Average Price of a Nondividend-Paying Stock as the Number of Time Steps and the Value of H Change

	Option	Number of Time Steps			
h	Type	20	40	60	80
0.100	American	5.197	5.311	5.360	5.377
	European	4.663	4.679	4.685	4.687
0.050	American	4.971	5.080	5.124	5.145
	European	4.588	4.605	4.612	4.614
0.010	American	4.823	4.906	4.941	4.962
	European	4.517	4.530	4.536	4.539
0.005	American	4.815	4.892	4.924	4.942
	European	4.513	4.522	4.526	4.529
0.003	American	4.814	4.890	4.920	4.936
	European	4.512	4.520	4.523	4.525

Notes: The initial stock price is $50, the strike price is $50, the risk-free interest rate is 10 percent per year, the stock price volatility is 30 percent per year, and the time to maturity is one year. Averaging is between the beginning of the life of the option and the exercise date. Calculations are carried out using the tree approach.

than three standard deviations from the LTW estimate. We can reject the hypothesis that the LTW values are the true values.

Exhibit 40–5 compares convergence of the tree procedure by varying h and the number of time steps for the option in Exhibit 40–4 where $X = 50$ and $T = 1$. We find our procedure to be at least 12 times as fast as Monte Carlo simulation at the same level of accuracy. For a given number of time steps, a value of h equal to 0.005 gives penny accuracy.

The number of time steps determines the frequency with which the asset price is observed in calculating the average. This affects the option's fair value. An American option is more sensitive to the number of time steps than a European option, presumably because the number of time steps also determines the number of early exercise opportunities.

The decline in option prices with declining values of h can be attributed to the interpolation procedure. Because option prices are a convex function of the average, the linear interpolation procedure in this case leads to overpricing that disappears only asymptotically.

MORTGAGE-BACKED SECURITIES

An application of our procedures is to the valuation of mortgage-backed securities (MBSs) and indexed-principal swaps (IPSs). An MBS is a fixed-rate debt security whose principal may be paid off prior to maturity. The usual assumption is that prepayments at a particular time are a function of the prevailing level of interest rates. An IPS is a fixed for floating-rate swap where the notional principal is reduced according to some contractually specified prepayment schedule that depends on the level of interest rates.

For both securities, the value at a particular time depends on the level of interest rates and the cumulative prepayments so far. Equivalently, it depends on the level of interest rates and the outstanding principal. The procedures we have outlined can be used with an interest rate tree replacing the stock price tree, with F defined as the outstanding principal. F satisfies the condition that its value at time $t + \Delta t$ can be calculated from the value at time t and interest rates at time $t + \Delta t$.

The first stage in the valuation of an MBS is to develop a prepayment function. This is the function that predicts how much of the principal will be prepaid under different circumstances. The function is estimated by observing the historic behavior of mortgage holders. In most cases, the prepayment function used for valuation purposes depends only on the current term structure.

To value an MBS, it is customary to model the evolution of the term structure using Monte Carlo simulation and to monitor the prepayments that are made on each run. Then the cash flows are discounted back down the interest rate path that has been simulated, in the following manner:

$$M_t = e^{-r\Delta t}[M_{t+\Delta t} + C_{t+\Delta t}] \quad 0 \leq t \leq T - \Delta t$$

where T is the mortgage maturity, M_t is the value of the MBS, r_t is the short-term interest rate, and C_t is the cash flow (interest plus repayment of principal) at time t in the simulation.

As an alternative to Monte Carlo simulation, the technique described in the second extension of CRR can be used to value an MBS, as an illustration will show. Consider a five-year, 10 percent semiannual payment mortgage with an initial \$100 principal prepaid according to the following schedule:

$$\text{Prepayment} = \begin{cases} 0 & R \leq 10\% \\ \dfrac{100}{3}\left(\dfrac{10}{R} - 1\right) & 4\% \leq R \leq 10\% \\ 50 & R \leq 4\% \end{cases}$$

where R is the six-month rate of interest (expressed as an annual percentage rate with continuous compounding). Prepayments are made only on the semi-annual interest payment dates, and the prepayment may not exceed the outstanding principal. When R is greater than 10 percent, there are no prepayments; as R decreases from 10 percent to 4 percent, prepayments increase from zero to $50; when R is less than 4 percent, $50 of the outstanding principal is prepaid.

The term structure evolution is modeled using the interest rate model described by J. Hull and A. White. In this model the short-term rate of interest, r, obeys

$$dr = (\theta(t) - ar) \, dt + \sigma dz$$

This is an arithmetic process similar to the one assumed by T. S. Y. Ho and S. B. Lee, but with mean reversion.

The drift parameter $\theta(t)$ is chosen to replicate the initial term structure, and the parameters σ and a determine the volatility structure. The standard deviation of the short-term interest rate is σ, and the standard deviations of longer-term rates decline exponentially from this value at rate a. For the purposes of our example, we assume that the initial term structure is flat (at 10 percent per year, quoted with semiannual compounding), the short rate volatility is 20 percent, and the volatility of the five-year rate is about 12 percent.

An n-time step trinomial tree on the short-term rate is constructed to replicate the initial term structure.[5] We let F be the value of the outstanding principal at each node in the tree and v be the value of the MBS.

First, the maximum and minimum possible values of F at each node in the interest rate tree are computed by forward induction through the tree. The set of possible F's is then approximated by m equally spaced representative values at each node.[6]

At time step $n - 1$, the value of the MBS is the discounted principal plus interest that will be paid at time n:

$$v_{n-1,j,k} = e^{-r_{i,j}\Delta t}[1.05F_{n-1,j,k}] \text{ for all } j,k$$

---

5 See Hull and White for the details of the construction of the interest rate tree. An interest rate tree is analogous to a CRR tree for stock prices. The principal difference is that the discount rate varies from node to node.

6 Here it proves appropriate to use equally spaced values of F. Note that we use a refinement of the procedure described in the second extension of CRR. The maximum and minimum F-values that are considered vary from node to node as well as from time to time.

At all earlier times t, the value of the MBS is the discounted expected value of coupon payments, prepayments, and the residual value of the MBS at $t + \Delta t$:

$$v_{i,j,k} = e^{-r_{ij}\Delta t}[Q_{i+1}F_{i,j,k} + (p_u(P_u + v_{i+1,j_u,k_u}) +$$
$$p_m(P_m + v_{i+1,j_m,k_m}) + p_d[P_d + v_{i+1,j_d,k_d}])]$$

In this equation, Q_{i+1} is the coupon rate that will be paid at $t + \Delta t$, so that Q_{i+1} equals 0.05 if time $(i + 1)\Delta t$ corresponds to a coupon payment date, and zero otherwise. The variables p_u, p_m, and p_d are, respectively, the (risk-neutral) probabilities that the short-term interest rate will move along the up (u), middle (m), and down (d) branch over the next time period Δt. P_x is the prepayment, if any, that takes place on branch x, and $v_{i+1,jx,kx}$ is the value of the MBS on branch x given that the principal was $F_{i,j,k}$ and a prepayment P_x took place. This value is generally interpolated from known values of $v_{i+1,jx,k}$.[7]

This procedure was implemented for 20-, 40-, 60-, and 80-step trees using 3, 6, 11, 16, and 21 different values of F at each node. Increasing the number of steps in the interest rate tree improves the accuracy of replication of the distribution of possible future term structures. Increasing the number of F-values at each node improves the approximation of the function v at each node.

For comparison purposes, a 10,000-sample Monte Carlo simulation was run through each interest rate tree to estimate the price of the MBS. For a tree of any particular size, a Monte Carlo simulation should in the limit perfectly replicate v.

The results are reported in Exhibit 40–6. In general, the results are not very sensitive to the number of steps in the tree or to the number of F-values considered, as long as $m \geq 6$. In only 1 out of 16 cases is the tree estimate more than two standard errors from the Monte Carlo estimate when $m \geq 6$. Even in that case, the discrepancy is only about 3 cents.

The results presented in Exhibits 40–4, 40–5, and 40–6 were produced using linear interpolation. In other words, v is assumed to be linear in F

---

7 At any time and interest rate, we are approximating the true value of the MBS, $v(F)$ for $F_{\min} \leq F \leq F_{\max}$, by interpolating between a limited number of estimates of the value, $v(F_i)$, $i = 1, 2, ..., m$. For one type of MBS, the prepayment is defined as a proportion of the principal currently outstanding. In this case $v(kF) = kv(F)$ and all problems of path-dependence can be avoided for this type of MBS by using the tree to calculate at each node the value of an MBS with \$1 of principal at the node.

EXHIBIT 40–6

Value of a Five-Year, 10 percent, Semiannual Pay Mortgage-Backed Security with an Initial Principal of $100

	Number of Time Steps			
m	20	40	60	80
3	98.3728	98.3818	98.3922	98.3935
6	98.3121	98.3065	98.3077	98.3065
11	98.3014	98.2862	98.2836	98.2816
16	98.2990	98.2814	98.2772	98.2747
21	98.2984	98.2795	98.2747	98.2718
Monte Carlo	98.2883	98.2934	98.2821	98.2715
	(0.0171)	(0.0171)	(0.0168)	(0.0170)

Notes: Prepayments are expected on interest payment dates according to the schedule:

$$\text{Prepayment} = \begin{cases} 0 & R \leq 10\% \\ \dfrac{100}{3}\left(\dfrac{10}{R} - 1\right) & 4\% \leq R \leq 10\% \\ 50 & R \leq 4\% \end{cases}$$

where R is the six-month rate of interest. The term structure is initially flat at 10 percent, so in the absence of prepayments the MBS would be priced at $100. The difference between $100 and the value of the MBS is the value of the prepayment option. Monte Carlo estimates of the value based on 10,000 samples using the control variate technique are included for reference purposes. The standard error of the estimate is shown in parentheses.

between any two computed values. In many instances, the derivative security price is a strongly nonlinear function of F so that linear interpolation leads to biased results.

In Exhibit 40–7, we test the effect of using quadratic interpolation to value the mortgage-backed securities in Exhibit 40–6. The evidence is that quadratic interpolation does produce significant improvements for small values of m.

The procedures suggested here can lead to significant improvements in computer speed. They are at least 10 times as fast as Monte Carlo simulation for the same level of accuracy. In some situations they are 100 times as fast.

CONCLUSION

We have explored a method of using the CRR binomial tree to value a wide range of path-dependent options on stocks, currencies, indexes, and futures contracts. The method can be extended to value path-dependent interest rate

EXHIBIT 40–7
Value of a Five-Year, 10 percent, Semiannual Pay Mortgage-Backed Security
with an Initial Principal of $100 When Quadratic Interpolation Is Used

	Number of Time Steps			
m	20	40	60	80
3	98.2924	98.2722	98.2636	98.2599
6	98.2973	98.2794	98.2739	98.2704
11	98.2976	98.2775	98.2718	98.2685
16	98.2975	98.2774	98.2715	98.2681
21	98.2974	98.2773	98.2714	98.2679
Monte Carlo	98.2883	98.2934	98.2821	98.2715
	(0.0171)	(0.0171)	(0.0168)	(0.0170)

Notes: Parameter values are the same as in Exhibit 40–6. The table shows that quadratic interpolation produces an improvement in accuracy for small values of m.

derivatives such as mortgage-backed securities, if the evolution of the term structure is modeled using a binomial or trinomial tree.

One important application is in the pricing of a class of options that have previously not been amenable to numerical analysis. These are American options where the payoff depends on the arithmetic average of an asset's price. Another important application is to mortgage-backed securities and indexed-principal swaps.

A key assumption in our analysis is that the value of the path function, F, at time $t + \Delta t$ can be calculated from its value at time t and the asset price at time $t + \Delta t$. Of course, this assumption does not hold for all path-dependent options. For example, it does not hold for American options where the payoff at time t depends on the average price of the asset over the previous six months. More generally, it does not hold when the average at time t is calculated between $t - \tau$ and t for a fixed τ. The pricing of these types of options presents ongoing challenges for analysts.

REFERENCES

Boyle, P.P. "Options: A Monte Carlo Approach." *Journal of Financial Economics*, 4 (1977), pp. 323–38.

Cox, J., S. Ross, and M. Rubinstein. "Option Pricing: A Simplified Approach." *Journal of Financial Economics*, 7 (1979), pp. 229–64.

Curran, M. "Beyond Average Intelligence." *RISK*, November 1992, p. 60.

Ho, T.S.Y., and S.B. Lee. "Term Structure Movements and Pricing Interest Rate Contingent Claims." *Journal of Finance*, 41 (December 1986), pp. 1011–29.

Hull, J., and A. White. "One-Factor Interest Rate Models and the Valuation of Interest-Rate Derivative Securities." *Journal of Financial and Quantitative Analysis*, 28 (June 1993), pp. 235–54.

Hull, J., and A. White. "Numerical Procedures for Implementing Term Structure Models I: Single-Factor Models." *Journal of Derivatives* 2, no. 1 (Fall 1996), pp. 7–16.

Levy, E. "Asian Arithmetic." *RISK*, May 1990, pp. 7–8.

Turnbull, S., and L. Wakeman. "A Quick Algorithm for Pricing European Average Options." *Journal of Financial and Quantitative Analysis*, 26 (September 1991), pp. 377–89.

Chapter Forty-One

Exotic Options
The Basic Building Blocks and Their Applications[1]

K. Ravindran

*Customized Solutions Group,
TD Securities Inc.,
and University of Waterloo*

Since the early 1970s, derivatives have been the most widely used hedging and investment vehicles in many financial markets. Due to the increasing level of sophistication in the financial markets, these vanilla-type derivatives, also known as first-generation derivatives, have led to a steady development of another generation of derivatives known as exotic derivatives.

As the derivatives market is very large and it would easily take a book to discuss these instruments, this chapter will focus only on the options segment of derivatives. The first section describes the limitations of vanilla options and how exotic options better address the complexity of modern day's risk exposure. The basic building blocks of these options and their practical use are described in the second section, keeping the level of mathematics to a bare minimum. Although most of this chapter's discussion is restricted to either the currency or the interest rate asset class, there is

___

1 The author is grateful to John Litwin and Karen Horcher for commenting on an earlier version of this material. © K. Ravindran 1995.

EXHIBIT 41–1
Payoffs of the European-Style Option

Type of Option	Payoff at Expiry Time T
$C_E(X,0,T,S_0)$	$\max[-P^*_{T,C}S_T-X-P^*_{T,C}]$
$P_E(X,0,T,S_0)$	$\max[-P^*_{T,P}X-S_T-P^*_{T,P}]$

where $C_E(X,0,T,S_0)$ and $P_E(X,0,T,S_O)$ represent the vanilla European-style call and put option respectively when the strike rate is X, the current time is 0, the option maturity time is T and the current spot rate is S_0, $P^*_{T,C}$ and $P^*_{T,P}$ represent the call and put option premiums that are future valued to the option expiry date; and *max* $[a,b]$ represents the maximum value of a and b.

nothing that prevents us from extending any part of the discussion to other asset classes such as equity, commodity, or credit.

VANILLA OPTIONS AND THEIR LIMITATIONS

The term *vanilla options* refers to the basic European- and American-style call and put options. More precisely, a European call (put) currency option buyer pays a premium at the inception of the option contract for the right to buy (sell) currency at a specified rate (also known as the strike rate) at the time of the option expiration. Letting T, X and S_T denote the life of the option, the strike rate of the currency option, and the value of the spot rate at time T, respectively, the buyer of a European-style call (put) option will only exercise the option at time T if $S_T > X$ ($S_T < X$). Throughout this chapter, the spot exchange rate represents the number of foreign currency units per U.S. dollar. The payoff to the buyer of the currency option at time T is shown in Exhibit 41–1; these payoffs also are depicted in Exhibits 41–2 and 41–3.

Unlike the buyer of an option who can choose to walk away from the contract, the seller (or writer) of the option is always obligated to perform his or her end of the contract if the option is exercised.[2]

In addition to possessing the properties of a European option, an American-style option allows the buyer to exercise the option at any time during the life of the option. Because the European option has only one exercise

---

2 See Hull (1993) for an excellent introduction to the fundamentals of options and Ravindran (1993) for a recreational approach to option pricing.

EXHIBIT 41–2
Call Option Buyer's Payoff at Maturity

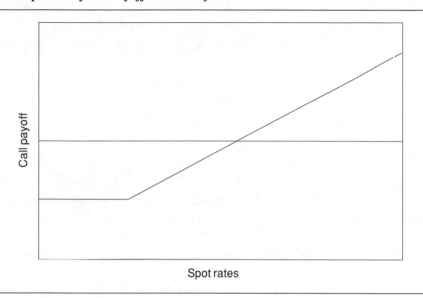

EXHIBIT 41–3
Put Option Buyer's Payoff at Maturity

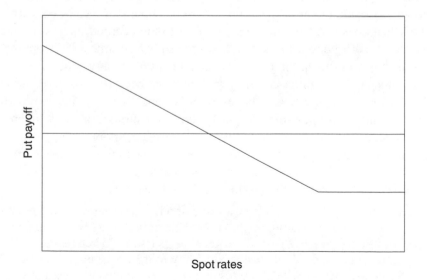

EXHIBIT 41–4
Payoffs of the American-Style Option

Type of Option	Payoff at Time t	Payoff at Expiry Time T
$C_A(X,0,T,S_0)$	$\max[S_t-X-P^*_{t,C}, C_{A,t}-P^*_{t,C}]$	$\max[-P^*_{T,C}, S_T-X-P^*_{T,C}]$
$P_A(X,0,T,S_0)$	$\max[X-S_t-P^*_{t,P}, P_{A,t}-P^*_{t,P}]$	$\max[-P^*_{T,P}, X-S_T-P^*_{T,P}]$

where $C_A(X,0,T,S_0)$ and $P_A(X,0,T,S_0)$ represent the American-style call and put options when X is the strike rate, the current time is 0, the life of the option is T, the current spot rate is S_0, and t lies in the time interval $[0,T]$; $P^*_{t,C}$ and $P^*_{t,P}$ represent the call and put option premiums that are future valued to time t; $C_{A,t}$ and $P_{A,t}$ represent the values of the American call and put options at time t when the strike rate is X, the current time is t, the option expiry time is T, and the current spot rate is S_t.

time (known as a decision node) at time T, and the American option has infinite decision nodes in the time interval O to T, it would be intuitively reasonable to expect the value of an American option to be at least as large as that of its European counterpart. The payoff to the buyer of an American-style currency option is given in Exhibit 41–4.

It is important to note that any currency option can be analogously viewed as an option on a stock that pays a continuous dividend. Furthermore, for a nondividend-paying stock, the value of a European-style vanilla call stock option can be shown to be the same as that of its American counterpart. An intuitive reason for this feature is that by exercising an American-style call option early, the buyer of the option has to pay up a strike value of X for a stock that does not pay any dividend. Due to the accrued interest on the strike that is forgone if the option is exercised before time T, it is optimal for the buyer of the option to delay exercising as much as possible.

Although only vanilla currency options have been discussed, offering vanilla options on other asset classes, such as equity, interest rate, commodity, or credit, is also possible. Despite the type of insurance or yield-enhancing opportunities that vanilla options can provide, more often than not clients, require solutions that manage their risk or monetize their market view more effectively and, if possible, at a lower cost.

As examples, consider the following three scenarios:

1. An investor has bought a new issue of a five-year semiannual bond with a 10 percent coupon that is callable at par by its issuer on any of its coupon dates after three years of its issue. To hedge against the issuer's call, the investor could buy four European-style bond options, each of which expires on every one of the callable dates

and exercises into a par value synthetic bond with a 10 percent coupon that matures on the same date as the callable bond.

Alternatively, the investor could buy a quasi–American-style bond option with both the option and the synthetic bond maturing in five years. The exercise of the option on any one of the coupon dates after three years would allow the investor to pay a par value for the synthetic 10 percent coupon bond. This solution, which would provide a cheaper and more effective means of insurance, is also known as a Mid-Atlantic/Bermudian option and is described in the section on Mid-Atlantic options.

2. An importer of Canadian goods has to make payments in Canadian dollars on prespecified future dates. The importer could either lock into a sequence of forward contracts on the Can./U.S. exchange rate or convert U.S. dollars into Canadian ones on the actual payment dates. If the U.S. dollar currently appears to be weaker than what the exchange rate has historically been, the latter alternative would seem the better choice. The only risk in the later alternative is encountered when the U.S. dollar gets even weaker. Here, the buying of put options on the U.S. dollar appears to be a good form of insurance because the put options would finish in the money when the U.S. dollar weakens. However, buying a series of put options for various option maturities may get expensive. A method of cheapening this cost would be to embed an extinguishing feature within the put options, so that if the U.S. dollar strengths during the life of the option past a certain level (called a barrier), the put option is extinguished. This type of insurance, which is also known as a knockout option, is described in the section on sudden birth/death options.

3. Based on the current shape of the yield curve, an asset manager believes that the spread between the five-year bond yield and the three-year bond yield would widen in three months (i.e., the yield curve would get steeper). Instead of buying a duration-weighted amount of each of the underlying bonds and then unwinding the positions in three months, which would involve huge cash positions and a large possible downside, the manager could alternatively buy a European option that pays off the maximum of the difference of the two bond yields (i.e., five-year bond yield less three-year bond yield) and zero at the end of the three months. To enter into such an option, the asset manager only needs to pay an up-front premium to monetize his view. This option, also known as a spread option, is discussed in the section on spread options.

The above examples describe only three of the numerous single and multivariate path dependent risks that investors and risk managers may wish to speculate upon or hedge. In each instance, the vanilla European- and American-style options are totally ineffective, clearly demonstrating the need for the use of nontraditional derivatives. In the next section, we will describe and use the various building blocks of exotic options.

DEMYSTIFYING EXOTIC OPTIONS THROUGH EXAMPLES

This section attempts to demystify the whole concept of exotic options by describing the characteristics of the basic building blocks of exotic land, which can be combined effectively to produce a complex but efficient financial instrument. In addition, the section also describes how these instruments are used in the marketplace either as yield enhancements or disaster insurances. Although each building block is presented in alphabetical order, it is very important to realize that marrying these products across asset classes to arrive at hybrid instruments could result in more effective and cost-efficient solutions.

Average Rate Options

A Canadian exporting company is exposed every week to the exchange rate risk between the Canadian and U.S. dollar. The treasurer of the company, in preparing a quarterly budget, has to forecast the cash inflows and outflows from the existing contracts of the company and state the company's expected net profit or loss for the upcoming quarter in Canadian funds. To make the conversion to Canadian funds, the treasurer picks an average exchange rate of 1.29 Can./U.S. Clearly, the treasurer does not have to worry about anything if the U.S. dollar gets stronger and the average of the weekly Can./U.S. exchange rates over the next quarter exceeds the 1.29 Can./U.S. level. However, if the Canadian dollar gets stronger over the next quarter, the treasurer will not be able to meet his budget. To hedge himself, or more precisely, his budget, he would need a currency put option on the U.S. dollar that is based on the weekly averaging of exchange rates for the next quarter and struck at 1.29 Can./U.S. This type of option is called an averaging put option.

An averaging or Asian put option is a derivative that gives the buyer at the maturity date an in-the-money payoff that is the difference between the strike rate and the average value of the exchange rates realized during the averaging period. The following example better illustrates the sequence of events depicting the nature of the transaction:

> **Time 0 months.** The Canadian dollar is currently trading at 1.33 Can./U.S. A treasurer, who has just submitted her quarterly budget, is worried about the Canadian dollar strengthening and pays a premium to buy an averaging put option on the U.S. dollar that is struck at 1.29 Can./U.S. and matures in four months. To do the averaging, the exchange rates are monitored once a week (also called a weekly sampling period) at noon, starting from today's spot rate of 1.33 Can./U.S. until and including the exchange rate at the expiration date of the option. An arithmetic average is calculated for all these observed rates and then compared with a strike rate of 1.29 Can./U.S.

> **Time 4 months.** *Case 1:* The Canadian dollar is currently trading at 1.30 Can./U.S. The arithmetic average of the weekly observed exchange rates (inclusive of the exchange rate at the option maturity date) turns out to be 1.2850 Can./U.S. The option finishes in the money and the payoff to the treasurer is:

> $(1.29 - 1.2850 - P^*_{4mths,PA})$ Can./U.S.

> where

> $P^*_{4mths,PA}$ represents the premium of the average rate put option future valued to four months.

Case 2: Currency is trading at 1.30 Can./U.S. The arithmetic average of the observed exchange rates turns out to be 1.2950 Can./U.S. The option goes out of the money and the treasurer loses the premium.

Four important observations should be made from the above example.

1. In dealing with vanilla currency options, it is not uncommon to see the terms U.S./Can. and Can./U.S. used interchangeably. Since a call option on the U.S. dollar is equivalent to a put option on the Canadian dollar, this interchangeability poses no problem. To extend this nomenclature to the averaging option, it is crucial to note that for a call or put (put or call respectively) option on the U.S. (Canadian) dollar, the averaging must be done on Can./U.S. (U.S./Can.) because the reciprocal of an average may not necessarily be equal to the average of the reciprocal. To better

understand this statement, consider the exchange rate triplet (1.28, 1.29, 1.30) Can./U.S., whose arithmetic average can be easily shown to be 1.29 Can./U.S. When these exchange rates are expressed in U.S./Can., the triplet (1.28, 1.29, 1.30) becomes (1/1.28, 1/1.29, 1/1.30), whose arithmetic average of 0.7752 U.S./Can. is not a reciprocal of the average 1.29 Can./U.S. This sort of ambiguity, however, does not exist in other asset classes.

2. The type of averaging discussed in the above example is arithmetic (i.e., the arithmetic average of the numbers 2, 3, 4 is $(2 + 3 + 4) \div 3 = 3$). The treasurer alternatively could have bought a put option, whose payoff on the option maturity date is based on a geometric average of the weekly observed rates, where the geometric average of the numbers 2, 3, 4 is defined as $(2 \times 3 \times 4)^{1/3} = 2.88$. In general, an arithmetic average rate put option can never be more expensive than a structurally similar geometric average rate put option. The converse is, however, true for an average rate call option.

3. If the notional sizes of the currency exposure vary over the weekly observed periods, a more customized hedge instrument would be a weighted averaging option on the currency rates. This can be further tailored to entertain either a daily averaging or an infrequent averaging (e.g., observing the daily exchange rates for the first month and then the biweekly exchange rates over the next three months). Finally, although the sampling period for computing the average starts in the above example at the inception of the option contract and ends at the option maturity date, nothing prohibits transacting on an average rate option whose sampling period is not a subset of the option life.

Letting S_i be the spot rate at time t_i (for $i = 1, 2, ..., n$) where the time intervals between the observation periods may not be the same (e.g., $t_n - t_{n-1}$ may not be necessarily equal to $t_{n-1} - t_{n-2}$), and w_i be the weight associated with spot rate S_i where $\sum w_i = w_1 + w_2 + ... + w_n = 1$, the payoffs of the averaging option can be more generally written as detailed in Exhibit 41–5.

By the nature of an average rate option, the contribution of a spot rate towards the averaging of the sampled points usually decreases as the option maturity date draws closer. This implies that the risk characteristics of an averaging option usually diminish as the option decays in time. When this happens, these options can be easily delta hedged. Exhibit 41–6 shows the effect of varying the sampling (averaging) frequency of a simple arithmetic averaging call option on the premium of such an option. Despite this, it is

EXHIBIT 41–5
Payoffs of the European-Style Average Rate Option

Type of Average Rate Option	Payoff at Expiry Time T
$C_{E,A}(X,0,T,S_0,w_1,...w_n,t_1,...t_n)$	$\max[-P^*_{T,CA}, \sum_{i=1}^{n} w_i S_{t_i} - X - P^*_{T,CA}]$
$P_{E,A}(X,0,T,S_0,w_1,...w_n,t_1,...t_n)$	$\max[-P^*_{T,PA}, X - \sum_{i=1}^{n} w_i S_{t_i} - P^*_{T,PA}]$
$C_{E,G}(X,0,T,S_0,w_1,...w_n,t_1,...t_n)$	$\max[-P^*_{T,CG}, \prod_{i=1}^{n} S_{t_i}^{w_i} - X - P^*_{T,CG}]$
$P_{E,G}(X,0,T,S_0,w_1,...w_n,t_1,...t_n)$	$\max[-P^*_{T,PG}, \prod_{i=1}^{n} S_{t_i}^{w_i} - P^*_{T,PG}]$

where $C_{E,A}(X,0,T,S_0,w_1,...,w_n,t_1,...,t_n)$ and $P_{E,A}(X,0,T,S_0,w_1,...,w_n,t_1,...,t_n)$ represent the arithmetic weighted averaging European-style call and put options respectively, $C_{E,G}(X,0,T,S_0,w_1,...,w_n,t_1,...,t_n)$ and $P_{E,G}(X,0,T,S_0,w_1,...,w_n,t_1,...,t_n)$ represent the geometric weighted averaging European-style call and put options when the strike rate is X, the current time is 0, the option maturity T, and the current spot rate is S_0; $P^*_{T,CA}$ and $P^*_{T,PA}$ represent the premiums of the weighted arithmetic average rate call and put option that are future valued to time T; $P^*_{T,CG}$ and $P^*_{T,PG}$ represent the premiums of the weighted geometric average rate call and put option that are future valued to time T; and

$\prod_{i=1}^{n} S_{t_i}^{w_i} = S_{t_1}^{w_1} \ldots S_{t_n}^{w_n}$. When the weights $w_i = 1/n$ and the time intervals $t_{i+1} - t_i$ are all equal (for $i = 1,...,n-1$), the above payoffs collapse to those of a simple arithmetic and a geometric average rate option.*

*The pricing formulas for standard arithmetic and geometric options are given in Levy (1992) and Kemna and Vorst (1990) respectively.

not necessarily true that the greater the sampling frequency, the cheaper the options, although these options would be cheaper than vanilla options expiring at the same time.

Although the discussion has so far been based on a currency transactions, treasurers can effectively use the concept of averaging options to cap their total annual borrowing costs. Averaging options also lends itself naturally to the commodity markets where the underlying price of a commodity trades as an average index (or price).

EXHIBIT 41–6
Effect of Averaging Frequency on Call Premium

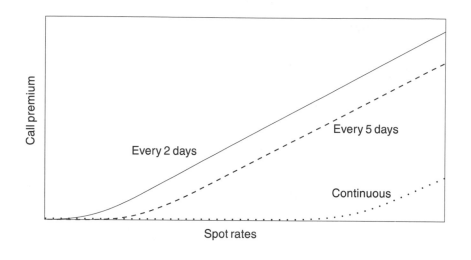

Basket Options

Although the Toronto Stock Exchange (TSE) 35, TSE 100, and TSE 300 represent three of the major equity market indices in Canada, none of the industries represented in these indexes has biased weighting. Thus, investors with a view on the forest sector stocks contained in the TSE 300 index cannot effectively monetize their view by simply purchasing any form of derivative on the TSE 300 index. Depending on the type of view or risk they are trying to manage, fundamentally they need a derivative on the forest sector stocks because the 18 stocks in the paper and forest sector contribute only 4.82 percent to the entire index.

Due to economic fundamentals and cyclic trends, suppose that the investors feel that the paper and forest sector stocks are going to increase in value over the next month. To monetize their view, they could purchase a call option on the TSE 300 index. As mentioned earlier, the disadvantage of this strategy is that the paper and forest sector constitute only a meagre 4.82 percent of the TSE 300 index. Their second alternative would be to purchase the 18 paper and forest stocks underlying the index, which would give them a large downside if their views turn out to be wrong. To protect themselves against this downside risk, the investors could alternatively choose to purchase 18 at-the-money call options underlying each of the 18 stocks. Given the investors' view that the paper and forest sector, as a whole, should increase in value, purchasing 18 at-the-money call options would be an expensive way of monetizing their view. A cheaper and a more effective way to achieve the same objective would be to purchase an at-the-money call option on the basket of 18 stocks. The cheapness of this strategy is due to the investors' employment of the notion of correlation between the 18 stocks to monetize their view. Options of this sort are known as basket or portfolio options. The following mechanics better illustrate how basket options work in practice.

Time 0 month.   Since the pipeline sector of the TSE 300 index has good economic fundamentals, an investor feels that the three stocks in this sector, symbolized by IPL, TRP, and W, should increase in value in a month. IPL, TRP, and W are currently trading at \$28, \$18, and \$23 respectively. To monetize her view, the investor pays a premium to purchase \$50 million worth of call options on a basket of three stocks that expire in one month. In purchasing this basket option, the investor desires each stock to be weighted by an amount proportional to the value of the stock. More precisely, each stock price would be weighted by an amount of $\frac{1}{28+18+23} = \frac{1}{69}$ and the strike price of the at-the-money option would be:

$$\left(\frac{1}{69} \times 28\right) + \left(\frac{1}{69} \times 18\right) + \left(\frac{1}{69} \times 23\right) = 1.$$

Time 1 month.   *Case 1.* The values of IPL, TRP, and W are \$35, \$16, and \$25 respectively, which implies that the index value of the basket is:

$$\left(\frac{1}{69} \times 35\right) + \left(\frac{1}{69} \times 16\right) + \left(\frac{1}{69} \times 25\right) = 1.1$$

Hence, the option finishes in the money and the investor gets a net payoff of:

$$\$50 * (1.1 - 1 - P^*_{1mth,C})$$

EXHIBIT 41–7
Payoffs of the European-Style Basket Option

Type of Basket Option	Payoff at Expiry Time T
$C_E(X,0,T,S_{10},...S_{no},w_1,...,w_n)$	$\max[-P^*_{T,C}, \sum_{i=1}^{n} w_i S_{iT} - X - P^*_{T,C}]$
$P_E(X,0,T,S_{10},...S_{no},w_1,...,w_n)$	$\max[-P^*_{T,P}, X - \sum_{i=1}^{n} w_i S_{iT} - P^*_{T,P}]$

where $C_E(X,0,T,S_{10},...,S_{n0},w_1...,w_n)$ and $P_E(X,0,T,S_{10},...,S_{n0},w_1...,w_n)$ represent the Euro-pean-style call and put basket options respectively, when the strike rate is X, the current time is 0, the option maturity T and the current spot rates are $S_{10},...,S_{n0}$ whose respective weights are $w_1,...,w_n$; $P^*_{T,C}$ and $P^*_{T,P}$ represent the premiums of the call and put basket options that are future valued to time T; $\sum_{i=1}^{n} w_i = 1$.

where

$P^*_{1mth,C}$ represents the basket option premium per dollar notional amount future valued to one month, and the payoff is in million of dollars.

Case 2. The values of IPL, TRP, and W are $30, $16, and $20 respectively, which implies that the index value of the basket is:

$$\left(\frac{1}{69} \times 30\right) + \left(\frac{1}{69} \times 16\right) + \left(\frac{1}{69} \times 20\right) = 0.95,$$

which is less than 1. The option finishes out of the money and the investor loses the premium.

Although the above example illustrates the use of an option on a basket of three stocks, the payoffs of an option on a basket of n stocks, where $n \geq 2$, can be more generally written as detailed in Exhibit 41–7.

The example discussed above is only one of the many variations that could be structured to suit the client's objective. Due to liquidity constraints, suppose that the client alternatively monetized her view by requesting instead that the stocks IPL, TRP, and W have contributing weights of 50 percent, 30 percent, and 20 percent respectively to the basket. The at-the-money strike value works out to be:

$(0.5 \times 28) + (0.3 \times 18) + (0.2 \times 23) = \$24$

Therefore, it makes sense for the purchaser to have an in-the-money payoff that is equal to the amount of the "in-the-moneyness" of the option multiplied by the number of option contracts, instead of simply multiplying the amount of the "in-the-moneyness" of the option by the notional principal amount of the trade as illustrated in the above example.

Exhibits 41–5 and 41–7 show that the payoffs of a basket option closely resemble those of an arithmetic average rate option. The only distinguishing feature between these two payoffs is that for an arithmetic average rate option, one asset is monitored n times during the life of the option and, hence, we can think of the average rate option as an option on n auto-correlated assets which are monitored sequentially at different points in time, where the auto-correlation coefficient can many times be implicitly calculated. For a basket option, on the other hand, n assets are monitored simultaneously on the expiration date of the option, which implies that the correlation between these asset prices can only be historically calculated. It is this observation that allows us to value a basket option, using the methods developed for pricing an arithmetic average rate option.[3]

Although basket options can be valued by modifying the arithmetic average rate option pricing formulas, the risk characteristics of a basket option are totally different from those of an averaging option, which typically diminish in magnitude as the option nears its maturity date. Furthermore, since there is only one variable or asset underlying the option, no element of correlation risk is present in an averaging option. Unlike the averaging option, the risk characteristics of a basket option do not diminish as the option nears its maturity date and the historical correlation coefficients between the underlying assets are crucial inputs to valuing the option. Furthermore, for an option written on a basket of n assets, the value of the option will be dependent on $\frac{n(n-1)}{2}$ historical correlation coefficients. Among these coefficients, it is intuitively reasonable to expect the correlation coefficient contribution from any two assets to be high as long as their individual contributing weights to the basket is large. Thus, in addition to delta hedging a basket option, the correlation risk component should be carefully managed with special consideration given to heavily weighted stocks.

---

3 Although this was the spirit of the methodology that was discussed by Huynh (1994), there is a simpler variation of the pricing formula produced by Huynh. More precisely, the algorithm of Levy (1992) could be modified to effectively and efficiently arrive at good approximate solutions for many practical situations.

Basket options can also be effectively used by foreign investors with views on specific sectors. Suppose, for example, that a Japanese investor believes that the utility component of the TSE 300 index is going to drop in value over the next two weeks. Since the Canadian dollar has been weakening relative to the Japanese yen, assume that the investor does not want this belief to be affected by any currency movements. We can structure a put option on a basket of stocks that make up the utility component of the TSE 300 index. This option should be a yen-denominated put on a basket of utility stocks, which if it finishes in the money, would also pay out in yen. Options of this sort allow the investor to take a view on a subindex of any foreign market without being subjected to the currency risk.

Binary Options

Based on current market conditions, an asset manager believes that the three-month LIBOR is at its all-time low. She thinks that the index will go up in a week after the announcement of the government budget, but she does not have a feel for the magnitude of the increase. Clearly, a vanilla call option is not going to be helpful in strictly reflecting the direction of a market movement. Binary options, also known as bet, digital, or all-or-nothing options, are instruments that allow the buyer to target the directional movement of the market. More precisely, if an investor believes that the market will not be trading below a certain level in a week and wants to receive a prespecified dollar amount if she is right, she could buy a binary option that will help monetize her view. The following sequence of events illustrate the nature of the product:

> **Time 0 weeks.**   Three-month LIBOR is currently trading at 3.5 percent. Despite the steepness of the yield curve on the short end, the investor feels that, given the current economic environment, this three-month LIBOR will never exceed 4.5 percent over the next two weeks. To monetize her view, she pays a premium to buy a binary option that pays out US $1 million if LIBOR trades below 4.5 percent at the end of two weeks. If the view turns out to be wrong, she gets no payoff from the option.

> **Time 2 weeks.**   *Case 1:* Three-month LIBOR is now trading at 3.8 percent. The option finishes in-the-money. The investor gets a net payoff of:

EXHIBIT 41–8
Payoffs of the European-Style Binary Option

Type of Binary Option	Payoff at Expiry Time T
$C_E(X,B,0,T,S_0)$	$-P^*_{T,C}$ if $S_T<X$
	$B-P^*_{T,C}$ if $S_T \geq X$
$P_E(X,B,0,T,S_0)$	$-P^*_{T,P}$ if $S_T>X$
	$B-P^*_{T,P}$ if $S_T \leq X$

where $C_E(X,B,0,T,S_0)$ and $P_E(X,B,0,T,S_0)$ represent the European-style binary call and put options when S_0 represents the current value of the index, strike value is X, B represents the dollar payoff the buyer of the option receives if he is right, the current time is 0 and the option maturity is T; $P^*_{T,C}$ and $P^*_{T,P}$ represent the binary call and put option premiums that are future valued to time T.

$$\$1 \text{ million} - P^*_{2\text{wks},P,}$$

where

$P^*_{2wks,P}$ represents the bet option premium future valued to two weeks.

Note. Regardless of how much the option finishes, in the money, the investor's payoff is a constant amount of $1 million $- P^*_{2\,wks,P}$

Case 2: Three-month LIBOR is now trading at 4.8 percent. The option finishes out of the money and the investor loses the premium.

The payoffs of a binary option can be more generally written as detailed in Exhibit 41–8.

Because the binary option has a payoff that is inherently a bet, it is easy to value this product. Furthermore, it is intuitively reasonable to expect the premium of such an option to be equal to the present value of the product of the bet payoff and probability that the option would finish in the money. Exhibit 41–9 shows the difference between the premiums of a binary call option for a varying B. It is intuitively reasonable to expect the option premiums to increase when the bet payoff increases.

Unlike the pricing, the hedging of this product is not easy. In practice, the purchase of a binary option is usually hedged by buying call options at a lower strike rate and selling the same amount of call options at a higher strike rate. Because of the discontinuous nature of the payoff, the above-mentioned static hedge strategy does not perfectly replicate the payoff

EXHIBIT 41–9
European-Style Binary Option Premium for Varying B

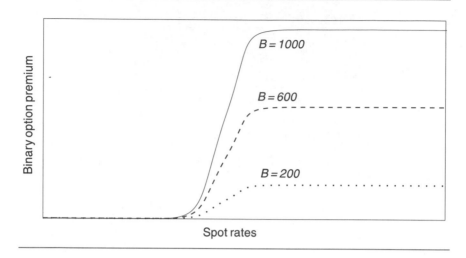

profile of a binary option. As such, these hedge amounts should be rebalanced as required during the life of the option.

Binary options have also been effectively used in note structures. For example, an investor, who thinks that the three-month LIBOR at the end of six months will be trading above 4.25 percent, can purchase a six-month note that pays off a coupon of 6.5 percent if he is right and no coupon if he is wrong. An alternative structure that protects the investor against a last-minute spike in LIBOR is a payoff that is a fraction of a coupon of 5 percent, where this fraction represents the proportion of the business days in the six-month period during which the three-month LIBOR exceeds 4.25 percent.[4]

Investors can also use the notion of a bet on spread options. To illustrate this, suppose that the difference between the current ten- and two-year U.S. Treasury bond yields is about 100 basis points and that the investor feels almost certain that, based on the current market conditions, this difference in yields will widen further in a month. He does not have a good feel for how much the widening is going to be and, as such, is only interested in betting that the spread between the ten and the two-year U.S. Treasury bond yields in a month will surpass the 100 basis point mark. To monetize his

---

4   See Ravindran (1993) and Das (1995) for examples of these structures.

views, he can buy a binary spread option that will pay $1 million if his view is right and nothing if he is wrong. The notion of betting on a yield curve spread can be easily extended to entertain the possibility of betting on the yield curve differential across different environments.

Binary options also lend themselves naturally to liability management in the form of contingent premium or pay-later options, which are essentially insurance products that allow the buyer to pay for the option only if the option finishes in the money. More precisely, suppose that the current three-month LIBOR is 4.5 percent and a liability manager wants to protect herself against the rise in interest rates by purchasing a one-year interest rate cap that is struck 150 basis points out of the money (or 6.0 percent) on the three-month LIBOR. Since the cost of this purchase turns out to be expensive due to a steeply upward sloping yield curve, the liability manager is reluctant to pay the premium. Furthermore, she believes that the three LIBOR resets over the next year will never be greater than the 6 percent level when the caplets expire. To monetize her view and protect herself against increasing interest rates, she could buy a one-year pay-later contingent premium cap that is struck at 6.0 percent. In purchasing such a cap, she does not have to pay any premium up front for the cap. In the event she is right and each of the caplets finishes out of the money, she would walk away without losing a cent. On the other hand, if she turns out to be wrong on any LIBOR reset, she would have to pay a prespecified premium for the appropriate caplet she ends up using. Note that in purchasing such an option, the manager ends up paying the premium for the protection even if the option finishes in the money by a fraction of a basis point.

Chooser Options

It is common for someone with strong views about the impact of a major event (e.g., election results, outbreak of a war) on a financial market to buy an option (e.g., a vanilla call option) that will help monetize these views. Come the event date, it is also common for the same person to realize that his or her views had been totally wrong and to wish that a vanilla put option had been purchased instead. For such a person, an option that gives the opportunity to choose between a vanilla call option and a vanilla put option on the event date would serve as a useful and valuable instrument. The chooser option, also known as the pay-now-choose-later option, is an option that allows the buyer to choose between a vanilla call option and a vanilla put option at a prespecified time in the future. More precisely, the investor pays an up-front premium to make a choice between a call and a put option, both of which are struck at the same level and expire on the same day. The following sequence of events better illustrate the mechanics involved with the purchase of a chooser option:

Time 0 months. The Canadian dollar is currently trading at 1.32 Can./U.S. and the federal election in Canada is to take place in three months. An investor who has no view about the impact of election results wants the ability to buy an instrument that will enable him or her to make a choice between a call and a put option at the end of the three months. The investor pays a premium to buy a European-style chooser option (i.e., an option to choose three months from now between a European call and a European put option on U.S. dollars with both the options being struck at 1.32 Can./U.S. and expiring three months after the choice date).

Case 1: A three-month European call option is chosen.

Time 3 months. Election results have been announced and currency is now trading at 1.35 Can./U.S. (i.e., the U.S. dollar is now stronger). The call option is now in the money and the put option is out of the money. Since the call option is more valuable than the put option, the investor chooses the call option on the U.S. dollar.

Time 6 months. *Case 1a:* The dollar is now trading at 1.34 Can./U.S. The option finishes in the money, and the payoff to the investor is:

$$(1.34 - 1.32 - P^*_{6\,mth,S})\ \text{Can./U.S.}$$

where

$P^*_{6mth,S}$ represents the premium of the chooser option future valued to six months.

Case 1b: Currency is now trading at 1.29 Can./U.S. The option finishes out of the money, and the investor has lost the option premium.

Case 2: A three-month European put option is chosen.

Time 3 months. Election results have been announced and the currency is now trading at 1.30 Can./U.S. (i.e., the U.S. dollar is now weaker). The put option is now in the money and the call option is out of the money. Because the put option is more valuable than the call option, the investor chooses the put option on the U.S. dollar.

Time 6 months. *Case 2a:* The dollar is now trading at 1.29 Can./U.S. The option finishes in the money, and the payoff to the investor is:

$(1.32 - 1.29 - P^*_{6\,mth,S})$ Can./U.S.

where

$P^*_{6\,mth,S}$ represents the premium of the chooser option future valued to six months.

Case 2b: Currency is now trading at 1.34 Can./U.S. The option finishes out of the money, and the investor has lost his option premium.

First, it is important to note from the above example that the investor, upon choosing the call option at the end of the three-month period, alternatively could have sold the chosen option in the market instead of holding it for another three months.

Second, the type of chooser option mentioned in the above example is known as a simple chooser option. Alternatively, the investor could have bought a complex chooser option that would have allowed him or her a choice between a European call option with strike X_1 and time to maturity T_1 and a European put option with strike X_2 and time to maturity T_2. Exhibit 41–10 details the payoffs of both the simple and complex chooser options.

Third, if the choice date in the above example of a simple chooser option was set to six months, which in our example is the maturity date of the option, the investor would have effectively bought a straddle (i.e., a call and a put both struck at 1.32 Can./U.S. and expiring in six months). Because of the ability to choose at the end of six months, the investor will always get a positive payoff. Thus, the closer the choice date to the option maturity, the more expensive the chooser option will be. Exhibit 41–11 shows the effect of varying the choice time t for a simple chooser option. The increase in premium is due to less uncertainty about the chosen option finishing in the money.

Fourth, although the above example illustrated choosing between a European-style call and put option, we could just as well have offered the investor a choice between an American-style call and put option. Furthermore, the added twist of offering the investor the ability to make a choice

EXHIBIT 41–10

Payoffs of the European-Style Chooser Option

Type of Chooser Option	Payoff at Choice time t	Payoff at Expiry Time
Simple	$\max[C_E(X,t,T,S_t),P_E(X,t,T,S_t)]$	If call chosen at time t: $\max[-P^*_{T,S},S_T-X-P^*_{T,S}]$ If put chosen at time t: $\max[-P^*_{T,S},X-S_T-P^*_{T,S}]$.
Complex	$\max[C_E(X_1,t,T_1,S_t),P_E(X_2,t,T_2,S_t)]$	If call chosen at time t: $\max[-P^*_{T_1,c},S_{T1}-X_1-P^*_{T_1,C}]$ If put chosen at time t: $\max[-P^*_{T_2,C},X_2-S_{T2}-P^*_{T_2,C}]$.

where $C_E(X_1,t,T_1,S_t)$ and $P_E(X_2,t,T_2,S_t)$ represent the European-style vanilla call and put option premiums when the strike rates are X_1 and X_2 respectively, the current (choice) time is t, the option maturity times are T_1 and T_2, and the current spot rate is S_t,; $P^*_{T,S}$ represents the simple chooser option premium that is future valued to time T, $P^*_{T_1,c}$ and $P^*_{T_2,c}$ represent the complex chooser option premiums that are future valued to times T_1 and T_2, respectively.

EXHIBIT 41–11

Simple Chooser Option Premiums for Varying t

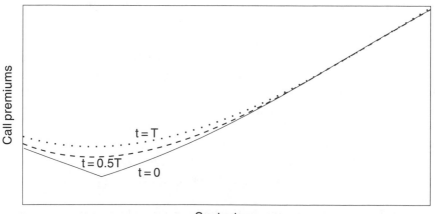

at any moment from the inception of the contract till the final choice time *t* has no value because market information increases as time decays and, as such, it is always beneficial for the investor to delay his or her decision of choice.

A chooser option is usually bought by someone who does not want to be affected by the uncertainty toward the run-up to a major event (e.g., elections, referendums, war). Buyers who want to avoid paying for the volatility caused by the event and are uncertain about the direction of the market should buy a chooser option with the choice date set about one day after the event. Furthermore, when buying a chooser option, the buyer should also be careful about the short-end volatility spiking up, which in turn would cause a straddle to be cheaper than a chooser option because as the event date draws closer and the outcome of the event becomes more uncertain (or equally split), the volatility of the market to the event date increases. Furthermore, since the outcome of the event will be realized on the event date, the volatility of the market out to a day past the event date becomes lesser, hence making a straddle cheaper.[5]

Compound Options

A manufacturer is bidding for a contract to manufacture a certain set of goods. If he is awarded the contract a month after the bid was submitted, for example, he is required to manufacture the goods at the bidded price. He also runs the risk of being exposed to the rising cost of raw materials if he waits until the date of award to purchase the raw materials. To hedge himself, he needs a call option on the price of the materials that is struck at the level of his tendered bid, only, if he is awarded the contract. Due to the hedging difficulties arising from nonmarket risk, it is usually difficult for an investment house to sell an option that is contingent on the buyer being awarded a contract. As such, the manufacturer's best alternative is to buy an option that would allow him to receive a call option at the award date for an extra premium. This option, also known as a compound option, option-on-option, or a split payment option, is a derivative that allows the buyer to pay an initial up-front premium for an option that he may need later. The buyer then pays an additional premium only if he decides that he needs this

---

5 Rubinstein (1991) covers the pricing of the chooser options, both simple and complex. These exotic options can be hedged using either the underlying asset or other appropriate vanilla options.

option. The mechanics associated with a compound option transaction are best illustrated with the following example:

> **Time 0 month.** The Canadian dollar is currently trading at 1.34 Can./U.S. The client bids on a contract based on today's exchange rate and will know the outcome of the bidding only one month from now. If the outcome is successful, she would be faced with a currency exposure six months after the results of the bidding. She is afraid that if the U.S. dollar strengthens seven months from now, she is bound to lose money on the contract which she tendered using an exchange rate of 1.34 Can./U.S. Thus, she needs a protection against a rising U.S. dollar in seven months only if she is awarded the contract. Her needs will be fulfilled if she had a call option on the U.S. dollar that has a strike rate of 1.34 Can./U.S., life of six months, and conditionally starting one month from now. To do this, she could purchase a call option (so that she can receive her second call option by paying an additional premium of 0.050 Can./U.S., which would be less than the amount prescribed by the market if the first call option goes in the money) on the call option.
>
> More precisely, she would pay a small initial premium today to buy a call option with a life of one month, which exercises into another call option (with strike rate 1.34 Can./U.S. and a life of six months) on the payment of an additional premium of 0.050 Can./U.S., which is prespecified at the inception of the contract. Since there is a possibility of not being awarded the contract, she obviously would not mind paying a smaller initial premium and a higher second premium upon winning the contract.
>
> *Case 1: The client is awarded the contract.*
>
> **Time 1 month.** The contract is now awarded to the client. She needs a call option on the U.S. dollar with a life of six months and a strike of 1.34 Can./U.S. She compares the second premium of 0.050 Can./U.S. that was prespecified at the inception of the contract with the premium required to buy the call option from the market. If the size of her second additional premium is smaller, she exercises the compound option. However, if it is cheaper for her to buy this option from the market, she does not exercise her compound option and forgoes the initial premium paid at the inception of the contract.

Time 7 months.   *Assuming that the compound option (or first call option) is exercised.*

Case 1a: Currency is now trading at 1.32 Can./U.S. The call option acquired by the client is out of the money, and as such she loses both her premiums.

Case 1b: The U.S. dollar is stronger and the exchange rate is now at a level of 1.35 Can./U.S. The call option finishes in the money, and the payoff to the client is:

$$(1.35 - 1.34 - P^*_{7\,mths,CP}) \text{ Can./U.S.}$$

where

$P^*_{7\,mths,CP}$ represent the sum of the two premiums that are future valued to a time of seven months.

Case 2: The client is not awarded the contract.

Time 1 month.   She does not receive the contract. Since she has no use for the call option, she does not exercise the compound option and forgoes her initial premium.

One should first note from the above example that the lower the initial compulsory payment, the higher the second optional payment and vice versa. Furthermore, when there is no second optional payment, it would be intuitively reasonable to expect the initial compulsory payment of a call-on-call option to be equal to the premium of a structurally similar vanilla call option with a life of seven months. Under this circumstance, it is also intuitively reasonable to expect that a structurally similar put-on-call option would be worthless. Exhibit 41–12 illustrates the effect of varying the second optional premium on the initial compulsory premium for a call-on-call option.

The curve $X_t - 0\%$ represents the premium (or the first compulsory payment) of a call-on-call option when there is no second installment. As discussed, this curve also represents the European-style vanilla call option premium. The curves $X_t - 20\%$ ($X_t - 50\%$) represent the premiums or the first compulsory payments of a call-on-call option when 20 percent (50 percent of the vanilla call option premium has been paid as a second installment. As illustrated in Exhibit 41–12, the higher this percentage, the lower the first compulsory premium.

Second, even if the client does not get awarded the contract, it may still be optimal for her to exercise her compound option and sell off the underlying call option as long as the second additional premium is lower

EXHIBIT 41–12
Effect of X_t on the Premium of a Call-on-Call Option

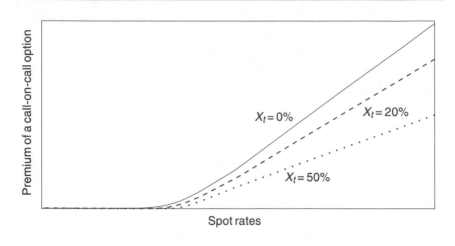

than the premium obtained by selling the call option in the market. Although, the example illustrates the use of a European-style call-on-call option, one can find justification for the use of put-on-call option, call-on-put option, and put-on-put option. The payoffs corresponding to these various compound options are given in Exhibit 41–13.

Although compound options can be priced using the binomial method, R. Geske (1979) and M. Rubinstein (1991) have provided analytical expressions for the pricing of European-style compound options. The concept of a compound option can be easily adapted to embed either a vanilla option exercising into any exotic option or any exotic option exercising into a vanilla option, depending on the type of risk the client is trying to manage. Furthermore, the philosophy of paying the option premium in two installments, with the first compulsory and the second optional, can be extended to paying the premium in n (where $n \geq 2$) installments with the first compulsory and the remaining $n - 1$ optional.

Extrema Options

A Canadian investor observes that the TSE 35 index is currently trading at 220 points and the TSE 100 index is currently trading at 250 points. Based on both current and historical levels, the investor feels that the Canadian

EXHIBIT 41–13
Payoffs of the European-Style Compound Option

Type of Compound Option	Payoff at Time t	Payoff at Expiry Time T if Compound Option is Exercised at Time t
$C_EC_E(X_t,X_T,0,t,T,S_0)$	$\max[-P^*_{t,CC},C_{E,t}-X_t-P^*_{t,CC}]$	$\max[-P^*_{T,CC},S_T-X_T-P^*_{T,CC}]$
$P_EC_E(X_t,X_T,0,t,T,S_0)$	$\max[-P^*_{t,PC},X_t-C_{E,t}-P^*_{t,PC}]$	$\max[-P^*_{T,PC},S_T-X_T-P^*_{T,PC}]$
$C_EP_E(X_t,X_T,0,t,T,S_0)$	$\max[-P^*_{t,CP},P_{E,t}-X_t-P^*_{t,CP}]$	$\max[-P^*_{T,CP},X_T-S_T-P^*_{T,CP}]$
$P_EP_E(X_t,X_T,0,t,T,S_0)$	$\max[-P^*_{t,PP},X_t-P_{E,t}-P^*_{t,PP}]$	$\max[-P^*_{T,PP},X_T-S_T-P^*_{T,PP}]$

where $C_EC_E(X_t,X_T,0,t,T,S_0)$, $P_EC_E(X_t,X_T,0,t,T,S_0)$, $C_EP_E(X_t,X_T,0,t,T,S_0)$ and $P_EP_E(X_t,X_T,0,t,T,S_0)$ represent the European-style call-on-call, put-on-call, call-on-put and put-on-put options respectively, when X_t is the strike rate (i.e. second additional premium) at time t, X_T is the strike rate at time T, 0 is the current time, t is the time that the first option expires, T is the time that the second option expires, and S_0 is the current exchange rate; $C_{E,t}$ and $P_{E,t}$ represent the European call and the put option premiums when the current time is t, option maturity time is T, the strike rate of the option is X_T and the current spot rate is S_t; $P^*_{t,CC}$, $P^*_{t,PC}$, $P^*_{t,CP}$, and $P^*_{t,PP}$ represent the initial premiums of the call-on-call, put-on-call, call-on-put, and put-on-put respectively that are future valued to time t, and $P^*_{T,CC}$, $P^*_{T,PC}$, $P^*_{T,CP}$, and $P^*_{T,PP}$ represent the sum of the initial and the second additional premiums (X_t) of these respective options that are future valued to time T.

equity market should rally enough over the next week, so that the maximum of the TSE 35 index and (0.88 * TSE 100 index) should easily exceed a level of 225 in a week, where 0.88 = 220/250. The instrument to help monetize this view is called an extrema option. An extrema option, also known as a rainbow or maxima/minima option, is a derivative that allows the buyer to pay an initial up-front premium for a call option. This call option provides a payoff that is the maximum of zero and the difference between the maximum of the two underlying variables and the strike rate. The mechanics associated with an extrema option transaction are best illustrated with the following example:

Time 0 weeks. The TSE 35 and TSE 100 indexes are currently trading at 220 and 250 points respectively. The investor pays a premium for a maxima call option that is struck at a level of 225 and expires in a week. If his view is right, ignoring the premium of the option paid, the investor would receive a payoff of the difference between the maximum of the TSE 35 index and (0.88*TSE 100 index) one week from now and a strike level of 225.

Time 1 week.   *Case 1:* The TSE 35 and the TSE 100 indexes are currently trading at 223 and 260 respectively. The maximum of the TSE 35 and (0.88*TSE 100) is:

max[223, (0.88*260)]=max[223,228.8]=228.8

The option finishes in the money and the payoff to the buyer is:

$(228.8 - 225) - P^*_{1\,wk,CMa}$,

where

$P^*_{1\,wk,CMa}$ represents the premium of the extrema option future valued to one week.

Case 2: The TSE 35 and TSE 100 indexes are currently trading at 223 and 250 points respectively. The maximum of the TSE 35 and (0.88*TSE 100) is

max[223,(0.88*250)]=max[223,220]=223.

The option finishes out of the money, and the buyer has lost his premium.

The payoffs relating to an extrema option can be more generally written as in Exhibit 41–14.

Although these options can be priced using the binomial method that has been illustrated in Rubinstein (1991), analytical expressions for valuing the above payoffs when $a - b - 1$ have been provided by Stulz (1982). Like the basket, product, and spread options, the correlation between asset S_{1T} and asset S_{2T} is an important input to the price of an extrema option. When X in the above payoffs in Exhibit 41–14 is set to zero, the call maxima option, for example, simplifies to a function of the exchange options. More precisely, when X is zero, the purchase of a call maxima option is equivalent to the purchase of an option that allows b times asset 2 to be exchanged for a times asset 1 at expiry time T and the purchase of b times asset 2. Furthermore, purchasing a call minima option is equivalent to purchasing b times asset 2 and selling an option that allows the buyer to exchange a times asset 1 for b times asset 2 at time T. Both the maxima and minima put options will be worthless when X is zero because an asset price cannot be negative. The section on spread option discusses the relationship between an exchange and a spread option.

Although, the above discussion was based on two underlying variables, nothing prohibits us from offering an extrema option on a basket of n

EXHIBIT 41–14
Payoffs of the European-Style Extrema Option

Type of Extrema Option	Payoff at Expiry Time T
$C_{E,Ma}(X,0,T,S_{10},S_{20},a,b)$	$-P^*_{T,CMa}$ if $\max[aS_{1T},bS_{2T}]<X$
	$\max[aS_{1T},bS_{2T}]-X-P^*_{T,CMa}$ if $\max[aS_{1T},bS_{2T}]\geq X$
$P_{E,Ma}(X,0,T,S_{10},S_{20},a,b)$	$-P^*_{T,PMa}$ if $\max[aS_{1T},bS_{2T}]>X$
	$X-\max[aS_{1T},bS_{2T}]-P^*_{T,PMa}$ if $\max[aS_{1T},bS_{2T}]\leq X$
$C_{E,Mi}(X,0,T,S_{10},S_{20},a,b)$	$-P^*_{T,CMi}$ if $\min[aS_{1T},bS_{2T}]<X$
	$\min[aS_{1T},bS_{2T}]-X-P^*_{T,CMi}$ if $\min[aS_{1T},bS_{2T}]\geq X$
$P_{E,Mi}(X,0,T,S_{10},S_{20},a,b)$	$-P^*_{T,PMi}$ if $\min[aS_{1T},bS_{2T}]>X$
	$X-\min[aS_{1T},bS_{2T}]-P^*_{T,PMi}$ if $\min[aS_{1T},bS_{2T}]\leq X$

where $C_{E,Ma}(X,0,T,S_{10},S_{20},a,b)$, $P_{E,Ma}(X,0,T,S_{10},S_{20},a,b)$, $C_{E,Mi}(X,0,T,S_{10},S_{20},a,b)$, and $P_{E,Mi}(X,0,T,S_{10},S_{20},a,b)$ represent the European-style call maxima, put maxima, call minima, and put minima options respectively when the strike rate is X, the current time is 0, the option maturity time is T, the current spot rates are S_{10} and S_{20}, and their corresponding nonnegative multiples are a and b respectively; $P^*_{T,CMa}$, $P^*_{T,PMa}$, $P^*_{T,CMi}$, and $P^*_{T,PMi}$ represent the call maxima, put maxima, call minima, and put minima option premiums that are future valued to time T.

indexes, where $n \geq 2$.[6] The philosophy of buying or selling derivatives on the best or the worst of n assets is apparent in certain exchange-traded derivative contracts. In selling a bond futures contract on either the Montreal or the Chicago exchange, the seller must typically deliver the cheapest of a basket of 25 bonds. Furthermore, although not very liquid, options on these cheapest-to-deliver contracts or extrema options on a basket of 25 bonds do trade in the exchanges.

Extrema structures can also be embedded into binary quanto options in the structuring of notes. A Canadian investor, for example, could buy a one-month note that pays off a coupon that is a fraction of 5 percent, where this fraction represents the proportion of business days in the six-month period during which the maximum of three-month Banker's Acceptance (BA) (1.15* three-month LIBOR) exceeds a level of 4 percent, where all the transactions are carried out in Canadian funds. Such a note can be similarly structured to pay out in U.S. funds.

---

6 See Boyle and Tse (1990) for a detailed discussion on the pricing of an extrema option on n assets.

Forward Start Options

Forward start options are paid for today but start at some prespecified time in the future. The simplest form of forward start options are caps and floors, which exist in abundance in capital markets. In this simplest form, the caplets and floorlets that make up a cap and floor respectively start at prespecified times in the future with the strike rates prespecified at the inception of the contract. Variations on the simplest form of forward start options have more recently developed in the interest rate market, where they take the form of periodic caps and floors, and in the equity and currency markets, where they take the form of cliquet or ratchet options. Instead of buying vanilla caps (where the strike rate of each caplet is prespecified in advance and may be different from one another), which could prove expensive during rapidly rising interest rates or a steeply upward sloping yield curve environment, liability managers could buy periodic caps where the strike rate of each caplet is set at a certain spread above the previous LIBOR setting. The following example better illustrates the mechanics behind the transaction of a period cap:

> **Time 0 months.** The client pays a premium to buy a one-year periodic cap where there are three caplets expiring at the three-month, six-month, and nine-month time periods. The strike rate of each caplet will be set equal to the sum of the previous three-month LIBOR setting and 50 basis points. The current three-month LIBOR is 3.5 percent. The strike rate of the first caplet expiring in three months is (3.5 percent + 50 basis points) = 4 percent.

> **Time 3 months.** LIBOR is 3.75 percent. The first caplet finishes out-of-the-money and the strike rate for the next caplet is set at (3.75 percent + 50 basis points) = 4.25 percent. The second caplet commences and matures in three months' time.

> **Time 6 months.** LIBOR is currently at 4.3 percent. The second caplet finishes in the money by five basis points and the strike rate for the third caplet is set at (4.3 percent + 50 basis points) = 4.8 percent. The third caplet commences and expires in three months.

> **Time 9 months.** LIBOR is at 4 percent. The third caplet finishes out of the money.

EXHIBIT 41–15
Payoffs of the European-Style Forward Start Option

Type of Forward Start Option	Payoff at Expiry Time T
$C_E(X,0,T,S_0,t,t_1)$	$-P^*_{T,C}$ if $S_T-S_t<X$
	$S_T-S_t-X-P^*_{T,C}$ if $S_T-S_t\geq X$
$P_E(X,0,T,S_0,t,t_1)$	$-P^*_{T,P}$ if $S_T-S_t>X$
	$X-(S_T-S_t)-P^*_{T,P}$ if $S_T-S_t\leq X$

where $C_E(X,0,T,S_0,t,t_1)$ and $P_E(X,0,T,S_0,t,t_1)$ represent the European-style forward start call and put options respectively when the strike value is X, the current time is 0, option starts at time t_1, the option maturity is T, floating strike is set at time t, and the current value of the index is S_0; $P^*_{T,C}$ and $P^*_{T,P}$ are the premiums of the call and put options that are future valued to time T.

Forward start options can also be used by investors to bet on reset LIBOR values. Suppose, for example, that the current yield curve environment is such that the 3×6 FRA (forward rate agreement) rate is higher than the 6×9 FRA rate, and investor's feel that this inversion in the yield curve is only temporary. To monetize their view, investors could buy a forward start call option on the three-month LIBOR starting three months from now. The strike rate on their option is the three-month LIBOR in three months' time, following which the vanilla option on the three-month LIBOR expires another three months later. Due to the current inversion in this part of the yield curve, the cost of this option would be minimal. It is important to note that the naive strategy of buying and selling the appropriate FRAs has a large downside–if the view turns out to be strong.[7]

The payoffs for a generic forward start option generally can be written as shown in Exhibit 41–15; the pricing expressions for these options when X (also called an offset in the context of a spread option) is zero and $t = t_1$ are given in Hull (1993). Hull shows that the premium of a forward start option is proportional to the premium of a vanilla European-style at-the-money option with life $T - t$. Furthermore, if the underlying asset does not pay any dividend, Hull shows that the purchase of the forward start option is equivalent to the purchase of a vanilla European-style at-the-money option with life $T - t$. These results can be extended to show that as long as $X = 0$, these valuation formulae hold true even if $t_1 \neq t$. To intuit this, consider

---

7 See, for example, Ravindran (1995).

the case where the underlying asset does not pay any dividend, $t_1 = 0$, and the option premium is paid today. In this instance, the buyer has effectively bought an option that expires at time T and whose strike price is set at time t. Since the value of this option is based solely on the difference in prices of the same asset at times T and t, this option has no value until the strike price is set. Thus, the effective life of the option is $T - t$. As long as the asset does not pay any dividend, this is equivalent to the buyer purchasing an option today with a life of $T - t$.

Because a forward start option is indeed a vanilla European-style option once the floating strike component has been set, risk management on a forward start option is identical to that of a vanilla option only after the floating strike is set. Prior to the fixing of the floating strike, we can still delta hedge a forward start option because we can implicitly calculate the correlation coefficient between S_T and S_t many times.

As long as $t_1 < t$, a forward start option described above can also be thought of as a spread option starting at time t_1. In the example of the 3×6 and the 6×9 FRAs given earlier, as long as the forward start option commences before the three-month period, this option can also be viewed as a spread option with the two variables being the three-month LIBOR six months from now and the three-month LIBOR three months from now. Unlike a typical spread option, in which the correlation coefficient can only be historically calculated, the auto-correlation can usually be implicitly calculated because we are actually monitoring a single variable at two different points in time rather than two variables at the same time. This phenomenon is similar to the discussion comparing the arithmetic average rate option to a basket option.

Despite the fact that the forward start option begins at a future time, it is important to note that the value of a forward start option will be exactly the same as that of a structurally similar vanilla option expiring at time T, as long as the floating component of the strike rate is absent from the option's payoff. To intuit this, observe that when the floating strike component is absent, the payoff of a forward start option depends only on the exchange rate at option maturity. Since this situation is exactly the same as that of a structurally similar vanilla option, an investor should not favor one structure over the other. Thus, we can expect both option premiums to be the same. Furthermore, when X is 0, the purchase of a forward start call option is equivalent to the purchase of a maxima call option with $a = 1, b = 1, S_{1T} = S_T$, and $S_{2T} = X = S_t$. See the discussion on extrema options.

Lookback Options

A U.S. manufacturer receives raw materials from Canada. Upon the receipt of his bills, he has until the end of the month to settle his accounts. He knows the total currency risk to which he is exposed at the end of every month and wants to protect himself against a weakening U.S. dollar. As such, the manufacturer wants to buy a one-month put option on the U.S. dollar and at the same time be able to lock in a better rate if the Canadian dollar strengthens during the life of the option. Since he has no view on the market, he needs to buy a European-style lookback put option on the U.S. dollar to address his concerns. A lookback option is a derivative that allows the buyer to pay an initial up-front premium for an option that provides maximum protection. The mechanics of a lookback option transaction are best illustrated with the following example:

> **Time 0 months.** The Canadian dollar is currently trading at 1.34 Can./U.S. A manufacturer who is faced with a currency exposure in a month is worried about the weakening of the U.S. dollar. At the same time, he wants to lock in the highest possible level reached by the Canadian dollar during this one-month period. As such, he wants to pay an up-front premium for a European-style lookback put option on the U.S. dollar that pays off in one month an amount that is the maximum of zero and the difference between the spot rate on the option maturity date and the lowest value the U.S. dollar reaches during the life of the option (inclusive of the spot rates at both the inception of the contract and the maturity of the option). The spot rates are observed at noon on each business day.

> **Time 1 month.** *Case 1:* The Canadian dollar is trading at 1.32 Can./U.S. The weakest value attained by the U.S. dollar during the one-month sampling period is at the maturity date of the option. The option therefore expires worthless and the manufacturer has lost his premium paid out at the inception of the contract.
>
> *Case 2:* The Canadian dollar is trading at 1.33 Can./U.S. The lowest value attained by the U.S. dollar during the sampling period was a level of 1.28 Can./U.S. The option finishes in the money and the payoff to the manufacturer is:

$$(1.33 - 1.28 - P^*_{1\,mth,PLo})\ \text{Can./U.S.}$$

EXHIBIT 41–16
European-Style Modified Lookback Call Option Premiums

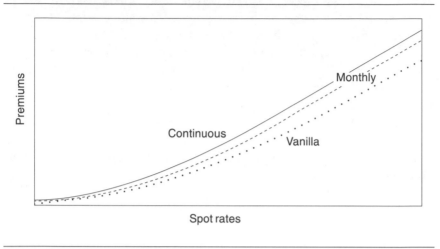

where

$P^*_{1\,mth,PLo}$ represents the premium of the lookback option future valued to one month.

First, it is important to note that the lookback option is not really an option. This follows from the observation that the sampling period that contains the exchange rates encountered during the life of the option also includes as its points the spot rate at the option maturity date. As such, one cannot do any worse than the spot rate at the option maturity date.

Second, we could have created an option that paid the buyer at the option maturity date a maximum of zero and the difference between a prespecified strike rate and the lowest exchange rate realized during the life of the option. Since it is possible for this difference in payoff to be negative, we will call these options modified lookback options.

Third, due to the high level of insurance provided, one can expect a lookback option to be costly. More precisely, the cost of a lookback option is directly proportional to the frequency of sampling. Thus, the greater the frequency of sampling (or the larger the sampling period), the more expensive the option. Exhibit 41–16 shows the difference in premiums between a modified lookback call option with continuous sampling frequency,

EXHIBIT 41–17
Payoffs of the European-Style Lookback Option

Type of Lookback Option	Payoff at Expiry Time T
$C_{E,F}(0,T,S_0,t_1,...,t_n)$	$-P^*_{T,CLo}$ if $S_T < \min S_{t_i}$
	$S_T - \min S_{t_i} - P^*_{T,CLo}$ if $S_T \geq \min S_{t_i}$
$P_{E,F}(0,T,S_0,t_1,...,t_n)$	$-P^*_{T,PLo}$ if $S_T > \max S_{t_i}$
	$\max S_{t_i} - S_T - P^*_{T,PLo}$ if $S_T \leq \max S_{t_i}$
$C_{E,M}(X,0,T,S_0,t_1,...,t_n)$	$-P^*_{T,CMLo}$ if $X > \max S_{t_i}$
	$\max S_{t_i} - X - P^*_{T,CMLo}$ if $X \leq \max S_{t_i}$
$P_{E,M}(X,0,T,S_0,t_1,...,t_n)$	$-P^*_{T,PMLo}$ if $X < \min S_{t_i}$
	$X - \min S_{t_i} - P^*_{T,PMLo}$ if $X \geq \min S_{t_i}$

where $C_{E,F}(0,T,S_0,t_1,...,t_n)$, $P_{E,F}(0,T,S_0,t_1,...,t_n)$, $C_{E,M}(X,0,T,S_0,t_1,...,t_n)$ and $P_{E,M}(X,0,T,S_0,t_1,...,t_n)$ represent the European-style lookback call, lookback put, modified lookback call, and modified lookback put options respectively, when the current time is 0, option maturity is T, current spot rate is S_0, strike rate of the modified lookback option is X, and the sampled times are t_i (where $i = 1,...,n$; $t_0 \leq 0$ and $t_n=T$); $P^*_{T,CLo}$, $P^*_{T,PLo}$, $P^*_{T,CMLo}$, and $P^*_{T,PMLo}$ represent the premiums of the lookback call, lookback put, modified lookback call and modified lookback put options that are future valued to time T, min S_{t_i} represents the smallest value of all the spot rates sampled and maxS_{t_i} represents the largest value of all the spot rates sampled. For the partial lookback options and the modified partial lookback options, the payoffs are essentially the same as above except the size of the sampling points are reduced.

modified lookback call option with discrete sampling frequency, and vanilla call option when the strikes and the times to maturity of the options are identical.

Furthermore, if the manufacturer has a strong view that the Canadian dollar over the last three of the four weeks is never going to get any stronger than the exchange rate at inception, he could use this view to lower the cost by purchasing a partial lookback option, where the sampling period for the lookback feature commences in a week's time and ends on the option maturity date. The payoffs for the various European-style lookback options can be more generally written as detailed in Exhibit 41–17.

Although both the European- and American-style lookback options can be priced using the binomial method regardless of the sampling frequency, Goldman, Sosin and Gatto (1979) have provided closed-form solutions to price European-style full lookback options on non–dividend-paying stocks when the assumption of a continuous time sampling period is used.[8] Look-back options can be easily hedged by using either the notion of delta hedging or by replicating the payoffs using European-style vanilla options.

The concept of a lookback strategy can also be embedded into a swap and used effectively by a liability manager. For example, suppose that based on the current yield curve, the three-year swap rate starting six months from now is 6.5 percent, which is higher than the current three-year spot swap rate of 4.73 percent. Clients who want to get into a three-year swap rate can receive the six-month LIBOR and pay a fixed rate of 4.73 percent. If they think that the realized three-year swap rate in six months is going to be less than 4.73 percent, they could get into a swap whereby they receive a floating rate of the six-month LIBOR plus some spread on each coupon date, and pay a fixed rate on the swap that will be the maximum of the current three-year swap rate and the three-year swap rate in six months' time.

Mid-Atlantic Options

A European-style vanilla option is an option that can be exercised only at the maturity date of the option. An American-style vanilla option is an option that can be exercised at any time during the life of the option. An intermediary between these two options is called the Mid-Atlantic option (or the quasi–American-style option, limited exercise option, and the Bermudan option). The Mid-Atlantic option can be exercised only at discrete points during the life of the option. Thus, at the inception of the contract, in addition to specifying the usual parameters of a vanilla European-style option, the buyer of a Mid-Atlantic option must also specify the times of exercise.

Mid-Atlantic options lend themselves naturally as hedge instruments in the interest rate market. The following example better illustrates the mechanics underlying the use of this option:

> **Time 0 years.** An investor owns a large amount of semiannual 8 percent coupon callable bonds issued by a corporation at $100. The bond has a five-year life and can be recalled by the issuer for $102 at any one of the coupon dates during the last year of the bond. More

---

8 These assumptions have been used by Garman (1987) to value European-style full lookback options on dividend-paying stocks, and by Conze and Viswanathan (1991) to value European-style modified lookback options on non–dividend-paying stocks.

precisely, the bond can be recalled by the issuer on the eighth or ninth coupon date at $102. To hedge against this recall, the investor pays an up-front premium to buy a Mid-Atlantic option on a synthetic bond with a 8 percent semiannual coupon that matures on the same day as the callable bond for $102.

Case 1: Bond is called at the end of four years.

Time 4 years. The bond is trading at $105 and the issuer pays the investor the coupon payment of $4 and recalls the bond at $102. The investor then pays $102 to exercise the Mid-Atlantic option into a one-year synthetic bond with a semiannual coupon of 8 percent.

Case 2: Bond is called at the end of four-and-one-half years.

Time 4 years. The bond is trading at $99.50. The investor receives the coupon payment of $4. The issuer does not recall the bond; hence, the investor does not exercise the option.

Time 4½ years. The bond is trading at $103. The issuer pays the investor the coupon payment of $4 and recalls the bond for $102. The investor exercises the Mid-Atlantic option into a six-month synthetic bond with a semiannual coupon of 8 percent by paying $102.

Case 3: Bond is not called.

Time 4 years. The bond is trading at $99.50. A coupon of $4 is paid to the investor. The issuer does not recall the bond; hence, the investor does not exercise the option.

Time 4½ years. The bond is trading at $101. The issuer does not recall the bond. The investor gets a coupon of $4 and does not exercise the option.

Time 5 years. The bond matures at par. In addition to the face value, the investor also receives the $4 coupon payment. The investor has lost the premium paid for the Mid-Atlantic option.

It is important to note that although the above example illustrates a scenario in which the issuer recalls the bonds only when they are in the

EXHIBIT 41–18
Payoffs of The Mid-Atlantic Option

Type of Option	Payoff at Time t	Payoff at Expiry Time T
$C_{MA}(X,0,T,S_0)$	$\max[S_t{-}X{-}P^*_{t,C}, C_{MA,t}{-}P^*_{t,C}]$	$\max[-P^*_{T,C}, S_T{-}X{-}P^*_{T,C}]$
$P_{MA}(X,0,T,S_0)$	$\max[X{-}S_t{-}P^*_{t,P}, P_{MA,t}{-}P^*_{t,PC}]$	$\max[-P^*_{T,P}, X{-}S_T{-}P^*_{T,P}]$

where $C_{MA}(X,0,T,S_0)$ and $P_{MA}(X,0,T,S_0)$ represent the Mid-Atlantic call and put options respectively when X is the strike rate, the current time is 0, the life of the option is T, the current spot rate is S_0, and t is one of the discrete exercise times $0{\leq}t_0,t_1,...,t_n{\leq}T$; $P^*_{t,C}$ and $P^*_{t,P}$ represent the call and put option premiums that are future valued to time t; $C_{MA,t}$ and $P_{MA,t}$ represent the values of the mid-Atlantic call and put options at time t when the strike rate is X, the current time is t, the option expiration time is T, and the current spot rate is S_t.

money, due to accounting or tax reasons it is not uncommon for the issued bonds to be recalled even when they are out of the money. Since the number of exercise points in a Mid-Atlantic option can never exceed that of an American-style option and can never be less than that of a European-style option, it is intuitively reasonable to expect the premium of a Mid-Atlantic option to be no less than that of a European option and no greater than that of an American option. Like the American-style options, Mid-Atlantic options can be easily priced using the binomial method, and making the times of exercise discrete can be easily implemented in other types of exotic options in any asset class. The hedging of a Mid-Atlantic option is no different from that of any vanilla option and the payoffs of a Mid-Atlantic option can be more succintly written as shown in Exhibit 41–18.

Non-linear Payoff Options

A vanilla option has a linear payoff if the derivative finishes in the money. More precisely, if S_T and X represent the exchange rates at the maturity of the option and the strike rate respectively, neglecting the cost of the option premium paid at the inception of the contract, a European-style vanilla call option would have a payoff of $S_T - X$ if the option goes in the money and zero otherwise. The in-the-money payoff in this instance is a linear function of the exchange rate at maturity. By the same token, a European-style nonlinear payoff option has an in-the-money payoff that is a nonlinear function of the exchange rate at maturity. Examples of these in-the-money payoffs at the maturity date are $e^{S_T} - X$, $S_T^2 - X$, $S_T0.5$ (see Exhibit 41–19).

EXHIBIT 41–19
Nonlinear Call Payoffs

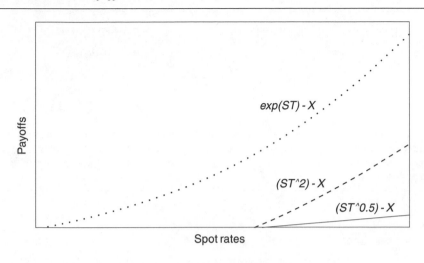

Nonlinear payoff options that have payoffs where S_T appears as a base instead of a power (e.g., $S_T^2 - X$ and $S_T 0.5 - X$) are also called power or turbo options. The following examples, although applied to a power option, can easily be modified for any nonlinear payoff option.

> **Time 0 weeks.** The Canadian dollar is currently trading at 1.30 Can./U.S. The investor is certain that in one week, the Canadian dollar is going to be much weaker, so he wants a payoff function at the expiration date to be $S_T 2 - 1.312$ if the option finishes in the money (i.e., if the U.S. dollar strengthens past the 1.31 mark). He pays a premium to buy the power option that is struck at 1.31^2 Can./U.S. and has a life of one week.

> **Time 1 week.** *Case 1:* Currency is now trading at 1.30 Can./U.S. The option finishes out of the money, and the investor loses his option premium.
> *Case 2:* Currency is now trading at 1.34 Can./U.S. The option finishes in the money and the payoff to the client is:

> $(1.34^2 - 1.31^2 - P*_{1\ wk,C})$ Can./U.S.

EXHIBIT 41–20
Payoffs of the European Style Nonlinear Payoff Option

Type of Nonlinear Payoff Option	Payoff at Expiry Time T
$C_E(X,0,T,S_0)$	$-P^*_{T,C}$ if $f(S_T)<X$
	$f(S_T)-X-P^*_{T,C}$ if $f(S_T)\geq X$
$P_E(X,0,T,S_0)$	$-P^*_{T,P}$ if $f(S_T)>X$
	$X-f(S_T)-P^*_{T,P}$ if $f(S_T)\leq X$

where $C_E(X,0,T,S_0)$ and $P_E(X,0,T,S_0)$ represent the European call and put nonlinear pay-off options when the strike rate is X, the current time is 0, the option maturity time is T, and the current spot rate is S_0; $P^*_{T,C}$ and $P^*_{T,P}$ represent the call and the put option premiums that are future valued to time T.

where

$P^*_{1\,wk,c}$ represents the premium of the power option future valued to the time of one week.

First it is important to note that—putting aside the premiums paid out for the options at the inception of the contract—if the investor had bought a vanilla call option instead, the payoff to the client would have been (1.34 – 1.31) Can./U.S., which is approximately 40 percent of the payoff value obtained from the purchase of the power option. The payoff to the investor can be further leveraged by increasing the index (or the power) of S_T in the above example from two to four.

Second, due to the high leveraging effect in the payoff function, we can expect the premium of the power option to be higher than that of a vanilla option. Letting $f(S_T)$ represent any nonlinear function of S_T and X be the strike rate of the option, the payoff to the investor can be more generally written as detailed in Exhibit 41–20.

As always, the binomial method can be easily used to price both European- and American-style nonlinear payoff options. Although a nonlinear payoff option can be hedged using the concept of delta hedging, due to the amount of leveraging involved, hedging the sale of a nonlinear payoff option can be quite expensive because of the high gamma feature in the option. This hedging cost can be reduced by alternatively hedging a nonlinear payoff option using a sequence of varying notional amounts of vanilla options struck at varying levels.

Nonlinear payoff options can also easily be used for liability or risk management. More precisely, a client could have a nonlinear risk profile for the various interest rate and foreign exchange levels due to their total borrowing costs and exchange rate risks. A perfect hedge for the client would be to buy a nonlinear payoff option that replicates his or her nonlinear risk profile.

Product Options

A Canadian investor observes that current five-year Canadian bond yields are 5.53 percent and U.S. government bond yields 5.10 percent. Based on the historical numbers, the current spread between these yields is relatively small compared to the historical values of this difference, which the investor feels will widen in a week. To monetize this view, the investor wants to buy an instrument that allows her to achieve her objective without being exposed to the currency risk. More precisely, she wants her payoff to be strictly the product of the notional amount of the contract and the difference in the bond yields. The instrument that she actually needs is called a quanto-spread option. To understand a quanto-spread option better, we must first discuss a simple quanto option. A quanto option, which is very loosely used to describe a guaranteed exchange rate option, is a member of the product option family, which allows the buyer to pay an initial up-front premium in domestic currency for an option that trades in a foreign country and to receive the payoff at a guaranteed exchange rate. The mechanics associated with a simple quanto option transaction are best illustrated with the following example:

> **Time 0 weeks.** The current five-year U.S. government bond yield is trading at 5.10 percent. A Canadian investor has a view that this yield will be higher in a week. To monetize her view, she wants to buy an option that will, if she is right, pay her the difference between the five-year bond yield in a week and 5.10 percent. However, she, wants to pay the premium and receive her payoff, if she is in the money, in Canadian funds and does not want to be exposed to the currency risk.

> **Time 1 week.** *Case 1:* The five-year U.S. Treasury bond is trading at a yield of 5.15 percent. The option finishes in the money and the payoff to the buyer in Canadian dollars is:

[Notional Principal * $(5.15 - 5.10)\%$] $- P^*_{1\,wk,CII}$

where

$P^*_{1\,wk,CII}$ represents the premium in Canadian dollars of the quanto option future valued to one week.

Case 2: The five-year Treasury bond is trading at 5.05 percent. The option finishes out of the money and the investor has lost the premium paid out at the inception of the contract.

It is important to note in the above example that although the investor did not have to undergo any currency exposure, the investor had implicitly bought an option guaranteeing her an exchange rate of 1 Can./U.S. Furthermore, it is just as easy to structure an instrument where the investor receives her payoff, if she is in the money, at any other guaranteed exchange rate or the exchange rate realized on the option maturity date. The payoffs for the product options family can be more generally written as shown in Exhibit 41–21.

Guaranteed exchange rate options, which are the category II options in the above exhibit, are usually priced like their vanilla counterparts with adjustments made to the drift term. As in basket, spread, and extrema options, correlation is a necessary input for valuing quanto options. In our example, this will be the correlation between the bond yield and the exchange rate. However, the effect of the correlation in the price of a quanto option is smaller than the contribution of the correlation component to the price of a spread option.[9]

As discussed earlier, quanto-spread options can be easily used by asset managers to help monetize views on relative movements between two different environments without exposure to currency risk. Due to the nature of the assets and liabilities in different environments, liability managers can also exploit the cheap borrowing cost in one environment (e.g., United States) to fund the activities in the other environment (e.g., Canada) by using a differential swap to swap from a Banker's Acceptance to a LIBOR in addition to some spread without undergoing any currency risk or exchange of principal.

---

9 Although both European- and American-style quanto options can be priced using the binomial method, Reiner (1992) and Wei (1995) have provided analytical expressions for pricing the payoffs of the product options given in Exhibit 40–21. Depending on the category, the hedging of certain product options can be complicated. Despite this, hedging any product option would imply hedging both the foreign asset and the currency risk. The static hedge parameters for all the categories have been given in Wei (1995).

EXHIBIT 41–21
Payoffs of the European-Style Product Option

Type of Product Option	Payoff at Expiry Time T
$C_{E,I}(X,0,T,S_0,F_0)$	$\max[-P_{T,CI}(S_T - X)F_T - P^*_{T,CI}]$
$P_{E,I}(X,0,T,S_0,F_0)$	$\max[-P^*_{T,PI}(X - S_T)F_T - P^*_{T,PI}]$
$C_{E,II}(X,0,T,S_0,F_0,F)$	$\max[-P_{T,CII}(S_T - X)F - P^*_{T,CII}]$
$P_{E,II}(X,0,T,S_0,F_0,F)$	$\max[-P_{T,PII}(X - S_T)F - P^*_{T,PII}]$
$C_{E,III}(X,0,T,S_0,F_0,F)$	$\max[-P^*_{T,CIII}S_TF - XF_T - P^*_{T,CIII}]$
$P_{E,III}(X,0,T,S_0,F_0,F)$	$\max[-P^*_{T,PIII}XF_T - S_{TF} - P^*_{T,PIII}]$
$C_{E,IV}(X,0,T,S_0,F_0,F)$	$\max[-P^*_{T,CIV}S_TF_T - X_F - P^*_{T,CIV}]$
$P_{E,IV}(X,0,T,S_0,F_0,F)$	$\max[-P^*_{T,PIV}X_F - S_TF_T - P^*_{T,PIV}]$
$C_{E,V}(X,0,T,S_0,F_0)$	$\max[-P^*_{T,CV}(F_T - X)S_T - P^*_{T,CV}]$
$P_{E,V}(X,0,T,S_0,F_0)$	$\max[-P^*_{T,PV}(X - F_T)S_T - P^*_{T,PV}]$

where $C_{E,I}(X,0,T,S_0,F0)$, $C_{E,II}(X,0,T,S_0,F_0,F)$, $C_{E,III}(X,0,T,S_0,F_0,F)$, $C_{E,IV}(X,0,T,S_0,F_0,F)$, and $C_{E,V}(X,0,T,S_0,F_0)$ represent the European-style category I, II, III, IV, and V call options respectively and $P_{E,I}(X,0,T,S_0,F_0)$, $P_{E,II}(X,0,T,S_0,F_0,F)$, $P_{E,III}(X,0,T,S_0,F_0,F)$, $P_{E,IV}(X,0,T,S_0,F_0,F)$, and $P_{E,V}(X,0,T,S_0,F_0)$ represent the European-style category I, II, III, IV, and V put options respectively when the strike rate is X, the current time is 0, the option maturity time is T, the current foreign asset value is S_0, the current (guaranteed) exchange rate expressed as the value of one unit of foreign currency in domestic dollars if F_0 (F), $P^*_{T,Ci}$ and $P^*_{T,Pi}$ represent the premium of the category i call and put option that is future valued to time T; where $i = $ I, II, III, IV, V.

Quanto structures can also be easily embedded into binary options and presented as structured notes. For example, a Canadian investor could buy a six-month note with a coupon that pays a fraction of 5 percent, where this fraction represents the proportion of business days in the six-month period during which the three-month LIBOR exceeds a level of 3.5 percent, where all the transactions are carried out in Canadian funds. One can similarly structure a binary note where the fraction depends instead on the proportion of business days in the life of the note during which the three-month BA exceeds the three-month LIBOR by 50 basis points.

Shout Options

A shout option is a hybrid of a European-style lookback option and an American-style vanilla option. To understand how a shout option works, it is useful to revisit the payoffs of a European-style vanilla option, lookback

EXHIBIT 41–22
Payoffs of the European-Style Call Option

Type of European Call Option	Payoff at Expiry Time T
vanilla	$\max[-P^*_{T,C}, S_T - X - P^*_{T,C}]$
lookback	$\max[-P^*_{T,CLo}, S_T - \min S_{t_i} - P^*_{T,CLo}]$
modified lookback	$\max[-P^*_{T,CMLo}, \max S_{t_i} - X - P^*_{T,CMLo}]$

where $P^*_{T,C}$, $P^*_{T,CLo}$, and $P^*_{T,CMLo}$ represent the premiums of the European-style vanilla, lookback, and modified lookback call options that are future valued to time T; T denotes the expiration time of the option, X denotes the strike rate of the option; S_{t_i} denotes the spot rate at time t_i; where $i = 1,2,...,n$; $t_0 = 0$, $t_n = T$.

option, and modified lookback option. A European-style vanilla call option on a currency gives the buyer of the contract, on the expiration date of the option, an exchange rate payoff that is the maximum of zero and the difference between the spot exchange rate at the expiration date and the strike rate. The buyer of a European-style lookback call option has a payoff on the option expiration date, which is the greater of zero and the difference between the spot rate at the option maturity date and the lowest exchange rate achieved by the currency during the life of the option. The buyer of a European-style modified lookback call option has a payoff on the expiration date of the option, which is the maximum of zero and the difference between the highest exchange rate achieved by the currency during the life of the option and a predefined strike rate. The payoffs corresponding to the above options are shown in Exhibit 41–22.

Unlike the above options, a shout option gives the buyer a payoff at the maturity date, which is the maximum of zero and the difference between the spot rate at the maturity date and the minimum of the spot rate at both the maturity date and the time of shout. The nature of this payoff is best illustrated by the following example:

Time 0 weeks. The Canadian dollar is currently trading at 1.35 Can./U.S. Due to an expected currency exposure in one month's time, a client wants to be protected against a weakening U.S. dollar. At the same time, the client wants to be able to lock in the best rate that the Canadian dollar might achieve during the life of the option. The cost incurred in buying a lookback put option on the U.S. dollar is high. The client feels that because he is good at calling the markets, he is not prepared to pay for an option that guarantees him a maximum payoff. However, he would not mind paying a lesser premium for a European-style shout put option on the U.S. dollar that matures in a month, with which he could possibly achieve the same payoff as the lookback option.

Time 1 week.   Currency is now trading at 1.30 Can./U.S. This has been the weakest U.S. level in the past week. The option holder feels that it is unlikely that the U.S. dollar will weaken any further and calls up the seller of the option to "shout" at the current level of 1.30 Can./U.S.

Time 1 month.   *Case 1:* The Canadian dollar is now trading at 1.34 Can./U.S. Since the min[1.34,1.30] Can./U.S. = 1.30 Can./U.S., the option finishes in the money and the payoff to the buyer of the option is:

$$(1.34 - 1.30 - P^*_{1\,mth,CSh})\ \text{Can./U.S.},$$

where

$P^*_{1\,mth,CSh}$ represents the premium of the option future valued to the time of one month, while 1.34 represents the spot rate at maturity and 1.30 represents the shout rate.

   Case 2: Currency is now trading at 1.28 Can./U.S. Since the min[1.28,1.30] Can./U.S. = 1.28 Can./U.S., the option finishes out of the money and the client loses his option premium.

From the example above, it should first be noted that in illustrating the payoffs at option maturity (i.e., one month), it was assumed that the owner of the option had an opportunity to shout. Ignoring the option premium paid at time 0, if the buyer had shouted at a level that was the strongest level of the Canadian dollar during the life of the option, the payoff to the buyer would be similar to that of a lookback option. On the other hand, if the shout had been made at a level that turns out to be equal to or less than the spot rate at maturity, the payoff would be equal to zero. Because the shout level can be either greater than or lesser than the spot rate at maturity, it readily follows that the premium of a shout option should be no larger than that of a lookback option.

Second, the shout option, like the lookback option, is not really an option because of the nonnegative nature of its payoff. By prespecifying a strike rate, however, the nonnegativity is removed and the modified shout option behaves like an option, where the premium of a modified shout option will be no less than the premium of a vanilla option that is struck at the same level and no greater than the premium of a modified lookback option that is also struck at the same level. Exhibit 41–23 illustrates the difference in premiums between a European-style vanilla call option and the European-style modified versions of a lookback and shout call options when the strike rates and option maturity times are identical.

The payoffs of the shout options can be more generally written as shown in Exhibit 41–24.

Although the buyer of a modified shout option can theoretically shout at any level that the exchange rate realizes during the life of the option, it is rational for the buyer to only consider shouting when the intrinsic value of the option is greater than zero. More precisely, it is rational for the buyer to shout at any time during the life of the option if the expected value of the option obtained by shouting is greater than the expected value of the option that can be obtained without shouting. It is crucial to note that this is analogous to the exercising of a vanilla American-style option. Although there is no notion of intrinsic value when dealing with a regular shout option, the buyer of such an option would again only shout at any given time if the expected value due to shouting at that time is greater than what he or she would get by not shouting. The shout option can be most easily valued using the binomial method and incorporating this rational behavior of shouting.[10]

Unlike the lookback option, which tends to be expensive, the shout option is cheaper and has the ability to give the buyer (typically an asset manager who is paid for his or her market calling abilities) the same payoff if the market is called correctly. This was illustrated in Exhibit 41–23. Thus, a shout option serves as a useful and inexpensive yield enhancement tool with a limited downside for someone who is good at predicting market movements. Because of its value, the shout option can also be used effectively for liability management by managers who are good at predicting market movements. For example, a liability manager could pay a fixed rate on a five-year swap and receive a six-month LIBOR. If his or her view over the

---

10 See Thomas (1993) for the use of a binomial method to value a shout option.

EXHIBIT 41–23
European-Style Call Option Premiums

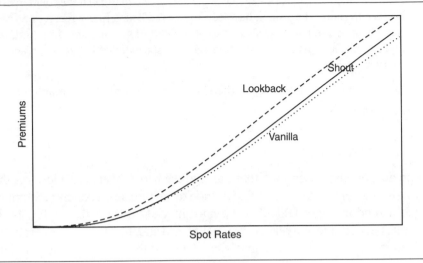

EXHIBIT 41–24
Payoffs of the European-Style Shout Option

Type of Shout Option	Payoff at Expiry Time T
$C_{E,F}(0,T,S_0)$	$\max[-P^*_{T,CSh}, S_T - \min[S^*, S_T] - P^*_{T,CSh}]$
$P_{E,F}(0,T,S_0)$	$\max[-P^*_{T,PSh}, \max[S^*, S_T] - S_T - P^*_{T,PSh}]$
$C_{E,M}(X,0,T,S_0)$	$\max[-P^*_{T,CMSh}, \max[S^*, S_T] - X - P^*_{T,CMSh}]$
$P_{E,M}(X,0,T,S_0)$	$\max[-P^*_{T,PMSh}, X - \min[S^*, S_T] - P^*_{T,PMSh}]$

where S^* represents the exchange rate at which the buyer of the option shouted; $P^*_{T,CSh}$, $P^*_{T,PSh}$, $P^*_{T,CMSh}$ and $P^*_{T,PMSh}$ represent the premiums of a call, put, modified call, and modified put shout options that are future valued to time T; $C_{E,F}(0,T,S_0)$, $P_{E,F}(0,T,S_0)$, $C_{E,M}(X,0,T,S_0)$, and $P_{E,M}(X,0,T,S_0)$ represent the European-style call shout, put shout, modified call shout, and modified put shout options respectively when X is the strike rate of the option, 0 the current time, T the time of option maturity, and S_0 the current spot rate.

next two months is that the five-year swap rate cannot get any higher, the manager can embed a shout option in the trade and end up with the following transaction:

The liability manager pays a fixed rate on a five-year swap with the fixed rate determined at the end of two months by setting it to the max[five-year swap rate at time of shout, five-year swap rate at the end of two months] if the counterparty decides to shout. If no shout has been made, the counterparty receives a fixed rate given by the five-year swap rate at the end of two months. In return, the liability manager receives a floating rate of (six-month LIBOR + spread) on every reset date.

Other variations of the uses of the shout options for liability management are also possible.

Spread Options

Spread options are options that can be used to monetize a view on the relative movement between any two indexes in the same economy. Suppose that a fund manager feels that the current yield differential of 100 basis points between the ten-year government bond and the two-year government bond is too narrow based on historical data and that this difference in yield will widen in a month. To monetize her view, as her first strategy, the fund manager could purchase the underlying bonds by going long and short the appropriate notional amount of the bonds. With this strategy, if she is wrong in a month's time, she has the potential for large losses when liquidating the position. Thus, the downside of replicating the spread using the underlying bonds can be costly and sometimes disastrous.[11]

An alternative way to monetize her view would be to buy on the one hand a spread option that pays at the end of one month the difference between the ten-year bond yield, the two-year bond yield, and an offset of 100 basis points if her view is right, and on the other hand a spread option that pays nothing if her view is wrong. More precisely, her payoff at the end of one month could be written as:

max[0, 10-year yield, −2-year yield − 0.01]

Clearly, if the market view was wrong, the only downside of this strategy is the loss of the premium that was paid at the inception of the contract.

The spread option can also be used to bet on the movement of the swap spreads (i.e., swap rate − bond yield). Suppose, for example, that an investor feels that based on current market conditions, the current three-year swap spread (i.e., the difference between the three-year swap rate and the three-

---

11 See Ravindran (1995) for a detailed discussion.

year on-the-run bond yield) is 28 basis points, and the investor thinks this will narrow in two months time by at least 5 basis points. She could easily monetize her view by purchasing a spread option on the three-year swap spread with an offset of 23 basis points that expires in two months. At the maturity of the option, the investor gets a payoff that is:

max[0,0.0023 – (3-year swap rate – 3-year bond yield)]

The following sequence of events helps illustrate this example better.

Time 0 months. The current swap spread is 28 basis points. The investor feels that in two months, the swap spread will narrow by at least 5 basis points. She pays a premium for a spread option on a $100 million notional amount with an offset of 23 basis points that allows her to monetize this view. Thus, for every basis point the option finishes in the money, the investor gets paid $10,000.

Time 2 months. *Case 1:* The current swap spread is 18 basis points. The option finishes in the money and the payoff to the buyer of the option is:

$100 million * $(0.0023 - 0.0018) - P^*_{2\,mth,CSp}$,

where

$P^*_{2\,mth,CSp}$ represents the premium of the spread option future valued to two months.

Case 2: The current swap spread is 35 basis points. The option finishes out of the money. Hence, the investor loses her premium.

It is important to note that although the above two examples illustrate the use of European-style spread options, we could just as well structure an American-style spread option where the buyer of the option is allowed to exercise at any time during the life of the option. Like the above examples, a spread option can easily be created to monetize a leveraged view on any part of the same yield curve. Exhibit 41–25 shows a generalized payoff structure for a spread option.

The payoff function showed in Exhibit 41–25 could be written more generally as:

max[0,(a*Yield$_1$) + (b*Yield$_2$) + c]

where

a, b and c are any three real numbers

EXHIBIT 41–25
Payoffs of the European-Style Spread Option

Type of Spread Option	Payoff at Expiry Time T
$C_E(a,b,c,0,T,S_{10},S_{20})$	$-P^*_{T,CSp}$ if $aS_{1T}+bS_{2T}<c$
	$aS_{1T}+bS_{2T}-c-P^*_{T,CSp}$ if $aS_{1T}+bS_{2T}\geq c$
$P_E(a,b,c,0,T,S_{10},S_{20})$	$-P^*_{T,PSp}$ if $aS_{1T}+bS_{2T}>c$
	$c-aS_{1T}-bS_{2T}-P^*_{T,PSp}$ if $aS_{1T}+bS_{2T}\leq c$

where $C_E(a,b,c,0,T,S_{10},S_{20})$ and $P_E(a,b,c,0,T,S_{10},S_{20})$ represent the European call and put spread options respectively when the current time is 0, the option maturity time is T, a and b are any two real numbers, c is a positive real number, and the current spot rates are S_{10} and S_{20}; $P^*_{T,CSp}$ and $P^*_{T,PSp}$ represent the premiums of the call and put spread options that are future valued to time T.

Yield$_1$ and Yield$_2$ represent the values of the two underlying variables describing the option.

These variables can represent the two different swap rates or bond yields or one of each on the same yield curve environment.

Although closed form solutions do exist,[12] when c (called the offset in the spread option) is zero and the two underlying assets are non–dividend-paying stocks, the spread option has to be generally evaluated numerically.[13] In addition to the volatilities of both the variables, the correlation between these variables is also an extremely important input into the price. Unlike volatilities, which can be easily traded, there is no market for correlation trading. Thus, the only means of getting a good estimate for the correlation number is to use the historical data. Hence, correlation estimation is very crucial to the pricing of a spread option. Like a vanilla option, the spread option can also be hedged using the delta hedging technique on each of the variables.[14]

---

12 See Margrabe (1978).

13 See Ravindran (1993) for an intuitive approach to spread option pricing.

14 As mentioned, when the offset c is zero, the spread option, also known as an exchange option, was first valued by Margrabe (1978). The pricing formulas of Margrabe can be extended to encompass dividend paying assets. This is given in Hull (1993). It is important to note that both Margrabe's and Hull's results do not contain the risk-free rate parameter. An intuitive explanation for this is given in the discussion portion of Gerber and Shiu (1994) by Kolkeiweitz and Ravindran (1994).

Sudden Birth/Death Options

When valuing any option, a fundamental input to the Black-Scholes equation is the life of the option, which has traditionally been assumed to be a known constant that is prespecified at the inception of the contract. An option that violates this assumption by allowing the maturity date to be a random variable is called a sudden birth/death option. Although the class of sudden birth/death options may at first glance appear to be somewhat impractical, careful examination shows that variations on the sudden birth/death theme have been and will continue to be widely used. An example of a sudden death option that is still quite popular in the insurance industry is the guaranteed minimum death benefit (GMDB). A GMDB is essentially a principal-guaranteed note that is linked to some index (e.g., TSE 35, S&P 500) and has an upside participation. The fundamental distinction between this note and any other structured note is that a GMDB expires only at the time of the purchaser's death.[15]

Another variation of the sudden birth/death option that is widely used in the financial markets is the barrier option. Although vanilla options serve as good disaster insurance, prevailing market conditions sometimes make such insurance costly. In these circumstances, the premium can be effectively reduced by using barrier options. A barrier option, alternatively known as a trigger or a knockin/knockout option, serves as a conditional insurance, which may suddenly come into effect (or cease to exist) upon the occurrence of an event. Although the investor pays a premium for such an instrument at the inception of the contract, the option would only come into existence (or cease to exist) if a prespecified barrier or level is triggered during the life of the option.

The following example better illustrates the use of a barrier option in practice:

> **Time 0 month.** The Canadian dollar is currently trading at 1.33 Can./U.S. Because of expected currency exposure in one month, the client is worried about the U.S. dollar weakening below the 1.31 Can./U.S. level. Buying a one-month put option on the U.S. dollar with a strike rate of 1.31 Can./U.S. would be an ideal solution.

---

15 The interested reader is referred to Bernard (1993), Gootzeit et. al. (1994), Mitchell (1994), Mueller (1992), and Ravindran and Edelist (1995) for in-depth discussions on valuing GMDBs and their variations.

Current market conditions, however, make this insurance costly. To overcome the cost, the put option can be purchased with the added feature that if the exchange rate during the life of the option exceeds a 1.36 Can./U.S. barrier, the put option would cease to exist. Presumably, if the U.S. dollar can strengthen to a level of 1.36 Can./U.S., it is unlikely to weaken below a level of 1.31 Can./U.S. by the time the option expires. This type of option is also called the up-and-out option; the term *up* refers to the fact that the current spot level must traverse up toward the barrier and the term *out* refers to the extinguishment of the option upon hitting the barrier. The up-and-out option has a smaller premium than the vanilla option.[16]

Case 1: Barrier is not breached during the one-month period. Because the exchange rate has not exceeded or gone beyond the 1.36 barrier level, the put option is still alive. Thus,

Time 1 month.   *Case 1a:* Currency is now trading at a level of 1.32 Can./U.S. The option finishes out of the money and the client has lost the premium paid at the inception of the contract.

Case 1b: U.S. dollar has now weakened to a level of 1.29 Can./U.S. The option finishes in the money and the payoff to the client is:

$$(1.31 - 1.29 - P^*_{1\,mth,PO})\ \text{Can./U.S.}$$

where

$P^*_{1\,mth,PO}$ is the premium of the option future valued to one month.

Case 2: Barrier is breached during the one-month period. Because the U.S. dollar has strengthened past 1.36 Can./U.S. (i.e., breached the barrier of 1.36) at some time during the one-month period, the put option gets extinguished and the client loses the premium.

Unlike a GMDB, which has a completely random expiration time, the knockout option has a random expiration time for only one month. Thus, if

---

16 The farther the barrier from the current exchange rate level, the more expensive the up-and-out option because the probability of the option extinguishing diminishes as the level of the barrier is raised.

EXHIBIT 41–26
Payoffs of the European-Style Barrier Option

Type of Barrier Option	Payoff at Expiry Time T if Barrier is Breached	Payoff at Expiry Time T if Barrier Is Not Breached
$C_{E,In}(X,H,0,T,S_0)$	$\max[-P^*_{T,CI},S_T-X-P^*_{T,CI}]$	$-P^*_{T,CI}$
$C_{E,Out}(X,H,0,T,S_0)$	$-P^*_{T,CO}$	$\max[-P^*_{T,CO},S_T-X-P^*_{T,CO}]$
$P_{E,In}(X,H,0,T,S_0)$	$\max[-P^*_{T,PI},X-S_T-P^*_{T,PI}]$	$-P^*_{T,PI}$
$P_{E,Out}(X,H,0,T,S_0)$	$-P^*_{T,PO}$	$\max[-P^*_{T,PO},X-S_T-P^*_{T,PO}]$

where $C_{E,In}(X,H,0,T,S_0)$, $C_{E,Out}(X,H,0,T,S_0)$, $P_{E,In}(X,H,0,T,S_0)$, and $P_{E,Out}(X,H,0,T,S_0)$ represent the European-style in-call, out-call, in-put, and out-put options respectively when the strike rate is X, the barrier level is H, the current time is 0, the life of the option is T, and the current spot rate is S_0; $P^*_{T,CI}$, $P^*_{T,CO}$, $P^*_{T,PI}$, and $P^*_{T,PO}$ represent the in-call, out-call, in-put, and out-put option premiums that are future valued to time T; the terms *in* and *out* describe the coming alive and dying, respectively, of an option upon breaching the barrier.

the option does not get extinguished during the one-month period, it will be forced to mature at the end of the one-month time period. Although the above example illustrates the use of an up-and-out put option, it is not difficult to construct practical examples where the up-and-in, down-and-out, and down-and-in call and put options can be effectively used. The payoffs of all these barrier options can be written as detailed in Exhibit 41–26.

Each of the above four payoffs can be decomposed further into the up-and-down options, depending on whether $S_0 < H$. Assuming a continuous trading market, the pricing formulas for the barrier options corresponding to the above payoffs has been given by Rubinstein and Reiner (1991). If a barrier option is bought on an underlying index that is trading in an illiquid market, the exact times of monitoring the breaching of the barrier by the index must be specified in the contract in advance. Furthermore, when the monitoring of the index is done at discrete times, no analytical expressions exist for the pricing of the barrier options and, as such, the prices can only be evaluated numerically. However, it can be shown that the cost of a continuously monitored knockout barrier option cannot be greater than the cost of a discretely monitored knockout barrier option. The converse is true for the knockin barrier options.

Although the barrier options are usually hedged using the classic delta hedging methodology, the effect of gamma is eminent in these options. To

EXHIBIT 41–27
In, Out, and Vanilla Option Premiums

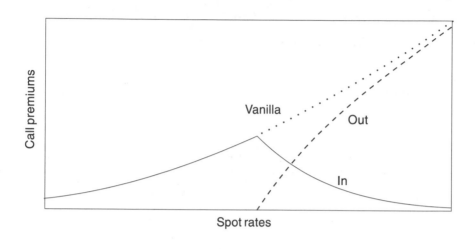

overcome this, a static hedging strategy that is philosophically motivated by the ability to replicate the payoff profile of a barrier option could be used. It should be noted that with the payoff structures given in Exhibit 41–26, going long a vanilla call option is equivalent to going long an up-and-in and up-and-out call option if $S_0 < H$, or going long a down-and-in and a down-and-out call option if $S_0 > H$ regardless of the barrier level, where we have implicitly assumed that all the options are struck at the same level and have the same time to maturity. Hence, we can conclude that the premium of any barrier option can never be greater than that of a corresponding vanilla option. Exhibit 41–27 illustrates this fact for a structurally similar vanilla call option, up-and-in call option, and up-and-out call option.

An alternative solution that addresses the client's concerns about high option premiums is an option with a knockout feature set only on the expiration date. More precisely, instead of monitoring the breaching of the barrier during the life of the option, one can monitor this breaching on the option expiration date itself. Unlike the example discussed earlier, if we set a barrier level of 1.36 Can./U.S. at the expiration date, there is no cheapening effect from the use of a barrier. To have a cheapening effect, we have to set the barrier to a level that is less than 1.31 Can./U.S., which is the strike rate of the option. We could, for example, set a barrier of 1.10 Can./U.S. at the expiration date such that if the exchange rate at the end of one month is above 1.31 Can./U.S. or less than 1.10 Can./U.S., the option expires worthless and the client loses his or her premium. In the range 1.10 Can./U.S. to 1.31 Can./U.S., in addition to losing the premium, the client's payoff will be the difference between the strike rate and the exchange rate at maturity. This type of one-point barrier strategy amounts to the client giving up some of the upside because in the event the U.S. dollar weakens below 1.31 Can./U.S. in a month, it will never weaken below the 1.10 Can./U.S. level. This strategy is different from simply buying and selling vanilla European-style put options on the U.S. dollar at strike levels 1.31 and 1.10 respectively. One can similarly create an example where the client buys a vanilla call option and gives away part of the upside.

One-point barrier options are also seen in the issues of the convertible/callable bonds and stock warrants where the issuer is forced to call (or convert) the bond (or warrant) if the price of the asset underlying the issues trades beyond/below a prespecified level on a certain date, which may not necessarily be the warrant maturity date. Single-barrier and dual-barrier options can also be used very effectively by technical analysis traders to monetize their market views.

CONCLUSION

To methodologically understand the dynamics, use, and the explosion of exotic options, it is important to first identify the basic blocks of the exotic options. Because a cutting-edge product can quickly become outdated, it makes more sense to philosophically understand the basic ingredients of the exotic options instead of all the products in the market. The building-block approach to exotic options presented in this chapter provides the ammunition to do just that. Any individual can use these building blocks as a platform to better understand and decompose complex option structures. With minor modifications, this platform can also be used effectively to understand complex derivatives structures that are currently available in the marketplace. It is our hope that the building-block approach will remove the mystery and fear of nontraditional derivatives, resulting in more participants in the both the over-the-counter and exchange-traded markets.

REFERENCES

Bernard, G. A. "A Direct Approach to Pricing Death Benefit Guarantees in Variable Annuity Products." *Product Develpoment News*, June, 1993. Society of Actuaries.

Boyle, P. P. and Y. K. Tse "An Algorithm for Computing Values of Options on the Maximum or Minimum of Several Assets." *Journal of Financial and Quantitative Analysis*, 25, no. 2 (1990), pp. 215–27.

Conze, A. and R. Viswanathan. "Path Dependent Options: The Case of Lookback Options. *Journal of Finance*, 26 (1991), pp. 1111–27.

Das, S. *Range Floaters. Handbook of Derivative Instruments*, 2nd ed. Irwin Professional Publishing, 1995.

Garman, M. "Recollection In Tranquility." *Risk* (March 1989).

Geske, R. "The Valuation of Compound Options." *Journal of Financial Economics*, 7 (1979), pp. 63–81.

Goldman, M. B., H. B. Sosin, and M. A. Gatto. "Path Dependent Options: Buy at the Low, Sell at the High. *Journal of Finance*, 34, no. 5 (1979), pp. 1111–27.

Gootzeit, A., D. Knowling, P. Schuster, and S. Sonlin. "Guaranteed Minimum Death Benefit Provisions—How Much Variable Annuity Risk Do We Want? Society of Actuaries. *Product Development News* (June 1994).

Hull, J. *Options, Futures, and Other Derivative Securities*. 2nd ed. Englewood Cliffs, N.J.: Prentice Hall, 1993.

Huynh, C. B. "Back to Baskets." *Risk* (May 1994), pp. 59–61.

Kemna, A. G. Z., and A. C. F. Vorst, "A Pricing Method for Options Based on Average Asset Values." *The Journal of Banking and Finance* 14 (1990), pp. 113–29.

Kolkiewicz, A., and K. Ravindran. "Option Pricing by Esscher Transforms by Gerber, H. U. and Shiu, E. S. W." *Transactions of the Society of Actuaries* XLVI (1994), pp. 157–62.

Levy, E. "Pricing European Average Rate Currency Options." *Journal of International Money and Finance* 11 (1992), pp. 474–91.

Margrabe, W. "The Value of an Option to Exchange One Asset for Another." *Journal of Finance* 33, no. 1 (1978), pp. 177–86.

Mitchell, G. T. "Variable Annuity Minimum Death Benefits—A Monte Carlo Pricing Approach." Society of Actuaries. *Product Development News* (February 1994).

Mueller, H. "Update on Variable Products." Society of Actuaries. *Product Development News* (July 1992).

Ravindran, K. "Effectively Riding the Yield Curve." *Journal of Derivatives Use, Trading, and Regulation,* 1, no. 2. pp. 211–14.

_____."Low Fat Spreads." *Risk* (October 1993).

_____."LIBOR Binary Notes." *Derivatives Week,* (December 6, 1993).

Ravindran, K. "Option Pricing: An Offspring of the Secretary Problem?" *Mathematicae Japonica* 38 (1993), pp. 905–912.

Reiner, E. "Quanto Mechanics. *Risk* (March 1992).

Rubinstein, M. "Double Trouble" *Risk* (Dec.–Jan. 1991) p. 73.

_____. "Options for the Undecided." *Risk* (April 1991).

_____. "Somewhere over the Rainbow." *Risk* (November 1991).

Rubinstein, M., and E. Reiner. "Breaking Down the Barriers." *Risk.* (Sept. 1991).

Stulz, R. "Options on the Minimum or Maximum of Two Risky Assets." Analysis and Applications, *Journal of Financial Economics* 10(1982), pp.161–185.

Thomas, B. "Something To Shout About." *Risk* (May 1993), pp. 56–58.

Index

A

ABN Amro Bank, 200
Abramowitz, Milton, 493
Absolute rate change, 513
Accreting swap, 173–175, 554
Accrual swap, 278
Accrued interest, and convertible bonds, 416–417
Active Total Return Management of Fixed Income Portfolios (Dattatreya and Fabozzi), 11, 179
Actuarial Standards of Practice, 661
Adjustable-rate mortgages; *See* ARMs
Advanced Interest Rate and Currency Swaps (Dattatreya and Hotta), 200, 215, 523, 567
Advances in Futures and Options Research (Stoll and Whaley), 461
Allen, Steven L., 13, 497
American currency options, 487–488, 880, 882
American Express, 304
American Financial Group, 787
American options, 736, 745, 870, 879–933
AMICA Mutual Insurance Group, 787
Amortization schedule, of indexed amortizing swaps, 201–202, 204, 212–213
Amortizing swaps, 173–174, 554, 822, 836
Annualized standard deviation, 99, 101–103
Arbitrage, anatomy of, 338–339
ARMs, 831–844
effect of increased rate volatility, 844

ARMs—*Cont.*
effect of market movements, 841
effect of yield curve shifts, 841–844
interest rate sensitivity of, 832–834
mechanics of, 834–836
rationale for restructuring, 834–836
restructuring a GNMA II, 836–837
risks in restructuring, 837–841
Arrears swap, 554
Asian option, 363, 369, 371, 374
Askin, 551
Asset allocation, 15, 694–747
pricing futures and options contracts, 726–746
setting up a tactical program, 711–722
shifts using futures, 698
using derivatives, 694–711, 722–726
Asset allocation swap, 391
Asset commitments, hedging, 671–673
Asset excess returns, 753–755
Asset hedging, 380–384
Asset/liability gap, 155–156
Asset-liability management (ALM), framework, 657–663
Asset Liability Management (Fabozzi and Konishi), 531
Assets
creating synthetic, 677–679
indexing, 781–782
Asset substitution, 384–391
Asset swaps, 168–171, 677
Attachment points, 793
At-the-money cap, 273–275

At-the-money-forward, 471
At-the-money options, 736, 889
At-the-money volatilities, 211
Average index level, 368
Average life profile method, 830
Average pricing feature, 388
Average rate options, 471, 884–888

B

Baber, Matthew C., 16, 831
Balance index, 216, 217
Bankers' Acceptances (BAs), 35, 905, 918
Bank for International Settlements (BIS), 193, 445, 689
Barone-Adesi, Giovanni, 488, 491, 493
Barrier options, 471, 602, 927, 929
Basis, 201–202, 204, 513
Basis limits, 564–565
Basis point, 72, 75, 81, 86, 89, 90, 92, 107, 116, 141
effect of drop in, 73
translating the advantage into, 97–98
value of, 84–85
Basis risk, 26, 31, 394, 396, 529, 561
Basis swap, 554
Basket hedging, 463, 466–468
Basket options, 888–892
Basle Accord of 1988, 193
Basle Committee on Banking Regulations and Supervisory Practices, 193, 561
Basle Risk Management Guidelines, 556
BBI, 122–123, 133, 135, 138
bonds used in calculating, 127

Other books of interest to you from Irwin Professional Publishing . . .

The Handbook of Exotic Options
Instruments, Analysis, and Applications
Edited by Israel Nelken

The first book to explain the theoretical applications of the exciting new instruments
known by such unusual names as collars, barriers, and compounds. Reflects some
of the innovative and creative thinking on Wall Street.
1-55738-904-7   350 pages

Derivatives Engineering
A Guide to Structuring, Pricing and Marketing Derivatives
The Globecon Group, Inc.

A comprehensive handbook which focuses on the instruments most commonly
traded, including characteristics, trading and portfolio management. Reviews the
financial techniques used by financial services firms in the booming drivatives
market.
1-55738-759-1   500 pages

The Derivatives Engineering Workbook
A Step-by-Step Guide to Structuring, Pricing and Marketing Derivatives
The Globecon Group, Ltd.

A companion to *Derivatives Engineering,* this hands-on guide provides the mechanism to reinforce product knowledge and practice transaction skills via a
combination of self-analysis tools and case studies. Focusing on the most commonly traded instruments, this book reviews the practical applications and use of
derivatives as well as selling and engineering techniques.
1-55738-760-5   200 pages

Advanced Interest Rates and Currency Swaps
State-of-the-Art Products, Strategies and Risk Management Applications
Ravi E. Dattatreya and Kensube Hotta

Written by leading experts in the field of swaps, this book analyzes and integrates
the latest developments in this rapidly changing field. It covers new products (both
indexed and cross-rate swaps); managing swap credit risk; liability hedging using
swaps; and risk management at major corporations and for developing countries.
1-55738-444-4   450 pages